Lecture Notes in Computer Science　　6633

Commenced Publication in 1973
Founding and Former Series Editors:
Gerhard Goos, Juris Hartmanis,

T0074363

Claudio A. Ardagna   Jianying Zhou (Eds.)

Information Security Theory and Practice

Security and Privacy of Mobile Devices
in Wireless Communication

5th IFIP WG 11.2 International Workshop, WISTP 2011
Heraklion, Crete, Greece, June 1-3, 2011
Proceedings

 Springer

Volume Editors

Claudio A. Ardagna
Università degli Studi di Milano
Dipartimento di Tecnologie dell'Informazione
Via Bramante, 65, 26013 Crema (CR), Italy
E-mail: claudio.ardagna@unimi.it

Jianying Zhou
Institute for Infocomm Research
1 Fusionopolis Way, #21-01 Connexis, South Tower, 138632 Singapore
E-mail: jyzhou@i2r.a-star.edu.sg

ISSN 0302-9743   e-ISSN 1611-3349
ISBN 978-3-642-21039-6   e-ISBN 978-3-642-21040-2
DOI 10.1007/978-3-642-21040-2
Springer Heidelberg Dordrecht London New York

Library of Congress Control Number: 2011927065

CR Subject Classification (1998): E.3, C.2, D.4.6, K.6.5, J.1, H.4

LNCS Sublibrary: SL 4 – Security and Cryptology

Typesetting: Camera-ready by author, data conversion by Scientific Publishing Services, Chennai, India

Printed on acid-free paper

Springer is part of Springer Science+Business Media (www.springer.com)

Preface

These proceedings include the papers selected for presentation at the 5th Workshop in Information Security Theory and Practice (WISTP 2011), held during June 1-3, 2011, in Heraklion, Crete, Greece.

In response to the call for papers, WISTP 2011 received 80 submissions. Each submission was evaluated on the basis of its significance, novelty, technical quality, and practical impact, and reviewed by at least three members of the Program Committee. The reviewing process was "double-blind," that is, the identities of the reviewers and of the authors were not revealed to each other. After an intensive discussion in a two-week Program Committee meeting held electronically, 19 full papers and 8 short papers were selected for presentation at the workshop. In addition to the technical program composed of the papers in the proceedings, the workshop included three keynotes by David Naccache, Reinhard Posch, and Pim Tuyls.

WISTP 2011 was organized in cooperation with the IFIP WG 11.2 Pervasive Systems Security. This workshop was also sponsored by FORTH, Institute of Computer Science, which took care of the organization under the aegis of ENISA, and by École Normale Supérieure (ENS) and Intrinsic-ID, who provided support for the invited speakers.

There is also a long list of people who devoted their time and energy to this workshop and who deserve acknowledgment. Thanks to all the members of the Program Committee, and the external reviewers, for all their hard work in reviewing the papers. We also gratefully acknowledge all the people involved in the organization process: the WISTP Steering Committee, and Damien Sauveron and Kostantinos Markantonakis in particular, for their advice; the General Chairs, Ioannis G. Askoxylakis and Demosthenes Ikonomou, for their support in the workshop organization; Cheng-Kang Chu and Sara Foresti, for their activity as Publicity Chairs. A special thanks to the three invited speakers for accepting our invitation and delivering invited talks at the workshop.

Last but certainly not least, our thanks are due to the authors for submitting the best results of their research to WISTP 2011 and to all the attendees. We hope you find the proceedings helpful for your future research activities.

June 2011

Claudio A. Ardagna
Jianying Zhou

Organization

The 5th Workshop in Information Security Theory and Practice (WISTP 2011) was held in Heraklion, Crete, Greece, June 1-3, 2011

General Chairs

Ioannis G. Askoxylakis	FORTH-ICS, Greece
Demosthenes Ikonomou	ENISA, Greece

Program Chairs

Jianying Zhou	Institute for Infocomm Research, Singapore
Claudio A. Ardagna	Università degli Studi di Milano, Italy

Workshop/Panel/Tutorial Chair

Damien Sauveron	University of Limoges, France

Publicity Chairs

Cheng-Kang Chu	Institute for Infocomm Research, Singapore
Sara Foresti	Università degli Studi di Milano, Italy

Steering Committee

Angelos Bilas	FORTH-ICS and University of Crete, Greece
Konstantinos Markantonakis	Royal Holloway University of London, UK
Jean-Jacques Quisquater	Catholic University of Louvain, Belgium
Pierangela Samarati	Università degli Studi di Milano, Italy
Damien Sauveron	University of Limoges, France
Michael Tunstall	University of Bristol, UK

Local Organizing Committee

Theodosia Bitzou	FORTH-ICS, Greece
Alison Manganas	FORTH-ICS, Greece
Nikolaos Petroulakis	FORTH-ICS, Greece (Chair)

Program Committee

Rafael Accorsi	University of Freiburg, Germany
Vijay Atluri	Rutgers University, USA
Angelos Bilas	FORTH-ICS and University of Crete, Greece
Carlo Blundo	University of Salerno, Italy
Marco Casassa Mont	HP Labs, UK
Cheng-Kang Chu	Institute for Infocomm Research, Singapore
Sabrina De Capitani di Vimercati	Università degli Studi di Milano, Italy
Xuhua Ding	Singapore Management University, Singapore
Josep Lluis Ferrer-Gomila	Universidad de las Islas Baleares, Spain
Sara Foresti	Università degli Studi di Milano, Italy
Bok-Min Goi	Universiti Tunku Abdul Rahman, Malaysia
Stefanos Gritzalis	University of the Aegean, Greece
Guofei Gu	Texas A&M University, USA
Jaap-Henk Hoepman	TNO and Radboud University Nijmegen, The Netherlands
Yih-Chun Hu	University of Illinois, USA
Michael Huth	Imperial College London, UK
Hongxia Jin	IBM Almaden Research Center, USA
Sokratis Katsikas	University of Piraeus, Greece
Miroslaw Kutylowski	Wroclaw University of Technology, Poland
Jin Kwak	Soonchunhyang University, Korea
Costas Lambrinoudakis	University of the Aegean, Greece
Peng Liu	Pennsylvania State University, USA
Javier López	University of Málaga, Spain
Wenjing Lou	Worcester Polytechnic Institute, USA
Mark Manulis	Technische Universität Darmstadt, Germany
Fabio Martinelli	IIT-CNR, Italy
Carlos Maziero	Pontifical Catholic University, Brazil
Chris Mitchell	Royal Holloway University of London, UK
Katerina Mitrokotsa	EPFL, Switzerland
Jose Onieva	University of Málaga, Spain
Ferruh Ozbudak	Middle East Technical University, Turkey
Stefano Paraboschi	University of Bergamo, Italy
Gerardo Pelosi	University of Bergamo, Italy
Raphael Phan	Loughborough University, UK
Joachim Posegga	University of Passau, Germany
Jean-Jacques Quisquater	Catholic University of Louvain, Belgium
Jason Reid	Queensland University of Technology, Australia
Kui Ren	Illinois Institute of Technology, USA

Reihaneh Safavi-Naini   University of Calgary, Canada
Kouichi Sakurai   Kyushu University, Japan
Gokay Saldamli   Bogazici University, Turkey
Pierangela Samarati   Università degli Studi di Milano, Italy
Jose Maria Sierra   Carlos III University of Madrid, Spain
Miguel Soriano   Technical University of Catalonia, Spain
Willy Susilo   University of Wollongong, Australia
Tsuyoshi Takagi   Kyushu University, Japan
Michael Tunstall   University of Bristol, UK
Wen-Guey Tzeng   National Chiao Tung University, Taiwan
Jian Weng   Jinan University, China
Chan Yeob Yeun   Khalifa University of Science,
                           Technology and Research, UAE
Heung-Youl Youm   Soonchunhyang University, Korea

External Reviewers

Isaac Agudo   Fengjun Li
Cristina Alcaraz   Ming Li
lessandro Barenghi   Yang Li
Lejla Batina   Bisheng Liu
Jung Hee Cheon   Jian Liu
Jihyuk Choi   Peng Liu
Sherman S.M. Chow   Hans Löhr
Gabriele Costa   Changshe Ma
Giampiero Costantino   Bilgin Metin
Eleni Darra   Alexander Meurer
Isao Echizen   Berna Ors
Dominik Engel   Pedro Peris-Lopez
Carmen Fernandez-Gago   Jing Qin
Kazuhide Fukushima   Panagiotis Rizomiliotis
Dimitris Geneiatakis   Rodrigo Roman
Johann Großschädl   Nashad Safa
Dongguk Han   Daniel Schreckling
Takuya Hayashi   Daniele Sgandurra
Luca Henzen   Zafar Shahid
Yoshiaki Hori   Thomas Stocker
Vincenzo Iovino   Donghai Tian
Keiichi Iwamura   Aggeliki Tsohou
Christos Kalloniatis   Nikos Vrakas
Markus Karwe   Witold Waligora
Young-Sik Kim   Jie Wang
Lukasz Krzywiecki   Pengwei Wang
Przemyslaw Kubiak   Kok-Sheik Wong
Hoi Le   Claus Wonnemann

Chao Yang
Yanjiang Yang
Artsiom Yautsiukhin

Ilsun You
Jialong Zhang
Wen Tao Zhu

Sponsoring Institutions

IFIP WG11.2 Pervasive Systems Security
FORTH, Institute of Computer Science, Greece
European Network and Information Security Agency (ENISA), Greece
École Normale Supérieure (ENS), France
Intrinsic-ID, The Netherlands

Table of Contents

Hardware Implementation

Security and Cryptography

Security Attacks and Measures (Short Papers)

Security Attacks

Security and Trust

Mobile Application Security and Privacy (Short Papers)

Can Code Polymorphism Limit Information Leakage?

Antoine Amarilli[1], Sascha Müller[2], David Naccache[1],
Daniel Page[3], Pablo Rauzy[1], and Michael Tunstall[3]

[1] École normale supérieure, Département d'informatique
45, rue d'Ulm, F-75230, Paris Cedex 05, France
{name.surname}@ens.fr
[2] Technische Universität Darmstadt, Security Engineering
Hochschulstraße 10, D-64289 Darmstadt, Germany
mueller@seceng.informatik.tu-darmstadt.de
[3] University of Bristol
Merchant Venturers Building, Woodland Road, Bristol, BS8 1UB, UK
{page,tunstall}@cs.bris.ac.uk

Abstract. In addition to its usual complexity assumptions, cryptography silently assumes that information can be physically protected in a single location. As one can easily imagine, real-life devices are not ideal and information may leak through different physical side-channels. It is a known fact that information leakage is a function of both the executed code F and its input x.

In this work we explore the use of polymorphic code as a way of resisting side channel attacks. We present experimental results with procedural and functional languages. In each case we rewrite the protected code code F_i before its execution. The outcome is a genealogy of programs $F_0, F_1, \ldots$ such that for all inputs x and for all indexes $i \neq j \Rightarrow F_i(x) = F_j(x)$ and $F_i \neq F_j$. This is shown to increase resistance to side channel attacks.

1 Introduction

From a security perspective, the advent of a software monoculture is an oft cited problem. Monoculture software is coarsely defined as programs (*e.g.*, Internet Explorer), generated from the same source code by the same compiler (*e.g.*, Visual Studio) and executed on the same processor family (*e.g.*, Intel x86) under control of the same operating system (*e.g.*, Windows). The premise is that monoculture makes attacks easier: an attack against any one member can be applied directly to the entire population; analogues exist in biology where monocultures and parthenogenesis are known to ease the spread of disease and lessen adaptation to environmental changes.

Various (seemingly different) protections attempt to break software monoculture through diversification. A simple example is that of Address Space Layout

C.A. Ardagna and J. Zhou (Eds.): WISTP 2011, LNCS 6633, pp. 1–21, 2011.

Randomization (ASLR): if each program is executed within a different address offset, then any assumptions an opponent makes on the location of a particular datum limits attacks to a smaller subset of the population.

This argument is equally relevant to embedded security and side-channel resilience, even if one accepts Kerckhoffs' principle (that cryptographic security should lay in the key alone). Defenders endeavor to make attacks harder by randomizing execution: even if opponents know the program being executed, their task of exploiting leakage is harder since they cannot focus their analysis with accuracy.

Background and Related Work. Focusing specifically on temporal randomization (*e.g.*, ignoring masking and related techniques), the term desynchronization is often used. The basic idea is to somehow alter normal program execution by "shuffling" instructions on-the-fly. This roughly means that the i-th instruction is no longer executed during the i-th execution cycle: the defender either swaps it with another instruction or inserts delays that cause the code to execute during a j-th cycle.

Consider the following randomization of the AES S-box layer [5]. Assuming that SBOX is a pre-computed table representing the AES S-box, a simple C implementation might resemble the following loop:

```
for( int i = 0; i < 16; i++ ) {
    S[ i ] = SBOX[ S[ i ] ];
}
```

To randomise the order of accesses to SBOX, one idea would be to maintain a table T where the i-th entry, *i.e.*, T[i], is initially set to i for $0 \leq i < 16$. This table can be used for indirection as follows:

```
for( int i = 0; i < 16; i++ ) {
    S[ T[ i ] ] = SBOX[ S[ T[ i ] ] ];
}
```

Note that this represents what one might term *online* overhead in the sense that the indirection's cost is paid during every program execution. Of course the trade-off is that table T can be updated, more specifically randomized, at regular intervals (*e.g.*, after each execution of the program) to ensure that S-box accesses are reordered. Such *re-randomization* is achievable using something as simple as:

```
t = rand() & 0xF;

for( int i = 0; i < 16; i++ ) {
    T[ i ] = T[ i ] ^ t;
}
```

This update of T represents what we term *offline* overhead: although the computational toll is not paid before run-time, the cost is offline in the sense that it is not borne during the execution of the program itself. Related work includes (but is certainly not limited to):

- Herbst *et al.* [7] describe the use of "randomization zones" within an AES implementation; the basic idea is to randomly reorder instructions within selected round functions, thus temporally skewing them in an execution profile.
- May *et al.* [12] describe NONDET, a processor design idiom that harnesses Instruction Level Parallelism (ILP) within a given instruction stream to issue instructions for execution in a random (yet valid) order. This essentially yields a hardware-supported and hence more fine-grained and more generic, version of the above.
- A conceptually similar idea is the design of re-randomizable Yao circuits by Gentry *et al.* [6]; the goal in both cases is to prevent leakage and in a sense construct per-use programs (circuits) via randomization.
- Many proposals have made use of random timing delays, *i.e.*, temporal skewing. For example Clavier *et al.* [3] describe a method which uses the interrupt mechanism while Tunstall and Benoît [16] describe a similar software-based approach.
- A vast range of program obfuscation techniques have appeared in the literature (see [4] for an overview) and are used in industry. The typical goals are to make reverse engineering harder and diversify the form of installed software; other applications include the area of watermarking.

Goals and Contribution. We consider the use of program self-modification as a means to allow a more general-purpose analogue of the above; we aim to describe an approach which

1. can be automated in a compiler (noting that parallelizing compilers can already identify light-weight threads in programs), and
2. can be composed with other countermeasures (*e.g.*, masking).

The basic idea is to (randomly) rewrite the program before execution and limit all overhead to being offline. The online overhead would be essentially nil: the overhead is associated purely with the number of static instructions in the program, *i.e.*, the cost of rewriting, rather than the number of dynamic instructions executed. A fully randomized rewriting approach would be costly since it demands analysis and management of instruction dependencies: in a sense, this would be trying to do in software what a NONDET processor does in hardware. We nonetheless explore this approach concretely using Lisp in Section 5. A conceptually simpler approach would be to follow the reasoning of Leadbitter [11] who imagines randomization as choices between threads which are *already* free from dependencies.

More formally, letting $c = F_0(k, m)$ denote a cryptographic program run on public input m and secret input k in a protected device, we explore ways to code F_0 in such a way that after each execution F_i will rewrite itself as F_{i+1} whose instructions differ from those of F_i before returning c.

In other words $\forall i, j, m, k, \quad F_i(k, m) = F_j(k, m)$, but $i \neq j \Rightarrow F_i \neq F_j$, a property that makes the attacker's signal collection task much harder.

2 Algorithmic Description

We represent the straight-line program fragment under consideration as a graph with n *levels*; each level contains a number of nodes which we term *buckets*. G_i denotes a list of buckets at the i-th level, with $|G_i|$ giving the length of this list. $G_{i,j}$ denotes a list of instructions in the j-th bucket at the i-th level, with $|G_{i,j}|$ giving the length of the list and $G_{i,j}[k]$ giving the k-th instruction.

Consider two instructions ins_1 and ins_2 that reside in buckets at the i-th and j-th level respectively: ins_1 *may* be dependant on ins_2 iff $i > j$, ins_1 and ins_2 *must* be independent if $i = j$. Informally, levels represent synchronization points: for some $i > j$, no instruction within the i-th level can be executed until every instruction within the j-th level has been executed. As such, buckets within a level can be viewed as threads and each level as a thread team: for some $i > j$ and k, instructions within buckets i and j can execute in parallel (or constituent instructions be scheduled in any order) if both buckets are at level k.

Our approach is to maintain in memory two copies of program instructions: a static version (*source program*) and a dynamic version (*target program*). The target program is actually executed at run-time. At some parameterized interval, the target program is rewritten using instructions extracted from the source program. The rewriting process is driven by the program graph which describes the source program structure: the goal is to use the structure to randomize the order according to which instructions are written into the target program while preserving dependencies. This is possible since the layer and buckets are essentially a pre-computed description of instructions inter(in)dependencies. The rewriting process is performed at run-time with a granularity matching the level of execution randomization (which relates loosely to the level of security) dictated by the context.

Algorithm 1. Initializes the indirection lists driving the program rewriting process.

Input: A program graph G with n levels representing a source program S.

```
1  for i = 0 upto n − 1 do
2      Let t be the type of buckets within Gᵢ.;
3      Rᵢ ← ∅;
4      if t = 1 then
5          for j = 0 upto |Gᵢ| − 1 do
6              |  Append j to the list Rᵢ.;
7          endfor
8      endif
9      else if t = 2 then
10         for j = 0 upto |Gᵢ| − 1 do
11             for k = 0 upto |Gᵢ,ⱼ| − 1 do
12                 |  Append j to the list Rᵢ.;
13             endfor
14         endfor
15     endif
16 endfor
```

2.1 Bucket Types

To facilitate rewriting we define two bucket-types. Where we previously denoted a bucket as $G_{i,j}$ we now write $G_{i,j}^t$ for a type-t bucket. Consider two buckets G and G', both at level i in the program graph:

Type-1 if the bucket is of type-1 this means we must extract *all* instructions in one go. This ensures that if we select G and then G', the instructions from G are written in a contiguous block within the target program and *then* instructions from G' are written in a second contiguous block.

Type-2 if the bucket is of type-2 this means we can extract a *single* instruction at a time. This means that if we select G and then G', instructions can be freely interleaved with each other.

The two bucket types represent a tradeoff. On one hand, using type-2 buckets is ideal since it allows fine-grained interleaving of instructions and therefore a higher degree of randomization. However, to preserve the program's functional behavior, such buckets must use a disjoint set of registers so that the instructions can be freely interleaved. Since a given register file is limited in size, this is sometimes impossible; to avoid the problem, one can utilize type-1 buckets as an alternative. Here, register pressure is reduced since buckets can use an overlapping set of registers.

2.2 Rewriting Algorithms

One can remove the restriction at extra cost, but to simplify discussion assume that all buckets at a particular level in the program graph are of the same type.

Algorithm 2. Randomly rewrites the source program into a target program.

Input: A program graph G with n levels representing a source program S.
Output: The target program T representing a valid, randomized reordering of instructions from S.

```
1  Set T ← ∅ ;
2  for i = 0 upto n − 1 do
3  │  Shuffle the list Rᵢ.;
4  endfor
5  for i = 0 upto n − 1 do
6  │  Let t be the type of buckets within Gᵢ.;
7  │  if t = 1 then
8  │  │  for j = 0 upto |Rᵢ| − 1 do
9  │  │  │  j' ← Rᵢ[j];
10 │  │  │  for k = 0 upto |Gᵢ,ⱼ'| − 1 do
11 │  │  │  │  Let I be the next unprocessed instruction in Gᵢ,ⱼ'.;
12 │  │  │  │  Append I to the target program T.;
13 │  │  │  endfor
14 │  │  endfor
15 │  endif
16 │  else if t = 2 then
17 │  │  for j = 0 upto |Rᵢ| − 1 do
18 │  │  │  j' ← Rᵢ[j];
19 │  │  │  Let I be the next unprocessed instruction in Gᵢ,ⱼ'.;
20 │  │  │  Append I to the target program T.;
21 │  │  endfor
22 │  endif
23 endfor
24 return T;
```

To drive the rewriting process, Algorithm 1 is first used to initialize n *indirection lists*: R_i is the i-th such list whose j-th element is denoted $R_i[j]$. This effectively sets $R_i = \langle 0, 1, \ldots, |G_i| - 1 \rangle$ if the buckets within G_i are of type-1, or

$$R_i = \langle \underbrace{0, 0, \ldots, 0}_{|G_{i,0}| \text{ elements}} , \underbrace{1, 1, \ldots, 1}_{|G_{i,1}| \text{ elements}} , \ldots \rangle$$

if buckets are of type-2. The lists relate directly to table T used within the example in Section 1.

When the program needs to be rewritten, Algorithm 2 is invoked: one level at a time, instructions from the source program S are selected at random, driven by the associated indirection list, to form the target program T. Note that before this process starts, each indirection list is randomly shuffled; this can be done, for example, by applying a Fisher-Yates shuffling [9, Page 145-146] driven by a suitable LCG-based PRNG [9, Page 10-26].

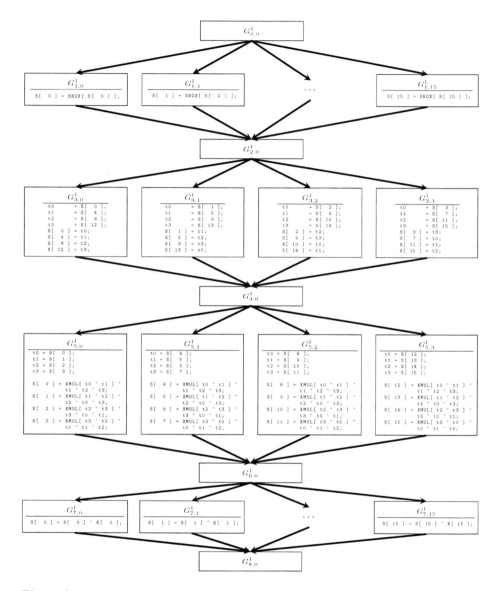

Fig. 1. A program graph for one AES round; the graph consists of 9 levels, with levels 0, 2, 4, 6 and 8 acting as synchronization points. Note that SBOX and XMUL represent precomputed tables for the AES S-box and xtime operation.

3   Concrete Implementation

As an example, consider an AES implementation [5] using an eight-bit software data-path; we represent the state matrix using a sixteen-element array S. One can describe instructions that comprise a standard, non-final AES round (*i.e.*, SubBytes⌢ShiftRows⌢MixColumns⌢AddRoundKey), as a program graph. Using both C and continuation dots for brevity, such a program graph is shown in Figure 1.

- For the example (and in general) one can specialize the program rewriting algorithm once the source program is fixed. *e.g.* all loops can be unrolled, empty levels or levels with a single bucket can be processed at reduced cost and special case treatment can be applied to levels with a single bucket type.
- The MixColumns layer houses buckets that can be split into smaller parts depending on register pressure. *e.g.* within level five one could split the second phase of each bucket into a further layer with sixteen buckets: each bucket would compute one element of the resulting state matrix (rather than the current formulation where four buckets each compute four elements).

4   Experimental Evaluation

Algorithm 2 was implemented on an ARM7 microprocessor. In this section we describe the performance of an unrolled reordered AES implementation and how one could attack such an implementation. We compare this with a straightforward unrolled AES implementation.

4.1   Performance

A standard (unprotected) unrolled AES implementation and a polymorphic AES code were written for an ARM7 microprocessor. The polymorphic version is only 1.43 times slower than the unrolled AES (7574 cycles *vs.* 5285), a time penalty which is not very significant for most practical purposes. This comparison is only indicative as faster polymorphic programs are possible (our rewriting function was written in C with no optimizations). Nonetheless, the polymorphic AES code requires a significant amount of extra RAM which might be problematic on some resource constrained devices.

4.2   Attacking a Standard AES Implementation

A standard AES code will call each sub-function deterministically. This typically involves constructing a loop that will go through all the indexes required to compute a given function in a fixed order. These loops are typically seen in the instantaneous power consumption, as a pattern of nine distinct patterns corresponding to the AES' first nine rounds. The last round is typically represented by a different pattern because of the absence of the MixColumn function.

The different sub-functions of an AES code can be identified by inspecting a power consumption trace. In the left hand part of Figure 2 two patterns of sixteen peaks can be seen. These correspond to the plaintext and secret key being permuted to enable efficient computation given the matrix representation in the AES' specification. This is followed by a pattern of four peaks that correspond to the exclusive or with the first key byte (the ARM7 has a 32-bit architecture). Following this there is a pattern of sixteen peaks that corresponds to the SubBytes function and two patterns of four peaks that correspond to the generation of the next subkey. ShiftRow occurs between these functions but is not visible in the power consumption. The exclusive or with this subkey can be seen on the right hand side of Figure 2, which means that the remaining area between this exclusive or and the generation of the subkey is where MixColumn is computed. However, no obvious pattern can be seen without plotting this portion of the trace with a higher resolution.

It is known that power consumption is typically proportional to the Hamming weight of the values being manipulated at a given point in time. This can be used to validate hypotheses on portions of the secret key being used in a given instance [2,10]. For example, the correlation between the Hamming weight of SubBytes's output the power consumption traces can be computed in a pointwise manner for a given key hypothesis, in this case we only need to form a hypothesis on one secret key byte. If the hypothesis is correct a significant correlation will be visible as shown in the right hand graphic of Figure 2, we note that the maximum correlation coefficient is ~ 0.6. If the key hypothesis is incorrect then no significant hypothesis will be present.

1000 encryption power consumption traces were taken where the secret key was a fixed value and the plaintext randomly changed for each trace. The right hand graphic of Figure 2 shows a trace of the correlation between the points of the power consumption traces and the Hamming weight of the result of the first byte produced by the SubBytes function given that the secret key is known. That is, the correlation is computed between the list of Hamming weights and the values of the first point of each trace, the values of the second point of each trace, *etc.* to form a trace of correlation values. The first peak corresponds to the point in time at which the first byte is produced in SubBytes and indicates which of the sixteen peaks corresponds to that byte being produced. The subsequent peaks in the correlation trace indicate the instants where the same byte is manipulated by MixColumns.

4.3 Attacking an Unrolled AES Implementation

The typical power consumption trace of an unrolled AES is shown in the left part of Figure 3.

In Figure 4, we note that the maximum correlation coefficient for an unrolled implementation is ~ 0.7.

Figure 4 is the analogous of 2 under identical experimental conditions (1000 traces *etc*). Interpretation remains the same: the subsequent peaks in the correlation trace indicate the instants at which the same byte is manipulated in MixColumns but have a lower correlation coefficient.

The left graph of Figure 6 shows the maximum observed correlation for all 256 possible hypotheses for one observed key for x power consumption traces.

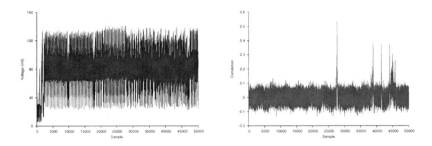

Fig. 2. Power consumption trace of a single round of an AES encryption performed by an ARM7 microprocessor (left) and a Differential Power Analysis signal (right)

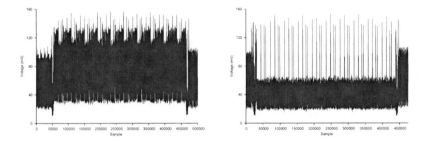

Fig. 3. Power consumption trace of an unrolled AES on ARM7. Unprotected (left) and polymorphic (right) codes.

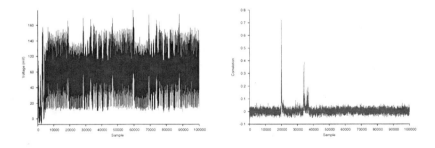

Fig. 4. The rightmost trace is the correlation between the power consumption and the output of the S-box that operates on the $\oplus$ of the first plaintext byte and the secret key. The leftmost trace shows a sample power consumption, in millivolts, during the same period of time.

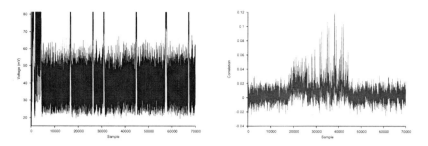

Fig. 5. The analogous of Figure 4 for the polymorphic code. In the leftmost trace the round functions are divided up by peaks in the power consumption.

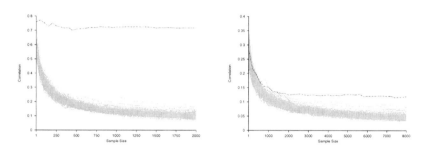

Fig. 6. Maximum correlation. Unrolled AES (left curve) and unrolled polymorphic AES (right curve).

Incorrect hypotheses are plotted in grey and the correct hypothesis is plotted in black. We note that ~ 100 traces suffice to distinguish the correct hypothesis from the incorrect hypotheses.

4.4   Attacking a Polymorphic AES Implementation

A polymorphic AES, as described in Section 3 was implemented on an ARM7. The power consumption for the round function changes considerably. In the implementation, the subset of opcodes used has a lower average power consumption and features local peaks in the power consumption caused by the call and return from the subfunctions in the individual round (right part of Figure 3). The individual round functions can only be identified by the time required to compute them as the patterns visible in Figure 2 are no longer present. These peaks can easily be removed by implementing the round function as one function. However, this feature is convenient for our analysis.

   Figure 5 is the equivalent of Figure 4 for a polymorphic AES. Figure 5 features two groups of peaks, the first of which has a correlation of ~ 0.06; this group is caused by the sixteen possible positions where the byte output from the SBOX indexed by the exclusive-or of the first plaintext byte and the first byte of the secret key is created. A second series of peaks representing a correlation of ~ 0.1

is visible. This series of peaks is caused by the sixteen possible positions where the same byte can be manipulated in the MixColumn function. We can note that these correlation coefficients are very low and 20, 000 power consumption curves were required to produce a correlation coefficient that is significantly larger than the surrounding noise.

The right graph of Figure 6 shows the maximum observed correlation for all 256 possible hypotheses for one observed key for x power consumption traces. The incorrect hypotheses are plotted in grey and the correct hypothesis is plotted in black. We note that $\sim 2,500$ traces are required to distinguish the correct hypothesis from the incorrect ones. This is considerably more than required to distinguish the correct hypotheses when attacking a non-polymorphic AES.

5   Can Lisp-Like Languages Help?

A further sophistication step consists in requiring F_i and F_{i+1} to have an extreme difference. While we do not provide a rigorous definition of the word *extreme*, the aim of our next experiment, nicknamed PASTIS, is to illustrate the creation of a program able to rewrite itself in a way that does not alter functionality but potentially changes *all its code*. We call a code *fully polymorphic* if any instruction of F_i can potentially change in F_{i+1}.

The code was designed with two goals in mind: illustrate the way in which fully polymorphic code is designed and provide a platform allowing to comfortably test the efficiency of diverse replacement rules as a step stone towards the design of a fully polymorphic AES code.

Such techniques can already be seen in polymorphic viruses as a way to foil signature-based detection attempts by anti-virus software; they also appear in code obfuscation systems. Readers can refer to [17] for more information on this topic.

PASTIS is written in Scheme for the MIT Scheme implementation [15]. The payload to transform (*e.g.* an AES) also has to be written in Scheme and is restricted to the subset of the Scheme syntax which the rewriting system is able to understand (Of course, since the rewriting engine has to rewrite itself, it is itself written using this limited subset of Scheme).

PASTIS is modular in a way making it easy to install new rewriting rules. Rules must change the source code's form while keeping it functionally equivalent. In this paper we voluntarily provide illustrative rules which could not work indefinitely because they tend to make the size of the code increase.

5.1   Structure

The top-level PASTIS function is pastis-generator. It creates the self-rewriting program from the payload and a rewriting function (which takes code as input and produces functionally equivalent rewritten code as its return value).

The produced code behaves functionally like the payload function; it will be evaluated to the same value if it gets the same parameters. However, it will additionally print, during the evaluation, a rewritten, equivalent version of itself.

Of course, the rewritten version is still functionally equivalent to the original payload and will also produce a rewritten version of itself, which, in turn, can be run, and so on, *ad infinitum* (forgetting about the growing size of the rewritten code, *i.e.*, assuming that we have an infinite amount of memory).

Internal Structure. The use of the `pastis-generator` function is quite straightforward; its role is to provide a convenient mechanism to weld the payload and rewriter together to make self-rewriting possible. Here is an example of the use of `pastis-generator`. The payload here is a simple function which adds 42 to its parameter and the rewriter is the identity function.

```
(pastis-generator
 '((payload . (lambda (x) (+ 42 x)))
   (rewriter . (lambda (x) x))))
```

The resulting code-blend produced by the `pastis-generator` function is given below.

```
(lambda (args)
  (define (pastis-rewrite x)
    ((lambda (x) x) x))
  (define (pastis-payload x)
    ((lambda (x) (+ 42 x)) x))
  (define (pastis-ls l)
    (map (lambda (x) (write (pastis-rewrite x)) (display " ")) l))
  (define (pastis-code l)
    (display "(")
    (pastis-ls l)
    (display "(pastis-code '(")
    (pastis-ls l)
    (display ")) (pastis-payload args))\n"))
  (pastis-code
   '(lambda (args)
      (define (pastis-rewrite x)
        ((lambda (x) x) x))
      (define (pastis-payload x)
        ((lambda (x) (+ 42 x)) x))
      (define (pastis-ls l)
        (map (lambda (x) (write (pastis-rewrite x)) (display " ")) l))
      (define (pastis-code l)
        (display "(")
        (pastis-ls l)
        (display "(pastis-code '(")
        (pastis-ls l)
        (display ")) (pastis-payload\nargs))\n"))))
  (pastis-payload args))
```

5.2   Step by Step Explanations

The code generated by `pastis-generator` seems complicated, but its structure is in fact very similar to that of the following classical quine[1].

```
(define (d l) (map write-line l))
(define (code l) (d l) (display "(code '(\n") (d l) (display "))\n"))
(code '(
(define (d l) (map write-line l))
(define (code l) (d l) (display "(code '(\n") (d l) (display "))\n"))))
```

Adding a payload to this quine is quite straightforward.

```
(define (payload) (write "Hello, World!\n"))
(define (ls l) (map write-line l))
(define (code l) (ls l) (display "(code '(\n") (ls l) (display "))\n"))
(payload)
(code '(
  (define (payload) (write "Hello, World!\n"))
  (define (ls l) (map write-line l))
  (define (code l) (ls l) (display "(code '(\n") (ls l) (display "))\n"))
  (payload)))
```

Given PASTIS's role, it is quite easy to see that it is related to quines. The only difference is that PASTIS has to modify its code before printing it, instead of printing it *verbatim* as regular quines do. This is also quite easy to do.

However, deeper technical changes are required if we want to be able to pass parameters to the payload because the classical quine's structure does not permit this. The solution is to make a quine that is also a λ-expression (instead of a list of statements). This is possible, thanks to S-expressions.

The way the quine works relies on the fact that its code is a list of statements and that the last one can take a list of the previous ones as arguments. Making the whole quine a λ-expression in order to accept arguments for the payload means making it a single expression. But thanks to the language used, it appears that this single expression is *still* a list. This enables us to solve our problem. Here is the result:

---

[1] A *quine* [8], named after Willard Van Orman Quine, is a program that prints its own code.

```
(lambda (args)
  (define (payload x) (+ x 42))
  (define (ls l) (map write-line l))
  (define (code l)
    (display "(")
    (ls l) (display "(code '(")
    (ls l) (display "))\n(payload x))"))
  (code '(lambda (x)
            (define (payload x) (+ x 42))
            (define (ls l) (map write-line l))
            (define (code l)
              (display "(")
              (ls l) (display "(code '(")
              (ls l) (display "))\n(payload x))"))))
  (payload args))
```

5.3 Rewriter

In addition to `pastis-generator`, we also provide a `rewriter` function. Its role is to call specialized rewriters for each keyword, which will call rewriters recursively on their arguments if appropriate.

Specialized rewriters randomly choose a way to rewrite the top-level construct. In our example, the implemented rules are any interchange between `if`, `case` and `cond` (*i.e.* if ⤳ cond ⤳ case ⤳ if) along with the transformation if (condition) {A} else {B} ⤳ if (!condition) {B} else {A}. It is easy and trivial to change these rules.

5.4 Results

PASTIS was tested with a simple payload and the example rewriter provided.

The code size increases steadily with generations, which seems to demonstrate that the `rewriter` function provided often adds new constructs, but seldom simplifies out the useless ones. As is clear from PASTIS' structure, code size grows linearly as generations pass (right-hand graphic of Figure 7). In our experiment code size in megabytes seemed to grow as $\sim 15.35 \times$ generation.

The produced code is still fairly recognizable: keywords are not rewritten and highly specific intermediate variables appear everywhere in the code. Furthermore, the numerous tautological conditional branches (of the form (if #t foo #!unspecific)) and useless nesting of operators are also a sure way to identify code produced by PASTIS. It is unclear if such artifacts could be used to conduct template power attacks to identify and remove polymorphic transformations. Given that a Lisp smart card does not exist to the best of that authors' knowledge, we could not practically test the effectiveness of this countermeasure *in vivo*.

Here is an example of the code produced by PASTIS after some iterations.

```
(lambda (args) (define (pastis-rewrite x) ((lambda (x) (define
(rewrite-if s) (define get-cond (rewrite (cadr s))) (define
get-then (rewrite (caddr s))) (define get-else (let ((
key9068561512430520509555138 (not (not (not (null? (cdddr s))))))))
(let ((key4506629534497774753790221 key9068561512430520509555138
))(let ((key3475303815763585605033413 (not (or (eq?
key4506629534497774753790221 (quote #f)))))) (let
((key7482276970755506992934025 9 (not (or (eq?
key3475303815763585605033413 (quote #f)))))) (cond ((not (not
(not (not (or (eq? key7482276970755506992934025 9 (quote #t))))))))
(let ((key1530095140490045361909209 6 #t)) (if (or (eq?
key1530095140490045361909209 6 (quote #t))) (begin (case #t ((#t) (let
((key8783884258550845645406647 (not (or (eq?
key7482276970755506992934025 9 (quote #t)))))) (case (not (or (eq?
key8783884258550845645406647 (quote #f))))((#t)(let ((
key4170147027488546012175938 5 key8783884258550845645406647))(if (not
(not (or (eq? key4170147027488546012175938 5 (quote #t)))))) (if (not
(or (eq? key4170147027488546012175938 5 (quote #t)))) (let ((
key9813414279311904186198070 7 #t)) (if (or (eq?
key9813414279311904186198070 7 (quote #t))) (begin 42)
```

It is interesting to note that the self-referencing nature of PASTIS makes it extremely hard to debug. When the third generation fails to run, for example, one needs to find the bug in the third generation code, identify what caused the second generation to produce it – and finally which code in the first generation caused the second generation to work this way. Several cases of bugs only occurring after several generations appeared during the development of PASTIS.

Readers wishing to experiment with the three main program modules[2] can download them from [14].

5.5 Possible Extensions

The current `rewriter` function only serves as an example. First, it leaves several recognizable features in the code. More importantly, the transformations it applies are not very deep, since one could simply decide to only use `cond` constructs, systematically rewrite all `if` and `case` constructs to `cond` and focus on the rewriting of `cond`. To be more precise, `if` and `case` can be seen as Scheme syntactic sugar; it would probably be better to restrict the rewriting to a bare bones subset of the Scheme syntax, convert everything to this subset before rewriting and possibly convert some things back to syntactic sugar forms to make the rewritten code look more natural.

Several transformations could be applied instead of the simplistic operations done by our `rewriter` function. Here are a few ideas:

α-Renaming. The current `rewriter` does not rename variables at all. A way to do this would be to keep an environment indicating current renamings. When we

---

[2] `rewriters.scm`, `rewrite.scm` and `generator.scm`

encounter a definition, we change the name and add the original and rewritten name to the environment. When we encounter a name, we change it to the appropriate rewritten name by a simple lookup in the environment. It is assumed that when the Scheme virtual machine processes names, power signatures caused by processing different names will differ as well.

β-Reduction and β-Expansion. A possible rewriting method would be to perform β-reductions (in the usual λ-calculus sense). Conversely, it would also be possible to perform β-expansions: select a sub-term, replace it by a variable and replace the whole expression by a function in this variable applied to the selected sub-term, taking all necessary care to prevent variable capture problems (roughly, ensuring that the operation does not bind other occurrences of the new variable and that the bindings of the sub-terms are still the same).

Of course, if we want to do such an operation without changing the semantics, we must ensure first that there is no breach of referential transparency in the code we are rewriting. Indeed, if side effects are taking place somewhere, the planned modifications could change the order of evaluation, or even the number of evaluations of some sub-terms.

Adding and Removing Definitions. This would be the ability for the rewriter to add or remove local definitions when possible. When the rewriter sees an expression $E(\text{expr})$ it could replace it with (let ((const expr)) $E(\text{const})$). This is very similar to the aforementioned β-reduction and expansion ideas and could be implemented in a similar way.

6   Avoiding Code Growth

While PASTIS is conceptually interesting, the code growth problem makes PASTIS useless for practical purposes. Let F_0 be the first generation of a self-rewriting program. Besides a payload representing the actual code's purpose, F_0 also contains a *non-deterministic* rewriting function H. H takes as input a version of the program and outputs another version, so that $\forall i \in \mathbb{N}$, $F_i = H(F_{i-1})$ with $i \neq j \Rightarrow F_i \neq F_j$ while retaining the code's core functionality, *i.e.* $F_i(m, k) = F_0(m, k)$ $\forall i, m, k$, as shown in the left hand-side of Figure 7.

As in the basic PASTIS example the size of F_i is monotonically increasing[3] (*i.e.*, size(F_{i+1}) $\geq$ size(F_i) with overwhelming probability), it is desirable to look for a different rewriting scheme[4].

An interesting alternative approach is to keep a representation of the original function F_0 within F_i and always rewrite F_0 differently. To ensure that each time a different program is created, the index i of the next version is passed to H: $F_i = H(F_0, i)$. Having F_i completely determined by F_0 and the index i

---

[3] Code size is monotonically increasing *on the average*, we neglect the unlikely cases where rewriting will cause a decrease in code size.

[4] Note that it is theoretically impossible to require that both $i \neq j \Rightarrow F_i \neq F_j$ and $\forall i$, size(F_i) < some bound.

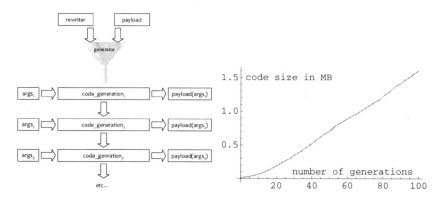

Fig. 7. Summary of the use of PASTIS (left) and typical evolution of code size with generations (right)

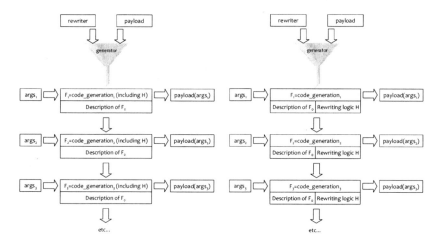

Fig. 8. Self-rewriting program without growth. Basic idea on the left, faster version on the right.

can be helpful, especially for debugging purposes. However, this approach has a crucial drawback: An attacker may be able pre-compute all F_i and analyze them for side channel information leakage, thereby weakening the polymorphic protection. Thus, it is advisable to have an additional randomness source that makes H non-deterministic. If H is truly non-deterministic, there is no need to pass i as an argument to H because each call of $H(F_0)$ creates a new, randomized version of F_0. The left-hand side of Figure 8 illustrates such a system.

Note that at each rewritten generation, F_i is *completely* discarded and only the description of F_0 is used again for the new code generation. In addition, the description of F_0 does not need to be included in clear. If desired by the setting, it can instead be encrypted with a random key. For this, the corresponding encryption and decryption function as well as the random key, must be included with F_i and upon each code rewrite, the encrypted description of F_0 must be decrypted, rewritten by H, and encrypted again with a new random key. Interestingly, if the payload itself contains a block-cipher code, this code can be also used for encrypting F_0; thus no additional encryption routine needs to be embedded in the program. This encryption approach bears some similarities to techniques used by polymorphic viruses.

6.1 Separating H From F_i

PASTIS is primarily meant for the protection of cryptographic functions from certain types of side-channel attacks. To this end, PASTIS' primary goal is to rewrite the payload, while the rewriting process H itself is not directly subject to such attacks and thus may not need to be rewritten at all. This is because the functionality of H is independent of the public message input m and the secret input k.

Thus, it may appear fit for purpose to rewrite only F_0 and keep H intact. Such an approach is interesting as in many cases, H will be much more complex than the payload and may become even more complex (and maybe less efficient) after being rewritten, as rewriting rules can have a detrimental effect on the size and the efficiency of H. However, in some cases side channels emanating from H may leak information about the rewriting process and thus about the code of F_i. If this is the case, then the information gained from the attack could be used to subsequently create attacks on F_i. If, however, such an indirect attack on F_i is considered infeasible or unlikely for a particular instance of polymorphic code, then the approach of not rewriting H can be a practicable way to improve code efficiency. This may also allow for more complex rewriting rules that would not be possible if H had to be expressed in the possibly restricted realm of rewritable code (for example, the limited subset of Scheme used in PASTIS).

This motivates the suggestion of yet another modification of our paradigm: Instead of having H be a part of F_i, we may consider H and F_i as *separate* functions. On each invocation H is called first. H loads the description of F_0 and takes as additional (implicit) input either an index i and/or a source of randomness and outputs F_i, which – as above – has the same functionality as F_0 but is rewritten.

After rewriting F_0 as F_i, H passes the inputs $\{m, k\}$ to F_i to execute the desired payload. This is illustrated in the right-hand side of Figure 8.

6.2   Randomizing Compilers: A Practical Approach

It remains to decide how such a "description of F_0" that is included in each code generation should be chosen. From an implementor's perspective, the form of F_0's description must be chosen such that it consists only of elements that are understood by the rewriting engine while at the same time allows for a fast creation of F_i for all i. While it may appear natural to use the same type for F_0 as for F_i (*i.e.*, code that can directly be executed), using a more abstract representation has some advantages: For example, if a program is represented under the form of a syntax tree, it can be straightforward to analyze to find permutations of code blocks (*i.e.*, subtrees) that do not change the code's semantics. This is similar to our *buckets* idea in Section 2. When, in contrast, the program is represented as virtual machine code, such code rearrangements may be much more difficult to identify. Thus, F_0 should be described in a more abstract way and converted by H to a more concrete representation. In fact, we may consider H as a *compiler* that transforms code from a high-level language into a less abstract one.

For example, F_0 may be represented by a GIMPLE tree. GIMPLE [13] is a rather simple language-independent tree-representation of functions used extensively by the GNU Compiler Collection (GCC) in various stages of the compilation process. Source code from any language supported by GCC is transformed into GIM-PLE which is then analyzed and optimized before being converted to the target language (for example, machine code)[5]. Representing functions under GIMPLE removes much of the complexity from the compiler that would be needed when working directly with a high-level language like C++. This makes compilation very fast.

GCC applies many optimizations to GIMPLE trees which may change their form in several ways. This can be used to create very powerful polymorphic code: randomizing which of these optimizations are done and how exactly they are applied to the tree leads to many different possible results, all of which yield semantically equivalent code. Randomization can also be applied to the next compilation steps which turn the GIMPLE tree into the target language. As there are many ways to encode constructs like an `if` or simple arithmetic expressions into machine code, a great variety of possible realizations of such constructs can be found.

Thus, an extensive polymorphic framework can be built by using a *randomizing* version of the parts of GCC that deal with GIMPLE trees and transform them to machine code as H. Such a framework would allow the execution of very elaborate rewriting rules while preserving efficiency by only dealing with GIMPLE instead of source code.

The implementation of this approach is an idea that is yet to be explored – left as future work.

---

[5] This description of GCC's inner workings is – of course – greatly simplified.

Acknowledgements

The work described in this paper has been supported in part by the European Commission IST Programme under Contract ICT-2007-216676 ECRYPT II and EPSRC grant EP/F039638/1.

References

1. Bertoni, G., Breveglieri, L., Fragneto, P., Macchetti, M., Marchesin, S.: Efficient Software Implementation of AES on 32-Bit Platforms. In: Kaliski Jr., B.S., Koç, Ç.K., Paar, C. (eds.) CHES 2002. LNCS, vol. 2523, pp. 159–171. Springer, Heidelberg (2003)
2. Brier, E., Clavier, C., Olivier, F.: Correlation Power Analysis with a Leakage Model. In: Joye, M., Quisquater, J.-J. (eds.) CHES 2004. LNCS, vol. 3156, pp. 16–29. Springer, Heidelberg (2004)
3. Clavier, C., Coron, J.-S., Dabbous, N.: Differential Power Analysis in the Presence of Hardware Countermeasures. In: Paar, C., Koç, Ç.K. (eds.) CHES 2000. LNCS, vol. 1965, pp. 252–263. Springer, Heidelberg (2000)
4. Collberg, C., Thomborson, C.: Watermarking, tamper-proofing, and obfuscation - tools for software protection. IEEE Transactions on Software Engineering 28(8), 735–746 (2002)
5. Daemen, J., Rijmen, V.: The Design of Rijndael. Springer, Heidelberg (2002)
6. Gentry, C., Halevi, S., Vaikuntanathan, V.: i-Hop Homomorphic Encryption and Rerandomizable Yao Circuits. In: Rabin, T. (ed.) CRYPTO 2010. LNCS, vol. 6223, pp. 155–172. Springer, Heidelberg (2010)
7. Herbst, C., Oswald, E., Mangard, S.: An AES Smart Card Implementation Resistant to Power Analysis Attacks. In: Zhou, J., Yung, M., Bao, F. (eds.) ACNS 2006. LNCS, vol. 3989, pp. 239–252. Springer, Heidelberg (2006)
8. Hofstadter, D.: Gödel, Escher, Bach: An Eternal Golden Braid. Basic Books, New York (1999) (1979)
9. Knuth, D.: The Art of Computer Programming, Seminumerical Algorithms, 3rd edn., vol. 2. Addison Wesley, Reading (1998)
10. Kocher, P.C., Jaffe, J., Jun, B.: Differential Power Analysis. In: Wiener, M. (ed.) CRYPTO 1999. LNCS, vol. 1666, pp. 388–397. Springer, Heidelberg (1999)
11. Leadbitter, P., Page, D., Smart, N.: Non-deterministic Multi-threading. IEEE Transactions on Computers 56(7), 992–998 (2007)
12. May, D., Muller, H.L., Smart, N.P.: Non-deterministic Processors. In: Varadharajan, V., Mu, Y. (eds.) ACISP 2001. LNCS, vol. 2119, pp. 115–129. Springer, Heidelberg (2001)
13. Merrill, J.: Generic and Gimple: A new tree representation for entire functions, Technical report, Red Hat, Inc., gcc Developer's Summit (2003)
14. http://pablo.rauzy.name/files/cryptomorph-sources.zip
15. http://www.gnu.org/software/mit-scheme/
16. Tunstall, M., Benoit, O.: Efficient Use of Random Delays in Embedded Software. In: Sauveron, D., Markantonakis, K., Bilas, A., Quisquater, J.-J. (eds.) WISTP 2007. LNCS, vol. 4462, pp. 27–38. Springer, Heidelberg (2007)
17. Xin, Z., Chen, H., Han, H., Mao, B., Xie, L.: Misleading Malware Similarities Analysis by Automatic Data Structure Obfuscation. In: Burmester, M., Tsudik, G., Magliveras, S., Ilić, I. (eds.) ISC 2010. LNCS, vol. 6531, pp. 181–195. Springer, Heidelberg (2011)

Mobile Electronic Identity: Securing Payment on Mobile Phones

Chen Bangdao and A.W. Roscoe

Oxford University Computing Laboratory and
James Martin Institute for the Future of Computing
{Bangdao.Chen,Bill.Roscoe}@comlab.ox.ac.uk

Abstract. The pervasive use of mobile phones has created a dynamic computing platform that a large percentage of the population carries routinely. There is a growing trend of integrating mobile phones with electronic identity, giving the phone the ability to prove or support the identity of the owner by containing, for example, a tuple of name, ID, photo and public key. While this helps phone owners prove who they are, it does not prove to them that they are giving their identities to intended parties. This is important in its own right for reasons of privacy and avoiding cases of "identity theft", but all the more important when identity is being provided to support the transfer of value (e.g. in mobile payment) or information. In this paper we show how Human Interactive Security Protocols can support this type of authentication in cases where PKIs are inappropriate, misunderstood or too expensive, concentrating on the case of payment.

1 Introduction

A report from International Telecommunication Union (ITU) earlier this year predicted that there would be 5 billion mobile phone subscribers by the end of 2010 [1]. This number is much larger than the number of personal computers (1,026 million in 2010) predicted by ITU [2]. At the same time, the computing power of mobile phones is ever improving: for example, the HTC Desire mobile phone has a 1 GHz CPU and 576 MB of RAM. In addition to the existing telephony functionalities, mobile phones, especially smart phones, are integrated with various kinds of sensors as well as powerful connectivity, typically on-board camera, GPS, motion sensor, light sensor, Bluetooth, NFC, WiFi, and 3G. Most importantly, they provide well designed convenience for people to use on a daily basis.

Such capabilities have made mobile phones a perfect electronic platform for various implementations. One of the most significant examples of these is the integration of different kinds of Electronic Identities (E-Identities), which helps reduce the number of cards and tokens a person usually carry, for example, ID card, door-access card/token, and bank card or other payment card. Such E-Identities may contain a person's name, photo, fingerprint, public/private keys, or banking/payment account details.

C.A. Ardagna and J. Zhou (Eds.): WISTP 2011, LNCS 6633, pp. 22–37, 2011.
© IFIP International Federation for Information Processing 2011

In Japan, the largest mobile operator NTT Docomo began deploying mobile phones containing the FeliCa contactless IC chip in 2004 [3]. The FeliCa contactless chip transforms mobile phones into carriers of various kinds of identities: transportation card, personal ID card and bank card.

It is reported that in 2012, banks and mobile phone operators in the Netherlands will launch a national NFC service which will enable users to use their mobile phones as payment card, tickets, coupons or membership cards [4].

In 2010, Chinese mobile phone operators started to implement a national mobile phone identification policy which requires users to register their mobile phone numbers under their real names and ID numbers. This will create the world's largest mobile phone identification system. At the same time, Chinese banks and mobile phone operators are working together to create a unified national platform for NFC based mobile payment service [5].

Thus there is a huge trend of integrating mobile phones with various kinds of identities, and the most significant use may lies in mobile payment. More generally, we may consider a mobile phone as a bank/payment card once it has logged onto a banking web-site or an e-money web-site like Paypal. Almost all major banks in the US and Europe have opened a mobile banking service.

E-Identities will be communicated between individuals who may or may not know each other, and from individuals to impersonal devices such as doors, merchant tills and web-sites. It is natural to require two things: that you only give your identity to the party that you wanted to give it to, and that you do not accept an identity which you believe attaches to one party when in fact it belongs to another. You may not know in advance the name of the party to whom you are trying to connect.

PKIs are expensive to implement, not usable in cases where the name of the intended connection is not known in advance, and are frequently misused by humans. We need a cheap method of authentication, that allows authentication by context (e.g. that the device you are connecting to is the one in front of you) and which is hard for humans to misuse. We must place into the last category any protocol which simply requires the human user to press a button to say "yes", because particularly in hurried mobile scenarios humans will become distracted and complacent. So while, in mobile-to-mobile connections, it may be a valuable security feature to show each human the photograph of the other, simply expecting them to say "yes" to the obvious enquiry will give only dubious security in practice. In this paper we propose what we think is an appropriate solution to this problem.

To securely transmit an E-Identity, we firstly need to ensure authenticity as well as integrity of the E-Identity, for example, the receiver can trust that the received E-Identity originates from the correct sender. Secondly, we must protect the private E-Identity, no one except from the dedicated sender and receiver can know the details of the transmitted private E-Identity. Thirdly, we have to achieve enough pervasiveness which enables a maximum coverage of mobile phones as well as an implementation of convenient user interfaces.

To satisfy such requirements, we firstly bootstrap an authentic electronic connection between the two parties by using a Human Interactive Security Protocol (HISP), and to fulfill the second requirement, we also bootstrap a session key during the establishment of the connection. In the mean time, a careful selection of an usable HISP can guarantee the satisfaction of the third requirement. Once we have a secure connection, an automatic downloading of such E-Identities is possible, which in some payment processes is made by manually inputting. This can further reduce the amount of human effort.

HISPs are explained in Section 3, which also presents two major mobile payment scenarios; The implementation of the two scenarios is discussed in Section 4, and a general security analysis is given in Section 5.

2   Present-Day Payment Solutions

At present, NFC, Bluetooth and SMS are the main channels used to carry authentication information in payment. Below we review how they are used.

2.1   NFC

NFC is based on a short range (<10cm) RF channel (13.6 MHz), which assumes that the proximity provides sufficient trust of the data transmitted over this channel. NFC is therefore regarded as a typical out-of-band (OOB) channel. OOB channels are sometimes termed as empirical channel or authentic channel, which assumes human trust but allows limited bandwidth of communication. Such channels are common in our daily life, for example, people talking, writing messages, typing words, handshaking, comparing images/words/digits.

An NFC enabled mobile phone can be used as a user-trusted touch point to display and check the received payment amount and the payee's details, as well as confirming the payment. Concrete designs of NFC-based mobile payment can be found in [6,7]. An NFC enabled mobile phone can act as a card or a terminal, and there is also a mode for peer-to-peer communication and therefore it enables peer-to-peer payment. It gives the convenience of simply touching our mobile phones to communicate securely. We also notice that NFC is currently not widely available among mobile phones, therefore it is not selected in our implementation in Section 4.

However, using proximity as the only authenticator can lead to attacks. For example, a practical NFC relay attack on mobile phones is demonstrated in [8]. In addition, a lack of proper protocols that against man-in-the-middle (MITM) attack may make the implementations of NFC based mobile payment an easier target to MITM attackers [9]. In addition, without link-level security, the transmission between two NFC devices may subject to eavesdropping and data modification [10]. As we were completing this paper there was a press report of a practical MITM attack on a proximity-based car key mechanism [44]. It is desirable that NFC based communication needs to be enhanced by introducing a security protocol that addresses the MITM attack [9]. For example, we can bootstrap a one-time session key between two NFC devices before transmitting any sensitive data. This key is independent to any existing security and it can be used as an add-on security to NFC.

2.2   Bluetooth

Bluetooth is probably the most popular short-range communication technology available now. According to the Bluetooth Special Interest Group (SIG), in 2014 Bluetooth will be found in 70 percent of all handsets and 83 percent of all netbooks [11]. There are many implementations [12,13] as well as researches [14,15]on using Bluetooth in mobile payments.

Bluetooth (v2.0 and older) is known to be subject to searching attack due to its reliance on an arbitrarily human selected passkey [16], and its pairing process generally require a long time which makes it not well user-friendly.

However, the new version Bluetooth v2.1 introduces a Secure Simple Pairing (SSP) scheme which is designed to solve the security problems and falls into the same class of HISPs that we will be studying later in this paper. But this immediately introduces a legacy problem: a communication between a v2.0 mobile phone and a v2.1 mobile phone will be eventually ended as a v2.0 communication.

Any Bluetooth which may fall short of v2.1 is too insecure to support payment. It will be possible to use v2.1 to support the same model of payment we propose in Section 3.

2.3   SMS

Telephony is regarded as a relatively secure communication technology in this paper despite some known attacks [19]. The attacks against telephony network usually require much larger strength in both resources and knowledge, and therefore may not be an "economic" attack against mobile payment. SMS is therefore frequently considered secure. It worries us, however, that this security has no logical basis and is based on purely economic and subjective arguments. Without a formal and provable basis for security it seems unwise to invest heavily in a payment technology.

SMS-based mobile payment methods can be laborious and difficult to learn, and sometimes may not be as instant as other types of mobile payment [17]. The best case for their use may be in long-distance communication in situations where the telephone service providers are able to give a good guarantee of authenticity.

2.4   Other Solutions

In [18], the authors discussed an empirical design called MP-Auth which uses mobile phones to protect online banking. Without any use of hardware supports, it is regarded as a typical example of using PKI in mobile payment.

MP-Auth uses two public keys, one is pk_B shared between the PC and the bank, the other is pk_T shared between the mobile phone and the bank. These public keys are used to bootstrap a symmetric key between the mobile phone and the bank.

In addition, two more procedures are needed: one is to secure the integrity of the data received from the PC, they use an OOB method which is by displaying a hashed result[1] on the mobile phone and the PC, and the user compares and selects the matching one on the mobile phone; the other is to install the correct public key pk_T on the mobile phone, which they recommend to use off-line methods, for example, at a bank branch, through in-branch ATM interfaces, or using telephony.

The use of public keys like this is appropriate in cases such as electronic banking when both parties know it in advance. We do not believe it is otherwise appropriate in the world of ad hoc connections, such as when making a payment to a previously unknown payee.

The solution we will propose can simplify the above processes by considering the two connections between the mobile phone and the bank as a single insecure connection by using an OOB channel between the bank and the mobile phone (see details in Section 3).

Another novel implementation is called Cronto[2]: by using the camera on the mobile phone, the user takes a photo of a square picture similar to a 2-D barcode displayed on his PC screen, and then the device translates the photo into payment details and generates a 6 digits number at the same time, once the user confirms the payment details, he enters the 6 digits number on his PC. By using the camera and the *https* web-site, they create an OOB channel between the user's mobile phone and the bank server. It is considered as a good example of using OOB channels in mobile payment.

3   Using a HISP: Mixing Context, Human Trust and Security

HISPs achieve what one might at first think impossible: they bootstrap security over insecure networks such as the Internet and WiFi without any pre-existing network of secrets. They do this via the transfer of a small amount of non-secret information, usually by human users, that is authenticated by context.

We hereby assume that in any mobile payment, a payer must have a way of identifying the proposed payee. This identification might arise from already-existing familiarity with the payee or from the context (presence in a shop, in front of a vending machine or through an E-commerce shopping session) in which the need for the payment arises. To understand this better, think of the scenarios in which you would be willing to hand over cash: you might trust a merchant by experience or reputation, you may choose to trust him by context, or you may "trust" him to receive payment because you have already received goods or services from him. Note that there is a weaker need for trust if, as with handing

---

[1] They use a correlation function to select the corresponding words to display based on the hashed results.

[2] http://www.cronto.com/

over cash, you know that the damage that can be caused by an abuse of trust is strictly limited (i.e. to losing a defined amount of cash).

Even when one trusts a large organisation by reputation, one still needs to know that a payment one is making to it is within the payment one thinks one is making.

Some of these means of identification might readily create secure channels: for example one might have retained a channel used for a previous payment to a familiar payee. However some do not, and in some cases there may be a secure channel from a different device (e.g. a browser session on a PC) to the mobile phone from which we want to make payment. However in the great majority of contexts where the need for payment arises, there is an opportunity for the payee to communicate a Short Authentication String (SAS) of 6 digits (say) to the payee in such a way that the payer knows it has come from the intended payee *within the intended payment*. Frequently this will be via an OOB channel such as those formed by the payee looking at a till display or at the *https* window on a browser.

The role of a HISP is to convert well-designed SASs, and the trust that the payee has in the sender, into robust security. An SAS is much more compact than other ways in which one might attempt to authenticate a payee, and much more amenable to incorporation into protocols in a way that is not vulnerable to human mis-use.

To demonstrate our solution, we give two scenarios of mobile phone payment applications:

1. peer-to-peer (phone-to-phone): user A wants to send A's public E-Identity to user B. For example, after verifying A's public E-Identity, B can then make a payment to A[3].
2. customer-to-merchant (phone-to-server): customer C wants to send C's private E-Identity to merchant server M. For example, C uploads C's payment account details to M. This can be an online or a point-of-sale (POS) mobile payment. A mobile phone can connect to the server via: A. a PC; B. telephony or GPRS/3G.

To simplify our discussion, Scenario 2 is discussed in this section, and Scenario 1 is discussed in Section 4.1. In this section, a mobile phone is connected to the server via a PC because this can demonstrate a POS mobile payment as well as an online mobile payment.

3.1 Choosing a HISP

Over the past few years, a new family of authentication protocols that are based on human trust and interaction have been introduced. These protocols are often referred to as HISPs. They use two kinds of channels: a high bandwidth channel

---

[3] This can be completed by sending B's private E-Identity (payment account details) to A, or by sending B's private E-Identity together with A's public E-Identity to a trusted third party, for example, a bank.

(denoted $\longrightarrow_N$) subject to the Dolev-Yao attack model [29] and a low bandwidth OOB channel (denoted $\longrightarrow_O$). Due to its limited bandwidth, the OOB channel transmits a Short Authentication String (SAS) that is used to authenticate data exchanged over the insecure high bandwidth channel.

By comparing an SAS on an OOB channel, human users can authenticate information received from an insecure high bandwidth channel. Nguyen and Roscoe wrote an extensive survey [28] of HISPs, comparing their cost and efficiency, of which [30,32,33] are good examples.

The Symmetric HCBK (SHCBK) protocol [31] is a typical HISP. This, the general description, connects an arbitrary-sized group.

1. $\forall A \longrightarrow_N \forall A' : A, INFO'_A, hash(A, hk_A)$
2. $\forall A \longrightarrow_N \forall A' : hk_A$
3. users compare $digest(hk^*, \{INFO'_A | A \in G\})$, where hk^* is the XOR of all hk_A's for $A \in G$

SHCBK has each node "publish" its name and a collection of information that it wishes to be authentically connected with that name. It also sends a hash[4] of a randomly generated key hk_A coupled with the name. Once it has received that information from all nodes, and therefore become committed to the set of identities, $INFO$ and hashed keys it will use, it publishes its previously secret hk_A. The point is that by the time of this last publication, it was in fact *committed* to all the data used in the above protocol, even though it does not yet *know* all the hk_As. HCBK stands for Hash Commitment Before Knowledge. A careful security analysis of this protocol (see [31], for example) demonstrates that any attacker is unable to profit from combinatorial analysis aimed at getting the SASs (i.e. digests) to agree even though nodes have difference views of the authenticated information. Good HISPs such as SHCBK therefore offer maximum security for a given amount of human effort.

3.2   Tailoring a HISP

In our payment scenario, only two parties are involved in the payment: customer and merchant. Therefore we have modified SHCBK into a pair-wise protocol which establishes a shared secret key. In the protocol, C represents the mobile phone, M represents a merchant, and U represents a user.

1. $C \longrightarrow_N M : ID_C, INFO_C, hash(hk_C, ID_C), hash(k)$
2. $M \longrightarrow_N C : ID_M, INFO_M, pk_M, hash(hk_M, ID_M)$
3. $C \longrightarrow_N M : \{k\}_{pk_M}, hk_C$
4. $M \longrightarrow_N C : hk_M$
5a. $M \longrightarrow_O C : digest(hk_C \oplus hk_M, (ID_C, ID_M, pk_M, k, hash(k), INFO_C, INFO_M))$
5b. C compares the *digest value*[5] with its own version.

---

[4] Hash means a standard cryptographic hash function that has two main properties: collision resistance, and inversion resistance.

[5] The *digest value* represents the SAS that is manually compared by humans.

In Messages 1 and 2, we have added 6 more components, k is a session key (a random number) generated by C, it is exchanged by using the uncertified public key pk_M provided by M. To avoid the intruder reflecting hk_C back to C as a supposed hk_M in a way that C would accept, we added ID_M and ID_C as two one-bit tags to distinguish the hashes generated by C and M. $INFO_M, INFO_C$ represent other information that the actual system would require, for example, date and time, part of the payment details, etc.

Naturally, if the protocol has proceeded uninterfered with, C's and M's values will be equal. If, however, an intruder has imposed his own values on the receivers of Messages 1–4, C and M will not agree on all four parameters. For security, what is important is that they agree on pk and k, so we will concentrate on what happens if the intruder interferes with these. What we are concerned about is the chance that the digests agree when these two values do not.

The digest function [30,31] is designed so that, as hk varies, the probability that $digest(hk, X) = digest(hk, Y)$ for $X \neq Y$ is less than ϵ, where typically ϵ is very close to 2^{-b} for b the number of bits in the output of $digest$. It must also have the property that for any fixed value d, the chance that $digest(hk, X) = d$ as hk varies is less than ϵ. The right value of ϵ is debatable because the larger it is, the more human effort is required. To maintain an acceptable security and usability, implementors need to examine carefully about the use case and the perceived risks between the user and the merchant. A standard [36] given by National Institute of Standards and Technology (NIST) requires that a successful guess of a secret value should be less than one in 1,000,000. Therefore, we put the number of digits of the digest value at 6 in our example[6].

3.3   The Human Contribution

Depending on human interaction can be dangerous because humans can become lazy, which can disable well designed security. To standardize the work flow of using a HISP, we need to clarify step (5a) and (5b).

In step (5a), when conducting online payments at home, those OOB channels U can directly interact with M are phone calls, SMSs, or using *https* web pages (as most of the banks/merchants are still using *https* service, this does not increase the risks by using it as an OOB channel). Therefore we use a dashed line to show the transmission of the digest value in Fig 1.

To remove the user's complacency[7] in step (5a), we force the user to type the digits of the received digest value into mobile phone[8]. If the comparison of digest

---

[6] The SAS here is not secret, but this provides a good analogy. In any case we believe that the use of HISPs in payments should usually be backed up by secondary security as discussed later. 6 digits happens to be the number used in the experiments reported in [35].

[7] A user may simply keep pressing the OK button regardless of what displayed on the mobile phone.

[8] [35] examines ways of performing this comparison and conclusively demonstrates that for security the best approach is for the customer to type the digits of the merchant's digest value into mobile phone, which then compares the two.

value failed at stage (5b), a warning will be displayed on the mobile phone, and we have designed what to do next. In our implementation, we prompt the user to check if he has entered the SAS incorrectly. If so, the protocol is restarted from the beginning. If not, the payment will be aborted, because there is a distinct possibility of the intruder being present.

After a successful run of the protocol, in which C verifies the digest value received from an OOB channel, and at the same time the protocol authenticates the uncertified pk_M and the one-time session key k. The user is convinced that a secure connection is established between him and M.

3.4   Demonstrating a HISP

Once the HISP above has been run, there is a channel between the payer's mobile phone and the payee that the payer trusts as both secret and authentic. We can therefore design payment methods which exploit this high-bandwidth secure channel, thereby increasing the amount of information that can be passed to (a) authenticate the identity of the payer and (b) secure the payment, for example against fraud by the payee.

We give an example of making a payment after successfully bootstrapped the session key k by using a HISP. This largely depends on the actual implementation of banks and merchants.

The session key can now be used to allow secure downloading of payment information from M. U is then asked to approve the payment by password entry. Following this, data necessary to complete the payment can be sent to M over the channel. This will vary depending on the payment protocol being used.

We recommend that an e-cheque is sent, which is encrypted under a bank key (and therefore not understandable by M), together with all information that is not secret from M. This e-cheque might contain M's E-Identity, date and time, amount, $hash(hash(Payment\ Info), Account\ Info)$. M sends $hash(Payment\ Info)$ to bank. An example protocol is given as below (also see Fig 1):

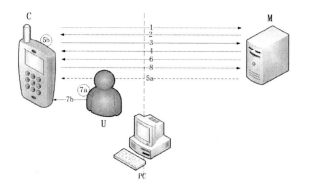

Fig. 1. Using a HISP (demonstration of a successful run)

6. $M \longrightarrow_N C :\{$*payment amount, M's E-Identity, date and time, other details*$\}_k$

7a. U checks payment amount, merchant's E-Identity, date and time, and other details displayed on C.

7b. If correct, U authorizes the payment by entering password on C.

8. $C \longrightarrow_N M :$ e-cheque

E-cheques provide a way of combatting sophisticated Man-in-the-Shop (MITS) attacks which is discussed in Section 5.3.

M can then forward this e-cheque to a bank to get cash.

In each case the fact that the payment details (amount, merchant's E-Identity, date and time) are downloaded onto the mobile phone and approved by the customer gives a considerable secondary security factor over and above that provided by HISP and password.

3.5   Reverse Authentication

As we have made clear, the unique feature of a HISP is that it gives the customer confidence that he or she is connected to the desired merchant within the context of the intended payment. This both gives extra security and enables us to make the traditional security goal of authenticating the customer to merchant/bank easier and more thorough. Because it goes in the opposite direction to the main/tranditional authentication accompanying payments, we have termed it *reverse authentication.*

In general, by using reverse authentication, we actually put the users' safety at the center of the security design.

4   Implementation

In demonstration implementations of Scenario 1 and 2 discussed at the beginning of Section 3, we have used the following approaches.

A. Two mobile phones are connected via Bluetooth: the protocol will start after the Bluetooth discover-and-connect process. An e-cheque is sent to the payee from the payer. As explained at the beginning of Section 3, it can be completed in two ways, and to simplify the demonstration, we do not show a second connection to a bank or a third party.

B. A mobile phone is connected to a server: because this can be remote/online or POS payment, we use a PC to act as the display on behalf of the server. To make the connection instant, the connection between the mobile phone and the server is made by initiating a data call from the server. This is slightly different from the example given in Section 3.4.

4.1   Implementation of Approach A

The photos above show the image of the users, and this is regarded as a useful supplement to the security we discussed in Section 3. By incorporating available biometrics or location information (GPS) into the protocol, we can further

Fig. 2. Peer-to-peer mobile payment implementation

enhance the security and provide the user more authentic information to verify each other.

There are two important factors in determining the practicability of this implementation. One is the set-up of connection between two mobile phones, the other is the input of the digest value. In our implementation, the set-up of Bluetooth connection takes around 10 seconds, and the inputing of the 6-digit digest value takes around 15 seconds. However, if one mobile phone can display the Bluetooth address as a 2D barcode, and the other mobile phone reads it by its camera, this can reduce the time of connection set-up. A similar approach can be taken to digest values when this technology is available. This function depends on the performance of specific mobile phones because not all mobile phone cameras can easily film a clear picture of 2D barcode, for example, low-end mobile phone camera can not auto-focus and have difficulty to take clear pictures when hands are shaking. It is, however, an important aspect of our technology that this function can be performed quickly and easily by humans alone.

This is implemented on Nokia N95 and Blackberry 9000: a J2ME Midlet is programmed to run on N95, and a JAVA (on RIM) application is programmed to run on Blackberry 9000. The Bluetooth is v2.0 and the profile is no security.

4.2   Implementation of Approach B

In this case, a mobile phone acts as a "trusted device", which is similar to the current Card Authentication Programme (CAP) readers. And it is required that the user must activate his or her online banking account or any other payment account before or during the payment process. By using reverse authentication,

Fig. 3. Customer-to-merchant mobile payment implementation

the merchant's E-Identity together with the payment information is downloaded onto the mobile phone, which can save the human effort of inputting those data required in most current mobile banking applications.

This is implemented on Nokia N70 and a PC (acting as the server): a Symbian C++ application is programmed to run on N70, and a C++ application is programmed to run on the PC.

The cryptography functions we have applied in the applications comply with the guidance published by NIST [37,38].

5 Security Analysis

The security attributes of a mobile payment solution usually include: confidentiality, authentication, integrity, authorization, availability and non-repudiation. Confidentiality and authentication is easily achieved by bootstrapping a secure connection prior the payment process. And the use of strong cryptographic functions protects integrity and can detect any data modification. Authorization is achieved by the verification of: A. user's password; B. user's private E-Identity (banking or payment account details). Non-repudiation is achieved by the use of an e-cheque: a bank will check and verify such an e-cheque, which contains the E-Identities of the two parties as well as the payment details. Availability is not discussed in this paper.

However, except for the above analysis, a few distinct security attributes and state-of-the-art attacks need to be considered carefully.

5.1 Phishing/Credential Harvesting

By means of disguised emails or web pages, attackers lure users to enter their credentials into a fake web form, for example, an online banking log-in form. This is a very common online attack and it is very difficult to defend once the users are tricked into such a web page.

Most mobile payments are immune to such attacks because they have independent applications that handle payment processes: the account details are input locally on the mobile phones rather than on web pages or web forms.

However, without the use of end-to-end security (for example, the use of e-cheque), sophisticated phishing attacks can be developed against mobile payment solutions, for example, a phishing attack can be applied against an NFC based mobile phone by modifying or replacing tags [20]: this can mislead the user to submit data to a wrong party. And some SMS based mobile payment solutions require users to submit their account details in clear text to a third party to log on, and this can lead to an SMS phishing attack: by luring users to submit their account details to a wrong phone number.

Our solution, which provides authentication as well as confidentiality, can ensure that the payer has approved the E-Identity of the payee, and the payee can not reuse anything from the payment. Therefore, it is resistant to the phishing attack.

5.2   Malware

Mobile malware is a serious security threat to all mobile phone based applications. A report from Kaspersky indicates that a total number of 514 pieces of mobile malware have been cataloged between 2006 and 2009 [21]. Such attacks can be detected by installing mobile anti-virus software, for example, Kaspersky, F-Secure and McAfee. And it can be further mitigated by forcing users to download software from the official web sites, for example, Android and iPhone require software to be installed from their official online application shops. However, it may become more difficult to maintain a high level of security with the increasing complexity of mobile phone systems. These issues need to be considered before deciding whether to impose an upper limit on the amount of money allowed in mobile payments. Some discussions about mobile malware can be found in [22,23].

5.3   Man in the Middle

Many NFC based mobile payment solutions are believed to be based on EMV [9,24], which has been found vulnerable to MITM attacks [25]. And the NFC in itself does lack of a link-level security which may result in eavesdropping, data corruption and data modification [10]. This may make them attractive to MITM attackers.

A HISP, which is designed to be resistant to MITM attack, can protect our solution against any MITM attack (see details in Section 3). However, different implementations may have different set-outs and policies, some MITM attacks need to be carefully examined, for example, the man-in-the-browser (MITB) attack and the MITS attack.

Other types of MITM attack can be found in *https* [41,42], Bluetooth [43]. [42] shows a more thorough discussion of MITM attacks in tunneled authentication protocols.

Man-in-the-browser attack. The MITB attack can be initiated by a MITB trojan embedded in the user's browser, for example, Zeus, Adrenaline, Sinowal and Silent Banker [27], which can then manipulate the online payment session in real-time and carry out legitimate online payments. Therefore, all the solutions that relies on or uses the security provided by web browsers to display payment details on PCs may become vulnerable to MITB attacks.

Defending against MITB attacks can be difficult. For example, the authors of MP-Auth have declared that such attacks are not addressed in their design. And a recent report [26] indicates Zeus trojan is now targeting mobile phones, and it can hijack SMS communication. This will endanger many mobile payment applications that based on SMS or use SMS authentication.

Our solution, which does not depend on any specific connection or display, can resist such attacks by carefully choosing an appropriate OOB channel (see details in Section 3.3). However, the attack on SMS (if successful) does increase the cost of security, for example, we may have to use phone call to deliver the digest value in case of an online/remote payment.

Man-in-the-shop attack. The merchant, the one we usually trust, can not guarantee the staff it hires are trustworthy. For example, we can find news like "Don't use cards at petrol stations" [39] or "Restaurant workers indicted in credit card scam" [40]. Same problem arises online – merchant might lose customers' card details or its staff steal data from the server. Various incidents of card data loss are reported on the web [34]. Therefore, users should not give out their card or account details to the merchant because of the MITS attack. Such attacks can be mitigated by using the concept of e-cheque which is discussed in Section 3.4. Or the payment may has to be made by a trusted third party: a bank or a mobile wallet service provider. And the merchant will be informed and invoiced by the trusted third party.

6   Conclusion

We have demonstrated that using a HISP on a mobile phone can help the customer to create a secure connection which "reversely authenticates" the merchant (the payee), while keeping a low-cost on human's effort. This solution helped by the flexibility of an OOB channel which assumes no existing security can be used to defeat MITM attacks as well as to allow an efficient and secure transmission of E-Identities. And the discussion of ϵ would be useful – the balance between security and usability, which can provide more guidance to future implementations of online payment solutions based on HISPs.

Acknowledgement

This project was funded in part by grants from US Office of Naval Research and the Oxford Martin School. We would like to thank Long Nguyen and Ronald Kainda for their contribution to the background of this work.

References

1. ITU Report, ITU sees 5 billion mobile subscriptions globally in 2010 (2010), http://www.itu.int/net/pressoffice/press_releases/2010/06.aspx
2. ITU Report, Personal Computers market, http://www.areppim.com/stats/stats_pcxfcst.htm
3. Srivastava, L.: Japan's ubiquitous mobile information society. J. Policy, Regulation and Strategy for Telecommunications 6(4) (2004)
4. Reuters. Dutch deal paves way for mobile payments in 2012 (2012), http://uk.reuters.com/article/idUKLDE68800C20100909
5. Finextra. China Telecom, Bank of China and China UnionPay launch mobile proximity payments, http://www.finextra.com/news/announcement.aspx?pressreleaseid=36776
6. Pasquet, M., Reynaud, J., Rosenberger, C.: Secure payment with NFC mobile phone in the smarttouch project. In: Symposium on Collaborative Technologies and Systems (2008)

7. Kadambi, K.S., Li, J., Karp, A.H.: Near-field communication-based secure mobile payment service. In: Proc. the 11th International Conference on Electronic Commerce (2009)
8. Francis, L., Hancke, G., Mayes, K., Markantonakis, K.: Practical NFC Peer-to-Peer Relay Attack Using Mobile Phones. In: Ors Yalcin, S.B. (ed.) RFIDSec 2010. LNCS, vol. 6370, pp. 35–49. Springer, Heidelberg (2010)
9. Anderson, R.: RFID and the Middleman. In: Proc. Financial Cryptography and Data Security (2007)
10. Haselsteiner, E., Breitfuss, K.: Security in Near Field Communication. In: Proc. Workshop on RFID Security (2006)
11. Bluetooth SIG. SPECIAL REPORT, Quarter 4 (2010),
    `http://signature.bluetooth.com/bluetoothsig/2010Q4?pg=22#pg22`
12. Chen, J.J., Adams, C.: Short-range wireless technologies with mobile payments systems. In: Proc. the 6th International Conference on Electronic Commerce (2004)
13. Pradhan, S., Lawrence, E., Zmijewska, A.: Bluetooth as an Enabling Technology in Mobile Transactions. In: Int'l Conference on Info. Tech.: Coding and Computing (2005)
14. Zolfaghar, K., Mohammadi, S.: Securing Bluetooth-based payment system using honeypot. In: Int'l Conference on Innovations in Info. Tech. (2009)
15. Gao, J., Edunuru, K., Cai, J., Shim, S.: P2P-Paid: A Peer-to-Peer Wireless Payment System. In: Proc. WMCS 2005 (2005)
16. Jakobsson, M., Wetzel, S.: Security Weaknesses in Bluetooth. In: Naccache, D. (ed.) CT-RSA 2001. LNCS, vol. 2020, pp. 176–191. Springer, Heidelberg (2001)
17. Mallat, N.: Exploring Consumer Adoption of Mobile Payments - A Qualitative Study. J. Strategic Information Systems 16(4), 413–432 (2007)
18. Mannan, M., van Oorschot, P.C.: Using a Personal Device to Strengthen Password Authentication from an Untrusted Computer. In: Proc. Financial Cryptography and Data Security (2008)
19. Mune, C., Gassira, R., Piccirillo, R.: Hijacking Mobile Data Connections (2009),
    `http://www.blackhat.com/presentations/bh-europe-09/Gassira_Piccirillo/`
    `BlackHat-Europe-2009-Gassira-Piccirillo-Hijacking-Mobile-Data-`
    `Connections-whitepaper.pdf`
20. Madlmayr, G., Langer, J., Kantner, C., Scharinger, J.: NFC Devices: Security and Privacy. In: Third Int'l Conference on Availability, Reliability and Security (2008)
21. Gotstev, A., Maslennikov, D.: Mobile Malware Evolution: An Overview, Part 3, `http://www.securelist.com/en/analysis/204792080/Mobile_Malware_`
    `Evolution_An_Overview_Part_3`
22. Lawton, G.: Is It Finally Time to Worry about Mobile Malware? J. Computer 41(5), 12–14 (2008)
23. Fleizach, C., Liljenstam, M., Johansson, P., Voelker, G.M., Mehes, A.: Can you infect me now?: malware propagation in mobile phone networks. In: Proc. WORM 2007 (2007)
24. Sanders, R.: From EMV to NFC: the contactless trail? J. Card Technology Today 20(3) (2008)
25. Adida, B., Bond, M., Clulow, J., Lin, A., Murdoch, S., Anderson, R.J., Rivest, R.: Phish and Chips. In: Security Protocols Workshop (2006)
26. S21sec. ZeuS Mitmo: Man-in-the-mobile, `http://securityblog.s21sec.com/`
    `2010/09/zeus-mitmo-man-in-mobile i.html`
27. RSA Lab. Making Sense of Man-in-the-browser Attacks, `http://www.rsa.com/`
    `products/consumer/whitepapers/10459_MITB_WP_0510.pdf`

28. Nguyen, L.H., Roscoe, A.W.: Authentication protocols based on low-bandwidth unspoofable channels: a comparative survey. J. Computer Security (2010)
29. Dolev, D., Yao, A.: On the security of public key protocols. IEEE Transactions on Information Theory 29(2), 198–208 (1983)
30. Nguyen, L.H., Roscoe, A.W.: Efficient group authentication protocol based on human interaction. In: Proc. FCS-ARSPA (2006)
31. Nguyen, L.H., Roscoe, A.W.: Authenticating ad hoc networks by comparison of short digests. J. Information and Computation 206 (2008)
32. Vaudenay, S.: Secure communications over insecure channels based on short authenticated strings. In: Shoup, V. (ed.) CRYPTO 2005. LNCS, vol. 3621, pp. 309–326. Springer, Heidelberg (2005)
33. Laur, S., Nyberg, K.: Efficient Mutual Data Authentication Using Manually Authenticated Strings. In: Proc. Cryptology and Network Security (2006)
34. Dataloss, http://datalossdb.org/search?query=card
35. Kainda, R., Flechais, I., Roscoe, A.W.: Usability and Security of Out-Of-Band Channels in Secure Device Pairing Protocols. In: Proc. SOUPS (2009)
36. NIST. Security Requirement for Cryptographic Modules. FIPS 140-2 (2002)
37. NIST. Recommendation for Key Management. SP 800-57 (2007)
38. NIST. Cryptographic Algorithms and Key Sizes for Personal Identity Verification. SP 800-78 (2010)
39. Times Online. Don't use cards at petrol stations, http://www.timesonline.co.uk/tol/money/consumer_affairs/article1400176.ece
40. Startribune. Metro restaurant workers indicted in credit card scam, http://www.startribune.com/local/west/102029153.html
41. Callegati, F., Cerroni, W., Ramilli, M.: Man-in-the-Middle Attack to the HTTPS Protocol. IEEE Security & Privacy (2009)
42. Asokan, N., Niemi, V., Nyberg, K.: Man-in-the-Middle in Tunnelled Authentication Protocols. In: Security Protocols Workshop (2005)
43. Kügler, D.: "Man in the middle" attacks on bluetooth. In: Wright, R.N. (ed.) FC 2003. LNCS, vol. 2742, pp. 149–161. Springer, Heidelberg (2003)
44. Tobin, D.: Open sesame: the magic car thieves. The Sunday Times (February 6, 2011)

Role-Based Secure Inter-operation and Resource Usage Management in Mobile Grid Systems

Antonios Gouglidis and Ioannis Mavridis

Department of Applied Informatics, University of Macedonia,
156 Egnatia Str., 54006, Thessaloniki, Greece
{agougl,mavridis}@uom.gr

Abstract. Dynamic inter-domain collaborations and resource sharing comprise two key characteristics of mobile Grid systems. However, inter-domain collaborations have proven to be vulnerable to conflicts that can lead to privilege escalation. These conflicts are detectable in inter-operation policies, and occur due to cross-domain role relationships. In addition, resource sharing requires to be enhanced with resource usage management in virtual organizations where mobile nodes act as resource providers. In this case the enforcement of resource usage policies and quality of service policies are required to be supported due to the limited capabilities of the devices. Yet, the ANSI INCITS 359-2004 standard RBAC model provides neither any policy conflict resolution mechanism among domains, nor any resource usage management functionality. In this paper, we propose the domRBAC model for access control in mobile Grid systems at a low administrative overhead. The domRBAC is defined as an extension of the standardized RBAC by incorporating additional functionality to cope with requirements posed by the aforementioned systems. As a result, domRBAC facilitates collaborations among domains under secure inter-operation, and provides support for resource usage management in the context of multi-domain computing environments, where mobile nodes operate as first-class entities.

Keywords: mobile Grid, role based access control (RBAC), secure inter-operation, resource usage management, cross-domain authorization.

1 Introduction

In recent years, Grid computing has become the focal point of science and enterprise computer environments. The Grid is an emergent technology that can be defined as a system able to share resources and provide problem solving in a co-ordinated manner within dynamic, multi-institutional virtual organizations [9]. This definition depends mostly on the sharing of resources and the collaboration of individual users or groups within the same or among different virtual organizations, in a service oriented approach. In turn, mobile Grid systems incorporate additional complexity and new challenges, due to the support of dynamic virtual organizations and the commercialization of Grid services [25]. Access control, in

C.A. Ardagna and J. Zhou (Eds.): WISTP 2011, LNCS 6633, pp. 38–53, 2011.

such computing systems, is an active research area given the challenges and complex applications. The role of access control is to control and limit the actions or operations in a system performed by a user on a set of resources. In brief, it enforces the access control policy of a system and it prevents the access policy from subversion [3]. An extensive research has been done in the area of access control in collaborative systems [24], [28]. Nonetheless, further examination is demanded. This is mainly due to the partial or weak fulfilment of access control requirements in the aforementioned systems [11].

In this paper, we propose a new access control model called domRBAC to provide secure inter-operation among domains and resource usage management in collaborative systems, as the mobile Grid computing paradigm, where mobile devices can participate as first-class entities. Specifically we examine an incremental integration of individual RBAC policies into a global policy, which is suitable for dynamic virtual organizations. This is achieved via the definition of cross-domain mappings between roles. Thus, any user authorized for a role $d_i r_m$ in a domain d_i is granted access to all the permissions of its mapped role $d_j r_n$ in domain d_j. Nevertheless, inter-domain collaborations is a challenging task since they can lead to various types of conflict. Research in [10] has shown that secure inter-operation in federated systems must conform to the principles of autonomy and security. The principle of autonomy states that any access permitted within an individual system must also be permitted under secure inter-operation. Regarding the principle of security, it states that any access not permitted within an individual system must also be denied under secure inter-operation [10]. The former principles can be preserved in a collaboration, if a number of violations are successfully identified. Violations in role-based approaches, possibly leading to privilege escalation, can occur due to conflicts in cyclic inheritance and in static and dynamic separation of duty relations. In regard to resource usage management, domRBAC provides the capability of applying usage policies and, thus, enforcing quality of service rules on sharable resources. The application of resource usage policies can greatly amplify the adoption of Grid systems. For instance, it can be applied in Grid systems where ad-hoc mobile devices operate as first-class entities, or in multi-tenant environments, where usage based pricing is required.

The structure of the remainder of this paper is as follows. Section 2 provides information on related work and presents our motivation. Section 3 discuss domRBAC model in a systematic manner. A demonstration of the proposed model is given in section 4. Finally, we present our concluding remarks in section 5.

2 Relevant Work and Motivation

The access control models implemented by the existing Grid authorization mechanisms are either role based or attribute based. Role based access control (RBAC) approaches have gained considerable attention among researchers, due to ease of administration and support of a significant number of principles, namely the least privilege, separation of administrative functions and separation of duty relationships [20]. However, RBAC handles better centralized architectures and is rather weak in inter-domain collaborations. Such functionality is absent from the ANSI INCITS 359-2004 [2]. Attribute based access control (ABAC) approaches have lately gained a lot of attention due to the development of internet based distributed systems. ABAC can provide access decisions on resources based on the requestor's owned attributes. A basic advantage of ABAC in comparison to RBAC is that in the former approach it is possible to provide access to users in a collaborative environment without the need for them to be known by the resource a priori. The UCON$_{ABC}$ model [15], [19] is a representative ABAC model, based on a modern conceptual framework, which encompasses traditional access control, trust management and digital rights management for the protection of digital resources.

Through time, numerous RBAC-based and ABAC-based models have been proposed trying to overcome some of the limitation of their initial implementations. In regard to RBAC and secure inter-operation, research in [21] proposed an integer programming (IP)-based approach for optimal resolution of the examined conflicts. A policy integration framework is used for the merging of the individual RBAC policies into a global policy. However, this approach is not dynamic, since the global policy is not a result of an incremental composition of the inter-domain policies. In [6] an inter-domain role-mapping approach based on the least privilege principle is suggested. Yet, the applied greedy algorithm may not compute optimal solutions, and from a security perspective may fail to find a safe solution. Research in [22] presents a protocol for secure inter-operation, which is based on the idea of access paths and access paths constraints. Nonetheless, the protocol does not check for violations during an inter-domain role assignment. Rather, it assumes that inter-domain role mappings already exist. In [26] the DRBAC is presented as a dynamic context-aware access control model for Grid applications. However, the management of inter-domain policies is not tackled. Resource usage management, to the best of our knowledge, is completely absent from the existing RBAC-based models. On the contrary, usage control was a subject of research in the UCON conceptual framework [15], [19], that is an ABAC model with the capability of enforcing RBAC policies. Nevertheless, UCON lacks administrative models and requires synchronized attribute acquisition and management that makes it more complex when applied to large systems.

In Grid systems, the existence of various access control models, inevitably led to the implementation of different Grid authorization mechanisms. Additionally, each mechanism tried to further implement features not intrinsically supported by the implemented model (i.e. support of inter-domain collaborations, quality of service and so on). Representative authorization mechanisms in Grid systems are the Community Authorization Service (CAS) [16], the Virtual Organization Membership Service (VOMS) [1], Akenti [23], PERMIS [4], [5], and Usage Based Authorization [27]. Regarding mobile Grid systems various architectures have been proposed to provide solutions, as the virtual cluster approach in [17], the mobile OGSI.NET [7] and the Akogrimo project [18]. Yet, the proposed authorization mechanisms are complementary to existing Grid authorization services, as the A4C infrastructure in Akogrimo.

So far we have outlined the key requirements of mobile Grid systems for access control operation and administration, which are explicitly identified by the need for support of dynamic and secure inter-operation and interaction among the participating entities. To this extent, the examined access control models do not provide a solid solution to cope with these requirements of mobile Grid systems. Nonetheless, they are mostly targeted to general-purpose collaborative systems. Furthermore, the support of resource usage policies, in order to tackle the enforcement of quality of service policies is absent from RBAC family of models and only supported by the UCON conceptual framework. However, as discussed, ABAC solutions are prone to complexity when applied to large systems and lack administrative models. Therefore, we propose the domRBAC model, which combines the virtues of RBAC-based models and provides in addition resource usage management functionality in order to support modern Grid systems, as described in detail in the next section.

3 The Proposed domRBAC Model for Modern Collaborative Systems

The domRBAC model is an access control model capable of enforcing restrictive access control policies in collaborative systems, as the mobile Grid computing paradigm. The domRBAC model is based on the ANSI INCITS 359-2004 [2]. Thus, it supports all the components of the RBAC model, namely the core RBAC, hierarchical RBAC, static separation of duty relations, and dynamic of duty relations. However, domRBAC is enriched with additional functionality to cope with the requirements posed by modern computing environments. In this section, we discuss domRBAC model in a systematic manner.

3.1 domRBAC Elements

The domRBAC model consists of the following six basic elements: users, roles, sessions, operations, objects, and containers. Furthermore, domRBAC can support access control among domains. A domain can be defined as a protected computer environment, consisted of users and resources under an access control policy. This is done to cope with the problem of governing inter-operations among domains. Figure 1 illustrates the proposed access control model.

Sessions, objects and operations are three concepts that are commonly used in access control. The latter two form a new element of permissions. A permission or a privilege is an approval to perform an operation on one or more RBAC protected objects. In domRBAC, the aforementioned elements provide the same functionality in their familiar sense. As in all role-based models, sessions are dynamic elements. They are used as intermediary entities between the users and roles elements. The user element usually depicts a physical person who interfaces with a computer system. User elements, in role-based models, are assigned to role elements and vice-versa. Sessions, in role-based models, are used to enforce dynamic security policies to computing systems. Each user can be

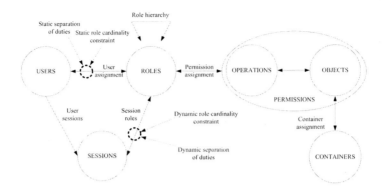

Fig. 1. The domRBAC access control model

associated with many sessions, and each session may have a combination of many active roles. Regarding objects, they are used to represent an entity in a computing system. Control of access to objects can be coarse-grained or fine-grained, depending on the computing system. For instance, the sharing of files and exhaustible system resources can be considered as an example of course-grained access control. On the contrary, the granting of access in a database on the level of record or field is an example of fine-grained access control. Yet, in domRBAC, an object can be associated with many container elements. The container element is explained in detail later in this section. Lastly, the element of operations provides a set of allowed operations on objects. Both operations and objects are system dependent. This means that different type of operations applies to different objects.

Roles in domRBAC are enriched with the notion of domains, and are expressed in pairs of domains and roles. For the naming of the roles, we use the *DomainRole* notation. Thus, the *Domain* prefix indicates the role's domain name, and the *Role* suffix indicates the name of the role. A formal definition is given later in definition 1.ii. The naming notation is used only for the element of roles. Nonetheless, when assigning users or permissions to roles, it is understood that the former two are also bound by the role's domain name. Through the role's naming convention, the domRBAC model can distinguish the security policies enforced among the autonomous domains.

The container is an abstract element that incorporates additional decision factors employed by the access decision function. The container can handle both environment and usage level information. The environment attributes are used to set time constraints, spatial information and so on and so forth. Yet, the usage level attributes can limit the usage of shared resources. The information specified in the container element is based on [14]. Thus, a container attribute can represent a certain property of the environment or usage levels. A container function provides a mechanism to obtain the current value of a specific container attribute. Lastly, a container condition is a predicate that compares the current value of a container attribute either with a predefined constant, or another container attribute of the same domain. A significant enhancement of domRBAC as compared to the ANSI INCITS 359-2004 is that the element of container can support resource usage policies.

Moreover, domRBAC can support additional constraints, namely static and dynamic role cardinality constraints, which can be applied to the process of role assignment and role activation, respectively. This means that the number of roles that can be assigned to and/or activated by the users of a system can be managed. The constraint of role cardinality is introduced to fulfil both requirements posed by the system administrators as well as resource owners. Administrators can use static role cardinality to limit the assignment of critical roles with users. Furthermore, dynamic role cardinality can be used for setting quality of service rules. Resource owners can manage the usage of their resources by limiting the number of users that utilizes them. Thus, it is feasible to create license agreements between users and resource owners. This leads users to receive high quality services in a computing system.

Furthermore, the domRBAC model supports the identification of inter-domain violations, in an automated way, to avoid privilege escalation. The inter-domain violations are caused due to new immediate inter-domain role inheritance relations. The supported violations are: cyclic inheritance, violation of static separation of duty relations in a domain, and violation of dynamic separation of duty relations in a domain. Formal definitions are given later in this section in the Z formal description language [12] as in the ANSI INCITS 359-2004.

3.2   domRBAC Definitions

Definition 1. The core domRBAC.

The formal definition of core domRBAC model is based on [2], and is extended as follows:

i. USERS, ROLES, OPS, OBS, CNTRS, stands for users, roles, operations, objects and containers, respectively.

ii. $d_{domain}r_{role} \in$ ROLES is a role expressed in a DomainRole format, where Domain denotes a domain name and Role denotes a role name. For example, if a role r_m belongs to a domain d_i, we write d_ir_m.

iii. UA $\subseteq$ USERS $\times$ ROLES, a many-to-many mapping user-to-role assignment relation.

iv. assigned_users(d_ir_m:ROLES) $\rightarrow 2^{USERS}$, the mapping of role d_ir_m onto a set of users.
    Formal definition: assigned_users(d_ir_m) = {u $\in$ USERS | (u,d_ir_m) $\in$ UA}.

v. PRMS $= 2^{(OPS \times OBS)}$, the set of permissions.

vi. PA $\subseteq$ PRMS $\times$ ROLES, a many-to-many mapping permission-to-role assignment relation.

vii. assigned_permissions(d_ir_m:ROLES) $\rightarrow 2^{PRMS}$, the mapping of role d_ir_m onto a set of permissions.
    Formal definition: assigned_permissions(d_ir_m)={p $\in$ PRMS | (p,d_ir_m) $\in$ PA}.

viii. $CA \subseteq CNTRS \times OBS$, a many-to-many mapping container-to-object assignment relation.

ix. assigned_containers(o: OBS) $\rightarrow 2^{CNTRS}$, the mapping of object o onto a set of containers.
   Formal definition: assigned_containers(o)={c $\in$ CNTRS | (c,o) $\in$ CA}.

x. Op(p: PRMS) $\rightarrow \{op \subseteq OPS\}$, the permission to operation mapping, which gives the set of operations associated with permission p.

xi. Ob(p: PRMS) $\rightarrow \{ob \subseteq OBS\}$, the permission to object mapping, which gives the set of objects associated with permission p.

xii. SESSIONS = the set of sessions.

xiii. session_user(s: SESSIONS) $\rightarrow$ USERS, the mapping of session s onto a corresponding user.

xiv. session_roles(s: SESSIONS) $\rightarrow 2^{ROLES}$, the mapping of session s onto a set of roles.
   Formal definition: session_roles$(s) \subseteq \{d_i r_m \in$ ROLES$|$(session_user$(s),d_j r_m)$ $\in UA\}$.

xv. avail_session_perms(s: SESSIONS) $\rightarrow 2^{PRMS}$, the permissions available to a user in a session $= \bigcup_{d_i r_m \in session\_roles(s)} assigned\_permissions(d_i r_m)$.

Definition 2. Hierarchical domRBAC.
The hierarchical domRBAC is defined to cope with inter-domain role inheritance relations, and is enriched with notations from the theory of graphs. The reason why we choose to use the latter type of notation is bilateral. Firstly, graphs help in the visualisation of inter-domain role inheritance relations. Secondly, adjacency matrixes make it easy to find sub-graphs and adjacency queries are fast. Henceforth, we use i and j to refer to domains, where $i = j$ if we refer to an intra-domain relation, and $i \overset{+}{=} j$ if we refer to inter-domain relations ($intra - domain \subseteq inter - domain$).

i. $RH \subseteq ROLES \times ROLES$ is a partial order on $ROLES$ called the inheritance relation, written as $\geq$, where $d_i r_m \geq d_j r_n$ only if all permissions of $d_j r_n$ are also permissions of $d_i r_m$, and all users of $d_i r_m$ are also users of $d_j r_n$, i.e., $d_i r_m \geq d_j r_n$.
   $\Rightarrow authorized\_permissions(d_j r_n) \subseteq authorized\_permissions(d_i r_m)$.

ii. $authorized\_users_{(i,j)}(d_i r_m : ROLES) \rightarrow 2^{USERS}$, the mapping of role $d_i r_m$ onto a set of users on the presence of a role hierarchy.
   Formal definition: $authorized\_users_{(i,j)}(d_i r_m) = \{u \in USERS | d_j r_n \geq d_i r_m, (u, d_j r_n) \in UA\}$.

iii. $authorized\_permissions_{(i,j)}(d_i r_m : ROLES) \rightarrow 2^{PRMS}$, the mapping of role $d_i r_m$ onto a set of permissions in the presence of a role hierarchy.
   Formal definition: $authorized\_permissions_{(i,j)}(d_i r_m) = \{p \in PRMS | d_j r_n \geq d_i r_m, (p, d_j r_n) \in PA\}$.

iv. $G = (V, E)$ is the inter-domain role hierarchy directed graph, which consists of a finite, nonempty set of role vertices $V \subset ROLES$ and a set of edges E. Each edge is an ordered pair $(d_i r_m, d_j r_n)$, $i \overset{+}{=} j$ of role vertices that indicates the following relation: $d_i r_m \geq d_j r_n$.

v. A path in a G graph is a sequence of edges $(d_i r_1, d_i r_2)$, $(d_i r_2, d_i r_3)$, ..., $(d_i r_{n-1}, d_i r_n)$. This path is from role vertex $d_i r_1$ to role vertex $d_i r_n$ and has length n-1. The path represents not immediate inheritance relation between role vertex $d_i r_1$ and $d_i r_n$.

vi. A_G is the adjacency matrix representation for graph $G = (V, E)$, which is a $|V| \times |V|$ matrix, where $A_G[d_i r_m, d_j r_n] = 1$ if there is an edge from role vertex $d_i r_m$ to role vertex $d_j r_n$, and $A_G[d_i r_m, d_j r_n] = 0$ otherwise.

vii. Given a directed graph $G = (V, E)$ with adjacency matrix A_G, we compute a boolean matrix T_G such that $T_G[d_i r_m, d_j r_n]$ is 1 if there is a path from $d_i r_m$ to $d_j r_n$ of length 1 or more, and 0 otherwise. We call T the transitive closure of the adjacency matrix. For the computation of the transitive closure, the algorithm in [13] can be used. The algorithm computes the transitive closure of G in $O(|V|^3)$ time and $O(|V|^2)$ space.

viii. An adjacency list representation for graph $G = (V, E)$ is an array L of $|V|$ lists, one for each role vertex in V. For each role vertex $d_i r_m$, there is a pointer $L_{d_i r_m}$ to a linked list containing all the role vertices that are adjacent to $d_i r_m$.

ix. $DESCENDANT\_ROLES_{d_i r_m} \subseteq ROLES$ is a set that contains the role vertices of adjacency list $L_{d_i r_m}$. Thus, $DESCENDANT\_ROLES_{d_i r_m}$ contains all the roles in the inter-domain collaboration that are immediate or not immediate descendant roles of a given role $d_i r_m$.

Definition 3. Constrained domRBAC.
Apart from the support of static and dynamic separation of duty constraints in each domain, domRBAC supports static and dynamic role cardinality constraints. Static role cardinality constraints can restrict the number of users assigned to a role, to a maximum number. Moreover, dynamic role cardinality constraints can restrict the number of users that activate a role, to a maximum number in all concurrent sessions. In the following, we redefine SSD and DSD in the presence of domains, and we define static and dynamic role cardinality.

i. **Static Separation of duty (SSD):** SSD $\subseteq (2^{ROLES} \times N)$ is a collection of pairs $(d_i rs,n)$ in SSD, where each $d_i rs$ is a role set in a domain d_i, t a subset of roles in $d_i rs$, and n is a natural number ≥ 2, with the property that no user of domain d_i is assigned to n or more roles from the set $d_i rs$ in each $(d_i rs,n) \in$ SSD.
Formal definition:
$\forall (d_i rs, n) \in SSD, \forall t \subseteq d_i rs : |t| \geq n \Rightarrow \bigcap_{d_i r_m \in t} assigned\_users(d_i r_m) = \emptyset.$

ii. **SSD in the presence of a hierarchy:** In the presence of a role hierarchy SSD is redefined based on authorized users rather than assigned users as follows:
Formal definition:
$\forall (d_i rs, n) \in SSD, i = j, \forall t \subseteq d_i rs : |t| \geq n$
$\Rightarrow \bigcap_{d_i r_m \in t} authorized\_users_{(i,j)}(d_i r_m) = \emptyset.$

iii. **Dynamic Separation of Duty (DSD):** DSD $\subseteq (2^{ROLES} \times N)$ is a collection of pairs (d_irs,n) in DSD, where each d_irs is a role set and n a natural number ≥ 2, with the property that no subject may activate n or more roles from the set d_irs in each dsd $\in$ DSD.

Formal definition:

$\forall d_irs \in 2^{ROLES}, n \in \mathbb{N}, (d_irs, n) \in DSD \Rightarrow n \geq 2.|d_irs| \geq n$, and

$\forall s \in SESSIONS, \forall d_irs \in 2^{ROLES}$,

$\forall role\_subset \in 2^{ROLES}, \forall n \in \mathbb{N}, (d_irs, n) \in DSD$,

$role\_subset \subseteq d_irs, role\_subset \subseteq session\_roles(s) \Rightarrow |role\_subset| < n$.

iv. **Static role cardinality (SRC):** If static role cardinality constraint is required for any role d_ir_m, then d_ir_m cannot be assigned to more than a maximum number of users.

SRC $\subseteq (ROLES \times N)$ is a collection of pairs (d_ir_m, n) in static role cardinality, where d_ir_m is a role r_m in a domain d_i and n is a natural number ≥ 0, with the property that the number of users assigned with role d_ir_m cannot exceed the number n in each $(d_ir_m, n) \in$ SRC.

Formal definition:

$d_ir_m \in ROLES, n \in \mathbb{N}, n \geq 0$,

$\forall (d_ir_m, n) \in SRC \Rightarrow |assigned\_users(d_ir_m)| \leq n$.

v. **SRC in the presence of a hierarchy:** In the presence of a role hierarchy static role cardinality constraint is redefined based on authorized users rather than assigned users as follows:

$d_ir_m \in ROLES, i \overset{+}{=} j, n \in \mathbb{N}, n \geq 0$,

$\forall (d_ir_m, n) \in SRC \Rightarrow |authorized\_users_{(i,j)}(d_ir_m)| \leq n$.

vi. **Dynamic role cardinality constraint (DRC):** If dynamic role cardinality is required for any role d_ir_m, then d_ir_m cannot be activated for more than a maximum number of authorized users in all concurrent sessions of a system.

DRC $\subseteq (ROLES \times N)$ is a collection of pairs (d_ir_m, n) in dynamic role cardinality, where d_ir_m is a role r_m and n is a natural number ≥ 0, with the property that the number of concurrent role activations by users authorized for role d_ir_m cannot exceed the number n.

Formal definition:

$d_ir_m \in ROLES, n \in \mathbb{N}, n \geq 0$,

$\forall s \in SESSIONS, (d_ir_m,n) \in DRC \Rightarrow \sum |d_ir_m \cap session\_roles(s)| \leq n$.

After defining both the container element and the DRC constraint, we elaborate on the supported types of resource usage policies. The first type is via the container element, by declaring the required attribute value, function and condition of the container. However, this type of resource usage policy is unable to provide quality of service to consumers, since each container element restricts the usage of a resource on per role activation. A second type of resource usage policy with quality of service capabilities is provided via the combination of the container element and DRC constraint. This type of resource usage policy enforcement restricts the usage of a resource on all concurrent role activations.

Definition 4. Role Inheritance Management in domRBAC.
The domRBAC model aims at providing a comprehensive solution to secure inter-operation based on the principles of autonomy, security and containment. In order to establish a secure inter-operation among the participating domains, domRBAC provides two new administrative commands for managing inter-domain role inheritance relations. The administrative commands can be used by the administrator of each domain, according to the inter-operability require-ments of each system. Their objective is to check for a number of violations before committing an inter-domain role inheritance relation. Thus, based on the defini-tions 4.i, 4.ii and 4.iii, we introduce the *InterdomainPolicyViolation* function for the checking of inter-domain violations due to the inter-domain role inheritance relations, and two new inter-domain administrative commands *AddInterdomain-Inheritance* and *DeleteInterdomainInheritance* for establishing and discarding immediate inter-domain inheritance relationships, respectively. Our approach utilizes algorithms derived from the theory of graphs. Intra-domain management not listed below is handled the same as in the ANSI INCITS 359-2004.

i. **Inter-domain violation of role assignment:** As stated in [21] an inter-domain policy causes a violation of role assignment constraint of domain d_i if it is allowed to a user u of domain d_i to access a local role $d_i r_m$ even though u is not directly assigned to $d_i r_m$ or any of the roles that are senior to $d_i r_m$ in the role hierarchy of domain d_i.

We identify role assignment violations by checking for cyclic inheritance in the inter-domain role hierarchy graph. Role assignment violations can occur due to the addition of a new immediate inter-domain inheritance relationship $d_i r_{m_{asc}} \gg d_j r_{n_{desc}}$ between existing roles $d_i r_{m_{asc}}, d_j r_{n_{desc}}$, where $d_i r_{m_{asc}}$ is a role ascendant of $d_j r_{n_{desc}}$.

The algorithm for detecting inter-domain violations of role assignment is given in Table 1.

ii. **Intra-domain violation of SSD relationships:** An inter-domain policy causes an intra-domain violation of SSD relationships of domain d_i if it is allowed to a user u of domain d_i to be assigned to any two conflicting roles

Table 1. Inter-domain violation of role assignment algorithm

1.	**ci_violation**$(d_i r_{m_{asc}}, d_j r_{n_{desc}})$: **boolean**
2.	**for each** $d_i r \in DESCENDANT\_ROLES_{d_i r_{m_{asc}}}$
3.	**for each** $d_j r \in DESCENDANT\_ROLES_{d_j r_{n_{desc}}}$
4.	**if not** $((T_G[d_i r_{m_{asc}}, d_i r] = 0$ **or**
5.	$(T_G[d_i r_{m_{asc}}, d_i r] = 1$ **and** $d_i r_{m_{asc}} \geq d_i r))$ **and**
6.	$(T_G[d_j r_{n_{desc}}, d_j r] = 0$ **or**
7.	$(T_G[d_j r_{n_{desc}}, d_j r] = 1$ **and** $d_j r_{n_{desc}} \geq d_j r)))$
8.	**then**
9.	**return true**
10.	**return false**

$d_i r_m$ and $d_i r_n$ of domain d_i. We identify violations of SSD relationships, using the following properties [8]:

Property 1: If there are two roles $d_i r_m$ and $d_j r_n$ that are mutually exclusive, then neither one should inherit the other, either directly or indirectly.

Property 2: If there are two roles $d_i r_m$ and $d_j r_n$ that are mutually exclusive, then there can be no third role that inherits both of them.

The algorithm for detecting intra-domain violations of SSD relationships is given in Table 2. Specifically, *Property 1* is maintained in lines 6-7, and *Property 2* in lines 8-9.

Table 2. Intra-domain violation of SSD relationships

1.   **ssd_violation**$(d_i r_{m_{asc}}, d_j r_{n_{desc}})$: **boolean**
2. $d_i r \in DESCENDANT\_ROLES_{d_i r_{m_{asc}}}$
3. $d_j r \in DESCENDANT\_ROLES_{d_j r_{n_{desc}}}$
4.   **for each** $(d_i r_m, d_i r_n) \in SSD_{d_i}$
5.   **for each** $(d_j r_m, d_j r_n) \in SSD_{d_j}$
6.   **if not** $(T_G[d_i r_m, d_i r_n] = 0$ **and** $T_G[d_i r_n, d_i r_m] = 0$ **and**
7. $T_G[d_j r_m, d_j r_n] = 0$ **and** $T_G[d_j r_n, d_j r_m] = 0$ **and**
8. $T_G[d_i r, d_i r_m] = 0$ **and** $T_G[d_i r, d_i r_n] = 0$ **and**
9. $T_G[d_j r, d_j r_m] = 0$ **and** $T_G[d_j r, d_j r_n] = 0)$
10.   **then**
11.   **return true**
12.   **return false**

iii. **Intra-domain violation of DSD relationships:** An inter-domain policy causes an intra-domain violation of DSD relationships of domain d_i if it is allowed to a user u of domain d_i to activate any two conflicting roles $d_i r_m$ and $d_i r_n$ of domain d_i. We identify violations of DSD relationships similarly to definition 4.ii due to the following property [8]:

Property 3: If SSD holds, then DSD is maintained. Thus, properties 1 and 2 must be guaranteed.

The algorithm for detecting intra-domain violations of DSD relationships is given in Table 3.

iv. **InterdomainPolicyViolation:** This function checks if violations 4.i, 4.ii and 4.iii occur during an inter-domain role inheritance relation. It returns **true** if a violation occurs from an inter-domain role association, and **false** otherwise. Table 4 presents the implementation of the function.

v. **AddInterdomainInheritance:** This command establishes a new immediate inter-domain inheritance relationship $d_i r_{m_{asc}} \gg d_j r_{n_{desc}}$ between existing roles $d_i r_{m_{asc}}, d_j r_{n_{desc}}$. The command is valid if and only if $d_i r_{m_{asc}}$ and $d_j r_{n_{desc}}$ are members of the $ROLES$ dataset, $d_i r_{m_{asc}}$ is not an immediate ascendant of $d_j r_{n_{desc}}$, and violations of role assignment and of SSD and DSD relationships do not occur.

Table 3. Intra-domain violation of DSD relationships

1.	**dsd_violation**$(d_i r_{m_{asc}}, d_j r_{n_{desc}})$: **boolean**
2.	$d_i r \in DESCENDANT\_ROLES_{d_i r_{m_{asc}}}$
3.	$d_j r \in DESCENDANT\_ROLES_{d_j r_{n_{desc}}}$
4.	**for each** $(d_i r_m, d_i r_n) \in DSD_{d_i}$
5.	**for each** $(d_j r_m, d_j r_n) \in DSD_{d_j}$
6.	**if not** $(T_G[d_i r_m, d_i r_n] = 0$ **and** $T_G[d_i r_n, d_i r_m] = 0$ **and**
7.	$T_G[d_j r_m, d_j r_n] = 0$ **and** $T_G[d_j r_n, d_j r_m] = 0$ **and**
8.	$T_G[d_i r, d_i r_m] = 0$ **and** $T_G[d_i r, d_i r_n] = 0$ **and**
9.	$T_G[d_j r, d_j r_m] = 0$ **and** $T_G[d_j r, d_j r_n] = 0)$
10.	**then**
11.	**return true**
12.	**return false**

Table 4. Inter-domain policy violation function

1.	**InterdomainPolicyViolation**$(d_i r_{m_{asc}}, d_j r_{n_{desc}})$: **boolean**
2.	**return ci_violation**$(d_i r_{m_{asc}}, d_j r_{n_{desc}})$ **or**
3.	**ssd_violation**$(d_i r_{m_{asc}}, d_j r_{n_{desc}})$ **or**
4.	**dsd_violation**$(d_i r_{m_{asc}}, d_j r_{n_{desc}})$

Formal definition:

$AddInterdomainInheritance(d_i r_{m_{asc}}, d_j r_{n_{desc}} : NAME) \lhd$

$d_i r_{m_{asc}}, d_j r_{n_{desc}} \in ROLES;$

$InterdomainPolicyViolation(d_i r_{m_{asc}}, d_j r_{n_{desc}}) = false;$

$\neg(d_i r_{m_{asc}} \gg d_j r_{n_{desc}}); \neg(d_j r_{n_{desc}} \ge d_i r_{m_{asc}})$

$\ge' = \ge \cup \{dr, dq : ROLES | dr \ge d_i r_{m_{asc}} \wedge d_j r_{n_{desc}} \ge dq \bullet dr \mapsto dq\} \rhd$

vi. **DeleteInterdomainInheritance:** This command deletes an existing immediate inter-domain inheritance relationship $d_i r_{m_{asc}} \gg d_j r_{n_{desc}}$. The command is valid if and only if the roles $d_i r_{m_{asc}}$ and $d_j r_{n_{desc}}$ are members of the $ROLES$ dataset, and $d_i r_{m_{asc}}$ is an immediate ascendant of $d_j r_{n_{desc}}$. The new inter-domain inheritance relation is computed as the reflexive-transitive closure of the immediate inheritance relation resulted after deleting the relationship $d_i r_{m_{asc}} \gg d_j r_{n_{desc}}$.

Formal definition:

$DeleteInterdomainInheritance(d_i r_{m_{asc}}, d_j r_{n_{desc}} : NAME) \lhd$

$d_i r_{m_{asc}}, d_j r_{n_{desc}} \in ROLES; (d_i r_{m_{asc}} \gg d_j r_{n_{desc}})$

$\ge' = (\gg \{d_i r_{m_{asc}} \mapsto d_j r_{n_{desc}}\})^* \rhd$

4   Use Cases

In this section, we describe two contrived use cases to demonstrate the newly introduced functionality of domRBAC. The first use case demonstrates how to enforce resource usage policies, and the second how to identify security violations in an inter-domain role inheritance relation.

4.1   Use Case 1: Resource Usage Management

Figure 2(a) shows a simple policy in a domain d_1. Role $d_1 r_a$ is a role senior to $d_1 r_b$. User Alice requires to share the CPU cycles of her mobile device. Since the CPU capabilities of the device are limited, she decides to share only 50% of her CPU cycles, and to provide to each consumer at most 5% of her sharable CPU cycles. In order to apply the aforementioned policy, role $d_1 r_b$ is assigned to permission $P_{UC} = (Usage, CPU)$. This means that a usage operation is assigned to a CPU object. A container c_B is assigned to object CPU. Container c_B has the following properties: a container attribute that defines the CPU usage value equal to 5%, a container function that returns the current CPU usage, and a container condition $\leq$. Moreover, a DRC constraint is applied to limit the number of active users to 10 ($DRC_{d_1 r_b} = (d_1 r_b, 10)$). The latter constraint assures that the number of concurrent active users cannot exceed the 10 users. Thus, in conjunction with the container element it is assured that the usage of CPU not exceed the 50%, and that each consumer receive at most 5% of CPU. If the DRC constraint was omitted, Alice would not be able to limit the usage of her resources, nor guarantee 5% of CPU usage to the consumers.

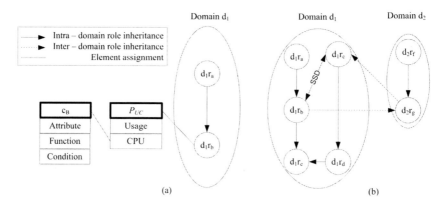

Fig. 2. (a) Resource usage management use case. (b) Security violation use case.

4.2   Use Case 2: Security Violation

Figure 2(b) shows a multi-domain policy that allows collaboration between domain d_1 and domain d_2. Domain d_1 has the following roles: $d_1 r_a$, $d_1 r_b$, $d_1 r_c$, $d_1 r_d$ and $d_1 r_e$. Role $d_1 r_a$ inherits all permissions of $d_1 r_b$ which further inherits $d_1 r_e$. Role $d_1 r_c$ inherits all permissions of $d_1 r_d$ which further inherits $d_1 r_e$. A static separation of duty relation is specified for $d_1 r_b$ and $d_1 r_c$ meaning that these roles cannot be assigned to the same user simultaneously. Domain d_2 has the following roles: d_2r_f and d_2r_g. Role d_2r_f inherits all permissions of d_2r_g. The policy defines the following inter-operation between domains d_1 and d_2.

  i. Role d_1r_b inherits all the permissions available to role d_2r_g.
  ii. Role d_2r_g inherits all the permissions available to role d_1r_c.

However, the multi-domain policy leads to a violation of a SSD relationship in domain d_1. It allows d_1r_b to access the permissions of role d_1r_c through d_2r_g. Policy i does not raise any of the discussed violations. Regarding policy ii we work as follows:

Step 1. We assume that policy ii can be enforced.
Step 2. We construct the adjacency matrix A_G, which contains the inter-domain role hierarchy and we compute the sets of descendant roles for the two roles used in the multi-domain policy.

$$A_G = \begin{array}{c} \\ d_1r_a \\ d_1r_b \\ d_1r_c \\ d_1r_d \\ d_1r_e \\ d_2r_f \\ d_2r_g \end{array} \begin{array}{ccccccc} d_1r_a & d_1r_b & d_1r_c & d_1r_d & d_1r_e & d_2r_f & d_2r_g \\ \left(\begin{array}{ccccccc} 0 & 1 & 0 & 0 & 0 & 0 & 0 \\ 0 & 0 & 0 & 0 & 1 & 0 & 1 \\ 0 & 0 & 0 & 1 & 0 & 0 & 0 \\ 0 & 0 & 0 & 0 & 1 & 0 & 0 \\ 0 & 0 & 0 & 0 & 0 & 0 & 0 \\ 0 & 0 & 0 & 0 & 0 & 1 & 0 \\ 0 & 0 & 1 & 0 & 0 & 0 & 0 \end{array}\right) \end{array}$$

$DESCENDANT\_ROLES_{d_2r_g} = \{d_1r_c, d_1r_d, d_1r_e\}$, and
$DESCENDANT\_ROLES_{d_1r_c} = \{d_1r_d, d_1r_e\}$.
Step 3. We call function $InterdomainPolicyViolation$ with function parameters d_2r_g and d_1r_c, and we compute the $ssd\_violation(d_2r_g, d_1r_c)$. Based on definition 4.ii: $T_G[d_1r_b, d_1r_c] = 1 \Rightarrow ssd\_violation(d_2r_g, d_1r_c) = true$. The identification of a inter-domain violation of SSD relation will discard the inter-domain inheritance relationship, assumed in the hypothesis of step 1.

5   Conclusion

The proposed domRBAC model is an extended RBAC model with enhancements stemmed from a list of requirements from mobile Grid systems and commercialized applications. The applied enhancements result in a robust, scalable and dynamic access control model. The domRBAC model takes advantage of all the virtues of RBAC family of models, and additionally, encompasses features from ABAC approaches such as multi-domain support and resource usage management. Opposed to existing solutions, secure inter-operation among domains in domRBAC is achieved by checking gradually and dynamically for violations in inter-domain role inheritance relations, as required by mobile Grid systems. Furthermore, resource usage management is firstly introduced in an RBAC-based access control model, as a requirement for enforcing quality of service policies. Future work includes the design of an architecture that will implement the proposed access control model and a performance study.

References

1. Alfieri, R., Cecchini, R.L., Ciaschini, V., dell'Agnello, L., Frohner, A., Gianoli, A., Lõrentey, K., Spataro, F.: VOMS, an authorization system for virtual organizations. In: Fernández Rivera, F., Bubak, M., Gómez Tato, A., Doallo, R. (eds.) Across Grids 2003. LNCS, vol. 2970, pp. 33–40. Springer, Heidelberg (2004)
2. American National Standard Institute, I.: Ansi incits 359-2004, role based access control (2004)
3. Benantar, M.: Access Control Systems: Security, Identity Management and Trust Models. Springer-Verlag New York, Inc., New York (2005)
4. Chadwick, D.: Authorisation in grid computing. Information Security Technical Report 10(1), 33–40 (2005)
5. Chadwick, D., Otenko, A., Ball, E.: Role-based access control with x. 509 attribute certificates. IEEE Internet Computing 7(2), 62–69 (2003)
6. Chen, L., Crampton, J.: Inter-domain role mapping and least privilege. In: SAC-MAT 2007: Proceedings of the 12th ACM Symposium on Access Control Models and Technologies, pp. 157–162. ACM, New York (2007)
7. Chu, D.C., Humphrey, M.: Mobile ogsi.net: Grid computing on mobile devices. In: IEEE/ACM International Workshop on Grid Computing, pp. 182–191 (2004)
8. Ferraiolo, D.F., Kuhn, D.R., Chandramouli, R.: Role-Based Access Control. Artech House, Inc., Norwood (2003)
9. Foster, I., Kesselman, C., Tuecke, S.: The anatomy of the grid: Enabling scalable virtual organizations. International Journal of High Performance Computing Applications 15(3), 200 (2001)
10. Gong, L., Qian, X.: Computational issues in secure interoperation. IEEE Trans. Softw. Eng. 22(1), 43–52 (1996)
11. Gouglidis, A., Mavridis, I.: On the definition of access control requirements for grid and cloud computing systems. In: Doulamis, A., Mambretti, J., Tomkos, I., Varvarigou, T. (eds.) GridNets 2009. Lecture Notes of the Institute for Computer Sciences, Social Informatics and Telecommunications Engineering, vol. 25, pp. 19–26. Springer, Heidelberg (2010)
12. ISO/IEC-13568: Information technology z - formal specification notation - syntax, type system and semantics, international Standard (2002)
13. Jonathan, L., Gross, J.Y. (eds.): Handbook of Graph Theory (Discrete Mathematics and Its Applications), 1st edn. CRC, Boca Raton (2003)
14. Neumann, G., Strembeck, M.: An approach to engineer and enforce context constraints in an rbac environment. In: SACMAT 2003: Proceedings of the Eighth ACM Symposium on Access Control Models and Technologies, pp. 65–79. ACM, New York (2003)
15. Park, J., Sandhu, R.: The ucon abc usage control model. ACM Trans. Inf. Syst. Secur. 7(1), 128–174 (2004)
16. Pearlman, L., Welch, V., Foster, I., Kesselman, C., Tuecke, S.: A community authorization service for group collaboration. In: Proceedings of the Third International Workshop on Policies for Distributed Systems and Networks., pp. 50–59. IEEE, Los Alamitos (2002)
17. Phan, T., Huang, L., Dulan, C.: Challenge: integrating mobile wireless devices into the computational grid. In: Proceedings of the 8th Annual International Conference on Mobile Computing and Networking, p. 278. ACM, New York (2002)
18. Racz, P., Burgos, J., Inacio, N., Morariu, C., Olmedo, V., Villagra, V, Aguiar, R., Stiller, B.: Mobility and qos support for a commercial mobile grid in akogrimo. In: 16th IST on Mobile and Wireless Communications Summit, pp. 1–5 (2007)

19. Sandhu, R., Park, J.: Usage control: A vision for next generation access control. In: Gorodetsky, V., Popyack, L.J., Skormin, V.A. (eds.) MMM-ACNS 2003. LNCS, vol. 2776, pp. 17–31. Springer, Heidelberg (2003)
20. Sandhu, R.S., Coyne, E.J., Feinstein, H.L., Youman, C.E.: Role-based access control models. IEEE Computer 29(2), 38–47 (1996)
21. Shafiq, B., Joshi, J.B.D., Bertino, E., Ghafoor, A.: Secure interoperation in a multidomain environment employing rbac policies. IEEE Trans. on Knowl. and Data Eng. 17(11), 1557–1577 (2005)
22. Shehab, M., Bertino, E., Ghafoor, A.: Serat: Secure role mapping technique for decentralized secure interoperability. In: SACMAT 2005: Proceedings of the Tenth ACM Symposium on Access Control Models and Technologies, pp. 159–167. ACM, New York (2005)
23. Thompson, M., Essiari, A., Mudumbai, S.: Certificate-based authorization policy in a pki environment. ACM Transactions on Information and System Security (TISSEC) 6(4), 566–588 (2003)
24. Tolone, W., Ahn, G.J., Pai, T., Hong, S.P.: Access control in collaborative systems. ACM Comput. Surv. 37(1), 29–41 (2005)
25. Waldburger, M., Stiller, B.: Regulatory issues for mobile grid computing in the european union. In: 17th European Regional ITS Conference, Amsterdam, The Netherlands, pp. 1–9 (2006)
26. Zhang, G., Parashar, M.: Dynamic context-aware access control for grid applications. In: Proceedings of the Fourth International Workshop on Grid Computing 2003, pp. 101–108. IEEE, Los Alamitos (2004)
27. Zhang, X., Nakae, M., Covington, M., Sandhu, R.: A usage-based authorization framework for collaborative computing systems. In: Proceedings of the 11th ACM Symposium on Access Control Models and Technologies, pp. 180–189. ACM, New York (2006)
28. Zhang, X., Nakae, M., Covington, M.J., Sandhu, R.: Toward a usage-based security framework for collaborative computing systems. ACM Trans. Inf. Syst. Secur. 11(1), 1–36 (2008)

SSL/TLS Session-Aware User Authentication Using a GAA Bootstrapped Key

Chunhua Chen[1,*], Chris J. Mitchell[2], and Shaohua Tang[3]

[1,3] School of Computer Science and Engineering
South China University of Technology
Guangzhou 510640, China
chunhua.chen@mail.scut.edu.cn, csshtang@scut.edu.cn
[2]Information Security Group
Royal Holloway, University of London
Egham, Surrey TW20 0EX, UK
c.mitchell@rhul.ac.uk

Abstract. Most SSL/TLS-based electronic commerce (e-commerce) applications (including Internet banking) are vulnerable to man in the middle attacks. Such attacks arise since users are often unable to authenticate a server effectively, and because user authentication methods are typically decoupled from SSL/TLS session establishment. Cryptographically binding the two authentication procedures together, a process referred to here as SSL/TLS session-aware user authentication (TLS-SA), is a lightweight and effective countermeasure. In this paper we propose a means of implementing TLS-SA using a GAA bootstrapped key. The scheme employs a GAA-enabled user device with a display and an input capability (e.g. a 3G mobile phone) and a GAA-aware server. We describe a simple instantiation of the scheme which makes the password authentication mechanism SSL/TLS session-aware; in addition we describe two possible variants that give security-efficiency trade-offs. Analysis shows that the scheme is effective, secure and scalable. Moreover, the approach fits well to the multi-institution scenario.

Keywords: man in the middle, SSL/TLS session-aware user authentication, Generic Authentication Architecture.

1 Introduction

Most current e-commerce applications (including Internet banking) employ the Secure Socket Layer (SSL) [12] or the Transport Layer Security (TLS) protocol[1] [9] to cryptographically protect the communication channel between the

---

* The author is a PhD student at the South China University of Technology. This work was performed during a visit to the Information Security Group at Royal Holloway, University of London, sponsored by the Chinese Scholarship Council and the Natural Science Foundation of Guangdong Province, China (No. 9351064101000003).

[1] The minor differences between SSL and TLS are not relevant here, and we thus refer to them jointly as SSL/TLS throughout.

C.A. Ardagna and J. Zhou (Eds.): WISTP 2011, LNCS 6633, pp. 54–68, 2011.

client and the server. Typically, when establishing the SSL/TLS session, the server authenticates itself to the client using a public key certificate. Although the client could also authenticate itself to the server using a public key certificate (an option in the SSL/TLS protocol), in practice this rarely takes place since very few clients have the necessary key pair and certificate [19]. Instead, SSL/TLS-based applications typically employ a separate user authentication protocol on top of SSL/TLS, e.g. using a password, personal identification number (PIN), or a more sophisticated mechanism such as a one-time password system.

The SSL/TLS protocol appears reasonably sound, and the security issues so far identified [20,26] appear to be relatively minor. However, in practice, the SSL/TLS protocol does not provide a high level of security because it requires the user to verify with whom the client system is communicating, a task that is often poorly performed [8]. Man in the middle attacks arise precisely because of this shortcoming and the fact that the user authentication process is decoupled from SSL/TLS session establishment. Consequently, any effective countermeasure against these man in the middle attacks in an SSL/TLS setting must either enforce proper server authentication or combine the user authentication process with SSL/TLS session establishment. Oppliger et al. [23,25] introduced the term SSL/TLS session-aware user authentication (TLS-SA) to describe the latter countermeasure, and proposed an approach of this type using a non-user-specific hardware token that shares a secret key with the server. However, this pre-shared key based approach has a number of disadvantages (see also section 3).

Universal Mobile Telecommunications System (UMTS) networks have been widely deployed, and there are a huge number of subscription holders across the world. The Generic Authentication Architecture (GAA) [3] exploits the UMTS authentication infrastructure to enable the provision of security services, including key establishment, to third party mobile and Internet applications. In essence, GAA makes use of the UMTS Authentication and Key Agreement (UMTS AKA) protocol [2] to bootstrap application-specific session keys between GAA-enabled devices and GAA-aware servers.

To avoid the disadvantages of the pre-shared key based approach, we propose a means of implementing TLS-SA using a GAA bootstrapped key. The scheme employs a GAA-enabled user device with a display and an input capability (e.g. a 3G mobile phone) and a GAA-aware server, and binds the user authentication process to the TLS session without modifying the operation of TLS. Analysis shows that the scheme is effective, secure, scalable and has a degree of flexibility enabling security-efficiency trade-offs. Moreover, the approach fits well to the multi-institution scenario. The rest of this paper is organised as follows. In section 2 we describe relevant background. In section 3 we survey related work with an emphasis on TLS-SA. In section 4 we propose the GAA-based approach, and also describe two possible variants that give security-efficiency trade-offs. In section 5 we present a security analysis, and in section 6 we draw conclusions.

2   Background

In this section we briefly describe the man in the middle attacks relevant to SSL/TLS-based applications, as well as relevant details of UMTS AKA and GAA.

2.1   Man in the Middle Attacks

A man in the middle attack targets associations between communicating entities. Typically, an adversary places itself between the client and the server and establishes separate associations with them. It then intercepts and selectively modifies communicated data to masquerade as the legitimate entities. Cryptographic protection does not in itself prevent such an attack, because the adversary engages in association establishment and possesses all the negotiated cryptographic keys.

We assume the following SSL/TLS setting in this paper:

1. the SSL/TLS protocol is only used to authenticate the server, and
2. user authentication is performed using username and password via an established SSL/TLS session.

When establishing the SSL/TLS tunnel, the user should verify the identity of the remote system with which the client system (e.g. a browser) is communicating. If not, then certain man in the middle attacks become possible.

Some classes of phishing attacks are examples of such man in the middle attacks, and attacks of this type have become widespread [1]. In these attacks, an adversary sets up a fake web site which imitates an existing legitimate site in order to mislead users and obtain their authentication credentials. Dhamija et al. [8] show that users often cannot distinguish a legitimate web site from a fake (including in the case where SSL/TLS server authentication is employed).

Against this background, and as discussed by Oppliger et al. [23], most currently deployed user authentication mechanisms fail to provide effective protection against man in the middle attacks, even when they run over the SSL/TLS protocol. There are two main reasons for this.

1. Verifying the identity of the SSL/TLS-authenticated server is usually done poorly by naïve end users, if at all.
2. SSL/TLS session establishment is usually decoupled from user authentication.

If both the above assumptions hold, an attacker can first establish a SSL/TLS session with the client, and fool the user into revealing his or her credentials. The attacker then establishes a separate SSL/TLS session with the server it has impersonated, and masquerades as the user by retransmitting the stolen credentials. Defeating this man in the middle attack requires either proper server authentication or a means of combining the user authentication process with SSL/TLS session establishment.

2.2 Generic Authentication Architecture

The information in this section is mainly derived from Holtmanns et al. [14].

The UMTS AKA protocol provides authentication and key establishment using a long-term secret subscriber key (K), shared by a user device (e.g. a 3G mobile phone) and a mobile network. After a successful UMTS AKA procedure, a pair of secret session keys is established which are shared by the device and the network. The established keys are CK, used for confidentiality protection, and IK, used for integrity protection. We note also that, in the UMTS AKA procedure, a random challenge ($RAND$) is sent by the mobile network to the user device.

The Generic Authentication Architecture (GAA) [3] has been standardised by the 3rd Generation Partnership Project (3GPP), and its North American counterpart, the 3rd Generation Partnership Project 2 (3GPP2). The 3GPP standard versions of GAA build on the widely established mobile authentication infrastructures (including the GSM and UMTS infrastructures). In this paper we focus on GAA as supported by the UMTS authentication infrastructure. GAA consists of two procedures: GAA bootstrapping and Use of bootstrapped keys.

GAA bootstrapping, also known as the Generic Bootstrapping Architecture (GBA), is the process by which UMTS AKA is used to set up a GAA master session key (MK) between a GAA-enabled device and a network, where MK is the concatenation of IK and CK. The network also sends a transaction identifier B-TID. B-TID is generated from the $RAND$ value and the network domain name of the mobile network, and can be used to identify MK and its lifetime to the GAA-enabled device. Both the GAA-enabled device and the network cache MK, the lifetime of MK and $RAND$ for later use. The master session key MK is not bound to a particular application, and can only be used to derive application-specific session keys.

Use of bootstrapped keys is the procedure by which a GAA-enabled device employs the bootstrapped keys to secure its exchanges in an application protocol with a particular GAA-aware application server. Once the GAA-enabled device decides to engage in an application protocol with a particular GAA-aware server, it derives an application-specific session key (SK) from MK, as follows:

$$SK = \mathrm{KDF}(MK, \mathrm{GBAvariant}, RAND, \mathrm{IMPI}, NAF\text{-}Id)$$

where KDF is a key derivation function, GBA_variant indicates the bootstrapping variant (such as GBA_ME or GBA_U), the IP Multimedia Private Identifier (IMPI) is derived from the International Mobile Subscriber Identity (IMSI) [6] which is unique to each mobile phone, and $NAF\text{-}Id$[2] is an application-specific value consisting of the Fully Qualified Domain Name (FQDN) of an application server and the identifier of the underlying application protocol. The device starts the application protocol by sending a request containing B-TID. The server fetches the same SK, the lifetime of SK, and other relevant information

---

[2] In the GAA specifications [3], the functionality of a GAA-aware application server is referred to as the Network Application Function (NAF).

from the corresponding mobile network by forwarding the received *B-TID* and its own identifier *NAF-Id*. Note that *B-TID* contains the network domain name of the mobile network, so the application server knows where to send the request. Normally the network has to authenticate that the requesting server is the genuine owner of FQDN, which forms a part of *NAF-Id*. In GAA, it is assumed that a confidential and authenticated channel between the server and the network has been set up by some means. At this point, the device and the server share the same value of *SK*. It is important to note that *SK* is bound to a specific application protocol and a particular application server.

In summary, UMTS GAA uses UMTS AKA to bootstrap application-specific session keys between GAA-enabled devices and GAA-aware servers.

3   Related Work

The incorporation of password authenticated key exchange (PAKE) schemes into the TLS protocol has been proposed by Steiner et al. [27] and, subsequently, by Abdalla et al. [7]. More recently, the use of the Secure Remote Password (SRP) protocol within TLS has been specified in an Internet draft [28]. Despite the potential advantages of such an approach, migrating from legacy user authentication to a PAKE-based system is non-trivial for a variety of technical and business reasons [10].

An application of GAA based on Pre-Shared Key (PSK) TLS [11] has been described in 3GPP documents [4,5]. GAA credentials are used to establish a TLS session by setting the Pre-Shared Key identity to be the *B-TID*, and the PSK to be the application-specific session key. Note the PSK TLS protocol is able to protect against man in the middle attacks.

Oppliger et al. [23] introduced SSL/TLS session-aware user authentication (TLS-SA), a lightweight and effective countermeasure [24] to man in the middle attacks. TLS-SA makes user authentication depend not only on the user's secret credentials, such as his or her password, but also on SSL/TLS session state information. As a result, the server can check whether or not the SSL/TLS session in which it receives the credentials matches the one employed by the user to send them. If the two sessions match, it is unlikely that a man in the middle is involved; however, if they differ, something abnormal must be taking place, e.g. a man in the middle attack is being performed.

TLS-SA is not a user authentication mechanism or system. Many different approaches can be used to make a given authentication mechanism SSL/TLS session-aware and hence resistant to man in the middle attacks. Oppliger et al. [23] proposed a pre-shared key based approach, and subsequently described a proof of concept implementation [25]. This scheme involves a hardware authentication token which shares a secret key with the server.

One disadvantage of this pre-shared key based approach is that every server needs to generate and securely distribute a key-bearing token to every user, which is likely to be a significant burden in practice. Another disadvantage is its poor scalability. A subsequent proposal [24] involves the use of a multi-institution token which is equipped with a separate secret key for each of a number of servers; however such a scheme may be difficult to market.

4   TLS-SA Using a GAA Bootstrapped Key

We now propose a means of implementing TLS-SA using a GAA bootstrapped key. The scheme employs a GAA-enabled user device with a display and an input capability (e.g. a 3G mobile phone) and a GAA-aware server. During the user authentication process, an application-specific session key (SK) is bootstrapped between the device and the server using GAA. The device uses this GAA boot-strapped key to compute a user authentication code from a combination of the user's secret credentials and state information for the current SSL/TLS session. The user authentication code is submitted to the server to authenticate the user, instead of the secret credentials. It is important to observe that, unlike previously proposed TLS-SA schemes, the system we describe does not require an initial-isation process. That is, the GAA-enabled mobile device is not user or server specific, and can be used in the protocol with no registration or configuration (except for the installation of the necessary application software).

The state information to be used in the computation of user authentication code must have the following properties: (1) it must be shared by the client and the server and be distinct for every SSL/TLS session, and (2) the state information established by a server operated by a man in the middle attacker must be different from the value established by the genuine server. In the scheme described below, this is achieved by using as state information a hash of all the messages exchanged during the underlying SSL/TLS Handshake, computed using a suitable cryptographic hash function.

In the remainder of this section we first describe a simple instantiation of the scheme. We then discuss two possible variants that give security-efficiency trade-offs.

4.1   The Basic Scheme

The following entities play a role in the scheme:

- A user U.
- A SSL/TLS-enabled and GAA-aware server S. We assume that the applica-tion supporting the scheme and executing in S can access certain elements of the SSL/TLS session information.
- A SSL/TLS-enabled client (e.g. a browser) C, used by U to access S. We assume that an application supporting the scheme has been installed in C (e.g. as a Java applet/browser plug-in). This application must have ability to access certain elements of the client's SSL/TLS session information and be aware of the FQDN of the underlying S and the identifier of the underlying application protocol.

- A GAA-enabled user device T (e.g. a 3G mobile phone) with a display and an input capability. We assume that an application supporting the scheme has been installed in T. This application must possess a means of communication with the scheme-specific application in C in order to get the necessary information, e.g. as provided by a USB cable or a Bluetooth link.
- A mobile network provider N that provides the GAA service, and that is trusted by users and servers.

These entities are equipped with various parameters and cryptographic keys. U is equipped with an identifier *username* and a *password* (pw), a secret shared with S. A long-term secret subscriber key (K) is shared by T (strictly its USIM) and its home mobile network as part of the subscription. Note that we also assume that S has the means to establish a secure authenticated channel (e.g. as provided by an SSL/TLS tunnel) with a mobile network as necessary to use GAA.

1. $C \leftrightarrow S$	: establish an SSL/TLS session,	
	: and generate H.	
2. $T \leftrightarrow N$	: B-TID, MK, RAND	
	: and the lifetime of MK ($[T_{start}, T_{end}]$).	
3. $C \rightarrow T$	: H, the FQDN of S, and the identifier	
	: of the application protocol.	
4. T	: derives a session key SK.	
5. T	: computes $uac = f(H, SK, pw, \ldots)$.	
6. $U(C) \rightarrow S$	: B-TID, *username*, and auc.	
7. $S \leftrightarrow N$	: SK and the lifetime of SK ($[T_{start}, T_{end}]$).	
8. S	: $T_{current} \in [T_{start}, T_{end}]$?	
	: if so, S recomputes auc for authentication;	
	: if not, S discards the request.	

Fig. 1. The GAA-based TLS-SA protocol

Figure 1 summarises the GAA-based TLS-SA protocol. We next give a more detailed description, referring to the step numbers shown in the figure.

When U wishes to access S, U directs its client C to S. C and S then establish an SSL/TLS session with server authentication using a public key certificate (step 1)[3]. Once the session has been established, C and S compute (and cache)

$$H = h(Msgs)$$

where h refers to a suitable cryptographic hash function, such as SHA-1 or one of the SHA-2 family [21] and $Msgs$ denotes all the messages exchanged within the SSL/TLS session establishment process[4].

---

[3] Whether or not the user verifies that S is indeed the server it wishes to communicate with is not critical to the security of the scheme.

[4] Enabling the application to gain access to these messages may require minor modifications to the SSL/TLS implementation. However, it requires no change to the SSL/TLS Handshake protocol itself.

T next checks whether it has a pre-established and valid master session key MK. If not, T triggers a GAA bootstrapping procedure with its home network. After successful execution of this process, the values B-TID, MK, the lifetime of MK, and $RAND$ are shared and cached by T and its home network (step 2).

U employs T to communicate with the scheme-specific application in C to get H, the FQDN of S and the identifier of the application protocol (step 3). T then constructs NAF-Id and derives a session key SK, as described in section 2.2 (step 4). Note that SK is not specific to U, and cannot be used to authenticate U to S.

After derivation of SK, T uses U's password pw (which must be input by U at some point) to compute a user authentication code uac as a function f of SK, H, pw, and other relevant parameters (step 5), i.e.

$$uac = f(SK||H||pw||\ldots),$$

where here and throughout $||$ is used to denote concatenation. The function f can be implemented in many ways. One possibility, which complies with clause 5.1.2 of ISO/IEC 9798-4 [16], is to instantiate f using HMAC [18] based on a suitable cryptographic hash function, where the various inputs to f are simply concatenated prior to applying HMAC. In this case, uac is computed as:

$$uac = \text{HMAC}_{SK}(H||pw||\text{"Client"}).$$

As discussed above, H is an SSL/TLS session-specific value, and it plays the role of the nonce in the ISO/IEC 9798-4 protocol. The fixed string "Client" plays the role of the entity identifier.

The server authenticates the user U by asking him or her to submit the values B-TID, $username$, and uac using the SSL/TLS-protected channel (step 6). Note that the user is not required to enter these values into the client, since they can be transferred electronically from T to C. To verify the received uac, S fetches the same SK, the lifetime of SK, and other relevant information from T's home network using the GAA bootstrapped key usage procedure (step 7). SK's lifetime can be set to be the same as that of MK. Before recomputing uac, S must check whether or not SK is valid. This is achieved by checking whether or not the current system time of S is within SK's lifetime[5]. If not, SK is invalid and U will be rejected; otherwise, S can now use the received SK to recompute uac for verification[6]. If the recomputed uac and the uac submitted by U match, U will be granted access (step 8).

Note that the SSL/TLS implementations in C and S need to provide access to session information to the application layer [13,17]. We propose that the SSL/TLS implementations compute H upon the completion of SSL/TLS Handshake session establishment, and cache it as part of the connection state for the SSL/TLS Record layer. However, how this is achieved is application and SSL/TLS implementation specific, and hence we do not discuss this further here.

---

[5] Note that we assume that the system time of the network and the server are synchronised with each other.

[6] S must retrieve H at some point.

4.2   Variants

In GAA, SK is typically used as a session key to secure application data sent between client and server. Using SK instead of MK reduces the risk of disclosing the master key MK, e.g. as a result of cryptanalysis. However, in our case SK is only used in the computation of the user authentication code, i.e. only a small amount of data is involved. Other application data is protected by transmission through an SSL/TLS-protected channel.

Examining the computation of SK (as above), it follows that, during the lifetime of the key MK, the value of SK only depends on $NAF\text{-}Id$. In practice, U could repeatedly access a particular server using the same application protocol[7]. In such a case, U would use the same $NAF\text{-}Id$ in the derivation of SK in multiple user authentication sessions. In fact, the GAA bootstrapping procedure can be avoided after the first use by setting the lifetime of MK to be sufficiently long. In this case, T uses the same MK in the derivation of SK in all subsequent authentication sessions, and hence a user can employ the same SK for all authentication sessions with a particular server which involve a specific application protocol. As a result, it is reasonable to propose that T and S both cache SK and use it as a long-term shared key to avoid frequent use of GAA and derivations of SK. We next describe two variants to achieve this.

In both variants, T and its home network first carry out a GAA bootstrapping procedure to establish a shared master key MK and other information. The lifetime of MK must be set to be sufficiently long. This process is performed before any user authentication processes.

A Straightforward Variant. The user device T can identify SK using $NAF\text{-}Id$, which is constructed from the FQDN of S and the identifier of the application protocol. When computing uac, T first tries to retrieve SK from its cache using the constructed $NAF\text{-}Id$ as index. If SK is not present, then T derives an SK from MK and the constructed $NAF\text{-}Id$, stores the pair $(NAF\text{-}Id, SK)$, and then uses the derived SK to compute uac. If SK is in the cache, T uses it directly in the computation of uac.

The server S needs to use both $B\text{-}TID$ and $NAF\text{-}Id$ to identify SK. U submits $username$, $B\text{-}TID$, and uac in the authentication process. Upon receiving an authentication request from C, S tries to retrieve SK from its cache using the received $B\text{-}TID$ and its own $NAF\text{-}Id$ as index. If SK is not present, S requests it from T's home network, stores the received triple $(B\text{-}TID, NAF\text{-}Id, SK)$, and then verifies the uac to authenticate the user. If SK is present, S uses it directly in the verification process.

A Separate Registration Procedure Variant. In the basic scheme and the first variant described above, U has to submit $username$, $B\text{-}TID$, and uac in order to be authenticated by S. $B\text{-}TID$ is submitted so that S can identify SK. In a standard password-based user authentication process, only $username$

---

[7] For example, the user might repeatedly interact with a browser to access his or her bank account via HTTPS.

and pw need to be submitted. Thus submitting $B\text{-}TID$ potentially significantly increases the traffic load (since $B\text{-}TID$ is much longer than a typical password), and increases the complexity of implementation in settings in which $B\text{-}TID$ must be input by U. In the variant we now describe, S is required to provide a service which allows U to register SK, enabling S to identify SK from just the *username*. As a result, U will only need to submit *username* and *uac* in the authentication process. The registration of SK can be done using a registration procedure of the type described below.

Before any user authentication process, T derives SK to be used by U to access a particular server S through a specified application protocol. T stores the pair $(username, SK)$. If $M = H\|pw$, then, in order to register SK, U submits *username*, $B\text{-}TID$, and $E_{SK}(M)$ via a previously established SSL/TLS-protected channel. Here E is an authenticated encryption technique, e.g. one of those standardised in ISO/IEC 19772 [15]. Upon receiving the request, S fetches the same SK, the lifetime of SK and other relevant information from T's home network using the GAA bootstrapped key usage procedure. S can now use the received SK to decrypt and verify the encrypted version of M to recover H and pw. S then checks whether the received H matches the current SSL/TLS session. Finally, S verifies whether *username* identifies a valid user and pw is the correct password for this user. If all the verifications succeed, then S registers the binding between *username* and SK.

After a successful registration procedure, T and S share the same SK which can be identified by *username*. Thus, in the user authentication process, U only needs to submit *username* and *uac*. However, it is important to note that the binding between U and SK remains weak, and is only useful for the purpose of identifying SK. That is, successful user authentication will require knowledge of both SK and pw.

5   Analysis

The GAA-based approach avoids the disadvantages of the pre-shared key approach discussed in section 3. To implement the GAA-based approach, the user only needs a GAA-enabled device with a display and an input capability. This can be implemented using a 3G mobile phone with a valid subscription, and there are a very large number of subscription holders across the world. The approach thus has good scalability. Moreover, since a GAA bootstrapped session key is used in the computation of the user authentication code, there is no need to generate and securely distribute a key-bearing token to every user. The approach also fits well to the multi-institution scenario. The system enables server-specific session keys to be generated using a single GAA-enabled device, where each such key can be used to help authenticate a user to the appropriate GAA-aware server. The GAA-enabled device thus acts as a non-institution-specific authentication token.

However, in deciding whether to use this GAA-based TLS-SA system, the server S and its users must trust the mobile network provider not to compromise its long-term password (see also section 5.1). Such a trust relationship could be supported by a contractual agreement between application service providers and mobile operators.

A limitation of the scheme is that use of the system will incur the cost of using the GAA service. The two variants described in section 4.2 are more cost-effective in this respect than the basic scheme.

We next give an informal security analysis. We then show that the GAA-based approach has a degree of flexibility, enabling the implementation of security-efficiency trade-offs.

5.1   Informal Security Analysis

We consider a threat model in which an attacker $\mathcal{A}$ is able to observe and make arbitrary modifications to messages exchanged between C and S, including replaying, blocking and inserting completely spurious messages. This allows a trivial denial of service attack which cannot be prevented. $\mathcal{A}$ is also assumed to be a legitimate user of the UMTS GAA service. However, $\mathcal{A}$ is not allows to compromise the implementations of T, C or S (e.g. using malware); such attacks on system integrity are not addressed by the schemes we propose.

The security of the schemes relies on the security of the underlying UMTS GAA and SSL/TLS protocol. In turn, the security of UMTS GAA is built on the assumption that learning the subscriber key and/or MK by attacking UMTS AKA is not possible [14].

We next provide a brief informal analysis of how the schemes meet the intended security goals.

1. *Resistance to user authentication code replay.*
   The GAA-based scheme, like the pre-shared key approach, involves authenticating a user via a user authentication code (uac). The user authentication code is cryptographically bound to the current SSL/TLS Handshake session state information. The state information (H) is a cryptographic hash of all the messages exchanged during SSL/TLS session establishment.

   Suppose $\mathcal{A}$ launches a man-in-the-middle attack by establishing two separate SSL/TLS sessions: one with S (masquerading as C) and one with C (masquerading as S). The value of the uac provided by C to $\mathcal{A}$ will be a function of the messages exchanged by C and $\mathcal{A}$ during SSL/TLS session establishment; similarly the uac expected by S will be a function of the messages exchanged by $\mathcal{A}$ and S during SSL/TLS session establishment. Even if they are otherwise identical, the first set of messages will include $\mathcal{A}$'s SSL/TLS server certificate, and the second set of messages will instead contains S's certificate. As a result the uac provided by C will be different to that expected by S, and hence the attack will fail.

2. *Resistance to compromise of a user password (pw).*
   $\mathcal{A}$ could set up an SSL/TLS session with C (impersonating a legitimate S) and request a uac. The uac is computed using a keyed one way hash function which takes as input the GAA bootstrapped session key; it is thus infeasible

to retrieve pw from a valid uac without knowing this session key. That is, $\mathcal{A}$ cannot succeed in a off-line dictionary attack against pw without knowing the corresponding SK or MK (using MK, $\mathcal{A}$ can derive SK). Similarly, in the registration procedure, $\mathcal{A}$ cannot retrieve pw from the encrypted string sent to S without knowing the corresponding SK or MK. We assume that the underlying UMTS GAA is secure [22], that is, it is impossible for $\mathcal{A}$ to learn SK (intended for a legitimate S) or MK established between T and its mobile network by attacking UMTS GAA.

Alternatively, $\mathcal{A}$ could attack the KDF algorithm used for SK derivation. In such an attack, $\mathcal{A}$ chooses and registers a value for $NAF\text{-}Id$ ($NAF\text{-}Id_{\mathcal{A}}$, say) which has the property that

$$\text{KDF}(MK, \text{GBAvariant}, RAND, \text{IMPI}, NAF\text{-} \\ Id_{\mathcal{A}}) = \text{KDF}(MK, \text{GBAvariant}, RAND, \text{IMPI}, NAF\text{-}Id_S)$$

for any master key MK, where $NAF\text{-}Id_S$ is the $NAF\text{-}Id$ for a legitimate server S. $\mathcal{A}$ then requests an SK from the mobile network by sending $B\text{-}TID$ and $NAF\text{-}Id_{\mathcal{A}}$. The mobile network derives an SK from $NAF\text{-}Id_{\mathcal{A}}$, which is equal to the SK derived from $NAF\text{-}Id_S$. As a result, the adversary learns the value of SK for U and S. However, the KDF algorithm used in GAA is based on HMAC-SHA-256, which is believed to be a secure MAC function [14], and hence such a collision attack is believed to be infeasible. The choice of a cryptographically strong KDF also means that even if $\mathcal{A}$ has discovered a number of SK values, they cannot be used to discover other keys derived from the same master key MK.

3. *Resistance to registration message replay (second variant only).*
   Note that S can detect such an attack by checking whether the H value matches the current SSL/TLS session. If not, S simply discards the request.

It is very important to note that the mobile network operator possesses the GAA bootstrapped session keys and must be trusted since, if it obtains the authenticator[8], it could perform a dictionary attack to find the user's long-term password. In practice, users already trust mobile operators not to intercept their phone calls. This is a high level of trust since operators could, for example, intercept and misuse a wide range of user secrets (e.g. credit card details).

5.2 Security-Efficiency Trade-Offs

In the pre-shared key approach outlined in section 3, a secret key is used in all authentication sessions. This is arguably more efficient, since there is no need for session key establishment (e.g. a GAA procedure) in the user authentication process. However, in a high security scenario it may be necessary to use a new key for each authentication session. Secret key re-configuration is highly non-trivial

---

[8] A malicious mobile network provider could potentially set up a phishing website to try to persuade a user to submit an authenticator. However, such a scenario seems rather far-fetched, particularly given that a user can choose which network operator to use.

in the pre-shared key approach, since tokens have to be distributed to users. As we show immediately below, the GAA-based approach has the flexibility to enable security-efficiency tradeoffs.

For a high-security scenario in which a new session key SK is needed for each authentication session, the basic GAA-based scheme can be used. By setting the lifetime of MK to be sufficiently short, a new master MK will be established between T and its home network in each authentication session. As a result, a new session key SK will be derived for the computation of each user authentication code. Of course, this will introduce a significant network traffic and computational overhead, including the establishment of MK using the GAA bootstrapping procedure, the derivation of the session key SK in T, and the fetching of SK from the mobile network by S. Such an approach therefore has relatively high security and low efficiency. In a scenario where security is not quite such a high priority, one of the variant schemes can be used in which the key SK is cached and used as a long-term key for multiple user authentication sessions. As a result, additional GAA procedures and calculations are avoided, and higher efficiency can be achieved.

6   Conclusions

SSL/TLS session-aware user authentication is a lightweight and effective countermeasure to man in the middle attacks. We propose a means of implementing SSL/TLS session-aware user authentication using a GAA bootstrapped key. The scheme employs a GAA-enabled user device with a display and an input capability (e.g. a 3G mobile phone) and a GAA-aware server. Importantly, the user device does not need to be registered with the server, and no server-specific details are stored in the device; that is, the user device is not specific to either the user or the server. Analysis shows that the scheme is effective, secure, scalable and has a degree of flexibility enabling security-efficiency trade-offs. Moreover, the scheme fits well to the multi-institution scenario.

References

1. Anti-phishing working group phishing archive,
   http://anti-phishing.org/phishing_archive.htm
2. 3rd Generation Partnership Project (3GPP). 3G Security: Access Secure for IP-based Services, Version 9.3.0 (2009)
3. 3rd Generation Partnership Project (3GPP). 3rd Generation Partnership Project, Technical Specification Group Services and Systems Aspects, Generic Authentication Architecture (GAA), Generic Bootstrapping Architecture, Version 9.2.0 (2009)
4. 3rd Generation Partnership Project (3GPP). Access to network application functions using Hypertext Transfer Protocol over Transport Layer Security (HTTPS), Version 9.0.0 (2009)
5. 3rd Generation Partnership Project (3GPP). Bootstrapping interface (Ub) and network application function interface (Ua); Protocol details, Version 9.0.0 (2009)

6. 3rd Generation Partnership Project (3GPP). Numbering, Addressing and Identification, Version 9.2.0 (2009)
7. Abdalla, M., Bresson, E., Chevassut, O., Möller, B., Pointcheval, D.: Provably secure password-based authentication in TLS. In: ASIACCS 2006: Proceedings of the 2006 ACM Symposium on Information, Computer and Communications Security, pp. 35–45. ACM, New York (2006)
8. Dhamija, R., Tygar, J.D., Hearst, M.: Why phishing works. In: CHI 2006: Proceedings of the SIGCHI Conference on Human Factors in Computing Systems, pp. 581–590. ACM, New York (2006)
9. Dierks, T., Rescorla, E.: The Transport Layer Security (TLS) Protocol Version 1.2. RFC 5246 (Proposed Standard) (August 2008)
10. Engler, J., Karlof, C., Shi, E., Song, D.: Is it too late for PAKE? In: W2SP 2009: Proceedings of the Web 2.0 Security and Privacy Workshop, Oakland, California, USA (May 2009)
11. Eronen, P., Tschofenig, H.: Pre-Shared Key Ciphersuites for Transport Layer Security (TLS). RFC 4279 (Proposed Standard) (December 2005)
12. Freier, A.O., Karlton, P., Kocher, P.C.: The SSL Protocol—Version 3.0. Internet Draft, Transport Layer Security Working Group (November 1996)
13. Gajek, S., Liao, L., Schwenk, J.: Stronger TLS bindings for SAML assertions and SAML artifacts. In: SWS 2008: Proceedings of the 5th ACM CCS Workshop on Secure Web Services, pp. 11–20. ACM, New York (2008)
14. Holtmanns, S., Niemi, V., Ginzboorg, P., Laitinen, P., Asokan, N.: Cellular Authentication for Mobile and Internet Services. John Wiley and Sons, Chichester (2008)
15. International Organization for Standardization, Genève, Switzerland. ISO/IEC 19772:2009 Information technology—Security techniques—Authenticated encryption (Feburary 2009)
16. International Organization for Standardization, Genève, Switzerland. ISO/IEC 9798-4:1999/Cor 1:2009 Information technology—Security techniques—Entity authentication—Part 4: Mechanisms using a cryptographic check function (September 2009)
17. Kohlar, F., Schwenk, J., Jensen, M., Gajek, S.: On cryptographically secure bindings of SAML assertions to TLS sessions. In: ARES 2010: Proceedings of the 5th International Conference on Availability, Reliability and Security, pp. 62–69. IEEE Computer Society, Los Alamitos (2010)
18. Krawczyk, H., Bellare, M., Canetti, R.: HMAC: Keyed-Hashing for Message Authentication. RFC 2104 (Informational) (February 1997)
19. Lopez, J., Oppliger, R., Pernul, G.: Why have public key infrastructures failed so far? Internet Research 15, 554–556 (2005)
20. Mitchell, J.C., Shmatikov, V., Stern, U.: Finite-state analysis of SSL 3.0. In: USENIX 1998: Proceedings of the 7th USENIX Security Symposium, pp. 201–216. USENIX Association, San Antonio (1998)
21. National Institute of Standards and Technology, Federal Information Processing Standards (FIPS) Publication 180-3. Secure Hash Standard (SHS) (October 2008)
22. Niemi, V., Nyberg, K.: UMTS Security. John Wiley and Sons, Chichester (2003)
23. Oppliger, R., Hauser, R., Basin, D.: SSL/TLS session-aware user authentication or how to effectively thwart the man-in-the-middle. Computer Communications 29(12), 2238–2246 (2006)
24. Oppliger, R., Hauser, R., Basin, D.: SSL/TLS session-aware user authentication revisited. Computers and Security 27(3-4), 64–70 (2008)

25. Oppliger, R., Hauser, R., Basin, D., Rodenhaeuser, A., Kaiser, B.: A proof of concept implementation of SSL/TLS session-aware user authentication (TLS-SA). In: Brauer, W., Braun, T., Carle, G., Stiller, B. (eds.) Kommunikation in Verteilten Systemen (KiVS). Informatik Aktuell, pp. 225–236. Springer, Heidelberg (2007)
26. Paulson, L.C.: Inductive analysis of the internet protocol TLS. ACM Transactions on Information and System Security (TISSEC) 2(3), 332–351 (1999)
27. Steiner, M., Buhler, P., Eirich, T., Waidner, M.: Secure password-based cipher suite for TLS. ACM Transactions on Information and System Security (TISSEC) 4(2), 134–157 (2001)
28. Taylor, D., Wu, T., Mavrogiannopoulos, N., Perrin, T.: Using the Secure Remote Password (SRP) protocol for TLS authentication. RFC 5054 (Informational) (November 2007)

An Almost-Optimal Forward-Private RFID Mutual Authentication Protocol with Tag Control

Paolo D'Arco

Dipartimento di Informatica
Università degli Studi di Salerno
I-84084 Fisciano (SA), Italy

Abstract. In this paper we propose an efficient forward-private RFID mutual authentication protocol. The protocol is secure under standard assumptions. It builds over a recent work, extends it to achieve mutual authentication, and improves it by introducing a resynchronization mechanism between tag and reader, through which the server-side computation from $O(N\omega)$ is reduced to $O(N + \omega)$, where N is the total number of tags in the system, and ω is the maximum number of authentications each single tag can afford during its lifetime. Moreover, the protocol enables the server to control how many times a tag has been read by legitimate and fake readers.

1 Introduction

Rfid Technology: basics, development and concerns. The Rfid technology enables *automatic object identification* without the need for physical access. Each object is labeled with a tiny integrated circuit equipped with a radio antenna, called *tag*, whose *information content* can be received by another device, called *reader*, at a distance of several meters. Usually the readers are connected to a *back-end server*: they forward to the server the read tag content, and get back the result of the server computation. The interest of the scientific community for the Rfid technology has grown a lot during the last years simultaneously to the wide diffusion of the technology and the deployment of applications which partially deal or embed Rfid components. Indeed, the indubitable advantages come with new challenges: *security* and *privacy*, due to the constrained computational capabilities of the tags, are non trivial properties to achieve. If some applications do not need stringent security and privacy measures, applications which have an impact on the people life style, raise more concerns: in some settings as users (e.g., in access control applications, in anti-theft tools) we would like to be sure that a certain tag cannot be impersonated by an adversary; as well as, there are uses in which tracking features (e.g., postal tracking, pet tracking, airline luggage tracking, waste disposal tracking) are very welcome but others (e.g., when buying tag-equipped goods from a shop) in which we would like to be sure that our privacy is preserved, and no adversary is able to build a preference profile by illegally reading the content of the tags attached to the goods we buy.

C.A. Ardagna and J. Zhou (Eds.): WISTP 2011, LNCS 6633, pp. 69–84, 2011.

State of art. We refer the interested reader to [14,13] for an overview of the applications of the RFID technology and of the main security issues, and to [1] for references to research papers dealing with RFID technology and its challenges[1].

Previous work. Roughly speaking, an Rfid authentication protocol enables tags and readers to be sure they are talking to each other, i.e., to identify and authenticate the other part. It is a key-component for building secure and private Rfid applications. An RFID authentication protocol is *forward-private* if an adversary, who tampers a tag and obtains its keys and state information, is unable to trace the tag, i.e., to associate the tag to previous transcripts of completed protocol executions he has eavesdropped. Obhuko et al. [15] proposed a simple and elegant forward-private scheme, which uses two hash functions. The scheme and its subsequent improvements, however, due to the costs of hash functions, are unsuitable for a real implementation on a tag. Moreover, such schemes are proven secure by using the random oracle methodology which is object of debate and criticism [2,6]. A recent paper [4] introduced a new Obhuko et al. like scheme, called PFP, which is efficient and is secure under standard assumptions, i.e., the existence of pseudorandom number generators and strongly universal hash function families.

Our contribution. In this paper we propose $EFPP$, a new forward-private RFID mutual authentication protocol. It builds over PFP and improves it by introducing a resynchronization mechanism between tag and reader, similar to the one used in [11,12], through which the server-side computation from $O(N\omega)$ is reduced to $O(N + \omega)$, where N is the total number of tags in the system, and ω is the maximum number of authentications each single tag can afford during its lifetime. Since the authors of [10], who focused on the design and the analysis of Rfid protocols based on symmetric-key primitives, showed that, if keys are chosen independently and uniformly at random, $\Omega(N)$ is a *lower bound* on the number of lookup operations the back-end server needs to authenticate a tag, then it follows that our forward-private scheme is *almost optimal*.

Related Work. Apart [4], which is our starting point, and [11,12], from which we borrow the resynchronization technique, other related papers are [17,5]. The $OFRAP$ mutual authentication scheme, proposed in [17], is elegant, efficient, and forward-private. It has been analyzed within the UC framework and proven secure and private under standard assumptions, i.e., the existence of pseudorandom functions. Moreover, it achieves an $O(N)$ overhead in terms of the number of lookup operations the server needs to authenticate a tag. Compared to ours, apart the computational tools, the main difference is that in $OFRAP$ the server has *no way* to control the total number of protocol executions a tag has been subject to, perhaps due to an adversary attack. In our scheme, on the other hand, we *gain* control by paying an additive ω factor within the asymptotic notation, which enables the back-end server to remove from the system a tag once its lifetime is over. On the other hand, the $PEPS$ scheme [5] also

---

[1] In the full version of the paper [8] are briefly mentioned the most significant efforts in order to provide *precise* notions of security and privacy, and to propose *efficient* constructions.

reduces the $O(N\omega)$ server-side computation of PFP [4] to $O(N)$. It has a design quite similar to $OFRAP$, and it is secure under the same assumptions. The main difference between $PEPS$ and $OFRAP$ is that $PEPS$ requires the tag to generate truly random numbers. We point out that also in $PEPS$ the server has *no way* to control the total number of protocol executions a tag has been subject to. In some applicative settings (e.g., access control, ticketing, automatic tolls ...) such a property is very welcome. The server could estimate the usage of the tag, as well as whether the tag has been target of attacks. $EFPP$ is a *true extension* of PFP, which is efficient and practical, and uses the same computational tools. To our knowledge, $EFPP$ is also the first efficient RFID forward-private authentication protocol enjoying the above tag-control feature.

2   Security Model

Every security model for evaluating Rfid authentication protocols focuses on three aspects: *correctness, security* and *privacy*. Loosely speaking, a protocol is correct if, with overwhelming probability, a legitimate tag and a legitimate reader successfully authenticate each other in an adversary-free protocol execution. Then, it is secure if an adversary has a negligible probability of impersonating a legitimate tag to the reader (vice versa, a reader to tag). Finally, it is private if a tag cannot be traced by analyzing the transcripts of protocol executions, and it is forward-private if the adversary does not succeed even if, at a certain point, gets access to the tag content and tries to trace the tag by using the transcript of previous completed executions.

Despite the properties we would like to get are intuitively clear, providing a suitable security and privacy model is a challenging task. Just to exemplify, the notion of correctness has to take into account a possible desynchronization attack tag and reader can be subject to at a certain point. What do we need to require from an adversary-free protocol execution *after* such an event has occurred? The models in [18,4,11] formalize this requirement in different ways. In this abstract, we do not deal with security model issues: since we basically use the same primitives of [4], for easiness of comparison, we refer to the same model (extended to deal with mutual authentication) which, as stated by the authors of [4], is a simplification and an adaptation of [18,16] to the symmetric setting[2].

The Model. Each tag T has an *internal state*, containing state information and secret keys. Tag secret keys are uncorrelated, chosen independently and uniformly at random. Part of the tag state is shared with the back-end server, which stores tag information in a database DB. Each tag can be used at most ω times. Readers are securely connected to the back-end server. During its lifetime, a tag enters authentication exchanges with the readers, following a *protocol* which specifies which messages have to be computed and exchanged, and how the internal states of the tag and the back-end server have to be updated. An authentication exchange between a tag and a reader either results inside the reader (resp. tag)

---

[2] An analysis of the protocol in different models is left as future work.

in an authentication success (together with a tag identity for the reader) or in an authentication failure. A tag cannot handle several authentication exchanges simultaneously. We assume that tags are exposed to an adversary during an exposure period, in which the adversary is able to observe and disturb all interactions involving the tag and possibly the reader, without confusing these interactions with exchanges involving other tags of the system. We also assume that no physical characteristics (e.g., radiation pattern, response time, et cetera) allow an adversary to recognize the tag and distinguish it from the other tags of the system, if the adversary observes it again in another exposure period.

Let A be an adversary with running time upper-bounded by T, allowed to trigger, observe, disturb and replace up to $q < \omega$ authentication exchanges involving the tag and the reader, and to access the outcome of the authentication protocol. We say that A is a (q, T)-adversary.

Definition 1. *An Rfid authentication protocol is said to be (q, T, ϵ)-correct iff the probability that a legitimate tag (resp. reader) is not successfully authenticated by a legitimate reader (resp. tag) in an undisturbed exchange at least once in its lifetime is upper-bounded by ϵ, even in the presence of a (q, T)-adversary. The probability is taken over the initial tag's secret values, the random numbers chosen during the protocol executions, and the random numbers chosen by the adversary.*

The definition states that a protocol is correct iff, even in presence of a (q, T)-adversary which tries to desynchronize tag and reader (i.e., so that they reach different states), the probability that in its lifetime there exists an adversary-free execution of the protocol in which the tag (resp. reader) is not authenticated by the reader (resp. tag), is at most ϵ. In other words, the protocol is robust against a (q, T)-adversary and it works almost always well.

Security requires resistance to impersonation attacks, which can be modeled as two-stage processes: during the first stage a (q, T)-adversary interacts both with a legitimate reader and a legitimate tag. During the second stage, the adversary only interacts with the reader (resp. tag) and initiates an authentication exchange to impersonate the tag (resp. the reader). The attack succeeds if the authentication is successful and the adversary is identified as the tag (resp. as the reader).

Definition 2. *An Rfid authentication protocol is said to be (q, T, ϵ)-secure (w.r.t. tag authentication/w.r.t. reader authentication) iff, for any (q, T)-adversary, the probability that an impersonation attack is successful is at most ϵ.*

The privacy requirement can be formalized through the following privacy experiment: during the first stage, a (q, T)-adversary A interacts with any two legitimate tags, T_0 and T_1, and a legitimate reader. At the end of this phase, a bit b (concealed to A) is chosen. Then, during the second stage, A again interacts with T_b. Then, A is given access to the internal state of T_b. Eventually, A outputs a guess bit b' for the value b, and it succeeds if b' is equal to b.

Definition 3. *An Rfid authentication protocol is said to be (q, T, ϵ)-private iff any (q, T)-adversary A has an advantage at most ϵ in winning the privacy experiment, i.e.,*

$$|Pr[A \; succeeds\;] - 1/2| \leq \epsilon.$$

Notice that, in the privacy experiment, we assume that A is given access to the internal state of the tag *when a protocol execution is completed*[3]. This precludes tag states following a failed protocol execution. The same approach was followed in [17] and, very recently, in [5], where the authors used the notion of *almost forward private protocol* to refer to the above setting with a restricted corruption capability for the adversary. However, we point out that, by using the same argument used in [16] (see Thm 1, page 294), it is possible to prove that if an adversary has the power to corrupt a tag *during* a protocol execution, then it easily wins the privacy experiment. Unfortunately, this issue *has no protocol solution without extra hardware assumptions* [16,9]. Therefore, the only possible goal is to look for a protocol which *safely locks* previous completed executions[4].

3   Tools

In this section we review some useful tools and properties needed to analyze the strength of the protocol. See [4] (Section 4 and the appendices) for proofs and details.

Let L, n and k be integers such that $L = n + k$, and let $g : \{0,1\}^n \rightarrow \{0,1\}^L$ be a binary function, which expands n-bit sequences into L-bit sequences. A distinguisher for g is a probabilistic algorithm A, which on input an L-bit sequence, outputs 0 or 1. The advantage of A in distinguishing g from a perfect random generator is defined as:

$$Adv_g(A) = |Pr[A(g(x)) = 1] - Pr[A(y) = 1]|$$

where the probabilities are taken over $x \in \{0,1\}^n$ (unknown to A) and $y \in \{0,1\}^L$, chosen uniformly at random, and over the random bits chosen by A. The advantage in distinguishing g in time T is:

$$Adv_g(T) = max_A\{Adv_g(A)\}$$

for all distinguishers A running in time at most T.

Definition 4. *The function $g : \{0,1\}^n \rightarrow \{0,1\}^L$ is a (T, ϵ)-secure pseudorandom number generator $((T, \epsilon)$-PRNG, for short) iff $Adv_g(T) \leq \epsilon$.*

---

[3] Using the language of [11], the tag is *clean* at the corruption time, i.e., an undisturbed protocol execution with the reader has been successfully completed and the tag is ready for a new protocol execution.

[4] Notice that similar constraints to get perfect forward-secrecy in the key-exchange setting were shown in [3] (see Remark 7). It is the same problem which appears in two different settings.

By using λ times the function g, we can define an iterated function G_λ. To this aim, let us denote $g(x) = g_1(x)\|g_2(x)$, where $g_1(x) \in \{0,1\}^n, g_2(x) \in \{0,1\}^k$, and $\|$ represents concatenation. Then, let λ be an integer greater than or equal to 1. The iterated function $G_\lambda : \{0,1\}^n \to \{0,1\}^{n+\lambda k}$ is defined by:

$$x \to (g_2(x), g_2(g_1(x)), \ldots, g_2(g_1^{\lambda-1}(x)), g_1^\lambda(x)).$$

Assuming that T_g is the time to compute g, it holds that:

Theorem 1. *If $g : \{0,1\}^n \to \{0,1\}^{n+k}$ is a (T, ϵ_g)-PRNG then, for any $\lambda \geq 1$, the associated iterated function G_λ is a $(T - (\lambda + 1)T_g, \lambda\epsilon_g)$-PRNG.*

Similarly, a duplicated function $G^N : \{0,1\}^{nN} \to \{0,1\}^{LN}$ is simply defined by $(x_1, \ldots, x_N) \to (G(x_1), \ldots, G(x_N))$. It holds that:

Lemma 1. *If G is a (T', ϵ_G)-PRNG, then G^N is a $(T', N\epsilon_G)$-PRNG.*

Finally, a duplicated iterated function $G_\lambda^N : \{0,1\}^{nN} \to \{0,1\}^{(n+\lambda k)N}$ is defined by $(x_1, \ldots, x_N) \to (G_\lambda(x_1), \ldots, G_\lambda(x_N))$.

Theorem 1 and Lemma 1 were proven in [4] by using standard hybrid arguments. From them, it follows that:

Theorem 2. *For any (T, ϵ_g)-PRNG $g : \{0,1\}^n \to \{0,1\}^{n+k}$, any $\lambda \geq 1$, and any $N \geq 1$, the associated duplicated function $G_\lambda^N : \{0,1\}^{nN} \to \{0,1\}^{(n+\lambda k)N}$ is a $(T - (\lambda + 1)T_g, N\lambda\epsilon_g)$-PRNG.*

The second key-tool we need in our construction are function families with special uniformity properties, referred to as universal classes of hash functions [7]. The idea of a universal class of hash functions is to define a collection $\mathcal{H}$ of hash functions in such a way that a random choice of a function $h \in \mathcal{H}$ yields a low probability that any two distinct inputs x and y will collide when their hashed values are computed using the function h. A more structured function family is defined as follows:

Definition 5. *A family $\mathcal{H} = \{h_s : \{0,1\}^\ell \to \{0,1\}^m\}$ of hash functions is called ϵ-almost strongly universal if and only if: $\forall a \in \{0,1\}^\ell, \forall b \in \{0,1\}^m$, it holds that $Pr_{s \in S}[h_s(a) = b] = 2^{-m}$, and $\forall a_1 \neq a_2 \in \{0,1\}^\ell, \forall b_1, b_2 \in \{0,1\}^m$, it holds that $Pr_{s \in S}[h_s(a_2) = b_2 | h_s(a_1) = b_1] \leq \epsilon$.*

Notice that, the first condition states that any input a is mapped to any hashed value b with probability $\frac{1}{2^m}$. The second states that, given that a_1 is mapped to b_1, the conditional probability that a_2 is mapped to b_2, for any $a_2 \neq a_1$, is at most ϵ. A 2^{-m}-almost strongly universal hash function family $\mathcal{H}$ is called a *strongly universal* hash function family. Further details and applications can be found in [20,19].

The following lemma was proven in [4]. It states that an adversary who knows a pair $(u_0, h_s(u_0))$ and a bunch of pairs (a_j, b_j), with $h_j \neq h_s(a_j)$, has a small probability of guessing the correct value of the function $h_s(a)$ on a new randomly chosen value a.

Lemma 2. *Let $\mathcal{H} = \{h_s : \{0,1\}^\ell \to \{0,1\}^m\}$ be an ϵ-almost strongly universal hash function family, let s^* be a (secret) value randomly chosen in S, and let A be a computationally unbounded adversary who tries to predict the value of h_{s^*} on a randomly chosen input value a. Suppose that A is given at most one pair (a_0, b_0) and at most $p \leq \frac{1}{2\epsilon}$ pairs (a_j, b_j) such that $h_{s^*}(a_0) = b_0$ and, for $0 < j \leq p$, it holds that $h_{s^*}(a_j) \neq b_j$. Then,*

$$Pr_{a \in \{0,1\}^\ell, s^*}[A(a) = h_{s^*}(a)] = 2^{-\ell} + \epsilon(1 + 2p\epsilon).$$

Lemma 3. *If s, s' are chosen independently, then $Pr_{s,s' \in S}[h_s(a) = h_{s'}(a)] = 2^{-m}$.*

In the following, we will denote with T_h the time to compute the function h_s.

4   Protocol Description

In this section we introduce our protocol. Let us briefly describe PFP, the forward-private protocol proposed in [4] we start from. Let $g : \{0,1\}^n \to \{0,1\}^{n+k}$ be a PRNG, and let $\mathcal{H} = \{h_s : \{0,1\}^\ell \to \{0,1\}^m\}$ be a strongly universal hash function family. Moreover, let $g(x) = g_1(x)\|g_2(x)$, where $g_1(x) \in \{0,1\}^n$ and $g_2(x) \in \{0,1\}^k$. Each tag can be used at most ω times. It stores the description of g and $\mathcal{H}$, and a state variable σ. The back-end server stores the same information for all tags in its database. The protocol works as follows:

1. The reader chooses uniformly at random a challenge $c \in \{0,1\}^n$ and sends c to the tag.
2. The tag, receiving c, *updates* its state σ and *chooses* a random function h_s from $\mathcal{H}$ by computing $(\sigma, s) = (g_1(\sigma), g_2(\sigma))$. Then, it computes $r = h_s(c)$, and sends r to the reader.
3. The reader, for each tag T, fetches into the database DB the last known state for tag T, say σ_j^T, and checks whether there exists an index $i \geq 0$ such that $j + i < \omega$ and $h_{g_2(g_1^i(\sigma_j^T))}(c) = r$. If such an index is found, then the tag is authenticated. Otherwise, it is refused.

In other words, at each protocol execution, the reader checks in DB along chains of at most ω elements if a match is found. The protocol is correct, secure and forward-private and, in a system with N tags, it has complexity $O(N\omega)$. In the following we show how to improve the scheme in order to get *mutual authentication* and to *reduce the complexity* from $O(N\omega)$ to $O(N + \omega)$.

Let us start by describing the information held by tags and readers in the new protocol.

Common public information: two d-bit values pad_1, pad_2, used for padding, and the descriptions of a pseudorandom number generator g (PRNG) and of a strongly universal hash function family H (SUHF, for short). The PRNG g is used for *identification* purposes, for *updating* tag information, and within the *authentication* process. The SUHF H is used within the *authentication* process.

As before, we split the values of $g : \{0,1\}^n \rightarrow \{0,1\}^{n+k}$ in two parts, i.e., $g(x) = g_1(x)||g_2(x)$.

Tag information: a $(n\text{-}d)$-bit randomizer CR, an identification key k, a state variable σ, the two d-bit values pad_1 and pad_2, and the descriptions of g and H

Reader information: a DB which stores the description of g and H, the two values pad_1 and pad_2, and, for each tag, the tag identifier ID, a counter CNT_{ID}, and two tuples: $< I_{old}, \sigma_{old}, k_{old}, CR_{DB}^{old} >$ and $< I, \sigma, k, CR_{DB} >$. Let us denote by $DB_{ID}[i]$, for $i = 0, 1$, the memory locations for the two tuples for tag ID. At the beginning, when DB is initialized, all counters and old tuples are set to zero, i.e., $CNT_{ID} = 0$ and $DB_{ID}[0] =< 0, 0, 0, 0 >$ for all N tags. The DB automatically removes tag ID when $CNT_{ID} = \omega$. Moreover, let us denote by $\sigma_{|n-d}$ the first $n - d$ bits of σ, and by rnd a value chosen uniformly at random.

Three-round authentication protocol overview:

1. The reader chooses uniformly at random a challenge $c \in \{0,1\}^n$ and sends c to the tag.
2. The tag updates its state, and computes and sends to the reader a *triple*, $(I, v_T, auth)$. The first two entries are used for identification and (if the synchronization is lost) to resynchronize tag and reader. More precisely, the value I can be seen as a sort of *pseudonym*, which changes at each invocation, while the value v_T contains information about the *current randomizer* CR of the tag. Finally, the value $auth$ is the *authenticator*, used to authenticate the tag to the reader.
3. The reader, once received $(I, v_T, auth)$, looks in DB for a tuple starting with pseudonym I. If a tuple is found, the reader checks the received values are computed correctly from the tag, overwrites the old tuple for the tag with the current tuple, updates the current tuple $< I, \sigma, k, CR_{DB} >$, and sends to the tag a value which acknowledges the received triple and authenticates the reader to the tag. Otherwise, it first tries to resynchronize with the tag and, then, it does the same check and update. If fails then it sends a random value to the tag.
4. The tag checks whether the received value is equal to the value it is expecting to receive and, accordingly, updates its key and outputs 1 or outputs 0.

A complete description of the protocol, referred to as $EFPP$, is given in Figure 1. The subroutines tag and reader invoke are described below.

Compute(c)	Verify($ID, c, I, v_T, auth$)
$I = g_1((CR||pad_1) \oplus k)$	$s = g_2(\sigma)$
$(v_0, v_1) = g((c \oplus I) \oplus k)$	if $auth \neq h_s(c \oplus I \oplus v_T)$ then return $(rnd, 0)$
$v_T = (CR||pad_2) \oplus v_0$	$(v_0, v_1) = g((c \oplus I) \oplus k)$
$CR = CR + \sigma_{|n-d}$	if $(CR_{DB}||pad_2) \neq v_T \oplus v_0$ then return $(rnd, 0)$
$(\sigma, s) = (g_1(\sigma), g_2(\sigma))$	return $(v_1, 1)$
$auth = h_s(c \oplus I \oplus v_T)$	
return $(v_1, I, v_T, auth)$	

Protocol steps:

1. Reader: chooses $c \in \{0,1\}^n$ uniformly at random, and sends c to the Tag.
2. Tag: sets $(v_1, I, v_T, auth) = \mathsf{Compute}(c)$ and sends $(I, v_T, auth)$ to the Reader.
3. Reader: if there exists a tuple $tp = (I, \sigma, k, CR_{DB})$ in DB for tag ID
   (a) computes $(v_1, b) = \mathsf{Verify}(ID, c, I, v_T, auth)$
   (b) if $(b == 1)$ then invokes $\mathsf{Update}(ID, tp)$ and outputs 1; else outputs 0
   (c) sets $v_R = v_1$ and sends v_R
   else, if no such a tuple exists, then
   (a) sets $(CR_N, ID) = \mathsf{Lookupkey}(I, c, v_T)$ and $d = \mathsf{Resynch}(CR_N, ID)$
   (b) if $(d == 0)$ then sets $v_1 = rnd$;
       else $(v_1, b) = \mathsf{Verify}(ID, c, I, v_T, auth)$
           if $(b == 1)$ then $\mathsf{Update}(ID, ID[1])$ and outputs 1; else outputs 0
   (c) sets $v_R = v_1$ and sends v_R
4. Tag: if $v_R == v_1$, then sets $k = g_1(k)$ and outputs 1; else outputs 0

Fig. 1. EFPP: Efficient Forward-Private Protocol

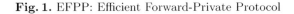

$\mathsf{Update}(ID, tp)$
$CNT_{ID} = CNT_{ID} + 1$
$DB_{ID}[0] = tp$
$CR_{DB} = CR_{DB} + \sigma_{|n-d}$
$\sigma = g_1(\sigma)$
$k = g_1(k)$
$I = g_1((CR_{DB}\|pad_1) \oplus k)$

$\mathsf{Lookupkey}(I, c, v_T)$	$\mathsf{Resynch}(CR_N, ID)$
look in DB for a key k for which	if $(0,0)$ then return 0
$(v_0, v_1) = g((c \oplus I) \oplus k)$ are such that	while $(CR_{DB} \neq CR_N$ and $CNT_{ID} < \omega)\{$
$v_T \oplus v_0 = (CR_N\|pad_2)$	$\quad CR_{DB} = CR_{DB} + \sigma_{|n-d}$
and $g_1((CR_N\|pad_1) \oplus k) = I$	$\quad \sigma = g_1(\sigma)$
if no k exists, then return$(0,0)$	$\quad CNT_{ID} = CNT_{ID} + 1$
else $DB_{ID}[1] = <I, \sigma, k, CR_{DB}>$	$\}$
$\quad$ return(CR_N, ID)	if $CNT_{ID} == \omega$ then return 0
	$\quad$ else return 1

5   Properties

The protocol enjoys several properties. Before going through formal proofs, and in order to get the ideas underlying the design, we provide some observations.

– **Desynchronization attacks.** An adversary might attack the system by sending multiple challenges c to the tag. In such a way, the tag updates CR and σ, which become different from CR_{DB} and σ stored in DB. However, notice that the identification key k, *stays the same*: it is updated *only* after a successful execution with the reader. In such a way, tag and reader, at the first adversary-free execution, recover the same value of CR and resynchronize their states. Similarly, an adversary might discard the last message from the reader to the tag. Again, the attack fails since the server stores new and old tag records in DB.

– Computational efficiency. PFP, to authenticate the tag to the reader, requires $O(N\omega)$ iterations of the PRNG g. Our scheme requires $O(N + \omega)$ iterations of g. The small extra-amount of tag-side computation at each protocol execution consistently reduces the server-side computation.

– Forward-privacy. If an adversary corrupts the tag *after* a successful execution with the reader has occurred, he gets the current state and identification key. The assumptions on g (i.e., it is a PRNG) guarantee the property[5].

6   Security Reductions

In this section we show that the protocol is private, secure and correct.

Privacy. We prove that the privacy property holds by showing that if there exists an adversary A_p which wins the privacy experiment for our protocol, then there exists an adversary B_p which wins the privacy experiment for PFP with the same advantage. Since PFP is private, we conclude that our protocol is private, too. Essentially B_p uses *the context of his privacy experiment*, to simulate *the context of the privacy experiment for adversary* A_p, which works against our protocol. Hence, we need to show *how* B_p simulates the context for A_p and *why* A_p does not distinguish the simulated context from the real one. Adversary B_p works as follows:

– B_p starts the simulation of 2 'augmented' tags, T_0' and T_1', for the adversary A_p, by using the real tags T_0 and T_1 of the privacy experiment for PFP he is interacting too.

– B_p runs A_p. B_p answers correctly all A_p's queries relaying modified queries to the tags and extending tags replies in phase 1. The modified queries and replies are constructed as follows: if A_p asks the reader to start a new execution, then B_p chooses a uniformly at random c and sends it to A_p. If A_p sends c to the tag, then B_p *chooses uniformly at random* the values I and v_T, and computes $c' = c \oplus I \oplus v_T$. Then sends c' to the tag and gets back $h_s(c')$. Hence, constructs the triple $(I, v_T, h_s(c'))$, stores it in a database of simulated transcripts $STDB$, and sends it to A_p. If A_p sends the triple to the reader, then B_p checks if the triple is in $STDB$, simulates acceptance of the reader and sends (and stores in $STDB$) v_1, *chosen uniformly at random*, to

---

[5] It is easy to see that, if an Adv corrupts the tag, for example, after sending it a challenge, then he gets the identification key k (which stays the same as long as an adversary-free execution tag/reader does not occur) and can trace the tag by re-computing the pseudonym I. As we have stressed before, such corruptions *during or after failed executions* are precluded by the model.

A_p. If A_p sends v_1 to the tag, B_p checks in $STDB$ and simulates acceptance by the tag. Therefore, B_p (using the real tags) is able to provide a *partially simulated* transcript to A_p.

- Let b be the bit chosen by the privacy experiment runner R for PFP, and let T_b be the target tag. Since B_p is simulating the privacy experiment for A_p, implicitly the choice of R holds for B_p. (Let us assume that R just removes from the scene $T_{b\oplus1}$.) Then, B_p keeps going with the simulation described before and, when A_p asks to corrupt T'_b, then B_p corrupts T_b, and forwards to A_p the state σ (read in T_b memory) and values *chosen uniformly at random* for CR and k to complete the amount of information which would be stored in a real tag T'_b. Finally, B_p outputs the same bit b' that A_p outputs.

B_p defeats the privacy of PFP exactly with the same probability with which A_p defeats the privacy of $EFPP$. What is left in the proof is to show that A_p *does not distinguish* the simulated transcript from a real transcript.

To this aim, notice that the transcript of a protocol execution is given by tuples of the form $(c, I, v_T, auth, v_1)$, where c is chosen uniformly at random, I, v_T and v_1 are computed through the PRNG g, and $auth$ is computed through the strongly universal hash function h_s, plus CR and k, obtained by corrupting the tag *after* a successful protocol execution. Let H_0, H_1, H_2 and H_3 (hybrid) distributions of tuples defined as follows:

- H_0 contains tuples $(c, I, v_T, auth, v_1)$ computed like in the real protocol
- H_1 contains tuples $(c, I, v_T, auth, v_1)$ where I is chosen uniformly at random
- H_2 contains tuples $(c, I, v_T, auth, v_1)$ where I and v_T are chosen uniformly at random
- H_3 contains tuples $(c, I, v_T, auth, v_1)$ where I, v_T and v_1 are chosen uniformly at random

Notice that H_3 is the distribution of sequences produced in our simulation by B_p. By showing that, for $i = 0, 1, 2$, it holds that H_i is indistinguishable from H_{i+1}, we infer that H_0 is indistinguishable from H_3. To show that, for $i = 0, 1, 2$, it holds that H_i is indistinguishable from H_{i+1}, we use the same technique: if there exists a distinguisher D_H between the two hybrids, then there exists a distinguisher D_g which distinguishes the outputs of the PRNG from truly random values. Let us report the proof for the first case.

Let H_i and H_j be two distributions over sequences of m tuples. We say that H_i and H_j are (T, ϵ)-indistinguishable, iff $Adv_{D_{H_i, H_j}}(T) \le \epsilon$, for any distinguisher D_{H_i, H_j} running in time at most T.

Lemma 4. *If g is a (T, ϵ_g)-secure PRNG, then H_0 and H_1 are (T_i, ϵ_i)-indistinguishable where $T_i = T - 3(m-1)T_g - (m-1)T_h$ and $\epsilon_i = \epsilon_g m^2$.*

Proof. Let $H_{0,0}$ be a sequence of m tuples, generated according to distribution H_0, and let $H_{0,m}$ be a sequence of m tuples, generated according to distribution H_1. Moreover, for $i = 1, \ldots, m - 1$, let $H_{0,i}$ be a sequence of m tuples, generated by choosing in the first i tuples the value I uniformly at random, and the remaining $m - i$ as in H_0. If there exists a (T_H, ϵ_H) distinguisher D_{H_0,H_1} for the distributions H_0 and H_1, then there exists an index i such that D_{H_0,H_1} distinguishes between $H_{0,i}$ and $H_{0,i+1}$ with advantage $\geq \epsilon_H/m$. We construct a distinguisher D_g, by using D_{H_0,H_1} as a subroutine, as follows:

- Let V be the challenge-value D_g has to decide (PRNG output or Random).
- Chooses uniformly at random an index $i \in \{1, \ldots, m - 1\}$.
- Constructs a sequence of tuples H_c by following the distribution $H_{0,i}$.
- Substitutes in the i-th tuple the value of I with the challenge-value V and provides H_c to D_{H_0,H_1}.
- If D_{H_0,H_1} outputs 0, then D_g outputs 0. Else D_g outputs 1.

Notice that, when $V = g_1((CR||pad_1) \oplus k)$ then $H_c = H_{0,i}$. On the other hand, when V is a random value, then $H_c = H_{0,i+1}$. It follows that D_g distinguishes the output of the PRNG from a random value with advantage $\geq \epsilon_H/m^2$. Moreover, D_g has running time upper bounded by $T_H + 3(m - 1)T_g + (m - 1)T_h$. Since by assumption g is (T, ϵ_g)-secure, if $T_H + 3(m - 1)T_g + (m - 1)T_h < T$, we get that $\epsilon_H/m^2 \leq \epsilon_g$, from which it follows that H_i and H_j are (T_i, ϵ_i)-indistinguishable, where $T_i = T - 3(m - 1)T_g - (m - 1)T_h$ and $\epsilon_i \leq \epsilon_g m^2$. $\triangle$

Similarly, we can show that if A_p distinguishes CR and k of the simulated transcript from CR and k obtained by opening a tag after a real successful protocol execution, then we can construct a distinguisher for the PRNG g. It follows that A_p does not distinguish a simulated transcript from a real one and we conclude that:

Theorem 3. *If PFP is (q, T, ϵ_p)-private, then EFPP is (q, T, ϵ_p)-private.*

Secure tag authentication. Notice that, restricting the attention to the first two rounds, our protocol generalises PFP. The first round is the same. In the second, the tag sends a triple (containing a value of h_s) instead of a single value h_s. Along the same line of the proof of [4], we show that, if there exists an efficient adversary A, which is able to impersonate a tag to the reader, then there exists an efficient distinguisher B capable of distinguishing outputs of the PRNG G_ω from random values in $\{0, 1\}^{\omega k}$. By suitably choosing the PRNG g, we show that the probability with whom B (and hence A) succeeds is small. More precisely, we construct B as follows:

- B receives in input the sequence of values $z_1, \ldots, z_\omega$ it has to decide from which source it comes from.
- Then, it uses the above values $z_1, \ldots, z_\omega$ to simulate the computations of the tag T (of unknown state) and the reader with whom A is supposed to interact. More precisely, B answers all A's queries in phase 1 as follows: if A asks the reader to start a new execution, then B chooses a uniformly at random c and sends it to A. If A sends c to the tag then, assuming it is the i-th execution, B chooses uniformly at random the values I, v_1 and v_T, sets $s = z_i$, and computes and sends to A the triple $(I, v_T, h_s(c \oplus I \oplus v_T))$. It also stores the triple and v_1 in $STDB$. If A sends the triple to the reader, then

B checks in $STDB$ whether there exists an entry which matches the triple, simulates acceptance of the reader and sends v_1 to A. If A sends v_1 to the tag, B checks in $STDB$ and simulates acceptance of the tag.

- Let c be the challenge on which A, in phase 2, tries to impersonate T. B gets back from A the triple $(I, v_T, h_s(c \oplus I \oplus v_T))$. B checks whether $h_s(c \oplus I \oplus v_T) = h_{z_{q+1}}(c \oplus I \oplus v_T)$ (A has interacted $q < \omega$ times with tag and reader in phase 1) and, if the check is satisfied then accepts and outputs 1; otherwise, it outputs 0.

Notice that, if $z_1, \ldots, z_\omega$ is pseudorandom (let us denote it as Z_{G_ω}), then B outputs 1 with probability p_A. Indeed, it is possible to show that the transcript of the simulated executions is *indistinguishable* from the transcript of real executions and, by assumption, on real transcripts, A impersonates the tag with probability p_A. The indistinguishability can be shown by using standard arguments: if A distinguishes between the transcripts, then can be constructed an efficient distinguisher for g. On the other hand, following the reasoning of [4] and applying Lemma 2, simple computations show that, if $z_1, \ldots, z_\omega$ are truly random values (let us denote them as Z_U), the probability that B outputs 1 is less than $\omega(2^{-\ell} + \epsilon(1 + 2q\epsilon))$. It follows that:

$$|Pr[B(Z_{G_\omega}) = 1] - Pr[B(Z_U) = 1]| \geq p_A - \omega(2^{-\ell} + \epsilon(1 + 2q\epsilon)).$$

However, if g is a (T, ϵ_g)-secure PRNG, applying Theorem 1, we get that the advantage $|Pr[B(Z_{G_\omega}) = 1] - Pr[B(Z_U) = 1]| \leq \omega\epsilon_g$. The last two equalities show that $p_A \leq \omega(\epsilon_g + 2^{-\ell} + \epsilon(1 + 2q\epsilon))$. Moreover, B's running time is equal to A's running time plus q computations of h_s for the tag simulation. Therefore, we can conclude that:

Theorem 4. *If $\mathcal{H}$ is an ϵ-almost strongly universal hash function family, g is a (T, ϵ_g)-secure PRNG, and $q \leq 1/2\epsilon$, then EFPP is (q, T', ϵ_s)-secure (w.r.t tag authentication) with $T' = T - (\omega + 1)T_g - qT_h$ and $\epsilon_s = \omega(\epsilon_g + 2^{-\ell} + \epsilon(1 + 2q\epsilon))$.*

Secure reader authentication. An adversary A, to be authenticated as reader from the tag T, has to send in the third round of the protocol the right value v_1 to T. By using the same argument and simulation we have used before we show that, if there is an efficient A who guesses v_1 with probability p_A, then there exists a distinguisher B which distinguishes outputs of the PRNG G_ω from random values in $\{0, 1\}^{\omega k}$, and then, by suitably choosing the PRNG g, we show that the probability p_A is small. The distinguisher B uses A as a subroutine and simulates A's interaction with tag and reader. Eventually, if A impersonates the reader, then B outputs 1. Otherwise, if A fails, then B outputs 0. When the sequence $z_1, \ldots, z_\omega$ is chosen uniformly at random, then B outputs 1 with probability at least $\frac{1}{2^k}$. On the other hand, if $z_1, \ldots, z_\omega$ is pseudorandom, then, B outputs 1 with probability p_A. Indeed, as argued before, the simulated values received by A from B are indistinguishable from the values of real executions with the tag T and, by assumption, on real transcripts, A impersonates the reader with probability p_A. It follows that:

$$Adv_{G_\omega}(B) = |Pr[B(Z_{G_\omega}) = 1] - Pr[B(Z_U) = 1]| \geq p_A - 1/2^k$$

Due to Theorem 1, if g is a (T, ϵ_g)-secure PRNG, then it follows that $Adv_{G_\omega}(B) \leq \omega\epsilon_g$. Hence, it holds that $p_A \leq 1/2^k + \omega\epsilon_g$. In conclusion:

Theorem 5. *If g is a (T, ϵ_g)-secure PRNG, then EFPP is $(q, T', \omega\epsilon_g)$-secure (w.r.t. reader authentication) where $T' = T - (\omega + 1)T_g - qT_h$.*

Correctness. In an adversary-free execution, a tag T (resp. reader) is not authenticated by the reader (resp. tag), only if the reader *updated twice* the tuple associated to the tag in the database DB and the tag did not or the tag updated its secret key k and the reader did not. Such events happen only if

1. The adversary is able to impersonate the tag T (resp. the reader).
2. Collisions of g and h occur.

Due to the security of the scheme, as we have seen before, the first possibility happens with small probability. Hence, we do not need to care about it. Regarding the second, collisions of g and h, we need to consider two separate cases: during an execution of the protocol, at a certain point, there exists a tuple in DB associated to *another* tag either with the same I and matching equations or with a different I' but a secret key k by means of which we get a collision on c, I, v_T, and $auth$. More precisely, in the first case there exists in DB a tuple $(I, k', \sigma', CR'_{DB})$, associated to tag $ID' \neq ID$, for which $(v_0, v_1) = g(c \oplus I \oplus k')$ are such that:

$$v_T \oplus v_0 = CR'_{DB}||pad_2 \bigwedge g_1((CR'_{DB}||pad_1) \oplus k') = I \bigwedge h_{s'}(c \oplus I \oplus v_T) = auth$$

while, in the second, there exists a tuple $(I', k', \sigma', CR'_{DB})$ for which $(v_0, v_1) = g(c \oplus I \oplus k')$ are such that:

$$v_T \oplus v_0 = CR_N||pad_2 \bigwedge g_1((CR_N||pad_1) \oplus k') = I \bigwedge h_{s'}(c \oplus I \oplus v_T) = auth$$

Notice that $g_1((CR'_{DB}||pad_1) \oplus k') = I$ implies that $g_1((CR_{DB}||pad_1) \oplus k) = g_1((CR'_{DB}||pad_1) \oplus k') = I$ i.e., g produces a collision. If g is a (T, ϵ_g)-secure PRNG, then it produces collisions with probability less than ϵ_g. Otherwise, it would possible to construct a simple distinguisher for g which distinguishes pseudorandom values from truly random values with probability higher than ϵ_g. Moreover, due to Lemma 3, the equality $h_s(c \oplus I \oplus v_T) = h_{s'}(c \oplus I \oplus v_T) = auth$, for $s \neq s'$, occurs with probability $1/2^m$. A similar analysis applies to the second case. In conclusion, it holds that:

Lemma 5. *If $\mathcal{H}$ is an ϵ-almost strongly universal hash function family and g is a (T, ϵ_g)-secure PRNG, a collision during an execution of the protocol occurs with probability $< 2 \cdot \epsilon_g/2^m = \epsilon_g/2^{m-1}$.*

We need to consider the probability of collisions within the lifetime of the protocol. If the system has N tags, since each tag can be used at most ω times, the protocol is useful for at most $N\omega$ authentications. By using the above result, we get that the probability of a collision within the system is $p_c \leq (N-1)\omega^2\epsilon_g/2^{m-1}$.

Let g be a (T, ϵ_g)-secure PRNG, where $T \geq (N-1)\omega^2 T_h + (\omega+1)T_g$. Theorem 2 shows that the PRNG G_ω^N, constructed from g (which models tag state updates and the generation of seeds for h_s,) is an $((N-1)\omega^2 T_h, N\omega\epsilon_g)$-secure PRNG. Applying the same steps of [4], we can conclude that the probability of failure of the protocol is $p < (N-1)\omega^2 \epsilon_g / 2^{m-1} + N\omega\epsilon_g + \epsilon_s$, where ϵ_s is the probability of impersonation. In conclusion:

Theorem 6. *Let g be a (T, ϵ_g)-secure PRNG where $T \geq (N-1)\omega^2 T_h + (\omega+1)T_g$, let $\mathcal{H}$ be an ϵ-almost strongly universal hash function family, and let $q \leq 1/2\epsilon$. The EFPP authentication protocol is (q, T', ϵ_c)-correct, with $T' = T - (\omega + 1)(3T_g + qT_h)$ and $\epsilon_c = (N-1)\omega^2 \epsilon_g / 2^{m-1} + N\omega\epsilon_g + \epsilon_s$.*

7 Conclusions

We have proposed an efficient forward-private RFID mutual authentication protocol, secure under the assumption that exist secure pseudorandom number generators and strongly universal hash function families. At each authentication, compared to PFP where the tag computes one time the PRNG g and one time the hash function h_s, the tag has to apply 3 times g and one time h_s. On the other hand, the server, to authenticate a tag, in the worst case, instead of $O(N\omega)$ evaluations of g and h_s as in PFP, needs only $O(N+\omega)$ evaluations, where N is the total number of tags in the system, and ω is the maximum number of authentications each single tag can afford during its lifetime. The server has full control over the number of protocol executions a tag has been subject to. The full version of this paper [8] reports an experimental comparison of PFP vs $EFPP$, obtained by implementing the protocols.

Acknowledgment

The work described in this paper has been supported in part by the European Commission through the ICT program under contract 216676 ECRYPT II, in part by the Italian Ministry of University and Research - Project PRIN 2008 PEPPER: Privacy and Protection of Personal Data (prot. 2008SY2PH4), and in part by Project MTM2010-15167 from the Spanish Ministry of Science and Technology.

References

1. Avoine, G.: RFID Security and Privacy Lounge, http://www.avoine.net/rfid/
2. Bellare, M., Rogaway, P.: Random oracles are practical: A paradigm for designing efficient protocols. In: Proceedings of the First Annual Conference on Computer and Communications Security. ACM, New York (1993)
3. Bellare, M., Pointcheval, D., Rogaway, P.: Authenticated key exchange secure against dictionary attacks. In: Preneel, B. (ed.) EUROCRYPT 2000. LNCS, vol. 1807, pp. 139–155. Springer, Heidelberg (2000)

4. Berbain, C., Billet, O., Etrong, J., Gilbert, H.: An Efficient Forward Private RFID Protocol. In: 16th ACM Conference on Computer and Communications Security (CCS 2009), pp. 43–53 (2009)
5. Billet, O., Etrog, J., Gilbert, H.: Lightweight Privacy Preserving Authentication for RFID Using a Stream Cipher. In: Hong, S., Iwata, T. (eds.) FSE 2010. LNCS, vol. 6147, pp. 55–74. Springer, Heidelberg (2010)
6. Canetti, R., Goldreich, O., Halevi, S.: The Random Oracle Methodology, Revisited. In: Proceedings of ACM STOC (1998)
7. Carter, J.L., Wegman, M.N.: Universal classes of hash functions. J. Computer and System Sci. 18, 143–154 (1979)
8. D'Arco, P.: An Almost-Optimal Forward-Private RFID Mutual Authentication Protocol with Tag Control, http://www.dia.unisa.it/paodar
9. D'Arco, P., Scafuro, A., Visconti, I.: Revisiting DoS Attacks and Privacy in RFID-Enabled Networks. In: 5th International Workshop on Algorithmic Aspects of Wireless Sensor Networks (ALGOSENSORS 2009). LNCS, vol. 5304, pp. 76–87 (2009)
10. Damgård, I., Østergaard, M.: RFID Security: Tradeoffs between Security and Efficiency. In: Proceedings of the RSA Conference, Cryptographers' Track, pp. 318–332 (2008)
11. Deng, R., Li, Y., Yao, A., Yung, M., Zhao, Y.: A New Framework for RFID Privacy, eprint archive, report no. 2010/059, http://eprint.iacr.org/
12. Deng, R., Li, Y., Yung, M., Zhao, Y.: A New Framework for RFID Privacy. In: Gritzalis, D., Preneel, B., Theoharidou, M. (eds.) ESORICS 2010. LNCS, vol. 6345, pp. 1–18. Springer, Heidelberg (2010)
13. Juels, A.: The Vision of Secure RFID. Proceedings of the IEEE 95(8), 1507–1508 (2007)
14. Juels, A., Pappu, R., Garfinkel, S.: RFID Privacy: An Overview of Problems and Proposed Solutions. IEEE Security and Privacy 3(3), 34–43 (2005)
15. Ohkubo, M., Suzuki, K., Kinoshita, S.: Efficient hash-chain based RFID privacy protection scheme. In: Proc. of the International Conference on Ubiquitous Computing Ubicomp Workshop Privacy: Current Status and Future Directions, Nottingham, England (September 2004)
16. Paise, R., Vaudenay, S.: Mutual Authentication in RFID: Security and Privacy. In: Proceedings of Aisaccs 2008, Lecture Notes in Computer Science, pp. 292–299 (2008)
17. Van Le, T., Burmester, M., de Medeiros, B.: Universally Composable and Forward-Secure Rfid Authentication and Authenticated Key Exchange. In: Proc. of ASIACCS 2007, pp. 242–252 (2007)
18. Vaudenay, S.: On Privacy Models for RFID. In: Kurosawa, K. (ed.) ASIACRYPT 2007. LNCS, vol. 4833, pp. 68–87. Springer, Heidelberg (2007)
19. Stinson, D.R.: Universal hashing and authentication codes. Designs, Codes and Cryptography (4), 369–380 (1994)
20. Wegman, M.N.: New hash functions and their use in authentication and set equality. Journal of Computer and System Sciences 22(3), 265–279 (1981)

Affiliation-Hiding Authentication with Minimal Bandwidth Consumption

Mark Manulis and Bertram Poettering

Cryptographic Protocols Group, TU Darmstadt & CASED, Germany
mark@manulis.eu, bertram.poettering@cased.de

Abstract. Affiliation-Hiding Authentication (AHA) protocols have the seemingly contradictory property of enabling users to authenticate each other as members of certain groups, without revealing their affiliation to group outsiders. Of particular interest in practice is the *group-discovering* variant, which handles multiple group memberships per user. Corresponding solutions were only recently introduced, and have two major drawbacks: high bandwidth consumption (typically several kilobits per user and affiliation), and only moderate performance in scenarios of practical application.

While prior protocols have $O(n^2)$ time complexity, where n denotes the number of affiliations per user, we introduce a new AHA protocol running in $O(n \log n)$ time. In addition, the bandwidth consumed is considerably reduced. We consider these advances a major step towards deployment of privacy-preserving methods in constraint devices, like mobile phones, to which the economization of these resources is priceless.

1 Introduction

In cryptography, Authenticated Key Establishment (AKE) protocols are an essential building block for creation of secure communication channels. Such schemes offer both the establishment of a strong session key and, simultaneously, mutual authentication of respective protocol partners. Usually, this authentication step is PKI-based and explicitly reveals to other users (including adversarial eavesdroppers) the identities and certificates of participants. This behavior can be considered a breach of users' privacy. To tackle this issue, Affiliation-Hiding Authentication (AHA) in form of Secret Handshakes (SH) [1, 2, 9, 15–17, 29–31] and key establishment protocols (AHA/KE) [13, 14, 19, 21, 22] emerged in the last decade.

Generally, in AHA protocols, users authenticate each other on basis of their affiliation to certain groups, and do so in a privacy-preserving manner: In the classical 'exact matching' approach [2, 9, 15, 17, 29–31], the own affiliation is revealed to the protocol partner if and only if the protocol partner is member of the same group. Users become members of groups by registering with the respective group's authority (GA). On admission of a new user, GA generates a corresponding membership certificate and gives it to the user. This credential allows the user to authenticate itself to other group members in later so-called

C.A. Ardagna and J. Zhou (Eds.): WISTP 2011, LNCS 6633, pp. 85–99, 2011.

'Handshake' sessions. We stress that the attempt to authenticate to non-members using such a group membership certificate not only fails, but in addition does not reveal any evidence or even hint about the group membership to given non-member. This is the pivotal property in affiliation-hiding security.

The main difference between the notions of Secret Handshakes and AHA/KE protocols is that the former are pure authentication protocols, i.e. are limited to perform the affiliation-hiding authentication of users, while the latter also succeed in the generation of a secure session key that may be used to protect further communication and exchange of digital data. In particular, AHA/KE protocols guarantee the usual key security properties of AKE protocols [3, 8] (including forward secrecy, etc).

These properties make AHA/KE protocols very attractive in various settings where privacy-preserving communication is needed. Their deployment in practice, especially on resource constraint devices and networks, requires, however, further research on efficient solutions. As we elaborate in the next sections, current proposals have efficiency limitations and are, therefore, less suitable in a mobile setting. To overcome these limitations we propose a novel AHA/KE protocol that outperforms existing approaches and minimizes the consumed communication bandwidth.

1.1   Linkable vs. Unlinkable AHA

Affiliation-Hiding Authentication protocols are either linkable or unlinkable. In *linkable* schemes [2, 9, 13, 14], users hold identities or have assigned pseudonyms which they actively reveal in protocol runs. Still, hiding of affiliations is considered valuable nonetheless, and remains an explicit security goal of those protocols. Linkable protocols are usually deployed in cases where participants are addressed by their identities anyway, e.g. in instant messaging, social networks, etc.

In *unlinkable* affiliation-hiding protocols [1, 15, 17, 31], however, sessions of users cannot be linked back to them. Obviously, these schemes offer a higher level of privacy. The challenging part in their design is the support of revocation, i.e. exclusion of members from the group: even though users do not have explicit identities, the schemes must provide methods for their individual exclusion.

In practice, linkable AHA protocols enjoy very efficient revocation by blacklisting pseudonyms on public revocation lists, while unlinkable AHA protocols support revocation either by restricting the number of unlinkable sessions of users [31], by regularly updating unrevoked membership credentials [15], or by the considerably costly verification of revocation tokens [17].

1.2   The Challenge of Group Discovery

Classical AHA schemes [1, 2, 9, 15, 17, 29–31] are mostly *single-group* protocols, i.e. it is assumed that the participating users are member of one group each, and the protocol execution checks whether these groups are identical or not. We argue, however, that this restriction to only one group may not be acceptable in practice. Consider, for instance, a social network where users are member of many, say n, groups. Now, when two participants of the network meet they may want to investigate in a privacy-preserving manner whether they have any group in common or not. If they used a classical AHA scheme, they would have to run $n \times n$ protocol instances in parallel to cover all possible combinations, spotting and reporting only the matching ones. This overhead is clearly unacceptable in practice for being inefficient, and justifies the need for special group-discovering (but still affiliation-hiding) protocols. The plurality of existing AHA schemes, however, ignores the *group-discovery* problem by design, and only two schemes, namely [16] and [19], support deployment of credentials for multiple groups in a single protocol run.

For AHA protocols that support multiple credentials, we need to define what we consider a successful authentication. It seems that the most useful notion is the following: If both users provide credentials for various groups in a specific protocol execution, the authentication is considered successful if there is at least one group in common. Output of the protocol would be this indication and, optionally, a list of all matching groups.

1.3   Related Work

The Secret Handshakes in [2, 9, 30] are linkable protocols that have been designed for the main purpose of authentication. While some of them, additionally, offer the generation of a session key, security of the latter is neither formally analyzed nor does it reach an adequate level of security in practice. In contrast, the schemes from [14, 21, 22] incorporate a secure key establishment protocol that satisfies accepted models of key security [3, 8]. Group Secret Handshakes are presented by Jarecki et al. in [12, 13], where the two-party setting is extended to multiparty authentication and key agreement. Both works achieve session group key establishment through a variant of the Burmester-Desmedt technique [7]. In [18, 21, 22], the impact of corrupt GAs on users' privacy is explored. In particular, while Manulis et al. [21, 22] act conservatively and harden protocols to withstand GA attacks, Kawai [18] deviates from the traditional setting by splitting the GA's role among an issue authority and a tracing authority (that are assumed not to collude).

We remark that unlinkable AHA schemes can generically be obtained from linkable protocols by using one-time pseudonyms; however, this approach is clearly impractical for not being scalable. Due to this restriction, several unlinkable Secret Handshakes [1, 15, 17, 29] based on reusable credentials have been proposed. Here, the challenging part is revocation of protocol participants: Ateniese's protocol [1] does not support revocation at all, Jarecki [15] presents a protocol in which participants need to regularly contact the GA for an update of users' internal state, Tsudik [29] introduces a heavy-weight framework that involves the use of group signatures and broadcast encryption techniques, while the state-of-the-art scheme [17] by Jarecki et al. uses group signatures with verifier-local revocation for group management and private conditional oblivious transfer for the handshake session, in the pairing-based setting.

Exclusively the protocols in [16, 19] offer support for multiple credentials per user, i.e. they solve the problem of efficient group-discovery. Still, the scheme in [16] by Jarecki et al. has the somehow weird and unusual property that GAs are in the position to fully impersonate any user that is registered to them: First step of the registration process to a group is that user sends its complete private key material to the corresponding GA, which then computes the appropriate user credential from it. Manulis' scheme in [19] is a rather efficient RSA-based protocol with two exponentiations per user and group, and can be considered the state-of-the-art protocol for group-discovering AHA/KE.

In the efficiency analyses, both [16] and [19] distinguish between the so-called asymmetric and symmetric workload of their protocols. While the former reflects the amount of (expensive) public key operations like exponentiations and pairing computations, the latter covers the remaining (relatively cheap) parts, including block cipher and hash function evaluations. Claiming that protocols' efficiency can be adequately estimated by taking into account only their asymmetric overhead, [16] and [19] promote their schemes as $O(n)$ protocols, where n is the number of group affiliations per user, although in both cases the real number of operations is $O(n^2)$. Contradicting this reasoning, recent results in [20] reveal that, in practice, the symmetric overhead of [16, 19] may not be neglected and limits protocols' applicability. We stress that our new protocol presented in Section 3 offers real $O(n \log n)$ performance, counting *all* computations, while the asymmetric workload remains to be $O(n)$, as in [16, 19].

1.4   Contributions and Organization

The contribution of this work is the construction of a new and highly-efficient linkable group-discovering AHA/KE protocol that outclasses existing schemes [16, 19] in several aspects: First, our protocol is the first real $O(n \log n)$ solution (consisting of $O(n)$ public key operations plus a simple sorting step in $O(n \log n)$). Second, the protocol's bandwidth requirements are impressively low. Specifically, as we will show in Section 3.3, our protocol consumes only 4% of the bandwidth when compared to [19].

We consider these improvements as a major step forward to make privacy-preserving techniques deployable in practice. In particular, on mobile devices, which are usually restricted in at least computing power or available bandwidth, without our improvements, execution of AHA protocols would be hardly feasible.

As an application, we envision users managing and exploring their social network relationships through their mobile phones that form ad hoc wireless networks of constraint range. In these scenarios, privacy-preserving techniques are of highest importance.

We start our work by giving insight into our main building block, a *Non-Interactive Key Distribution Scheme* (NIKDS), in Section 2. In Section 3 we present our new protocol, and discuss its efficiency and the selection of reasonable parameters for deployment in practice. We support the security of our protocol by giving a formal analysis in form of a model specification (Section 4) and proof of security (Section 5), in respect to this model.

2 Non-Interactive Key Distribution

In a multi-user setting, the purpose of a Non-Interactive Key Distribution Scheme (NIKDS) [5, 11, 23] is the assignment of a (fixed) symmetric key to each pair of users. The intrinsic property and advantage of NIKDS over (authenticated) key establishment protocols is that NIKDS are non-interactive, i.e. users can compute the particular keys shared with other users without any (prior) communication with them.

Typically, NIKDS are identity based schemes, i.e. users are 'addressed' by their identities, which may be arbitrary strings. In NIKDS, users first register their particular identity $id \in \{0,1\}^*$ with an authority called *Key Generation Center* (KGC) to obtain their specific user credential $sk[id]$. With this credential they can compute, without any interaction, a key shared between id and id', for any other user identity $id' \in \{0,1\}^*$. The notion of NIKDS and its security properties are formalized next.

2.1 Definition and Security Model of NIKDS

Definition 1. *A* Non-Interactive Key Distribution Scheme *is a tuple* NIKDS = (Setup, Register, GetKey) *of efficient algorithms as follows:*

Setup(1^λ) :
> *This algorithm initializes a* KGC. *On input security parameter* 1^λ, *it outputs a secret key* sk.

Register(sk, id) :
> *On input* KGC*'s secret key* sk *and user identity* $id \in \{0,1\}^*$, *this algorithm outputs private user credential* $sk[id]$.

GetKey($sk[id], id'$) :
> *On input user credential* $sk[id]$ *and user identity* $id' \in \{0,1\}^*$, *this algorithm outputs a key* $K \in \{0,1\}^\lambda$.

A NIKDS *is called* correct *if for all* $\lambda \in \mathbb{N}$, *all* $sk \leftarrow$ Setup(1^λ), *all user identities* $id, id' \in \{0,1\}^*$, *all* $sk[id] \leftarrow$ Register(sk, id) *and* $sk[id'] \leftarrow$ Register(sk, id'), *and all* $K \leftarrow$ GetKey($sk[id], id'$) *and* $K' \leftarrow$ GetKey($sk[id'], id$) *we have* $K = K'$. *We consider this key as a* shared key *between parties* id *and* id'. *For convenience, we denote it by* SharedKey($sk; id, id'$).

The following security property adopts the classical key indistinguishability requirements of interactive key agreement protocols [3] to the non-interactive setting. Note that in [11] an even stronger but less natural computational variant of this model is analyzed.

Definition 2 (Indistinguishability of NIKDS). *A* NIKDS = (Setup, Register, GetKey) *is called* indistinguishable under adaptive chosen-identity attacks *(IND-CIA), if for all efficient adversaries* $\mathcal{A} = (\mathcal{A}_1, \mathcal{A}_2)$ *the advantage function*

$$\mathbf{Adv}_{\mathsf{NIKDS}, \mathcal{A}}^{\text{ind-cia}}(\lambda) = \left| \Pr\left[\mathbf{Exp}_{\mathsf{NIKDS}, \mathcal{A}}^{\text{ind-cia},1}(\lambda) = 1 \right] - \Pr\left[\mathbf{Exp}_{\mathsf{NIKDS}, \mathcal{A}}^{\text{ind-cia},0}(\lambda) = 1 \right] \right|$$

is negligible in λ, *where* $\mathbf{Exp}_{\mathsf{NIKDS},\mathcal{A}}^{\mathsf{ind\text{-}cia},b}$ *denotes the following experiment:*

$\mathbf{Exp}_{\mathsf{NIKDS},\mathcal{A}}^{\mathsf{ind\text{-}cia},b}(\lambda)$:

- $sk \leftarrow \mathsf{Setup}(1^\lambda)$
- $(id, id', state) \leftarrow \mathcal{A}_1^{\mathsf{Register}(sk,\cdot)}(1^\lambda)$
- $K_0 \stackrel{\$}{\leftarrow} \{0,1\}^\lambda$ *and* $K_1 \leftarrow \mathsf{SharedKey}(sk; id, id')$
- $b' \leftarrow \mathcal{A}_2^{\mathsf{Register}(sk,\cdot)}(state, K_b)$
- *output* 0 *if* $\mathcal{A}$ *queried* $\mathsf{Register}(sk, id)$ *or* $\mathsf{Register}(sk, id')$ *to its oracle*
- *else output* b'

2.2   A Construction of NIKDS Based on Bilinear Maps (Pairings)

The first efficient NIKDS was constructed in [23] and analyzed in [11] (although the notion of NIKDS was introduced to cryptography about 20 years earlier, in [25]). The scheme is described as follows:

$\mathsf{Setup}(1^\lambda)$:
> Specify cyclic groups $G = \langle g \rangle$ and G_T of prime order q, for which an efficient non-degenerate bilinear pairing $\hat{e} : G \times G \to G_T$ is known (see also [5, Chapter X]). In addition, specify hash functions $H : \{0,1\}^* \to G$ and $H^* : G_T \to \{0,1\}^\lambda$. Pick $s \stackrel{\$}{\leftarrow} \mathbb{Z}_q \setminus \{0\}$ randomly and return secret key $sk = s$.

$\mathsf{Register}(sk, id)$:
> On input secret key $sk = s$ and identity $id \in \{0,1\}^*$, user credential $sk[id] = H(id)^s$ is output.

$\mathsf{GetKey}(sk[id], id')$:
> This algorithm outputs key $K = H^*\big(\hat{e}(sk[id], H(id'))\big)$.

Proof of Correctness. For arbitrary $id, id' \in \{0,1\}^*$, let $h \leftarrow H(id)$ and $h' \leftarrow H(id')$. We then have $sk[id] = h^s$ and $sk[id'] = (h')^s$, and correctness is implied by $\hat{e}(h^s, h') = \hat{e}(h, h')^s = \hat{e}(h', h)^s = \hat{e}((h')^s, h)$. Note that $\hat{e}(h, h') = \hat{e}(h', h)$ follows for all $h, h' \in G$ from $\hat{e}(g^a, g^b) = \hat{e}(g, g)^{ab} = \hat{e}(g^b, g^a)$. $\square$

Security of this scheme was established in [11] as follows:

Theorem 1. *NIKDS is IND-CIA secure under the Bilinear Diffie-Hellman assumption (BDH) [6] in the Random Oracle Model (ROM) [4].*

3   Our Affiliation-Hiding Authentication Protocol

In this section, we present our Affiliation-Hiding Authentication and Key Agreement protocol (AHA/KE). We kept the scheme's syntax consistent with [19], where the first practical AHA in the multi-group setting is proposed. Still, we improve considerably on that protocol in both asymptotic computational performance and bandwidth consumption. In particular, while in both [19] and our protocol the number of public key operations is linear in the number of affiliations n, the remaining 'symmetric' workload of [19] is $O(n^2)$, in contrast to $O(n \log n)$ in our protocol.

3.1   Syntax of AHA

An AHA scheme $\mathsf{AHA} = (\mathsf{CreateGroup}, \mathsf{AddUser}, \mathsf{Handshake}, \mathsf{Revoke})$ consists of four efficient algorithms and protocols:

$\mathsf{CreateGroup}(1^\lambda)$:

This algorithm is executed by a Group Authority (GA) to set up a new group G. On input security parameter 1^λ, a public/secret group key pair $(G.pk, G.sk)$ is generated, the group's pseudonym revocation list $G.prl$ is initialized to $\emptyset$, and public group parameters $G.par = (G.pk, G.prl)$ and private key $G.sk$ are output.

$\mathsf{AddUser}(G, id)$:

This algorithm is executed by the GA of group G to add user pseudonym $id \in \{0,1\}^*$ to its group. A private membership credential $sk_G[id]$ is created and confidentially handed over to the particular user. Note that users are allowed to register the same pseudonym id in different groups.

$\mathsf{Handshake}(U_i \leftrightarrow U_j)$:

This is the key exchange protocol (handshake), executed between two users U_i and U_j, that have pseudonyms id_i and id_j, respectively. Input of U_i is a set $\mathcal{G}_i$ of pairs of the form $(sk_G[id_i], G.prl)$, where all $sk_G[id_i]$ are credentials on pseudonym id_i obtained from the GA of particular G (computed by the AddUser algorithm), and $G.prl$ is the corresponding revocation list. For user U_j, the protocol's input is $\mathcal{G}_j$, analogously.

Users keep track of the state of created $\mathsf{Handshake}(\mathcal{G})$ sessions π through session variables that are initialized as follows: $\pi.\mathsf{state} \leftarrow \mathsf{running}$, $\pi.id \leftarrow id$, $\pi.\mathcal{G} \leftarrow \mathcal{G}$, and $(\pi.\mathsf{key}, \pi.\mathsf{partner}, \pi.\mathsf{groups}) \leftarrow (\bot, \bot, \emptyset)$. At some point the protocol will complete and $\pi.\mathsf{state}$ is then updated to either $\mathsf{rejected}$ or $\mathsf{accepted}$. In the latter case, $\pi.\mathsf{key}$ is set to the established session key (of length λ), the handshake partner's pseudonym is assigned to $\pi.\mathsf{partner}$, and $\pi.\mathsf{groups}$ holds a non-empty set of group identifiers.

$\mathsf{Revoke}(G, id)$:

This algorithm is executed by the GA of G and results in the update of G's pseudonym revocation list $G.prl$.

Definition 3 (Correctness of AHA). *Assume that two users with pseudonyms id_i and id_j participate in a $\mathsf{Handshake}$ protocol on inputs $\mathcal{G}_i$ and $\mathcal{G}_j$, respectively, and let π_i and π_j denote the corresponding sessions. By $\mathcal{G}_\cap$ we denote the set of groups that appear in both $\mathcal{G}_i$ and $\mathcal{G}_j$ with the restriction that neither id_i nor id_j are contained in the respective group's revocation lists $G.prl$. The AHA scheme is called* correct *if (1) π_i and π_j complete in the same state, which is $\mathsf{accepted}$ iff $\mathcal{G}_\cap \neq \emptyset$, and (2) if both sessions accept then $\pi_i.\mathsf{key} = \pi_j.\mathsf{key}$, $(\pi_i.\mathsf{partner}, \pi_j.\mathsf{partner}) = (id_j, id_i)$, and $\pi_i.\mathsf{groups} = \pi_j.\mathsf{groups} = \mathcal{G}_\cap$.*

3.2   Protocol Definition

We are ready to specify our new AHA protocol with implicit group discovery. As a major building block it uses a generic NIKDS. In particular, the scheme presented in Section 2 is suitable. Recall that the algorithms of NIKDS are denoted Setup, Register, and GetKey.

CreateGroup(1^λ) Algorithm. To create a new group, the Group Authority (GA) sets up a new KGC of a NIKDS by running $sk \leftarrow$ Setup(1^λ). In addition, the group's pseudonym revocation list $G.prl$ is emptied. This algorithm outputs $G.par = (G.prl)$ and $G.sk = sk$. Note that a group's public key is not needed, and it hence is not specified.

AddUser(G, id) Algorithm. A new user with pseudonym id is added to group G by registering id to the NIKDS's KGC: the user's private membership credential in group G will be $sk_G[id] \leftarrow$ Register(sk, id), where $sk = G.sk$.

Handshake($\mathcal{G}$) Protocol. The specification of our Handshake protocol is given in Figure 1. The protocol makes use of the following building blocks:

- To achieve forward security of the established session key, a standard Diffie-Hellman key exchange is incorporated into the protocol (cf. lines 1 and 3). Hence, we require existence of a cyclic group $\mathbb{G} = \langle g \rangle$ of prime order q in which the Computational Diffie-Hellman Problem (CDH) is hard (in respect to security parameter λ).
- By $H : \{0,1\}^* \rightarrow \{0,1\}^\ell$, where $\ell = \ell(\lambda)$ is polynomially dependent on security parameter λ, we denote a hash function. It will be modeled as random oracle in the security analysis of the protocol.
- By $Sort(\mathcal{M})$, for a set $\mathcal{M} \subseteq \{0,1\}^\ell$ of strings of length ℓ, we denote the lexicographic ordering of $\mathcal{M}$. It is well-known that $Sort(\ )$ is an $O(n \log n)$ algorithm (e.g. 'Quicksort'), and that look-up in an ordered set is an $O(\log n)$ operation.

We briefly explain the design principles of the protocol from the point of view of user U_i. For all groups G in which id_i is registered (line 5) and in which id_j is not revoked (line 6), the NIKDS key K_G shared by id_i and id_j is computed (line 7) and used to derive two authentication tags $c_{G,0}, c_{G,1}$ in lines 8 and 9 (that also will serve for key confirmation). One of the tags is sent to U_j (line 12), while the other one is stored in state variable $\mathcal{S}_i$ for later use (line 10). Note that U_j computes the same tags for all groups that both U_i and U_j are member of. This intersection set (named groups) is determined in lines 13–16, by recording all matches of group-specific authentication tags. If U_i and U_j have at least one group in common (line 17), then the protocol accepts with a secure session key (lines 1, 3, and 18). Observe that the purpose of the sorting step (center of line 12) is not only to enable an $O(\log n)$ look-up of authentication tags in line 15, but also to hide the order in which these tags have been computed. This is an important prerequisite to make the protocol affiliation-hiding.

Notice that the scheme is displayed as four-message protocol for reasons of better readability. By combining messages m_j and $Sort(\mathcal{M}_j)$ into a single datagram, the scheme can be relieved by one message transmission.

	USER U_i ON INPUT id_i AND $\mathcal{G}_i$:		USER U_j ON INPUT id_j AND $\mathcal{G}_j$:
1	$r_i \leftarrow_R \mathbb{Z}_q$	$\xrightarrow{m_i = (id_i, g^{r_i})}$ $\xleftarrow{m_j = (id_j, g^{r_j})}$	$r_j \leftarrow_R \mathbb{Z}_q$
2	sid $\leftarrow m_i \,\|\, m_j$		sid $\leftarrow m_i \,\|\, m_j$
3	$K \leftarrow$ sid $\|\, g^{r_i r_j}$		$K \leftarrow$ sid $\|\, g^{r_i r_j}$
4	$\mathcal{M}_i \leftarrow \emptyset$. $\mathcal{S}_i \leftarrow \emptyset$		$\mathcal{M}_j \leftarrow \emptyset$. $\mathcal{S}_j \leftarrow \emptyset$
5	FOR ALL $(sk_G[id_i], G.prl) \in \mathcal{G}_i$:		FOR ALL $(sk_G[id_j], G.prl) \in \mathcal{G}_j$:
6	IF $id_j \notin G.prl$:		IF $id_i \notin G.prl$:
7	$K_G \leftarrow$ GetKey$(sk_G[id_i], id_j)$		$K_G \leftarrow$ GetKey$(sk_G[id_j], id_i)$
8	$c_{G.0} \leftarrow H(K_G \,\|\, K \,\|\, 0)$		$c_{G.0} \leftarrow H(K_G \,\|\, K \,\|\, 0)$
9	$c_{G.1} \leftarrow H(K_G \,\|\, K \,\|\, 1)$		$c_{G.1} \leftarrow H(K_G \,\|\, K \,\|\, 1)$
10	$\mathcal{S}_i \leftarrow \mathcal{S}_i \cup \{(G, c_{G.1})\}$		$\mathcal{S}_j \leftarrow \mathcal{S}_j \cup \{(G, c_{G.0})\}$
11	ELSE: $c_{G.0} \leftarrow_R \{0,1\}^\ell$		ELSE: $c_{G.1} \leftarrow_R \{0,1\}^\ell$
12	$\mathcal{M}_i \leftarrow \mathcal{M}_i \cup \{c_{G.0}\}$	$\xrightarrow{Sort(\mathcal{M}_i)}$ $\xleftarrow{Sort(\mathcal{M}_j)}$	$\mathcal{M}_j \leftarrow \mathcal{M}_j \cup \{c_{G.1}\}$
13	groups$_i \leftarrow \emptyset$		groups$_j \leftarrow \emptyset$
14	FOR ALL $(G, c_{G.1}) \in \mathcal{S}_i$:		FOR ALL $(G, c_{G.0}) \in \mathcal{S}_j$:
15	IF $c_{G.1} \in Sort(\mathcal{M}_j)$:		IF $c_{G.0} \in Sort(\mathcal{M}_i)$:
16	groups$_i \leftarrow$ groups$_i \cup \{G\}$		groups$_j \leftarrow$ groups$_j \cup \{G\}$
17	IF groups$_i \neq \emptyset$ THEN		IF groups$_j \neq \emptyset$ THEN
18	key$_i \leftarrow H(K)$		key$_j \leftarrow H(K)$
19	partner$_i \leftarrow id_j$		partner$_j \leftarrow id_i$
20	TERMINATE WITH "ACCEPT"		TERMINATE WITH "ACCEPT"
21	ELSE		ELSE
22	TERMINATE WITH "REJECT"		TERMINATE WITH "REJECT"

Fig. 1. Specification of Handshake$(U_i \leftrightarrow U_j)$. We consider the left party as initiator and the right party as responder. We intentionally left out indices i, j for variables sid, $K, K_G, c_{G.0}, c_{G.1}$ as they are expected to have the same value in both U_i's and U_j's computations.

Revoke(G, id) Algorithm. By setting $G.prl \leftarrow G.prl \cup \{id\}$, the group's pseudonym revocation list $G.prl$ is extended by the new entry. The updated prl is distributed authentically to all group members.

3.3   Correctness, Efficiency, and Parameter Selection

Our AHA scheme is correct in the sense of Definition 3. This follows from correctness of deployed NIKDS and inspection of Figure 1. Recall also the exposition of design rationale in Section 3.2.

Asymptotically, the protocol is an $O(n \log n)$ protocol, where $n = |\mathcal{G}|$ denotes the number of groups per user. This is due to the fact that both the sorting step (line 12) and the tag-matching step (lines 14–16) are $O(n \log n)$. However, the number of expensive public key operations (i.e. pairing evaluations in the NIKDS) is linear in the number of affiliations. More precisely: A user that deploys credentials for n groups has to compute n pairings to complete the protocol (or even less, when considering the possibility of revoked users). Note that the AHA schemes from [16] and [19] have $O(n^2)$ workload of 'symmetric operations'. Although these can be considered rather fast in comparison to big-integer exponentiations or pairing evaluations, for large n (e.g. $n \gg 100$), the quadratic overhead of [16, 19] will be clearly noticed [20].

Especially in respect to bandwidth consumption, our protocol impressively outperforms state-of-the-art protocol [19]. In the latter, for being an RSA-based protocol, more than 4000 bits have to be sent and received per user, affiliation, and session. In our protocol, however, this number drops to about 160 bits (80 bits for each authentication tag), for a comparable level of security. Hence, our protocol consumes only 4% of the bandwidth, when compared to [19].

For practical security, we suggest to use Diffie-Hellman and pairing groups of about 2^{160} elements, authentication tags of length 80 bit (lines 8–9), and a 128 bit KDF for key derivation (line 18).

The selection of parameters for an efficient pairing suitable in practice will not be too complicated. Note that in NIKDS group elements are never transmitted from one party to the other. Hence, care does not have to be taken to find pairing-friendly curves with 'nice' element representations. Although, for reasons of convenience, only symmetric pairings were considered in Section 2 to build NIKDS, they can be built from asymmetric pairings as well [11]. At the time of writing this article, ηT-pairing evaluations on desktop machines in under 500 μs were feasible [26, 27], i.e. for a user with about 100 affiliations[1] we estimate the total running time of a Handshake execution below 50 ms. Recall from Section 2 that in our NIKDS scheme the first input element to the pairing is always $sk[id]$, which can be considered a fixed long-term parameter. See [10, 24] for considerable optimizations on fixed-argument pairing evaluations. Finally note that all NIKDS computations are session-independent and can be cached: If the same two users run the Handshake protocol multiple times they can fall back to previously computed K_G to considerably save computation time.

4   Security Model for AHA

In this section we present the security model for AHA protocols. It takes into account the challenges implied by the group discovery problem and bases on the current state-of-the-art model from [19]. Essentially, there exist two central security properties for AHA: Linkable Affiliation-Hiding security, and Authenticated Key Exchange security (with forward secrecy). Both requirements are defined with regard to multiple input groups per user and session. As the model for the latter goal is very similar to standard definitions of AKE security [3, 8], and only minor modifications are necessary to fit the LAH setting, we abstain from giving a full description of the model in this article, and refer to [19] for a detailed exposition. In contrast, LAH security is a non-standard goal and was only recently modeled [19]. We describe it in full detail below.

---

[1] Note that an average Facebook user is member of about 80 communities or groups [28].

4.1 Adversary Model

The adversary $\mathcal{A}$ is modeled as a PPT machine that interacts with protocol participants and can mount attacks via the following set of queries.

Handshake$(id, \mathcal{G}, r)$: This query lets the holder of pseudonym id start a new session π of the Handshake protocol. It receives as input a set $\mathcal{G}$ of groups G and a role identifier $r \in \{\text{init}, \text{resp}\}$ that determines whether the session will act as protocol initiator or responder. If there is a group G listed in $\mathcal{G}$ for which id has no private credential $sk_G[id]$ then this query is ignored. Optionally, this query returns a first protocol message M.

Send(π, M) : Message M is delivered to session π. After processing M, the eventual output is given to $\mathcal{A}$. This query is ignored if π is not waiting for input.

Reveal(π) : If $\pi.\text{state} = \text{running}$ then this query is ignored. Otherwise $(\pi.\text{state}, \pi.\text{key}, \pi.\text{groups})$ is returned.

Corrupt(id, G) : Membership credential $sk_G[id]$ of pseudonym id in group G is passed to the adversary. Note that this query models the possibility of selective corruptions.

Revoke(G, id) : This query lets the GA of G include id in its revocation list $G.prl$.

4.2 Linkable Affiliation-Hiding Security

We now define the property of Linkable Affiliation-Hiding (LAH). At a high level, the goal here is to protect from disclosure of non-shared affiliations to handshake partners. We model LAH-security using the indistinguishability approach (similar to that used for encryption schemes). The goal of the adversary is to decide which of two sets of affiliations, $\mathcal{G}_0^*$ or $\mathcal{G}_1^*$, some challenge session π^* is running on. The adversary specifies these sets himself, and, additionally, is allowed to invoke any number of handshake sessions, and ask Reveal and Corrupt queries at will. This intuition is formalized as follows.

Definition 4 (LAH-Security). *Let* AHA = {CreateGroup, AddUser, Handshake, Revoke}, *b be a randomly chosen bit, and* $\mathcal{Q}$ = {Handshake, Send, Reveal, Corrupt, Revoke} *denote the set of queries the adversary* $\mathcal{A}$ *has access to. We consider the following experiment between a challenger and an efficient adversary* $\mathcal{A}$:

$\mathbf{Exp}_{\text{AHA},\mathcal{A}}^{\text{lah},b}(\lambda, n, m)$:

- *the challenger creates users* $U_1, \ldots, U_n$ *and pseudonyms* ID = $\{id_1, \ldots, id_n\}$;
- *the challenger creates* m *groups* $\mathcal{G} = \{G_1, \ldots, G_m\}$ *and registers user* U_i *with pseudonym* id_i *in group* G_j *for all* $(i, j) \in [1, n] \times [1, m]$;
- $\mathcal{A}^{\mathcal{Q}}$ *interacts with all participants using the queries in* $\mathcal{Q}$; *at some point* $\mathcal{A}^{\mathcal{Q}}$ *outputs a tuple* $(id^*, \mathcal{G}_0^*, \mathcal{G}_1^*, r^*)$ *where* $id^* \in$ ID, $\mathcal{G}_0^*, \mathcal{G}_1^* \subseteq \mathcal{G}$ *with* $|\mathcal{G}_0^*| = |\mathcal{G}_1^*|$, *and* $r^* \in \{\text{init}, \text{resp}\}$. *The set* $\mathcal{D}^* = (\mathcal{G}_0^* \setminus \mathcal{G}_1^*) \cup (\mathcal{G}_1^* \setminus \mathcal{G}_0^*) = (\mathcal{G}_0^* \cup \mathcal{G}_1^*) \setminus (\mathcal{G}_0^* \cap \mathcal{G}_1^*)$ *is called the* distinguishing set;
- *the challenger invokes a* Handshake$(id^*, \mathcal{G}_b^*, r^*)$ *session* π^* *(and provides all needed credentials)*;

- $\mathcal{A}^{\mathcal{Q}}$ continues interacting via queries (including on session π^*) until it terminates and outputs bit b';
- the output of the game is b' if all of the following hold; else the output is 0:
  - (a) if π^* accepted and there is a Handshake session π' with $\mathcal{D}^* \cap \pi'.\mathcal{G} \neq \emptyset$ which was in state running while π^* was in state running, then no Reveal(π^*) query was asked, and
  - (b) no Reveal(π') query was asked for any Handshake session π' with $\mathcal{D}^* \cap \pi'.\mathcal{G} \neq \emptyset$ and $\pi'.$partner $= id^*$ that was in state running while π^* was in state running, and
  - (c) no Corrupt(id, G) query with $(id, G) \in \mathsf{ID} \times \mathcal{D}^*$ was asked.

We define $\mathbf{Adv}_{\mathsf{AHA},\mathcal{A}}^{\mathsf{lah}}(\lambda, n, m) :=$

$$\left| \Pr\left[\mathbf{Exp}_{\mathsf{AHA},\mathcal{A}}^{\mathsf{lah},0}(\lambda, n, m) = 1 \right] - \Pr\left[\mathbf{Exp}_{\mathsf{AHA},\mathcal{A}}^{\mathsf{lah},1}(\lambda, n, m) = 1 \right] \right|$$

and denote with $\mathbf{Adv}_{\mathsf{AHA}}^{\mathsf{lah}}(\lambda, n, m)$ the maximum advantage over all PPT adversaries $\mathcal{A}$. We say that AHA is LAH-secure if this advantage is negligible in λ (for all n, m polynomially dependent on λ).

Conditions (a)–(c) exclude some trivial attacks on affiliation hiding. Condition (a) thwarts the attack where $\mathcal{A}$ starts a Handshake($id', \mathcal{G}', r'$) session π' with $\mathcal{G}' \cap \mathcal{D}^* \neq \emptyset$, relays all messages between π^* and π' and finally asks Reveal(π^*). By protocol correctness $\pi^*.$groups would contain elements from $\mathcal{D}^*$ and it would be trivial to correctly decide about b. Condition (b) handles the same attack, but from the point of view of π'. Condition (c) prevents $\mathcal{A}$ to corrupt a pseudonym in a group in $\mathcal{D}^*$, to impersonate that user, and to decide about bit b from the output of its protocol run.

5   Security Analysis of Our Protocol

Following the definitions in Section 4, we claim that our AHA protocol from Section 3 satisfies the desired security goals.

Theorem 2 (Linkable Affiliation-Hiding Security). The AHA protocol presented in Section 3.2 is LAH-secure in the Random Oracle Model (ROM) [4], given that NIKDS is IND-CIA secure.

Proof (Sketch). We prove LAH security of our AHA protocol by using the 'game-hopping' technique, i.e. by presenting a sequence of games that are 'neighbor-wise' computationally indistinguishable from adversary's point of view. The first game, $G_{0,b}$, is identical with $\mathbf{Exp}_{\mathsf{AHA},\mathcal{A}}^{\mathsf{lah},b}(\lambda, n, m)$.

Let $G_{1,b}$ denote the game that is identical with $G_{0,b}$, except that the challenger, before even starting the simulation, makes guesses for $\mathcal{A}$'s (future) choice of attacked identity id^* and protocol partner π^* partner. The simulation is aborted if these guesses are not consistent with adversary's actions, i.e. with probability at most $1/n^2$, as n denotes the number of simulated users.

Let $G_{2,b}$ denote the game that is identical with $G_{1,b}$, except that, for all groups in $\mathcal{G}_b^* \cap \mathcal{D}^*$, the NIKDS keys K_G shared between id^* and π^*.partner are replaced by random values in $\{0,1\}^\lambda$ (see Figure 1, line 7). As condition (c) in Definition 4 assures that adversary $\mathcal{A}$ did not obtain a corresponding user credential $sk_G[id^*]$ or $sk_G[\pi^*.\text{partner}]$ by corruption, the probability for $\mathcal{A}$ to detect a difference between $G_{2,b}$ and $G_{1,b}$ can be bound by $|\mathcal{G}_b^* \cap \mathcal{D}^*| \cdot \mathbf{Adv}_{\text{NIKDS},\mathcal{A}}^{\text{ind-cia}}(\lambda)$ (see Definition 2), which is assumed to be negligible in λ.

Now note that in messages and keys of the protocol simulated in game $G_{2,b}$ no information about the groups in $\mathcal{G}_b^* \cap \mathcal{D}^*$ remains (all relevant keys K_G have been replaced by random strings). We hence argue that experiments $G_{2,b}$ and $G_{2,(1-b)}$ are not distinguishable (the stochastic distance is zero).

We conclude the proof by noticing that we have shown

$$G_{0,b} \approx G_{1,b} \approx G_{2,b} = G_{2,(1-b)} \approx G_{1,(1-b)} \approx G_{0,(1-b)},$$

where relation '$\approx$' expresses that two games are only computationally distinguishable by an adversary with negligible probability. It follows that

$$\Pr\left[\mathbf{Exp}_{\text{AHA},\mathcal{A}}^{\text{lah},1}(\lambda, n, m) = 1\right] \approx \Pr\left[\mathbf{Exp}_{\text{AHA},\mathcal{A}}^{\text{lah},0}(\lambda, n, m) = 1\right],$$

and hence $\mathbf{Adv}_{\text{AHA},\mathcal{A}}^{\text{lah}}(\lambda, n, m)$ is negligible in λ (cf. Definition 4). $\square$

As we abstained from formally defining AKE-security in Section 4, we here only give a qualitative result about key security of our protocol. We refer the interested reader to [19] for the state-of-the-art key security model that considers the affiliation-hiding setting. The proof given for the protocol of [19] can easily be adapted to fit our new scheme.

Theorem 3 (Authenticated Key Exchange Security). *The* AHA *protocol presented in Section 3.2 is AKE-secure [19] under the CDH assumption in the Random Oracle Model (ROM) [4], given that* NIKDS *is IND-CIA secure.*

6 Conclusion

We gave a construction of a new and impressively efficient Affiliation-Hiding Authentication scheme with included Key Establishment (AHA/KE). Its asymptotic computational performance of $O(n \log n)$ compares very favorably to $O(n^2)$ of its predecessors [16, 19]. The same holds for bandwidth consumption, which amounts to only 4% of that of [19]. Still, the protocol's syntax and security properties remain in consistency with accepted security notions for AHA [19].

We consider this work crucial in respect to deployment of privacy-preserving techniques in devices with limited resources, such as mobile phones in ad hoc wireless networks. Without the improvements described in the preceding sections, implementations of AHA protocols would hardly run at acceptable speed on such equipment.

Acknowledgments

The authors are supported in part by the DAAD PPP grant Nr. 50743263 (Project PACU) and by the BMBF grant AUS 10/046 (Project POC).

References

1. Ateniese, G., Kirsch, J., Blanton, M.: Secret Handshakes with Dynamic and Fuzzy Matching. In: Network and Distributed System Security Symposium (NDSS 2007). The Internet Society, San Diego (2007)
2. Balfanz, D., Durfee, G., Shankar, N., Smetters, D.K., Staddon, J., Wong, H.-C.: Secret Handshakes from Pairing-Based Key Agreements. In: IEEE Symposium on Security and Privacy 2003, pp. 180–196. IEEE CS, Los Alamitos (2003)
3. Bellare, M., Rogaway, P.: Entity Authentication and Key Distribution. In: Stinson, D.R. (ed.) CRYPTO 1993. LNCS, vol. 773, pp. 232–249. Springer, Heidelberg (1994)
4. Bellare, M., Rogaway, P.: Random Oracles are Practical: A Paradigm for Designing Efficient Protocols. In: 1st ACM Conference on Computer and Communications Security (CCS 1993), pp. 62–73. ACM, New York (1993)
5. Blake, I., Seroussi, G., Smart, N., Cassels, J.W.S.: Advances in Elliptic Curve Cryptography. London Mathematical Society Lecture Note Series. Cambridge University Press, New York (2005)
6. Boneh, D., Franklin, M.K.: Identity-Based Encryption from the Weil Pairing. SIAM J. Comput. 32(3), 586–615 (2003)
7. Burmester, M., Desmedt, Y.G.: A Secure and Efficient Conference Key Distribution System. In: De Santis, A. (ed.) EUROCRYPT 1994. LNCS, vol. 950, pp. 275–286. Springer, Heidelberg (1995)
8. Canetti, R., Krawczyk, H.: Analysis of Key-Exchange Protocols and their use for Building Secure Channels. In: Pfitzmann, B. (ed.) EUROCRYPT 2001. LNCS, vol. 2045, pp. 453–474. Springer, Heidelberg (2001)
9. Castelluccia, C., Jarecki, S., Tsudik, G.: Secret Handshakes from CA-Oblivious Encryption. In: Lee, P.J. (ed.) ASIACRYPT 2004. LNCS, vol. 3329, pp. 293–307. Springer, Heidelberg (2004)
10. Costello, C., Stebila, D.: Fixed Argument Pairings. In: Abdalla, M., Barreto, P.S.L.M. (eds.) LATINCRYPT 2010. LNCS, vol. 6212, pp. 92–108. Springer, Heidelberg (2010)
11. Dupont, R., Enge, A.: Provably Secure Non-interactive Key Distribution Based on Pairings. Discrete Applied Mathematics 154(2), 270–276 (2006)
12. Jarecki, S., Kim, J.H., Tsudik, G.: Authentication for Paranoids: Multi-party Secret Handshakes. In: Zhou, J., Yung, M., Bao, F. (eds.) ACNS 2006. LNCS, vol. 3989, pp. 325–339. Springer, Heidelberg (2006)
13. Jarecki, S., Kim, J.H., Tsudik, G.: Group Secret Handshakes or Affiliation-Hiding Authenticated Group Key Agreement. In: Abe, M. (ed.) CT-RSA 2007. LNCS, vol. 4377, pp. 287–308. Springer, Heidelberg (2006)
14. Jarecki, S., Kim, J.H., Tsudik, G.: Beyond Secret Handshakes: Affiliation-Hiding Authenticated Key Exchange. In: Malkin, T. (ed.) CT-RSA 2008. LNCS, vol. 4964, pp. 352–369. Springer, Heidelberg (2008)
15. Jarecki, S., Liu, X.: Unlinkable Secret Handshakes and Key Private Group Key Management Schemes. In: Katz, J., Yung, M. (eds.) ACNS 2007. LNCS, vol. 4521, pp. 270–287. Springer, Heidelberg (2007)

16. Jarecki, S., Liu, X.: Affiliation-Hiding Envelope and Authentication Schemes with Efficient Support for Multiple Credentials. In: Aceto, L., Damgård, I., Goldberg, L.A., Halldórsson, M.M., Ingólfsdóttir, A., Walukiewicz, I. (eds.) ICALP 2008, Part II. LNCS, vol. 5126, pp. 715–726. Springer, Heidelberg (2008)

17. Jarecki, S., Liu, X.: Private Mutual Authentication and Conditional Oblivious Transfer. In: Halevi, S. (ed.) CRYPTO 2009. LNCS, vol. 5677, pp. 90–107. Springer, Heidelberg (2009)

18. Kawai, Y., Yoneyama, K., Ohta, K.: Secret Handshake: Strong Anonymity Definition and Construction. In: Bao, F., Li, H., Wang, G. (eds.) ISPEC 2009. LNCS, vol. 5451, pp. 219–229. Springer, Heidelberg (2009)

19. Manulis, M., Pinkas, B., Poettering, B.: Privacy-Preserving Group Discovery with Linear Complexity. In: Zhou, J., Yung, M. (eds.) ACNS 2010. LNCS, vol. 6123, pp. 420–437. Springer, Heidelberg (2010)

20. Manulis, M., Poettering, B.: Practical Affiliation-Hiding Authentication from Improved Polynomial Interpolation. In: ACM Symposium on Information, Computer and Communications Security (ASIACCS 2011). ACM, New York (2011)

21. Manulis, M., Poettering, B., Tsudik, G.: Affiliation-Hiding Key Exchange with Untrusted Group Authorities. In: Zhou, J., Yung, M. (eds.) ACNS 2010. LNCS, vol. 6123, pp. 402–419. Springer, Heidelberg (2010)

22. Manulis, M., Poettering, B., Tsudik, G.: Taming Big Brother Ambitions: More Privacy for Secret Handshakes. In: Atallah, M.J., Hopper, N.J. (eds.) PETS 2010. LNCS, vol. 6205, pp. 149–165. Springer, Heidelberg (2010)

23. Sakai, R., Ohgishi, K., Kasahara, M.: Cryptosystems Based on Pairings. In: Symposium on Cryptography and Information Security, SCIS (2000)

24. Scott, M.: Computing the Tate Pairing. In: Menezes, A. (ed.) CT-RSA 2005. LNCS, vol. 3376, pp. 293–304. Springer, Heidelberg (2005)

25. Shamir, A.: Identity-Based Cryptosystems and Signature Schemes. In: Blakely, G.R., Chaum, D. (eds.) CRYPTO 1984. LNCS, vol. 196, pp. 47–53. Springer, Heidelberg (1985)

26. Shigeo, M.: A Fast Implementation of ηT Pairing in Characteristic Three on Intel Core 2 Duo Processor. Cryptology ePrint Archive, Report 2009/032 (2009)

27. Takahashi, G., Hoshino, F., Kobayashi, T.: Efficient $GF(3^m)$ Multiplication Algorithm for ηT Pairing. Cryptology ePrint Archive, Report 2007/463 (2007)

28. The Facebook (2010), http://www.facebook.com/press/info.php?statistics

29. Tsudik, G., Xu, S.: A Flexible Framework for Secret Handshakes. In: Danezis, G., Golle, P. (eds.) PETS 2006. LNCS, vol. 4258, pp. 295–315. Springer, Heidelberg (2006)

30. Vergnaud, D.: RSA-Based Secret Handshakes. In: Ytrehus, Ø. (ed.) WCC 2005. LNCS, vol. 3969, pp. 252–274. Springer, Heidelberg (2006)

31. Xu, S., Yung, M.: k-Anonymous Secret Handshakes with Reusable Credentials. In: 11th ACM Conference on Computer and Communications Security (CCS 2004), pp. 158–167. ACM, New York (2004)

Formal Framework for the Evaluation of Waveform Resynchronization Algorithms

Sylvain Guilley[1], Karim Khalfallah[2],
Victor Lomne[2], and Jean-Luc Danger[1]

[1] TELECOM-ParisTech, CNRS LTCI, France
[2] ANSSI (Agence Nationale pour la Sécurité des Systèmes d'Information), France

Abstract. In side-channel analysis, the waveforms can be acquired misaligned. Several algorithms have been put forward to resynchronize signals, as a pretreatment before the attack proper. In this article, we examine two of them, namely amplitude-only and phase-only correlation (abridged AOC and POC), and introduce a third one, called threshold-POC (T-POC) that corrects a flaw of the phase-only correlation. Those three resynchronization algorithms are computationally efficient insofar as they find the correct displacement in $\mathcal{O}(n \log n)$ steps per waveform made up of n samples.

Former studies on resynchronization algorithms quantified their quality by their indirect effect on side-channel attacks. We introduce in this article a formal framework for the evaluation of the resynchronization algorithms *per se*. A benchmarking on representative waveforms shows that there is an adequation between the waveforms and the most suitable resynchronization algorithm. On unprotected circuits, the intra-waveform similarity in amplitude or in phase determines the choice for either the AOC or the POC algorithm. Circuits protected by hiding countermeasures have their amplitude made as constant as possible. Therefore, the intra-waveform similarity in amplitude is lowered and the POC is better. Circuits protected by masking countermeasures have their amplitude made as random as possible. Therefore, even if the intra-waveform similarity in amplitude is high, the inter-waveform similarity is reduced; hence a trade-off between AOC and POC, namely T-POC, is the most adequate resynchronization algorithm.

1 Introduction

Side-channel analysis starts with the acquisition of a collection of waveforms, corresponding typically to the measurement of the power or to the radiated electromagnetic (EM) field of a targeted device. However, these measurements can be desynchronized for several reasons. Very often, the attacker does not have an access to a signal that indicates that the operation to be spied is beginning. Instead, the attacker can approximate the operation boundaries indirectly, for instance by sending a request and observing the response. Most embedded systems react in non-deterministic timing because they must handle internally asynchronous buffering and interruptions. In some other cases, the delay between

C.A. Ardagna and J. Zhou (Eds.): WISTP 2011, LNCS 6633, pp. 100–115, 2011.

the external trigger and the operation processing results from a countermeasure, such as *instructions shuffling* [17] or *random delay insertion* [21,3].

Strictly speaking, misalignment of measurements, either due to approximate synchronization between the acquisition apparatus and target or to intentional desynchronization, does not prevent attacks. It is shown in [2] that the averaging of the curves is a solution to get round these drawbacks. Let us assume the desynchronization results from a displacement of the waveforms by a number of clock periods that varies in the interval $[\![0, t[\![$. We say that $t \in \mathbb{N}^*$ is the size of the desynchronization window. Then, in the extreme case where the desynchronization is uniformly distributed over $[\![0, t[\![$ (which is almost achieved by [3]), the correlation ρ between the waveforms and a leakage model with the misalignment is equal to $1/\sqrt{t}$ times that without any misalignement. Now, the speed of a correlation power analysis (CPA [1]) is directly linked to these correlation coefficients. More precisely, the average number of waveforms required to break a cryptographic implementation is equal to [12,13]:

$$3 + 8 \left(\frac{Z_{1-\alpha}}{\ln\left(\frac{1+\rho}{1-\rho}\right)} \right)^2 , \tag{1}$$

where $Z_{1-\alpha}$ is the quantile of a normal distribution for the 2-sided confidence interval with error $1 - \alpha$. For low values of ρ, the Eqn. (1) is $\propto \rho^{-2}$. Therefore, all in one, the number of traces to break a cryptographic implementation with a misalignment window t is roughly multiplied by $\left(1/\sqrt{t}\right)^{-2} = t$. This shows that the countermeasure is not very impeding.

Nonewithstanding, it is better for an attacker to get rid off the misalignement, so as to attack in the best conditions. Conversely, from the evaluator's standpoint, it is important to know if a prospective attacker can indeed manage to revert the misalignement. Therefore, we focus in this article on the algorithms to resynchronize the side-channel waveforms, and forget the attack or the analysis that follows.

In the sequel, we are interested in resynchronizing waveforms that have been translated in time by an integer number n of acquisition samples. This is a more general case than the abovementioned displacements of integer number of clock cycles. Indeed, modern oscilloscopes digitize waveforms at a very high sampling rate, so that many samples are captured per clock period. Additionally, we assume the clock frequency is stable and we do not address the reversal of the varying clock (VC [16,8,22]).

The rest of the article is organized as follows. In Sec. 2, the state-of-the-art resynchronization algorithms, namely AOC and POC, are introduced. One flaw of POC is described, and the threshold-POC (called T-POC) is defined. The complexity of the three algorithms is shown to be optimal. A formal framework for the evaluation of resynchronization algorithms is described in Sec. 3. The three algorithms are evaluated based on real side-channel waveforms captured from representative circuits, without and with side-channel countermeasures. Finally, the conclusions and the perspectives are given in Sec. 4.

2   Resynchronization Algorithms

2.1   Problem Statement

Theoretically, a waveform X is a series of real values, *i.e.* an element of $\mathbb{R}^{\mathbb{Z}}$. We note X_i the sample of X at date $i \in \mathbb{Z}$. Now, the measured waveform Y is said be desynchronized by an offset of k samples with respect to X if it satisfies: $\forall i, Y_i = X_{i-k}$. In practice, the (unshifted) reference X is unknown and the acquisition is limited in time. Thus, a waveform will rather be a finite set of n samples, belonging to $\mathbb{R}^n$. Given a collection of misaligned waveforms, the resynchronization problem consists in finding the correct offset for each of them. In fact, a relative offset is sufficient, because it allows to bring all the waveforms in phase; whether they are collectively offset by a constant time shift is generally not an issue. Indeed, most side-channel attacks consist in validating an hypothesis based on the maximization of a distinguisher over both time samples and key hypotheses. Thus an arbitrary collective offset in time does not change the side-channel attack's outcome. More specifically, in this paper, we focus on the resynchronization with respect to one reference waveform. The resynchronization thus comes down to the unitary problem of resynchronizing waveform Y knowing one reference waveform X.

2.2   AOC: Amplitude-Only Correlation

The cross-correlation $X \star Y$ between two waveforms X and Y is a new waveform, whose sample $i \in [\![0, n[\![$ is defined as: $(X \star Y)_i \doteq \sum_{j \in \mathbb{Z}_n} X_j \cdot Y_{j+i}$. In this notation, the time indices are considered not in the bounded interval $[\![0, n[\![$, but in the additive group $\mathbb{Z}_n$. Strictly speaking, we choose to consider the sample indexes modulo n to ease the computations, for instance in the identity involved in Eqn. (4). But in practice, it also makes "physical" sense, for instance if a waveform consists in the superposition of the clock activity and some extra signal incurred by cryptographic operations. This likely scenario is sketched in the leftmost part of Fig. 1. The straightforward cross-correlation algorithm would discard non-overlapping samples, resulting in a cross-correlation estimation over $n - k$ samples when testing for a k-sample offset. This sub-optimal solution is depicted in the middle part of Fig. 1. To avoid this loss of samples in the cross-correlation, we suggest to fold the shifted wave. The folded part, provided it contains only non-cryptographic information, will consistently match the beginning of the waveform, all the more so as the number of samples n divides the number of clock periods in the waveform. This advantageous situation is described in the right part of Fig. 1. We focus on this strategy in rest of the article.

The cross-correlation[1] can be used to recover the offset by guessing $\hat{k}$, as the offset that maximizes the cross-correlation between X and Y. Formally,

$$\hat{k} = \mathrm{argmax}_{k \in \mathbb{Z}_n} (X \star Y)_k \ . \tag{2}$$

---

[1] We would like to make clear that we name $X \star Y$ *auto-correlation* and not *correlation* to avoid the confusion with Pearson correlation coefficient.

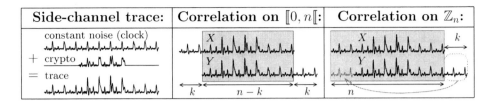

Side-channel trace:	Correlation on $[\![0, n[\![$:	Correlation on $\mathbb{Z}_n$:

Fig. 1. Typical trace, exhibiting a special cryptographic zone (*left*), cross-correlation-based resynchronization without folding (*center*) and *idem* with folding (*right*). The shaded zone is the interval on which the "scalar product" can be computed between X and Y shifted by k samples.

Let us note ROR_k the samples circular right shift operation: $\forall i, \mathrm{ROR}_k(X)_i = X_{i-k}$, and $A \cdot B$ the coordinate-wise product: $(A \cdot B)_i = A_i \cdot B_i$. The resynchronization algorithm of Eqn. (2) is said sound, since it indeed recovers the correct offset when Y is equal to the reference waveform X circularly shifted by k':

$$\mathrm{argmax}_{k \in \mathbb{Z}_n} \left(X \star \mathrm{ROR}_{k'}(X) \right)_k = \mathrm{argmax}_{k \in \mathbb{Z}_n} \sum_{j \in \mathbb{Z}_n} X_j \cdot X_{j+(k-k')} = k' \ .$$

This result comes from the application of the Cauchy-Schwarz theorem to an auto-correlation.

The cross-correlation between two curves can be computed very efficiently using the discrete Fourier transform (DFT). The definition of the DFT and of the inverse DFT (IDFT), as per the library FFTW3 [4], is:

$$\begin{cases} \mathrm{DFT}(X)_i \doteq \sum_{j=0}^{n-1} X_j \cdot \exp\left(-2\pi j i \sqrt{-1}/n\right) , \\ \mathrm{IDFT}(X)_i \doteq \sum_{j=0}^{n-1} X_j \cdot \exp\left(+2\pi j i \sqrt{-1}/n\right) . \end{cases} \tag{3}$$

The definition of Eqn. (3) is not normalized, since it implies that: $\mathrm{DFT} \circ \mathrm{IDFT} = \mathrm{IDFT} \circ \mathrm{DFT} = n\mathrm{Id}$. In these equations, expressions are waveforms, *i.e.* elements of $\mathbb{R}^n$. Then, we have the following property: $\mathrm{DFT}(X \star Y) = \overline{\mathrm{DFT}(X)} \cdot \mathrm{DFT}(Y)$. It allows to rewrite the cross-correlation as:

$$X \star Y = \mathrm{IDFT}\left(\overline{\mathrm{DFT}(X)} \cdot \mathrm{DFT}(Y)\right) / n \ .$$

We also call the algorithm presented in this section the "amplitude-only correlation" (AOC):

$$\mathrm{AOC}(X; Y) \doteq X \star Y = \mathrm{IDFT}\left(\overline{\mathrm{DFT}(X)} \cdot \mathrm{DFT}(Y)\right) / n \ . \tag{4}$$

2.3   POC: Phase-Only Correlation

The AOC can be contrasted with the phased-only correlation (POC), described in [6,15,7]. In POC, the DFT of the reference X and desynchronized Y waveforms are normalized prior to being multiplied. The computed quantity is:

$$\text{POC}(X;Y) \doteq \text{IDFT}\left(\frac{\overline{\text{DFT}(X)} \cdot \text{DFT}(Y)}{\left|\overline{\text{DFT}(X)}\right| \cdot |\text{DFT}(Y)|}\right) / n. \tag{5}$$

The POC is also sound, since if $Y = \text{ROR}_{k'}(X)$, then:

$$\text{argmax}_{k \in \mathbb{Z}_n} \text{POC}\left(X; \text{ROR}_{k'}(X)\right)_k = k' . \tag{6}$$

Indeed, $\text{DFT}\left(\text{ROR}_{k'}(X)\right)_i = \text{DFT}(X)_i \cdot \exp\left(-2\pi k' i \sqrt{-1}/n\right)$. Let us note U the vector of components $U_i = \exp\left(-2\pi k' i \sqrt{-1}/n\right) \in \mathbb{C}$. Then

$$\text{POC}(X; \text{ROR}_{k'}(X)) = \text{IDFT}\left(\frac{\overline{\text{DFT}(X)} \cdot \text{DFT}(X) \cdot U}{\left|\overline{\text{DFT}(X)}\right| \cdot |\text{DFT}(X) \cdot U|}\right) / n = \text{IDFT}(U)/n.$$

The result of Eqn. (6) comes from the fact that:

$$\text{IDFT}(U)_i = \sum_{j=0}^{n-1} \exp\left(+2\pi j(i-k')\sqrt{-1}/n\right) = n \cdot \delta_{i-k'} , \tag{7}$$

where δ is the Kronecker symbol, that satisfies $\delta_i = 0$ if $i \neq 0$ and 1 otherwise.

Compared to the AOC, the authors of the POC underline that the former is able to resynchronize with a resolution that is below the sampling rate. In this article, we consider only the resynchronization problem stated in Sec. 2.1, *i.e.* with an accuracy equal to that of the sample. We address the comparison of the AOC and POC algorithms empirically in the next section 2.4.

2.4   POC Flaw and Threshold-POC

We base our empirical study on waveforms taken from the DPA contest [20]. The first line of Fig. 2 shows three waveforms to resynchronize. The leftmost waveform, called $X[0]$, is the reference. On its right, $X[1]$ and $X[2]$ are two other waveforms from the same campaign that use different plaintexts, and that have been shifted artificially in time by respectively 31 and 195 samples. The exact details of these acquisitions is given in Tab. 1. These curves represent one DES encryption, that computes one round per clock period. The sampling rate is 20 Gsample/s and the DES is cadenced at a clock frequency of 32 MHz. Hence, one clock period lasts 625 samples. The waveforms are made up of $n = 20,000$ samples, thus representing 32 clock periods. The 16 clock periods where the DES hardware accelerator is computing are in the middle of the waveforms.

In this section, we compare AOC and POC algorithms on $X[q]$, $q \in \{0, 1, 2\}$. The application of the first method is illustrated on the second line of Fig. 2. The three figures show the amplitude of the correlation for various offsets in $[\![0, n[\![$. It appears clearly that the auto correlation $\text{AOC}(X[0]; X[0])$ is the greatest for

Table 1. Detail of the encryption whose side-channel is represented in the first line of Fig. 2

Waveform	Key	Message	Ciphertext	Offset
$X[0]$	0x6a65786a65786a65	0x67c6697351ff4aec	0xc54baee5fc80756a	0
$X[1]$	0x6a65786a65786a65	0x29cdbaabf2fbe346	0x857f106855100811	31
$X[2]$	0x6a65786a65786a65	0xabb2cdc69bb45411	0x04385795f886e215	195

a null offset. However, the auto-correlation features peaks, of smaller amplitude, for non-zero offsets: there is a peak (local maximum) at each clock period.

Therefore, the computation of the correlations with the shifted curves is maximal at the "correct" offsets (31 and 195), but reveals also a local maximum at the same offsets modulo the clock period. We also notice an especially large peak at the correct offset plus 16 clock periods: the reason is that DES executes in 16 clock periods and that the acquisition window happens, by chance, to be exactly equal to 32 clock periods. There is therefore an ambiguity in the correct phase to choose for the resynchronization. Nonetheless, the maximum peak (indicated by a "$\oplus$" sign) coincides with the actual offset.

The POC's results are shown on the line below in Fig. 2. The POC alignment of the reference waveform $X[0]$ versus itself is, as expected, a real Dirac function. This was indeed proved theoretically in Eqn. (7). Hence, the POC might look better than AOC to distinguish the correct offset from offsets modulo one clock period. Indeed, the graphs POC$(X[0]; X[1])$ and POC$(X[0]; X[2])$ show a clear peak at the correct offsets. Although the noise of the POC is high, the correct offset clearly stands out. But spurious peaks appear at high offsets, especially for POC$(X[0]; X[2])$, where the greatest peak occurs at an offset of $n-1$ (indicated by a "$\otimes$" sign). The reason is the numerical instability, during the computation, of the ratio:

$$\frac{\overline{\mathrm{DFT}(X)} \cdot \mathrm{DFT}(Y)}{|\mathrm{DFT}(X)| \cdot |\mathrm{DFT}(Y)|}$$

for small modulus values of $\mathrm{DFT}(X)$ or $\mathrm{DFT}(Y)$, because of a floating point values resolution problem (we use the C type `double`).

In order to make up for this computational artifact, we resort to a trick that consists in preventing the division by too small a quantity if the DFT modulus is small. To make up for this issue, the denominator is added a small quantity $\epsilon > 0$. Thus, the threshold-POC is defined as:

$$\text{T-POC}(X;Y) \doteq \mathrm{IDFT}\left(\frac{\overline{\mathrm{DFT}(X)} \cdot \mathrm{DFT}(Y)}{\left|\overline{\mathrm{DFT}(X)}\right| \cdot |\mathrm{DFT}(Y)| + \epsilon} \right) / n. \tag{8}$$

The same empirical protection of the normalization has already been used in the correlation calculation [11]. Results are shown in Fig. 2 for $\epsilon = 10^{-3}$.

The auto-correlation has a less sharp contrast, but the spurious peaks have disappeared. From a theoretical perspective, the T-POC synchronization algorithm cannot be proved sound any longer.

The value of the positive constant ϵ to be added at the denominator in Eqn. (8) is not trivial to find. To have a better idea of the normalization factor, we have computed the spectrum of a waveform. It is shown in the left part of Fig. 3. The frequency range is limited to $[0, n/2[$ because on the other half $[n/2, n[$, the curve would simply be mirrored. This is due to the fact $X[0]$ is a real waveform; thus: $\text{DFT}(X[0])_{n-i} = \overline{\text{DFT}(X[0])_i}$, hence $|\text{DFT}(X[0])_{n-i}| = |\text{DFT}(X[0])_i|$. To choose ϵ methodically, we could opt to have it equal (by convention) to a fraction of the maximum peak. The log graph on the right of Fig. 3 shows that $|\text{DFT}(X[0])|$ spans 10 decades: a reasoned choice for ϵ is not obvious. Therefore, in the sequel, ϵ is rather considered an empirical parameter.

2.5   Complexity of AOC, POC and T-POC

The computation of $(X \star Y)_i$ for a given i requires n multiplications. The naive algorithm to compute the n correlations $X \star Y$ corresponding to all the possible offsets (there are n of them) runs in $\mathcal{O}(n^2)$. Now, the DFT approach reduces this complexity down to $\mathcal{O}(n \log n)$.

Indeed, one DFT or one IDFT costs $\mathcal{O}(n \log n)$. We note that for all three formulas (Eqn. (4), (5) & (8)), the $\text{DFT}(X)$ on the reference waveform X can be factored for the synchronization of all the other waveforms. For the AOC, the recurrent computations consist thus only in one component-wise multiplication (n operations), one DFT and one IDFT. Regarding the POC, one additional component-wise division (n operations) is required, which does not change the computation complexity. Eventually, the T-POC also runs in $\mathcal{O}(n \log n)$, but is however the slowest method. Nonetheless, we mention that the three resynchronizations algorithms run very efficiently in practice; the resynchronization using the DFT is not the limiting operation in side-channel analysis: the attack that follows the resynchronization is the real bottleneck.

For the experiences presented in the article, we have used FFTW3, that computes Fourier transforms efficiently for every $n \in \mathbb{N}^*$. This is important as the number of samples in typical campaigns is rather a power of 10 and not a power of 2. With this FFTW3 library, all the computations can be done in complex numbers, which has the advantage of simplicity. However, the speed factor and the memory footprint can be divided by two if we consider the input is real data. The operations involve an n-sample real-to-complex DFT, that turns an array of n real numbers into an array of $n/2+1$ complex numbers. Thus the products and the divisions in the frequency domain are conducted with complex arrays of size $n/2 + 1$. Then, n-(logical) sample complex-to-real inverse DFT transforms the $n/2+1$ complex array into an array of $2 \times (n/2+1)$ real numbers. The elements strictly above index $n - 1$ are "padding", and thus ignored for the maximum peak research.

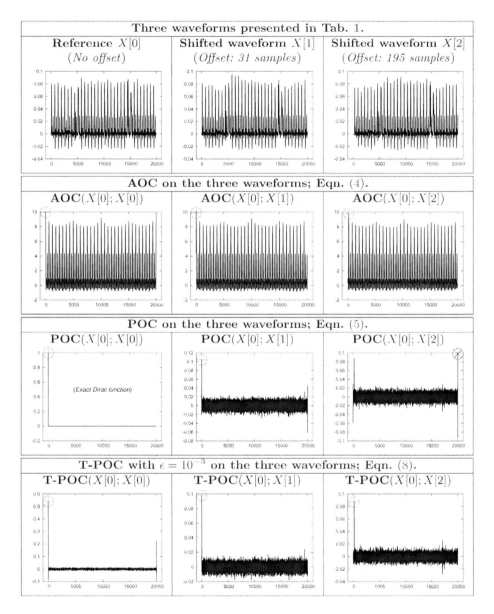

Fig. 2. Three waveforms (*topmost*) and empirical test for the resynchronization, with, from 2nd line to the 4th, respectively AOC, POC and T-POC with $\epsilon = 10^{-3}$. In these campaigns, the number of samples is $n = 20,000$. The colored circle indicates the maximum of the resynchronization algorithm. When it is green ($\oplus$), the resynchronization is successful, whereas when it is red ($\otimes$), it is not.

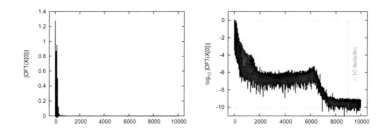

Fig. 3. Spectral power of $X[0]$, in regular scale (*left*) and in log-scale (*right*)

3 Evaluation of Resynchronization Algorithms

3.1 Formal Framework

To evaluate the several resynchronization methods fairly, we need a formal framework based on a figure of merit. Basically, such a framework assumes the knowledge of a correct synchronization and needs to assess the performance of resynchronisation algorithms based on a relative notion of resynchronization correction. The general approach is similar to the formal framework introduced in [18] in the sibling field of side-channel attacks, that introduced a "success rate" or a "guessing entropy". These metrics are fully relevant in the context of key recovery attacks, insofar as only the exact solution for the key is informative for the attacker. Indeed, an approximation on the key is useless in cryptanalysis, since all keys are equiprobable. In addition, the other way round, the key ranked second by a side-channel attack is typically decorrelated from the correct key.

The situation is different for the synchronization problem. Indeed, an approximate resynchronization (*i.e.* with an error of only one or few samples) is nearly as good as an exactly correct resynchronization, because very often the side-channel leakage remains consistent over some samples. This is all the more true as data is acquired at a large sampling rate. In the examples of the Fig. 2, a correlation power analysis (CPA [1]) leads to peaks that are about 50 samples large. This width, illustrated in Fig 4, is caused by an impedance mismatch between the side-channel sensor and the spied circuit. Thus a resynchronization algorithm still performs well if it predicts an offset a few tens of samples away from the correct offset. This means that the resynchronization cannot be solely evaluated by its success or failure rates. Indeed, we need a qualitative appreciation.

Obviously, it is better to synchronize by reducing the offset than to still make it worse. We introduce a factor of merit for the resynchronization accuracy: it is equal to the average distance to the correct resynchronization value.

This notion can be formalized. We denote by A an algorithm that rates each possible offset. In this study, A is either AOC, POC or T-POC (defined in Eqn. (4), (5) or (8)). Given two synchronized waveforms X and Y, and a maximal offset K, we set up an experiment called "**ResynchError**", in which Y is artificially shifted in time by a uniformly distributed random quantity in

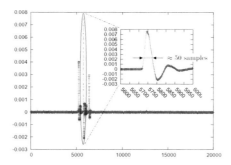

Fig. 4. Correlation power analysis (CPA) on the first round of the DES [20]. The approximate width of the peak indicates the tolerated inaccuracy of the resynchronization algorithms.

$[0, K[$. The experiment returns the distance between the actual offset and the best rated by A. This procedure can be expressed as:

Experiment ResynchError$_\mathsf{A}(X; Y; K)$

$$\left[\begin{array}{l} k' \xleftarrow{R} [0, K[; \\ \text{Return } \left| k' - \text{argmax}_{k \in \mathbb{Z}_n} \mathsf{A}\left(X; \text{SRL}_{k'}\left(Y\right)\right)_k \right|; \end{array} \right.$$

where $\text{SRL}_{k'}$ operates as $\text{ROR}_{k'}$, with the sole difference it inputs k' zeros on the left end instead of reinjecting the k' samples flushed outside from the right end. A synchronized acquisition campaign C is a collection of $Q \in [2, +\infty[$ waveforms. Every waveform $C[q]$, $1 \le q < Q$ is synchronized. The quality of the resynchronization algorithm A for waveforms randomly misaligned by offsets uniformly distributed in $[0, K[$ is assessed by:

$$\mathbf{AvgResynchError_A}(C; K) \doteq \frac{1}{Q-1} \sum_{q=1}^{Q-1} \mathbf{ResynchError_A}(C[0]; C[q]; K) \ .$$

$$(9)$$

Resynchronization algorithm A is said better than A' if

$$\mathbf{AvgResynchError_A}(C; K) \quad \le \quad \mathbf{AvgResynchError_{A'}}(C; K) \ .$$

We will see in the next Sec. 3.2 that this notion does depend on the campaign C and on the maximal offset K.

We recall that the POC can be used to resynchronize with a resolution inferior than the sampling rate. Incidentally, such a method could also be applied to AOC. However, we have not tested this option, because, as will be shown in Sec. 3.2, the distinction between the resynchronization algorithm can already be clearly seen at a resolution equal to the clock period. Furthermore, modern oscilloscopes digitize waveforms at a very fast sample rate, thereby reducing the interest of fractional sample resynchronization.

3.2   Benchmarking of Representative Waveforms

We validate the average resynchronization error introduced in Eqn. (9) on five representative campaigns, corresponding to three setups. One setup is an experimental evaluation environment. On the three setups, the same DES algorithm (*i.e.* synthesized from the same VHDL source code) is run. The first setup is that of the DPA contest first edition [20], where the DES is an ASIC and where the acquisitions are averaged 64 times by the oscilloscope. The second one is carried out on an ASIC but with unaveraged acquisitions. Eventually, the third setup is identical to the second one, except that the device under analysis is an FPGA, and not an ASIC. More details are provided in Tab. 2. We have selected very different setups on purpose to gather various representative side-channel types.

Table 2. The three setups studied

Setup	Samples/clk	Fclk [MHz]	Nature	Device
#1	625	32.000	Power	ASIC (0.13 μm technology, 1.2 Volt)
#2	150	33.333	Power	ASIC (0.13 μm technology, 1.2 Volt)
#3	120	8.333	EM	FPGA (0.13 μm technology, 1.5 Volt)

The second and third setups are also used to implement side-channel resistant versions of DES. On the second setup, one campaign is done on a hiding countermeasure [13, Chp. 7]. On the third setup, one campaign is done on a masking countermeasure [13, Chp. 9]. In the sequel, we represent the five studied campaigns as per Fig. 5, that gives one raw trace for each campaign.

The average resynchronization error is represented in Fig. 6 for those five campaigns, based on $Q = 1,000$ artificial shifts. It gives, for the AOC and the POC (with 4 values of ϵ) the mean absolute error of resynchronization **AvgResynchError** as a function of the synchronization error window K.

The figure 6 reveals very different behaviors of resynchronization performance $K \mapsto$ **AvgResynchError**$(C; K)$. Notably, the setups #1 and #3 fail to have their unprotected designs properly resynchronized for some algorithms.

In SETUP1_REF, large errors occur for the POC and the T-POC with the smallest correction value $\epsilon = 10^{-6}$. These errors increase almost linearly with the desynchronization amplitude. More precisely, there is an improvement when the desynchronization maximal value is not a multiple of half the clock period. This observation shows that the computational flaw identified in the POC in Sec. 2.4 is the main limitation to the resynchronization on this campaign.

Interestingly enough, the campaign SETUP3_REF features an opposite behaviour. The AOC and the T-POC with a large $\epsilon = 10^3$ coefficient both fail. We notice that when ϵ becomes larger and larger, then T-POC tends towards AOC, since the denominator in Eqn. (8) becomes negligible. The reason for the AOC to fail can be accounted by the nature of the setup: the measurements are noisy, which makes the identification of the correct phase by the analysis of the wave-

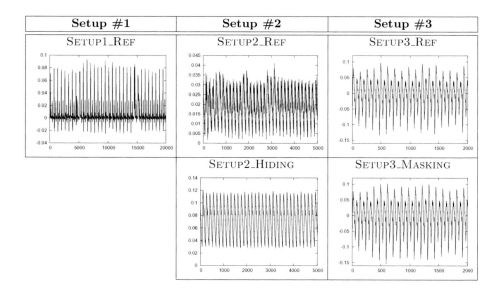

Fig. 5. Raw traces examples for the five investigated campaigns

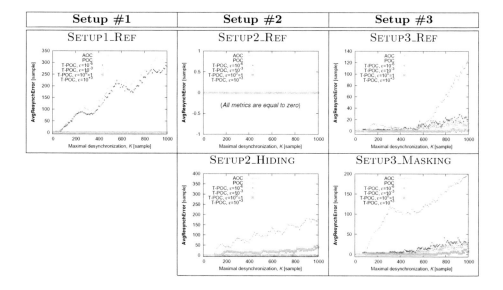

Fig. 6. Average resynchronization performance for the five campaigns presented in Tab. 5

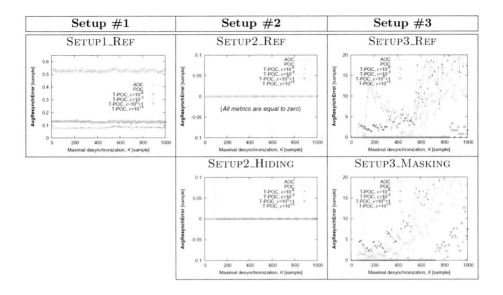

Fig. 7. Average resynchronization performance for the five campaigns; vertical zoom on Fig. 6, that focuses on errors that do not diverge with K

forms amplitude very error-prone. The cause of high noise in the measurement setup #3 is threefold:

1. Unaveraged measurements have a greater quantification noise than traces that have been averaged;
2. FPGAs activate a lot of logic per single logical event in the netlist, which increases the algorithmic noise [1];
3. EM measurements are notoriously more noisy than power measurements.

Nonetheless, this noise is independently and identically distributed (*iid*) over the samples. Therefore, the phase information, which is collective over one clock period, is less affected. In particular, because of the high level of noise, the DFT transform of the setup #3 waveforms is rich in frequencies, and therefore varies less than that of Fig. 3. Therefore the POC flaw does not manifest. We observe in this campaign that the pure POC neither succeeds in resynchronizing well the curves, but that T-POC with $\epsilon = 1$ is almost successful 100% of the time. Thus, for this campaign, the best resynchronization algorithm is a tradeoff between amplitude- and phase-correlation.

The campaign SETUP2_REF is perfectly resynchronized with all the studied algorithms. The explanation clearly stands out by looking at the sample waveform provided for this campaign in Fig. 5. Every waveform has both a very clear shape (which favors amplitude-related matching techniques) and an elaborate spectrum (both clock-level and higher frequencies are already visible on the time-domain trace, which is beneficial for phase-related matching techniques).

It is interesting to zoom on the resynchronization performance for the campaigns carried out on unprotected circuits. These graphs are provided with in Fig. 7. AOC definitely best realigns the campaign SETUP1_REF. This is due to the extremely accurate acquisition in amplitude; notably, the averaging of the waveforms helps make resynchronization with vertical values reliable. The characteristic shape for these waveforms, associated with their high resolution, makes each of them very recognizable. The resemblance (intra-waveform similarity) outperforms the difference between the waveforms (acquired with different plaintexts). The opposite conclusion can be drawn for the noisy SETUP3_REF campaign: even if we manage to identify some points of larger amplitude than others in each individual waveform, the noise makes each waveform dissimilar in amplitude. As the phase is noisy too, the T-POC is the best tool to extract the synchronization between waveforms of campaign SETUP3_REF.

Let us now study the two campaigns on protected implementations, namely SETUP2_HIDING and SETUP3_MASKING. It is straightforward to see in the corresponding graphs of Fig. 6 that the AOC is the worst resynchronization algorithm. Two compelling arguments can explain this. On power-constant circuits, the goal of the countermeasure is to balance the side-channel leakage, by having its amplitude as constant as possible. Thus, it is expected that resynchronization based on amplitude-matching fail. However, it has been noted in [19,10] that small (much beneath the clock period) discrepancies in evaluation dates could exist. This phenomenon is referred to as "early propagation effect" in the specialized literature. The success of the resynchronization using the phase information of the waveforms might be a confirmation of this effect. On masked circuits, the shapes of the waveforms are forced to look random in a view to mitigate first-order side-channel attacks. It is therefore no surprise if AOC is ineffective in average. Nonetheless, it is noteworthy that the phase of the signals carry information about the algorithm scheduling. We conjecture that despite the additional amount of noise carried out by the masking countermeasure, the sequence of operations (registers evaluation, then maybe the addressing of a RAM, or the activity that comes from the control block, *etc.*) might be a characteristic signature of the DES operations.

All in one, the Fig. 7 shows that campaigns acquired from a protected circuit are more difficult to synchronize than those acquired from unprotected circuits implemented on the same setups. Nevertheless, our general noting is that the two prominent countermeasures (hiding and masking) aim at dissimulating the information in amplitude, but that unexpectedly the phase is still useful to achieve a correct waveforms realignment. Those conclusions are in line with many papers focusing on DFT attacks [5,9,14]. They all conclude that the side-channel waveforms exhibit extremely distinguishable features once turned into the frequency domain. We note that the best value for ϵ happens to be small ($\epsilon \leq 1$) for SETUP2_HIDING: all the information lays in the waveforms phase. The optimal ϵ for SETUP3_MASKING is exactly the same as for SETUP3_REF. Indeed, the masking simply increases the algorithmic noise level, but does not fundamentally affect the acquisition.

4   Conclusions and Perspectives

Side-channel measurements can be desynchronized for various reasons, especially in the common case of acquisitions where a reliable trigger signal is not available. This study introduces a formal practice-oriented evaluation framework for resynchronization algorithms. In this article, we compare several approaches to realign the waveforms. We conclude that, in the absence of countermeasures, if the acquired signal is of excellent vertical quality, then the amplitude should be used to resynchronise the signals. Otherwise, in the case of noisy measurements, the phase-based correlations are better techniques. We notice that under some circumstances, the genuine version of the phase-only correlation (POC) is not efficient, and we introduce the threshold POC (*aka* T-POC). If a countermeasure is employed, then, undoubtedly, the T-POC (including T-POC with $\epsilon = 0$, *i.e.* the original POC) is the best realignment algorithm. The reason is that state-of-the-art side-channel countermeasures aim at impeding amplitude-level waveforms variation, but neglect to protect the information carried by the phase. Therefore, using POC or T-POC algorithms, we show how to successfully resynchronize protected waveforms.

Several questions remain however open. For instance, what is the optimal threshold value ϵ involved in T-POC? Also, we wonder if a mixed resynchronization techniques (for instance based on wavelets, that feature a compromise between time and frequency) could bridge the gap between amplitude-only and phase-only correlation algorithms.

References

1. Brier, É., Clavier, C., Olivier, F.: Correlation Power Analysis with a Leakage Model. In: Joye, M., Quisquater, J.-J. (eds.) CHES 2004. LNCS, vol. 3156, pp. 16–29. Springer, Heidelberg (2004)
2. Clavier, C., Coron, J.-S., Dabbous, N.: Differential power analysis in the presence of hardware countermeasures. In: Paar, C., Koç, Ç.K. (eds.) CHES 2000. LNCS, vol. 1965, pp. 252–263. Springer, Heidelberg (2000)
3. Coron, J.-S., Kizhvatov, I.: Analysis and improvement of the random delay countermeasure of CHES 2009. In: Mangard, S., Standaert, F.-X. (eds.) CHES 2010. LNCS, vol. 6225, pp. 95–109. Springer, Heidelberg (2010)
4. Frigo, M., Johnson, S.G.: The design and implementation of FFTW3. Proceedings of the IEEE 93(2), 216–231 (2005)
5. Gebotys, C.H., Ho, S., Tiu, C.C.: EM Analysis of Rijndael and ECC on a Wireless Java-Based PDA. In: Rao, J.R., Sunar, B. (eds.) CHES 2005. LNCS, vol. 3659, pp. 250–264. Springer, Heidelberg (2005)
6. Homma, N., Nagashima, S., Imai, Y., Aoki, T., Satoh, A.: High-resolution side-channel attack using phase-based waveform matching. In: Goubin, L., Matsui, M. (eds.) CHES 2006. LNCS, vol. 4249, pp. 187–200. Springer, Heidelberg (2006)
7. Homma, N., Nagashima, S., Sugawara, T., Aoki, T., Satoh, A.: A High-Resolution Phase-Based Waveform Matching and Its Application to Side-Channel Attacks. IEICE Transactions 91-A(1), 193–202 (2008)

8. Kafi, M., Guilley, S., Marcello, S., Naccache, D.: Deconvolving Protected Signals. In: ARES/CISIS, March 16-19, pp. 687–694. IEEE Computer Society Press, Fukuoka (2009)
9. Kasper, T., Oswald, D., Paar, C.: EM Side-Channel Attacks on Commercial Contactless Smartcards Using Low-Cost Equipment. In: Youm, H.Y., Yung, M. (eds.) WISA 2009. LNCS, vol. 5932, pp. 79–93. Springer, Heidelberg (2009)
10. Kulikowski, K.J., Karpovsky, M.G., Taubin, A.: Power Attacks on Secure Hardware Based on Early Propagation of Data. In: IOLTS Como, Italy, pp. 131–138. IEEE Computer Society, Los Alamitos (2006)
11. Le, T.-H., Clédière, J., Canovas, C., Robisson, B., Servière, C., Lacoume, J.-L.: A Proposition for Correlation Power Analysis Enhancement. In: Goubin, L., Matsui, M. (eds.) CHES 2006. LNCS, vol. 4249, pp. 174–186. Springer, Heidelberg (2006)
12. Mangard, S.: Hardware countermeasures against DPA – A statistical analysis of their effectiveness. In: Okamoto, T. (ed.) CT-RSA 2004. LNCS, vol. 2964, pp. 222–235. Springer, Heidelberg (2004)
13. Mangard, S., Oswald, E., Popp, T.: Power Analysis Attacks: Revealing the Secrets of Smart Cards. Springer, Heidelberg (2006), http://www.dpabook.org/ ISBN 0-387-30857-1
14. Mateos, E., Gebotys, C.H.: A new correlation frequency analysis of the side channel. In: Proceedings of the 5th Workshop on Embedded Systems Security, WESS 2010, pp. 4:1–4:8. ACM, New York (2010)
15. Nagashima, S., Homma, N., Imai, Y., Aoki, T., Satoh, A.: DPA Using Phase-Based Waveform Matching against Random-Delay Countermeasure. In: ISCAS, May 27-20, pp. 1807–1810. IEEE Computer Society, Los Alamitos (2007), doi:10.1109/ISCAS.2007.378024
16. Réal, D., Canovas, C., Clédière, J., Drissi, M., Valette, F.: Defeating classical Hardware Countermeasures: a new processing for Side Channel Analysis. In: DATE, Munich, Germany, March 10-14, pp. 1274–1279. IEEE Computer Society, Los Alamitos (2008)
17. Rivain, M., Prouff, E., Doget, J.: Higher-order masking and shuffling for software implementations of block ciphers. In: Clavier, C., Gaj, K. (eds.) CHES 2009. LNCS, vol. 5747, pp. 171–188. Springer, Heidelberg (2009)
18. Standaert, F.-X., Malkin, T.G., Yung, M.: A unified framework for the analysis of side-channel key recovery attacks. In: Joux, A. (ed.) EUROCRYPT 2009. LNCS, vol. 5479, pp. 443–461. Springer, Heidelberg (2009)
19. Suzuki, D., Saeki, M.: Security evaluation of DPA countermeasures using dual-rail pre-charge logic style. In: Goubin, L., Matsui, M. (eds.) CHES 2006. LNCS, vol. 4249, pp. 255–269. Springer, Heidelberg (2006)
20. TELECOM ParisTech SEN research group. DPA Contest, 1st. edn. (2008–2009), http://www.DPAcontest.org/
21. Tunstall, M., Benoit, O.: Efficient Use of Random Delays in Embedded Software. In: Sauveron, D., Markantonakis, K., Bilas, A., Quisquater, J.-J. (eds.) WISTP 2007. LNCS, vol. 4462, pp. 27–38. Springer, Heidelberg (2007)
22. van Woudenberg, J.G.J., Witteman, M.F., Bakker, B.: Improving Differential Power Analysis by Elastic Alignment, http://www.riscure.com/fileadmin/images/Docs/elastic_paper.pdf

Solving DLP with Auxiliary Input over an Elliptic Curve Used in TinyTate Library

Yumi Sakemi[1], Tetsuya Izu[2], Masahiko Takenaka[2],
and Masaya Yasuda[2]

[1] Okayama University
3-1-1, Tsushima-naka, Kita-ku, Okayama, 700-8530, Japan
[2] FUJITSU LABORATORIES Ltd.,
4-1-1, Kamikodanaka, Nakahara-ku, Kawasaki, 211-8588, Japan
{izu,takenaka,myasuda}@labs.fujitsu.com

Abstract. The discrete logarithm problem with auxiliary input (DLP-wAI) is a problem to find α from G, αG, $\alpha^d G$ in an additive cyclic group generated by G of prime order r and a positive integer d dividing $r - 1$. The infeasibility of DLPwAI assures the security of some cryptographic schemes. In 2006, Cheon proposed a novel algorithm for solving DLP-wAI. This paper shows our experimental results of Cheon's algorithm by implementing it with some speeding-up techniques. In fact, we succeeded to solve DLPwAI in a group with 128-bit order in 45 hours with a single PC on an elliptic curve defined over a prime finite field with 256-bit elements which is used in the TinyTate library.

1 Introduction

Let $\mathbb{G}$ be an additive cyclic group generated by G of prime order r. The discrete logarithm problem with auxiliary input (DLPwAI) is a problem to find α from G, αG, $\alpha^d G \in \mathbb{G}$ and a positive integer d dividing $r - 1$. The infeasibility of DLPwAI assures the security of some cryptographic schemes including Boneh-Boyen's ID-based encryption scheme [2] and Boneh-Gentry-Waters' broadcast encryption scheme [5]. In 2006, Cheon proposed a novel algorithm for solving DLPwAI [7,8]. The time complexity of Cheon's algorithm (with KKM improvement) is $O\left(\sqrt{(r-1)/d} + \sqrt{d}\right)$, and especially when $d \approx \sqrt{r}$, the complexity becomes $O(\sqrt[4]{r})$, which is much efficient than that for solving DLP in general groups (which requires $O(\sqrt{r})$).

This paper implements Cheon's algorithm combined with the baby-step giant-step algorithm [16] as a sub-algorithm and some speeding-up techniques. Then, this paper reports experimental results of our implementation. In fact, we have successfully solved a DLPwAI in 45 hours with a single PC in a group with 128-bit order defined on an elliptic curve over a prime finite field with 256-bit elements, which is used in the TinyTate library [14] for implementing pairing cryptosystem in the embedded devices (see also Table 1. Note that Jao-Yoshida's

C.A. Ardagna and J. Zhou (Eds.): WISTP 2011, LNCS 6633, pp. 116–127, 2011.
© IFIP International Federation for Information Processing 2011

Table 1. Required time for solving DLPwAI

	Size of r	Required Time
Jao, Yoshida [11]	60 bit	3 hours
Izu et al. [10]	83 bit	14 hours
This paper	**128 bit**	**45 hours**

result was not dedicated to an efficient implementation. Also note that Izu et al.'s result was implemented over a finite field with characteristics 3). Here, solving DLP on the elliptic curve is regarded to be infeasible (since the order is 128-bit). As a feedback of our experimental results, it is better to avoid such elliptic curve when some cryptographic schemes are implemented. We also estimated the required time and memory for solving DLPwAI with larger r. According to our estimations, it would be difficult to solve DLPwAI with larger r by the same approach, namely, Cheon's algorithm combined with the baby-step giant-step algorithm.

2 Preliminaries

This section introduces the discrete logarithm problem with auxiliary input (DLPwAI) and Cheon's algorithm for solving DLPwAI [7,8]. Implications of DLPwAI and Cheon's algorithm on cryptographic schemes are also explained.

2.1 Discrete Logarithm Problem with Auxiliary Input (DLPwAI)

Let $\mathbb{G} = \langle G \rangle$ be an additive group generated by G of prime order r. The discrete logarithm problem (DLP) in $\mathbb{G}$ is to find $\alpha \in \mathbb{Z}/r\mathbb{Z}$ on input G, $\alpha G \in \mathbb{G}$. In the general setting, the most efficient algorithms for solving DLP require $O(\sqrt{r})$ in time. In fact, Shanks' baby-step giant-step (BSGS) algorithm [16] requires $O(\sqrt{r})$ group operations in time and $O(\sqrt{r})$ group elements in space. On the other hand, Pollard's λ-algorithm also requires $O(\sqrt{r})$ in time, but much smaller elements in space.

In 2006, Cheon defined the discrete logarithm problem with auxiliary input (DLPwAI) as a variant of DLP [7,8], where DLPwAI is a problem to find α on input G, αG, $\alpha^d G$ and an integer d dividing $r - 1$[1]. At the same time, Cheon proposed a novel algorithm for solving DLPwAI [7,8]. Cheon's algorithm (together with Kozaki-Kutsuma-Matsuo's improvement [12]) requires $O\left(\sqrt{(r-1)/d} + \sqrt{d}\right)$ group operations in time. Especially, when $d \approx \sqrt{r}$, it only requires $O(\sqrt[4]{r})$ operations, which is much smaller than that required in the baby-step giant-step algorithm or in the λ-algorithm for solving DLP.

---

[1] There are many possible variations of DLPwAI. However, this paper only deals with this type.

Algorithm 1. Cheon's Algorithm

Input: : G, $G_1 = \alpha G$, $G_d = \alpha^d G \in \mathbb{G}$, $d \in \mathbb{Z}$ dividing $r - 1$
Output: : $\alpha \in \mathbb{Z}/r\mathbb{Z}$
1: Find a generator $\zeta \in (\mathbb{Z}/r\mathbb{Z})^*$
2: Set $\zeta_d \leftarrow \zeta^d$, $d_1 = \left\lceil \sqrt{(r-1)/d} \right\rceil$
3: [Step 1] Find $0 \leq k_1 < (r-1)/d$ such that $G_d = \zeta_d^{k_1} G$
4:    Find $0 \leq u_1, v_1 < d_1$ such that $\zeta_d^{-u_1} G_d = \zeta_d^{v_1 d_1} G$
5:    $k_1 \leftarrow u_1 + v_1 d_1$
6: Set $\zeta_e \leftarrow \zeta^{(r-1)/d}$, $d_2 \leftarrow \left\lceil \sqrt{d} \right\rceil$, $G_e \leftarrow \zeta^{-k_1} G_1$
7: [Step 2] Find $0 \leq k_2 < d$ such that $G_e = \zeta_e^{k_2} G$
8:    Find $0 \leq u_2, v_2 < d_2$ such that $\zeta_e^{-u_2} G_e = \zeta_e^{v_2 d_2} G$
9:    $k_2 \leftarrow u_2 + v_2 d_2$
10: Output $\zeta^{k_1 + k_2 (r-1)/d}$

2.2 Cheon's Algorithm

A goal of Cheon's algorithm is to find an integer $k \in \mathbb{Z}/r\mathbb{Z}$ such that $\alpha = \zeta^k$ for a generator of the multiplicative group $\zeta \in (\mathbb{Z}/r\mathbb{Z})^*$ (Note that finding the generator ζ is easy). Here, such k is uniquely determined. To do so, Cheon's algorithm searches two integers k_1, k_2 such that $k = k_1 + k_2(r-1)/d$ satisfying $0 \leq k_1 < (r-1)/d$, $0 \leq k_2 < d$ in the following two steps (see Algorithm 1).

Step 1 searches an integer k_1 such that $\alpha^d = \zeta_d^{k_1}$ for $\zeta_d = \zeta^d$, or equivalently, searches two integers u_1, v_1 such that

$$\alpha^d \zeta_d^{-u_1} = \zeta_d^{v_1 d_1}$$

satisfying $0 \leq u_1, v_1 < \sqrt{(r-1)/d}$. Here, such u_1, v_1 are uniquely determined. In practice, Step 1 searches u_1, v_1 such that $\zeta_d^{-u_1} G_d = \zeta_d^{v_1 d_1} G$.

Then, Step 2 searches an integer k_2 such that $\alpha = \zeta^{k_1} \zeta_e^{k_2}$ for $\zeta_e = \zeta^{(r-1)/d}$ in the similar way, or equivalently, searches integers u_2, v_2 such that

$$\alpha \zeta^{-k_1} \zeta_e^{-u_2} = \zeta_e^{v_2 d_2}$$

satisfying $0 \leq u_2, v_2 < \sqrt{d}$ (where $G_e = \zeta^{-k_1} G$). Here, such u_2, v_2 are uniquely determined. In practice, Step 2 searches u_2, v_2 such that $\zeta_e^{-u_2} G_1 = \zeta_e^{v_2 d_2} G$.

In Cheon's algorithm, searching u_1, v_1 in Step 1 and searching u_2, v_2 in Step 2 require another sub-algorithm. Since these problems are very similar to DLP in the general setting, the baby-step giant-step algorithm or the λ-algorithm can be used as a subroutine. Since this paper is interested in Cheon's algorithm combined with the baby-step giant-step algorithm only, the next section briefly describes its outline.

Baby-step Giant-step Algorithm. The baby step giant step (BSGS) algorithm was introduced by Shanks in 1971 for solving DLP [16]. Instead of finding α directly, on input G and $G_1 = \alpha G$, BSGS searches two integers i, j such that $\alpha = i + jm$ and $0 \le i,\ j < m = \lceil \sqrt{r} \rceil$. Here, such i, j are uniquely determined. Since $\alpha G = (i + jm)G = iG + jG'$ for $G' = mG$, we have a relation $G_1 - iG = jG'$.

BSGS consists of two steps: in the 1st step (the baby-step), we compute

$$G_1,\ G_1 - G,\ G_1 - 2G, \ldots, G_1 - (m-1)G$$

successively and store them in a database. In the 2nd step (the giant-step), we compute

$$G',\ 2G', \ldots, (m-1)G'$$

successively and store them in another database. Then, we search a collision $G_1 - iG = jG'$ among these databases and thus a solution $\alpha = i + jm$ is obtained. Since $O(m)$ group operations and $O(m)$ group elements are required in both steps, the time and space complexity of BSGS are $O(\sqrt{r})$ group operations and $O(\sqrt{r})$ group elements, respectively.

When BSGS algorithm is used in Step 1 of Cheon's algorithm, we establish two databases

$$\zeta_d^0 G_d,\ \zeta_d^{-1} G_d,\ \zeta_d^{-2} G_d,\ \ldots,\ \zeta_d^{-d_1} G_d$$

and

$$\zeta_d^0 G,\ \zeta_d^{d_1} G,\ \zeta_d^{2d_1},\ \ldots,\ \zeta_d^{d_1^2} G,$$

and searches a collision satisfying $\zeta_d^{-u_1} G_d = \zeta_d^{v_1 d_1} G$ among these databases. Thus, Step 1 in Cheon's algorithm combined with BSGS algorithm requires $2d_1 = 2\sqrt{(r-1)/d}$ elements in space. Similarly, Step 2 requires $2d_2$ elements in space.

KKM Improvement. Cheon's algorithm requires the number of scalar multiplications for fixed elements G, G_1 and G_d. In 2007, Kozaki, Kutsuma and Matsuo introduced a precomputation table for such multiplications and reduced the time complexity of Cheon's algorithm from $O\left(\log r \left(\sqrt{(r-1)/d} + \sqrt{d}\right)\right)$ to $O\left(\sqrt{(r-1)/d} + \sqrt{d}\right)$.

Let us describe KKM improvement for a scalar multiplication γP ($\gamma \in \mathbb{Z}/r\mathbb{Z}$, $P \in \mathbb{G}$) in the followings. For a fixed integer c (which will be optimized later) and $n = \lceil \sqrt[c]{r} \rceil$, obtain the n-array expansion of the scalar $\gamma = \sum_{i=0}^{c-1} \gamma_i n^i$ ($0 \le \gamma_i < n$). For all $0 \le i < c$ and $0 \le j < n$, compute $S(i, j) = jn^i P$ and store them in a table in advance to the scalar multiplication. Then, the scalar multiplication γP is computed by the following way:

$$\begin{aligned} \gamma P &= \gamma_0 P + \gamma_1 n P + \cdots + \gamma_{c-1} n^{c-1} P \\ &= S(0, \gamma_0) + S(1, \gamma_1) + \cdots + S(c-1, \gamma_{c-1}). \end{aligned} \quad (1)$$

Since the precomputation table can be computed by at most c scalar multiplications and cn additions, KKM improvement reduces the time complexity of Cheon's algorithm by a factor of $\log r$.

Complexity of Cheon's Algorithm. As a summary of this section, when Cheon's algorithm is combined with the baby-step giant-step algorithm and KKM improvement, the time complexity T and the space complexity S are evaluated by the followings:

$$T = O\left(\sqrt{(r-1)/d} + \sqrt{d}\right) \quad \text{(group operations)},$$

$$S = O\left(\max\left(\sqrt{(r-1)/d}, \sqrt{d}\right)\right) \quad \text{(group elements)}.$$

2.3 DLPwAI in Cryptographic Schemes

In recently proposed cryptographic schemes, new mathematical problems have been proposed and the infeasibility of such problems assure the security of the schemes. For example, ℓ-BDHE problem was introduced in Boneh-Gentry-Waters' broadcast encryption system [5]. Here, ℓ-BDHE problem is a problem to find $e(G, \hat{G})^{\alpha^{\ell+1}}$ for a given bilinear map $e : \mathbb{G} \times \hat{\mathbb{G}} \to \mathbb{G}_T$ on input $G, \alpha G, \ldots, \alpha^\ell G, \alpha^{\ell+2} G, \ldots, \alpha^{2\ell} G \in \mathbb{G}$ and $\hat{G} \in \hat{\mathbb{G}}$, where $\mathbb{G} = \langle G \rangle$, $\hat{\mathbb{G}} = \langle \hat{G} \rangle$, and $\mathbb{G}_T$ is a multiplicative group with order r. When $\ell > d$, Cheon's algorithm can be applied to the scheme: by finding α as DLPwAI, an answer of ℓ-BDHE problem is obtained. Thus, Cheon's algorithm is an attacking algorithm for such cryptographic schemes. Note that there are many other recently proposed problems to which Cheon's algorithm can be allied such as ℓ-SDH problem [3], ℓ-sSDH problem [4], ℓ-BDHI problem [2].

3 Implementation

This section describes our strategy for implementing Cheon's algorithm. We adopted the baby-step giant-step (BSGS) algorithm as a subroutine, and KKM improvement for the speeding-up.

3.1 BSGS Algorithm

Databases. In step 1 of Cheon's algorithm, when BSGS algorithm is used, two databases

$$\text{DB}_{1,\text{B}} = \{\zeta_d^0 G_d, \ \zeta_d^{-1} G_d, \ldots, \ \zeta_d^{-i} G_d, \ldots, \zeta_d^{-d_1} G_d\}$$

and

$$\text{DB}_{1,\text{G}} = \{\zeta_d^0 G, \zeta_d^{d_1} G, \ldots, \ \zeta_d^{jd_1} G, \ldots, \ \zeta_d^{d_1^2} G\}$$

should be established. In our implementation, an element $\zeta_d^{-i} G_d$ in the database $\text{DB}_{1,\text{B}}$ is expressed by the following 12-byte representation

$$\underbrace{i}_{\text{4-byte}} \ || \ \underbrace{\text{LSB}_{64}(\text{MD5}(x(\zeta_d^{-i} G_d)||y(\zeta_d^{-i} G_d)))}_{\text{8-byte}}$$

where i is assumed to be 4-byte, $\text{LSB}_{64}(\cdot)$ represents the least 64-bit (8-byte) of the data, MD5 is the hash function, and $x(G)$, $y(G)$ represent x- and y-coordinate values of a point G on an elliptic curve. In the following, i is identified as the index part and the rest is as the data part. Similarly, in the database $\text{DB}_{1,\text{G}}$, an element $\zeta_d^{jd_1} G$ is expressed by the following 12-byte representation

$$\underbrace{j}_{\text{4-byte}} \,\|\, \underbrace{\text{LSB}_{64}(\text{MD5}(x(\zeta_d^{jd_1} G)\|y(\zeta_d^{jd_1} G)))}_{\text{8-byte}} \,.$$

Thus, the databases $\text{DB}_{1,\text{B}}$ and $\text{DB}_{1,\text{G}}$ requires $12d_1$ bytes, respectively.

Database Search. Then, in step 1 of Cheon's algorithm, it is needed to find two integers u_1, v_1 satisfying $\zeta_d^{-u_1} G_d = \zeta_d^{v_1 d_1} G$ among the databases $\text{DB}_{1,\text{B}}$ and $\text{DB}_{1,\text{G}}$. Since a straight-forward search (namely, compare all $\zeta_d^{-i} G_d$ in $\text{DB}_{1,\text{B}}$ and $\zeta_d^{jd_1} G$ in $\text{DB}_{1,\text{G}}$) is inefficient, we used the following bucket-sort like algorithm [1].

1. Divide each database into 64 sub-databases depending on the most significant 6-bit of the index part. When the most significant 6-bit of data $\zeta_d^{-i} G_d$ in $\text{DB}_{1,\text{B}}$ is ℓ ($0 \leq \ell \leq 63$), it is stored in the sub-database $\text{DB}_{1,\text{B}}^{(\ell)}$. Similarly, when the most significant 6-bit of data $\zeta_d^{jd_1} G$ in $\text{DB}_{1,\text{G}}$ is ℓ ($0 \leq \ell \leq 63$), it is stored in the sub-database $\text{DB}_{1,\text{G}}^{(\ell)}$.
2. Sort all sub-database $\text{DB}_{1,\text{G}}^{(\ell)}$ ($\ell = 0, \dots, 63$). by the comb-sort algorithm [6], which sorts N elements in $O(\log N)$.
3. For each ℓ, search a collision among $\text{DB}_{1,\text{B}}^{(\ell)}$ and $\text{DB}_{1,\text{G}}^{(\ell)}$. To do so, pick up an element $\zeta_d^{jd_1} G$ from the sub-database $\text{DB}_{1,\text{B}}^{(\ell)}$ and check whether the same element is in $\text{DB}_{1,\text{G}}^{(\ell)}$ by the binary search algorithm.

If a collision is found in step 3 for a certain ℓ, then, their indexes are what we required: set $u_1 \leftarrow i$ and $v_1 \leftarrow j$.

3.2 KKM Improvement

In our implementation, KKM improvement is also used for speeding-up Cheon's algorithm. Since our target group $\mathbb{G}$ is on an elliptic curve defined over a prime finite field with a mediate size, the affine coordinate system is used rather than the projective coordinate system. In the affine coordinate, every elliptic curve addition requires an inversion computation in the finite field. In order to avoid heavy operations, we used the Montgomery trick [13], which converts N inversion computations into 1 inversion and $3(N-1)$ multiplication computations. When the Montgomery trick is used in KKM improvement, only $O(\log_2 c)$ inversions are required.

4   Experimental Results

This section describes our experimental results of Cheon's algorithm for an elliptic curve used in the TinyTate library [14]. We successfully solved DLP-wAI by our implementation in a group $\mathbb{G}$ with 128-bit order. Strongly note that DLP has been believed to be secure in the same group.

4.1   Parameters

We used an addition cyclic group $\mathbb{G} = \langle G \rangle$ with order r on an elliptic curve $y^2 = x^3 + x$ defined over a prime finite field $\mathbb{F}_p$ used in the TinyTate library [14] which was developed by Oliveria et al. for implementing the pairing-based cryptosystem in the embedded devices. Concrete values of these parameters are summarized in the following:

$$
\begin{aligned}
p &= \text{0x5387a1b6 93d85f28 8f131dd5 e7f9305c f4436019 a00f3181} \\
&\quad \text{168d7b20 8934d073}\ \ (256\text{-bit}) \\
&= 3778160688\ 9598235856\ 7455764726\ 5839472148\ 1625071533 \\
&\quad 3029839574\ 7614203820\ 7746163 \\
\#E &= \text{0x5387a1b6 93d85f28 8f131dd5 e7f9305c f4436019 a00f3181} \\
&\quad \text{168d7b20 8934d074}\ \ (256\text{-bit}) \\
&= 3778160688\ 9598235856\ 7455764726\ 5839472148\ 1625071533 \\
&\quad 3029839574\ 7614203820\ 7746164 \\
&= 2^2 \cdot 3^2 \cdot 1227703 \cdot 50242951607062233279866689772851 \cdot r \\
r &= \text{0x80000040 00000000 00000000 00000001}\ \ (128\text{-bit}) \\
&= 1701411885\ 3107163264\ 4604909702\ 696927233 \\
r-1 &= \text{0x80000040 00000000 00000000 00000000}\ \ (128\text{-bit}) \\
&= 2^{102} \cdot 3 \cdot 11 \cdot 251 \cdot 4051
\end{aligned}
$$

where $\#E$ denotes the number of points in $E(\mathbb{F}_p)$. In our implementation of Cheon's algorithm, we used the following parameters:

$$
\begin{aligned}
d &= 12682136550675316736\ \ (64\text{-bit}) \\
&= 2^{60} \cdot 11 \\
\zeta &= 5 \\
\zeta_d &= \zeta^d = 1243133183\ 1021416944\ 7902414199\ 634645036 \\
d_1 &= \left\lceil \sqrt{(r-1)/d} \right\rceil = 3662760472\ \ (32\text{-bit}) \\
d_2 &= \left\lceil \sqrt{d} \right\rceil = 3561198752\ \ (32\text{-bit})
\end{aligned}
$$

Here, d is chosen to minimize the time complexity of Cheon's algorithm, and it is estimated that our implementation requires about $O(2^{32.75})$ group operations

Table 2. Computational Environment

CPU	Intel(R) Core^{TM} i7 2.93 GHz
OS	Ubuntu 10.04
Compiler	gcc 4.2.2
Library	GNU MP 4.1.2 [9]

and elements for solving DLPwAI. The generator ζ is chosen as the minimum generator of the multiplicative group $(\mathbb{Z}/r\mathbb{Z})^*$.

A base point G is randomly chosen from points in $E(\mathbb{F}_p)$ with order r. Then, coordinate values of G, $G_1 = \alpha G$, $G_d = \alpha^d G$ for our solution $\alpha = 3$ are as follows:

$$x(G) = 2120028877\ 3256318148\ 7254387784\ 2136477705\ 5392159948$$
$$4324389949\ 0272291266\ 930386$$
$$y(G) = 2676162370\ 5989368931\ 2040187896\ 9265522293\ 1214614323$$
$$9140635788\ 4068972949\ 5767328$$
$$x(G_1) = 1406565621\ 3797322149\ 8774526987\ 0546365700\ 1853001649$$
$$7338926577\ 6415100308\ 801614$$
$$y(G_1) = 3868330857\ 4106521926\ 0782358744\ 6121629591\ 2909889285$$
$$5061671768\ 3614580548\ 353865$$
$$x(G_d) = 3249689782\ 1175066681\ 3828703556\ 2385974940\ 1559994074$$
$$9555201487\ 6205365160\ 5880230$$
$$y(G_d) = 2017849900\ 8260892062\ 0757985589\ 8849092692\ 3717554232$$
$$0859082745\ 3474597173\ 7681072$$

4.2   Results

In the experiment, our implementation of Cheon's algorithm successfully found the solution $\alpha = 3$ in about 45 hours and 246 GByte by using a single PC (other environmental information are summarized in Table 2).

KKM Improvement. In our implementation, the Montgomery trick is used for KKM improvement part. By experimental optimizations, we used parameters $n = 2^{16}$ and $c = 8$. The precomputation requires about 4 seconds, and each scalar multiplication requires about 27 μseconds. About 1.03 $m$seconds is required for a multiplication without KKM improvement, about 38 times speed-up was established. Also, about 54 μseconds is required with KKM improvement but without the Montgomery trick, about 2 times speed-up was established.

Step 1. Two databases $DB_{1,B}$ and $DB_{1,G}$ are generated in about 14.5 hours and 82 GByte memory with 4 parallel computations. Then, 1 hour is required to divide these databases into 64 sub-databases $\mathrm{DB}_{1,\mathrm{B}}^{(\ell)}$ and $\mathrm{DB}_{1,\mathrm{G}}^{(\ell)}$ ($0 \leq \ell \leq 63$). Since the parent databases $\mathrm{DB}_{1,\mathrm{B}}$ and $\mathrm{DB}_{1,\mathrm{G}}$, and their cache are stored in this divisions, $82 \times 3 = 246$ GByte are required.

Sorting a sub-database $\mathrm{DB}_{1,\mathrm{B}}^{(\ell)}$ required about 8 minutes, and searching a collision among $\mathrm{DB}_{1,\mathrm{B}}^{(\ell)}$ and $\mathrm{DB}_{1,\mathrm{G}}^{(\ell)}$ required about 2 minutes. In our experiment, we found a collision when $\ell = 39$ and obtained $u_1 = 2170110422$ and $v_1 = 846301393$. Thus, we found a partial solution

$$k_1 = u_1 + v_1 d_1$$
$$= 3099799291849047918$$

in about 22.1 hours.

Step 2. Similarly to Step 1, the database generation required about 14.2 hours and 80 GByte. Dividing databases required about 1 hour and $80 \times 3 = 240$ GByte. Sorting a sub-database required about 7 minutes and searching a collision among sub-databases required about 2 minutes. We found a collision when $\ell = 52$ and obtained $u_2 = 1609744154$ and $v_2 = 718704617$. Thus, we found a partial solution

$$k_2 = u_2 + v_2 d_2$$
$$= 2559449986726782138$$

in about 23.2 hours.

Consequently, we successfully obtained

$$k = k_1 + k_2(r - 1)/d$$
$$= 34337105659404196008394232931084369774$$

and the solution

$$\alpha = \zeta^k \bmod r = 3$$

in about 45.3 hours and 246 GByte memory.

4.3   Estimations

Based on our experimental results described in the previous section, we estimate required time (in the worst case) and memory for solving DLPwAI with larger r. Here, we do not consider the parallel processing. We assume that the parameter d can be chosen as large as $\sqrt{r}$, namely, required time in Step 1 and Step 2 are almost same.

Let T_{C} be the required time for generating databases. Since a scalar multiplication is computed in 27 μseconds, T_{C} can be evaluated by

$$T_{\mathrm{C}} = 2 \times 27 \times 10^{-6} \times 2\sqrt[4]{r} \ \ [\text{Seconds}]. \tag{2}$$

Table 3. Cost Estimations

r	T_C	T_S	$T = T_C + T_S$	S_C
128 bit	6 Days	17 Hours	7 Days	288 GByte
132 bit	11 Days	35 Hours	13 Days	576 GByte
136 bit	22 Days	74 Hours	25 Days	1152 GByte
140 bit	45 Days	6 Days	51 Days	2304 GByte

Table 4. Estimated Time for 128-bit r

	Estimated Time
Jao, Yoshida [11]	16384 Days
Izu et al. [10]	1195 Days
This paper	7 Days

Then, let us evaluate the required time T_S for the database search. Since the sorting are dominant procedures, we neglect time for other parts. In our implementation, the comb-sort algorithm requires $O(\log N)$ for sorting N elements, and a sort in a sub-database requires 8 minutes for 128-bit r, T_S can be evaluated by

$$T_S = 2 \times 64 \times (8 \times 60) \times \frac{(\sqrt[4]{r}) \log (\sqrt[4]{r}/64)}{(2^{32}) \log (2^{26})} \quad [\text{Seconds}].$$

On the other hand, the required memory S_C can be evaluated by

$$S_C = 12 \times \sqrt[4]{r} \times 3 \times 2 \; [\text{Bytes}].$$

By using these evaluations, estimated required time and memory for various sizes of r are summarized in Table 3.

According to Table 3, solving DLPwAI seems to be feasible even if r is 140-bit since the required time is about 50 days. However, the required memory is beyond 2 TByte in this case. In the computational environment we used, and in most environments, dealing with such huge memory is too difficult to proceed. Thus, it is concluded that solving DLPwAI with 140-bit r is infeasible by Cheon's algorithm combined with BSGS algorithm. In order to solve such larger problems, Cheon's algorithm combined with the λ-algorithm or the kangaroo algorithm would be employed.

Next, let us compare our results to the previous experiments (summarized in Table 1) when r is 128-bit by the extrapolation. According to the time complexity of Cheon's algorithm, Jao and Yoshida's implementation[2] would require $3 \times \sqrt{2^{64}/2^{30}} = 393216$ hours (16384 days) and Izu et al.'s implementation would require $14 \times \sqrt{2^{64}/2^{42}} = 28672$ hours (1195 days) (Table 4). Even if the parallel computation is applied, solving DLPwAI is infeasible with 128-bit r by these implementations.

---

[2] Note that Jao-Yoshida's result was not dedicated to an efficient implementation.

5   Concluding Remarks

This paper succeeded to solve a discrete logarithm problem with auxiliary input (DLPwAI) in 45 hours with a single PC in a group with 128-bit order defined on an elliptic curve over a prime finite field with 256-bit elements, which are used in TinyTate library for implementing pairing cryptosystem in the embedded devices. If cryptographic schemes based on problems such as ℓ-BDE problem, ℓ-SDH problem, ℓ-sSDH problem or ℓ-BDHI problem are implemented, TinyTate library should avoid using such weak parameters. However, there are pairing-based cryptographic schemes which are not effected by Cheon's algorithm such as Boneh-Franklin's ID-based encryption scheme.

Acknowledgements

The authors would like to thank Yoshitaka Morikawa and Yasuyuki Nogami in Okayama University for their supports on this research.

References

1. Aoki, K., Ueda, H.: Sieving Using Bucket Sort. In: Lee, P.J. (ed.) ASIACRYPT 2004. LNCS, vol. 3329, pp. 92–102. Springer, Heidelberg (2004)
2. Boneh, D., Boyen, X.: Efficient Selective-ID Secure Identity-Based Encryption Without Random Oracles. In: Cachin, C., Camenisch, J.L. (eds.) EUROCRYPT 2004. LNCS, vol. 3027, pp. 223–238. Springer, Heidelberg (2004)
3. Boneh, D., Boyen, X.: Short Signatures Without Random Oracles. In: Cachin, C., Camenisch, J.L. (eds.) EUROCRYPT 2004. LNCS, vol. 3027, pp. 56–73. Springer, Heidelberg (2004)
4. Boneh, D., Boyen, X., Goh, E.-J.: Hierarchical Identity Based Encryption with Constant Size Ciphertext. In: Cramer, R. (ed.) EUROCRYPT 2005. LNCS, vol. 3494, pp. 440–456. Springer, Heidelberg (2005)
5. Boneh, D., Gentry, C., Waters, B.: Collusion Resistant Broadcast Encryption with Short Ciphertexts and Private Keys. In: Shoup, V. (ed.) CRYPTO 2005. LNCS, vol. 3621, pp. 258–275. Springer, Heidelberg (2005)
6. Box, R., et al.: A Fast Easy Sort. Computer Journal of Byte Magazine 16(4), 315–320 (1991)
7. Cheon, J.H.: Security Analysis of the Strong Diffie-Hellman Problem. In: Vaudenay, S. (ed.) EUROCRYPT 2006. LNCS, vol. 4004, pp. 1–11. Springer, Heidelberg (2006)
8. Cheon, J.H.: Discrete Logarithm Problems with Auxiliary Inputs. Journal of Cryptology 23(3), 457–476 (2010)
9. GNU MP, http://gmplib.org/
10. Izu, T., Takenaka, M., Yasuda, M.: Experimental Results on Cheon's Algorithm. In: WAIS 2010 in the Proceedings of ARES 2010, pp. 625–630. IEEE Computer Science, Los Alamitos (2010)
11. Jao, D., Yoshida, K.: Boneh-Boyen Signatures and the Strong Diffie-Hellman Problem. In: Shacham, H., Waters, B. (eds.) Pairing 2009. LNCS, vol. 5671, pp. 1–16. Springer, Heidelberg (2009)

12. Kozaki, S., Kutsuma, T., Matsuo, K.: Remarks on Cheon's Algorithms for Pairing-Related Problems. In: Takagi, T., Okamoto, T., Okamoto, E., Okamoto, T. (eds.) Pairing 2007. LNCS, vol. 4575, pp. 302–316. Springer, Heidelberg (2007)
13. Montgomery, P.: Speeding the Pollard and Elliptic Curve Methods of Factorization. Math. Comp. 48(177), 243–264 (1987)
14. Oliveira, L., López, J., Dahab, R.: TinyTate: Identity-Based Encryption for Sensor Networks, IACR Cryptology ePrint Archive, Report 2007/020 (2007)
15. Pollard, J.: Monte Carlo Methods for Index Computation (mod p). Math. Comp. 32, 918–924 (1978)
16. Shanks, D.: Class Number, a Theory of Factorization, and Genera. In: Proc. of Symp. Math. Soc., vol. 20, pp. 41–440 (1971)

Information Leakage Discovery Techniques to Enhance Secure Chip Design

Alessandro Barenghi[1], Gerardo Pelosi[1,2], and Yannick Teglia[3]

[1] DEI – Dipartimento di Elettronica e Informazione
Politecnico di Milano, Via Ponzio 34/5, I-20133 Milano, Italy
{barenghi,pelosi}@elet.polimi.it
[2] DIIMM – Dipartimento di Ingegneria dell'Informazione e Metodi Matematici
Università degli Studi di Bergamo, Viale Marconi 5, I-24044 Dalmine (BG), Italy
gerardo.pelosi@unibg.it
[3] STMicroelectronics, ZI de Rousset BP2, 13106 Rousset Cedex, France
yannick.teglia@st.com

Abstract. Side channel attacks analyzing both power consumption and electromagnetic (EM) radiations are a well known threat to the security of devices dealing with sensitive data. Whilst it is well known that the EM emissions of a chip represent an information leakage stronger than the overall dynamic power consumption, the actual relation between the emissions and the computations is still a subject under exploration. It is important for the chip designer to be able to distinguish which portions of the measured EM emissions are actually correlated with the sensitive information. Our technique obtains a detailed profile of the information leakage, identifying which harmonic components carry the largest part of the it on the measured signals. It may be successfully integrated in a design workflow as a post-testing feedback from the prototype chip, in the form of additional constraints aimed at reducing the local wires congestion up to a point where the emissions are no longer sufficient to conduct an attack. The analysis allows the design of ad-hoc countermeasures (shields and/or EM jammers), which do not require architectural changes to the chip. We provide a validation of the proposed technique on a commercial grade ARM Cortex-M3 based System on Chip (SoC), executing a software implementation of AES-128. The proposed approach is more efficient than a search of the whole frequency spectrum, allowing to conduct a deeper analysis with the same timing constraints.

Keywords: Side-Channel Attacks, Embedded Systems Security, Differential Power Attacks, Differential Electromagnetic Attacks.

1 Introduction

A significant part of the security margin provided by a cryptographic device is represented by its resistance to side channel attacks. Side channel attacks aim at disclosing the secret key of cryptographic primitives, through measuring environmental parameters during their computation. Typical environmental parameters from which it is possible to extract information relative to the values being

C.A. Ardagna and J. Zhou (Eds.): WISTP 2011, LNCS 6633, pp. 128–143, 2011.

processed are: power consumption [6,10], electromagnetic radiation [1,9] and execution timing [5]. Depending on the environmental parameter being measured, the attack techniques are called respectively Differential Electromagnetic Analysis (DEMA), Differential Power Analysis (DPA) and Timing analysis (TA).

A regular Differential Electromagnetic Analysis (DEMA) or a DPA attack aims at modeling the variation of the EM emissions or the dynamic power consumption of a chip caused by the different inputs fed to the cryptographic primitive executed on it. Assuming all the values undergoing computation are known, it is possible to accurately predict the values of the aforementioned environmental parameters, but, since the value of the secret key is not known to the attacker, an alternative strategy is devised. The attacker creates a family of a-priori models, each one depending on a *key hypothesis*, i.e. an hypothetical value of a small part of the key. The most common way of modelling either the power consumption or the EM emissions of a digital circuit is taking into account either the Hamming Weight (HW) of the values being computed or the Hamming Distance between two subsequent values, during a part of the cryptographic primitive involving the secret key. After building the models, the attacker correlates each of the predicted results with each sample in the time series of an experimental measurement (*trace*) of the environmental parameter related to the execution of the targeted part of the cryptographic primitive. Since only one of the models will fit, it is possible for the attacker to deduce the right key hypothesis. In order to obtain a significant estimate of the relation between the models and the physical parameters being measured, a large number of traces are taken while employing different inputs (plaintexts or ciphertexts). Pearson's linear correlation coefficient is the most common figure of merit employed to assess the goodness of fit of the a-priori models against the actual measurements [3]. Pearson's correlation coefficient turns out to be rather effective in practice since the strength of both the EM-emissions and the dynamic power consumption depend linearly on the switching activity of the underlying circuitry [8].

The analysis of EM emissions has proven an effective side channel able to yield efficient attacks [1, 4, 12], although it implies a quadratic increase in the number of chip spots to be considered when compared to a DPA technique. A significant factor for this efficiency is the use of small probes with a consequent precise spatial localization of the sources of the measured signal.

The signals collected through these kinds of measurements have a high correlation with the data computed by the cryptographic primitive operation considered in the a-priori models. For example, in [13] the authors show that recording the emission traces over a particular spot of an FPGA programmed with an implementation of the AES block cipher (identified as the places where the S-Box function was synthesized) resulted in an effective reduction of the number of traces required. Therefore, this kind of enhancements may be expected also when the device under test is either an ASIC implementation or a general purpose CPU running the same cryptographic primitive. Moreover, an important advantage of EM analysis is the possibility to bypass common power analysis countermeasures, such as voltage pumps, and to ignore the presence of static dummy cycles inserted to rebalance timing issues.

Within this context, we propose an enhancement of the testing methodology for a circuit in order to include evaluation of the resistance to EM side channel analysis as a design step. We propose an information leakage finding algorithm aiming at recognizing which harmonic components of the measured signals actually convey the significant part of the exploitable side channel information. The proposed algorithm is faster than an exhaustive brute force sweeping the whole frequency range, while preserving the same accuracy for real world scenarios. The proposed analysis enables to design countermeasures targeted to the specific leakage pattern of the device and may be conducted also on simulated traces without any change in the procedure. At the best of the authors' knowledge, this is not currently possible due to the lack of publicly available EM emission estimation tools from any pre-prototype description of the chip. The availability of such tools would allow a pre-prototyping evaluation of the EM leakage and would allow to properly tune the post place-and-route procedure in order to mitigate the EM leakage. This may be achieved through proper routing of the wires, which represent the most EM radiating part of the circuit.

The paper is organized as follows: Sect. 2 describes how the proposed methodology integrates within the current chip design workflow. Sect. 3 explains the proposed information leakage finding algorithm and provides insights on its inner workings. Sect. 4 reports a practical validation of the proposed technique on a commercial grade Cortex-M3 SoC running an industrial grade implementation of AES-128. Finally, Sect. 5 presents our conclusions.

2   EMA Analysis as a Design Phase

A typical digital circuit design flow is composed of a fixed chain of stages following the high level specification of the device, in the form of a netlist description of the chip. The first steps in tackling the transformation of a netlist into an accurate blueprint of the chip are: performing a preliminary consumption analysis on the design, and adding the Built In Self Test (BIST) additional logic required to perform functional testing of the circuit. After these steps, the chip description is accurate enough to perform a full placement through the wire routing and clock tree design process. The obtained description is accurate up to a full three dimensional representation of the design at single wire level, stored in the Graphic Database System II (GDSII) common interchange format in order to control the integrated circuit photolithographic etching. After completing the whole design of the chip, a first prototype of the actual device is realized and packaged in order to be sent to the testing stage. The prototype chips are still subject to a series of compliance tests among which the Electromagnetic compatibility (EMC) ones, aimed at ascertaining that the EM radiations of the device are not strong enough to disturb the regular functioning of neighbouring devices. Electromagnetic compatibility tests are oriented to obtain a quantitative measure of the radiated energy, regardless of the information which may

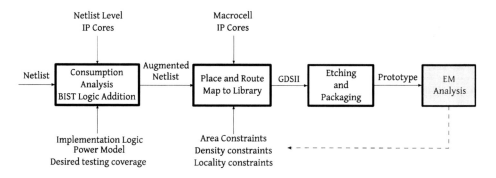

Fig. 1. Description of a typical digital chip design flow. The proposed EM analysis stage is highlighted in gray

be carried by the wavefronts. In particular, since the die emits significantly less than the bonding wires which connect it to the package pins, its emissions are usually regarded as harmless by the common EM compatibility standards. The security testing methodology proposed in this paper can easily be integrated in the EMC compatibility testing phase, since it requires the same equipment to be performed, and does not add a prohibitive amount of time to be spent at the workbench. The target of the EM analysis is to provide a more accurate information on both the spatial location and the informative content of the EM radiation of the silicon die, through checking if there is a viable side channel for attacks. After performing the proposed analysis, it is possible for the designer to employ the gathered information for introducing countermeasures during the place-and-route (p&r) step. In particular, it is possible to either exploit the free space on the top layer of the chip, after all the p&r operations have been performed, to introduce a grounded metallic shield over the most radiative zones or to reroute partially the wires in order to avoid excessive local congestions. A further possible countermeasure is the introduction of a jamming resonator tuned on the frequencies which carry sensitive informations out of the chip. Such a resonator may be easily realised as a simple tuned wire antenna and does not need to interact with other circuits related to the chip. Thus it is possible to design it without having any concerns on the actual chip architecture thus, helping a late-stage introduction, with only a negligible area overhead.

2.1 Electromagnetic Emission Analysis

The first step in the testing methodology is to obtain a map of the intensity of the electromagnetic emissions of the silicon die. In a region of space close to the chip surface, it is possible to model the EM emitting components as a set of wires lying on the die plane. Since the radiated field of a single wire is emitted perpendicularly to direction of the current flow, a probe constituted by a wire coil placed parallel to the die surface will not be sensitive to crosstalk from nearby wires[1], thus resulting in a reliable measure of the EM field intensity per underlying area unit. As a consequence, the parts of the chip which will be radiating more strongly are the ones characterized by a high wiring density. At the moment, the routing tools are not considering excessive wiring density as a problem because the power estimate is usually done before the wires are placed[2]. Consequently, it is possible to have strongly radiating zones which are not de-congestioned automatically by the tool, resulting in EM radiating hotspots. Round coil probes are already in use to perform EMC testing[3] on packaged chips, and may be used to perform the mapping of the EM emissions as well, thus enabling equipment reuse during the testing methodology. It is possible to obtain a precise mapping of the intensity of the EM emissions of a chip per area unit during the computation of a software cryptographic primitive through recording the field emitted in a spot and repeating the measurements while sweeping with the probe all over the die surface.

A kind of chip areas which may be of particular interest to be mapped are the so-called *glue logic* areas: sections of the chip where the placement tool is allowed complete freedom over the component and wire layout thus possibly causing large wire skeins. Since the recorded emission signals provide the evolution of the field intensity over time, it also is possible for the designer to locate exactly which part is emitting through checking either where the chip was active during a certain time instant or which instruction is being executed on a mapped CPU. This is particularly interesting in order to focus the analysis only on the instructions of the running cryptographic primitive dealing with the secret values thus, avoiding unnecessary concerns about strong EM emissions in unrelated time instants. We point out that the EM testing is performed in a white-box environment, where the designer knows all the implementation details of the chip, including the software running on the general purpose CPU in case the algorithm is not directly implemented as an ASIC. This kind of analysis is the one warranting the strongest security on the final product, since it already assumes that the attacker is able to know all the details of the device he will target, thus considering the position of utmost advantage for him. Indeed, motivated attackers may apply hardware reverse engineering techniques in order to fully reconstruct the structure of a chip[4]. After the strongest emitting spots of the chip have been located, a set of traces T is collected on top of them in order to proceed to the frequency analysis of the EM radiation.

---

[1] In a circular wire coil, placed parallel to the surface of the chip, the induced voltage drop at the ends of the wire is proportional derivative of the sensed magnetic flux ($\Delta V = -\frac{d\phi}{dt}$).

[2] Cadence Design Systems, Inc., *Physical Prototyping–Key to Nanometer SoC Chip Design*, Whitepaper. Dec. 2010, http://www.cadence.com

[3] International Electrotechnical Commission, *IEC/TS 61967-3 ed1.0*, ISO-Standard, Dec. 2010, http://webstore.iec.ch/webstore/webstore.nsf/artnum/035659

[4] Chipworks, *Report Library & Technical Competitive Analysis*, Technical Report, Dec. 2010, http://www.chipworks.com/Report_search.aspx

---

Algorithm 1. Leaked Information Finding Algorithm

Globals: T: set of traces, b: branching factor,
γ: confidence level of the correlation attack

Input: δ: frequency interval on which traces are evaluated; $|\delta|$ denotes the length of the frequency interval
Output: L: list of pairs (δ, n_δ), where δ is a frequency interval used to set up a filter for the measured traces, and n_δ is the minimum number of filtered traces so that the correlation attack succeed with the given confidence level. Initially, $L \leftarrow \emptyset$

1 **begin**
2   **if** $(|\delta| \geq \eta\ N_{threshold})$ **then**
3        $T_\delta \leftarrow \text{FILTER}(\delta,\ T)$
4        $n_\delta \leftarrow \text{CORRELATIONATTACK}(\gamma,\ T_\delta)$
5        $L \leftarrow L\ \cup\ \{\ (\delta,\ n_\delta)\ \}$
6   **if** $(n_\delta = \bot)$ **then**
7   **return**
8   **else**
9           $\{\delta_0,\ \ldots,\ \delta_{b-1}\} \leftarrow \text{SPLITUP}(\delta)$
10   **for** i **from** 0 **to** $b-1$ **do**
11   **Call Algorithm** $\mathbf{1}(\delta_i)$

---

3   Information Finding Algorithm

In order to automatically determine the harmonic components of the recorded signals that actually carry the exploitable information, we devised an information finding method reported in Alg. 1. This computation is intended to improve the information leakage characterization by lowering the ratio between the energies $\mathcal{E}_f$ and $\mathcal{E}_t$ of the filtered and unfiltered version of any trace, respectively. The output of the algorithm provides all the information required to build an optimum multi-bandpass filter in order to both maximize the aforementioned energy ratio, and discard the signal components not related to the key-dependent computation. The effect on leakage estimation efficiency and precision is measured through considering the decrease in the minimum number of traces needed to carry out a successful attack with a reasonable confidence margin. The key idea is to split the spectrum in equally sized shares and filter the EM traces with a Finite Impulse Response (FIR) filter whose bandpass keeps only one share at a time. The shape of the filtering window is driven by the necessity of having a maximum flat bandpass while retaining moderate aliasing in the time domain and a reasonable roll-off in the frequency domain. Reasonable choices are either a Chebyshev (type II) window or a tapered cosine window [11]. Subsequently, a series of attacks on the filtered traces is performed to understand which is the minimum number of measurements needed to distinguish, with a reasonable statistic confidence, the correct key hypothesis from the other ones. In order to perform a computationally efficient search in the frequency space, Alg. 1 exploits a b-ary split search strategy. The algorithm employs the previously

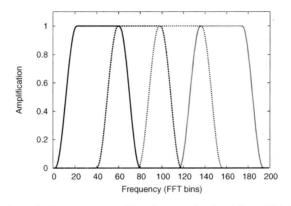

Fig. 2. Overlapping windows generated by the search algorithm. This example depicts the amplitude of four tapered cosine windows, as it could happen on the first run of the algorithm with $b = 4$.

collected trace set T as a test bench for the efficiency of the attacks. Let N be the number of samples in the time series of each trace or, equivalently, the number of *bins* of the Fast Fourier Transform (FFT) of the trace, and η the frequency interval corresponding to a single bin ($\eta=2\,f_{Ny}/N$). The frequency interval below which considering the energy of the signal is still appropriate may be defined as $\eta\,N_{threshold}$, $N_{threshold}> 1$, therefore the FFT bins of each trace may be thought as a sequence of $B=N/N_{threshold}$ slices. The algorithm receives the frequency interval δ, on which traces are evaluated, as a parameter. If the length of the frequency interval in input, $|\delta|$, is greater or equal than $\eta\,N_{threshold}$, a digital filter with such a support is applied to each trace in the set T, thus obtaining a new set of filtered traces T_δ (lines 1–3). Given the set T_δ, a correlation attack on the filtered traces is carried out in order to obtain either the minimum number of traces n_δ (which enable to recover the secret key) or a null value $\perp$ (in case of a failure of the attack) (line 4). Subsequently, the pair (δ, n_δ) is inserted in a global list L in order to record the shortest frequency intervals where the correlation attack either succeeded or failed (line 5). In case the figure of merit n_δ is different from $\perp$ (line 8), the interval δ is split up in b shares, with a 50% mutual overlap, (as depicted in Fig. 2) and the same procedure is recursively called on each share (lines 8–11), otherwise the algorithm returns from the call.

At the end of the execution, the list L will contain both the shortest frequency intervals for which the correlation attack is able to recover the secret key and the largest frequency intervals for which the measured traces T do not provide enough information to retrieve the key. The use of a larger trace set may lead the algorithm to spot more leaking intervals than the ones obtained with less traces at the cost of a longer computation. After obtaining the output of the algorithm, the designer is able to exploit the information to design an ad-hoc filter which will remove all the harmonic components not containing any relevant information. In order to design the filter, the designer may choose to keep all the parts of the spectrum where the attack has succeeded with the number of traces at his disposal. A more restrictive choice is to keep only the harmonic components where the attack succeeds with a number of traces smaller than the one needed for an attack with unfiltered traces. The rationale behind this choice is the fact that the stricter filtering will yield a higher ratio between the energy of the filtered signal $\mathcal{E}_f$ and the total energy of the signal $\mathcal{E}_t$, while retaining most of the informative content. On the other hand, discarding harmonic components which are still carrying some information, although more polluted than the original unfiltered signal, may be detrimental to the analysis, in case the leakage is not concentrated in a precise number of slices. In the following sections we will refer to the former spectrum slices as the *good* ones, while the latter will be indicated as the *acceptable* ones.

3.1 Complexity Analysis

Let the running time of the algorithm be expressed as the number of FILTER, and CORRELATIONATTACK operations being executed. Assuming the shortest possible frequency interval ($\eta\,N_{threshold}$) for the application of every digital filter and correlation attack, a linear scan of the spectrum $[0, B\,\eta\,N_{threshold}]$ would have a temporal complexity equal to $\Theta(B)$. It is possible to obtain a significant reduction of the computational effort needed to detect the leaking components of the signal through exploiting their sparsity and clustering over the whole spectrum, since real world scenarios commonly exhibits such a behaviour.

The best case of Alg. 1 happens when the useful information in each measured trace is concentrated in at most 1 out of b frequency sub-intervals for each call of the recursive procedure, thus giving a computational complexity of $\mathcal{T}(B)=\Omega(b\log_b B)$.

The worst case of Alg. 1 gives an upper bound to the temporal complexity $\mathcal{T}(B)$ and corresponds to a balanced configuration of the b-tree where at leaves level each group of sub-intervals has at least a slice where the attack succeeds. We note that the worst case condition implies the information is uniformly spread on the entire spectrum. Although this scenario is highly unlikely, it is possible to mitigate the additional computational complexity that a tree-based search algorithm would imply in such a case. A sensible trade-off is to modify the algorithm, so that the execution will halt in case the slices reach a size of $b\,N_{threshold}$, while all the attacks are still successful. This yields a temporal complexity proportional to $\mathcal{T}(B)=O(\sum_{i=0}^{\lceil\log_b B\rceil-1} b^i)=O(\frac{B-1}{b-1})$ at the cost of a reduction of a factor b in the precision of the analysis, while in turn avoiding the only case where the algorithm is slower than a linear scan.

The average-case running time requires a more accurate analysis. Intuitively, the information is very clustered over the entire frequency domain, thus the average running-time is expected to be much closer to the best case than to the worst case for most part of the practical cases. Let $p(j)$ the probability of mounting a successful CORRELATIONATTACK when considering the harmonic components of the traces in T on a single slice of the frequency spectrum:

$[j \eta N_{threshold}, (j+1) \eta N_{threshold})$, where $j \in \{0, \ldots, B-1\}$, consequently the probability that the attack does not succeed is: $1 - p(j)$.

Let X_j be the indicator random variable associated with such an event. Hence, $X_j = 1$ if the CORRELATION ATTACK is successful through filtering the traces on the interval $[j \eta N_{threshold}, (j+1) \eta N_{threshold})$, $j \in \{0, \ldots, B-1\}$. Assume each call of Alg. 1 to be bound to a b-tree node, corresponding to a determined share of the frequency spectrum B. Denote with $X_{j_t}^{[h-t]}$ the indicator random variable associated with the event of executing a successful CORRELATION ATTACK when considering the harmonic components of the traces in T on the frequency interval: $[j_t b^{h-t} \eta N_{threshold}, (j_t+1) b^{h-t} \eta N_{threshold})$, where $j_t \in \{0, \ldots, B/b^{h-t}-1\}$, $t \in \{0, \ldots, h\}$, $h = \lceil \log_b B \rceil$. Therefore, $X_{j_h}^{[h]}$, $X_{j_{h-1}}^{[h-1]}$, $\ldots$, $X_{j_0}^{[0]}$ may denote the random variables (from the leaf level to the root level) associated with each node of the aforementioned b-tree, respecting the following relations:

$$\Pr(X_{j_h}^{[h]} = 1) = p(j_h); \qquad\qquad j_h \in \{0, \ldots, B-1\}$$

$$\Pr(X_{j_{h-1}}^{[h-1]} = 1) = \sum_{j_h = j_{h-1} \cdot b}^{j_{h-1} \cdot b + b - 1} \Pr(X_{j_h}^{[h]} = 1); \qquad j_{h-1} \in \{0, \ldots, \tfrac{B}{b} - 1\}$$

$$\Pr(X_{j_{h-2}}^{[h-2]} = 1) = \sum_{j_{h-1} = j_{h-2} \cdot b}^{j_{h-2} \cdot b + b - 1} \Pr(X_{j_{h-1}}^{[h-1]} = 1); \quad j_{h-2} \in \{0, \ldots, \tfrac{B}{b^2} - 1\}$$

$$\cdots \qquad\qquad\qquad \cdots$$

$$\Pr(X_{j_1}^{[1]} = 1) = \sum_{j_2 = j_1 \cdot b}^{j_1 \cdot b + b - 1} \Pr(X_{j_2}^{[2]} = 1); \qquad j_1 \in \{0, \ldots, \tfrac{B}{b^{h-1}} - 1\}$$

$$\Pr(X_{j_0}^{[0]} = 1) = \sum_{j_1 = j_0 \cdot b}^{j_0 \cdot b + b - 1} \Pr(X_{j_1}^{[1]} = 1); \qquad j_0 \in \{0\}$$

The probability density function $p(0), p(1), \ldots$ in the above formula must be either estimated or modelled taking into account (i) the specific operation of the targeted cryptographic primitive, (ii) the hardware design of the target device and (iii) the physical characteristics of the environmental parameter measured by the attack. In common practical cases such as the analysis of EM emissions, the harmonic components carrying information are usually restricted to a relatively small bandwidth, since it is reasonable to assume that the resonating conductors will have reasonably close impedances. The same narrow band consideration may be made for power consumption measurements, since a synchronous circuit dissipates most of the dynamic power at each clock edge, thus resulting in a large part of the informative signal being concentrated on the same frequencies. Therefore, the probability density function $p(0), p(1), \ldots$ it is expected to be highly clustered (i.e., there are only a few $p(k) \neq 0$, $k \in \{0, \ldots, B-1\}$). Such a probability density function results in a low number of branches requiring a full depth exploration. Thus the proposed algorithm is faster than a linear scan in the best and average case and as fast as the linear scan in the worst case.

4 Experimental Validation

4.1 Workbench

The device under exam was a commercial grade Cortex-M3 based SoC[5], endowed with on die SRAM and Flash memory, both coupled to the CPU, and USB, RS-232 and GPIO interfaces. The Cortex macrocell is synthesized together with 10+ other IP cores in a single block of glue logic, thus it is not possible to identify through optical inspection any of the components, nor to infer the placement of any of IP cores through looking at die surface with an optical microscope. In order to get as close as possible to the die surface during the measurements, the top of the chip package was removed through a combination of nitric and sulphuric acid. The device under profiling was mounted on a regular development board and affixed to a gas suspended X–Y moving table controlled by the same computer gathering the data from the oscilloscope. We chose to map the chip area by moving in $100\mu m$ steps and covering the whole zone to be mapped scanning it line by line. The equipment employed to collect all the measures was a LeCroy WavePro 7300a digital oscilloscope[6] sampling at $f_{s,DEMA}$=10Gsample/s (thus resulting in a Nyquist limit for the sampled components at $f_{Ny}=f_s/2$=5GHz), and an EM-profiling oriented Langer ICR H probe[7] made of an horizontally oriented coil with an inner diameter of $150\mu m$, placed roughly at 0.8mm from the die surface. The signal picked up by the probe was amplified by a low noise differential amplifier and fed directly into the oscilloscope sampling channel. We targeted the `load` operation executed for the first look up in the S-Box. The start of the acquisition was triggered by the device under test through the use of a GPIO pin asserted by the enciphering program before the start of the execution of the first AES-128 round. All the recorded traces was obtained through averaging 16 measurements taken with the same settings and the same plaintext in order to reduce the environmental noise.

In order to provide comparative results on Alg. 1, we also conducted a power consumption measurements campaign. The measurements were collected with a LeCroy Waverunner WavePro 7100A with a maximum sampling rate of 20Gsamples/s with a LeCroy AP034 differential probe[8] connected to a 2Ω shunt inserted on the only power supply line available for the Cortex-M3 SoC. The sampling rate was set to $f_{s,DPA}$=5Gs/sec (f_{Ny}=2.5GHz) in order to provide a sound safety margin on the sampling of fast dynamics which may be useful during the analysis. All the signals measured are recorded in an 8-bit per sample raw format and all signal treatment on a Core i7 920 running 64-bit Linux Gentoo 2010.1.

---

[5] ARM, *Cortex-M3 Processor*, Technical Specifications, Dec. 2010,
   http://www.arm.com/products/processors/cortex-m/cortex-m3.php
[6] LeCroy, *WavePro 7000 Series*, Technical Specifications, Dec. 2010,
   http://www.lecroy.com/france/press/articles/images/WavePro7000_DS.pdf
[7] Langer EMV-Technik, *IC Test Systems–Near Field Microprobes (ICR probes)*,
   Technical Specifications, Dec 2010,
   http://www.langer-emv.de/en/products/ic-measurement/
[8] LeCroy, *AP034 Differential Probe*, Technical Specifications, Dec. 2010,
   http://www.lecroy.com/Options/

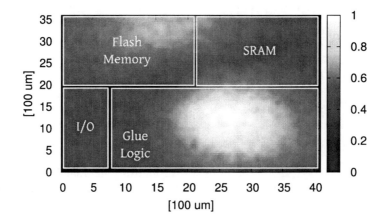

Fig. 3. Intensity of the Cortex-M3 SoC EM emissions during the time lapse when the first round key addition of AES-128 is performed. Clearer zones represent a stronger EM activity. The magnitude of the current measured by the probe has been normalized for visual enhancement.

4.2   Experimental Results

Employing the described setup, the silicon die of the device under attack was fully mapped in order to determine which components were emitting and which parts of the device logic were most active during the computation. The collected traces were processed in order to obtain a temporal sequence of maps of the emissions of the chip through adding the values of the emitted signal for 50 consecutive samples at once. The result of this preprocessing was a movie depicting the evolution of the emission during the whole running time of the AES-128, with a time accuracy of 5ns per frame. Through the knowledge of the code running on the chip, and thanks to the synchronization provided by the trigger raised by the Cortex-M3 board, it was possible to locate when the CPU was doing active computation at the beginning of the first AES round thus, obtaining the frame depicted in Fig. 3. Figure 3 depicts the amount of emitted EM radiation, measured as the intensity of the current running through the probe, where clearer colours indicate a higher EM activity. The overlain boxes point out which areas of the chip are optically recognizable. Through examining the map, it is possible to distinguish which zone of the glue logic is occupied by the Cortex-M3 core, thanks to the higher radiation caused by the ongoing switching activity. The second zone having non negligible radiating activity is the flash memory: this activity can be ascribed to the ongoing instruction fetch operation, performed in pipeline with the CPU execution phase. A possible cause of the lower radiation activity shown by the flash memory is the metal tiling added at manufacturing time to flatten the photolithographic layers which partially shields the emissions. Nonetheless, the memory electromagnetic activity is still strong enough to be measured by the probe. Placing the probe directly above the center of the hotspot (at the bottom right of the map) we collected 1100 traces of the EM emissions of the chip during

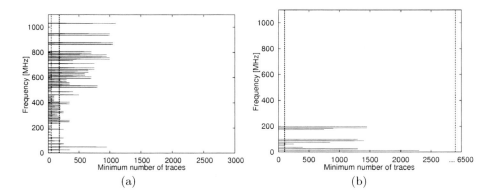

Fig. 4. Minimum number of traces necessary to perform an attack in Alg. 1 considering a single slice. Figure (a) depicts the results for the EM traceset, while Fig.(b) for the power consumption traceset. The leftmost dashed line indicates the least number of traces employed per slice, the rightmost the number of traces necessary with the unfiltered traces. The omitted part of the spectrum has no slices where the attack succeeds.

the execution of the AES-128 algorithm employed in the previous phase, while changing the input plaintexts. Each of the 1100 measurements is obtained as the average of 16 measurements taken with the same plaintext in input to the cipher. In order to perform efficiency analyses also on the power consumption traces, 10000 traces of the power consumption of the same chip were collected. Each recorded trace was the result of the averaging of 64 executions of the first round of AES-128 with the same plaintext.

During the execution of Alg. 1, all the attacks were performed considering the Hamming weight of the output of one byte of the S-Box as the emission intensity model of the observable value. The branching factor of the b-tree was set to $b=20$ and the branching depth employed was 2. The precision achieved for the EM spectrum leakage detection was $N_{threshold,DEMA} \cdot \eta_{DEMA}=80 \cdot 1.25\text{MHz}=100\text{MHz}$, while for the power spectrum was $N_{threshold,DPA} \cdot \eta_{DPA}=250 \cdot 0.2\text{MHz}=50\text{MHz}$. Figure 4(a) shows the minimum number of traces required to successfully perform an attack on a specific slice of the spectrum (indicated on the y-axis). For the sake of clarity, all the slices where the attack does not succeed have been represented having 0 as the minimum number of traces (instead of the maximum number available for each traceset). The two vertical dashed lines, for each picture, represent the minimum number of traces required to perform an attack keeping only a single slice of the spectrum (leftmost line) and the number of traces required to perform an attack with the unfiltered traceset (rightmost line). Both figures show that the effective part of the spectrum carrying information is rather small and, in particular, concentrated towards the low end of the spectrum. In particular, the power traces (Fig. 4(b)) show only two zones containing significant information for the analysis, while the EM spectrum (Fig. 4(a)) is richer in terms of leaking components. We note that many components of the EM spectrum contain more

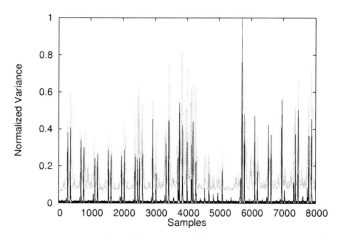

Fig. 5. Time-wise variance of the whole traceset for EM emission before (grey) and after (black) the filtering with the filter encompassing both *good* and *acceptable* slices

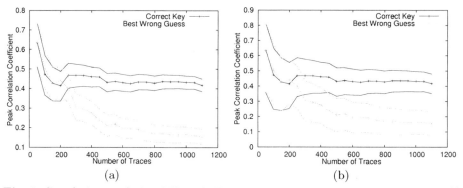

Fig. 6. Correlation analysis of filtered EM traces assuming a confidence level γ=80% (a), and γ=99% (b)

noise than information with respect to the unfiltered traces. Indeed, a significant number of attacks succeed with a greater number of traces than the one needed for the unfiltered ones (this is indicated by the horizontal bars exceeding the second dashed threshold).

Figure 5 depicts the variance of the whole EM trace set, computed sample-wise. The black plot depicts the variance of the traces where a filter keeping both good and acceptable slices has been applied, while the grey plot depicts the variance of the unfiltered traces. It can be easily seen that evicting all the frequency components found to be unrelated by the Alg. 1 yields a time series where it is easy to spot which time instants have a large variation among different inputs, and are thus expected to leak a significant amount of information. This allows the designer to spot the other temporal locations where the information is leaked by the same physical location of the chip. After obtaining the two filters,

Table 1. Comparison among the efficiency of the filter construction technique on EM and power consumption traces

	Statistical Confidence	No Filtering Min. Num. of Traces	Good Slices Min. Num. of Traces	$\mathcal{E}_f/\mathcal{E}_t$	Accept.+Good Slices Min. Num. of Traces	$\mathcal{E}_f/\mathcal{E}_t$
DEMA	80%	310	240	-63.8 dB	210	-61.6 dB
	99%	660	400		410	
DPA	80%	5800	300	-62.4 dB	450	-55.8 dB
	99%	5800	800		800	

one containing only the good slices, the other containing both the good and the acceptable ones, we compared the attacks run with both the filtered and the raw traces. In order to obtain a robust evaluation of the precision of the characterization performed, we chose *the minimum number of traces* necessary for the attack to succeed as a figure of merit. Since this figure is dependent on a point estimate of a statistical value (Pearson's coefficient) it is important to take into account its level of confidence in order to properly evaluate the results. This, in turn, implies that, instead of comparing the correlation coefficient of the correct key with the best guess among the wrong ones (i.e., the most likely error for an attacker), we checked when the two confidence intervals for the two values are disjoint. This occurs when the value of the estimate of the correlation coefficient for the correct key is above the one for the best mistake an attacker will make, with a statistical significance (80% and 99%, respectively, in Tab. 1) given by the width of the confidence interval. An example of the trend of the correlation coefficient when employing a growing number of traces is presented in Fig. 6. The figure depicts how the estimate of the correlation coefficients of filtered traces stabilizes with respect to the number of traces employed to perform the attack: the value of the figure of merit can be directly read (240 traces at 80% confidence level (see Fig. 6(a)) and 410 at 99% confidence level (see Fig. 6(b)). The correlation values for the DPA attacks follow the same pattern, except for the required number of traces which is higher. This may be attributed to the large amount of uncorrelated power consumption which happens on the SoC during the computation.

Table 1 reports the quantitative improvements obtained through the application of the profiling technique to both DEMA and DPA. The first row of the table shows how employing the automatically designed filters improves the efficiency of the attack on a set of measurements. The eviction of the part of the frequency spectrum unrelated to the observed value reduces the number of measurements needed to detect the leakage by 22.5% employing only dense zones and by 32% employing also the sparse ones thus, enhancing the quality of the analysis of the radiated emissions. The quantity of noise removed by the filtering is particularly relevant: the ratio between the energy of the filtered signal $\mathcal{E}_f$ and the one of the raw acquisition $\mathcal{E}_t$ is in the -60 dB range, implying that only a small part of the radiated emission is actually correlated with the critical computation. Nonetheless, EM attacks are still able to succeed, if more resources are devoted to take a large number of measurements from the chip. The second row of the table reports the gains when the automatic filtering design methodology is applied to power traces. The results suggest that also the correlation analysis on the power consumption signals benefits from employing proper filtering on the measured signals. The number of measurements is reduced by an order of magnitude, coherently with the fact that the power traces, taking into account the consumption of the whole chip, are expected to contain more content unrelated to the attack. In both cases, the enhancement in the efficiency allows the designer to take into account the real entity of the threat, which would have been masked by the environmental and systematic noise. One particular effect is that, while DPA attacks benefit from employing only harmonic components where the obtained information is dense, DEMA attacks perform better when including also sparse ones. This may be ascribed to the fact that the leakage in power consumption is concentrated in a few harmonic components [2].

The running time of the algorithm was sensibly lower than the linear scanning of the spectrum for both cases. In particular, the analysis of the EM traces required only 20 attacks at the first level and 40 at the second level of the b-tree (thus 60 calls to CorrelationAttack instead of 400), while the analysis of the power traces required 20 attacks at the first level and 20 at the second (40 calls versus the 400 needed for a linear scan). Taking into account the time for a single attack the overall running time of Alg. 1 was of 2.5 hours (against a 16.6 for a full linear scan) for the power consumption profiling and of 19 minutes for the EM profiling (against a 3 hours and 10 minutes long linear scan).

5   Conclusion

In this work we proposed a new technique able to obtain a characterization of the information of the EM leakage and demonstrated its viability employing an ARM Cortex-M3 chip running an implementation of AES-128. The proposed algorithm is able to obtain a precise characterization of the harmonic components of the side channel measurements (up to a 1/400th of the measured bandwidth in our experiments), within an acceptable time frame on a single desktop. We note that the information obtained from the spatial and frequency profiling of the EM traces allows the designer to introduce ad-hoc countermeasures to the information leakage. This results either in savings in terms of shielded area or in the introduction of non-architecturally invasive active countermeasures into the chip to selectively choke up the EM emitted information. As future developments for reinforcing the security of cryptographic devices, through employing signal processing techniques, we plan to investigate topics about blind source separation (BSS) methods [7]. After a proper mapping of the targeted device, these techniques provide an interesting tool to separate the signal components bound to the cryptographic primitive computation from the signals emitettcd from other active parts of the device.

References

1. Agrawal, D., Archambeault, B., Rao, J.R., Rohatgi, P.: The EM side-channel(s). In: Kaliski Jr., B.S., Koç, Ç.K., Paar, C. (eds.) CHES 2002. LNCS, vol. 2523, pp. 29–45. Springer, Heidelberg (2003)
2. Barenghi, A., Pelosi, G., Teglia, Y.: Improving First Order Differential Power Attacks Through Digital Signal Processing. In: Elçi, A., Makarevich, O.B., Orgun, M.A., Chefranov, A., Pieprzyk, J., Bryukhomitsky, Y.A., Örs, S.B. (eds.) SIN, pp. 19–29. ACM, New York (2010)
3. Brier, E., Clavier, C., Olivier, F.: Correlation Power Analysis with a Leakage Model. In: Joye, M., Quisquater, J.-J. (eds.) CHES 2004. LNCS, vol. 3156, pp. 16–29. Springer, Heidelberg (2004)
4. Gebotys, C.H., White, B.A.: EM analysis of a Wireless Java-based PDA. ACM Trans. Embedded Comput. Syst. 7(4) (2008)
5. Kocher, P.C.: Timing Attacks on Implementations of Diffie-Hellman, RSA, DSS, and Other Systems. In: Koblitz, N. (ed.) CRYPTO 1996. LNCS, vol. 1109, pp. 104–113. Springer, Heidelberg (1996)
6. Kocher, P.C., Jaffe, J., Jun, B.: Differential Power Analysis. In: Wiener, M. (ed.) CRYPTO 1999. LNCS, vol. 1666, pp. 388–397. Springer, Heidelberg (1999)
7. Le, T.H., Clediere, J., Serviere, C., Lacoume, J.L.: How can Signal Processing benefit Side Channel Attacks? In: Workshop on Signal Processing Applications for Public Security and Forensics 2007. SAFE 2007, pp. 1–7. IEEE, Los Alamitos (2007)
8. Mangard, S., Oswald, E., Popp, T.: Power Analysis Attacks: Revealing the Secrets of Smart Cards (Advances in Information Security). Springer-Verlag New York, Inc., Secaucus (2007)
9. Mangard, S.: Attacks on Cryptographic ICs Based on Radiated Emissions. In: Proceedings of Austrochip, pp. 13–16 (2003)
10. Messerges, T.S., Dabbish, E.A., Sloan, R.H.: Investigations of Power Analysis Attacks on Smartcards. In: WOST 1999: Proceedings of the USENIX Workshop on Smartcard Technology, p. 17. USENIX Association, Berkeley (1999)
11. Oppenheim, A.V., Schafer, R.W., Buck, J.R.: Discrete-Time Signal Processing, 2nd edn. Prentice-Hall, Englewood Cliffs (1999)
12. Peeters, E., Standaert, F.X., Quisquater, J.J.: Power and Electromagnetic Analysis: Improved Model, Consequences and Comparisons. Integr. VLSI J. 40(1), 52–60 (2007)
13. Réal, D., Valette, F., Drissi, M.: Enhancing Correlation Electromagnetic Attack Using Planar Near-Field Cartography. In: DATE, pp. 628–633. IEEE, Los Alamitos (2009)

A Cryptographic Processor for Low-Resource Devices: Canning ECDSA and AES Like Sardines

Michael Hutter[1], Martin Feldhofer[1], and Johannes Wolkerstorfer[2]

[1] Institute for Applied Information Processing and Communications (IAIK),
Graz University of Technology, Inffeldgasse 16a, 8010 Graz, Austria
{Michael.Hutter,Martin.Feldhofer}@iaik.tugraz.at
[2] xFace, Plüddemanngasse 39, 8010 Graz, Austria
Johannes.Wolkerstorfer@xface.at

Abstract. The Elliptic Curve Digital Signature Algorithm (ECDSA) and the Advanced Encryption Standard (AES) are two of the most popular cryptographic algorithms used worldwide. In this paper, we present a hardware implementation of a low-resource cryptographic processor that provides both digital signature generation using ECDSA and encryption/decryption services using AES. The implementation of ECDSA is based on the recommended $\mathbb{F}_{p192}$ NIST elliptic curve and AES uses 128-bit keys. In order to meet the low-area requirements, we based our design on a sophisticated hardware architecture where a 16-bit datapath gets heavily reused by all algorithms and the memory is implemented as a dedicated RAM macro. The proposed processor has a total chip area of 21 502 GEs where AES needs only 2 387 GEs and SHA-1 requires 889 GEs.

Keywords: Cryptographic Processor, ECDSA, ECC, AES, SHA-1, ASIC Implementation, Low-Resource Constraints.

1 Introduction

In a world where an innumerable amount of pervasive devices communicate with each other, the need for security increases heavily. Cryptographic services like secure symmetric and asymmetric authentication as well as confidentiality build the basis for contactless security applications like access control, mobile payment, and product authentication.

Most of the published hardware implementations of cryptographic services optimize a single algorithm or even a part of it and often do not account for higher-level protocols and applications. Turning such cryptographic primitives into a working product turns out to require a multiple of resources in the end. In this paper, we investigate the implementation of a cryptographic processor for low-resource devices. We present a complete integrated solution which is based only on standardized algorithms and protocols.

In particular, using standardized algorithms and protocols with an appropriate level of security is important to assure the interoperability between devices

C.A. Ardagna and J. Zhou (Eds.): WISTP 2011, LNCS 6633, pp. 144–159, 2011.
© IFIP International Federation for Information Processing 2011

and to allow reuse of existing infrastructures in back-end applications. Even in the very cost-sensitive market, people get more and more convinced that standardized solutions are inevitable. Two of the most important standardized algorithms are the Elliptic Curve Digital Signature Algorithm (ECDSA) [23] and the Advanced Encryption Standard (AES) [21]. ECDSA, which is for example used for secure identification in e-passports, generates digital signatures for message and entity authentication. AES is the successor of the Data Encryption Standard (DES) and today the most frequently used symmetric block cipher for encryption and authentication.

Hence, we target the implementation of our cryptographic processor on these two algorithms. The reason why we have chosen to implement both algorithms in one module is that the public-key scheme ECDSA can be used for offline authentication in open-loop applications while AES is much faster when the verifier has online access especially in closed-loop scenarios. Furthermore, with our approach of reusing components like the memory and the controlling engine we want to demonstrate that these high-security algorithms can be migrated to very resource-constrained devices such as mobile devices, embedded systems, wireless sensors, and RFID devices.

In this paper, we present the first ASIC hardware implementation of a cryptographic processor that is able to perform both the ECDSA using the NIST elliptic curve over $\mathbb{F}_{p192}$ and the AES (encryption and decryption) with 128-bit keys. Our implementation targets low-resource devices which implies fierce requirements concerning chip area (costs) and power consumption (due to a possible contactless operation). We meet the ambitious design goals by using a sophisticated hardware architecture where the main components memory, datapath, and controlling engine are reused by all implemented algorithms. Using a 16-bit datapath with a multiply-accumulate unit and a dedicated RAM macro instead of a flip-flop based memory minimizes the chip area. Next to several algorithmic-level improvements, we present a very efficient arithmetic-level implementation of a modular multiplication with interleaved NIST reduction over $\mathbb{F}_{p192}$. The entire processor needs 21 502 GEs where 2 387 GEs are required to support AES and 889 GEs are needed for SHA-1. This is because AES and SHA-1 reuse several components of our processor such as the microcontroller and the common memory.

The article is structured as follows. Section 2 summarizes related work on AES and elliptic-curve hardware implementations. An overview of the system is given in Section 3 and the hardware architecture is described in detail. Arithmetic-level implementation are given in Section 4 where we describe the NIST modular multiplication. Section 5 shows the implemented algorithms such as SHA-1, AES, and ECDSA. Results of our work are presented in Section 6. Conclusions are drawn in Section 7.

2   Related Work

There exist many articles that describe hardware architectures for AES and elliptic-curve based algorithms. One landmark paper that reports a low-resource implementation of AES is due to M. Feldhofer et al. [4] in 2004. Their implementation needs 3 595 GEs and performs a 128-bit encryption within 1 016 clock cycles. P. Hämäläinen et al. [7] presented an encryption-only AES architecture in 2006. Their design needs only 3 100 GEs. Similar results have been reported also by J.-Kaps et al. [14] and M. Kim [15] who presented an encryption-only AES implementation with around 4 000 GEs.

In view of elliptic-curve cryptography (ECC) there exist several implementations that propose efficient hardware architectures for scalar multiplication, e.g. S. Kumar et al. [17] and L. Batina et al. [1]. Architectures with implementations of also higher-level protocols have been proposed by A. Satoh et al. [24] and J. Wolkerstorfer [27] who proposed a dual-field ECC processor for low-resource devices. Y. K. Lee et al. [18] and D. Hein et al. [9] presented an ECC co-processor over binary fields $\mathbb{F}_{2^{163}}$. The work of Lee integrates a tiny microcontroller for higher-level arithmetics while the work of Hein includes a digital RFID front-end supporting the ISO 18000-3-1 standard protocol. ECDSA implementations have been realized by J. Wolkerstorfer [27], F. Fürbass et al. [5], and E. Wenger et al. [26]. They based their design on prime-field arithmetics to support ECDSA.

Our work is based on an ECDSA implementation of M. Hutter et al. [10]. We extended the work by implementing AES-128 (supporting encryption and decryption) as a main contribution and show that it can be integrated into the processor with low resources. We further give a detailed description of the arithmetic-level and algorithmic-level implementation of the processor and discuss the results in Section 6.

3   System Overview

The implementation of our proposed processor is based on the recommended NIST Weierstrass elliptic curve over $\mathbb{F}_{p192}$. This has mainly two reasons. First, our processor should be as flexible and scalable as possible while keeping the required chip area low. A processor over $\mathbb{F}_p$ allows us to support different protocols and algorithms on the processor without the need of any additional logic circuits. However, the costs for that choice are a lower performance compared to binary-extension field processors. Second, fixing the implementation to a standardized elliptic curve provides interoperability with existing applications like X.509 public-key infrastructures (PKI), citizen cards, and e-passports. Furthermore, it allows several optimizations in hardware like the NIST modular reduction [8] to gain additional performance.

We decided to implement a 16-bit architecture. During our investigations, it has shown that a 16-bit data width provides an optimum for reducing the chip area and the power consumption while keeping the required number of clock cycles within limitations.

3.1   Hardware Architecture

In order to design a low-resource processor, we minimized the required hardware resources by reusing components like the memory and the controller for all

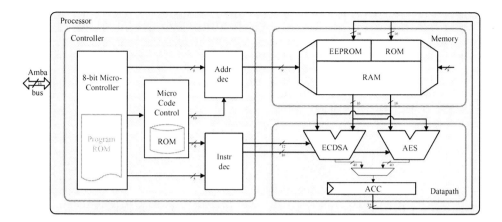

Fig. 1. Architecture of the Cryptographic Processor

implemented algorithms. Especially for the AES this means that the overhead is very low because the ECDSA dominates the memory requirements and the controlling effort.

The cryptographic processor consists of three main components as depicted in Figure 1. The first component is the controller, which is responsible for sequencing the desired algorithms and the generation of the control signals for the memory and the datapath unit. The second module is the memory, which holds data during computation, constants like curve parameters, and also non-volatile data like the private key (for ECDSA) and the secret key (for AES). The third module is the datapath, which performs the arithmetic and logic operations for ECDSA and AES.

The memory of the processor can be accessed by a memory-mapped I/O. Via an AMBA interface it is possible to write and read data to and from the RAM (e.g. the message to sign or the generated signature) but also to access the EEPROM or the instruction register. In very complex algorithms and protocols like ECDSA with implicit SHA-1 calculation and random-number generation, the controlling effort in terms of design complexity and chip area gets more and more dominant. Hence, we investigated a totally new concept where a microcontrolled approach makes the implementation more flexible but keeps also the hardware complexity low compared to dedicated finite-state machines.

Memory Unit. The memory unit comprises the three types RAM, ROM, and EEPROM in a 16-bit linear addressable dual-port memory space. The 128×16-bit dual-port RAM is realized as a dedicated macro block. This halves the chip area of this memory resource. In detail, ECDSA needs 7×192 bits for calculating the point multiplication, one 192-bit value to store the message that has to be signed, and one 192-bit value for the ephemeral key k. Additionally, we reserved 192 bits for storing the seed that is used in both ECDSA and AES to generate the needed random numbers. The ROM circuit stores 128 16-bit

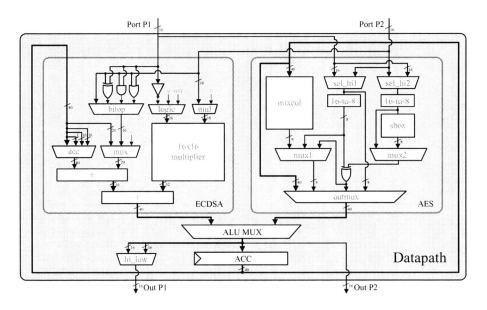

Fig. 2. Architecture of the ECDSA and AES Datapath

constants like ECC parameters, SHA-1, and AES constants. It is implemented as an unstructured mass of standard cells. The EEPROM stores non-volatile data like the ECDSA private key, the public-key certificate, the AES secret key, and potentially other user-specific data up to 4K bits, which can be written in a personalization phase or during the protocol execution.

Datapath Unit. The datapath of our processor is shown in Figure 2. It is mainly composed of an ECDSA and AES datapath. Both datapaths share one single 40-bit accumulator register which pursues the strategy of reusing components for ECDSA and AES. The 40-bit register is used as accumulator for ECDSA (multiply-accumulate unit) as well as intermediate storage for AES.

The AES datapath is mainly composed of an S-box submodule, a MixColumns submodule, five multiplexers, one XOR gate, and two 16-to-8 bit converters. The converters are used since we decided to implement the AES operations with 8 bits instead of 16. The remaining 8 bits are used to store random values which are required to perform dummy operations[1]. The AES datapath has been implemented similar to the work of M. Feldhofer et al. [4]. For the S-box operation, we calculated the substitution values using combinatorial logic instead of a look-up table, which reduces the number of additional gates. Furthermore, the MixColumns operation has been realized as an individual submodule which generates one byte of the AES *State* using one single clock cycle. The ShiftRows and AddRoundKey operations, in contrast, have been realized without expensive logic circuits. These operations

---

[1] Dummy operations are types of *hiding* countermeasure techniques against side-channel attacks (see [19] for more details).

need several controlling signals and one XOR gate. The AES constant *Rcon* has been externally stored in the ROM memory. In addition, we integrated an *operand-isolation* technique (also often referred to as *sleep logic*) to reduce the power consumption of the processor. If AES in enabled, the operands for AES get isolated from the ECDSA datapath. This eliminates unnecessary power dissipation and reduces the power consumption of the processor by about 13 %.

The ECDSA datapath is mainly composed of a 16 × 16-bit multiplier, two 40-bit adders, and five multiplexers. For low-area reasons, we decided to use a 16-bit multiply-accumulate (MAC) architecture to perform a finite-field multiple-precision multiplication. For this, partial products are calculated and accumulated in the common register to perform a multiplication. The implemented algorithm for the multiple-precision modular multiplication is described in Section 4.

SHA-1 is an integral part of ECDSA and is used to hash digital messages. Thus, we decided to integrate all needed components to perform SHA-1 operations into the ECDSA datapath. These are four additional 16-bit logic gates, i.e. AND, OR, XOR, and NOT. The logic operations are directly connected to port A and port B of the entire datapath. The *bitop* and *mux* multiplexer are then used to output the result of the appropriate operation. For a detailed description of the SHA-1 standard see the FIPS-180-3 [22] standard.

Low-Resource Microcontroller. A sophisticated two-layer approach was necessary to efficiently implement the controlling of the cryptographic processor. The generation of control signals for various irregular algorithms and protocols, which require in total several 100 000 clock cycles, is very complex. The highest layer of the controller comprises an 8-bit microcontroller with a highly optimized instruction set. It performs higher-level functions like protocol handling, point multiplication, and invocation of round functions for SHA-1 and AES, for instance, due to its ability for looping and subroutine calls. The advantage of having a microcontroller is that it is very flexible because of extending the functionality by simple Assembler programming. Basically the microcontroller sets up and calls certain instructions which lie in a subsequent microcode ROM table (the second control layer). For the execution of such instructions, which can take up to 102 clock cycles, the start address in the microcode ROM has to be provided. While the microcode ROM provides instructions for the datapath and the memory via the instruction and the address decoder, the microcontroller can set up the next instruction. This avoids idle cycles of the datapath during execution of the algorithm.

Our proposed microcontroller is based on a Harvard architecture, *i.e.* program memory and data memory are separated. Such a design has the advantage that the program memory can have a different word size than the data memory. The microcontroller is a Reduced Instruction Set Computer (RISC) supporting 32 instructions that have a width of 16 bits. The instructions are mainly divided into four groups: logical operations like XOR and OR, arithmetic operations like addition (ADD) and subtraction (SUB), control-flow operations like GOTO and CALL, and microcode instructions (MICRO).

4   Arithmetic-Level Implementation

Modular multiplication is the most resource-consuming operation in an ECC implementation. In fact, more than 80 % of the execution time is due to finite-field multiplications. In the following, we describe the implemented modular multiplication with interleaved NIST reduction. Modular addition and subtraction have a minor impact on the overall performance and they have been implemented according to [8].

NIST P-192 Modular Multiplication. The given algorithm is based on a product scanning (Comba) method and performs a modular multiplication using t^2 single-precision multiplications, where t represents the number of words of the processor, *i.e.* 12 in our case. In general, a multiplication by two 192-bit integers $a, b \in [0, p < 2^{Wt})$ will result in a 384-bit result c, where W represents the number of bits of a word (e.g. 16) and p represents the NIST prime $p = 2^{192} - 2^{64} - 1$. Instead of storing the 384-bit result in memory, we reduced the result during the multiplication (interleaved reduction and multiplication). Thus, no additional memory is needed for the multiplication. We make use of the following congruency [25], *i.e.*

Algorithm 1. Modular multiplication with interleaved NIST P-192 reduction.

Require: $a, b \in [0, p - 1], S \in [0, 2^{3W} - 1], \varepsilon \in [0, t + t/3 - 1]$.
Ensure: $c = a * b \pmod{2^{192} - 2^{64} - 1}$.

1. $S \leftarrow 0$.
2. **for** i **from** 0 **to** $t - 1$ **do**
3.   **for** j **from** $t - 1$ **to** i **do**
4. $S \leftarrow S + A[j]*B[i + t - j]$.
5.   **end for**
6. $C[i] \leftarrow (S \bmod 2^W); S \leftarrow (S \gg W)$.
7. **end for**
8. $C[t - 1] \leftarrow (S \bmod 2^W). S \leftarrow 0$.
9. **for** i **from** 0 **to** $t/3$ **do**
10. $S \leftarrow (S + C[i] + C[i + 2t/3])$.
11. $C[i] \leftarrow (S \bmod 2^W); S \leftarrow (S \gg W)$.
12. **end for**
13. **for** i **from** 0 **to** $t/3$ **do**
14. $S \leftarrow (S + C[i] + C[i + t/3])$.
15. $C[i+t/3] \leftarrow (S \bmod 2^W); S \leftarrow (S \gg W)$.
16. **end for**
17. **for** i **from** 0 **to** $t/3$ **do**
18. $S \leftarrow (C[i+t/3] - C[i] - S) + C[i+2t/3]$.
19. $C[i + 2t/3] \leftarrow (S \bmod 2^W)$;
20. $S \leftarrow (S \gg W) \pmod 2$.
21. **end for**
22. $\varepsilon \leftarrow S$

23. **for** i **from** 0 **to** $t - 1$ **do**
24.   **for** j **from** 0 **to** i **do**
25. $S \leftarrow S + A[i - j]*B[j]$.
26.   **end for**
27.   **if** $(\varepsilon = t/3)$ **then**
28. $S \leftarrow S + C[i] + \varepsilon$.
29.   **else**
30. $S \leftarrow S + C[i]$.
31.   **end if**
32. $C[i] \leftarrow (S \bmod 2^W)$.
33. $S \leftarrow (S \gg W)$.
34. **end for**
35. $\varepsilon \leftarrow S$
36. **for** i **from** 0 **to** $t - 1$ **do**
37.   **if** $(\varepsilon = t/3)$ **then**
38. $S \leftarrow S + C[i] + \varepsilon$.
39.   **else**
40. $S \leftarrow S + C[i]$.
41.   **end if**
42. $C[i] \leftarrow (S \bmod 2^W)$.
43. $S \leftarrow (S \gg W)$.
44. **end for**

    return (c).

$$
\begin{aligned}
c \equiv \quad & c_5 2^{128} + c_5 2^{64} + c_5 \\
+ \, & c_4 2^{128} + c_4 2^{64} \\
+ \, & \qquad\quad c_3 2^{64} + c_3 \\
+ \, & c_2 2^{128} + c_1 2^{64} + c_0 \qquad (\mathrm{mod}\ p),
\end{aligned}
\tag{1}
$$

where c_i are 64-bit integers. Equation (1) shows that c can be reduced by simple additions. The first three lines reduce the higher part $c_{high} = c_5 2^{320} + c_4 2^{256} + c_3 2^{192}$. The result is then added to the lower part $c_{low} = c_2 2^{128} + c_1 2^{64} + c_0$.

The algorithm for the modular multiplication with interleaved NIST reduction is given in Algorithm 1. First, the higher part of the 384-bit result is calculated (line 1-8). Second, the higher part is reduced by subsequent additions to the lower part of c (line 9-21). After that, the lower part of the 384-bit result is calculated and added to the already reduced result (line 23-34). In line 27-31, the carry ε is reduced by adding ε to the accumulator variable S at word index 0 (line 22) and $t/3 = 4$ (line 28). Finally, a last reduction is performed in line 35-44 to reduce the final carry ε.

The modular multiplication has been implemented as a fully unrolled microcode instruction. It needs 204 clock cycles to perform a modulo multiplication of two 192-bit numbers. Modular addition and subtraction need 31 clock cycles.

5   Algorithm-Level Implementation

5.1   The SHA-1 Algorithm

For our ECDSA processor, we decided to sign messages with a fixed length of 16 bytes. This constraint allows us to reduce the SHA-1 implementation to only one 512-bit message block W. In addition, the message padding can be implemented *a priori* by storing the length of the message in ROM. Thus, the 16-byte message can be simply copied into the RAM before signature generation. Message padding is done during the computation of ECDSA by copying the length of the message at the end of the input block W.

We implemented 13 different microcode instructions for SHA-1 and made several modifications to improve the performance (see Algorithm 2). First, since line 13 and line 20 are the same, *i.e.* F $\leftarrow$ (B $\oplus$ C $\oplus$ D), we implemented only one microcode instruction that is invoked two times during the computation. Second, instead of copying the values of the state variables (A,B,C,D,E,T) as shown in line 25+26, we simple rotated the addressing of the variables. Thus, no additional clock cycles are needed and the addresses get shifted by the microcontroller in every loop iteration. Third, all bit-shift operations are realized by multiplication. A left shift by one (line 6) is a simple multiplication with the constant 2, a shift by five (line 8) is a multiplication by 32, and a shift by 30 (line 24) is realized by a multiplication with 16 384. Thus, no dedicated shifting unit is necessary in the datapath of the processor and the multiplier of the ECDSA datapath gets simply reused by the design. Fourth, the constants K0...K4 and the initial values for H0...H4 are stored in ROM and are loaded by the microcode instructions.

Algorithm 2. The Secure Hash Algorithm (SHA-1) [22].

Require: 512-bit block W; $H0, H1, H2, H3, H4, T, F, A, B, C, D, E \in [0, 2^{32} - 1]$.
Ensure: $h = \text{SHA-1}(W)$.

1. $A = H0; B = H1; C = H2;$	16. $F \leftarrow (B \wedge C) \vee (B \wedge D) \vee$
2. $D = H3; E = H4.$	17. $(C \wedge D).$
3. **for** i **from** 0 **to** 79 **do**	18. $T \leftarrow T + 0x8F1BBCDC.$
4. **if** $(i \geq 16)$ **then**	19. **else**
5. $W[i] \leftarrow W[i\text{-}3] \oplus W[i\text{-}8] \oplus$	20. $F \leftarrow (B \oplus C \oplus D).$
6. $W[i\text{-}14] \oplus W[i\text{-}16] \ll 1.$	21. $T \leftarrow T + 0xCA62C1D6.$
7. **end if**	22. **end if**
8. $T \leftarrow (A \ll 5) + W[i].$	23. $T \leftarrow E + F.$
9. **if** $(i < 20)$ **then**	24. $B \leftarrow B \ll 30.$
10. $F \leftarrow (B \wedge C) \vee (\overline{B} \wedge D).$	25. $E \leftarrow D; D \leftarrow C; C \leftarrow B;$
11. $T \leftarrow T + 0x5A827999.$	26. $B \leftarrow A; A \leftarrow T.$
12. **else if** $(i < 40)$ **then**	27. **end for**
13. $F \leftarrow (B \oplus C \oplus D).$	28. $H0 \leftarrow H0 + A; H1 \leftarrow H1 + B;$
14. $T \leftarrow T + 0x6ED9EBA1.$	29. $H2 \leftarrow H2 + C; H3 \leftarrow H3 + D;$
15. **else if** $(i < 60)$ **then**	30. $H4 \leftarrow H4 + E;$

   return $(H0, H1, H2, H3, H4).$

Fourth, the round loop i is done by the microcontroller which also performs the branching at certain loop indices. Since the microcontroller can prepare the loop-index calculation during the execution of a microcode instruction, additional clock cycles are saved. In total, our processor needs 3 639 clock cycles to hash a 512-bit message.

5.2   The AES Algorithm

For AES, we implemented 11 microcode instructions. As already stated in Section 3.1, we extended the 16×8-bit AES *State* to 16×16-bit where 8 bits are used to store the real *State* and the other 8 bits store random values ($r_0...r_{15}$).

Figure 3 shows the processing of the first AES *State*. The first operations are SubBytes and ShiftRows which transform the *State* column-wise, *i.e.* four byte blocks. First, each byte of the *State* is loaded and substituted by the S-box unit. In order to implicitly shift the bytes of the *State* for the ShiftRows operation, we simply addressed the appropriate bytes in the *State*. Thus, each byte of a column is addressed accordingly (address 0, 5, 10, and 15 in our example) and substituted afterwards. The result is stored in the accumulator of the datapath. After that, the bytes are loaded from the accumulator and processed by the MixColumns operation. The output is then XORed with the key within the AddRoundKey operation. Finally, the result is stored back into the AES *State*. Since we processed the bytes of a column without the ShiftRows operation (in fact the bytes have not been shifted before MixColumns), we stored the resulting bytes in the correct position within the *State*. However, to avoid overwriting of data, we simply swap the values of the real and dummy *State*. Thus, after the first round, the dummy values are stored in the lower 8 bits and the real values are stored in the higher 8 bits of the *State*.

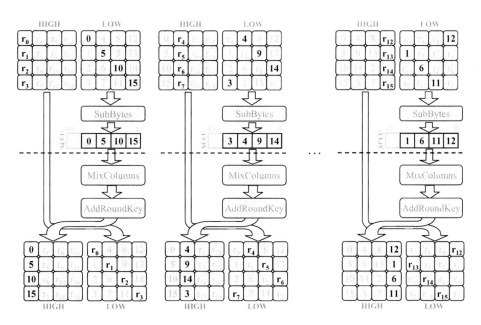

Fig. 3. The processing of the *State* in the first AES round

In order to make the implementation less attractive to side-channel attacks, we integrated several countermeasures described in the following. As a first countermeasure, we integrated dummy operations before and/or after the actual AddRoundKey operation. 16 dummy operations are performed in total where the actual operation is widespread over 17 different locations in time.

As a second countermeasure, we randomized the processing of the bytes in the AES *State* which is often referred as *byte-shuffling* countermeasure. For this, we randomized the byte position after the SubBytes operation. The transformed bytes are stored in the accumulator with a random offset. After MixColumns and AddRoundKey transformation, the offset is incorporated through the right addressing of the *State*.

As a third countermeasure, we added 16 dummy rounds to the actual rounds. In fact, we performed dummy rounds only in the first and second round and the last two rounds of AES. This has its reason in the fact that side-channel attacks need to target intermediate values which can be generated by a model with less computational effort. Targeting intermediates of higher rounds would increase the computational effort significantly to generate values for each possible key. It is therefore sufficient to consider only the first and last two rounds of AES to obtain an appropriate protection.

All implemented countermeasures are commonly used in practice and provide a state-of-the-art protection for cryptographic devices. For a more detailed description about dummy operations and shuffling (*hiding* techniques), see the work of Mangard et al. [19].

5.3   ECC Scalar Multiplication

We applied the Montgomery ladder as scalar multiplication method given in Algorithm 3. This is due to the fact that it provides security against several attacks, e.g. Simple Power Analysis (SPA) attacks [16,19] and safe-error attacks [28]. Furthermore, it allows to perform all group operations with x-coordinate only formulae [12].

We applied the idea of N. Meloni [20] and Y. Lee et al. [18] and performed the computations in a common-Z coordinate representation. The idea is to satisfy that the Z coordinate of each curve point is the same during each Montgomery ladder iteration. Only three coordinates have to be maintained during every *differential addition and doubling* operation instead of normally four, i.e. X_0, X_1, and Z. By applying the method, we did not reduce the needed number of intermediate registers but rather improved the point-multiplication performance. One Montgomery loop iteration needs therefore 12 finite-field multiplications, 4 squarings[2], 9 additions, and 7 subtractions. The memory stores three coordinates (X_0, X_1, and Z) and four intermediate values of 192 bits.

Algorithm 3. The implemented ECC scalar multiplication method based on the Montgomery ladder.

Require: Base point $P = (x_P, y_P) \in E(\mathbb{F}_{p192}), k \in [1, n-1]$, random λ
Ensure: $Q = kP$, where $Q = (x_Q, y_Q) \in E(\mathbb{F}_{p192})$
1: $(X_0, Z_0) \leftarrow (\lambda x_P, \lambda)$.
2: $(X_1, Z_1) \leftarrow Dbl(P)$.
3: $X_0 \leftarrow X_0 \cdot Z_1, X_1 \leftarrow X_1 \cdot Z_0, Z \leftarrow Z_0 \cdot Z_1$.
4: **for** $i = 190$ **downto** 0 **do**
5:     $(X_{k_i \otimes 1}, X_{k_i}, Z) \leftarrow DifferentialAdditionAndDoubling(X_{k_i}, X_{k_i \otimes 1}, Z)$.
6: **end for**
7: $(X_0, Y_0, Z_0) \leftarrow Yrecovery(X_0, X_1, Z, P)$.
8: **if** $Z_0'(Y_0'^2 - bZ_0'^2) \neq X_0'(X_0'^2 + aZ_0'^2)$ **abort.**
9: $x_Q \leftarrow X_0 \cdot Z_0^{-1}$.
10: **Return** (x_Q).

As a side-channel countermeasure, we applied the randomized projective coordinate (RPC) countermeasure as proposed by S. Coron [2] in 1999. Before starting a point multiplication, we generate a random number λ and performed one finite-field multiplication to randomize the affine x-coordinate of the base point x_P to obtain the randomized projective coordinates $(X_0, Z_0) = (\lambda x_P, \lambda)$.

After scalar multiplication, we perform a check if the point is still a valid point on the elliptic curve. For this, we recovered the coordinates (X_0, Y_0, Z_0) according to Izu et al. [11] and evaluated $Z_0'(Y_0'^2 - bZ_0'^2) = X_0'(X_0'^2 + aZ_0'^2)$ according to N. Ebeid and R. Lambert [3]. Finally, the projective coordinates (X_0, Z_0) are transformed back into affine coordinates by applying a finite-field inversion and multiplication, *i.e.* $x_Q \leftarrow X_0 \cdot Z_0^{-1}$.

---

[2] The squaring operation is realized by a simple multiplication operation.

5.4 ECDSA Implementation

After scalar multiplication, all performed operations are done modulo the prime n. The implemented ECDSA signature generation algorithm is shown in Algorithm 4. Modulo multiplication has been implemented according to the Montgomery multiplication algorithm proposed by G. Hachez and J. J. Quisquater [6]. We implemented five microcode instructions to perform the operation. The Montgomery inversion has been implemented by the algorithm proposed by B. Kaliski [13]. For that operation we implemented seven microcode instructions.

Algorithm 4. Signature Generation using ECDSA.

Require: Domain parameters $D = (q, FR, S, a, b, P, n, h)$, private key d, message m.
Ensure: Signature (r, s)
  1: Select $k \in [1, n-1]$
  2: Compute $Q = kP = (x_Q, y_Q)$.
  3: Compute $r = x_Q \mod n$. If $r = 0$ then go to step 1.
  4: Compute $e = \text{SHA-1}(m)$.
  5: Compute $s = k^{-1}(e + dr) \pmod{n}$. If $s = 0$ then go to step 1.
  6: Return (r, s).

Random numbers have been generated according to the FIPS 186-2 [23] standard. The standard describes a hash-based pseudo-random number generator that can be realized with the SHA-1 algorithm. Our decision has mainly two reasons. First, the process of random number generation is based on a standard specification and is considered to be cryptographically secure. Second, we already need a hash calculation for the message-digest calculation in ECDSA and we can simply reuse the implementation of the SHA-1 algorithm for that purpose. The prerequisite is to load a true-random seed from an external source into RAM. The random number is hashed and the message digest is stored as a seed key (XKEY). This seed key is then used in any higher-level protocol to generate any random numbers needed to provide the cryptographic service.

6 Results

We implemented our processor in a $0.35\,\mu\text{m}$ CMOS technology using a semi-custom design flow with Cadence RTL Compiler as synthesis tool. The summarized results are shown in Table 1 and Table 2. The total chip area of 21 502 GEs includes datapath, ROM, RAM macro, and controller for ECDSA, SHA-1, and AES (including microcontroller and microcode control and ROM). Note that we included a standard RAM macro needing 8 727 GEs that can be further minimized using an area-optimized RAM block.

We also synthesized our processor without the AES datapath and microcode entries resulting in 19 115 GEs. This means that the integration of AES needs 2 387 GEs which is lower than existing stand-alone (and finite-state machine based) AES modules. The same has been done with SHA-1. Even though ECDSA

Table 1. Area of chip components

Component	GE
Datapath	3 393
Memory without RAM	729
RAM macro (128x16-bit)	8 727
Controller	8 653
ECDSA+SHA1+AES Total	**21 502**
Overhead of AES	**2 387**
Overhead of SHA-1	**889**

Table 2. Cycle count of operations

Component	Cycles
PRNG generation (4× SHA-1)	14 947
Point multiplication	753 393
Point-validity check	29 672
Final signing process	65 097
ECDSA Total	**863 109**
SHA-1	**3 639**
AES with shuffling	**4 529**

required SHA-1 for signing of messages, we removed any SHA-1 related implementation to validate the overhead. These are program-ROM entries, microcode instructions, decoder circuits, and the logic operations in the ECDSA datapath. After synthesis, we obtain 20 613 GEs which means that SHA-1 needs an area of 889 GEs (180 GEs for program ROM, 546 GEs for microcode instructions, and 163 GEs for the datapath).

In view of ECC, our processor needs 753 393 clock cycles for one point multiplication. The entire ECDSA signing process needs 863 109 clock cycles including side-channel and fault-attack countermeasures (RPC and point-validity check). AES with byte shuffling needs 4 529 clock cycles and 15 577 cycles with 10 dummy-round operations enabled. Note that the number of clock cycles for AES thus varies depending on the number of added dummy rounds. The more dummy rounds, the higher the security level and the higher the needed number of clock cycles. SHA-1 needs 3 639 clock cycles for hashing a 512-bit message block. The SHA-1 algorithm has also been used to generate random numbers. For ECDSA, four SHA-1 computations are performed to generate the needed random numbers which needs 14 947 clock cycles. We also evaluated the critical path of our processor and determined a maximum clock frequency of 33 MHz.

The mean current of the circuit is 485 μA at 847 kHz and 3.3 V and has been simulated using Synopsis NanoSim. This value includes the power consumption of the entire processor including microcontroller, ECDSA, SHA-1, and AES datapath, and memory. Note that we based our design on a rather old CMOS process technology (0.35 μm) so that further power reductions can be achieved by using a smaller process technology (for example CMOS 0.13 μm).

We compare our implementation with existing ASIC solutions over prime-field arithmetic. Since there does not exist any implementation of both ECDSA and AES within one processor, we have to compare it with ECC (or ECDSA) only implementations. The processor of F. Fürbass et al. [5] needs 23 656 GEs and 502 000 clock cycles, J. Wolkerstorfer [27] needs 23 800 GEs and 677 000 clock cycles, and M. Hutter et al. [10] need 19 115 GEs and 859 188 clock cycles. The work of A. Satoh et al. [24] needs 29 655 GEs and 4 165 000 clock cycles for the same size of prime-field arithmetic and E. Wenger et al. [26] need 11 686 GEs and 1 377 000 clock cycles. Note that a fair comparison is largely infeasible since the implementations differ in several ways, for example they do not use RAM macros and do not contain an AES implementation.

7 Conclusions

In this article we presented the first stand-alone cryptographic processor which performs ECDSA using the recommended NIST elliptic curve over $\mathbb{F}_{p192}$ and AES-128. We improved the state-of-art of building cryptographic processors for low-resource devices on the arithmetic level, on the architectural level (combined ECDSA, SHA-1, and AES module), and on the implementation level. The processor's architecture has an optimized 16-bit datapath and a controller with an integrated 8-bit microcontroller, both implemented in standard-cells. The entire chip has an area of 21 502 GEs where AES requires 2 387 GEs and SHA-1 requires 889 GEs. Currently, we are about to manufacturing the chip on a 0.35 μm CMOS process technology. The chip will be integrated in a passively powered Near Field Communication (NFC) device.

Acknowledgements

The work has been supported by the Austrian Government through the research program FIT-IT Trust in IT Systems (Project CRYPTA, Project Number 820843), and by the IAP Programme P6/26 BCRYPT of the Belgian State (Belgian Science Policy).

References

1. Batina, L., Mentens, N., Sakiyama, K., Preneel, B., Verbauwhede, I.: Low-Cost Elliptic Curve Cryptography for Wireless Sensor Networks. In: Buttyán, L., Gligor, V.D., Westhoff, D. (eds.) ESAS 2006. LNCS, vol. 4357, pp. 6–17. Springer, Heidelberg (2006)
2. Coron, J.-S.: Resistance against Differential Power Analysis for Elliptic Curve Cryptosystems. In: Koç, Ç.K., Paar, C. (eds.) CHES 1999. LNCS, vol. 1717, pp. 292–302. Springer, Heidelberg (1999)
3. Ebeid, N., Lambert, R.: Securing the Elliptic Curve Montgomery Ladder Against Fault Attacks. In: Proceedings of the Workshop on Fault Diagnosis and Tolerance in Cryptography - FDTC 2009, Lausanne, Switzerland, pp. 46–50 (September 2009)
4. Feldhofer, M., Dominikus, S., Wolkerstorfer, J.: Strong Authentication for RFID Systems Using the AES Algorithm. In: Joye, M., Quisquater, J.-J. (eds.) CHES 2004. LNCS, vol. 3156, pp. 357–370. Springer, Heidelberg (2004), http://springerlink.metapress.com/content/26tmfjfcju58upb2/fulltext.pdf, doi:10.1007/b99451
5. Fürbass, F., Wolkerstorfer, J.: ECC Processor with Low Die Size for RFID Applications. In: Proceedings of 2007 IEEE International Symposium on Circuits and Systems. IEEE, Los Alamitos (2007)
6. Hachez, G., Quisquater, J.-J.: Montgomery Exponentiation with no Final Subtractions: Improved Results. In: Paar, C., Koç, Ç.K. (eds.) CHES 2000. LNCS, vol. 1965, pp. 91–100. Springer, Heidelberg (2000), http://www.springerlink.com/content/n2m6w6b0kg3elaxu/

7. Hämäläinen, P., Alho, T., Hännikäinen, M., Hämäläinen, T.D.: Design and Implementation of Low-Area and Low-Power AES Encryption Hardware Core. In: Proceedings of the 9th EUROMICRO Conference on Digital System Design: Architectures, Methods and Tools (DSD 2006), Dubrovnik, Croatia, August 30-September 1, pp. 577–583. IEEE Computer Society, Los Alamitos (2006)

8. Hankerson, D., Menezes, A.J., Vanstone, S.: Guide to Elliptic Curve Cryptography, p. 332. Springer, Heidelberg (2004)

9. Hein, D., Wolkerstorfer, J., Felber, N.: ECC Is Ready for RFID – A Proof in Silicon. In: Avanzi, R.M., Keliher, L., Sica, F. (eds.) SAC 2008. LNCS, vol. 5381, pp. 401–413. Springer, Heidelberg (2009)

10. Hutter, M., Feldhofer, M., Plos, T.: An ECDSA Processor for RFID Authentication. In: Ors Yalcin, S.B. (ed.) RFIDSec 2010. LNCS, vol. 6370, pp. 189–202. Springer, Heidelberg (2010)

11. Izu, T., Möller, B., Takagi, T.: Improved Elliptic Curve Multiplication Methods Resistant against Side Channel Attacks. In: Menezes, A., Sarkar, P. (eds.) INDOCRYPT 2002. LNCS, vol. 2551, pp. 296–313. Springer, Heidelberg (2002)

12. Joye, M., Yen, S.-M.: The Montgomery Powering Ladder. In: Kaliski Jr., B.S., Koç, Ç.K., Paar, C. (eds.) CHES 2002. LNCS, vol. 2523, pp. 291–302. Springer, Heidelberg (2003),
http://www.springerlink.com/content/1eupwrx4c4xayyyv/fulltext.pdf

13. Kaliski, B.: The Montgomery Inverse and its Applications. IEEE Transactions on Computers 44(8), 1064–1065 (1995)

14. Kaps, J.-P.: Cryptography for Ultra-Low Power Devices. PhD thesis, ECE Department, Worcester Polytechnic Institute, Worcester, Massachusetts, USA (May 2006)

15. Kim, M., Ryou, J., Choi, Y., Jun, S.: Low Power AES Hardware Architecture for Radio Frequency Identification. In: Yoshiura, H., Sakurai, K., Rannenberg, K., Murayama, Y., Kawamura, S.-i. (eds.) IWSEC 2006. LNCS, vol. 4266, pp. 353–363. Springer, Heidelberg (2006),
http://www.springerlink.com/content/1pk7q6621xj2422r/fulltext.pdf,
doi:10.1007/11908739

16. Kocher, P.C., Jaffe, J., Jun, B.: Differential Power Analysis. In: Wiener, M. (ed.) CRYPTO 1999. LNCS, vol. 1666, pp. 388–397. Springer, Heidelberg (1999)

17. Kumar, S.S., Paar, C.: Are standards compliant Elliptic Curve Cryptosystems feasible on RFID? In: Workshop on RFID Security 2006 (RFID Sec 2006), Graz, Austria, July 12-14 (2006)

18. Lee, Y.K., Sakiyama, K., Batina, L., Verbauwhede, I.: Elliptic-Curve-Based Security Processor for RFID. IEEE Transactions on Computers 57(11), 1514–1527 (2008), doi:10.1109/TC.2008.148

19. Mangard, S., Oswald, E., Popp, T.: Power Analysis Attacks – Revealing the Secrets of Smart Cards. Springer, Heidelberg (2007) ISBN 978-0-387-30857-9

20. Meloni, N.: Fast and Secure Elliptic Curve Scalar Multiplication Over Prime Fields Using Special Addition Chains. Cryptology ePrint Archive, Report 2006/216 (2006)

21. National Institute of Standards and Technology (NIST). FIPS-197: Advanced Encryption Standard (November 2001), http://www.itl.nist.gov/fipspubs/

22. National Institute of Standards and Technology (NIST). FIPS-180-3: Secure Hash Standard (October 2008), http://www.itl.nist.gov/fipspubs/

23. National Institute of Standards and Technology (NIST). FIPS-186-3: Digital Signature Standard, DSS (2009), http://www.itl.nist.gov/fipspubs/

24. Satoh, A., Takano, K.: A Scalable Dual-Field Elliptic Curve Crypto-graphic Processor. IEEE Transactions on Computers 52(4), 449–460 (2003), doi:10.1109/TC.2003.1190586
25. Solinas, J.A.: Generalized mersenne numbers. Technical Report CORR 99-39, Centre for Applied Cryptographic Research, University of Waterloo (1999)
26. Wenger, E., Feldhofer, M., Felber, N.: Low-Resource Hardware Design of an Elliptic Curve Processor for Contactless Devices. In: Chung, Y., Yung, M. (eds.) WISA 2010. LNCS, vol. 6513, pp. 92–106. Springer, Heidelberg (2011), http://dx.doi.org/10.1007/978-3-642-17955-6_7
27. Wolkerstorfer, J.: Is Elliptic-Curve Cryptography Suitable for Small Devices? In: Workshop on RFID and Lightweight Crypto, Graz, Austria, July 13-15, pp. 78–91 (2005)
28. Yen, S.-M., Joye, M.: Checking Before Output May Not Be Enough Against Fault-Based Cryptanalysis. IEEE Transactions on Computers 49, 967–970 (2000)

An Evaluation of Hash Functions on a Power Analysis Resistant Processor Architecture

Simon Hoerder, Marcin Wójcik, Stefan Tillich, and Daniel Page

Department of Computer Science, University of Bristol
{hoerder,wojcik,tillich,page}@compsci.bristol.ac.uk

Abstract. Cryptographic hash functions are an omnipresent component in security-critical software and devices; they support digital signature and data authenticity schemes, mechanisms for key derivation, pseudo-random number generation and so on. A criterion for candidate hash functions in the SHA-3 contest is resistance against side-channel analysis which is a major concern especially for mobile devices. This paper explores the implementation of said candidates on a variant of the Power-Trust platform; our results highlight a flexible solution to power analysis attacks, implying only a modest performance overhead.

1 Introduction

Within the cryptographic community, open "contests" to evaluate, select and standardise the use of secure and efficient primitives have become de rigueur. The most high-profile example is the Advanced Encryption Standard (AES) contest run by NIST from 1997 to 2000 to find a replacement for DES, the incumbent block cipher design. This model was repeated in 2007 when, partly motivated by increasingly able attacks [1, 2] on SHA-1 [3], NIST launched the SHA-3 contest [4] to develop a new cryptographic hash function. Briefly, a hash function

$$H : \{0,1\}^* \longrightarrow \{0,1\}^n$$

maps an arbitrary-length input (or message) to a fixed-length, n-bit output (or digest). Hash functions support, for example, digital signature and data authenticity schemes, mechanisms for key derivation and pseudo-random number generation and are indispensable for security-critical devices. As such, various security requirements (e.g., the need for H to be collision resistant) are outlined in [5]. However, in common with the AES contest, other metrics are important for SHA-3; specifically, efficiency in hardware and on a variety of software-based platforms is paramount.

Within the context of embedded and mobile computing, such metrics are particularly pertinent: they represent the exact resources in short supply. The same context may imply additional requirements in the sense that physical security (e.g., against side channel and fault attacks) is also a valid metric. Example attacks on hash functions are given by [6, 7, 8, 9, 10, 11]; these are exacerbated by the wide range of use cases. Ideally one has an idea of the trade-offs different

C.A. Ardagna and J. Zhou (Eds.): WISTP 2011, LNCS 6633, pp. 160–174, 2011.

countermeasures offer so as to select the right one before deployment, but in practice this topic has not drawn much attention (for example, note the discussion triggered by Rivest's question [12] on the matter).

Keeping this difficulty in mind, one attractive approach is to provide a "generic" countermeasure. For power analysis based attacks, and focusing on hardware implementation, this can be realised by utilising a so-called secure logic style. The idea is to take a generic circuit and automatically replace CMOS cells with alternatives such as SABL [13] or WDDL [14]. To consider a similar approach for software, one must instrument a generic countermeasure so that each instruction is prevented from leaking information during execution. Several proposals exist, such as NONDET [15], but a more concrete and complete implementation is provided by Power-Trust [16,17]. The SPARC V8-based Power-Trust platform houses a secure zone, implemented in a secure logic style, and security-critical instructions are executed only by this zone to avoid leakage; the result is a generic countermeasure, mounted in a general-purpose processor, which offers an extremely flexible solution. The question is, how does this solution fare wrt. the SHA-3 use-case? Does it, for example, imply a performance overhead low enough to allow secure deployment of the selected SHA-3 candidate in embedded and mobile applications?

Focusing on 6 of the 14 remaining (as per round two) SHA-3 candidates, this paper addresses three points all stemming from the same underlying work, namely investigation of said candidates on the Power-Trust platform:

Performance of candidates, i.e., assuming that Power-Trust provides an adequate countermeasure against power analysis attacks, what overhead does this imply and is this the best approach? Section 2.1 presents a concrete attack scenario; the criteria for performance includes throughput and instruction mix (e.g., any bias toward memory access).

Agility of SPARC V8 analogous instructions, i.e., given a set of protected instructions required for one SHA-3 candidate, can we implement another candidate with the same set?

Potential for advanced Instruction Set Extensions (ISEs), i.e., for which candidates can we find useful ISEs? For example, we suggest several generic (i.e., not Power-Trust-specific) instruction set extensions which could be used to accelerate BMW.

One can view the second and third points as evaluating the Power-Trust design itself; the novel aspect in this respect is the workload used (namely the SHA-3 candidates), which is more diverse than previously studied.

2   Background

2.1   Side-Channel Attacks on Hash Functions

There are numerous examples of successful side-channel attacks on specific hash functions, and a variety of specific countermeasures have been proposed [6,7,8,9, 10,11]. However, within the context of developing hash functions it is attractive

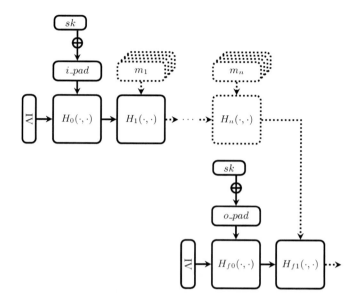

Fig. 1. Protecting HMAC from side-channel attack: only the operations and values drawn with solid lines need to be protected

to be more general (both for attacks and countermeasures) since this allows far easier high-level comparison. As such, we keep our model of side-channel attack as generic as possible within practical limits:

Simple Power Analysis (SPA) is possible whenever the sequence of operations performed during execution of H depends on a fixed, security-critical input.

Differential Power Analysis (DPA) is possible when the input to an invocation of H combines fixed security-critical data and variable data which can be controlled by the attacker. That is, invocation resembles $H(s, m)$ for a fixed, security-critical s and variable m.

Timing Attacks are possible whenever a security-critical input affects the time taken to execute H; examples include conditional branches or cached table look-ups based on said input.

Additionally, for all three types of attacks we allow the attacker to perform a profiling step to create templates. In the following, $H_i(s_{i-1}, m_i)$ denotes the i-th invocation of the compression function used by H with the state (or chaining variable) s and message m as input.

Neither SPA nor timing attacks matter for the hash functions that we are considering: they always use the same instruction sequence (i.e., there are no input-dependant branches), and do not use any table look-ups. Indeed, CubeHash [18, Page 3] makes this an explicit design criterion. On the other hand, DPA *does* matter. Fig. 1 illustrates this fact for H used within the popular HMAC construction. The outputs of H_0 and H_{f0} are intermediate states; they are both fixed (they depend only on constant values) and security-critical (since they are derived directly from sk, the key used to authenticate messages). Thus, H_1 and H_{f1} fall squarely into our attack scenario:

$$H_1\big(\underbrace{H_0(IV, sk \oplus i\_pad)}_{\text{constant, secret}} , \underbrace{m_1}_{\text{variable}} \big)$$

$$H_{f1}\big(\underbrace{H_{f0}(IV, sk \oplus o\_pad)}_{\text{constant, secret}} , \underbrace{H((sk \oplus i\_pad) \parallel m)}_{\text{variable}} \big)$$

To roughly outline a potential DPA attack, notice that the attacker can repeatedly invoke the HMAC construction with an m of his choice. By observing the power consumption during execution, correlation between the data-dependent interaction of m and the secret constant allows him to hypothesise about the value of the constant and ultimately to recover it, thus undermining security.

This scenario demonstrates the value of an agile solution via two points. First, an inflexible solution dictates the H to be used; this is unattractive because if H is (seriously) broken, one might hope to change it without incurring significant cost. Second, notice that the vulnerable invocations are H_1 and H_{f1} only, while $H_{2,...,n}$ need no protection as long as the compression function is one-way. An inflexible hardware-oriented approach might implement a countermeasure for *all* invocations, hence incurring a performance overhead in each. A more flexible solution would apply the countermeasure only where necessary, and potentially provide a performance advantage in other cases.

2.2   The Power-Trust Platform

The so-called "Power-Trust platform" is a SPARC V8-based ASIC prototype of a side-channel resistant embedded processor implementing the security concept developed in the context of the Power-Trust project [16, 17]; its main goal is to evaluate the validity and effectiveness of the security concept as a whole. Furthermore, the prototype allows to investigate various design options and trade-offs in practice, e.g., different management instructions, exception handling features, and secure logic styles. The Power-Trust prototype has integrated support for AES and ECC, but the security concept itself is principally suited for handling a wide range of cryptographic workloads.

The basic idea of the security concept used in Power-Trust is to combat side-channel leakage directly in the processor hardware. The main concern are power and EM analysis attacks, but also timing attacks are mitigated. As a first measure, the circulation of potentially vulnerable datums is restricted to a tiny portion of the processor (essentially the functional units) by masking them whenever they are not required. This includes values which pass through various pipeline stages or which are written to caches and memories. The second measure protects all remaining vulnerable parts of the processor containing the unmasked data values themselves, the masks, and any values related to mask generation, by implementing them in a secure logic style. This part of the processor is referred to as "secure zone" and shown in Fig. 2. The secure zone offers a range

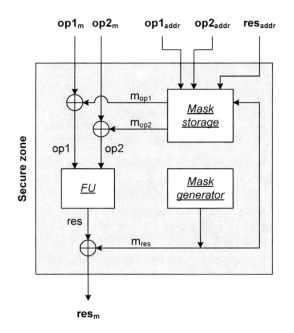

Fig. 2. The secure zone of the Power-Trust platform

of instructions which can be executed within its boundaries. From its interface, the secure zone looks very similar to a regular functional unit, which facilitates integration into the processor.

In the following, we explain the secure zone concept from a programmer's point of view. In order to implement a cryptographic algorithm in a power-analysis resistant manner, the following steps are necessary:

- Before execution, the inputs to the cryptographic algorithm are masked explicitly by the caller.
- Any instructions which produce potentially vulnerable values must be executed within the secure zone.
- Depending on the implementation and the secure zone capabilities, it might be required to save some masks to memory and restore them later on to the secure zone.
- Once the output of the cryptographic algorithm has been calculated, the mask is removed by the caller.

Explicit masking and unmasking of inputs and outputs can be seen as transferring values between "normal" domain and "masked" domain. In the masked domain, values can only be manipulated by instructions of the secure zone (in the following denoted as *secure zone instructions*)[1], and consequently a

---

[1] Of course, masked values could be manipulated by "normal" processor instructions, but this would mean that masked values and masks become desynchronised, leading to erroneous output from the algorithm.

cryptographic algorithm can only be protected if it can be implemented with secure zone instructions. The number of masked values which are readily available for processing is limited by the number of masks that the secure zone can actually store. However, masks can be swapped in and out of the secure zone in order to extend the number of masked values at the expense of some additional *mask management instructions* and storage.

In relation to the workload of typical cryptographic algorithms, masking and unmasking constitute only a minor overhead. Implementations using secure zone instructions can even see a considerable speed-up in comparison to the use of native processor instructions, since secure zone instructions can be tailor-made to fit specific algorithms or classes of algorithms. However, the management of masks might entail overheads, especially if a large number of masked values is required. Thanks to the flexibility of the mask management instruction set, this overhead can often be minimised by exploiting the structure of the protected cryptographic algorithm.

A mask may never directly leave the protection of the secure zone, as otherwise an attacker might launch a higher-order attack [19] on masked data and the corresponding mask. However, masks need to be extracted if the secure zone runs out of storage entries for masks or if there is a task switch. For this case, masks can be represented as a specific state of the mask generator unit which originally produced the mask and the number of steps the mask generator has taken till it produced the mask. The secure zone features mask management instructions for extracting the state of the mask generator and the step count. Similarly, instructions for setting the mask generator state and regenerating masks from a given step count exist for restoring masks to the secure zone.

In the Power-Trust prototype, the mask generator state consists of 128 bits and the step count (including some additional meta-information) is another 32 bits; therefore in the worst case a 32-bit mask requires five 32-bit words of storage. However, several stored masks can relate to the same state of the mask generator, thus greatly reducing the required memory. Similarly, the software can take steps to ensure the step count from a given mask generator state is low when a mask is written out to memory. In this way, when the mask is then restored, the required number of instructions is limited.

2.3 Our Variant of the Power-Trust Platform

We made two additional choices at the architectural level in order to ensure realistic and comparable results:

– We needed to decide on the number of masks that can be held within the mask storage, selecting 32 as a trade-off between 8 masks supported by the current IC prototype and the upper bound of 2^{10} which could principally be supported by the architecture. We believe this to be at the upper-edge of economic possibilities, but will demonstrate that some candidates can be implemented with a much smaller mask store.

- We only add instructions to the secure zone if they can be executed in one cycle and do not affect the critical path. Designing more elaborate functional units (e.g., multipliers) for the secure zone is principally possible but would require considerable design effort and is left for further research.

Based on these choices, we are confident that any subsequent prototypes can support our candidates without significant differences in performance from the original.

A third choice had to be made on the software level; any consideration of operating system influences such as trap handling, interrupts and context switches would have biased our results towards a specific use case, e.g., toward smartcards. However, we want our results to be as generic as possible, and therefore did not consider any operating system.

3   Implementation of Hash Functions on the Power-Trust Platform

To make comparison easier, we chose the following hash functions for implementation on the Power-Trust platform:

- BLAKE-32 and its third round version BLAKE-32v3 ([20], [21])
- BlueMidnightWish−256 ([22], [23])
- CubeHash160+16/32+160-256 and CubeHash16+16/32+32-256 which was suggested for the third round ([18], [24])
- Keccak[1088, 512, 32] ([25], [26])
- SHA-256 ([27])
- Shabal-256 ([28], [29])
- Skein-256-256 (this is the "low-memory" proposal of [30])

In the following we will motivate these choices, and highlight noteworthy specifics in our implementations. Where possible we follow the notation of the original submissions.

BLAKE-32 *and* SHA-256 were easy to implement for us due to their small internal states; for BLAKE-32 we followed the example of the "Optimized_32bit" implementation provided by the BLAKE team. We also give numbers for the third round version BLAKE-32v3 which increases the number of rounds from 10 to 14.

CubeHash operates on a state that is too large to fit completely into the registers, and uses a large number of round function iterations within each H_i; this is a bad combination for Power-Trust because masked data has to be swapped in and out of memory frequently. However, by choosing a suitable memory layout the number of memory accesses can be reduced. The 1024-bit CubeHash state is represented as a 5-dimensional cube state [] [] [] [] [] of two 32-bit words per dimension but can be split into four 3-dimensional subcubes state $[x_1]$ [] [] [] $[x_5]$ with $x_{1,5} \in \{0, 1\}$ requiring 8 masked registers each. The first 9 steps of the round function can be computed first on the two subcubes $\text{state}\,[\mathsf{x_1}]\,[]\,[]\,[]\,[0]$, and then on the two subcubes $\text{state}\,[\mathsf{x_1}]\,[]\,[]\,[]\,[1]$ since there are no interdependencies during these 9 steps. Therefore, no more than two of these subcubes have to be kept in registers at any point of time. The 10-th (and last) step swaps the subcubes $\text{state}\,[1]\,[]\,[]\,[]\,[\mathsf{x_5}]$ which can be implemented simply by swapping pointers. Overall, this means that only three subcubes have to be loaded and stored per iteration of the round function.

Keccak[1088, 512, 32] allows a separation in the memory layout similar to that afforded by CubeHash if one follows the example given by the unrolled "Optimized_32bit" implementation by the Keccak team. However, one has to deal with ten memory blocks of five 32-bit values, using 10 masked registers for each of the intermediate variables $\mathsf{D[5][2]}$ and $\mathsf{C[5][2]}$.

BMW256 had to be implemented without optimisation regarding memory usage since its internal state can not be separated into bigger blocks, as it was for CubeHash or Keccak, due to its high interdependency. However, we were able to identify two possible sets of generic ISEs that implement the six $s_{0,\ldots,5}$-functions

$$s_{i\in\{0,\ldots,3\}}(x) := \text{SHR}(x, c_{i,0}) \oplus \text{SHL}(x, c_{i,1}) \oplus \text{ROTL}(x, c_{i,2}) \oplus \text{ROTL}(x, c_{i,3})$$
$$s_{i\in\{4,5\}}(x) := \text{SHR}(x, c_{i,0}) \oplus x$$

where SHR, SHL, and ROTL denote right shift, left shift, and left rotate, respectively, and $c_{i,j}$ are constants specifying the number of bits to shift or rotate. Furthermore, they always occur in combination with a modular addition

$$z \leftarrow s_i(x) + y \bmod 2^{32}$$

where y in some cases is the output of another s-function. Thus we implemented and compared three versions of BMW256:

BMW **Plain:** This implementation of BMW256 uses no ISEs.
BMW **"generic s":** This implementation uses one ISE, namely

$$\text{SZ\_BMWS } \%x, \%i, \%z$$

to compute

$$z \leftarrow s_i(x).$$

BMW **"special s":** This implementation uses six ISEs, namely

$$\text{SZ\_BMWS}_i \%x, \%y, \%z$$

to compute

$$z \leftarrow s_{i\in\{0,\ldots,5\}}(x) + y \bmod 2^{32}.$$

Shabal-256 , according to our results, has significantly worse performance on Power-Trust than other SHA-3 candidates. One of the main reason is the relatively large internal state comprising forty-eight 32-bit words which exceeds the number of processor registers. Additionally, it requires a relatively large amount of iterations with a high interdependency between the internal state variables. The resulting memory accesses for masked values generate considerable overhead on the Power-Trust platform.

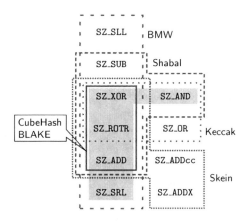

Fig. 3. Generic commands required from the secure zone to implement SHA-3 candidates. With the exception of SZ_ROTR they have an unprotected equivalent in the SPARC V8 instructions (see appendix B, [31]).

Skein offers two replacements for SHA-256, a "primary proposal" Skein-512-256 and a "low-memory" proposal Skein-256-256 targeted at embedded devices; since our platform is intended for mobile and embedded devices we chose to implement Skein-256-256. The Skein family is optimised for 64-bit architectures, but most of the Skein-256-256 kernel can be easily implemented on our 32-bit architecture; the exception is addition of 64-bit values. To implement it, we use SZ_ADDcc and SZ_ADDX commands analogous to the SPARC V8 ADDX and ADDcc instructions which require a carry flag within the secure zone[2]. The flag has to be taken care of by the scheduling algorithm of the operating system and is not reflected in our analysis any further.

Other hash functions. We did not consider the AES-based candidates (e.g., ECHO) since we expect they can be implemented using variants of the existing AES-oriented ISEs within Power-Trust. In addition, we did not consider candidates requiring multiplication (e.g., SIMD); as mentioned before, implementation of sufficiently efficient multipliers for the Power-Trust secure zone is a non-trivial task which we reserve for future work.

4   Results

4.1   Instruction Set Agility

Many SHA-3 candidates have been developed with ISEs in mind: CubeHash, for example, can capitalise on the availability of SSE-based ISEs on x86 platforms.

---

[2] One straight forward possibility to do this is to provide a command that reads the value of the flag (and all other flags if there are any) into a masked registers which can then be stored to memory and another command to restore the flags from a masked register.

Table 1. Total number of instructions required for one iteration of the compression function $H_i(\cdot, \cdot)$, to hash a one-block message (denoted by H) and the register usage of the implementations

Hash Function	#Ops		#Ops/byte		#Registers		code size
	$H_i(\cdot, \cdot)$	H	$H_i(\cdot, \cdot)$	H	masked	in total	$H_i(\cdot, \cdot)$
BLAKE-32	4142	4142	64.72	64.72	18	23	17.28kB
BLAKE-32v3	5678	5678	88.72	88.72	18	23	23.53kB
BMW256	6042	15068	94.41	235.44			25.44kB
BMW256, "generic s" ISE	4686	12356	73.22	193.06	29	32	20.15kB
BMW256, "specialised s" ISEs	4622	12228	72.22	191.06			19.90kB
CubeHash160+16/32+160-256	14880	160540	465.00	5016.88	17	21	62.00kB
CubeHash16+16/32+32-256	14880	44444	465.00	1388.88			62.01kB
Keccak[1088, 512, 32]	107960	107960	812.35	812.35	30	32	456.68kB
SHA-256	6833	6833	106.77	106.77	22	27	27.12kB
Shabal-256	128387	513548	2006.05	8024.19	31	32	556.66kB
Skein-256-256 ("low-memory" variant)	13222	39666	413.19	1239.56	28	31	54.72kB
	see Fig. 4		see Fig. 5				

Table 2. Total number of load and store instructions required for one iteration of the compression function $H_i(\cdot, \cdot)$ and to hash a one-block message (denoted by H)

Hash Function	#load		#store		#load+store	
	$H_i(\cdot, \cdot)$	H	$H_i(\cdot, \cdot)$	H	$H_i(\cdot, \cdot)$	H
BLAKE-32	192	192	26	26	**218**	**218**
BLAKE-32v3	256	256	26	26	**282**	**282**
BMW256	512	1634	302	757	**814**	**2391**
CubeHash160+16/32+160-256	1256	13814	1668	17544	**2924**	**31358**
CubeHash16+16/32+32-256	1256	3830	1668	4872	**2924**	**8702**
Keccak[1088, 512, 32]	14674	14674	9810	9810	**24484**	**24484**
SHA-256	328	328	48	48	**376**	**376**
Shabal-256	20268	81072	12111	48444	**32379**	**129516**
Skein-256-256 ("low-memory" variant)	544	1632	541	1623	**1085**	**3255**
					see Fig. 6	

In a similar way, certain candidates can exploit ISEs available in the Power-Trust platform. For example, it already provides AES-oriented ISEs and, in Section 3, we outlined various extensions for BMW256.

Despite the advantage this implies on platforms which support such ISEs, the approach is a potential disadvantage on platforms which do not: on many mobile and embedded platforms, for example, SIMD ISEs are missing (unless one counts packed arithmetic within word-sized values). As a result, it is useful to consider the agility of a minimal instruction set as a design metric for Power-Trust. That is, given there is an inherent cost associated with adding an ISE to Power-Trust, it is attractive to support a broad workload (i.e., many different SHA-3 candidates) using as few secure zone instructions as possible. This is especially important when considering the need to support migration from SHA-256 to SHA-3 within the device lifetime. With this in mind, we investigated which Power-Trust instructions are required by each candidates; the result is shown in Fig. 3. A major feature of the results is that a secure zone processor that provides instructions which can implement SHA-256, also provides all instructions needed for BLAKE-32 and CubeHash as well. For all the other candidates considered,

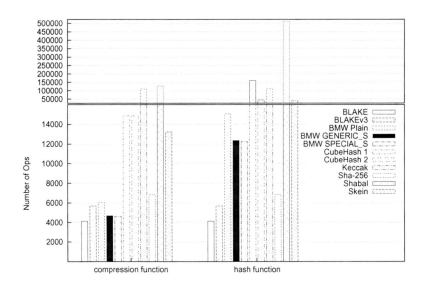

Fig. 4. Total number of instructions (including loads and stores) for one block (see Table 1)

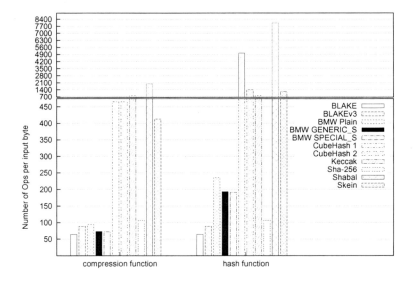

Fig. 5. Number of instructions per byte of input for one block (see Table 1)

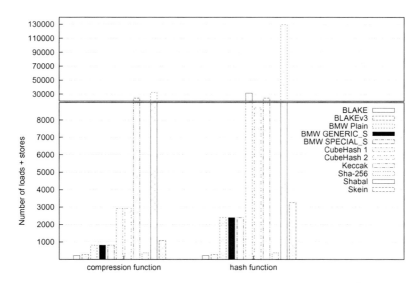

Fig. 6. Total number of load and store instructions for one block (see Table 2)

additional instructions must be implemented in the secure zone and will incur additional expenses.

4.2   Performance

To optimise performance, we fully unrolled all implementations, hard-coded any constants and ran them on a cycle-accurate simulator of the platform. We did not implement message padding; instead we assumed having a padded but un-masked message block stored in memory which is loaded when appropriate and then masked. As shown in Section 2.1, the most common case for hash function implementations with countermeasures against side-channel attack will have a preformatted, unmasked message in memory which has to be hashed without leaking information on the previous states. The code can easily be adopted to hash masked messages and the costs of loading a masked message block is to some extent absorbed by the then superfluous message masking. However, this would have required a convention with the calling function how to store a masked message and the related mask information.

The performance results of our implementations are shown in Table 1; the instruction counts show the candidates separated into three distinct but constant groups. The first group is formed by BLAKE-32, BLAKE-32v3, SHA-256 and all three BMW256 implementations. The second group comprises CubeHash16+16/32+32-256, Keccak[1088, 512, 32] and Skein-256-256; the ranking within this group varies depending on the performance criteria. Most notably, it shows the performance disadvantage CubeHash16+16/32+32-256 and Keccak[1088, 512, 32] incur in software implementations for supporting only one state size for all security parameters. The third group comprises

CubeHash160+16/32+160-256 (which has been superseded by CubeHash16+16/32+32-256) and Shabal-256. Both are not competitive on this platform. (See also Fig. 4 and Fig. 5.)

Another interesting metric are the number of load and store instructions contained within the total number of instructions; these are listed in Table 2. The ISEs for BMW256 have, as expected, no influence on the number of memory accesses. The ranking of algorithms in respect to memory access is not very different from the ranking in respect to instructions per byte; while Keccak[1088, 512, 32] ranks better on the number of instructions per byte than Skein-256-256 and CubeHash16+16/32+32-256, it is behind them in the number of memory access. The poor ranking of Shabal-256 with respect to any of the instruction counts is easily explained by the high number of memory access required to implement it; about 28% of all instructions are memory accesses.

Working in the design phase of a processor architecture, we can only present operation counts that do not represent the costs of load and store instructions properly. Therefore we decided not to compare our results with other studies such as eBASH [32] as they measure their results in processor cycles.

5   Conclusions

In this paper we demonstrated the flexibility of the Power-Trust platform wrt. to provision of generic countermeasures against side-channel attacks at reasonable costs; these metrics are paramount in the design and deployment of hash functions on secure embedded and mobile devices. Furthermore, our analysis contributes to the SHA-3 competition by highlighting, for the first time, the cost each candidate incurs from hardware protection. We additionally provided the first example of (non-AES) ISEs for BMW256, and outlined design requirements for general ISEs in this area. Furthermore, the effort to produce human-optimized code for these hash functions highlights the need to develop a compiler for this platform in the future; this work will then provide a good base to measure the compiler's efficiency.

Acknowledgements. The research described in this paper has been supported by EPSRC grant EP/H001689/1, and, in part by the European Commission through the ICT Programme under contract ICT-2007-216676 ECRYPT II. The information in this document reflects only the author's views, is provided as is, and no guarantee or warranty is given that the information is fit for any particular purpose. The user thereof uses the information at its sole risk and liability.

References

1. Wang, X., Yu, H., Yin, Y.: Efficient Collision Search Attacks on SHA-0. In: Shoup, V. (ed.) CRYPTO 2005. LNCS, vol. 3021, pp. 1–16. Springer, Heidelberg (2005)
2. Wang, X., Yin, Y., Yu, H.: Finding Collisions in the Full SHA-1. In: Shoup, V. (ed.) CRYPTO 2005. LNCS, vol. 3621, pp. 17–36. Springer, Heidelberg (2005)

3. National Institute of Standards and Technology (NIST): Secure Hash Standard (SHS). Federal Information Processing Standards Publication 180-2 (August 2002), http://csrc.nist.gov/publications/fips/fips180-2/fips180-2withchangenotice.pdf

4. National Institute of Standards and Technology (NIST): Cryptographic Hash Algorithm Competition, http://csrc.nist.gov/groups/ST/hash/sha-3/index.html

5. Rogaway, P., Shrimpton, T.: Cryptographic Hash-Function Basics: Definitions, Implications, and Separations for Preimage Resistance, Second-Preimage Resistance, and Collision Resistance. In: Roy, B., Meier, W. (eds.) FSE 2004. LNCS, vol. 3017, pp. 371–388. Springer, Heidelberg (2004)

6. Dent, A., Dottax, E.: An overview of side-channel attacks on the asymmetric NESSIE encryption primitives. NESSIE Public Report NES/DOC/RHU/WP5/020/a (May 2002), https://www.cosic.esat.kuleuven.be/nessie/reports/phase2/sidechannels.pdf

7. Lemke, K., Schramm, K., Paar, C.: DPA on n-Bit Sized Boolean and Arithmetic Operations and Its Application to IDEA, RC6, and the HMAC-Construction. In: Joye, M., Quisquater, J.J. (eds.) CHES 2004. LNCS, vol. 3156, pp. 205–219. Springer, Heidelberg (2004), http://dx.doi.org/10.1007/978-3-540-28632-5_15

8. Okeya, K.: Side Channel Attacks Against HMACs Based on Block-Cipher Based Hash Functions. In: Batten, L.M., Safavi-Naini, R. (eds.) ACISP 2006. LNCS, vol. 4058, pp. 432–443. Springer, Heidelberg (2006)

9. McEvoy, R., Tunstall, M., Murphy, C., Marnane, W.: Differential Power Analysis of HMAC Based on SHA-2, and Countermeasures. In: Sehun, K., Yung, M., Lee, H.W. (eds.) WISA 2007. LNCS, vol. 4867, pp. 317–332. Springer, Heidelberg (2008) ISBN: 3-540-77534-X

10. Gauravaram, P., Okeya, K.: Side Channel Analysis of Some Hash Based MACs: A Response to SHA-3 Requirements. In: Chen, L., Ryan, M., Wang, G. (eds.) ICICS 2008. LNCS, vol. 5308, pp. 111–127. Springer, Heidelberg (2008)

11. Fouque, P.A., Leurent, G., Réal, D., Valette, F.: Practical Electromagnetic Template Attack on HMAC. In: Clavier, C., Gaj, K. (eds.) CHES 2009. LNCS, vol. 5747, pp. 66–80. Springer, Heidelberg (2009), http://dx.doi.org/10.1007/978-3-642-04138-9_6

12. Rivest, R.: Side-channel-free timings?, E-Mail to the hash-forum@nist.gov mailing list (November 2010), http://www.cio.nist.gov/esd/emaildir/lists/hash-forum/msg02189.html

13. Tiri, K., Akmal, M., Verbauwhede, I.: A Dynamic and Differential CMOS Logic with Signal Independent Power Consumption to Withstand Differential Power Analysis on Smart Cards. In: European Solid-State Circuits Conference (ESSCIRC), pp. 403–406 (2002)

14. Tiri, K., Verbauwhede, I.: A Logic Level Design Methodology for a Secure DPA Resistant ASIC or FPGA Implementation. In: Design, Automation, and Test in Europe (DATE), pp. 246–251 (2004)

15. May, D., Muller, H., Smart, N.: Non-deterministic processors. In: Varadharajan, V., Mu, Y. (eds.) ACISP 2001. LNCS, vol. 2119, pp. 115–129. Springer, Heidelberg (2001)

16. IAIK, Graz University of Technology: Power-Trust project website, http://www.iaik.tugraz.at/content/research/implementation_attacks/prj_powertrust/

17. Tillich, S., Kirschbaum, M., Szekely, A.: SCA-Resistant Embedded Processors—The Next Generation. In: 26th Annual Computer Security Applications Conference (ACSAC 2010), Austin, Texas, USA, December 6-10, pp. 211–220. ACM, New York (2010)

18. Bernstein, D.: CubeHash specification (2.B.1). Submission to NIST, (Round 2) (2009)

19. Kocher, P., Jaffe, J., Jun, B.: Differential Power Analysis. In: Wiener, M. (ed.) CRYPTO 1999. LNCS, vol. 1666, pp. 388–397. Springer, Heidelberg (1999)

20. Aumasson, J.P., Henzen, L., Meier, W., Phan, R.W.: SHA-3 proposal BLAKE. Submission to NIST (2008)

21. Aumasson, J.P., Henzen, L., Meier, W., Phan, R.W.: OFFICIAL COMMENT: BLAKE tweak. E-Mail to the `hash-forum@nist.gov` mailing list (November 2010), `http://www.cio.nist.gov/esd/emaildir/lists/hash-forum/msg02233.html`

22. Gligoroski, D., Klima, V., Knapskog, S., El-Hadedy, M., Amundsen, J., Mjølsnes, S.: Cryptographic Hash Function BLUE MIDNIGHT WISH. Submission to NIST (Round 2) (2009)

23. Gligoroski, D., Klima, V., Knapskog, S., El-Hadedy, M., Amundsen, J., Mjølsnes, S.: Clarification on the rotation constant for the variable M_15. Official Comment to `hash-forum@nist.gov` (Round 2) (November 2009), `http://csrc.nist.gov/groups/ST/hash/sha-3/Round2/documents/BMW_Comments.pdf`

24. Bernstein, D.: CubeHash parameter tweak: $10 \times$ smaller MAC overhead. Submission to NIST (Round 2) (2010)

25. Bertoni, G., Daemen, J., Peeters, M., Assche, G.V.: Keccak sponge function family main document. Submission to NIST (Round 2) (2009)

26. Bertoni, G., Daemen, J., Peeters, M., Assche, G.V.: Keccak specifications. Submission to NIST (Round 2) (2009)

27. National Institute of Standards and Technology (NIST): Secure Hash Standard (SHS). Federal Information Processing Standards Publication 180-3 (October 2008), `http://csrc.nist.gov/publications/fips/fips180-3/fips180-3_final.pdf`

28. Bresson, E., Canteaut, A., Chevallier-Mames, B., Clavier, C., Fuhr, T., Gouget, A., Icart, T., Misarsky, J.F., Naya-Plasencia, M., Paillier, P., Pornin, T., Reinhard, J.R., Thuillet, C., Videau, M.: Shabal, a Submission to NIST's Cryptographic Hash Algorithm Competition. Submission to NIST (2008)

29. Bresson, E., Canteaut, A., Chevallier-Mames, B., Clavier, C., Fuhr, T., Gouget, A., Icart, T., Misarsky, J.F., Naya-Plasencia, M., Paillier, P., Pornin, T., Reinhard, J.R., Thuillet, C., Videau, M.: Indifferentiability with Distinguishers: Why Shabal Does Not Require Ideal Ciphers. Cryptology ePrint Archive, Report 2009/199 (2009)

30. Ferguson, N., Lucks, S., Schneier, B., Whiting, D., Bellare, M., Kohno, T., Callas, J., Walker, J.: The Skein Hash Function Family. Submission to NIST (Round 2) (2009)

31. SPARC International, Inc.: The SPARC Architecture Manual, Version 8, 535 Middlefield Road, Suite 210, Menlo Park, CA 94025, Revision SAV080SI9308 (1992)

32. eBACS: ECRYPT Benchmarking of Cryptographic Systems: ECRYPT Benchmarking of All Submitted Hashes, `http://bench.cr.yp.to/results-sha3.html`

A Comparison of Post-Processing Techniques for Biased Random Number Generators

Siew-Hwee Kwok[1], Yen-Ling Ee[1], Guanhan Chew[1], Kanghong Zheng[1], Khoongming Khoo[1], and Chik-How Tan[2]

[1] DSO National Laboratories, 20 Science Park Drive, S118230, Singapore
{ksiewhwe,eyenling,cguanhan,zkanghon,kkhoongm}@dso.org.sg
[2] Temasek Laboratories, National University of Singapore
tsltch@nus.edu.sg

Abstract. In this paper, we study and compare two popular methods for post-processing random number generators: linear and Von Neumann compression. We show that linear compression can achieve much better throughput than Von Neumann compression, while achieving practically good level of security. We also introduce a concept known as the adversary bias which measures how accurately an adversary can guess the output of a random number generator, e.g. through a trapdoor or a bad RNG design. Then we prove that linear compression performs much better than Von Neumann compression when correcting adversary bias. Finally, we discuss on good ways to implement this linear compression in hardware and give a field-programmable gate array (FPGA) implementation to provide resource utilization estimates.

Keywords: bias, linear correcting codes, entropy, random number generators, post-processing.

1 Introduction

Hardware-based random number generators (HRNGs) are sometimes preferred over algorithm-based bit generators. The randomness in the raw bitstream generated by HRNGs depend on the highly unpredictable nature of certain physical processes and are therefore less prone to the risks of cryptanalytic attacks, which are more applicable on deterministic bit generators. However, the raw output of HRNGs tends to be slightly biased and may even deteriorate over time.

To address this problem, HRNG implementations typically add an additional post-processing step to ameliorate symptoms of non-randomness in the raw bitstream. Basically, a compression function is applied to the raw bitstream before it is output at the user's end. If the raw bitstream starts out with an unusually high bias, the post-processing step would transform the bitstream such that the bias becomes more acceptable. Sometimes this may come at the expense of throughput, for example, the processed bitstream of [4] is half as long as the raw bitstream.

C.A. Ardagna and J. Zhou (Eds.): WISTP 2011, LNCS 6633, pp. 175–190, 2011.
© IFIP International Federation for Information Processing 2011

Common techniques used in the post-processing step include hashing or block-wise XOR-ing. A well-known method that makes use of the Von Neumann corrector [3] is sometimes used. Each of these methods has its pros and cons. Another technique, proposed by several authors [4,6,9] recently, uses linear compression functions based on good linear codes. Since there is a large pool of linear codes to choose from, it becomes possible to trade-off different aspects of a HRNG's performance, unlike in the other methods. For example, we show in Section 3 that if a RNG has random bias 0.001, using Von Neumann compression will produce perfect correction with bias= 0 but throughput equal to 25% of its original. However, if we use a $[255, 191, 17]$ BCH code, we could get a good bias of 2^{-153} and three times the throughput at 75% of the original transmission speed.

In Section 4, we introduce a concept called the adversary bias, which measures how accurately an adversary can guess the output of a RNG. This may occur, for example, if a user buys a RNG from a dishonest vendor who installed a trapdoor; or it may arise from an inherent weakness/bad design of a RNG. We show that linear compression can lower the adversary bias by much more than Von Neumann compression. In [6,9], the authors suggested using BCH codes with parameters $[255, 21, 111]$ and $[256, 16, 113]$ for linear compression, which do not seem to offer any advantage over Von Neumann compression in terms of throughput and correction of random bias. However, we show that these BCH codes are many times more effective than Von Neuman compression for correcting the adversary bias.

In addition, we look at two explicit constructions for implementing linear corrector functions based on BCH codes. One is based on multiplication by the generator polynomial, while the other is based on taking the remainder after division by the parity check polynomial. We compare the two methods and show when one is more advantageous over the other for different parameters. Finally, we implement this post-processing function in field-programmable gate array (FPGA) hardware circuitry to provide some resource utilization figures.

2   Known Techniques for De-Biasing

2.1   Compression with Cryptographic Hash

A cryptographic hash function is a deterministic algorithm that takes in an arbitrary block of data as input and returns a string of fixed size as output. When the size of the data input is larger than the stipulated size of the output, a compression is done on the data block by the hash function. The fundamental requirements of a cryptographic hash function are one-wayness, pre-image resistance, second pre-image resistance and collision-resistance. Examples of cryptographic hash functions include the SHA family of hash functions [1].

In [2], it is stated that if the data input has high entropy, the cryptographic hash output on this data will be close to a uniform distribution, thus de-biasing the input. However, it is hard to quantify how good the output bias is with respect to the input bias. Moreover, as hash functions are non-linear functions, there are hardware limitations and they may not be efficient to implement.

It is common to use hash functions for post-processing RNG output. However, because it is hard to quantify their strength and compare with other de-biasing methods, we shall leave hash functions out of our discussion in this paper.

2.2   Compression Using the Von Neumann Corrector

The Von Neumann corrector [3] is a well known method for post-processing a biased random stream. It is a simple method that produces perfectly unbiased outputs. Suppose an input stream has independent but biased bits. The corrector processes the stream of bits as a stream of non-overlapping pairs of successive bits and generates outputs as follows:

(1) If the input is "00" or "11", the input is discarded (no output),
(2) If the input is "01" or "10", output the first bit only.

Suppose the input bits have bias e , this means that for an input bit x,

$$Pr(x = 0) = \frac{1}{2} + e \text{ and } Pr(x = 1) = \frac{1}{2} - e. \tag{1}$$

Then for a given output bit y,

$$
\begin{aligned}
Pr(y = 1) &= Pr(y = 1| \text{ there is an output }) \\
&= \frac{Pr(\text{"10"})}{Pr(\text{"01" or "10"})} \\
&= \frac{(\frac{1}{2} - e)(\frac{1}{2} + e)}{(\frac{1}{2} + e)(\frac{1}{2} - e) + (\frac{1}{2} - e)(\frac{1}{2} + e)} \\
&= \frac{\frac{1}{4} - e^2}{2(\frac{1}{4} - e^2)} \\
&= \frac{1}{2}.
\end{aligned}
$$

Thus the Von Neumann corrector output bits with zero bias.

However, the rate of such a corrector is fairly slow. The rate a desirable pair (i.e. "01" and "10") occurs is $2(\frac{1}{2} + e)(\frac{1}{2} - e)$ which is $2(\frac{1}{4} - e^2)$. However, each pair gives an output half its length. Hence the rate of the corrector is given by $\frac{1}{4} - e^2$. Thus the rate of the Von Neumann corrector is at best $\frac{1}{4}$ with at least 75% of the input bits discarded. This means that the input size needs to be much larger than the output size and there may be a long wait before there is an output (in the event where there is a long stream of 'undesirable' bits of "00"s and "11"s). Thus, despite its excellent de-biasing property, the Von Neumann method is not ideal.

2.3   Compression Based on Good Linear Codes

In this section, we describe a technique proposed by Lacharme [6], which derives good linear compression for random number generation based on good error correcting codes. The input is a random stream where each input bit has bias e. The output will be a "more" random stream where each output bit has bias $e' < e$.

The method is a generalization of a construction by Dichtl [4]. An example of Dichtl's construction is given by $L : GF(2)^8 \times GF(2)^8 \to GF(2)^8$:

$$L(X, Y) = X \oplus (X \lll 1) \oplus (X \lll 2) \oplus (X \lll 4) \oplus Y.$$

The above function takes 16 independent random bits, each with bias e, and compresses it to 8 bits. In the process, the bias of each compressed bit becomes $2^4 \times e^5$. Thus a RNG which has deteriorated over time, say to give output streams having a bias of 0.05 can be corrected to give a bias of $2^4 \times 0.05^5 = 0.000005$, which is more random. The compression rate is $1/2$ which is the same as XOR: $L(X, Y) = X \oplus Y$. However, XOR only improves the bias from e to $2e^2$.

Thus we see that constructing better linear correctors can achieve better bias while maintaining the same compression rate. Moreover, these compression functions are linear, which makes them efficient to implement on both hardware and software. While Dichtl constructed specific 16 to 8 bit linear correctors, Lacharme generalized his method to apply to more scenarios:

Proposition 1. *([6, Theorem 1]) Let G be a linear corrector mapping n bits to m bits. Then the bias of any non zero linear combination of the output bits is less than or equal to $2^{d-1}e^d$, where e is the bias of each input bit and d is the minimal distance of the linear code constructed by the generator matrix G.*

The above result can be proved by noticing that each output bit of G is an XOR-sum of at least d input bits each with bias e, and then we apply the well-known Piling-Up lemma [5] to get the resulting bias $2^{d-1}e^d$.

Thus we can deduce by Proposition 1 that the linear corrector $L(X, Y)$ gives output streams with bias $2^4 \times e^5$ because L is the generator matrix of a $[16, 8, 5]$ error correcting code.

3   Comparison of Random Bias of Different Post-Processing Functions

In the existing literature, the idea of using post-processing functions based on linear codes is not new. Examples of this can be found, in [6] and [9], where BCH and extended BCH codes were used to construct linear corrector functions. We note, however, that the particular codes picked in these papers do not offer significant advantages over the Von Neumann corrector. We shall illustrate this point numerically.

The codes $[255, 21, 111]$ and $[256, 16, 113]$ codes were used in [6] and [9] respectively. Suppose that the bias of the input bit stream is 0.25, then the bias and throughput, on applying the $[255, 21, 111]$ corrector, is $2^{110} \times (0.25)^{111} = 2^{-112}$ and $\frac{21}{255} - 0.0824$ respectively. In comparison, we get zero bias and a throughput of $\frac{1}{4} - 0.25^2 = 0.1875$ if we had used the Von Neumann corrector. Clearly, the

Table 1. Rate and Output Bias

	XOR	Von Neumann	Linear Code $[n, k, d]$
Rate	$\frac{1}{2}$	$\frac{1}{4} - e^2$	$\frac{k}{n}$
Output Bias	$2e^2$	0	$\leq 2^{d-1} e^d$

corrector based on the $[255, 21, 111]$ code has no advantage over the well-known Von Neumann corrector in these aspects.

The same can be said of the corrector based on the $[256, 16, 113]$ code. With the same input bit stream bias of 0.25, we get an output bias and throughput of $2^{112} \times (0.25)^{113} = 2^{-114}$ and $\frac{16}{256} = 0.0625$. Again, the Von Neumann corrector is better in these aspects.

Linear code based correctors still have their merits despite what the above examples suggest. We shall show that if the linear code is chosen wisely, such correctors can be preferred over other forms of post-processing methods.

Although we can achieve zero output bias with the Von Neumann corrector, the rate is at best $\frac{1}{4}$, which may be inadequate if there are stringent demands on the output bit throughput. For this reason, it may be desirable to use a different corrector that has a better rate if we are willing to tolerate a small bias in the output bits. The other two methods we looked at in the previous section, hashing and linear compression, can both achieve better throughput than Von Neumann compression. However, hashing is an intuitive approach in which we cannot quantify the bias reduction of the output stream and we therefore leave it out in our analysis. We shall concentrate on the comparison between Von Neumann and linear compression method in the rest of our paper.

To recap, let us suppose that the bias of the input bits is e, then we have the following results for the various correctors described thus far:

We can observe from Table 1 that the rate for the XOR corrector is at least twice that of the Von Neumann corrector, while the output bias for the latter is much better than for the former. However, the weaknesses of these correctors are as outstanding as their strengths. The Von Neumann corrector has a low throughput of at most $\frac{1}{4}$, while the XOR corrector does not improve the output bias very significantly. It is desirable to construct a corrector that offers a better trade-off between the rate and the output bias. We shall demonstrate that with proper choices of n, k, and d, the Linear Code (more specifically, BCH code) corrector fulfills this purpose.

In Table 2, we have compared the rate and output biases for the XOR, Von Neumann, linear correctors based on various BCH codes with $n = 255$ and different input bias values, e. The numbers in square brackets are in the usual $[n, k, d]$ notation used to represent BCH codes. The linear codes we have chosen are such that they produce a throughput greater than that of the Von Neumann method. Table 2 lists the rate and output bias for values of $e = 0.25, 0.1, 0.01$ and 0.001.

The throughputs for the BCH code correctors vastly outperform that of the XOR and Von Neumann correctors. The output biases are also very much smaller

Table 2. Rate and Output Bias for Various Input Bias, e

$e = 0.25$	XOR	Von Neumann	$[255, 223, 9]$	$[255, 171, 23]$	$[255, 107, 45]$	$[255, 55, 63]$
Rate	0.5	0.1875	0.875	0.671	0.420	0.216
Output Bias	0.0625	0	$\leq 2^{-10}$	$\leq 2^{-24}$	$\leq 2^{-46}$	$\leq 2^{-64}$
$e = 0.1$	XOR	Von Neumann	$[255, 231, 7]$	$[255, 171, 23]$	$[255, 115, 43]$	$[255, 63, 61]$
Rate	0.5	0.24	0.906	0.671	0.451	0.247
Output Bias	0.01	0	$\leq 2^{-17.3}$	$\leq 2^{-54.4}$	$\leq 2^{-100.8}$	$\leq 2^{-142.6}$
$e = 0.01$	XOR	Von Neumann	$[255, 247, 3]$	$[255, 191, 17]$	$[255, 131, 37]$	$[255, 71, 59]$
Rate	0.5	0.2499	0.967	0.749	0.514	0.278
Output Bias	0.0001	0	$\leq 2^{-17.9}$	$\leq 2^{-96.9}$	$\leq 2^{-209.8}$	$\leq 2^{-334.0}$
$e = 0.001$	XOR	Von Neumann	$[255, 247, 3]$	$[255, 191, 17]$	$[255, 131, 37]$	$[255, 71, 59]$
Rate	0.5	0.249999	0.969	0.749	0.514	0.278
Output Bias	0.000001	0	$\leq 2^{-27.9}$	$\leq 2^{-153.4}$	$\leq 2^{-332.7}$	$\leq 2^{-529.0}$

than that of the XOR corrector. In all cases, to just outperform the throughput of Von Neumann corrector, d only needs to be at most 63. If the input bias is small, i.e. 0.1 or 0.01, we can use a code with very low d to obtain a throughput of nearly 1 at the cost of a small output bias of less than 2^{-17}. The near quadrupling of the throughput is a large improvement over the Von Neumann method.

We have shown that with a proper choice of BCH code, a better trade-off between the throughput and output bias can be achieved. Although the output bias is non-zero, it is small enough to be acceptable in some applications.

4   Comparison of Adversary Bias of Different Post-Processing Functions

Sometimes, an adversary might be able to predict the output of a random number generator with probability more than $1/2$. The reasons might be due to:

(1) A black box random number generator might be bought from a dishonest vendor, who planted some bugs/backdoor to leak information on the random stream output.
(2) The random number generator designer might make an honest mistake and design a weak RNG, where the output stream is predictable.

Because of the above scenarios, we make the following definition.

Definition 1. *Suppose an adversary can predict the output of a random number generator with probability p_A. Then the adversary bias $e_A = |p_A - 1/2|$.*

4.1   Adversary Bias after Linear Compression

Next we shall show that using linear correctors for random stream compression is better than using Von Neumann compression to lower the adversary bias. First we shall demonstrate the effect with a numerical example.

Example 1. Suppose a random number generator produces the following 16-bit random stream and the adversary knows $12/16 = 75\%$ of the random output:

$$\begin{aligned} \text{Random stream:} \quad & 0101101010001101 \\ \text{Adversary stream:} \quad & 0101\mathbf{0}1\mathbf{1}010\mathbf{1}11101. \end{aligned}$$

Then Von Neumann on the random stream gives 001110 while Von Neumann on the adversary's stream gives 000110. Now the adversary knows $5/6 = 83\%$ of the compressed stream, the adversary bias actually increase during Von Neumann compression!

If we had used the linear corrector $L(X, Y) = X \oplus (X \lll 1) \oplus (X \lll 2) \oplus (X \lll 4) \oplus Y$, then the random stream compresses to 10101111 while the adversary's stream compresses to 01111011. Now he only knows $4/8 = 50\%$ of the random stream.   □

The reason why the linear corrector outperforms Von Neumann compression when correcting adversary bias is as follows. Let $L(\cdot)$ be the linear corrector, AS denote the output stream known to the adversary and RS be the actual random stream. Also let e_L be the adversary bias after compression and e_A be the adversary bias before compression, then

$$\begin{aligned} e_L &= |Pr(L(AS) = L(RS)) - 1/2| \\ &= |Pr(L(AS) \oplus L(RS) = 0) - 1/2| \\ &= |Pr(L(AS \oplus RS) = 0) - 1/2| \\ &= 2^{d-1}e_A^d \text{ where } e_A = |Pr(AS = RS) - 1/2|. \end{aligned}$$

This computation shows that the reduction in adversary bias is as good as the reduction in random bias for linear compression. However, we showed in the previous example that the adversary bias after Von Neumann compression can become worse (higher), although we have perfect correction for the random bias.

4.2   Adversary Bias after Von Neumann Compression

Von Neumann compression can be deemed as irregular due to the irregularity of the production of outputs. According to the definition of the Von Neumann compression in Section 2.2, we see that there is a probability of $\frac{1}{2}$ where the compression gives no output.

In the worst case assumption, we assume a knowledgeable adversary who is able to have information on the timing when there is no output after Von Neumann compression. This is a possible scenario due to trapdoors or lack of buffer in the generator, or in side channel attacks where the difference in timing of outputs is analysed. When there is no output from the compression in the middle of the stream, the timing between a first output and a second output is longer due to the missing output in the middle. This constitutes a valid analysis on the Von Neumann output stream.

Table 3. Adversary Stream Prediction Probabilities

RS input	01	10	00	11	Total probability
AS input $(= RS$ input$)$	01	10	00	11	p_A^2
AS input $(\neq RS$ input$)$	-	-	11	00	$q_A^2(p_R^2 + q_R^2)$
VN output	"0"	"1"	"X"	"X"	$p_A^2 + q_A^2(p_R^2 + q_R^2)$

In these cases, the adversary will be able to guess the nonproduction of output and hence, have auto-correlation in the output streams for comparison. Thus, we will consider this condition in this section. We will also show in Section 4.3 that, in the worst case assumption, linear compression will still outperform Von Neumann compression even if the adversary is resourceful enough to know the timing when no output is produced from the compression.

A theoretical bound on Von Neumann compression can be derived if we consider 3 types of output, namely "0", "1" and "X" (no output). Let $VN(\cdot)$ be the Von Neumann corrector, AS denote the output stream known to the adversary and RS be the actual random stream. Also let e_R be the bias of the random stream and e_A be the adversary bias before compression. Since the bias of the random stream e_R is the bias of the input bits to the Von Neumann corrector, this means that for an input bit x of the random stream,

$$p_R = Pr(x = 0) = \frac{1}{2} + e_R \text{ and } q_R = Pr(x = 1) = \frac{1}{2} - e_R. \qquad (2)$$

Similarly for adversary bias e_A and an input bit x' of the adversary stream,

$$p_A = Pr(x' = x) = \frac{1}{2} + e_A \text{ and } q_A = Pr(x' \neq x) = \frac{1}{2} - e_A. \qquad (3)$$

Every two input bits will give one output bit through the Von Neumann corrector. Therefore, the probabilities of the adversary predicting the Von Neumann output correctly under the two conditions, $AS = RS$ and $AS \neq RS$, are given in Table 3 below.

It is clear that if the adversary guessed the input bits correctly, the probability of getting the same output as with the random stream is the same as the probability of guessing the two input bits correctly, which is p_A^2.

$$Pr(VN(AS) = VN(RS)| \text{ AS} = \text{RS}) = p_A^2. \qquad (4)$$

In the case of adversary guessing the wrong input bits, there are only two situations where the adversary gets the same output. That is, when the random stream input is "00" and the adversary's guess is "11", or vice versa. In this case,

$$Pr\left(VN(AS) = VN(RS)| \text{ AS} \neq \text{RS} \right)$$
$$= Pr(RS = \text{"11"}, AS = \text{"00"}) + Pr(RS = \text{"00"}, AS = \text{"11"})$$
$$- q_R^2 q_A^2 + p_R^2 q_A^2$$
$$= q_A^2(p_R^2 + q_R^2).$$

Hence, the total probability p_V of the adversary guessing the output of the Von Neumann corrector correctly is given by

$$
\begin{aligned}
p_V &= Pr(VN(AS) = VN(RS)) \\
&= Pr(VN(AS)=VN(RS)|\ AS=RS\ )+Pr(VN(AS)=VN(RS)|\ AS \neq RS\ ) \\
&= p_A^2 + q_A^2(p_R^2 + q_R^2) \\
&= (\frac{1}{2} + e_A)^2 + (\frac{1}{2} - e_A)^2[(\frac{1}{2} + e_R)^2 + (\frac{1}{2} - e_R)^2] \\
&= (\frac{1}{4} + e_A + e_A^2) + (\frac{1}{4} - e_A + e_A^2)[(\frac{1}{4} + e_R + e_R^2) + (\frac{1}{4} - e_R + e_R^2)] \\
&= (\frac{1}{4} + e_A + e_A^2) + (\frac{1}{4} - e_A + e_A^2)(\frac{1}{2} + 2e_R^2) \\
&= (\frac{3}{2} + 2e_R^2)e_A^2 + (\frac{1}{2} - 2e_R^2)e_A + \frac{1}{2}e_R^2 + \frac{3}{8}.
\end{aligned}
$$

As a result, the adversary bias e_V of the output after Von Neumann compression will be

$$
e_V = |p_V - \frac{1}{2}| = |(\frac{3}{2} + 2e_R^2)e_A^2 + (\frac{1}{2} - 2e_R^2)e_A + \frac{1}{2}e_R^2 - \frac{1}{8}|. \tag{5}
$$

4.3 Linear Compression Outperforming the Von-Neumann Compression

Let us define some notations and also give a summary of the results we have derived at so far.

In section 3, it is shown that although the random bias after linear compression is always greater than that after Von Neumann, we can have the random bias lowered to a value close to zero which makes it comparable to the Von Neumann compression. In other words, although $e_{RL} > e_{RV}$ but by choosing a large enough d, we can have $e_{RL} \approx e_{RV}$.

Next we compare the adversary bias after each compression. Figure 1 below illustrates the adversary bias after each compression for the case where $e_R = 0.1$. The modulus graph denoted by e_{AV} shows the adversary bias after Von Neumann compression while the e_{AL} graph shows the adversary bias after linear compression for $d = 3, 4$ and 20.

Table 4. Bias after Compression

	Bias After Von Neumann Compression	Bias After Linear Compression
Random Bias, e_R	$e_{RV} = 0$	$e_{RL} \leq 2^{d-1}e_R^d$
Adversary Bias, e_A	$e_{AV} =$ $\|(\frac{3}{2} + 2e_R^2)e_A^2 + (\frac{1}{2} - 2e_R^2)e_A + \frac{1}{2}e_R^2 - \frac{1}{8}\|$	$e_{AL} \leq 2^{d-1}e_A^d$

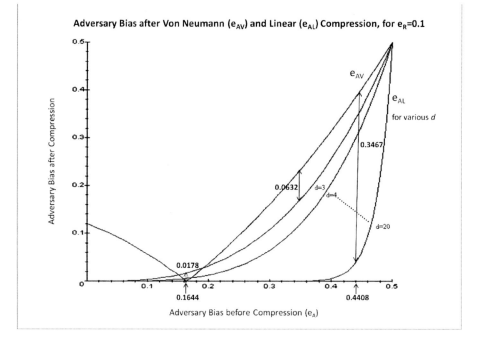

Fig. 1. Impact of compression on adversary bias

Consider the case $d = 3$. The graph shows that linear compression gives a better reduction of adversary bias most of the time except for $0.15025 \leq e_A \leq 0.19219$. Linear compression can outperform Von-Neumann compression (i.e. e_{AL} is smaller than e_{AV}) by as much as 0.0632 while Von-Neumann compression outperforms linear compression (i.e. e_{AV} is smaller than e_{AL}) by at most 0.0178. As d increases, the range of e_A where Von Neumann compression outperforms linear compression will get narrower where its size tends to zero, the advantage of Von Neumann compression in this range will also tend to zero while the advantage of linear compression will increase substantially. For the case where $d = 20$, linear compression is comparable to Von Neumann compression when $e_A = 0.1644$ while it outperforms Von Neumann compression for all other values of e_A. The maximum advantage occurs when $e_A = 0.4408$, where the advantage of linear compression is $e_{AV} - e_{AL} = 0.3869 - 0.0402 = 0.3467$. Table 5 summarizes our discussion and compare the advantage of linear compression for different d.

Similar results hold for varying values of e_R. Summarising, the linear compression reduces the adversary bias much more than the Von Neumann, except over a negligible range of e_A with d suitably large, say $d = 20$. Moreover, in the unlikely event that the Von Neumann outperforms the linear compression, the large d will reduce the adversary bias to a value close to zero, which makes it comparable to the Von-Neumann . Thus we conclude that the linear compression is much more effective in lowering the adversary bias than the Von Neumann.

Table 5. Maximum Advantage of Linear Compression over Von Neumann Compression, $e_R = 0.1$

d	Small Range where Von Neumann outperforms Linear	Max Advantage of Von Neumann	Max Advantage of Linear
3	$0.1502 < e_A < 0.1922$	0.0178	0.0632
4	$0.1594 < e_A < 0.1714$	0.0058	0.1158
5	$0.1625 < e_A < 0.1665$	0.0019	0.1551
6	$0.1638 < e_A < 0.1651$	0.0006	0.1859
$\vdots$	$\vdots$	$\vdots$	$\vdots$
20	$0.1644 - \delta < e_A < 0.1644 + \delta$, δ negligible	10^{-5}	0.3467

4.4   The Use of Linear Codes with Large d

In Section 3, we pointed out that the codes $[255, 21, 111]$ and $[256, 16, 113]$ does not offer any advantage over Von Neumann compression in terms of both throughput and random bias correction. However, it is very effective for correcting adversary bias.

Suppose we have a RNG whose random bias is $e_R = 0.005$, which is not too bad. But it is bought from a dishonest vendor who planted a trapdoor and is able to guess the RNG output with bias $e_A = 0.3$. Using the formulae from Sections 4.1 and 4.2, linear compression with $[255, 21, 111]$ would give adversary bias:

$$e_{AL} = 2^{110} \times (0.3)^{111} = 2^{-82.8},$$

while Von Neumann compression would give adversary bias (Table 3):

$$e_{AV} = (0.8)^2 + (0.2)^2 \times (0.505^2 + 0.495^2) - 0.5 = 0.16.$$

I.e. the probability of the adversary guessing the output is reduced from 80% to very close to $1/2$ for linear compression while it is still 66% for Von Neumann compression.

5   Implementation

In this section, we describe two constructions for implementing linear corrector functions based on BCH codes. We also aim to estimate the resources required to implement the linear codes in ASIC technology, as well as provide resource utilization results for our FPGA implementation.

5.1   Construction of Linear Corrector Functions Based on Cyclic Codes

BCH code is a family of cyclic codes with high hamming distance that can be derived from a generator polynomial. As such the generator matrix can be easily derived and the code is efficient in lowering both the random bias and adversary

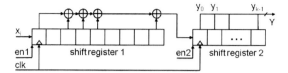

Fig. 2. $[255, 247, 3]$ hardware implementation using the generator polynomial

bias when used as a linear compression. A list of generator polynomials and their corresponding parity check polynomials of $[n, k, d]$ BCH codes with $n = 255$ is given in Appendix A for reference.

Either the generator polynomial or the parity-check polynomial can be used in the implementation. Both methods provide efficient hardware implementation. We first describe the generator polynomial method.

For input $X = (x_{n-1}, \cdots, x_0)^T$, the output $Y = (y_{k-1}, \cdots, y_0)^T$ is defined as the product of the generator matrix G and the vector X:

$$Y = \begin{pmatrix} g_{n-k} & \cdots & \cdots & \cdots & g_0 & 0 & \cdots & 0 \\ 0 & g_{n-k} & \cdots & \cdots & \cdots & g_0 & \cdots & 0 \\ \vdots & \ddots & & \ddots & & & \ddots & \vdots \\ 0 & \cdots & 0 & g_{n-k} & \cdots & \cdots & \cdots & g_0 \end{pmatrix}_{k \times n} \begin{pmatrix} x_{n-1} \\ x_{n-2} \\ \vdots \\ x_0 \end{pmatrix}_{n \times 1}$$

where $g_{n-k}, \cdots, g_0$ are the coefficients of the generator polynomial $g(x)$.

This transformation mapping can be implemented using the circuit shown in Fig. 2 [10]. In the first $n - k + 1$ cycles, the input bits are shifted (MSB first) into a register of $n - k + 1$ bits (shift register 1). In the next k cycles, while the remaining input bits are shifted into shift register 1, the output bits are produced by XOR-ing certain bits of shift register 1 and fed into a register of k bits (shift register 2). The position of the XOR taps is determined by the generator polynomial $g(x)$. In this example of the $[255, 247, 3]$ BCH code with generator polynomial $g(x) = x^8 + x^4 + x^3 + x^2 + 1$, a total of 256 registers and 4 XOR gates are required for the implementation.

Next, we describe the parity-check polynomial method, which is a modular polynomial reduction [6]. By definition, parity-check polynomial $h(x) = (x^n - 1)/g(x)$ is at most of degree k. Using polynomial modulo under $h(x)$, the output has at most k bits. The function for this mapping from input vector X to output vector Y is defined by:

$$Y = X \bmod h(x)$$

The circuit for this method is similar to a Galois LFSR, shown in Fig. 3. Again, the position of the XOR taps is determined by the parity-check polynomial $h(x)$. In this example of the $[255, 21, 111]$ BCH code with parity-check polynomial $h(x) = x^{21} + x^{19} + x^{14} + x^{10} + x^7 + x^2 + 1$, a total of 21 registers and 6 XOR gates are utilized.

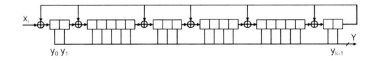

Fig. 3. $[255, 21, 111]$ hardware implemention using the parity-check polynomial

5.2   Resource Utilization

As the linear corrector function can be constructed using either the generator polynomial or the parity-check polynomial, the implementation which uses fewer resources is preferred. In ASIC technology, a rough comparison can be made by estimating the Gate Equivalent (GE) of the resources used. Consider the $[255,$ $247, 3]$ code in Appendix A. Its generator polynomial is of weight 5 whereas its parity check polynomial is of weight 128. Implementing with the generator polynomial, we need 256 registers and 4 XORs. Suppose a XOR uses 2.67 GE while a register uses 6 GE [11], the total resources required is then 1,546.68 GE. On the other hand, implementing the parity check polynomial will require 1,821.09 GE. The resources for the two different implementations of the codes in Appendix A is calculated and summarized in Table 6 below. As observed in the table, generating the whole codespace using $g(x)$ is better than using $h(x)$, in terms of resources usage, only for the first 3 codes of dimension $[255, 247, 3]$, $[255, 231, 7]$ and $[255, 223, 9]$. Using $h(x)$ for the other codes is better as fewer resources are required for implementation.

In FPGA technology, the same comparison cannot be made easily. This is because different FPGA devices have different logic cell architectures, and FPGA design tools may apply optimizations automatically. Therefore, the more efficient construction to use for the FPGA in interest is best found out through actual implementation.

Table 6. Comparison of estimated Gate Equivalents for $n = 255$

k	$w_1 =$ $wt(g(x)) - 1$	$w_2 =$ $wt(h(x)) - 1$	Using $g(x)$, # GE = $6(n+1) + 2.67w_1$	Using $h(x)$, # GE = $6k + 2.67w_2$	Polynomial requiring less GE
247	4	127	$1,546.68$	$1,821.09$	
231	14	111	$1,573.38$	$1,682.37$	$g(x)$
223	20	123	$1,589.40$	$1,666.41$	
191	38	87	$1,637.46$	$1,378.29$	
171	42	85	$1,648.14$	$1,252.95$	
131	58	67	$1,690.86$	964.89	
115	74	57	$1,733.58$	842.19	$h(x)$
107	72	47	$1,728.24$	767.49	
71	84	47	$1,760.28$	551.49	
63	104	31	$1,813.68$	460.77	
55	92	27	$1,781.64$	402.09	

Table 7. Comparison of FPGA implementation resources for $n = 255$

k	Using $g(x)$, # slices	Using $h(x)$, # slices
247	148	145
231	148	136
223	149	132
191	149	112
171	141	101
131	140	77
115	145	67
107	140	63
71	135	42
63	142	37
55	128	32

We implemented the codes in Appendix A on a Xilinx Spartan 3A-DSP XC3SD1800A. The number of slices utilized is shown in Table 7. From the table, we can see that the implementation using the parity-check polynomial uses fewer resources than that of the generator polynomial for all cases. This can be explained as follows. As the number of XOR gates required is always less than the number of registers, the slice utilization is largely dominated by the number of registers required. Thus, since the parity-check polynomial (k registers) always uses less registers than the generator polynomial ($n + 1$ registers), its slice utilization is also less.

In general, for Xilinx FPGA, the implementation with the parity-check polynomial should utilize fewer resources in most cases. However, this may not hold true for FPGA devices from other vendors. Therefore, as mentioned earlier, the construction which is more resource-efficient for a particular FPGA is best found out through actual implementation.

6   Conclusion

In this paper, we studied the benefits of using linear compression for postprocessing random number generators over the Von Neumann and XOR corrector. We find that when suitable linear codes of dimension $[n, k, d]$ are selected, the random bias and adversary bias can be greatly lowered while maintaining a high throughput. The general idea is to select a d large enough to lower both biases to acceptable values. In our study, we found that for $e_R = 0.1$, $d = 20$ is generally sufficient to reduce both random and adversary bias to approximately zero. Also, the rate given by $\frac{k}{n}$ will be more efficient compared to the Von Neumann corrector. For instance, using $[255, 171, 23]$-BCH code as a linear corrector reduces biases to approximately zero after linear compression with a higher throughput of $\frac{171}{255} \approx 67\%$, compared to Von Neumann compression with zero bias of throughput 24%. A suggested list of BCH codes for $n = 255$, their generator and parity check polynomials are given in the appendix. Implementation issues and results of resource utilization are discussed in the last section.

References

1. NIST Approved Algorithms for Secure Hashing,
   `http://csrc.nist.gov/groups/ST/toolkit/secure_hashing.html`
2. Halevi, S.: Cryptographic Hash Functions and their many applications. In: USENIX Security Symposium (2009),
   `http://people.csail.mit.edu/shaih/pubs/Cryptographic-Hash-Functions.ppt`
3. Von Neumann, J.: Various Techniques used in Connection with Random Digits. National Bureau of Standards Applied Mathematics Series 12, 36–38 (1951)
4. Dichtl, M.: Bad and Good Ways of Post-processing Biased Physical Random Numbers. In: Biryukov, A. (ed.) FSE 2007. LNCS, vol. 4593, pp. 127–152. Springer, Heidelberg (2007)
5. Matsui, M.: Linear Cryptanalysis Method for DES Cipher. In: Helleseth, T. (ed.) EUROCRYPT 1993. LNCS, vol. 765, pp. 386–397. Springer, Heidelberg (1994)
6. Lacharme, P.: Post-Processing Functions for a Biased Physical Random Number Generator. In: Nyberg, K. (ed.) FSE 2008. LNCS, vol. 5086, pp. 334–342. Springer, Heidelberg (2008)
7. Menezes, A.J., van Oorschot, P.C., Vanstone, S.A.: Handbook of Applied Cryptography. CRC Press, Boca Raton (1997)
8. Grassl, M.: Code tables: bounds on the parameters of various types of codes,
   `http://www.codetables.de`
9. Sunar, B., Stinson, D.: A Provably Secure True Random Number Generator with Built-In Tolerance to Active Attacks. IEEE Transactions on Computers 56(1) (2007)
10. Schellekens, D., Preneel, B., Verbauwhede, I.: FPGA Vendor Agnostic True Random Number Generator. In: International Conference on Field Programmable Logic and Applications (2006)
11. Poschmann, A.: Lightweight Cryptography - Cryptographic Engineering for a Pervasive World (2009), `http://eprint.iacr.org/2009/516.eps`

A   Appendix: BCH Codes

The generator polynomials $g(x)$ and parity-check polynomials $h(x) = (x^n - 1)/g(x)$ are represented in hexadecimals such that in the binary form, the rightmost bit represents the coefficient of the constant term 1 and the leftmost nonzero bit represents the degree of the polynomial.

Example 2. The generator polynomial $g(x)$ for BCH code $[255, 247, 3]$ is represented as 11D in Table 8. In binary form, hexadecimal 11D is $(000100011101)_2$, which represents $x^8 + x^4 + x^3 + x^2 + 1$ in polynomial form. The rightmost bit represents the coefficient of the constant term (x^0) and the leftmost non-zero bit is in the 9th position from the right, representing the degree of the polynomial as 8.   □

Table 8. Generator and Parity Check Polynomials of BCH Codes

Code Parameters $[n, k, d]$	Generator Polynomial $g(x)$	Parity-check Polynomial $h(x)$
$[255, 247, 3]$	11D	8E25C0C93720ADACB0FB7 AE886C79CC5A452A7767B F4CD460EABE509FE178D
$[255, 231, 7]$	1BBA1B5	E7400884547D0D3D1A82 98CB0B2497ECD4CAD9 60F1F70B471667357EE5
$[255, 223, 9]$	1EE5B42FD	CA1E95439F31F12A925E 61E1BF5DE175C668DA 9B159BC7A1F93FF66D
$[255, 191, 17]$	16CE707E26B6F9977	BF5F0B83A04CF7C58047CBF0 B8C8A5D8E28C2C4609020D6B
$[255, 171, 23]$	1B0E46229C4EE1F8C7319F	E3E79B7AFE3243AA9A400A CAB2138885EBF0B40BBE3
$[255, 131, 37]$	11BCB6CCE6906958 AA17F2231050EB39	8D493EDCA6106BE2A FA4F85A2A3DE6879
$[255, 115, 43]$	1855B6B7A2029D679E 826017CEAB732E75DF	FDD74802A09D1F 88718D4B97B1EA3
$[255, 107, 45]$	1242FE9A4365732A1EC 04EB9E207EBE7A0D921	905F8D71982A80 0DE9456B55D21
$[255, 71, 59]$	140A722A1A468D36D87A2536 4E685922A1E56FD1A478C1D	AAFC7EA6FFFBEF0A8D
$[255, 63, 61]$	11EC9E8B4E7646AB351EEFE38 0F6C49EB4B56F8BD770AC6C1	8FC22EFA9CC296C1
$[255, 55, 63]$	1D9B1541D04805B06AF58C1A1 635618D6F6822DE248B076778F	D466E1C119DAB3

AES Variants Secure against Related-Key Differential and Boomerang Attacks*

Jiali Choy[1], Aileen Zhang[1], Khoongming Khoo[1], Matt Henricksen[2], and Axel Poschmann[3]

[1] DSO National Laboratories
20 Science Park Drive, Singapore 118230
{cjiali,zyinghui,kkhoongm}@dso.org.sg
[2] Institute for Infocomm Research,
A*STAR, Singapore
mhenricksen@i2r.a-star.edu.sg
[3] Division of Mathematical Sciences, School of Physical and Mathematical Sciences
Nanyang Technological University, Singapore
aposchmann@ntu.edu.sg

Abstract. In this paper, we present a framework for protection against the recent related-key differential and boomerang attacks on AES by Biryukov et al. Then we study an alternative AES key schedule proposed by May et al. at ACISP 2002 as a possible candidate to protect against these related key attacks. We find that there exist equivalent keys for this key schedule and in response, we propose an improvement to overcome this weakness. We proceed to prove, using our framework, that our improved May et al.'s key schedule is secure against related-key differential and boomerang attacks. Since May et al.'s key schedule is not on-the-fly (which is a requirement for some hardware implementations), we propose an on-the-fly AES key schedule that is resistant against related-key differential and boomerang attacks.

Keywords: Related-key attacks, differential cryptanalysis, boomerang attacks, AES key schedule.

1 Introduction

In [4], Biryukov et al. launched the first known key-recovery attack on AES-256. It is a related-key differential attack that exploits a differential characteristic path of high probability, where we allow both the plaintext and key to have non-zero differentials. The attack has a time/data complexity of 2^{131} and requires 2^{65} memory in addition to 2^{35} related key pairs. Later in [3], Biryukov and Khovratovich used a shortened version of the related-key differential characteristic of [4] to construct a distinguisher for the related-key boomerang attack on AES-256. This allowed the authors to avoid the majority of the active S-boxes in the differential characteristic of [4], which resulted in a much improved attack with time

---

* The extended version of this paper shall appear on the eprint archive.

C.A. Ardagna and J. Zhou (Eds.): WISTP 2011, LNCS 6633, pp. 191–207, 2011.
© IFIP International Federation for Information Processing 2011

and data complexity of $2^{99.5}$, requiring 2^{77} memory and just 4 related keys. A similar approach was used to derive a related-key boomerang attack on AES-192 with data complexity 2^{123}, time complexity 2^{176}, and memory complexity 2^{152} in addition to 4 related keys. This is also the first known key-recovery attack on full AES-192. However, we need adaptive ciphertext decryption for the attack of [3] whereas only chosen plaintext encryption is needed for the attack of [4]. In our paper, we present a framework for practical resistance against Biryukov et al.'s related-key differential attacks from [3,4].

The structure of the AES-256 cipher is still very secure as the best non related-key attacks can work up to at most 8 of the 14 rounds [9]. The more devastating related key attacks [3,4] exploits the high linearity in the AES-256 key schedule. If we look only at a key schedule differential characteristic path, it is possible to find paths which involve only one active S-box. Thus a key point in securing AES against the latest related-key differential/boomerang attacks is to make the key schedule more nonlinear, so that any related-key differential path would involve more active S-boxes in the subkey differences[1].

1.1   Our Contribution

We design two new AES variants to protect against the related-key attacks of [3,4] by making the AES key schedule more nonlinear, while keeping the main AES cipher the same. Thus we retain the strong security of AES against non related-key attacks.

Construction 1: In Section 3, we consider the possibility of using an alternative AES key schedule by May et al. [11]. This key schedule was shown to have good statistical properties while achieving the strong property of round key irreversibility and resistance against previously known related-key attacks [1]. However, we show in Section 3.1 that there are pairs of equivalent keys that produce the same encryption functions. We propose an improvement of their key schedule in Section 3.2 that avoids this weakness. Based on our framework, we prove in Sections 3.3 and 3.4 that the improved May et al.'s key schedules for AES have practical resistance against related-key differential and boomerang attacks. This key schedule is also secure against related-cipher attacks and slide attacks, and has round key irreversibility.

Construction 2: However, our improved May et al.'s design uses three AES rounds to derive a subkey. This is too expensive for hardware implementation, which requires on-the-fly key schedule. In Section 4, we propose an on-the-fly key schedule design for AES-128, AES-192, and AES-256, where the time needed to derive each round key is no more than the computation of 1.25 (amortized) AES rounds. Furthermore, we prove that this new key schedule has practical resistance against related-key differential and boomerang attacks. This key schedule is also

---

[1] Our observations also correspond with those made by Kim et al. in Section 2.6 of [10] where it is mentioned that if the key schedule of the cipher is complex enough and does not have "good" differential properties, then the number of keys required for the attack becomes infeasibly large.

secure against related-cipher attacks and slide attacks, and has partial round key irreversibility.

2   Framework for Protection against Related Key Differential and Boomerang Attacks

2.1   Some Definitions and Notation

We first define some notation and concepts which form the basis of differential attacks.

Given a block cipher, the plaintext, secret key and ciphertext are denoted by P, K and C respectively. The encryption and decryption processes are denoted by $C = E_K(P)$ and $P = E_K^{-1}(C)$ respectively. We denote the input of the first round by P_0, and the output of the ith round by P_i, $i = 1, \ldots, NR$, where NR is the number of rounds. Similarly, we write K_i, $i = 0, \ldots, m$, for the $m + 1$ subkeys generated by the key schedule.

To launch a differential attack, one attempts to find a pair of differences in the plaintext and ciphertext that occur with high probability. This usually involves finding a sequence of round inputs and outputs that occur with high probability. We write ΔP and ΔC to denote a plaintext and ciphertext difference respectively, and ΔP_i to denote the difference in the round output of round i. A differential characteristic refers to a sequence of input differences to the rounds

$$(\Delta P_0 \longrightarrow \Delta P_1 \longrightarrow \cdots \longrightarrow \Delta P_{NR})$$

We abbreviate the above expression to $(\Delta P \xrightarrow{dc} \Delta C)$.

Similarly, to launch a related-key differential attack, one attempts to find a set of differences for (P, K, C) that hold with high probability. We shall see that this can be done by finding a sequence of differences in the key and subkeys generated by the key schedule, and the plaintext and round outputs generated by the main cipher, such that these differences occur with high probability.

We first consider a differential characteristic in the key schedule alone. We denote a difference in the key by ΔK, and differences in the subkeys ΔK_i, $i = 0, \ldots, m$. We note that the subkeys are not necessarily derived sequentially from each other, so the concept of a differential characteristic 'path' may not exist in this sense. We therefore write $(\Delta K \xrightarrow{dc} \Delta K_0, \ldots, \Delta K_m)$ for a differential characteristic in the key schedule.

Now we consider a differential characteristic in the key schedule and the main cipher. We write this as

$$(\Delta K \xrightarrow{dc} \Delta K_0, \ldots, \Delta K_m, \ \Delta P_0 \longrightarrow \cdots \longrightarrow \Delta P_{NR})$$

which we abbreviate to $(\Delta P, \Delta K \xrightarrow{dc} \Delta C)$. We also define:

$$p_k = Prob(\Delta K \xrightarrow{dc} \Delta K_0, \ldots, \Delta K_m),$$
$$p_{c|k} = Prob(\Delta P \xrightarrow{dc} \Delta C | \Delta K \xrightarrow{dc} \Delta K_0, \ldots, \Delta K_m).$$

It is easy to see that $Prob(\Delta P, \Delta K \xrightarrow{dc} \Delta C) = p_k \times p_{c|k}$ by Bayes' Theorem.

2.2   Protection against Related-Key Differential Attack of [4]

The attacker must run through p_k^{-1} key pairs on average in order to find one that satisfies the specified differential characteristic in the key schedule. For each key pair, the differential attack has complexity $O(p_{c|k}^{-1})$ and needs the same number of chosen plaintexts, so in total the complexity is $O((p_{c|k}p_k)^{-1})$. In the attack of [4], we have $p_k = 2^{-35}$, $p_{c|k} = 2^{-93}$, and with some computational overheads get an attack complexity of 2^{131}. The interested reader should refer to [4] for the details.

We can defend against this attack by having $p_k \times p_{c|k} < 2^{-NK}$ where NK is the key size of the cipher, for any related-key differential characteristic, i.e. no good distinguisher can be found that can be exploited in a related-key differential attack. The attack also cannot be applied if $p_{c|k} < 2^{-NB}$, where NB is the block size of the cipher, as there would be insufficient plaintexts to launch the attack.

2.3   Protection against Related-Key Boomerang Attack of [3]

The main idea behind the boomerang attack [2,15] is to use two short differential characteristics of high probabilities instead of one long differential characteristic of low probability. We assume that a block cipher $E : \{0,1\}^{NB} \times \{0,1\}^{NK} \rightarrow \{0,1\}^{NB}$ can be described as a composition of two sub-ciphers, i.e. $E = E_1 \circ E_0$. Here, NB and NK denote the block size and key size of the cipher respectively. Suppose we have a related-key differential characteristic $\alpha \rightarrow \beta$ of E_0 (excluding a couple of rounds at the beginning of the cipher) under a key difference ΔK_0 with probability p and another related-key differential characteristic $\gamma \rightarrow \delta$ for E_1 under key difference ΔK_1 with probability q. Here, $p = p_k \times p_{c|k}$ where p_k is the probability that the differential characteristic path in the key schedule corresponding to E_0 will be satisfied while $p_{c|k}$ is the probability that the differential characteristic path in the main cipher, $\alpha \rightarrow \beta$ in E_0, will be satisfied given that the key differential characteristic is satisfied. Likewise, $q = q_k \times q_{c|k}$ with similar definitions pertaining to E_1. The differential characteristic trails of E_0 and E_1 are called *upper* and *lower* trails respectively.

The related-key boomerang process involves four different unknown but related keys. The relation between the keys can be an arbitrary bijective function R chosen in advance by the attacker. A plaintext pair results in a *quartet* with probability p^2q^2 whereas for a random permutation, the probability of obtaining a good quartet is 2^{-NB}.

The attacker must run through $(p_kq_k)^{-2}$ quartets of related keys on average in order to find one that satisfies the specified differential characteristic in the key schedule. For each quartet, the attack has complexity $O((p_{c|k}q_{c|k})^{-2})$, so in total the complexity is $O(1/(p_{c|k}p_k))$. In the attack of [3], we have $(p_kq_k)^2 = 1$, $(p_{c|k}q_{c|k})^2 = 2^{-96}$, and with some computational overheads get an attack complexity of $2^{99.5}$. The interested reader should refer to [3] for the details.

We can defend against this attack by having $(p_kq_k)^2(p_{c|k}q_{c|k})^2 < 2^{-NK}$ where NK is the key size of the cipher, for all decompositions of the cipher into two smaller sub-ciphers and for all differential characteristics for these sub-ciphers. This would mean that there do not exist any boomerang quartets of high probability that can be exploited. The attack also cannot be applied if $(p_{c|k}q_{c|k})^{-2} < 2^{-NB}$, where NB is the block size of the cipher, as there would be insufficient plaintexts to launch the attack.

3   Security of Improved May et al.'s AES Key Schedule against Related-key Attack

To protect AES against related-key differential and boomerang attacks, one strategy is to use a strengthened key schedule with good differential properties. One possible candidate is an alternative key schedule for AES proposed by May et al. in [11] in 2002. At that time, there was already a 9-round related-key square attack [9] on AES-256 which exploited the slow diffusion of relatively few non-linear elements in the key schedule. May et al. wanted to design an efficient key schedule with more nonlinear components and better diffusion to defend against such attacks.

Their key schedule for AES-256 is shown below. Here, $NR=14$ is the number of rounds; a, b are 128-bit values derived from the Master Key $MK = MK_0|MK_1|\ldots|MK_{32}$, $a = a_0|a_1|\ldots|a_{15}$ (the MK_i and a_i are 8-bit values, and $|$ represents concatenation), r is the round number and K_r is the 128-bit round subkey for Round q. Each round subkey is the 128-bit output after the execution of three rounds of the cipher algorithm, using the master key (with the addition of different round constants) as both data and key input.

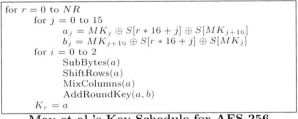

```
for r = 0 to NR
    for j = 0 to 15
        a_j = MK_j ⊕ S[r ∗ 16 + j] ⊕ S[MK_{j+16}]
        b_j = MK_{j+16} ⊕ S[r ∗ 16 + j] ⊕ S[MK_j]
    for i = 0 to 2
        SubBytes(a)
        ShiftRows(a)
        MixColumns(a)
        AddRoundKey(a, b)
    K_r = a
```

May et al.'s Key Schedule for AES-256

In [11], the authors conducted statistical tests to show that for their proposal, there is no bit leakage between round subkeys. Furthermore, each round key satisfies both the frequency and Strict Avalanche Criterion (SAC) tests, indicating good pseudorandomness properties such as bit confusion and diffusion. The authors concluded that previously published attacks that exploit the key schedule such as the standard related-key attacks [1] will not work on their proposed key schedule.

Moreover, the key schedule achieves the property of round key irreversibility, by which we mean that given any subset of the round keys, it is hard to derive the remaining round keys. This forces an adversary to attack all the round keys. This is in contrast to the AES key schedule, which is reversible - given any two round keys, one can derive all the other round keys. The obvious countermeasures for preventing related-key attacks on AES, such as increasing the number of rounds and hashing the key before expanding it, also produce key schedules which are also reversible.

3.1 Equivalent Keys in May et al.'s Key Schedule

Despite the good cryptographic properties of May et al.'s key schedule as mentioned in the previous section, we shall show that their key schedule has equivalent keys as shown in the following proposition.

Proposition 1. *In May et al.'s key schedule for AES-256, there are 2^{271} equivalent key pairs $\{(MK, MK') : MK \neq MK'\}$ such that $AES_{MK}(\cdot) = AES_{MK'}(\cdot)$, i.e. they produce the same encryption output.*

Proof. Consider the 4-byte tuple $(MK_i, MK'_i, MK_{i+16}, MK'_{i+16})$ for each index i. We look for those that satisfy the equations:

$$MK_i \oplus MK'_i = S[MK_{i+16}] \oplus S[MK'_{i+16}], \ \ S[MK_i] \oplus S[MK'_i] = MK_{i+16} \oplus MK'_{i+16}. \ \ (1)$$

By a computer simulation, there are 65644 tuples $(MK_i, MK'_i, MK_{i+16}, MK'_{i+16})$ that satisfy equation (1). In that case,

$$\Delta a_i = \Delta MK_i \oplus \Delta S[MK_{i+16}] = 0 \text{ and } \Delta b_i = \Delta MK_{i+16} \oplus \Delta S[MK_i] = 0$$

Thus for $i = 0, 1, 2, \ldots, 15$, if we let $(MK_i, MK'_i, MK_{i+16}, MK'_{i+16})$ satisfy equation (1) for $s \geq 1$ of the indices i and let $(MK_i, MK_{i+16}) = (MK'_i, MK'_{i+16})$ for the rest of the $16 - s$ indices, we will have $\Delta a = 0 = \Delta b$. From the definition of May et al.'s key schedule, this implies the subkeys derived from MK and MK' are the same and they will produce the same encryption output. The number of such equivalent key pairs are given by:

$$\sum_{s=1}^{16} \binom{16}{s} \times 65644^s \times (256^2)^{16-s} \approx 2^{272}.$$

When (MK, MK') is an equivalent key pair, (MK', MK) is also an equivalent key pair. Thus we divide the total number of equivalent key pairs by 2 to get 2^{271}. $\qquad\square$

3.2 An Improved May et al.'s Key Schedule

From Section 3.1, we have seen that the three AES rounds used to generate each round key in May et al.'s key schedule help to ensure that the round keys have good statistical properties and attain round key irreversibility. The problem is the initialization of a and b which allows an adversary to force a, b to have zero differential by choosing an appropriate pair of related secret keys.

Below, we propose an improved version of the May et al.'s key schedule. Basically, we simplify the initialization of a, b so that each byte of a and b only depends on one instead of two bytes of the secret key. This prevents an adversary from using the technique in Proposition 1 to force Δa and Δb to be zero. We also make use of key-length-dependent counters *keylen* to defend against the related-cipher attack [16], which was first applied to the alternative AES key schedule proposed by May et al. In the algorithm shown, *keylen* $- 1$ refers to the key length of the cipher (minus 1) encoded as a byte. A more detailed explanation of the related-cipher attack can be found in [16].

This key schedule, as with the original key schedule by May et al., has the property of round key irreversibility.

Next, we shall show in the following section that the improved May et al.'s key schedule can protect AES against related-key differential and boomerang attacks.

```
for r = 0 to NR
    for j = 0 to 15
        a_j = S[MK_j] ⊕ S[r * 16 + j] ⊕ (keylen − 1)
        b_j = S[MK_{j+16}] ⊕ S[r * 16 + j] ⊕ (keylen − 1)
    for i = 0 to 2
        SubBytes(a)
        ShiftRows(a)
        MixColumns(a)
        AddRoundKey(a, b)
    K_r = a
```

Improved May et al.'s Key Schedule AES-256

3.3 Improved May et al.'s Key Schedule is Secure against Related-Key Differential Attack

Our aim in this section is to study the security of our improved May et al.'s key schedule against the related-key differential attack which was recently used by Biryukov et al. [4,3,5] to attack full-round AES-256.

We have the following technical lemma which will be used to prove the main results of this section later on.

Lemma 1. *For any round subkey generation using the key schedule proposal described above, if we have a pair of master keys with nonzero difference, then the differential characteristic path either has at least four active S-boxes, or it has at least three active S-boxes and an additional four active S-boxes resulting from the generation of a and b.*

The proof of this lemma can be found in Appendix A of this paper. Based on the above result, we may deduce the following corollary.

Corollary 1. *If we have a pair of master keys with nonzero difference, then our improved May et al.'s key schedule for AES-256 has at least 43 active S-boxes involved in the generation of 13 subkeys.*

Proof. By Lemma 1, the differential characteristic path for each subkey generation has at least three active S-boxes, and if there exists a subkey whose differential characteristic path produces only three active S-boxes occurs, then there will be four additional S-boxes involved in generating a and b. This would give at least $13 \times 3 + 4 = 43$ S-boxes in total. On the other hand, if the differential characteristic path for each subkeys produces at least four active S-boxes, there are at least $13 \times 4 > 43$ S-boxes in total. $\square$

In the attacks on AES, we always consider an $(NR-2)$-round attack involving $NR-1$ subkeys, in keeping with [4] where the attack is based on an $(NR-2)$-round related-key differential characteristic.

Theorem 1. *AES-256 using our improved May et al.'s key schedule is resistant to related-key differential attack.*

Proof. We apply Corollary 1 for AES-256 assuming an $NR-2$ round attack, i.e. a 12-round attack which involves 13 subkeys. Since each active S-box has probability at most 2^{-6}, this gives a probability of at most $p_k \times p_{c|k} = (2^{-6})^{43} \times p_{c|k} = 2^{-258} \times p_{c|k} < 2^{-256}$. Therefore, we may conclude that AES-256 with the strengthened key schedule is indeed resistant to related-key differential attacks.   □

May et al. also proposed alternative key schedules for AES-128 and AES-192. The key schedules proposed by May et al. in [11] for AES-128 and AES-192 are largely the same as that for AES-256, except that a and b are generated in slightly different ways: for $r = 0$ to NR, $j = 0$ to 15.

(1) For AES-128: $a_j = b_j = MK_j \oplus S[r * 16 + j]$.
(2) For AES-192: $a_j = MK_j \oplus S[r * 16 + j] \oplus S[MK_{j+8}]; b_j = MK_{j+8} \oplus S[r * 16 + j] \oplus S[MK_j]$.

It is easy to see that equivalent keys similar to those in Proposition 1 exist for May et al.'s key schedule for AES-192. Thus we propose a similar improvement to May et al.'s key schedule for AES-192 below. As before, we also tweaked the key schedules a bit by introducing key-length-dependent counters *keylen* for protection against the related-cipher attack [16].

(1) Improvement for AES-128: $a_j, b_j = MK_j \oplus S[r * 16 + j] \oplus (keylen - 1)$.
(2) Improvement for AES-192: $a_j = MK_j \oplus S[r * 16 + j] \oplus (keylen - 1); b_j = MK_{j+8} \oplus S[r * 16 + j] \oplus (keylen - 1)$.

Based on the above description of the schedules for AES-128 and AES-192, it is easy to deduce the following corollary from the proof of Lemma 1.

Corollary 2. *If we have a pair of master keys with nonzero difference in our proposed improvement of the key schedule of [11] for AES-128 and AES-192, then there are at least 3 active S-boxes involved in the generation of each subkey.*

Corollary 2 allows us to prove Theorem 2.

Theorem 2. *AES-128 and AES-192 using the key schedule of [11] for AES-128 and our improvement for AES-192 are also resistant to related-key differential attack.*

Proof. In our improved key schedule for AES-128 and AES-192, we see that if a pair of master keys has non-zero difference, then one of Δa or Δb is non-zero. Thus we can use the fact that every differential characteristic path of a round subkey generation has at least 3 active S-boxes (excluding the generation of a and b) from the proof of Lemma 1.

For AES-128, an 8-round attack involves 9 subkeys. Assuming that each active S-box has probability 2^{-6}, this gives a probability of at least $p_k \times p_{c|k} = (2^{-6})^{(9 \times 3)} \times p_{c|k} = 2^{-162} \times p_{c|k} < 2^{-128}$.

Similarly for AES-192, a 10-round attack involves 11 subkeys. The differential characteristic probability is at least $p_k \times p_{c|k} = (2^{-6})^{(11 \times 3)} \times p_{c|k} = 2^{-198} \times p_{c|k} < 2^{-192}$.

Therefore, AES-128 and AES-192 with the strengthened key schedule are resistant to differential related-key attacks. $\qquad\square$

Remark 1. Our proofs show that the original May et al.'s key schedule is also resistant against related-key differential attack. This is because if a pair of keys is an equivalent weak key pair, then they produce the same roundkeys and we have normal differential attack instead of related-key differential attack. If they are not an equivalent key pair, then Δa or Δb is non-zero and we can apply[2] Lemma 1 to prove Theorem 1 for May et al.'s key schedule.

3.4 Improved May et al.'s Key Schedule is Secure against Related-Key Boomerang Attack

We consider an arbitrary decomposition of AES, with our improved key schedule, into two smaller sub-ciphers. The generation of the subkeys by the key schedule will be split between the two sub-ciphers. Since the subkeys are independently generated, $p_k q_k$ is simply the product of the probabilities that the differential characteristics hold for the generation of each subkey.

We note that it may be possible to bypass one subkey for the round at which the cipher is split into two using a boomerang switch. Furthermore, we assume that two rounds at the start can be ignored by not specifying the differences in the differential trail (as in [3], where one round at the start is ignored). Hence, for AES-128, we consider the generation of 7 subkeys; for AES-192, 9; and for AES-256, 11.

By Lemma 1 and Corollary 2, we see that there are at least 3 active S-boxes involved in the generation of each subkey for all three versions of AES. For t subkeys, the product of the probabilities that the differential characteristics hold for each subkey is $(2^{-6})^{3t}$. Since $p_k q_k \leq 2^{-18t}$, $(p_k q_k)^2 < 2^{-NK}$ holds if $(2^{-18t})^2 < 2^{-NK}$.

If $t \geq 4$, we have $(p_k q_k)^2 < 2^{-128}$; if $t \geq 6$, we have $(p_k q_k)^2 < 2^{-192}$; and if $t \geq 8$, we have $(p_k q_k)^2 < 2^{-256}$. For AES-128, $t = 7$; for AES-192, $t = 9$; and for AES-256, $t = 11$. Hence, for AES with the strengthened key schedule, for any decomposition into two sub-ciphers, there does not exist a boomerang quartet of high probability which can be exploited. Therefore, we have proved that AES-128, AES-192 and AES-256 using the strengthened key schedule of [11] are resistant to related-key boomerang attack.

By a reasoning similar to Remark 1, the original May et al.'s key schedule is also resistant against related-key boomerang attack.

---

[2] We can apply Lemma 1 because both the improved and original May et al.'s key schedule uses the same 3-round AES structure to generate each roundkey.

4 A New On-the-fly Key Schedule for AES Secure against Related-Key Differential and Boomerang Attacks

We present here a new key schedule for AES that offers several advantages over both the original key schedule (security against related-key differential and boomerang attacks) and that proposed by May et al. [11] (better efficiency).

The key schedule shown below generates fifteen 128-bit round keys $K_i, 0 \leq i \leq NR = 14$ from a 256-bit master key or thirteen 128-bit round keys $K_i, 0 \leq i \leq NR = 12$ from a 192-bit master key. Round key K_i is used in the ith round of encryption. For a 256-bit master key, one subkey SK_0 is not converted into a usable round key, and for a 192-bit master key, three subkeys $SK_{0..2}$ are not converted into usable round keys.

Here, C_j denote 128-bit strings which are initialized by equating them to integers j encoded as 128-bit strings. $keylen - 1$ refers to the key length of the cipher (minus 1) also encoded as a 128-bit string. $1R\_AES(x)$ refers to one round of unkeyed AES with the plaintext x. The $AddRoundKey$ operation in the AES round can be omitted or provided with a null key.

These proposed key schedules for AES-192 and AES-256 are partially irreversible, by which we mean that, given two round keys, it is hard to derive the rest of the round keys. However, given certain combinations of three or more round keys, it may be possible to derive the rest of the round keys. For example, if we have SK_i, SK_{i+1} for $i = 1$ or 2, as well as SK_4, then we can obtain $K1$ from SK_i, SK_{i+1}, and then we either have, or can compute SK_3, and then use SK_4 to get $K2$. In this sense, this proposed key schedule is weaker than the original and improved key schedules by May et al. Nonetheless, partial irreversibility is a desirable property which is lacking in the original AES-192 and AES-256 key schedules.

```
if AES-192
        f = 1
if AES-256
        f = 2

for j = 0 to 15
        K1_j = MK_j
        K2_j = MK_{j+(8*f)}

for j = 0 to 15
        C_j = j
C_0 = C_0 ⊕ K1 ⊕ (keylen − 1)
C_4 = C_4 ⊕ K2
C_8 = C_8 ⊕ K1
C_12 = C_12 ⊕ K2

SK_{−1} = K1, I_{−1} = 0
for i = 0 to 15
        I_i = 1R_AES(I_{i−1} ⊕ C_i)
        SK_i = I_i ⊕ SK_{i−1}
        if AES-192
                K_{i−3} = SK_i
        if AES-256
                K_{i−1} = SK_i
```

New key schedule proposal for 192-bit and 256-bit keys

The following key schedule shown generates eleven 128-bit round keys $K_i, 0 \le i \le NR = 10$ from a 128-bit master key. One subkey SK_0 is not converted into a usable round key.

```
for j = 0 to 11
      C_j = j
C_0 = C_0 ⊕ MK ⊕ (keylen − 1)
C_4 = C_4 ⊕ MK
C_8 = C_8 ⊕ MK

SK_{-1} = MK, I_{-1} = 0
for i = 0 to 11
      I_i = 1R_AES(I_{i-1} ⊕ C_i)
      SK_i = I_i ⊕ SK_{i-1}
      K_{i-1} = SK_i
```

New key schedule proposal for 128-bit keys

Our proposed key schedule for AES-128 is also partially irreversible in that at least two round keys are needed to derive the rest of the round keys, and only certain combinations of keys can work. In contrast, the original AES-128 key schedule requires only one round key to derive all the other round keys.

Theorem 3. *AES-128, AES-192 and AES-256 with the key schedules proposed in this section are resistant against related-key differential and boomerang attacks.*

Proof. In this proof, we use the fact that the differential characteristic probability of four consecutive AES rounds is bounded by 2^{-150} [8, page 33]. This result holds only when the input differential is non-zero and encryption is under a fixed key, i.e. the subkey differentials are zero.

For an attacker to control the round key differences ΔK_i to launch a related-key attack, he would need to control the output differential ΔI_i of the key schedule internal state. Thus we need to prove that the differential probability of this internal state is low enough to prevent related-key differential and boomerang attacks. Since we are considering related key differential attack, we assume $\Delta MK \ne 0$.

Key schedule for AES-128: $\Delta MK \ne 0$ implies the input differential to the first four AES rounds of the internal state is non-zero. Therefore the differential characteristic probability of the key schedule internal state I_i is bounded by 2^{-150}.

Key schedule for AES-192, AES-256: $\Delta MK \ne 0$ implies $\Delta(K1, K2) \ne 0$. Thus, we consider the three cases $\Delta K1 \ne 0, \Delta K2 = 0$; $\Delta K1 = 0, \Delta K2 \ne 0$ and $\Delta K1 \ne 0, \Delta K2 \ne 0$.

When $\Delta K1 \ne 0, \Delta K2 = 0$, the first round corresponding to internal state I_0 will have a non-zero differential input $\Delta K1$. Rounds 2 to 8 corresponding to I_1 to I_7 will have zero input key differences. Thus the differential characteristic probability of these eight rounds, and consequently, of the entire key schedule internal state I_i is at most $(2^{-150})^2 = 2^{-300}$.

When $\Delta K1 = 0$, $\Delta K2 \neq 0$, the first four rounds corresponding to I_0 to I_3 will have zero differential characteristic probability since there is a zero input difference and no input key differences for all four rounds. The fifth round corresponding to I_4 will have a non-zero differential input $\Delta K2$. Following this, rounds 6 to 12 corresponding to internal state I_5 to I_{11} will have zero input key differences. Thus the differential characteristic probability of these eight rounds, and consequently, of the entire key schedule internal state I_i is at most $(2^{-150})^2 = 2^{-300}$.

When $\Delta K1 \neq 0$, $\Delta K2 \neq 0$, the first round corresponding to internal state I_0 will have a non-zero differential input $\Delta K1$ while rounds 2 to 4 corresponding to I_1 to I_3 will have zero input key differences. This gives a differential characteristic probability of at most 2^{-150} for the first four rounds. The differential output after these four rounds is ΔI_3. If $\Delta I_3 \oplus \Delta K2 \neq 0$, then we have a non-zero differential input to the next four AES rounds corresponding to I_4 to I_7. Since rounds 6 to 8 corresponding to internal states I_5 to I_8 have zero key differences, this gives a differential characteristic probability of at most 2^{-150} for rounds 5 to 8. If $\Delta I_3 \oplus \Delta K2 = 0$, then there is no differential characteristic probability associated with rounds 5 to 8. But $\Delta K1$ will be a non-zero differential input to the next four AES rounds while rounds 10 to 12 corresponding to internal states I_8 to I_{11} have zero input key differences. This gives a differential characteristic probability of at most 2^{-150} for rounds 9 to 12. In both cases, the differential characteristic probability of the key schedule internal state I_i is at most $(2^{-150})^2 = 2^{-300}$.

For protection against related-key boomerang attack, when we split the cipher into two sub-ciphers E_0, E_1, the corresponding internal state I_i of the key schedule for one of the sub-cipher will contain 4 unkeyed AES rounds with a non-zero input differential. This means one of p_k or q_k is bounded by 2^{-150} and that $(p_k q_k)^2 \leq 2^{-300}$. Thus our cipher is secure against related-key boomerang attack.   □

For protection against other attacks on the key schedule, the use of round counters defeats slide attacks [6,7]. As in the case for the improved May et al.'s key schedule, the use of key-length-dependant counters *keylen* defeats the related-cipher attack [16].

The key schedule offers better efficiency than the proposal by May et al. which invokes three AES rounds and a few S-box lookups per round key. Our key schedule proposal invokes at most an (amortized) 1.25 AES rounds per round key, making it more suitable for hardware implementation. If two AES round functions are implemented in parallel, it is three times as fast as the May et al. key schedule to encrypt; or if a single AES round function is implemented, it is twice as fast.

4.1   Hardware Implementation

Usually hardware implementations of encryption algorithms are optimized for high throughput, i.e. first for speed and then for area. If we look on these typically round-based architectures, our proposed new AES key schedule introduces only minor timing overheads compared to the original AES key schedule. Then for the encryption of one block with a 128-bit key 11 clock cycles are required (compared to 10 clock cycles for standard AES) and for 192-bit and 256-bit keys we need 15 clock cycles compared to 12 and 14 clock cycles, respectively. Note that for AES-256 -which suffers most from recent related key attacks and needs to be fixed most urgently- this is an overhead of only 7%.

At the same time, the similarity of the key schedule and the data path allows a better time-area trade-off and thus more flexibility for implementation. A designer can choose to implement both data paths (as described above, variant A) or to share resources between them (variant B). The latter variant B allows to save area at the cost of additional clock cycles (21 for AES-128, 25 for AES-192 and 29 for AES-256). The proposal by May *et al.* invokes three AES rounds and a few S-box lookups per round key. Therefore it cannot compute the round keys on-the-fly and will never achieve the same speed as the standard AES or our proposal, regardless of the hardware spent. Using a shared data path (variant B), our proposal is twice as fast as the proposal by May *et al.*, and using two separate data paths (variant A) it is three times faster.

Also the area overhead of our proposal is very moderate as the following estimations, which are based on the 180 nm *UMCL18G212D3* standard-cell library from UMC [14], indicate. In a round-based implementation, we need two 128-bit XOR gates to add MK and SK (600 GE) and a 4-bit XOR gate to add C_i (10 GE). Depending on the key length we need a 7-bit XOR gate (17 GE) or an 8-bit XOR gate (19 GE) and for AES-192 and AES-256 we also need a 128-bit MUX (342 GE). Finally a 128-bit AND gate (170 GE) is required to handle the proper addition of MK and the variables I and SK need to be stored in flip-flops (1536 GE). If the master key is never changed, it can be hardwired and requires no gates. Otherwise we have an additional storage overhead of 768 GE for AES-128, 1152 GE for AES-192, and 1536 GE for AES-256. For variant A an additional complete round of AES is required. Since the gate count for an AES round depends on a wide variety of design choices, an estimation of the total overhead for variant A is difficult. We therefore concentrate on variant B, which only needs an additional 128-bit AND gate (170 GE). For variant B our proposal introduces an overhead of 2505 GE with a hardwired MK and 3270 GE with a flexible MK for AES-128. For AES-192 it sums up to 2850-4000 GE and for AES-256 to 2850-4385 GE.

To put these overhead figures into perspective, please note that a typical throughput-optimized co-processor implementation of AES-128 requires tens of thousands of GE: Satoh *et al.* report such an implementation on a 0.11 μm technology with 54,000 GE [13], while the implementation of Pramstaller *et al.* on a 0.6 μm technology requires 85,000 GE [12].

Acknowledgements

We would like to thank the anonymous reviewers of our previous paper submission for their valuable comments.

References

1. Biham, E.: New Types of Cryptanalytic Attacks Using Related Keys. In: Helleseth, T. (ed.) EUROCRYPT 1993. LNCS, vol. 765, pp. 398–409. Springer, Heidelberg (1994)
2. Biham, E., Dunkelman, O., Keller, N.: Related-Key Boomerang and Rectangle Attacks. In: Cramer, R. (ed.) EUROCRYPT 2005. LNCS, vol. 3494, pp. 507–525. Springer, Heidelberg (2005)
3. Biryukov, A., Khovratovich, D.: Related-Key Cryptanalysis of the Full AES-192 and AES-256. In: Matsui, M. (ed.) ASIACRYPT 2009. LNCS, vol. 5912, pp. 1–18. Springer, Heidelberg (2009)
4. Biryukov, A., Khovratovich, D., Nikolić, I.: Distinguisher and Related-Key Attack on the Full AES-256. In: Halevi, S. (ed.) CRYPTO 2009. LNCS, vol. 5677, pp. 231–249. Springer, Heidelberg (2009)
5. Biryukov, A., Dunkelman, O., Keller, N., Khovratovich, D., Shamir, A.: Key Recovery Attacks of Practical Complexity on AES Variant with Up To 10 Rounds, IACR eprint server, 2009/374 (July 2009), http://eprint.iacr.org/2009/374
6. Biryukov, A., Wagner, D.: Slide attacks. In: Knudsen, L.R. (ed.) FSE 1999. LNCS, vol. 1636, pp. 245–259. Springer, Heidelberg (1999)
7. Biryukov, A., Wagner, D.: Advanced Slide Attacks. In: Preneel, B. (ed.) EURO-CRYPT 2000. LNCS, vol. 1807, pp. 589–606. Springer, Heidelberg (2000)
8. Daemen, J., Rijmen, V.: Rijndael. In: First Advanced Encryption Standard Conference (August 1998), http://csrc.nist.gov/encryption/aes/
9. Ferguson, N., Kelsey, J., Lucks, S., Schneier, B., Stay, M., Wagner, D., Whiting, D.: Improved Cryptanalysis of Rijndael. In: Schneier, B. (ed.) FSE 2000. LNCS, vol. 1978, pp. 213–230. Springer, Heidelberg (2001)
10. Kim, J., Hong, S., Preneel, B., Biham, E., Dunkelman, O., Keller, N.: Related-Key Boomerang and Rectangle Attacks, IACR eprint server, 2010/019 (January 2010), http://eprint.iacr.org/2010/019
11. May, L., Henricksen, M., Millan, W., Carter, G., Dawson, E.: Strengthening the Key Schedule of the AES. In: Batten, L.M., Seberry, J. (eds.) ACISP 2002. LNCS, vol. 2384, pp. 226–240. Springer, Heidelberg (2002)
12. Pramstaller, N., Mangard, S., Dominikus, S., Wolkerstorfer, J.: Efficient AES Implementations on ASICs and FPGAs. In: Dobbertin, H., Rijmen, V., Sowa, A. (eds.) AES 2005. LNCS, vol. 3373, pp. 98–112. Springer, Heidelberg (2005)
13. Satoh, A., Morioka, S., Munetoh, S.: A Compact Rijndael Hardware Architecture with S-Box Optimization. In: Boyd, C. (ed.) ASIACRYPT 2001. LNCS, vol. 2248, pp. 239–254. Springer, Heidelberg (2001)
14. Virtual Silicon Inc. 0.18 μm VIP Standard Cell Library Tape Out Ready, Part Number: UMCL18G212T3, Process: UMC Logic 0.18 μm Generic II Technology: 0.18μm (July 2004)
15. Wagner, D.: The Boomerang Attack. In: Knudsen, L.R. (ed.) FSE 1999. LNCS, vol. 1636, pp. 156–170. Springer, Heidelberg (1999)
16. Wu, H.: Related-Cipher Attacks. In: Deng, R.H., Qing, S., Bao, F., Zhou, J. (eds.) ICICS 2002. LNCS, vol. 2513, pp. 447–455. Springer, Heidelberg (2002)

A   Proof of Lemma 1

A.1   Notation

Referring to Figure 1 in Appendix B, for $i = 0, 1, 2$, let $\Delta a_0^{(i)}$, $\Delta a_1^{(i)}$, and $\Delta a_2^{(i)}$ be the input differences to the SubBytes, MixColumns, and AddRoundKey operations respectively in the ith round of the subkey generation. Also, let Δb be the difference in b at each round. Therefore, $\Delta a_0^{(0)}$ is the data input difference to the subkey generation function and Δb is the key input difference to each round of the subkey generation function, where $(\Delta a_0^{(0)})_j = \Delta a_j = \Delta S(MK_j)$ and $(\Delta b)_j = \Delta S(MK_{j+16})$. The output difference $\Delta a_0^{(3)}$ is the difference in the round subkey.

We make a few observations about these differences.

(1) After applying the SubBytes operation to the state, the positions of the active bytes are unchanged. The ShiftRows operation preserves the number of active bytes, so the input difference to the SubBytes operation $\Delta a_0^{(i)}$ and the output difference of the ShiftRows operation $\Delta a_1^{(i)}$ have the same number of active bytes.

(2) Furthermore, if $\Delta a_1^{(i)}$ has one active column, and it contains more than one active byte, ShiftRows^{-1} spreads them to different columns, so $\Delta a_0^{(i)}$ must have more than one active column, each containing one active byte.

(3) $\Delta a_2^{(i)} = \mathrm{MixColumns}(\Delta a_1^{(i)})$. The MixColumns function is maximal distance separable, so its branch number is 5. Thus t active bytes in one column of $\Delta a_1^{(i)}$ spread to at least $5 - t$ active bytes in the same column of $\Delta a_2^{(i)}$. In particular, one active byte in $\Delta a_0^{(i)}$ gives one active byte in $\Delta a_1^{(i)}$ which spreads to one column of at least four active bytes in $\Delta a_2^{(i)}$.

(4) The AddRoundKey operation gives $\Delta a_0^{(i+1)} = \Delta a_2^{(i)} \oplus \Delta b$.

A.2   Proof of Lemma 1

Proof. We denote n and m to be the number of nonzero bytes in Δa and Δb respectively, and we write k and l for the number of nonzero bytes in $\Delta a_0^{(1)}$ and $\Delta a_0^{(2)}$ respectively. Then the number of active S-boxes in the differential characteristic path is $n + k + l$. We also note that if $\Delta MK \neq 0$, then $\Delta(a, b) \neq (0, 0)$. We consider the various cases below.

(1) $n = 0$

We have $\Delta a = 0$, so $\Delta b \neq 0$ and $m \neq 0$. Since $\Delta a_0^{(1)} = \Delta b$, we must have $k = m$.

If $\Delta a_2^{(1)}$ has one active column, then it has at least $5 - m$ active bytes, and the active bytes of $\Delta a_0^{(1)} = \Delta b$ are all in different columns. Then $\Delta a_0^{(2)} = \Delta a_2^{(1)} \oplus \Delta b$ has at least $5 - m - 1$ active bytes, i.e. $l \geq 4 - m$. Then $n + k + l \geq 0 + m + 4 - m = 4$.

If $\Delta a_2^{(1)}$ has more than one active column, then, $\Delta a_2^{(1)}$ has at least $8 - m$ active bytes. If $m \geq 4$, we have $n + k + l \geq 4$. If $m \leq 3$, then $\Delta a_0^{(2)} = \Delta a_2^{(1)} \oplus \Delta b$ has at least $8 - 2m$ active bytes, i.e. $l \geq 8 - 2m$, which gives $n + k + l \geq 0 + m + 8 - 2m = 8 - m \geq 5$.

(2) $k = 0$

We have $\Delta b = \Delta a_2^{(0)}$, so $m \geq 5 - n$. We also have $\Delta a_0^{(2)} = \Delta b$, so $l = m$. Then $n + k + l \geq n + 0 + 5 - n = 5$.

(3) $n \geq 1, k \geq 1, l = 0$

From $l = 0$ we have $\Delta b = \Delta a_2^{(1)} = \text{MixColumns}\left(\Delta a_1^{(1)}\right)$.

If $k = 1$, $\Delta a_0^{(1)} = \Delta a_2^{(0)} \oplus \Delta b$ has one active byte. We have $\Delta a_0^{(0)} = \text{MixColumns}\left(\Delta a_1^{(0)}\right)$, and we can write $\Delta a_0^{(1)} = \text{MixColumns}(\alpha)$, where α has four active bytes. Equating the two expressions for Δb, we get $\Delta a_2^{(1)} = \Delta a_0^{(1)} \oplus \Delta a_2^{(0)}$, and by the linearity of MixColumns we get $\Delta a_1^{(0)} = \Delta a_1^{(1)} \oplus \alpha$. Then $\Delta a_1^{(0)}$ has at least three active bytes, as does $\Delta a_0^{(0)}$, and so $n \geq 3$, giving $n + k + l \geq 3 + 1 + 0 = 4$.

If $k = 2$, $\Delta b = \Delta a_2^{(1)}$ has either one or two columns active. If it has two columns active, then all eight bytes in the two columns are active, and we also know that $\Delta a_0^{(1)}$ has two active bytes. If $\Delta a_0^{(1)}$ has one column active, then at least three of the bytes in that column active, and the two bytes of $\Delta a_0^{(1)}$ must be in different columns. Either way, $\Delta a_2^{(0)} = \Delta a_0^{(1)} \oplus \Delta b$ has at least two active columns, so we must have $n \geq 2$. Then $n+k+l \geq 2+2+0 = 4$. If $k \geq 3$, then because $n \geq 1$, we have $n + k + l \geq 4$.

(4) $n \geq 1, k \geq 1, l \geq 1$

We either have $n = k = l = 1$, or $n + k + l \geq 4$. Assume $n = k = l = 1$. Then $n + k + l = 3$, and since $\Delta a_2^{(0)}$ has four active bytes and $\Delta a_0^{(1)}$ has one active byte, $\Delta b = \Delta a_2^{(0)} \oplus \Delta a_0^{(1)}$ has at least three active bytes, i.e. $m \geq 3$. Since $n + m \geq 4$, we have at least four active S-boxes from the generation of a and b. $\qquad \square$

B   Figures

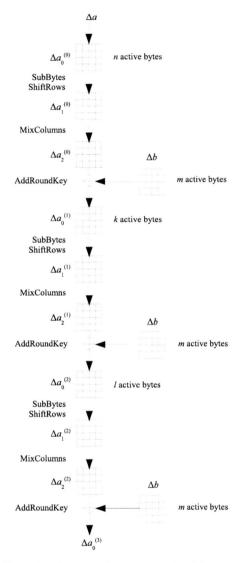

Fig. 1. Flow of differences for one round subkey generation

Leakage Squeezing Countermeasure against High-Order Attacks

Houssem Maghrebi, Sylvain Guilley, and Jean-Luc Danger

TELECOM-ParisTech, Crypto Group,
37/39 rue Dareau, 75 634 PARIS Cedex 13, France

Abstract. In the recent years, side channel attacks have been widely investigated. In particular, second order attacks (2O-attacks) have been improved and successfully applied to break many masked implementations. In this context we propose a new concept to hinder attacks of all order: instead of injecting more entropy, we make the most of a single-mask entropy. With specially crafted bijections instantiated on the mask path, we manage to reduce the inter-class variance (method we call "leakage squeezing") so that the leakage distributions become almost independent from the processed data. We present two options for this countermeasure. The first one is based on a recoded memory with a size squared w.r.t. the unprotected requirement, whilst the second one is an enhancement alleviating the requirement for a large memory. We theoretically prove the robustness of those implementations and practically evaluate their security improvements. This is attested by a robustness evaluation based on an information theoretic framework and by a 2O-DPA, an EPA and a multi-variate mutual information analysis (MMIA) attack metric. As opposed to software-oriented 3O-DPA-proof countermeasures that seriously impact the performances, our is hardware-oriented and keeps a complexity similar to that of a standard 2O-attack countermeasure with an almost untouched throughput, which is a predominant feature in computing-intensive applications.

Keywords: Higher-Order Differential Power Analysis, Variance-based Power Attack (VPA), Multi-variate Mutual Information Analysis (MMIA), Masking Countermeasure, Leakage Squeezing, FPGA.

1 Introduction

During the last ten years, a lot of effort has been dedicated towards the research about side-channel attacks [1, 10] and the development of corresponding countermeasures. In particular, there have been many endeavors to develop effective countermeasures against differential power analysis (DPA) [11] attacks.

Amongst the two major countermeasures against DPA, hiding and masking, the latter is certainly the least complex to implement when applied at the algorithmic level. The idea of masking the intermediate values inside a cryptographic algorithm has been suggested in several papers [2, 4, 12] as a possible countermeasure to power analysis attacks. Masking ensures that every single variable

C.A. Ardagna and J. Zhou (Eds.): WISTP 2011, LNCS 6633, pp. 208–223, 2011.

is masked with at least one random value so that a classical (first order) DPA attack cannot be successfully carried out anymore. However other attacks, such as the Higher Order DPA attacks [19, 20, 24], exist that can defeat masking.

In fact, masking can be defeated if the attacker knows how to combine the leakages corresponding to the masked data and its mask. This is known as second-order, or more generally higher-order, power analysis (abridged 2O-DPA and HO-DPA) and was originally suggested by Thomas S. Messerges in [19]. Investigating 2O-DPA, however, is of major importance for practitioners as it remains a good alternative that is powerful enough to break real-life, DPA-protected security products.

The attacker is allowed to profile the leakage in order to exhibit a relationship between the statistical distribution of the leakage and the value of a sensitive variable. Once this relationship is determined, the likelihood of key guesses is estimated given the distribution of the leakage. Such attacks are based on the same principle as the template attacks introduced by Suresh Chari *et al.* in [5]. These attacks have been successfully applied by Éric Peeters *et al.* in [20] to break some masked implementations more efficiently than any combining 2O-DPA. Moreover, Houssem Maghrebi *et al.* in [14] proposed a 2O-DPA based on variance analysis, called Variance Power Analysis (VPA), which is powerful enough to practically break a masked DES implemented in an FPGA. More recently, a generic multi-variate attack called MMIA has been introduced by Benedikt Gierlichs *et al.* [8] to attack high-order countermeasures. Therefore, there is a need for countermeasures thwarting 2O-DPA in particular and HO-DPA in general. We describe in the present paper a methodology to squeeze the leakage distributions so that any partitioning becomes almost indistinguishable.

The paper is organized as follows. Section 2 presents the state-of-the-art of first order masking and describes its weaknesses against 2O-DPA. The description of the concept of leakage squeezing is provided in section 3. The section 4 presents two variants of implementations and includes the experimental results about the complexity and robustness evaluation. Finally, section 5 concludes the paper and opens some perspectives.

2   State of the Art

2.1   First Order Masking Overview

Let us consider the masked DES studied at UCL [23], whose principle is illustrated in Fig. 1. This algorithmic masking associates a mask ML, MR to the plaintext L, R.

At each round $i \in [1 : 16]$ an intermediate mask ML_i, MR_i is calculated in parallel with the intermediate cipher word L_i, R_i. If we let apart the expansion E and the permutation P, the DES round function f is implemented in a masked way by using a set of functions S and a set of functions S':

$$\begin{cases} \text{masked data: } S(x_m \oplus k) = S(x \oplus m \oplus k) = S(x \oplus k) \oplus m', \\ \text{mask} \qquad\quad m' = S'(x_m \oplus k, m) = S'(x \oplus m \oplus k, m). \end{cases} \tag{1}$$

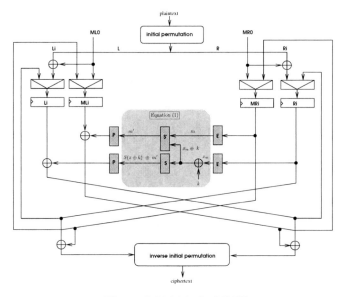

Fig. 1. ROM Masked DES

The variable m' is a new mask reusable for the next round. The set of functions S contains the traditional S-boxes applied on masked intermediate words. The size of each S is 64 words of 4 bits when implemented with a ROM. S' is a new table which has a much greater ROM size of $4K$ words of 4 bits, as there are two input words of 6 bits.

The two operations of Eq. (1) can be executed sequentially, as in software. In hardware, they can be executed simultaneously. We call it "zero-offset" masking, and it will be our case of study in the rest of this article.

2.2   Vulnerability of the Masking against 1O-Attacks

It has been reported in [17] that first order DPA could be conducted on masked circuits. As investigated in [18], it happens that the leakage does not come from the registers, but from the combinational parts of the design. This logic is susceptible to produce glitches, whose appearance can be correlated with unmasked data during the internal demasking of the variables.

In this article, we reduce the number of glitches by confining the sensitive combinational logic in ROMs. The same approach has already been suggested in other papers, such as [9, §IV.1] Although this is not formally a guarantee that sensitive glitches disappear, we benefit all the same from the low-power design of the memory blocks that suppresses most of the non-functional activity.

For the proposed countermeasure to be evaluated clearly, we focus the rest of the article on the protection of registers: we assume a toggle count leakage model (*aka* Hamming distance model), and we consider only attacks targeting this model.

2.3   Vulnerability of the Masking against 2O-Attacks

Implementations were studied to thwart attacks of high order, as that of Mehdi-Laurent Akkar [3] which uses constant masks. However to obtain an important robustness the price to be paid is a strong increase of the complexity. As illustration, it has been demonstrated by Jiqiang Lv in [13] that the DES algorithm requires at least three different masks and six additional S-boxes for every S-box to be resistant against high order attacks using this method. Another method, such as that used by François-Xavier Standaert *et al.* [23], consists in recomputing a new mask in every iteration at the same time as S-box, as Fig. 1 shows for the DES algorithm. The masked variable $x \oplus m$ of the register R is associated in every round with a new mask m stemming from the register M. So at the end of a round the variable $x \oplus m$ is transformed in $S'(x) \oplus m$ and the new mask m' which is calculated according to m and $x \oplus m$ by means of new S-box S'. This method offers a good compromise of complexity because it associates only a new S-box S' with every existing S-box S.

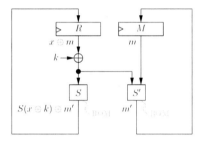

Fig. 2. Masked DES using two paths, implemented with ROM

This implementation remains subject to the 2O-DPA of Éric Peeters [20]. The figure 2 represents the S-box implementation S' in ROM. For reasons of simplicity the figure disregards the expansion and permutation functions appropriate for the DES algorithm. The so-called "zero-offset" HO-DPA attack of Éric Peeters [20] concerns variables $x \oplus m$ and m which are stored in R and M registers. The principle consists in studying the distributions of the activity at the register outputs for various values of x. In CMOS logic, a model of activity, noted A, can be the Hamming distance, noted HD, between two consecutive words:

$$A(x \oplus m, m) \doteq HD(x \oplus m, S(x \oplus k) \oplus m') + HD(m, m')$$
$$= HW(x \oplus S(x \oplus k) \oplus m \oplus m') + HW(m \oplus m')$$
$$= HW(\Delta(x) \oplus \Delta(m)) + HW(\Delta(m)),$$

where HW corresponds to the Hamming Weight and Δ is the difference between two consecutive values of a register output:

$$\Delta(x) \doteq x \oplus S(x \oplus k) \text{ and } \Delta(m) \doteq m \oplus m'. \tag{2}$$

If x and m fit on a single bit, the corresponding activity is $2 \cdot HW(\Delta(m))$ if $HW(\overline{\Delta(x)}) = 0$, whereas if $HW(\Delta(x)) = 1$, the corresponding activity is $HW(\overline{\Delta(m)}) + HW(\Delta(m))$ and is thus constantly equal to 1. The knowledge of the consumption distributions for every $HW(\Delta(x))$ values allows to build the HO-DPA attack by observing the consumption distributions and by comparing them with the predicted activity for a key hypothesis included in x.

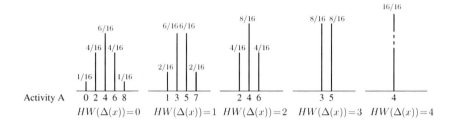

Fig. 3. Ideal (*i.e.* noise-free) probability density functions (pdf) corresponding to the five possible values of $HW(\Delta(x))$ without 2O-DPA protection [14]

Considering 4-bit registers, there are five possible distributions depending on the $HW(\Delta(x))$ values. They are shown in Fig. 3. It appears a clear difference between the five distributions, which could be exploited by a HO-DPA attack.

In [20], Éric Peeters proposed an improved higher-order technique to bypass the masking countermeasure. It is based on the efficient use of the statistical distributions of the power consumption described in figure 3 and it consists in computing the maximum likelihood of key guesses. Another alternative is to take advantage of the fact that the distributions showed in figure 3 all have the same mean value and only differ in their variances. This fact allows to understand the origin of previous attacks, as the one in [14], so-called Variance-based Power Attack where it is proposed to compute the difference of variance between the five possible distributions depending on the secret state of the implementation $HW(\Delta(x))$ values. This attack is quite efficient on "zero-offset" implementation and requires a reasonable number of traces (200K) [14]. Moreover, in [15] a novel approach to information-theoretic HO attacks, called the Entropy-based Power Analysis (EPA) was introduced using a weighted sum of conditional entropies as a distinguisher. It is designed to ease the distinguisability between hypotheses on candidate keys by computing the difference of conditional entropies between the distributions. Moreover, a novel approach, Multivariate Mutual Information Analysis MMIA, was proposed in [8]. This attack works in software masking but has never been applied on zero-offset implementations.

Therefore, there is a need for countermeasures thwarting 2O-DPA in particular and HO-DPA in general, by balancing the leakage distributions described in figure 3 so that any partitioning becomes almost indistinguishable whatever the secret state $HW(\Delta(x))$.

3   Proposed Masking Method for "Leakage Squeezing"

Indeed, we implement the S-boxes in (synchronous) ROMs of FPGA, which are much less if not totally immune to spurious glitching activity. We have checked that with a standard masking scheme, 2O-DPA succeeds but not 1O-DPA [14]. Also, unlike other initiatives, we do not attempt to add extra masks to increment the order n of resistance against n^{th}-order DPA; our philosophy has been to stick with one sole mask, but to adapt the masking scheme and the leakage function. This approach is deliberately pragmatic and tightly linked to a specific leakage model, namely the "transition count" model, which has been experimentally verified for registers in FPGAs and ASICs. Such a methodology is of high practical interest for practitioners, because some theoretically backed countermeasures have been shown to present vulnerabilities and because most of them are almost impossible to implement in throughput-driven circuits due to excessive overhead.

3.1   Masking Principle

The "leakage squeezing" approach is not a countermeasure dedicated only to fight 2O-Attacks (for instance by making the distribution second order indiscernible, but by opening the door to an attack of still higher order). Instead, it consists in making the overall leakage indiscernible in order to reduce the information leakage provided by the countermeasure, thereby anticipating any adversarial strategy. The principle is somehow similar to static power balancing countermeasures (information hiding, with dual-rail for instance [16, Chp. 7]): this methodology is also attack-agnostic.

Following this philosophy, we do not concentrate on a particular characteristic of the squeezed leakages (such as the nth momentum) but instead consider a global metric.

The principle consists mainly in making the activity of the register storing the mask m independent from the activity of the register containing the masked variable $x \oplus m$. A second action is to use ROMs for the implementations in order to avoid or at least strongly reduce the glitching activity. The first point is that if the variable x does not influence the consumption distributions for the variable and the mask register, we obtain similar (and ideally identical) distributions for every $HW(\Delta(x))$ values, and as a result it is not possible any more to mount a successful 2O-DPA as that of Peeters [20] or the VPA attack [14].

The similarity between the five consumption distributions can be made by modifying the structure of the mask path without touching the path of the masked variable.

A simple approach consists in modifying the mask m by using a bijective transformation B before storing $B(m)$ in the mask register M. It is shown in Fig. 4. Indeed, the presence of $\Delta(m)$ twice in the leakage function, (Eqn. (2)), tends to reduce the effect of the masking countermeasure as the two terms compensate partially so that there remains a residual dependency in $HW(\Delta(x))$. To decorrelate those two terms, we need a Boolean function that implements

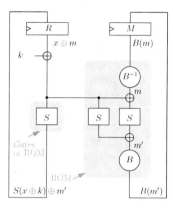

Fig. 4. Mask path with bijections for "Leakage squeezing"

good confusion, namely an S-box B. The activity of the variables $x \oplus m$ and $B(m)$ should be ideally decorrelated. This activity of the registers R and M is expressed by:

$$
\begin{aligned}
A_B &= HW(x \oplus S(x \oplus k) \oplus m \oplus m') + HW(B(m) \oplus B(m')) \\
&= HW[\Delta(x) \oplus \Delta(m)] + HW[\Delta B(m)]\,.
\end{aligned} \tag{3}
$$

With the bijection, the leakage (Eqn. (3)) is squeezed because $\Delta(m)$ and $\Delta(B(m))$ do not cancel as easily as previously.

The bijection and its inverse can be implemented as internal encodings in a table. The figure 4 describes a hardware architecture, where the registers R and M are protected against Hamming distance attack via a squeezing of their leakage. The rest of the schematic is combinational logic : either gates or memory blocks.

By choosing the appropriate bijection B we can obtain very close distributions which should not allow the adversary to take advantage of the residual mismatches.

3.2   Formal Security Assessment and Motivation for Some Bijections

In order to evaluate the information revealed by the squeezing countermeasure, we follow the information theoretic approach suggested in [22]. Namely we compute the mutual information between the sensitive variable k and the leakage function A_B of Eqn. (3).

In our experiments, we will consequently assume that the leakage is affected by some Gaussian noise. Thus, the physical observations are represented by a variable : $O = A_B + \mathcal{N}(0, \sigma^2)$.

For comparison purposes, we compute the mutual information value ($I(k; O)$) as proposed in [22] for several bijection functions. The lower the mutual information, the better the countermeasure.

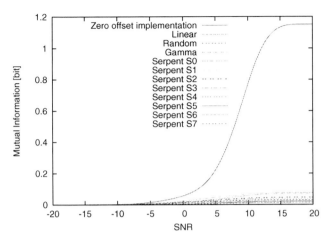

Fig. 5. Mutual information for some bijections

The mutual information is represented in figure 5 for the different bijections, in function of the signal-to-noise ratio ($SNR = 10 \cdot \log_{10} \frac{\epsilon^2}{\sigma^2}$), where ϵ and σ respectively denote the standard deviation of the signal and the noise emanated from the implementation.

These results demonstrate the information leakage reduction implied by the use of bijections functions. The linear function already decreases significantly the mutual information. Then, the non-linear functions still achieve a better improvement. It appears that Serpent S-boxes are leaking less than the randomly generated bijection or than the Gamma function of Noekeon. This justifies the use of the S-boxes crafted for strong symmetric algorithms.

This first analysis allows us to observe that the gain is high when the leakage squeezing is applied, because the mutual information is almost zero whatever the SNR. On the other hand, these results justify the best choice of the bijection to be used in our implementation. Indeed, the knowledge of this bijection (that can even be made public) is of no help for the attacker since the mask is unknown. Therefore, in all the cases, we assume a partitioning according to $HW(\Delta(x))$, that is independent of B.

4   Experiments on Masked DES Implementations

In this section, we apply the principle of leakage squeezing introduced in section 3.1 to DES. It requires an adaptation since its round function is more elaborate than $x \mapsto S(x \oplus k)$. Also, it is unrealistic to use 32-bits bijections. Therefore, we show how to split the bijection B (refer to Fig. 4) into smaller bijections. Two implementations are proposed: a ROM based architecture and a simpler structure called "Universal S-box Masking" (USM).

4.1   ROM Implementation

For DES we can use eight different bijections[1], denoted B_1, one for each S-box. To further protect the new mask m', we compose the DES parts by using external encodings with bijections B_2, for instance:

$$\underbrace{B_1^{-1} \circ E \circ S \circ P \circ \mathrm{XOR}(L) \circ B_1}_{\mathrm{ROM}} = \underbrace{B_1^{-1} \circ E \circ S \circ B_2}_{\mathrm{ROM}} \circ P \circ \underbrace{B_2^{-1} \circ \mathrm{XOR}(L) \circ B_1}_{\mathrm{LUT\ network}},$$

(4)

where B_1 and B_2 are 4-bit bijections, E, S, P and $\mathrm{XOR}(L)$, respectively the Expansion, S-Box, Permutation and Left part recombination of the DES algorithm. As the expansion E needs 6 bits, specific care has to be taken for the 4-bit bijections. This point is discussed further.

This principle of internal encodings has already been proposed by Chow *et al.* in [6] in the context of white box cryptography. This protection method has already been attacked for the DES and for the AES. However these attacks should not apply for the mask path as it is random and consequently no values can be imposed at the table inputs.

The general ROM implementation is given in figure 6. With respect to figure 4, the intermediate data (*e.g.* Sboxes output) have been protected by the same strategy, so as to provide a seamless "squeezing" throughout the combinational logic.

The bijection B_2 is constrained to be a *xor* operation with a constant, as the permutation P on 32 bits causes the ROM output bits to be split for the next round. The implementation of the mixing L with the left part can be done by a Look Up Table (LUT) network in FPGAs rather than a ROM in order to reduce the complexity. This requires that the bijections are a set of three 2-bit bijections to take advantage of LUT having 4 inputs (LUT4) in FPGAs, or two 3-bit bijections if LUT6 are available.

If we compare this implementation to the one proposed in [23] and described in figure 1, we have the same ROM complexity which is of eight 2^{12} words of four bits.

4.2   USM Implementation

The ROM implementation can be replaced by a more simple structure which is the Universal S-box Masking (USM) studied in [14]. This implementation presents some security weaknesses as discussed in [14]; the weakness can be exploited successfully by a classical CPA. If we apply function compositions as for Eq. (4) with new bijection encodings, the CPA and second order DPA attacks could be thwarted. Figure 7 illustrates the mask path of DES with USM implementation taking advantage of the "leakage squeezing" method. It is made up four stages which can be protected by using bijections B_1, B_2, B_3 and B_4. All the bijection are on four bits except B_2 which is on six bits.

---

[1] The same bijection can be reused eight times without compromising the security.

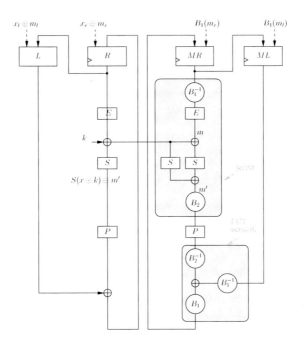

Fig. 6. Leakage squeezing of DES with a masked ROM implementation

Every stage can be implemented by a set of LUT networks or a ROM.

The bijection B_4 is constrained to be a *xor* operation with a constant, as the permutation P on 32 bits causes the output bits to be split.

All the stages can be implemented with a LUT network based on sets of 2-bit bijections. The second stage with the S-box could also be implemented in a small 64×4 ROM.

In this stage the mask m is xored with the masked data $x \oplus k \oplus m$ and the expansion E is performed as 6 bits of masks are considered.

4.3   Complexity and Throughput Results

The proposed implementations have been tested in a STRATIXII FPGA which is based on Adaptative LUT Module (ALM) cell. They have been compared with non protected DES, masked ROM and masked USM implementations without any leakage squeezing.

The table 1 summarizes the memories needed for each implementation and the estimated throughput.

These results show that the leakage squeezing method on hardware implementations has little impact on complexity and speed compared with software implementation against HO-DPA [21]. Moreover the USM implementation is particularly efficient as it avoids the use of large ROMs while keeping a high throughput.

Table 1. Complexity and speed results. "l. s." denotes the "leakage squeezing" countermeasure.

Implementation	ALMs	Block mem-ory [bit]	M4Ks	Throughput [Mbit/s]
Unprotected DES (*reference*)	276	0	0	929.4
DES masked USM	447	0	0	689.1
DES masked ROM	366	131072	32	398.4
DES masked ROM with l. s.	408	131072	32	320.8
DES masked USM with l. s.	488	0	0	582.8

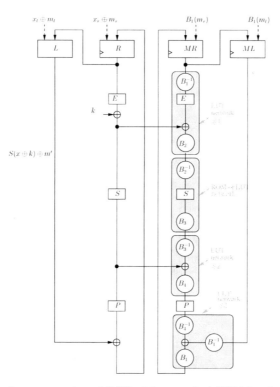

Fig. 7. Leakage squeezing of DES with a masked USM implementation

In order to validate our implementations, we conduct in the next sections an evaluation of the leakages resulting from the leakage squeezing implementation. In [22], a theoretical framework was consequently introduced and suggests analyzing side-channel attacks with a combination of information theoretic and security metrics. These metrics respectively aim at evaluating the amount of information provided by a leaking implementation and the possibility to turn this information into a successful key recovery.

4.4   Information-Theoretic Evaluation of the Proposed Solutions

As it was suggested in [22], we computed the mutual information between the secret state k and the leakage function in the Hamming weight model with Gaussian noise for our two implementations and the others for comparison purposes.

Figure 8 (a) shows the mutual information values obtained for each kind of leakage with respect to an increasing noise standard deviation over $[0.1, 10]$ (*i.e.* an increasing SNR over $[-20 , 20]$)

These results demonstrate the information leakage reduction implied by the use of the leakage squeezing technique. As expected, the two implementations based on leakage squeezing leak less information than the zero offset implementation and the unprotected DES for all SNRs. The somewhat surprising conclusion of our experiments is that the mutual information is almost zero which proves the robustness of this technique. In figure 8 (b), we zoom on the evolution of the mutual information in the case of the implementations based on the leakage squeezing technique in order to make a comparison between them.

We clearly see that when the SNR increases the mutual information for the USM implementation tend asymptotically to the value $1e^{-4}$ bit and remains below the mutual information leaked in the case of the ROM implementation (*i.e.* $5e^{-4}$) and then is the most robust implementation.

We can explain this results by the fact that the leakage squeezing techniques, (*i.e.* by applying bijection), aim at balancing the leakage distributions described in figure 3 so that any partitioning becomes almost distinguishable whatever the secret state $HW(\Delta(x))$ and as a consequence the information leakage is reduced. We showed in figure 9 the five possible values of $HW(\Delta(x))$ for the USM implementation with the squeezing leakage technique using the sixteenth serpent S-Box (*i.e.* proved to be the most appropriate bijection, see subsection 3.2). These distributions are clearly identical.

4.5   Evaluation of the Implementations against 2O-Attacks

After the information theoretic evaluation, the second step to evaluate the robustness of a leaking device is the security evaluation using various distinguishers

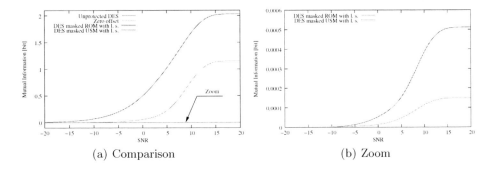

(a) Comparison   (b) Zoom

Fig. 8. Mutual information metric computed on several DES implementations

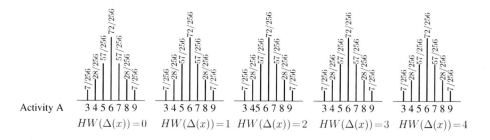

Activity A

$HW(\Delta(x))=0$ $HW(\Delta(x))=1$ $HW(\Delta(x))=2$ $HW(\Delta(x))=3$ $HW(\Delta(x))=4$

Fig. 9. Probability density functions (pdf) corresponding to the five possible values of $HW(\Delta(x))$ with Leakage Squeezing protection

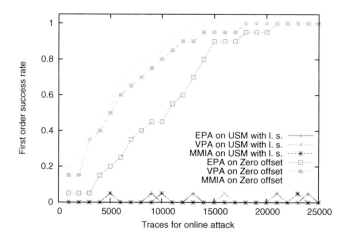

Fig. 10. First order success rate of 3 distinguishers, FPGA implementation

to see how the information leakages translate into success rate under different assumptions.

First, we applied several side-channel distinguishers to leakage measurements simulated in the Hamming weight model with Gaussian noise. We not only applied (HO)-DPA, but also other kinds of attacks, namely MMIA. We chose to test these three side channel distinguishers against different kinds of masking, firstly because they are the most widely used in the literature, and secondly because they represent a brand spectrum of adversary capabilities.

Afterward, we performed these attacks against real power consumption measurements of our FPGA implementations in order to check them in a real-world context.

For each scenario, we acquired a set of 25,000 power consumption traces using random masks and plaintexts. We performed the first order success rate as in [22].

We showed in figure 10 our experimental results also for these attacks on the "zero offset" hardware implementation used here for comparison purposes with our hardware solution based on the leakage squeezing technique.

We can see that the attacks based on various distinguishers perform well in the case of the "zero offset" implementation. About $5,000$ traces suffice to achieve a success rate of 50% and starting from about $13,000$ traces the MMIA attack reveals the correct key with success rate of 100%. The VPA and EPA attack perform well also. For the EPA, the success rates stay well above 50% even when using $11,000$ measurements, but eventually reaches success rate of 95% using $18,000$ traces.

For our proposed countermeasure, the attacks perform worse. The success rates stay under 10% even when using $25,000$ measurements.

We conclude that the experiments on a real circuit shows the evidence of benefit of our countermeasure since it leaks little information which are not exploited by the adversary to mount a successful attack.

5   Conclusion and Perspectives

Second order DPA attacks not only allow to theoretically invalidate some countermeasures, but can break them in practice. We presented in this paper a method called "leakage squeezing" which aims at balancing the power consumption distribution on hardware masked implementations. This method consists in using bijective encodings composed of functional operations and implemented in ROMs or LUT networks. Two implementations have been proposed and evaluated. They provide a great robustness against 2O-DPA (VPA, EPA) and MMIA as none of the subkeys have been guessed using 25k traces. The robustness is corroborated by an information theoretic analysis of the leakage. Moreover the performances decrease in terms of complexity and speed are very limited, which is particularly true for the USM implementation which does not require large memories.

The main perspective of this work is to compare our countermeasure based fundamentally on Boolean masking with others solutions such the affine masking [7] scheme which also provides good performance-security against HO attacks.

Acknowledgment

This work has been supported by the french Agency "Agence Nationale de la Recherche" in the frame of the SECRESOC project ANR-09-SEGI-013.

References

1. Agrawal, D., Archambeault, B., Rao, J.R., Rohatgi, P.: The EM side-channel(s). In: Kaliski Jr., B.S., Koç, Ç.K., Paar, C. (eds.) CHES 2002. LNCS, vol. 2523, pp. 29–45. Springer, Heidelberg (2003)
2. Akkar, M.-L., Giraud, C.: An Implementation of DES and AES, Secure against Some Attacks (Paris, France). In: Koç, Ç.K., Naccache, D., Paar, C. (eds.) CHES 2001. LNCS, vol. 2162, pp. 309–318. Springer, Heidelberg (2001)

3. Akkar, M.-L., Goubin, L.: A Generic Protection against High-Order Differential Power Analysis. In: Johansson, T. (ed.) FSE 2003. LNCS, vol. 2887, pp. 192–205. Springer, Heidelberg (2003)
4. Chari, S., Jutla, C.S., Rao, J.R., Rohatgi, P.: Towards Sound Approaches to Counteract Power-Analysis Attacks. In: Wiener, M. (ed.) CRYPTO 1999. LNCS, vol. 1666, p. 398. Springer, Heidelberg (1999) ISBN: 3-540-66347-9
5. Chari, S., Rao, J.R., Rohatgi, P.: Template attacks. In: Kaliski Jr., B.S., Koç, Ç.K., Paar, C. (eds.) CHES 2002. LNCS, vol. 2523, pp. 13–28. Springer, Heidelberg (2003)
6. Chow, S., Eisen, P.A., Johnson, H., van Oorschot, P.C.: A White-Box DES Implementation for DRM Applications. In: Feigenbaum, J. (ed.) DRM 2002. LNCS, vol. 2696, pp. 1–15. Springer, Heidelberg (2003)
7. Fumaroli, G., Martinelli, A., Prouff, E., Rivain, M.: Affine masking against higher-order side channel analysis. Cryptology ePrint Archive, Report 2010/523, http://eprint.iacr.org/2010/523 To be published at SAC 2010 (2010),
8. Gierlichs, B., Batina, L., Preneel, B., Verbauwhede, I.: Revisiting higher-order DPA attacks: In: Pieprzyk, J. (ed.) CT-RSA 2010. LNCS, vol. 5985, pp. 221–234. Springer, Heidelberg (2010)
9. Kim, C., Schläffer, M., Moon, S.: Differential Side Channel Analysis Attacks on FPGA Implementations of ARIA. ETRI Journal 30(2), 315–325 (2008), doi:10.4218/etrij.08.0107.0167
10. Kocher, P.C., Jaffe, J., Jun, B.: Timing Attacks on Implementations of Diffie-Hellman, RSA, DSS, and Other Systems ((PDF)). In: Koblitz, N. (ed.) CRYPTO 1996. LNCS, vol. 1109, pp. 104–113. Springer, Heidelberg (1996)
11. Kocher, P.C., Jaffe, J., Jun, B.: Differential Power Analysis. In: Wiener, M. (ed.) CRYPTO 1999. LNCS, vol. 1666, pp. 388–397. Springer, Heidelberg (1999)
12. Goubin, L., Patarin, J.: DES and Differential Power Analysis - The "Duplication" Method (1999)
13. Lv, J., Han, Y.: Enhanced DES implementation secure against high-order differential power analysis in smartcards. In: Boyd, C., González Nieto, J.M. (eds.) ACISP 2005. LNCS, vol. 3574, pp. 195–206. Springer, Heidelberg (2005)
14. Maghrebi, H., Danger, J.-L., Flament, F., Guilley, S.: Evaluation of Countermeasures Implementation Based on Boolean Masking to Thwart First and Second Order Side-Channel Attacks. In: SCS, Jerba, Tunisia, November 6-8, pp. 1–6. IEEE, Los Alamitos (2009), http://hal.archives-ouvertes.fr/hal-00425523/en/, doi:10.1109/ICSCS.2009.5412597
15. Maghrebi, H., Guilley, S., Danger, J.-L., Flament, F.: Entropy-based Power Attack. In: HOST, Anaheim Convention Center, Anaheim, CA, USA, June 13-14, pp. 1–6. IEEE Computer Society, Los Alamitos (2010), doi:10.1109/HST.2010.5513124
16. Mangard, S., Oswald, E., Popp, T.: Power Analysis Attacks: Revealing the Secrets of Smart Cards. Springer, Heidelberg (December 2006), http://www.dpabook.org/ ISBN 0-387-30857-1
17. Mangard, S., Pramstaller, N., Oswald, E.: Successfully Attacking Masked AES Hardware Implementations. In: Rao, J.R., Sunar, B. (eds.) CHES 2005. LNCS, vol. 3659, pp. 157–171. Springer, Heidelberg (2005)
18. Mangard, S., Schramm, K.: Pinpointing the Side-Channel Leakage of Masked AES Hardware Implementations. In: Goubin, L., Matsui, M. (eds.) CHES 2006. LNCS, vol. 4249, pp. 76–90. Springer, Heidelberg (2006)
19. Messerges, T.S.: Using Second-Order Power Analysis to Attack DPA Resistant Software. In: Paar, C., Koç, Ç.K. (eds.) CHES 2000. LNCS, vol. 1965, pp. 71–77. Springer, Heidelberg (2000)

20. Peeters, E., Standaert, F.-X., Donckers, N., Quisquater, J.-J.: Improved Higher-Order Side-Channel Attacks with FPGA Experiments. In: Rao, J.R., Sunar, B. (eds.) CHES 2005. LNCS, vol. 3659, pp. 309–323. Springer, Heidelberg (2005)
21. Rivain, M., Prouff, E., Doget, J.: Higher-order masking and shuffling for software implementations of block ciphers. In: Clavier, C., Gaj, K. (eds.) CHES 2009. LNCS, vol. 5747, pp. 171–188. Springer, Heidelberg (2009)
22. Standaert, F.-X., Malkin, T., Yung, M.: A unified framework for the analysis of side-channel key recovery attacks. In: Joux, A. (ed.) EUROCRYPT 2009. LNCS, vol. 5479, pp. 443–461. Springer, Heidelberg (2009)
23. Standaert, F.-X., Rouvroy, G., Quisquater, J.-J.: FPGA Implementations of the DES and Triple-DES Masked Against Power Analysis Attacks. In: Proceedings of FPL 2006. IEEE, Madrid (2006)
24. Waddle, J., Wagner, D.: Towards efficient second-order power analysis. In: Joye, M., Quisquater, J.-J. (eds.) CHES 2004. LNCS, vol. 3156, pp. 1–15. Springer, Heidelberg (2004)

Differential Fault Analysis of the Advanced Encryption Standard Using a Single Fault

Michael Tunstall[1], Debdeep Mukhopadhyay[2], and Subidh Ali[2]

[1] Department of Computer Science, University of Bristol,
Merchant Venturers Building, Woodland Road,
Bristol BS8 1UB, United Kingdom
`tunstall@cs.bris.ac.uk`
[2] Computer Sc. and Engg, IIT Kharagpur, India
`{debdeep,subidh}@cse.iitkgp.ernet.in`

Abstract. In this paper we present a differential fault attack that can be applied to the AES using a single fault. We demonstrate that when a single random byte fault is induced at the input of the eighth round, the AES key can be deduced using a two stage algorithm. The first step has a statistical expectation of reducing the possible key hypotheses to 2^{32}, and the second step to a mere 2^8.

Keywords: Differential Fault Analysis, Fault Attack, Advanced Encryption Standard.

1 Introduction

The Advanced Encryption Standard (AES) [10] has been a de-facto standard for symmetric key cryptography since October 2000. Smart cards and secure microprocessors, therefore, typically include implementations of AES to protect the confidentiality and the integrity of sensitive information. To satisfy the high throughput requirements of such applications, these implementations are typically VLSI devices (crypto-accelerators) or highly optimized software routines (crypto-libraries).

Several applications of DFA to AES have been reported in the literature. In [3], authors describe an analysis based on faults induced in one byte of the ninth round of AES that requires 250 faulty ciphertexts. An attack reported in [1] allows an attacker to recover the secret key with around 128 to 256 faulty ciphertexts. In [2], Dusart et al. show that using a fault which affects one byte anywhere between the eighth round MixColumn and ninth round MixColumn, an attacker would be able to derive the secret key using 40 faulty ciphertexts. The authors of [12] describe an attack on AES with single byte faults that requires two faulty outputs, where a fault is induced in the input of the eighth or ninth round, extended to one 32-bit fault in the ninth round in [8].

We can note that when the assumptions are on the value of a byte (either it being faulty or uncorrupted) the number of faulty pairs is quite small. However, it is difficult to be able to affect a given value with any certainty. When numerous

C.A. Ardagna and J. Zhou (Eds.): WISTP 2011, LNCS 6633, pp. 224–233, 2011.

faulty ciphertexts are required this problem is amplified, since an attacker needs to find a method of determining which faulty ciphertexts correspond to the desired model. We can, therefore, state that the attacks that are most likely to be realizable require the least faulty ciphertexts and assumptions on the effect of the fault.

In [9] a fault attack against AES was proposed, which suggested that a secret key can be derived using a single *byte* fault induction at the input of the eighth round. The attack exploited the inter-relations between the fault values in the state matrix after the ninth round `MixColumn` operation and reduced the number of possible keys to around 2^{32}. However it may be noted that this work, like the previous fault attacks on AES does not use the effect of the fault maximally in an information theoretic sense [7]. The work proposed in this paper improves the previous fault analysis on AES-128 and reduces the key space to its minimal possible set of hypotheses attainable using a single byte fault. In this paper, we describe the extended version of this attack, where an attacker could reduce the exhaustive search to 2^8.

Notation

In this paper, multiplications are considered to be polynomial multiplications over $\mathbb{F}_{2^8}$ modulo the irreducible polynomial $x^8 + x^4 + x^3 + x + 1$. It should be clear from the context when a mathematical expression contains integer multiplication.

Organization

The paper is organized as follows: In Section 2 we describe the background to this paper. In Section 3 we describe an attack based on one of the fault models given in Section 2. In Section 3 we extend this attack. In Section 4 we compare this paper to work described in the literature, and we conclude in Section 5.

2   Background

2.1   The Advanced Encryption Standard

The structure of the Advanced Encryption Standard (AES) , as used to perform encryption, is illustrated in Algorithm 1. Note that we restrict ourselves to considering AES-128 and that the description above omits a permutation typically used to convert the plaintext $P = (p_1, p_2, \ldots, p_{16})_{(256)}$ and key $K = (k_1, k_2, \ldots, k_{16})_{(256)}$ into a 4×4 array of bytes, known as the state matrix. For example, the 128-bit plaintext input block P which produces fault free (CT) and faulty ciphertexts (CT') are arranged in the following fashion

$$P = \begin{pmatrix} p_1 & p_5 & p_9 & p_{13} \\ p_2 & p_6 & p_{10} & p_{14} \\ p_3 & p_7 & p_{11} & p_{15} \\ p_4 & p_8 & p_{12} & p_{16} \end{pmatrix} \quad \mathbf{CT} = \begin{pmatrix} x_1 & x_5 & x_9 & x_{13} \\ x_2 & x_6 & x_{10} & x_{14} \\ x_3 & x_7 & x_{11} & x_{15} \\ x_4 & x_8 & x_{12} & x_{16} \end{pmatrix} \quad \mathbf{CT'} = \begin{pmatrix} x'_1 & x'_5 & x'_9 & x'_{13} \\ x'_2 & x'_6 & x'_{10} & x'_{14} \\ x'_3 & x'_7 & x'_{11} & x'_{15} \\ x'_4 & x'_8 & x'_{12} & x'_{16} \end{pmatrix}$$

Algorithm 1. The AES-128 encryption function.

Input: The 128-bit plaintext block P and key K.
Output: The 128-bit ciphertext block C.

$X \leftarrow \text{AddRoundKey}(P, K)$
for $i \leftarrow 1$ **to** 10 **do**
  $\quad X \leftarrow \text{SubBytes}(X)$
  $\quad X \leftarrow \text{ShiftRows}(X)$
  $\quad$ **if** $i \neq 10$ **then**
    $\quad\quad \mid \quad X \leftarrow \text{MixColumns}(X)$
  $\quad$ **end**
  $\quad K \leftarrow \text{KeySchedule}(K)$
  $\quad X \leftarrow \text{AddRoundKey}(X, K)$
end
$C \leftarrow X$

return C

---

where $x_i \in \{0, \dots, 255\} \ \forall i \in \{1, \dots, 16\}$. We also define the key matrix for the subkeys used in the ninth and tenth round as $K_{10} = \{k_1, \dots, k_{16}\}$ and $K_9 = \{k'_1, \dots, k'_{16}\}$ that are arranged in a state matrix as described above.

The encryption itself is conducted by the repeated use of a number of round functions:

- The SubBytes function is the only non-linear step of the block cipher. It is a bricklayer permutation consisting of an S-box applied to the bytes of the state. Each byte of the state matrix is replaced by its multiplicative inverse, followed by an affine mapping. Thus the input byte x is related to the output y of the S-Box by the relation, $y = A\,x^{-1} + B$, where A and B are constant matrices. In the remainder of this paper we will refer to the function S as the SubBytes function and S^{-1} as the inverse of the SubBytes function.
- The ShiftRows function is a byte-wise permutation of the state.
- The KeySchedule function generates the next round key from the previous one. The first round key is the input key with no changes, subsequent round keys are generated using the SubBytes function and XOR operations. This is shown in Algorithm 2 which shows how the rth round key is computed from the $(r-1)^{th}$ round key. The value h_r is a constant defined for the rth round, and $<<$ is used to denote a bitwise left shift.
- The MixColumn is a bricklayer permutation operating on the state column by column. Each column of the state matrix is considered as a 4-dimensional vector where each element belongs to $\mathbb{F}(2^8)$. A 4×4 matrix M whose elements are also in $\mathbb{F}(2^8)$ is used to map this column into a new vector. This operation is applied on all the 4 columns of the state matrix. Here M and its inverse M^{-1} are defined as:

$$M = \begin{pmatrix} 2 & 3 & 1 & 1 \\ 1 & 2 & 3 & 1 \\ 1 & 1 & 2 & 3 \\ 3 & 1 & 1 & 2 \end{pmatrix} \qquad M^{-1} = \begin{pmatrix} 14 & 11 & 13 & 9 \\ 9 & 14 & 11 & 13 \\ 13 & 9 & 14 & 11 \\ 11 & 13 & 9 & 14 \end{pmatrix}$$

All the elements in M and M^{-1} are elements of $\mathbb{F}(2^8)$ expressed as a decimal digit.

- AddRoundKey: Each byte of the array is XORed with a byte from a corresponding array of round subkeys.

Algorithm 2. The AES-128 KeySchedule function.

Input: $(r-1)^{th}$ round key ($X = x_i$ for $i \in \{1, \ldots, 16\}$).
Output: r^{th} round key X.

for $i \leftarrow 0$ **to** 3 **do**
   | $x_{(i<<2)+1} \leftarrow x_{(i<<2)+1} \oplus S(x_{(((i+1)\wedge 3)<<2)+4})$;
end
$x_1 \leftarrow x_1 \oplus h_r$;
for $i \leftarrow 1$ **to** 16 **do**
   | **if** $(i-1) \mod 4 \neq 0$ **then**
   | | $x_i \leftarrow x_i \oplus x_{i-1}$;
   | **end**
end

return X

2.2 The Fault Model

The implementation of AES we target is an iterative one, i.e. where a round function is executed in a loop as described in Algorithm 1. An attacker can typically predict at what point in time certain events take place, e.g. when a particular round commences. Moreover, the time certain events take can often be determined by analyzing a suitable side channel.

The fault model that we consider is the same as that used in many other papers, for example [9], where we assume that the effect of an induced fault is to change one byte to a random value.

For example, an attacker could attempt to use a glitch in the clock to create a fault at the input of a particular round with a certain probability. An iterative design helps in this regard, as the attacker is able to control the timing of fault induction by simply counting the number of clock edges from the start of an encryption.

3 The Fault Analysis

3.1 The First Step of the Fault Attack

If a fault is induced in a byte of the state matrix, which is then input to the eighth round, the MixColumn operation at the end of the round propagates this fault to the entire column of the state. The ShiftRow operation at the beginning of the following round will then shift these bytes to occupy different columns. The next MixColumn operation will then propagate the fault to the remaining twelve bytes.

This process is shown in Figure 1 where we show the diffusion of a byte fault induced at the input of the eighth round. The XOR difference of the state matrices of the two results, one fault free and the other faulty, is shown. This is what we use as basis for a differential fault analysis.

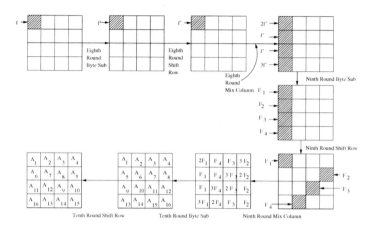

Fig. 1. Propagation of Fault Induced in the input of eighth round of AES

If, given a fault in the input to the eighth round, we consider the state of the differences after the ninth round shift row, we can obtain the following set of equations that include the values of the key bytes k_1, k_8, k_{11} and k_{14}, thus giving an expression for 32 bits of $\mathbf{K_{10}}$.

$$2\,\delta_1 = S^{-1}(x_1 \oplus k_1) \oplus S^{-1}(x'_1 \oplus k_1)$$
$$\delta_1 = S^{-1}(x_{14} \oplus k_{14}) \oplus S^{-1}(x'_{14} \oplus k_{14})$$
$$\delta_1 = S^{-1}(x_{11} \oplus k_{11}) \oplus S^{-1}(x'_{11} \oplus k_{11})$$
$$3\,\delta_1 = S^{-1}(x_8 \oplus k_8) \oplus S^{-1}(x'_8 \oplus k_8)$$

Where δ_1, k_1, k_8, k_{11} and k_{14} are all unknown values $\in \{0, \ldots, 255\}$.

The above system of equations can be used to reduce the possibilities for these 32 bits of the key. An attacker would select a value for δ_1 and determine which values of k_1, k_8, k_{11} and k_{14} satisfy the equations using four independent exhaustive searches. Each equation will return 0, 2, or 4 hypotheses [11]. If any of the four equations cannot be satisfied, i.e. there is an impossible differential [6], then any hypotheses for that value of δ_1 can be discarded.

As noted in [4,8] one can apply the same technique to recover information on the remaining bytes of the last sub key. That is, information on the remaining key bytes can be derived by using the following sets of equations: In order to obtain information on k_2, k_5, k_{12} and k_{15} an attacker can use

$$3\,\delta_2 = S^{-1}(x_5 \oplus k_5) \oplus S^{-1}(x'_5 \oplus k_5)$$
$$2\,\delta_2 = S^{-1}(x_2 \oplus k_2) \oplus S^{-1}(x'_2 \oplus k_2)$$
$$\delta_2 = S^{-1}(x_{15} \oplus k_{15}) \oplus S^{-1}(x'_{15} \oplus k_{15})$$
$$\delta_2 = S^{-1}(x_{12} \oplus k_{12}) \oplus S^{-1}(x'_{12} \oplus k_{12})$$

In order to obtain information on k_3, k_6, k_9 and k_{16} an attacker can use the following equations:

$$\delta_3 = S^{-1}(x_9 \oplus k_9) \oplus S^{-1}(x'_9 \oplus k_9)$$
$$3\,\delta_3 = S^{-1}(x_6 \oplus k_6) \oplus S^{-1}(x'_6 \oplus k_6)$$
$$2\,\delta_3 = S^{-1}(x_3 \oplus k_3) \oplus S^{-1}(x'_3 \oplus k_3)$$
$$\delta_3 = S^{-1}(x_{16} \oplus k_{16}) \oplus S^{-1}(x'_{16} \oplus k_{16})$$

Finally, in order to obtain information on k_4, k_7, k_{10} and k_{13} an attacker can use the following equations:

$$\delta_4 = S^{-1}(x_{13} \oplus k_{13}) \oplus S^{-1}(x'_{13} \oplus k_{13})$$
$$\delta_4 = S^{-1}(x_{10} \oplus k_{10}) \oplus S^{-1}(x'_{10} \oplus k_{10})$$
$$3\,\delta_4 = S^{-1}(x_7 \oplus k_7) \oplus S^{-1}(x'_7 \oplus k_7)$$
$$2\,\delta_4 = S^{-1}(x_4 \oplus k_4) \oplus S^{-1}(x'_4 \oplus k_4)$$

It can be noted that the equations have an identical structure, and, therefore, the solutions are of similar nature. An evaluation of each set of equations will be expected to return 2^8 unique hypotheses for the key bytes concerned. Therefore, an attacker would expect to have 2^{32} key hypotheses for the secret key used.

3.2   Analysis of the First Step of the Fault Attack

The first step of the fault attack uses four sets of equations to reduce the key space of AES. In this section we determine the expected number of key hypotheses that an attacker will have at each stage of an attack.

In order to analyze the number of valid hypotheses in the first stage of the attack we consider the first set of equations given in Section 3.1. In this set of equations δ_1 is $\in \{1, \ldots, 255\}$. If δ_1 is equal to zero then one could say that the expected fault has not been injected. If δ_1 is zero it would imply that x_1 is equal to x'_1 and all 256 key hypotheses are possible. Let us first consider the first equation in this set:

$$2\,\delta_1 = S^{-1}(x_1 \oplus k_1) \oplus S^{-1}(x'_1 \oplus k_1)$$

We know the values of x_1 and x'_1 from the correct and faulty ciphertexts respectively. For a given value of $2\,\delta_1$ there will 0, 2 or 4 valid key hypotheses. The mean hypotheses for all $\delta_1 \in \{1, \ldots, 255\}$ is approximately one, and, therefore, 256 key hypotheses when all $\delta_1 \in \{1, \ldots, 255\}$ are considered.

The same can be said for each of the four equations in the set given above. However, for a given value of δ_1 each of the four equations would be expected to return approximately one hypothesis for a key byte. These values will give one hypothesis for the quartet of key bytes $\{k_1, k_8, k_{11}, k_{14}\}$. Given that an attacker will have to take into account all the values in $\{0, \ldots, 255\}$ there will be 256 possible values for the quartet $\{k_1, k_8, k_{11}, k_{14}\}$. After an attacker has analyzed the four equations defined in Section 3.1 there would be an expected 2^{32} key hypotheses.

3.3 The Second Step of the Fault Attack

In order to further reduce the key hypotheses we use the relationship between the ninth round key and the tenth round key.

We consider the key-scheduling algorithm (see Algorithm 2), the ninth round key, K_9, generates the tenth round key, K_{10}. The key schedule is invertible and $\mathbf{K_9}$ can be expressed in terms of elements of $\mathbf{K_{10}}$. The value of $\mathbf{K_9}$ can be expressed as

$$
\begin{pmatrix}
k_1 \oplus S(k_{14} \oplus k_{10}) \oplus h_{10} & k_5 \oplus k_1 & k_9 \oplus k_5 & k_{13} \oplus k_9 \\
k_2 \oplus S(k_{15} \oplus k_{11}) & k_6 \oplus k_2 & k_{10} \oplus k_6 & k_{14} \oplus k_{10} \\
k_3 \oplus S(k_{16} \oplus k_{12}) & k_7 \oplus k_3 & k_{11} \oplus k_7 & k_{15} \oplus k_{11} \\
k_4 \oplus S(k_{13} \oplus k_9) & k_8 \oplus k_4 & k_{12} \oplus k_8 & k_{16} \oplus k_{12}
\end{pmatrix} .
$$

We can observe that the fault values in the first column of the state matrix at the output of the eighth round MixColumn is $(2 f', f', f', 3 f')$, where f' is a non-zero arbitrary value in $\mathbb{F}_{2^8}$. Using the InverseMixColumn operation and using the inter-relations between the fault values, we can define the following equation:

$$
\begin{aligned}
2 f' = S^{-1}\Big(& 14\left(S^{-1}(x_1 \oplus k_1) \oplus ((k_1 \oplus S(k_{14} \oplus k_{10}) \oplus h_{10}))\right) \oplus 11\left(S^{-1}(x_8 \oplus k_8) \oplus \right. \\
& (k_2 \oplus S(k_{15} \oplus k_{11}))\big) \oplus 13\left(S^{-1}(x_{11} \oplus k_{11}) \oplus (k_3 \oplus S(k_{16} \oplus k_{12}))\right) \oplus \\
& 9\left(S^{-1}(x_8 \oplus k_8) \oplus (k_4 \oplus S(k_{13} \oplus k_9))\right)\Big) \oplus S^{-1}\Big(14\left(S^{-1}(x'_1 \oplus k_1)\right. \\
& \oplus ((k_1 \oplus S(k_8 \oplus k_{10}) \oplus h_{10}))\big) \oplus 11\left(S^{-1}(x'_8 \oplus k_8) \oplus (k_2 \oplus S(k_{15} \oplus k_{11}))\right) \oplus \\
& 13\left(S^{-1}(x'_{11} \oplus k_{11}) \oplus (k_3 \oplus S(k_{16} \oplus k_{12}))\right) \oplus 9\left(S^{-1}(x'_8 \oplus k_8) \oplus\right. \\
& (k_4 \oplus S(k_{13} \oplus k_9))\big)\Big)
\end{aligned}
$$

Similarly, we can define the following equations:

$$
\begin{aligned}
f' = S^{-1}\Big(& 9\left(S^{-1}(x_{13} \oplus k_{13}) \oplus (k_{13} \oplus k_9)\right) \oplus 14\left(S^{-1}(x_{10} \oplus k_{10}) \oplus (k_{10} \oplus k_{14})\right) \oplus \\
& 11\left(S^{-1}(x_7 \oplus k_7) \oplus (k_{15} \oplus k_{11})\right) \oplus 13\left(S^{-1}(x_4 \oplus k_4) \oplus (k_{16} \oplus k_{12})\right)\Big) \oplus \\
& S^{-1}\Big(9\left(S^{-1}(x'_{13} \oplus k_{13}) \oplus (k_{13} \oplus k_9)\right) \oplus 14\left(S^{-1}(x'_{10} \oplus k_{10}) \oplus (k_{10} \oplus k_{14})\right) \oplus \\
& 11\left(S^{-1}(x'_7 \oplus k_7) \oplus (k_{15} \oplus k_{11})\right) \oplus 13\left(S^{-1}(x'_4 \oplus k_4) \oplus (k_{16} \oplus k_{12})\right)\Big)
\end{aligned}
$$

$$f' = S^{-1}\Big(13\left(S^{-1}(x_9 \oplus k_9) \oplus (k_9 \oplus k_5)\right) \oplus 9\left(S^{-1}(x_6 \oplus k_6) \oplus (k_{10} \oplus k_6)\right)\Big) \oplus$$
$$14\left(S^{-1}(x_3 \oplus k_3) \oplus (k_{11} \oplus k_7)\right) \oplus 11\left(S^{-1}(x_{16} \oplus k_{16}) \oplus (k_{12} \oplus k_8)\right)\Big) \oplus$$
$$S^{-1}\Big(13\left(S^{-1}(x'_9 \oplus k_9) \oplus (k_9 \oplus k_5)\right) \oplus 9\left(S^{-1}(x'_6 \oplus k_6) \oplus (k_{10} \oplus k_6)\right)\Big) \oplus$$
$$14\left(S^{-1}(x'_3 \oplus k_3) \oplus (k_{11} \oplus k_7)\right) \oplus 11\left(S^{-1}(x'_{16} \oplus k_{16}) \oplus (k_{12} \oplus k_8)\right)\Big)$$

$$3\,f' = S^{-1}\Big(11\left(S^{-1}(x_2 \oplus k_2) \oplus (k_2 \oplus k_1)\right) \oplus 13\left(S^{-1}(x_5 \oplus k_5) \oplus (k_6 \oplus k_5)\right)\Big) \oplus$$
$$9\left(S^{-1}(x_{12} \oplus k_{12}) \oplus (k_{10} \oplus k_9)\right) \oplus 14\left(S^{-1}(x_{15} \oplus k_{15}) \oplus (k_{14} \oplus k_{13})\right)\Big) \oplus$$
$$S^{-1}\Big(11\left(S^{-1}(x'_2 \oplus k_2) \oplus (k_2 \oplus k_1)\right) \oplus 13\left(S^{-1}(x'_5 \oplus k_5) \oplus (k_6 \oplus k_5)\right)\Big) \oplus$$
$$9\left(S^{-1}(x'_{12} \oplus k_{12}) \oplus (k_{10} \oplus k_9)\right) \oplus 14\left(S^{-1}(x'_{15} \oplus k_{15}) \oplus (k_{14} \oplus k_{13})\right)\Big)$$

The second stage of the attack is coupled with the first stage, and can be used to further reduce the number of key hypotheses.

3.4 Analysis of the Second Step of the Fault Attack

The expected number of hypotheses produced by the second step of the attack follows a similar reasoning to the analysis of the first step, given in Section 3.2.

If we consider the second equation defined in Section 3.3, it can be rewritten as

$$f' = A \oplus B\,,$$

where A and B are defined as

$$A = S^{-1}\Big(9\left(S^{-1}(x_{13} \oplus k_{13}) \oplus (k_{13} \oplus k_9)\right) \oplus$$
$$14\left(S^{-1}(x_{10} \oplus k_{10}) \oplus (k_{10} \oplus k_{14})\right)\Big) \oplus 11\left(S^{-1}(x_7 \oplus k_7) \oplus$$
$$(k_{15} \oplus k_{11})\right) \oplus 13\left(S^{-1}(x_4 \oplus k_4) \oplus (k_{16} \oplus k_{12})\right)\Big)$$

and

$$B = S^{-1}\Big(9\left(S^{-1}(x'_{13} \oplus k_{13}) \oplus (k_{13} \oplus k_9)\right) \oplus$$
$$14\left(S^{-1}(x'_{10} \oplus k_{10}) \oplus (k_{10} \oplus k_{14})\right)\Big) \oplus 11\left(S^{-1}(x'_7 \oplus k_7) \oplus\;.$$
$$(k_{15} \oplus k_{11})\right) \oplus 13\left(S^{-1}(x'_4 \oplus k_4) \oplus (k_{16} \oplus k_{12})\right)\Big)$$

We can consider A and B to be random values in $\mathbb{F}_{2^8}$. For a given values of f' the difference between A and B will be equal to f' with a probability of $\frac{1}{2^8}$. Using the same reasoning, the probability of all four equations being valid is $\left(\frac{1}{2^8}\right)^4 = \frac{1}{2^{32}}$.

We have to consider all the possible values of f', i.e. $\{0, \ldots, 255\}$. A given key hypothesis will, therefore, be valid for some arbitrary value of f' with a probability of $2^8 \times \frac{1}{2^{32}} = \frac{1}{2^{24}}$. The first step of the attack is expected to return 2^{32} hypotheses each of which still be under consideration at the end of the second step with a probability of $\frac{1}{2^{24}}$. One would, therefore, expect the second step of the attack to produce 2^8 possible key hypotheses.

3.5 Attacking other Bytes

In the previous sections we describe an attack where we base our Differential Fault Analysis on the knowledge that a fault has been induced in the first byte of the state matrix. However, we can note that the analysis returns a very small number of hypotheses. We can, therefore, conduct 16 independent analyses under the assumption that a fault is induced each of the 16 bytes of of the state at the beginning of the eighth round. An attacker would expect this to produce $2^4 \times 2^8 = 2^{12}$ valid key hypotheses, which is still a trivial exhaustive search.

4 Comparison with Previous Work

There are several versions of fault-based differential cryptanalysis that are able to reduce the number of key hypotheses from two faults injected into an implementation of AES, as described in [5, 9, 12]. However, the analysis proposed in this paper is more effective, since the resulting exhaustive search can be reduced to a trivial size using one fault. The number of key hypotheses returned by previous work would be somewhat time consuming. The advantage of the proposed attack is that it does not need to reproduce a successful attack in order to able to determine a secret key. Acquiring multiple faulty ciphertexts can be problematic as faults are only successful with a certain probability, and the effect cannot always be predetermined. This would mean that an attacker could potentially have to search among numerous faulty ciphertexts to find a pair that both have the desired fault.

5 Conclusion

This paper proposes a fault-based differential cryptanalysis of AES, that is an extended version of the attack described in [9]. An attacker would expect to be able to reduce the number of key hypotheses from 2^{128} to 2^8 with one well placed fault. As noted in [8], these attacks can be conducted without any knowledge of the plaintext being enciphered, as an attacker would just need to know the plaintexts were the same.

There are many descriptions of a fault-based differential cryptanalysis of AES that could be prevented by repeating the last two or three rounds of an implementation of AES, to verify that no exploitable fault has been inserted [1,2,3,12,13]. However, to prevent the attack described in this paper the last four rounds would need to be repeated to check no fault was injected. Moreover, given how much information can be gleaned from one fault, one would expect there are attacks that require more faulty ciphertexts that would be able to make use of faults in earlier rounds. One would, therefore, suggest that in order to protect an implementation of AES the last five rounds should be protected against fault injection.

Acknowledgements

The work described in this paper has been supported in part by the European Commission IST Programme under Contract ICT-2007-216676 ECRYPT II and EPSRC grant EP/F039638/1 "Investigation of Power Analysis Attacks". The second author would like to acknowledge the support of Department of Science and Technology (DST) India under the Fast Track Proposals for Young Scientists for the proposal entitled "Design and Analysis of Side Channel Attack Resistant Symmetric Key Cryptosystems".

References

1. Blömer, J., Seifert, J.-P.: Fault based cryptanalysis of the advanced encryption standard (AES). In: Wright, R.N. (ed.) FC 2003. LNCS, vol. 2742, pp. 162–181. Springer, Heidelberg (2003)
2. Dusart, P., Letourneux, G., Vivolo, O.: Differential fault analysis on A.E.S. In: Zhou, J., Yung, M., Han, Y. (eds.) ACNS 2003. LNCS, vol. 2846, pp. 293–306. Springer, Heidelberg (2003)
3. Giraud, C.: DFA on AES. In: Dobbertin, H., Rijmen, V., Sowa, A. (eds.) AES 2005. LNCS, vol. 3373, pp. 27–41. Springer, Heidelberg (2005)
4. Giraud, C., Thillard, A.: Piret and Quisquater's DFA on AES revisited. Cryptology ePrint Archive, Report 2010/440 (2010), http://eprint.iacr.org/
5. Kim, C.H., Quisquater, J.-J.: New differential fault analysis on AES key schedule: Two faults are enough. In: Grimaud, G., Standaert, F.-X. (eds.) CARDIS 2008. LNCS, vol. 5189, pp. 48–60. Springer, Heidelberg (2008)
6. Knudsen, L.: Deal — a 128-bit block cipher. Technical report no. 151. Department of Informatics, University of Bergen, Norway (1998)
7. Li, Y., Gomisawa, S., Sakiyama, K., Ohta, K.: An information theoretic perspective on the differential fault analysis against aes. Cryptology ePrint Archive, Report 2010/032 (2010), http://eprint.iacr.org/
8. Moradi, A., Shalmani, M.T.M., Salmasizadeh, M.: A generalized method of differential fault attack against AES cryptosystem. In: Goubin, L., Matsui, M. (eds.) CHES 2006. LNCS, vol. 4249, pp. 91–100. Springer, Heidelberg (2006)
9. Mukhopadhyay, D.: An improved fault based attack of the advanced encryption standard. In: Preneel, B. (ed.) AFRICACRYPT 2009. LNCS, vol. 5580, pp. 421–434. Springer, Heidelberg (2009)
10. National Institute of Standards and Technology (NIST). Advanced Encryption Standard (AES). FIPS Publication 197 (2001), http://www.itl.nist.gov/fipspubs/
11. Nyberg, K.: Differentially uniform mappings for cryptography. In: Helleseth, T. (ed.) EUROCRYPT 1993. LNCS, vol. 765, pp. 55–64. Springer, Heidelberg (1994)
12. Piret, G., Quisquater, J.-J.: A differential fault attack technique against SPN structures, with application to the AES and KHAZAD. In: Walter, C.D., Koç, Ç.K., Paar, C. (eds.) CHES 2003. LNCS, vol. 2779, pp. 77–88. Springer, Heidelberg (2003)
13. Takahashi, J., Fukunaga, T., Yamakoshi, K.: DFA mechanism on the AES schedule. In: Fault Diagnosis and Tolerance in Cryptography 2007 — FDTC 07, pp. 62–72 (2007)

Entropy of Selectively Encrypted Strings

Reine Lundin and Stefan Lindskog

Department of Computer Science
Karlstad University
Sweden
{reine.lundin,stefan.lindskog}@kau.se

Abstract. A feature that has become desirable for low-power mobile devices with limited computing and energy resources is the ability to select a security configuration in order to create a trade-off between security and other important parameters such as performance and energy consumption. Selective encryption can be used to create this trade-off by only encrypting chosen units of the information. In this paper, we continue the investigation of the confidentiality implications of selective encryption by applying entropy on a generic selective encryption scheme. By using the concept of run-length vector from run-length encoding theory, an expression is derived for entropy of selectively encrypted strings when the number of encrypted substrings, containing one symbol, and the order of the language change.

Keywords: computer security, security measures, selective encryption, entropy.

1   Introduction

The ability to select a security configuration is a feature that has become desirable for low-power mobile devices acting in heterogeneous wireless network environments with limited computing and energy resources. A selective security service is a service that provides various security configuration at run-time to create a trade-off between security and other important parameters such as performance and energy consumption. Selective security is also a way to comply with the principle of adequate security, which states that resources should only be protected to a degree consistent with their value and only until they lose their value.

The concept of selective encryption was introduced in 1995 and 1996 for the purpose of reducing the amount of encrypted MPEG data in a video stream while still providing an acceptable level of confidentiality [9]. Selective encryption has also been used to save energy and processing time for H.264/AVC video streams [7], JPEG images [6], speech compressed with the G.729 speech encoding standard [10], and a wireless video camera [3]. Previous work on selective encryption has mainly focused on performance and/or energy saving issues and on making selectively encrypted information perceptively secure to a certain protection level: that is, to determine which parts of the information to encrypt to distort its perception beyond a desired threshold. In this paper, we continue the investigation in [5]

C.A. Ardagna and J. Zhou (Eds.): WISTP 2011, LNCS 6633, pp. 234–243, 2011.

of the confidentiality implications of selective encryption by applying entropy on the generic selective encryption scheme presented in [4]. Using the concept of run-length vector from run-length encoding theory, an expression is derived for entropy of selectively encrypted strings when the number of encrypted substrings, containing one symbol, and the order of the language change.

The remainder of the paper is organized as follows. Sect. 2 introduces terminology and definitions of languages and entropy. Selective encryption is discussed in Sect. 3, and this section also presents the concept of run-length vector from run-length encoding. The expression for entropy of selectively encrypted strings is derived in Sect. 4. Finally, Sect. 5 concludes the paper.

2   Terminology and Definitions

Terminology and definitions of languages and entropy are introduced in this section.

2.1   Languages

In language theory an alphabet Σ is a finite non-empty set of symbols and a string s over Σ is a finite sequence of symbols drawn from that alphabet. The length of a string, $|s|$, is the number of symbols in the string. If no symbol is drawn from the alphabet, the empty string ϵ is created, having $|\epsilon| = 0$. The concatenation operator $|$ is used to join two strings together by appending. Hence, the string $s_1|s_2$ is produced by appending s_2 to s_1. This is often written as s_1s_2 without the concatenation operator. Concatenation of a string with the empty string yields the string itself, $s\epsilon = \epsilon s = s$; thus ϵ is the identity string during concatenation.

The set of all strings over an alphabet Σ is called the transitive closure Σ^* and every set $L \subset \Sigma^*$ is called a language. The size of a language, $|L|$, is the number of strings in the language. An n-language, L^n, is a subset of a language L containing the strings of length n, hence

$$L^n = \{s \in L; |s| = n\} \tag{1}$$

Note that the union of all n languages constitutes the whole language, hence $L = \bigcup_{n=0}^{k} L^n$, where k is an arbitrarily large integer. Furthermore, $L^0 = \{\epsilon\}$ and $L^1 = \Sigma$. Thus, L^1 can both refer to a language with strings of length one and the constructing alphabet.

The symbols in a language will normally have different probabilities that depend on preceding symbols. Orders of languages, ω, to approximate the originally language were proposed in [8]. The idea is shown in the following list.

L_0 Zero-order language, symbols are independent and uniformly distributed.
L_1 First-order language, symbols are independent and distributed as in L.
L_2 Second-order language, symbols are dependent on one preceding symbol with probabilities as in L.
L_n n-order language, symbols are dependent on $n-1$ preceding symbols with probabilities as in L.

2.2   Entropy

Entropy $H(X)$ [8] is a measure that gives the average amount of information of a discrete random variable X. However, entropy can also be seen as a measure giving the average number of guesses in an optimal binary search attack. The discrete random variable X is a variable that attains values from finite sample space $\mathcal{X} = \{x_1, \ldots, x_n\}$ with probability distribution $p_i = p(X = s^i) = p(X^i)$. From this, entropy is defined as follows.

Definition 1. *The entropy $H(X)$ of a random variable X with probability distribution p_i is defined as*

$$H(X) = -\sum_i p_i \log_2 p_i \tag{2}$$

Definition 1 can be extended to joint and conditional entropy [1].

Definition 2. *The joint entropy $H(X_0, X_1)$ of a pair of random variables (X_0, X_1) with joint probability distribution p_{ij} is defined as*

$$H(X_0, X_1) = -\sum_{i,j} p_{ij} \log_2 p_{ij} \tag{3}$$

Definition 3. *The conditional entropy $H(X_1|X_0)$ of the random variable X_1 given the random variable X_0 with conditional probability distribution $p_{j|i}$ is defined as*

$$H(X_1|X_0) = \sum_i p_i H(X_1|X_0^i) = -\sum_{i,j} p_{ij} \log_2 p_{j|i} \tag{4}$$

Definition 2 can be generalized to n random variables that are related in the chain rule as follows.

$$H(X_0, \ldots, X_{n-1}) = H(X_0) + \sum_{i=1}^{n-1} H(X_i|X_0, \ldots, X_{i-1}) = \sum_{i=0}^{n-1} H^i \tag{5}$$

3   Selective Encryption

As stated above, the main idea of selective encryption is to create a trade-off between confidentiality and performance by encrypting chosen substrings of a string while leaving the remaining substrings unencrypted, compressed or encrypted with another encryption algorithm. In this paper, the substrings are assumed to be of equal size, containing one symbol, and the remaining substrings are assumed to be unencrypted and given in position.

The generic selective encryption scheme presented in [4] consists of three basic entities: the string s to be selectively encrypted, the bit vector b that controls which substrings of s to encrypt and the selectively encrypted message $E(s)$. In the scheme, s is divided into n equally sized substrings s_i, $0 \leq i < n$, hence

$$s = \overset{n-1}{\underset{i=0}{|}} s_i \tag{6}$$

Furthermore, s_i is encrypted if $b_{i \bmod |b|} = 1$ and left unencrypted if $b_{i \bmod |b|} = 0$. Without a loss of generality it can be assumed that $n = |b|$, hence the modulus operator can be removed. The selectively encrypted string $E(s)$ is now constructed as follows.

$$E(s) = \overset{n-1}{\underset{i=0}{|}} \begin{cases} s_i & \text{if } b_i = 0 \\ E(s_i) & \text{if } b_i = 1 \end{cases} \tag{7}$$

From the number of encrypted substrings in $E(s)$, controlled by b, the encryption level is defined as

$$EL = \frac{\sum_{i=0}^{n-1} b_i}{n} \tag{8}$$

The concept of run-length vector from run-length encoding theory [1] is used in this paper in order to capture the distribution of zeros and ones in the bit vector. In run-length encoding, information is stored as a run-length value and a single instance of the corresponding data entity, where a run is the longest substring from the current position containing identical data entities. Thus the description length of information containing long runs will decrease. However, if the information does not contain long runs, the description length of the information might instead increase. The sequence of run-length values of the information is called the run-length vector r. For instance, the bit vector $(0, 0, 0, 1, 1, 0, 0)$ can be written as (302120), with the corresponding run-length vector $r = (3, 2, 2)$. Note how r captures the distribution of runs of zeros and ones in the bit vector. By using the convention of letting the first element in the run-length vector express the run-length of zeros at the beginning of the bit vector, even if there are none, r_{2j} will then give the run-length of zeros and r_{2j+1} will give the run-length of ones in the bit vector. The elements in r will thus alternate between giving the run-lengths of zeros and ones of the bit vector, starting with zeros.

From the notation of the 1-norm [2], also called the taxicab geometry or Manhattan distance, the partial cumulative sum of a vector v will be denoted

$$||v_{[k,l]}|| = \sum_{i=k}^{l} |v_i| \tag{9}$$

where k is the starting position and l the ending position of the vector. Note that $||v_{[k,l]}|| = 0$ if $k > l$, and if $|v| = n$ then $||v_{[0,n-1]}|| = ||v||_1$. From this notation the run-length vector can be calculated from the bit vector as

$$r_i = \max\{k + 1 \; ; \; ||\neg^i b_{[||r_{[0,i-1]}||, ||r_{[0,i-1]}||+k]}|| = 0\} \tag{10}$$

where $\neg^i$ is the negation operator to the power of i. In a similar way, the bit vector can be calculated from the run-length vector as

$$b_i = \min\{k \,;\, ||r_{[0,k]}|| > i\} \mod 2 \tag{11}$$

The elements in the bit vector will be one when k is an odd integer. By setting $\alpha_j = ||r_{[0,2(j-1)]}||$ and $\beta_j = ||r_{[0,2j-1]}||$, this will happen for the index sets $I_j = [\alpha_j, \beta_j)$ where $J = [1, \lfloor \frac{|r|}{2} \rfloor]$. Since $I_{j_1} \cap I_{j_2} = \emptyset$ if $j_1 \neq j_2$, the union of all index sets

$$I = \bigcup_{j \in J} I_j \tag{12}$$

indexes all ones in the bit vector while still preserving the uniqueness of the indexing.

4   Confidentiality of Selective Encryption

To investigate how the entropy changes for selectively encrypted strings, let each of the n equally sized substrings of a selectively encrypted string be associated with a random variable as

$$X_0, \ldots, X_{n-1} = E(s) = \prod_{i=0}^{n-1} \begin{cases} X_i = s_i & \text{if } b_i = 0 \\ X_i = E(s_i) & \text{if } b_i = 1 \end{cases} \tag{13}$$

Since the entropy is affected only when $b_i = 1$, unencrypted substrings only affect the entropy indirectly; it is sufficient to use the index set I in (12) to describe how entropy changes. Hence, by using (5), (12) and (13), the entropy of selectively encrypted strings can be written as

$$H_\omega(X_0, \ldots, X_{n-1}) = \sum_{i \in I} H_\omega^i = \sum_{j \in J} \sum_{i \in I_j} H_\omega^i = \sum_{j \in J} H_\omega^{I_j} = H_\omega^I \tag{14}$$

4.1   Zero- and First-Order Languages

The random variables are independent for L_1 languages. Hence, the conditional entropies in (14) becomes

$$H_1^i = H(X_i) \tag{15}$$

By using (15) in (14)

$$H_1^I = \sum_{i \in I} H(X_i) = |I| H(X_0) \tag{16}$$

where the last step comes from the fact that the random variables are identically distributed. In [5] it was shown for first-order languages that the entropy is given by the expression $H(X_0) \sum_{i=0}^{n-1} b_i$. However, since $|I| = \sum_{i=0}^{n-1} b_i$, the expressions are equal. The symbols are also uniformly distributed for L_0 languages, hence (16) transforms to

$$H_0^I = |I| \log_2 |L_0^1| \tag{17}$$

From the derived expression, no confidentiality can be achieved for L_1 or L_0-languages if the number of encrypted units is zero, $|I| = 0$, or if the alphabet contains only one symbol, $|L^1| = 1$. Furthermore, intuitively and obviously, encrypting more substrings or having a larger alphabet will increase the level of confidentiality. Note also that the entropy tends to infinity as the number of encrypted substrings or the number of symbols in the alphabet tends to infinity.

4.2   Second-Order Languages

For L_2 languages the probability distribution of the symbols depends on one preceding symbol. Thus, when deriving an expression for H_2^I, the symbol preceding a run of ones must be taken into consideration. In [5], two cases were shown to affect the expression of H_2^I. The first case deals with a run of ones starting at the beginning of the bit vector, $i \in I_1 = [0, \beta_1)$, and the second case deals with runs of ones not starting at the beginning of the bit vector, $i \in I_j = [\alpha_j, \beta_j)$ with $\alpha_j \neq 0$ and $X_{\alpha_j-1}^{h_j}$. However, a single expression for H_2^I combining the two cases was not derived in the paper.

The conditional entropies in Definition 3 is defined as the average of the entropies of the conditional distributions, averaged over the conditioning distribution. Hence, in the first case, the conditional entropies in (14) can for L_2 languages be written as

$$H_2^i = p(X_0, \ldots, X_{i-1}^l) H(X_i|X_{i-1}^l) = p(L_2^{i-1} X_{i-1}^l) H(X_i|X_{i-1}^l) \tag{18}$$

where $p(L_2^{i-1} X_{i-1}^l)$ is a row vector of the second-order probabilities of the strings ending with the substring X_{i-1}^l and $H(X_i|X_{i-1}^l)$ is a column vector of the conditional entropies. By using (18) in (14), the expression of the first case becomes

$$H_2^{I_1} = H(X_0) + \sum_{i=1}^{\beta_1-1} p(L_2^{i-1} X_{i-1}^l) H(X_i|X_{i-1}^l) \tag{19}$$

In the second case, the conditional entropies in (14) can for L_2 languages be written as

$$H_2^i = p(X_{\alpha_j-1}, \ldots, X_{i-1}^l | X_{\alpha_j-1}^{h_j}) H(X_i|X_{i-1}^l)$$
$$= p(L_2^{i-\alpha_j} X_{i-1}^l | X_{\alpha_j-1}^{h_j}) H(X_i|X_{i-1}^l) \tag{20}$$

By using (20) in (14), the expression of the second case becomes

$$H_2^{I_j} = \sum_{i \in I_j} p(L_2^{i-\alpha_j} X_{i-1}^l | X_{\alpha_j-1}^{h_j}) H(X_i|X_{i-1}^l) \tag{21}$$

Table 1. The probability distribution that gives $H_1^I < H_2^I$ if X_0^1 and $H_2^I < H_1^I$ if X_0^2

p_{ij}	X_1^1	X_1^2
X_0^1	0.2	0.2
X_0^2	0.2	0.4

If $\alpha_1 \neq 0$, then it is only necessary to sum over all I_j in (21) to derive H_2^I. However, if $\alpha_1 = 0$, then (19) needs to be included in the sum. To combine the two cases, the alphabet L^1 must be extended with a new special symbol δ to $\mathbb{L}^1 = L^1 \bigcup \{\delta\}$. Language $\mathbb{L}^2$ is constructed as an extension to language L_2 by setting $p(\delta) = 1$, $p(\delta|\gamma_i) = 0$ and $\forall \gamma_i \in L^1 \ p(\gamma_i|\delta) = p(\gamma_i)$. Thus, all strings in $\mathbb{L}_2$ start with the to L_2 independent substring δ and then continue as in L_2. Now, by setting $X_{-1}^{h_1} = \delta$, it is possible to rewrite (19) as follows.

$$H_2^{I_1} = p(X_{-1}^l|X_{-1}^{h_1})H(X_0|X_{-1}^l) + \sum_{i=1}^{\beta_1-1} p(L_2^{i-1}X_{i-1}^l|X_{-1}^{h_1})H(X_i|X_{i-1}^l)$$

$$= \sum_{i \in I_1} p(L_2^{i-\alpha_1}X_{i-1}^l|X_{\alpha_1-1}^{h_1})H(X_i|X_{i-1}^l) \qquad (22)$$

Note that (22) is a special case of (21) with $j = 1$, hence

$$H_2^I = \sum_{j \in J}\sum_{i \in I_j} p(L_2^{i-\alpha_j}X_{i-1}^l|X_{\alpha_j-1}^{h_j})H(X_i|X_{i-1}^l) \qquad (23)$$

For L_1 languages (23) transforms as

$$H_2^I = \sum_{j \in J}\sum_{i \in I_j} p(L_1^{i-\alpha_j}X_{i-1})H(X_i) = \sum_{i \in I} H(X_i) = H_1^I \qquad (24)$$

Furthermore, H_2^I can be larger or smaller than H_1^I. For instance, the probability distribution in Table 1 gives $H_1^I < H_2^I$ if X_0^1 and $H_2^I < H_1^I$ if X_0^2. In Fig. 1 the eight different states of a selectively encrypted string containing three substrings are illustrated with encrypted substrings colored gray and unencrypted substrings colored white. The states are grouped into columns according to the encryption level, with arrows pointing towards the next state containing the encrypted substrings of the current state. By using (23) the entropy of the different states becomes

1. $H_2^I = 0$
2. $H_2^I = H(X_0)$
3. $H_2^I = H(X_1|X_0^{h_1})$
4. $H_2^I = H(X_2|X_1^{h_1})$
5. $H_2^I = H(X_0, X_1)$
6. $H_2^I = H(X_0) + p(X_1^l|X_1^{h_2})H(X_2|X_1^l)$
7. $H_2^I = p(X_0^l|X_0^{h_1})H(X_1|X_0^l) + p(L_2^1X_1^l|X_0^{h_1})H(X_2|X_1^l)$
8. $H_2^I = H(X_0, X_1, X_2)$

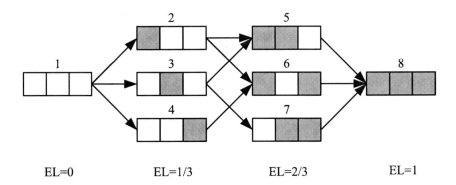

Fig. 1. The eight states of a selectively encrypted string containing three substrings

4.3   Third-Order Languages

For L_3 languages, the probability distribution of the symbols depends on the two preceding symbols. Thus, when deriving an expression for H_3^I, two symbols preceding a run of ones must be taken into consideration. Note that it is only the first preceding symbol of a run of ones that is known with certainty to be unencrypted. The second preceding symbol could either be encrypted or unencrypted; this will be denoted $X_i^\dagger$.

From the alphabet $\mathbb{L}^1 = L^1 \bigcup \{\delta\}$, language $\mathbb{L}_3$ is constructed as an extension of language L_3 by setting $p(\delta^2) = 1$, $p(\delta|\gamma_i) = 0$ and $\forall \gamma_i \in L^1$, $p(\gamma_i|\delta^2) = p(\gamma_i)$. Thus, all strings in $\mathbb{L}_3$ start with the independent substring δ^2 and then continue as in L_3. The conditional entropies in (14) can now be written for L_3 languages as

$$H_3^i = p(X_{\alpha_j-2}, \dots X_{i-2}^{l_1}, X_{i-1}^{l_2}|X_{\alpha_j-2}^\dagger, X_{\alpha_j-1}^{h_j})H(X_i|X_{i-2}^{l_1}, X_{i-1}^{l_2})$$
$$= p(L_3^{i-\alpha_j} X_{i-2}^{l_1}, X_{i-1}^{l_2}|X_{\alpha_j-2}^\dagger, X_{\alpha_j-1}^{h_j})H(X_i|X_{i-2}^{l_1}, X_{i-1}^{l_2}) \qquad (25)$$

Hence,

$$H_3^I = \sum_{j \in J}\sum_{i \in I_j} p(L_3^{i-\alpha_j} X_{i-2}^{l_1}, X_{i-1}^{l_2}|X_{\alpha_j-2}^\dagger, X_{\alpha_j-1}^{h_j})H(X_i|X_{i-2}^{l_1}, X_{i-1}^{l_2}) \qquad (26)$$

By using (26), the entropy of the different states in Fig. 1 becomes

1. $H_3^I = 0$
2. $H_3^I = H(X_0)$
3. $H_3^I = p(X_0^{l_2}|X_0^{h_1})H(X_1|X_0^{l_2})$
4. $H_3^I = p(X_0^{l_1}, X_1^{l_2}|X_0^\dagger, X_1^{h_1})H(X_2|X_0^{l_1}, X_1^{l_2})$
5. $H_3^I = H(X_0, X_1)$
6. $H_3^I = H(X_0) + p(X_0^{l_1}, X_1^{l_2}|X_0^\dagger, X_1^{h_2})H(X_2|X_0^{l_1} X_1^{l_2})$
7. $H_3^I = p(X_0^{l_2}|X_0^{h_1})H(X_1|X_0^{l_2}) + p(X_0^{l_1}, X_1^{l_2}|X_0^{h_1})H(X_2|X_0^{l_1}, X_1^{l_2})$
8. $H_3^I = H(X_0, X_1, X_2)$

4.4 n-Order Languages

For L_n languages the probability distribution of the symbols depends on $n-1$ preceding symbol. Thus, as before, from the alphabet $\mathbb{L}^1 = L^1 \bigcup \{\delta\}$, language $\mathbb{L}_n$ is constructed as an extension of language L_n by setting $p(\delta^{n-1}) = 1$, $p(\delta|\gamma_i) = 0$ and $\forall \gamma_i \in L^1$, $p(\gamma_i|\delta^{n-1}) = p(\gamma_i)$ Thus, all strings in $\mathbb{L}_n$ start with the independent substring δ^{n-1} and then continue as in L_n.

To shorten the notation in the following expressions

$$\mathbb{X}_{i-1}^{n-1} = X_{i-(n-1)}^{l_1}, \ldots, X_{i-1}^{l_{n-1}} \tag{27}$$

and

$$\mathbb{Y}_{\alpha_j-1}^{n-1} = X_{\alpha_j-(n-1)}^{\dagger}, \ldots, X_{\alpha_j-1}^{h_j} \tag{28}$$

By using (27) and (28) the conditional entropies in (14) can now be written for L_n languages as

$$H_n^i = p(L_n^{i-\alpha_j} \mathbb{X}_{i-1}^{n-1} | Y_{i-1}^{n-1}) H(X_i | \mathbb{X}_{i-1}^{n-1}) \tag{29}$$

Hence,

$$H_n^I = \sum_{j \in J} \sum_{i \in I_j} p(L_n^{i-\alpha_j} \mathbb{X}_{i-1}^{n-1} | \mathbb{Y}_{\alpha_j-1}^{n-1}) H(X_i | \mathbb{X}_{i-1}^{n-1}) \tag{30}$$

5   Concluding Remarks

We have in this paper continued the investigation of the confidentiality implications of selective encryption by applying entropy on a generic selective encryption scheme. By using the concept of run-length vector from run-length encoding theory, an expression was derived for entropy of selectively encrypted strings when the number of encrypted substrings, containing one symbol, and the order of the language change.

To further understand the confidentiality implication of selective encryption we will investigate how entropy changes when the substrings are of different sizes larger than one. Moreover, the conditional probabilities in the paper are used left to right. That is, if $b = (0,1)$, then the first string gives information about the second string. However, if $b = (1,0)$, then the second string also gives information about the first string. In our future work we will also aim to investigate how the entropy changes for different sources of information and appearances of the bit vector.

References

1. Cover, T., Thomas, J.: Elements of Information Theory. John Wiley & Sons, New York (1991)
2. Folland, G.B.: Real Analysis, Modern Techniques and Their Applications. John Wiley & Sons, New York (1999)

3. Goodman, J., Chandrakasan, A.P.: Low power scalable encryption for wireless systems. Wireless Networks 4(1), 55–70 (1998)
4. Lindskog, S., Lundin, R., Brunstrom, A.: Middleware support for tunable encryption. In: Proceedings of the 5th International Workshop on Wireless Information Systems, WIS 2006 (May 23, 2006)
5. Lundin, R., Lindskog, S.: Security implications of selective encryption. In: Proceedings of the 6th International Workshop on Security Measurements and Metrics (MetriSec 2010), Bolzano, Italy (September 15, 2010)
6. Podesser, M., Schmidt, H.P., Uhl, A.: Selective bitplane encryption for secure transmission of image data in mobile environments. In: Proceedings of the 5th IEEE Nordic Signal Processing Symposium (NORSIG 2002), Tromsø/Trondheim, Norway, October 4-6 (2002)
7. Shahid, Z., Chaumont, M., Puech, W.: Fast protection of H.264/AVC by selective encryption of CABAC for I & P frames. In: Proceedings of the 17th European Signal Processing Conference (EUSIPCO 2009), Glasgow, Scotland, August 24–28, pp. 2201–2205 (2009)
8. Shannon, C.E.: Claude Elwood Shannon: Collected Papers. IEEE Press, Piscataway (1993)
9. Spanos, G.A., Maples, T.B.: Performance study of a selective encryption scheme for security of networked, real-time video. In: Proceedings of the 4th International Conference on Computer Communications and Networks (ICCCN 1995), Las Vegas, Nevada, USA, pp. 72–78 (September 1995)
10. Su, Z., Jiang, J., Lian, S., Zhang, G., Hu, D.: Hierarchical selective encryption for G.729 speech based on bit sensitivity. Journal of Internet Technology 10(5), 599–608 (2010)

Practical Attacks on HB and HB+ Protocols[*]

Zbigniew Gołębiewski, Krzysztof Majcher, Filip Zagórski,
and Marcin Zawada

Institute of Mathematics and Computer Science, Wrocław University of Technology
{zbigniew.golebiewski,k.majcher,filip.zagorski,marcin.zawada}@pwr.wroc.pl

Abstract. HB and HB+ are a shared secret-key authentication protocols designed for low-cost devices such as RFID tags. HB+ was proposed
by Juels and Weis at Crypto 2005. The security of the protocols relies
on the "learning parity with noise" (LPN) problem, which was proven to
be NP-hard.

The best known attack on LPN by Levieil and Fouque [13] requires
sub-exponential number of samples and sub-exponential number of operations, which makes that attack impractical for the RFID scenario (one
cannot assume to collect exponentially-many observations of the protocol
execution).

We present a passive attack on HB protocol in detection-based model
which requires only linear (in the length of a secret key) number of
samples. Number of performed operations is exponential, but attack is
efficient for some real-life values of the parameters, i. e. noise $\frac{1}{8}$ and key
length 152-bits. Passive attack on HB can be transformed into active one
on HB+.

Keywords: lightweight cryptography, RFID, authentication, LPN problem, learning parity with noise, HB, HB+.

1   Introduction

The HB/HB+ Scheme. HB [12] is a lightweight secret-key protocol for RFID
tag identification. It is based on the human-to-computer authentication protocol
designed by Hopper and Blum (HB, [11]). The security of the HB/HB+ schemes
is provable – it is based on the "learning parity with noise" (LPN) problem,
which was proved to be NP-hard [2].

Previous Attacks. Over the last years, several attacks on the LPN problem have
been proposed. Most of them (e.g. *LF2* from [13] or [14]) are tune-ups of the
BKW algorithm (Blum, Kalai, Wasserman 2003) [3].

   The BKW algorithm takes a sub-exponential (in the size of the secret key)
number of samples and then tries to find out a secret key by adding up sample
vectors to obtain vectors from a canonical basis of a vector space. An algorithm

---

[*] This paper was supported by funds from Polish Ministry of Science and Higher
Education – grant No. N N206 2573 35.

C.A. Ardagna and J. Zhou (Eds.): WISTP 2011, LNCS 6633, pp. 244–253, 2011.

proposed in [14] manages from a small number of samples to generate exponentially many of them and then use the BKW algorithm.

HB+ is vulnerable to man-in-the-middle attack proposed by Gilbert, Robshaw, and Silbert [7]. Since then, many other schemes have been proposed to design an LPN-based protocol which is secure against man-in-the-middle attacks [4,15,9] and some of them have been already broken – see [6,8,16].

Our Results. We present a different approach to attack LPN problem. Our attack has worse asymptotic time-complexity that the best algorithms solving LPN problem, but it is efficient for real-life sizes of the parameters – parameters that may be used in RFID devices. Some ideas of our algorithm are already used as a sub-protocol in [6] to attack LPN-based protocols.

We need only to collect two successful executions of the HB protocol in order to start an attack (while other solutions need much larger samples). We assume that a single execution of the HB protocol uses parameters suggested in [13], i. e. number of bits sent during a single execution of the protocol is $O(n^2)$, where n is the length of a secret key. Number of bits required by the best known algorithm is $\Omega(2^n)$ while we need only to collect $O(n^3)$ bits (i. e. $O(n)$ protocol executions).

Our first implementation of the algorithm breaks 88-bit HB with noise parameter $\frac{1}{4}$ and 152-bit HB with noise parameter $\frac{1}{8}$. We estimate that algorithm presented is able to practically break HB for noise parameter $\frac{1}{4}$ for keys of the length up to $n = 96$.

Let us also notice that the presented passive attack on HB can be transformed into active one on HB+.

2   Description of the HB and HB+ Protocols

The HB Protocol. The Tag and the Reader share public values: $n, \varepsilon, \eta(\varepsilon)$ and a secret key x of the length n. The protocol proceeds in r 2-move rounds as shown in Figure 1: the tag generates a challenge $a^{(i)} \in_R \{0,1\}^n$ and sends it to the tag; the tag computes $(\mathbf{a^{(i)}} \cdot \mathbf{x}) \oplus \nu^{(i)}$, where $\nu^{(i)} \sim Ber(\varepsilon)$. The reader authenticates the tag if the number of i's, for which $z^{(i)} \neq a^{(i)} \cdot x$ does not exceed ηr.

Public parameters: $n, \varepsilon, \eta(\varepsilon)$
Shared secret key: $\mathbf{x} \in \{0,1\}^n$

Reader		**Tag**

choose $\mathbf{a}^{(i)} \in_R \{0,1\}^n$ $\xrightarrow{\mathbf{a}^{(i)}}$

$$\nu^{(i)} := \begin{cases} 1 \text{ with probability } \varepsilon \\ 0 \text{ with probability } 1 - \varepsilon \end{cases}$$

check $z^{(i)} \overset{?}{=} \mathbf{a}^{(i)} \cdot \mathbf{x}$ $\xleftarrow{z^{(i)}}$ $z^{(i)} := (\mathbf{a}^{(i)} \cdot \mathbf{x}) \oplus \nu^{(i)}$

Fig. 1. The i-th round of HB protocol

Efficiency of the HB. Efficiency of the HB protocol depends on three values: n, ε, r (in fact $r = r(n, \eta)$). The number of bits sent during an authentication process by the reader is equal to $N_r(n, \eta) = n \cdot r(\eta)$, the tag responds with $N_t = r(\eta)$ bits. Unfortunately, the simplicity in hardware design influences on the communication complexity. The number of bits sent required by a <u>reliable</u> authentication, according to [13], are presented in the table below (all values in KB, $1KB = 8192b$).

Table 1. Number of bits sent during the authentication (in KB)

n	$\eta = 1/20$	$\eta = 1/8$	$\eta = 1/4$
128	4	7	18
512	16	28	73

So, for some parameters of the HB/HB+ protocol, it may take seconds to authenticate even an expensive tag. The meaning of the "high-speed data rate" for RFIDs depends on the manufacturer and varies usually from $20KB/s$ to $40KB/s$. Low-end RFIDs are even 10-times slower.

This leads to the observation that for cheap RFIDs a key length and a number of rounds and thus a noise parameter ε should be adjusted at the relatively low level.

The HB+ Protocol. The HB+ was proposed as a protocol robust against active attacks (while HB is immune against passive attacks). Use of the blinding factor y turns an active attack on HB+ into a passive attack on HB.

In the HB+ scheme the tag and the reader share public values: $n, \varepsilon, r(n, \varepsilon)$ and secret keys x, y. The protocol proceeds in r 3-move rounds as shown on Figure 2.

Let us notice that if an attacker wants to break actively the HB+ tag i. e. by sending appropriate values of a, she has to be able to passively break HB.

Public parameters: $n, \varepsilon, \eta(\varepsilon)$
Shared secret keys: $\mathbf{x}, \mathbf{y} \in \{0, 1\}^n$

Reader		Tag
choose $\mathbf{a}^{(i)} \in_R \{0,1\}^n$	$\xrightarrow{\mathbf{a}^{(i)}}$	
	$\xleftarrow{\mathbf{b}^{(i)}}$	choose $\mathbf{b}^{(i)} \in_R \{0,1\}^n$
		$\nu^{(i)} := \begin{cases} 1 \text{ with probability } \varepsilon \\ 0 \text{ with probability } 1 - \varepsilon \end{cases}$
check $z^{(i)} \stackrel{?}{=} (\mathbf{a}^{(i)} \cdot \mathbf{x}) \oplus (\mathbf{b}^{(i)} \cdot \mathbf{y})$	$\xleftarrow{z^{(i)}}$	$z^{(i)} := (\mathbf{a}^{(i)} \cdot \mathbf{x}) \oplus (\mathbf{b}^{(i)} \cdot \mathbf{y}) \oplus \nu^{(i)}$

Fig. 2. The i-th round of HB+ protocol

3 Passive Attacks on HB Protocol

Basic notation. Let $\mathbf{x} \in \{0,1\}^n$ be a n-bit shared secret between the tag and reader. Suppose that a passive adversary has collected m authentications of the HB protocol. Let us consider that $\mathbf{A} = \{\mathbf{a}_i \in \{0,1\}^n : i = 1, \ldots, m\}$ be a matrix of challenges sent by a reader (each challenge is a row of the matrix) and let $\mathbf{z} = \{z_i \in \{0,1\} : i = 1, \ldots, m\}$ be a vector of collected responses for the tag.

The subset $\mathbf{B} = \{\mathbf{b}_i \,|\, i = 1, \ldots, n\} \subseteq \mathbf{A}$ is called a *basis* of $\{0,1\}^n$ treated as an n-dimensional vector space over $GF(2)$ if vectors $\mathbf{b}_i$ for $i = 1, \ldots, n$ are linearly independent and span whole space $\{0,1\}^n$.

Problem. We re-formulate the HB protocol as follows. The reader sends matrix $\mathbf{A}$ of challenges to the tag. The tag responses with a vector $\mathbf{z} = (\mathbf{A} \cdot \mathbf{x}) \oplus \mathbf{v}$, where $\mathbf{v}$ is m-bit vector of "noise". Then the reader checks if $|(\mathbf{A} \cdot \mathbf{x}) \oplus \mathbf{z}| \leq \eta \cdot m$, where $|\cdot|$ is the Hamming weight.

During eavesdropping, an attacker collects samples $\mathcal{S} = (\mathbf{A}, \mathbf{z})$ as a matrix $\mathbf{A}$ of challenges and vector of responses $\mathbf{z}$, therefore the problem of breaking HB is: to find a vector $\mathbf{x}'$ such that $|(\mathbf{A} \cdot \mathbf{x}') \oplus \mathbf{z}| \leq \eta \cdot m$.

Further we show that such $\mathbf{x}'$ has to be equal to the secret-key $\mathbf{x}$ with high probability. This problem is know in the literature as the Learning Parity in the present of Noise (LPN problem).

k-Basis Property. Let us assume that we have collected m samples $\mathcal{S} = (\mathbf{A}, \mathbf{z})$ of the HB protocol. Further, we have found such a matrix $\mathbf{B} \subseteq \mathbf{A}$ of size $n \times n$ with vector of responses $\mathbf{z_B}$ such that $\mathbf{B}$ is a basis and vector $\mathbf{z_B}$ has all correct responses ($\mathbf{z_B} = \mathbf{B} \cdot \mathbf{x}$). In such a case we can easily find a secret $\mathbf{x}$. Since we have a system of linear equations over $GF(2)$, thus we can solve it very fast by Gaussian elimination. Let us notice that linear equations have exactly one solution since $\mathbf{B}$ form a basis. The secret can also be found by possessing inverse matrix of $\mathbf{B}$ as follows: $\mathbf{x} = \mathbf{B}^{-1} \cdot \mathbf{z_B}$. However situations that we are capable to find such a basis are quite rare. Thus we introduce the notion of k-basis. A k-basis is a basis with exactly k responses wrong.

Definition 1. *A k-basis for a HB protocol instance $(n, \mathbf{x}, \varepsilon, \eta, r)$ and samples $\mathcal{S} = (\mathbf{A}, \mathbf{z})$ is a subset $\mathbf{B} \subseteq \mathbf{A}$ with a vector of responses $\mathbf{z_B}$ which satisfies the following conditions:*

- *$\mathbf{B}$ is a basis of an n-dimensional vector space $\{0,1\}^n$,*
- *$|(\mathbf{B} \cdot \mathbf{x}) \oplus \mathbf{z_B}| = k$.*

We call a *k-basis test* a procedure of verification if both conditions of the definition of k-basis hold.

3.1 Simple Walker Algorithm

Our first algorithm (called a Simple Walker Algorithm) is quite simple probabilistic algorithm which implements the idea presented in previous subsection

i. e. one collects samples and then finds 0-basis. As we mentioned before, possessing 0-basis is equivalent to finding a secret key $\mathbf{x}$. Simple Walker Algorithm can be treated as a slightly different version of the natural brute-force algorithm. However simulations show that even such simple algorithm works quite well in practical settings and there is still room for improvements. In Algorithm 1 we presents pseudo-code of the algorithm which finds secret $\mathbf{x}$ and needs only $m \geq n + C$ samples of the "single authentication step of HB protocol" (Fig. 1), where C is a small constant needed to assure that one can find a basis of n dimensional space in a set of $m = n + C$ vectors each of the length n (for more information see [10]). Input of the algorithm is a set of samples $\mathcal{S} = (\mathbf{A}, \mathbf{z}), n, \varepsilon, \eta$) and the output is a secret vector $\mathbf{x}$.

Algorithm 1. SIMPLEWALKER($\mathcal{S} = (\mathbf{A}, \mathbf{z}), n, \varepsilon, \eta$)

1: $m \leftarrow$ length of the vector $\mathbf{z}$
2: find subset $\mathbf{B} \subseteq \mathbf{A}$ such that it is a basis with responses $\mathbf{z_B}$
3: $\mathbf{A}' \leftarrow \mathbf{A} \cdot \mathbf{B}^{-1}$
4: **repeat**
5:     $\boldsymbol{\nu} \leftarrow$ choose a random vector $\in \{0, 1\}^n$, provided that $|\boldsymbol{\nu}| \sim Bin(n, \varepsilon)$ (i.e. the number of 1's in $\boldsymbol{\nu}$ is Binomially distributed with parameters n, ε)
6:     $\mathbf{z}'_{\mathbf{B}} \leftarrow \mathbf{z_B} \oplus \boldsymbol{\nu}$
7: **until** $|(\mathbf{A}' \cdot \mathbf{z}'_{\mathbf{B}}) \oplus \mathbf{z}| \leq \eta \cdot m$
8: **return** $\mathbf{x} \leftarrow \mathbf{B}^{-1} \cdot \mathbf{z}'_{\mathbf{B}}$

The SIMPLEWALKER could be impractical even a few years ago, but since it can be very easily implemented in distributed fashion collecting even small number of samples and access to computers, an adversary can easily find a secret key. Moreover, remarkable progress in multi-core processors makes the HB protocol even more vulnerable to SIMPLEWALKER. Further, it is worth to mention that SIMPLEWALKER has very low memory requirements.

3.2 k-Basis Walker Algorithm

The main drawback of SIMPLEWALKER algorithm is that it is purely probabilistic and do not try to take advantage of using data that were already computed in previous attempts. Therefore, we introduce second algorithm k-BASISWALKER. Let us describe the main idea behind the algorithm. The algorithm takes a set of the samples $\mathcal{S} = (\mathbf{A}, \mathbf{z})$, where $\mathbf{A}$ is a set of challenges, $\mathbf{z}$ is a set of responses. Then it divides $\mathcal{S}$ into two parts $(\mathbf{U}, \mathbf{z_U})$ and $(\mathbf{V}, \mathbf{z_V})$. The samples $(\mathbf{U}, \mathbf{z_U})$ are used as a "universe" from which the algorithm picks at random potential 0-Basis. It is called *the testing set* while the samples $(\mathbf{V}, \mathbf{z_V})$ are used for k-Basis-testing and are called *the observations set*. It is important to make this division correctly i.e. in a way that does not change the fraction of incorrect responses. For instance, let $\mathcal{W}(\mathbf{z})$ denote an expected percentage of the incorrect bits in vector $\mathbf{z}$, then the division of the samples set has to satisfy: $\mathcal{W}(\mathbf{z}) = \mathcal{W}(\mathbf{z_U}) = \mathcal{W}(\mathbf{z_V})$.

Notice, that performing such division can be done as follows. Let α be some adjustable parameter. Thus, if one eavesdropped l correct executions of the HB protocol then $\lfloor \alpha l \rfloor$ of these executions could be treated as $(\mathbf{U}, \mathbf{z_U})$ and the rest of executions $\lceil (1-\alpha)l \rceil$ could be treated as $(\mathbf{V}, \mathbf{z_V})$.

As we show later, we need that the sample set has to contain at least $|\mathbf{A}| \geq n + \frac{n}{1-\eta} = O(n)$ vectors. The size of the testing set should be at least of the size of the length of authentication packet n. We also need about $\frac{n}{1-\eta}$ samples (vectors) to be sure that in the sample space there exists at least one 0-Basis. For parameters suggested in [13] and small keys (length smaller than 128), it occurs that our algorithm needs to collect observations from only 2 successful executions of the HB.

Input of the algorithm is a set of samples $\mathcal{S} = (\mathbf{A}, \mathbf{z}), n, \varepsilon, \eta, k)$ and the output is a secret vector $\mathbf{x}$.

Algorithm 2. k-BASISWALKER($\mathcal{S} = (\mathbf{A}, \mathbf{z}), n, \varepsilon, \eta, k$)

1: divide $(\mathbf{A}, \mathbf{z})$ into $(\mathbf{U}, \mathbf{z_U})$ and $(\mathbf{V}, \mathbf{z_V})$
2: $m \leftarrow$ length of the vector $\mathbf{z_V}$
3: **loop**
4:    **repeat**
5:       $\mathbf{B} \in_R \mathbf{U}$ draw at random n row vectors and the corresponding vector $\mathbf{z_B} \subseteq \mathbf{z_U}$
6:    **until** $\mathbf{B}$ is a basis of an n-dimensional vector space $\{0, 1\}^n$
7:    $\mathbf{V'} \leftarrow \mathbf{V} \cdot \mathbf{B}^{-1}$
8:    **for** $1 \leq i_1 \leq n$ **do**
9:       $\boldsymbol{\nu} \leftarrow n$-bits vector with 1 at position i_1
10:      $\mathbf{z'_B} \leftarrow \mathbf{z_B} \oplus \boldsymbol{\nu}$
11:      **if** $|(\mathbf{V'} \cdot \mathbf{z'_B}) \oplus \mathbf{z_V}| \leq \eta \cdot m$ **then**
12:         **return** $\mathbf{B}^{-1} \cdot \mathbf{z'_B}$
13:      **end if**
14:    **end for**

15:    $\vdots$
16:    **for** $1 \leq i_1 < i_2 < \ldots < i_k \leq n$ **do**
17:       $\boldsymbol{\nu} \leftarrow n$-bits vector with 1's at positions $i_1, i_2, \ldots, i_k$
18:      $\mathbf{z'_B} \leftarrow \mathbf{z_B} \oplus \boldsymbol{\nu}$
19:      **if** $|(\mathbf{V'} \cdot \mathbf{z'_B}) \oplus \mathbf{z_V}| \leq \eta \cdot m$ **then**
20:         **return** $\mathbf{B}^{-1} \cdot \mathbf{z'_B}$
21:      **end if**
22:    **end for**
23: **end loop**

After execution of the above algorithm we get a basis $\mathbf{B}$ and the corresponding set of responses $\mathbf{z_B}$. Because one has to check if the 0-Basis test holds, one has to find a representation of the testing-vectors. It takes a while, so is worth to use the same basis several times. To find a representations of test vectors in a basis $\mathbf{B}$ it takes $O(n^2 \cdot |\mathbf{V}|)$, so it is worth to check if the set $\mathbf{B}$ is 1-Basis or 2-Basis, because checking i-Basis property requires $\binom{n}{i} \cdot |\mathbf{B}|$ operations.

Let us call by 012-*Basis Walker Algorithm (012-BWA, BWA)* a modification of the 0-*Basis Walker Algorithm* which checks also 1- and 2-Basis property for every picked set. As we will see later this has a good influence on the efficiency of the algorithm.

4   Algorithm Analysis

First, let us find a probability that k-BASISWALKER finds a k-basis (line 4–6 of the Algorithm 2).

Lemma 1. *Let $(n, \mathbf{x}, \varepsilon, \eta, r)$ be a instance of HB protocol. Let $\mathcal{S} = (\mathbf{A}, \mathbf{z})$ be a sample of the HB protocol divided into $(\mathbf{U}, \mathbf{z_U})$ and $(\mathbf{V}, \mathbf{z_V})$ such that $|\mathbf{U}| = t$. Then, the probability that the matrix $\mathbf{B}$ picked uniformly at random from $\mathbf{U}$ is k-basis equals to*

$$p_k = p_B \binom{n}{k} \sum_{j=k}^{\lfloor \eta \cdot t \rfloor} \binom{t-n}{j-k} \varepsilon^j (1-\varepsilon)^{t-j}, \tag{1}$$

where $p_B \approx 0.2887$ denote the probability that randomly chosen set $\mathbf{B}$ is a basis of an n-dimensional vector space $\{0,1\}^n$.

Proof. The probability that random chosen set $\mathbf{B}$ of size n from $\mathbf{U}$ is k-basis can be calculated as follows. Let C_j denotes an event that there are exactly j incorrect responses in $(\mathbf{U}, \mathbf{z_U})$. Then from the Bernoulli trails we have: $\Pr[C_j] = \binom{t}{j} \varepsilon^j (1-\varepsilon)^{t-j}$. Let A be an event that $\mathbf{B} \in_R \mathbf{U}$ is a basis and B_k be an event that $\mathbf{B}$ has exactly k incorrect responses. Thus, the probability that $\mathbf{B}$ is k-basis is equal to $p_k = \Pr[A \wedge B_k]$. By the law of total probability we obtain that $\Pr[A \wedge B_k] = \sum_{j=k}^{\lfloor \eta \cdot t \rfloor} \Pr[A \wedge B_k \wedge C_j] = \sum_{j=k}^{\lfloor \eta \cdot t \rfloor} \Pr[A|B_k \wedge C_j] \cdot \Pr[B_k|C_j] \cdot \Pr[C_j]$.

Since $\mathbf{B}$ is k-basis, then $\mathbf{U}$ must have at least k incorrect responses, thus the sum starts from $j = k$. The upper bound of the sum is $\lfloor \eta \cdot t \rfloor$ because we assume that $\mathbf{U}$ comes from successful authentications. The probability p_B that set B is a basis of $\{0,1\}^n$ is independent on the choices of the responses and $p_B \approx 0.2887$ has been already calculated in the paper [5]. Thus $\Pr[A|B_k \wedge C_j] = p_B$. The probability that one taking n bits from the vector of $\mathbf{z_U}$ responses of length t, takes exactly k wrong responses is equal to $\Pr[B_k|C_j] = \binom{t-j}{n-k} \cdot \binom{j}{k} \cdot \binom{t}{n}^{-1}$. After elementary simplifications, we obtain that $\frac{\binom{t-j}{n-k}\binom{j}{k}}{\binom{t}{n}} \cdot \binom{t}{j} = \binom{n}{k} \cdot \binom{t-n}{j-k}$.

Thus, the proof of the lemma follows.   □

The expected value and the variance of basis that should be tested. Let X_k denote a random variable that counts the number of basis that should be tested before at most one k-basis is found. It easy to see that the variable X_k is geometrically distributed with the success probability $p_{X_k} = \sum_{i=0}^{k} p_i$. Thus the expected value for geometrically distributed random variable is $\mathbf{E}[X_k] = 1/p_{X_k}$ and the variance $\mathbf{Var}[X_k] = (1 - p_{X_k})/p_{X_k}^2$. Notice that we are not interested in asymptotic

Table 2. The expected number of basis that should be tested in case of the 012-BWA

n	Size of a sample $m = 3 \cdot n$		Size of a sample $m = n^2$	
	$\varepsilon = 0.125$, $\eta = 0.256$	$\varepsilon = 0.25$, $\eta = 0.348$	$\varepsilon = 0.125$, $\eta = 0.256$	$\varepsilon = 0.25$, $\eta = 0.348$
48	68	24172	44	5271
64	348	$1.39 \cdot 10^6$	167	146704
80	1963	$9.04 \cdot 10^7$	694	$4.55 \cdot 10^6$
96	11865	$6.33 \cdot 10^9$	3062	$1.51 \cdot 10^8$
112	75287	$4.67 \cdot 10^{11}$	14108	$5.30 \cdot 10^9$
128	495413	$3.59 \cdot 10^{13}$	67206	$1.92 \cdot 10^{11}$
144	$3.35 \cdot 10^6$	$2.84 \cdot 10^{15}$	328581	$7.21 \cdot 10^{12}$
160	$2.32 \cdot 10^7$	$2.30 \cdot 10^{17}$	$1.64 \cdot 10^6$	$2.76 \cdot 10^{14}$

behavior, since in practice the size of the secret key is at most 512. Thus, in Table 2 we present only the numerical results of $\mathbf{E}[X_k]$ for different value of protocol parameters.

Finding Wrong Secrets. Now we deal with the problem of getting secret keys different from the searched ones. In the Lemma 3 we show how often a "bad" basis passes the test.

Lemma 2. *Let* $\mathbf{x}$ *be* n-*bit secret key. Let* $\mathbf{A}$ *be a matrix of challenges and* $\mathbf{z_A}$ *be a* m-*bit vector of responses. We assume that* $\mathbf{B} \subseteq \mathbf{A}$ *is a* k-*basis with vector* $\mathbf{z_B} \subseteq \mathbf{z_A}$ *of responses and* $\mathbf{x}' = \mathbf{B}^{-1} \cdot \mathbf{z_B}$ *is a potential secret key. Then*

$$\Pr[(\mathbf{a} \cdot \mathbf{x}) \oplus \nu \neq \mathbf{a} \cdot \mathbf{x}'] = \begin{cases} \varepsilon & \text{if } k = 0, \\ \frac{1}{2} & \text{if } k \geq 1, \end{cases} \tag{2}$$

where $\mathbf{a} \in_R \{0,1\}^n$ *and* ν *is* $0-1$ *random variable such that* $\Pr[\nu = 1] = \varepsilon$.

Proof. By the law of total probability we get

$$\Pr[(\mathbf{a} \cdot \mathbf{x}) \oplus \nu \neq \mathbf{a} \cdot \mathbf{B}^{-1} \cdot \mathbf{z_B}] =$$
$$\Pr[\mathbf{a} \cdot \mathbf{x} \neq \mathbf{a} \cdot \mathbf{B}^{-1} \cdot \mathbf{z_B}] \cdot \Pr[\nu = 0] + \Pr[\mathbf{a} \cdot \mathbf{x} = \mathbf{a} \cdot \mathbf{B}^{-1} \cdot \mathbf{z_B}] \cdot \Pr[\nu = 1].$$

Notice that if $\mathbf{B}$ is 0-basis then $\mathbf{x} = \mathbf{B}^{-1} \cdot \mathbf{z_B}$. Thus $\Pr[\mathbf{a} \cdot \mathbf{x} \neq \mathbf{a} \cdot \mathbf{B}^{-1} \cdot \mathbf{z_B}] = 0$ and $\Pr[\mathbf{a} \cdot \mathbf{x} = \mathbf{a} \cdot \mathbf{B}^{-1} \cdot \mathbf{z_B}] = 1$. Therefore for 0-basis we obtain

$$\Pr[(\mathbf{a} \cdot \mathbf{x}) \oplus \nu \neq \mathbf{a} \cdot \mathbf{B}^{-1} \cdot \mathbf{z_B}] = \Pr[\nu = 1] = \varepsilon .$$

Let $k > 0$. Consider that $\mathbf{B}$ is k-basis. We need to calculate the probability $\Pr[\mathbf{a} \cdot \mathbf{x} \neq \mathbf{a} \cdot \mathbf{B}^{-1} \cdot \mathbf{z_B}]$. Let $\mathbf{z}_{corr} = \mathbf{B} \cdot \mathbf{x}$ be a vector of correct responses. Then

$$\Pr[\mathbf{a} \cdot \mathbf{x} \neq \mathbf{a} \cdot \mathbf{B}^{-1} \cdot \mathbf{z_B}] = \Pr[\mathbf{a} \cdot \mathbf{B}^{-1} \cdot \mathbf{z}_{corr} \neq \mathbf{a} \cdot \mathbf{B}^{-1} \cdot \mathbf{z_B}]$$
$$= \Pr[\mathbf{a} \cdot \mathbf{B}^{-1} \cdot (\mathbf{z}_{corr} - \mathbf{z_B}) \neq 0] .$$

Since $\mathbf{z}_{corr} - \mathbf{z_B}$ has 1's on $k \geq 1$ positions and $\mathbf{B}^{-1}$ has linearly independent vectors. Then, by fact that if $(X_i)_{i=1,\ldots,k}$ are independent random 0-1 variables

$\Pr[X_i = 1] = 1/2$, then $\Pr[\bigoplus_{i=1}^{k} X_i \neq 0] = 1/2$. Moreover, notice that $\Pr[X_i \oplus \nu = 0] = \Pr[X_i = 0] \cdot \Pr[\nu = 1] + \Pr[X_i = 1] \cdot \Pr[\nu = 0] = (1/2) \cdot \varepsilon + (1 - \varepsilon) \cdot (1/2) = 1/2$. Therefore $\Pr[\mathbf{a} \cdot \mathbf{x} \neq \mathbf{a} \cdot \mathbf{B}^{-1} \cdot \mathbf{z_B}] = \frac{1}{2}$. Thus, the proof is complete.   □

Lemma 3. *Let $\mathcal{S} = (\mathbf{A}, \mathbf{z})$ be a sample of the HB protocol divided into $(\mathbf{U}, \mathbf{z_u})$ and $(\mathbf{V}, \mathbf{z_v})$ such that $|\mathbf{V}| = m$. Let $\mathbf{B} \subseteq \mathbf{U}$ be a k-basis for $k \geq 1$ with vector $\mathbf{z_B}$ of responses. Thus $\mathbf{x}' = \mathbf{B}^{-1} \cdot \mathbf{z_B}$ is a wrong secret key. Then the probability that $\mathbf{x}'$ passes a test $|(\mathbf{V} \cdot \mathbf{x}') \oplus \mathbf{z}| \leq \eta \cdot m$ is given by $\frac{1}{2^m} \cdot \sum_{i=0}^{\eta \cdot m} \binom{m}{i}$.*

Proof. By Lemma 2 for $k \geq 1$, we obtain that single vector gives us a correct response with probability $1/2$. Then the probability p_i that exactly i vectors from $\mathbf{V}$ disagree is equal to $\binom{m}{i} \left(\frac{1}{2}\right)^i \left(1 - \frac{1}{2}\right)^{m-i} = \binom{m}{i} \left(\frac{1}{2}\right)^m$. Therefore, the probability that at most $\eta \cdot m$ out of m vectors passes a test we can obtain by adding the probabilities p_i for $i = 0, 1, \ldots, \eta \cdot m$.   □

5   Experimental Results

We have implemented and tested our algorithm for several values. We have broken HB for the parameter $\varepsilon = 0.125, \eta = 0.256, n = 144$ and it took about 3 hours on home PC. For the parameters $\varepsilon = 0.25, \eta = 0.348, n = 80$ it takes on average 10 hours on home PC.

This results and the values in the Table 2 suggest, that we are able to break $n = 96$ bit version of 0.25-HB and $n = 154$ bit version of 0.125-HB protocol.

Parallelization of the presented algorithm is very easy. We are currently working on the CUDA-version of the implementation. First results show that even a cheap GPU allow for about 8-time speedup of a protocol compared to the execution times run on CPU. The new graphic cards that have been recently appeared on the marked can run 8-times more threads than the one which we used for "pre"-testing. Use of GPUs allows to break keys that are few bits longer (≈ 10).

6   Conclusions

We have shown a passive attack for the HB protocol which allow to perform an active attack for HB+ scheme (not man-in-the middle). Our attack needs only $O(n)$ eavesdropped pairs of challenge-response, where n is the length of a secret key, while the best known algorithm *LF2* ([13]) needs exponential number of samples.

References

1. Chekuri, C., Jansen, K., Rolim, J.D.P., Trevisan, L. (eds.): APPROX 2005 and RANDOM 2005. LNCS, vol. 3624. Springer, Heidelberg (2005)
2. Berlekamp, E.R., McEliece, R.J., van Tilborg, H.C.A.: On the inherent intractability of certain coding problems. IEEE Trans. Info. Theory, 384–386 (1978)

3. Blum, A., Kalai, A., Wasserman, H.: Noise-tolerant learning, the parity problem, and the statistical query model. Journal of the ACM 50(4), 506–519 (2003)
4. Bringer, J., Chabanne, H., Kevenaar, T.A.M., Kindarji, B.: Extending match-on-card to local biometric identification. In: Fierrez, J., Ortega-Garcia, J., Esposito, A., Drygajlo, A., Faundez-Zanuy, M. (eds.) BioID MultiComm2009. LNCS, vol. 5707, pp. 178–186. Springer, Heidelberg (2009)
5. Cichon, J., Klonowski, M., Kutylowski, M.: Privacy protection for rfid with hidden subset identifiers. Pervasive Computing (2008)
6. Frumkin, D., Shamir, A.: Un-trusted-hb: Security vulnerabilities of trusted-hb. Cryptology ePrint Archive, Report 2009/044 (2009)
7. Gilbert, H., Sibert, H., Robshaw, M.: An active attack against a provably secure lightweight authentication protocol. IEEE Electronic Letters 41, 1169–1170 (2005)
8. Gilbert, H., Robshaw, M.J.B., Seurin, Y.: Good variants of hB+ are hard to find. In: Tsudik, G. (ed.) FC 2008. LNCS, vol. 5143, pp. 156–170. Springer, Heidelberg (2008)
9. Gilbert, H., Robshaw, M.J.B., Seurin, Y.: Hb# Increasing the security and efficiency of hb+. In: Smart, N.P. (ed.) EUROCRYPT 2008. LNCS, vol. 4965, pp. 361–378. Springer, Heidelberg (2008)
10. Golebiewski, Z., Majcher, K., Zagórski, F.: Attacks on CKK family of RFID authentication protocols. In: Coudert, D., Simplot-Ryl, D., Stojmenovic, I. (eds.) ADHOC-NOW 2008. LNCS, vol. 5198, pp. 241–250. Springer, Heidelberg (2008)
11. Hopper, N.J., Blum, M.: Secure human identification protocols. In: Boyd, C. (ed.) ASIACRYPT 2001. LNCS, vol. 2248, p. 52. Springer, Heidelberg (2001)
12. Juels, A., Weis, S.A.: Authenticating pervasive devices with human protocols. In: Shoup, V. (ed.) CRYPTO 2005. LNCS, vol. 3621, pp. 293–308. Springer, Heidelberg (2005)
13. Levieil, É., Fouque, P.-A.: An improved LPN algorithm. In: De Prisco, R., Yung, M. (eds.) SCN 2006. LNCS, vol. 4116, pp. 348–359. Springer, Heidelberg (2006)
14. Lyubashevsky, V.: The parity problem in the presence of noise, decoding random linear codes, and the subset sum problem. In: APPROX-RANDOM [1], pp. 378–389
15. Munilla, J., Peinado, A.: Hb-mp: A further step in the hb-family of lightweight authentication protocols. Comput. Netw. 51(9), 2262–2267 (2007)
16. Ouafi, K., Overbeck, R., Vaudenay, S.: On the security of hB# against a man-in-the-middle attack. In: Pieprzyk, J. (ed.) ASIACRYPT 2008. LNCS, vol. 5350, pp. 108–124. Springer, Heidelberg (2008)

Attacks on a Lightweight Mutual Authentication Protocol under EPC C-1 G-2 Standard

Mohammad Hassan Habibi, Mahdi R. Alagheband, and Mohammad Reza Aref

EE Department, ISSL Laboratory, Sharif University of Technology, Tehran, Iran
mohamad.h.habibi@gmail.com, m.alaghband@srbiau.ac.ir,
aref@sharif.edu

Abstract. Yeh et al. have recently proposed a mutual authentication protocol based on EPC Class-1 Gen.-2 standard. They claim their protocol is secure against adversarial attacks and also provides forward secrecy. In this paper we show that the proposed protocol does not have cited security features properly. A powerful and practical attack is presented on this protocol whereby the whole security of the protocol is broken. Furthermore, Yeh et al.'s protocol does not assure the *untraceabilitiy* and *backwarduntraceabilitiy* attributes. We also will propose our revision to safeguard the Yeh et al.'s protocol against cited attacks.

Keywords: RFID, authentication, EPC C-1 G-2 standard, Security analysis, Traceability attack.

1 Introduction

Nowadays Radio Frequency Identification (RFID) technology has been incorporated in our daily life and employed in many applications e.g. public transportation passes [1], supply chain management [2], e-passport [3] etc. RFID systems include tags, readers and back-end server. The tag is a low cost device with a constraint microchip, small memory and antenna to communicate with the reader. The readers are placed between tags and back-end server as an intermediary for message transmission. Not surprisingly, the back-end server has the whole information and secret values of all tags.

EPC Class-1 Gen.-2 standard is a framework for RFID communications, defined by EPC global (Electronic Product Code) organization [4, 5] but RFID authentication protocols based on it have undergone noticeable difficulties to satisfy the perfect security characteristics.

In order to have secure authentication protocols, an adversary should not be able to obtain any information about the target tag. Privacy and untraceability are two important issues relevant to RFID systems. Thus, an authentication protocol should assure the privacy characteristics including *untraceability* and *backward untraceability* for tags and their holders [6]. On the other side, RFID authentication protocols are under different threats, defined as follows.

Information leakage: the tag and reader perform an authentication protocol and exchange some messages with each other. Since the wireless communication channel is insecure, it can be eavesdropped by an adversary. Hence, each authentication protocol

C.A. Ardagna and J. Zhou (Eds.): WISTP 2011, LNCS 6633, pp. 254–263, 2011.
© IFIP International Federation for Information Processing 2011

should be designed in a way that the adversary, with reasonable computational capabilities, does not be able to exploit the exchanged messages [7].

Tag Tracing and tracking: Tag tracing and tracking are damaging problems in RF-ID systems. Even when the leakage of information isimpossible, the untraceability of tag and its holder is not guaranteed in RFID systems. Untraceability means that if an adversary eavesdrops message transmission between a target tag and a reader at time t, he does not be able to distinguish an interaction of that tag at time t' >t [8].

DoS attack: denial-of-Service (*DoS*) is another attack on RFID systems. An adversary tries to find ways to fail target tag from receiving services, e.g. in the desynchronization attack, as one kind of *DoS* attacks, the shared secret value between the tag and the back-end server is made inconsistentby an adversary. Then, the tag and back-end server cannot recognize each other in future and tag becomes disabled [9].

Many RFID authentication protocols have been proposed [10, 11, 12, 13, 14, 15]. Although these protocols tried to provide secure and untraceable communication for RFID systems, however many weaknesses have been found in them [16, 17, 18, 19, 20, 21]. In this context, Yeh et al. have recently proposed a RFID mutual authentication protocol compatible with EPC C-1 G-2 standard [22] that we name SRP (Securing RFID Protocol) in this paper. The authors have claimed that not only SRP does not reveal any information but also it has forward secrecy and robustness against *DoS* attack. In this paper, we prove that SRP is vulnerable to a powerful and fatal attack that needs only 2^{16} off-line PRNG (pseudo random number generator) computations. Furthermore, the whole security of this protocol will be destroyed inasmuch as the RFID system is most vulnerable to tag and reader impersonation, *DoS* attack, *untraceability* and *backward untraceability*. Finally we propose our revision to prevent the mentioned attacks.

2   Review SRP

2.1   Initialization Phase

The nine secret values K_{old}, P_{old}, C_{old}, K_{new}, P_{new}, C_{new}, EPC_s, RID and DATA corresponding to each tag is loaded in database. Besides, random values K_0, P_0 and C_0 are generated by manufacturer and the recorded values are set in a way that $K_{old}=K_{new}=K_0$, $P_{old}=P_{new}=P_0$ and $C_{old}=C_{new}=C_0$. Each tag records four values $K_i=K_0$, $P_i=P_0$, $C_i=C_0$ and EPC_s.

2.2   The (i+1)th Authentication Round

In this part, the SRP protocol is briefly described. The following steps explain the protocol in the round $(i+1)$.

1. The reader generates number N_R randomly and sends it to the tag.
2. Receiving N_R, the tag generates random number N_T and computes:
    $M1 = PRNG(EPC_s \oplus N_R) \oplus K_i$, $D = N_T \oplus K_i$ and $E = N_T \oplus PRNG(C_i \oplus K_i)$. Then the tag forwards $(C_i, M1, D, E)$ to the reader.
3. The reader computes $V = H(RID \oplus N_R)$ and sends $(C_i, M1, D, E, N_R, V)$ to the database.

Receives $(C_i, M1, D, E, N_R, V)$, the database performs the following procedure:

  a) For each stored RID, computes $H(RID \oplus N_R)$ and compares it with V to find whether the computed value is equal to V. If it is true, the database will authenticate the reader.

  b) Based on value C_i, one of the two following procedures is occurred:

  i. The database computes $PRNG(EPC_s \oplus N_R)$, $I_{old} = M1 \oplus K_{old}$ and $I_{new} = M1 \oplus K_{new}$ provided that $C_i = 0$, because it means the first access. Then it checks whether I_{old} or I_{new} correspond to $PRNG(EPC_s \oplus N_R)$. This process is regularly repeated until a match equality is founded. X is set to either *old* or *new* provided that either I_{old} or I_{new} is the match, respectively.

  ii. If $C_i \neq 0$, the database uses C_i as an index to find the corresponding recorded entry. When the database finds an entry correspondent to C_i, then the value of X is determined either *old* or new provided that $C_i = C_{old}$ or C_{new} respectively. Corresponding K_X and EPC_s are extracted to check whether $PRNG(EPC_s \oplus N_R) \oplus K_X$ is equal to $M1$ or not.

The database obtains N_T with the aid of K_X and D, and ensures whether $N_T \oplus PRNG(C_X \oplus K_X)$ is equal to the received E.

  c) Computes $M2 = PRNG(EPC_s \oplus N_T) \oplus P_X$ and $Info = (DATA \oplus RID)$, and sends them to the reader.

  d) If $X = new$, it updates the stored values as follows: $K_{old} = K_{new}$, $K_{new} = PRNG(K_{new})$, $P_{old} = P_{new}$, $P_{new} = PRNG(P_{new})$, $C_{old} = C_{new}$, $C_{new} = PRNG(N_T \oplus N_R)$. But if $X = old$, it just updates C_{new} as $C_{new} = PRNG(N_T \oplus N_R)$.

4. The reader does XOR operation with RID and the received $Info$ and extracts $DATA$, and sends $M2$ to the tag. The tag picks up the stored P_i and computes $P_i \oplus M2$ to find whether it is equal to $PRNG(EPC_s \oplus N_T)$. If the matching is found, the database is authenticated and the tag updates as follows: $K_{i+1} = PRNG(K_i)$, $P_{i+1} = PRNG(P_i)$, $C_{i+1} = PRNG(N_T \oplus N_R)$.

3   Vulnerabilities of SRP

In this section we show the vulnerabilities of SRP. First a practical and powerful attack on SRP is presented. Then, we show that an adversary obtains the most important secret value of a tag which called EPC_s, and show that SRP is vulnerable to tracing attacks. Hence, we show that the SRP does not provide *backward untraceability* and *untraceability*.

3.1   Reveal EPC_s

Since N_R and N_T are XORed with EPC_s, we can conclude the N_R and N_T bit lengths are the same as EPC_s bit length. Furthermore, K_i, P_i and C_i bit length must be equal to the PRNG bit length inasmuch as they are updated by PRNG. Due to the fact that the

EPC_s bit length is very short and fix in all rounds of the SRP, an adversary can exploit this subject to get EPC_s. He just needs to perform two consecutive sessions with the target tag and calculate 2^{16} off-line PRNG computations. The procedure of our attack is explained as follows.

1. The adversary starts a session with the target tag $\mathcal{T}_i$ in the round $(i+1)$ by sending random number N_{R1} and $\mathcal{T}_i$ replies with $(C_i, M1_1, D_1, E_1)$. The adversary reserves $M1_1$ and terminates the session. He performs the second session with $\mathcal{T}_i$ by transmission of N_{R2} and gets tag's response as $(C_i, M1_2, D_2, E_2)$.
2. Since the first session is not completed, $\mathcal{T}_i$ does not update its secret key K_i for the second session. Hence $M1_1$ and $M1_2$ are constructed as follows:

$$M1_1 = PRNG(EPC_s \oplus N_{R1}) \oplus K_i, M1_2 = PRNG(EPC_s \oplus N_{R2}) \oplus K_i.$$

3. $\mathcal{A}$ omits K_i by XORing $M1_1$ and $M1_2$: $M1_1 \oplus M1_2 = PRNG(EPC_s \oplus N_{R1}) \oplus K_i \oplus PRNG(EPC_s \oplus N_{R2}) \oplus K_i = PRNG(EPC_s \oplus N_{R1}) \oplus PRNG(EPC_s \oplus N_{R2}) = \beta$, Where β is a 16-bit string as a result of $M1_1 \oplus M1_2$.
4. Let $L = \{l_1, l_2, \ldots, l_{2^{16}}\}$ be the set of all bit strings with length 16. Since EPC_s is a bit string with length 16, $EPC_s \in L$. Therefore, the adversary with the aid of β, N_{R1} and N_{R2}, executes below algorithm to reach correct EPC_s the adversary proceeds according to the below algorithm:

Algorithm 1

For $1 \le i \le 2^{16}$

Choose $l_i \in L$

$\alpha = PRNG(l_i \oplus N_{R1}) \oplus PRNG(l_i \oplus N_{R2})$, If $\alpha = \beta$ then return l_i as EPC_s

End for

After at most 2^{16} execution of the algorithm, the adversary finds the correct EPC_s. As a result of the above attack, we present three noticeable attacks on SRP including tag impersonation, reader impersonation and DoS attack.

3.1.1 Tag Impersonation

An adversary simply gets the secret key K_i by a passive attack. Indeed, he listens to the communication channelbetween the legitimate reader $\mathcal{R}$ and the target tag $\mathcal{T}_i$ in the round $(i+1)$ to obtain N_{R3} and $(C_i, M1_3, D_3, E_3)$. Since the adversary has EPC_s, he computes PRNG $(EPC_s \oplus N_{R3})$. Thus the secret key K_i is computed as: $K_i = M1_3 \oplus (EPC_s \oplus N_{R3})$ and $K_{i+1} = PRNG(K_i)$. The random number N_{T3} is computed as: $N_{T3} = D \oplus K_i$ and finally the index for the next session is computed as $C_{i+1} = PRNG(N_{T3} \oplus N_{R3})$.

Now, the adversary starts a new session with the reader. $\mathcal{R}$ sends N_{R4} to him and he replies $(C_i, M1_4, D_4, E_4)$ where $M1_4 = PRNG(EPC_s \oplus N_{R4}) \oplus K_i$, $D_4 = N'_{T4} \oplus K_i$ and $E_4 = N'_{T4} \oplus PRN(C_i \oplus K_i)$. Since these values are correctly computed, the database accepts the adversary and authenticates him.

3.1.2 Reader Impersonation and DoS Attack

SRP is also vulnerable by two other attacks. By revealing EPC_s, the adversary can forge a legitimate reader and then desynchronize the target tag. The procedure of these attacks is explained as follows.

1. The adversary listens to the communication between $\mathcal{R}$ and $\mathcal{T}_i$ in the round $(i+1)$ to obtain N_{R5}, $(C_i, M1_5, D_5, E_5)$ and $M2_5$. As the adversary has EPC_s, he computes $\text{PRNG}(EPC_s \oplus N_{R5})$ and gets the secret key K_i as: $K_i = M1_5 \oplus \text{PRNG}(EPC_s \oplus N_{R5})$ and $K_{i+1} = \text{PRNG}(K_i)$. The secret key P_i is gotten as: $P_i = M2_5 \oplus \text{PRNG}(EPC_s \oplus N_{T5})$ and $P_{i+1} = \text{PRNG}(P_i)$ where $N_{T5} = D_5 \oplus K_i$.
2. He begins a new session with $\mathcal{T}_i$ and sends N_{R6} to it. $\mathcal{T}_i$ replies with $(C_{i+1}, M1_6, D_6, E_6)$, created by EPC_s, N_{R6}, K_i, N_{T6} and C_{i+1}.
3. After receiving the tag's response, the adversary extracts N_{T6} $(N_{T6} = D_6 \oplus K_i)$, computes $M2_5 = \text{PRNG}(EPC_s \oplus N_{T6}) \oplus P_{i+1}$ and sends it to the tag.
4. $\mathcal{T}_i$ checks whether $M2_5 \oplus P_{i+1}$ is equal to $\text{PRNG}(EPC_s \oplus N_{T6})$ or not. $\mathcal{T}_i$ authenticates the adversary and updates its secret values provided that the equation will be true: $K_{i+2} = \text{PRNG}(K_{i+1})$, $P_{i+2} = \text{PRNG}(P_{i+1})$, $C_{i+2} = \text{PRNG}(N_{R6} \oplus N_{T6})$.

Eventually, the stored secret values on $\mathcal{T}_i$ are $(K_{i+2}, P_{i+2}, C_{i+2}, EPC_s)$ whereas the database has stored $(K_i, P_i, C_i, K_{i+1}, P_{i+1}, C_{i+1}, RID, EPC_s, DATA)$. Therefore, the tag and reader have been desynchronized because the secret stored values in database are completely different from the values stored in the tag.

3.2 Privacy Analysis

The authors of SRP have specified that not only their protocol have forward secrecy, but also SRP is resistant to the tracing attacks. We show that SRP does not have forward secrecy and we also present a *traceability* attack on SRP.

3.2.1 Privacy Model

There are privacy models for the evaluation of RFID protocols [6, 23, 24, 25, 26]. We analyze SRP protocol based on Ouafi and Phan model [26] which is based on [24] and [6]. The model is summarized as follows.

The protocol parties are tags ($\mathcal{T}$) and readers ($\mathcal{R}$) which interact in protocol sessions. In this model an adversary $\mathcal{A}$ controls the communication channel between all parties by interacting either passively or actively with them. The adversary $\mathcal{A}$ is allowed to run the following queries:

*   **Execute** ($\mathcal{R}, \mathcal{T}, i$) query. This query models the passive attacks. The adversary $\mathcal{A}$ eavesdrops on the communication channel between $\mathcal{T}$ and $\mathcal{R}$ and gets read access to the exchanged messages between the parties in session i of a truthful protocol execution.
*   **Send** ($\mathcal{U}, \mathcal{V}, m, i$) query. This query models active attacks by allowing the adversary $\mathcal{A}$ to impersonate some reader $\mathcal{U} \in \mathcal{R}$ (respectively tag $\mathcal{V} \in \mathcal{T}$) in some protocol session i and send a message m of its choice to an instance of

some tag $\mathcal{V} \in \mathcal{T}$(respectively reader $\mathcal{U} \in \mathcal{R}$). Furthermore the adversary $\mathcal{A}$ is allowed to block or alert the message m that is sent from $\mathcal{U}$ to $\mathcal{V}$ (respectively $\mathcal{V}$ to $\mathcal{U}$) in session i of a truthful protocol execution.

- **Corrupt**$(\mathcal{T}, K')$ query. This query allows the adversary $\mathcal{A}$ to learn the stored secretK of the tag$\mathcal{T} \in \mathcal{T}$, and which further sets the stored secret toK'. **Corrupt** query means that the adversary has physical access to the tag, i.e. the adversary can read and tamper with the tag's permanent memory.
- **Test** $(i, \mathcal{T}_o, \mathcal{T}_1)$ query. This query does not correspond to any of $\mathcal{A}$'s abilities, but it is necessary to define the untraceability test. When this query is invoked for session$i$, a random bit $b \in \{0, 1\}$ is generated and then, $\mathcal{A}$ is given$\mathcal{T}_b \in \{\mathcal{T}_0, \mathcal{T}_1\}$. Informally, $\mathcal{A}$wins if he can guess the bit b.

Untraceable privacy (*UPriv*) is defined using the game $\mathcal{G}$played between an adversary $\mathcal{A}$ and a collection of the reader and the tag instances. The game $\mathcal{G}$isdivided into three following phases:

- **Learning phase:**$\mathcal{A}$ is given tags $\mathcal{T}_0$ and $\mathcal{T}_1$ randomly and he is able to send any **Execute**, **Send** and **Corrupt** queries of its choice to $\mathcal{T}_0$, $\mathcal{T}_1$ and reader.
- **Challenge phase:** $\mathcal{A}$ chooses two fresh tags $\mathcal{T}_0$, $\mathcal{T}_1$ to be tested and sends a **Test** $(i, \mathcal{T}_0, \mathcal{T}_1)$ query. Depending on a randomly chosen bit $b \in \{0, 1\}$, $\mathcal{A}$ is given a tag $\mathcal{T}_b$ from the set $\{\mathcal{T}_0, \mathcal{T}_1\}$.$\mathcal{A}$continues making any **Execute**, and **Send** queries at will.
- **Guess phase:** finally, $\mathcal{A}$ terminates the game $\mathcal{G}$ and outputs a bit $b' \in \{0, 1\}$, which is its guess of the value of b.

The success of$\mathcal{A}$ in winning game $\mathcal{G}$ and thus breaking the notion of *UPriv*is quantified in terms $\mathcal{A}$ advantage in distinguishing whether$\mathcal{A}$received$\mathcal{T}_0$ or $\mathcal{T}_1$ and denoted by **Adv** $_{A}^{UPriv}$ (k) where k is the security parameter.

$$\mathbf{Adv}_{A}^{UPriv}(k) = |\text{pr}(b = b') - \text{pr}(\text{random flip coin})| = |\text{pr}(b' = b) - \frac{1}{2}| \quad \text{where}$$
$$0 \leq \mathbf{Adv}_{A}^{UPriv}(k) \leq \frac{1}{2}.$$

Besides, the notion *backward untraceability* is defined as: "*backward untraceability* states that even if given all the internal states of a target tag at time t, the adversary shouldn't be able to identify the target tag's interactions that occur at time t' < t" [6].

3.2.2 Backward Traceability
In this section we show how to break the notion *backward untraceability* in the SRP protocol. Because EPC_s is constant in the all rounds of SRP, an adversary $\mathcal{A}$ can track the target tag with doing the following steps:

- **Learning phase:** $\mathcal{A}$ sends a **Corrupt**$(\mathcal{T}_0, K')$ query in the round $(i+1)$ and obtains $(K_i^{T_0}, P_i^{T_0}, C_i^{T_0}, EPC_{s,i}^{T_0})$.

- **Challenge phase:** $\mathcal{A}$ chooses two fresh tags $(\mathcal{T}_0, \mathcal{T}_1)$ to be tested and sends a **Test** $(i, \mathcal{T}_0, \mathcal{T}_1)$ query. Depending on a randomly chosen bit $b \in \{0, 1\}$, $\mathcal{A}$ is given a tag $\mathcal{T}_b$ from the set $\{\mathcal{T}_0, \mathcal{T}_1\}$. $\mathcal{A}$ makes an **Execute** $(\mathcal{R}, \mathcal{T}_b, i)$ query in the round (i) and as a result, $\mathcal{A}$ is given messages $\{N_{R,i-1}^{T_b}, (M1_{i-1}^{T_b}, D_{i-1}^{T_b}, C_{i-1}^{T_b}, E_{i-1}^{T_b})\}$.

- **Guess phase:** finally, $\mathcal{A}$ terminates the game $\mathcal{G}$ and outputs a bit $b' \in \{0, 1\}$ as its guess of the value of b. In particular, $\mathcal{A}$ performs the following procedure to obtain the value b':

1. He computes $\mathrm{PRNG}(EPC_{s,i}^{T_0} \oplus N_{R,i-1}^{T_b}) \oplus M1_{i-1}^{T_b} = \theta$ where θ is a 16-bit string.

2. $\mathcal{A}$ utilizes the following simple decision rule:

$$b' = \begin{cases} if\, D_{i-1}^{T_b} \oplus E_{i-1}^{T_b} = \theta \oplus \mathrm{PRNG}(C_{i-1}^{T_b} \oplus \theta)\, b' = 0 \\ otherwise\, b' = 1 \end{cases}$$

Hence we have:

Adv $_{\mathbf{A}}^{\mathbf{UPriv}}$ (k) $= |\mathrm{pr}\,(b' = b) - \mathrm{pr}\,(\text{random flip coin})| = |\mathrm{pr}(b'=b) - \frac{1}{2}| = |1 - \frac{1}{2}| = \frac{1}{2}$

Proof: By the fact that EPC_s is a permanent value in the all rounds of the protocol, we have $\mathrm{EPC}_{s,i}^{T_0} = \mathrm{EPC}_{s,i-1}^{T_0}$. Thus we have the following procedure:

If $\mathcal{T}_b = \mathcal{T}_0 \Rightarrow \mathrm{PRNG}(\mathrm{EPC}_{s,i}^{T_0} \oplus N_{R,i-1}^{T_b}) = \mathrm{PRNG}(EPC_{s,i}^{T_0} \oplus N_{R,i-1}^{T_0})$ (1)

If $\mathcal{T}_b = \mathcal{T}_0 \Rightarrow M1_{i-1}^{T_b} = M1_{i-1}^{T_0} = \mathrm{PRNG}(\mathrm{EPC}_{s,i}^{T_0} \oplus N_{R,i-1}^{T_0}) \oplus K_{i-1}^{T_0}$ (2)

(1), (2) $\Rightarrow \mathrm{PRNG}(\mathrm{EPC}_{s,i}^{T_0} \oplus N_{R,i-1}^{T_b}) \oplus M1_{i-1}^{T_b} = \mathrm{PRNG}(\mathrm{EPC}_{s,i}^{T_0} \oplus N_{R,i-1}^{T_0}) \oplus M1_{i-1}^{T_0} =$

$\mathrm{PRNG}(\mathrm{EPC}_{s,i}^{T_0} \oplus N_{R,i-1}^{T_0}) \oplus \mathrm{PRNG}(\mathrm{EPC}_{s,i}^{T_0} \oplus N_{R,i-1}^{T_0}) \oplus K_{i-1}^{T_0} = K_{i-1}^{T_0} = \theta$ (3)

If $\mathcal{T}_b = \mathcal{T}_0 \Rightarrow D_{i-1}^{T_b} \oplus E_{i-1}^{T_b} = D_{i-1}^{T_0} \oplus E_{i-1}^{T_0} = N_{T,i-1}^{T_0} \oplus K_{i-1}^{T_0} \oplus N_{T,i-1}^{T_0} \oplus \mathrm{PRNG}(C_{i-1}^{T_0} \oplus K_{i-1}^{T_0}) =$

$K_{i-1}^{T_0} \oplus \mathrm{PRNG}(C_{i-1}^{T_0} \oplus K_{i-1}^{T_0}) = \theta \oplus \mathrm{PRNG}(C_{i-1}^{T_0} \oplus \theta) = \theta \oplus \mathrm{PRNG}(C_{i-1}^{T_b} \oplus \theta)$ (4)

3.2.3 Traceability Attack

An authentication protocol for RFID systems should assure the privacy of a tag and its holder. However, many RFID protocols put it at risk by designing protocols where tags answer reader's queries with permanent values. Thus performing traceability attacks not only possible but trivial.

Now, we prove the SRP does not guarantee privacy location and allows tags tracking.

- **Learning phase:** $\mathcal{A}$ sends an **Execute** $(\mathcal{R}, \mathcal{T}_0, i+1)$ query in the $(i+1)th$ round by sending N_{RI} and obtains $(M1_i^{T_0}, D_i^{T_0}, C_i^{T_0}, E_i^{T_0})$.

- **Challenge phase:** $\mathcal{A}$ chooses two fresh tags $(\mathcal{T}_0, \mathcal{T}_1)$ to be tested and sends a **Test** $(i+1, \mathcal{T}_0, \mathcal{T}_1)$ query. Depending on a randomly chosen bit $b \in \{0, 1\}$, $\mathcal{A}$ is given a tag $\mathcal{T}_b$ from the set $\{\mathcal{T}_0, \mathcal{T}_1\}$. $\mathcal{A}$ makes an **Execute** $(\mathcal{R}, \mathcal{T}_b, i+1)$ query by sending N_{RI} and as a result, $\mathcal{A}$ is given messages $(M1_i^{Tb}, D_i^{Tb}, C_i^{Tb}, E_i^{Tb})$.

- **Guess phase:** finally, $\mathcal{A}$ terminates the game $\mathcal{G}$ and outputs a bit b' $\in\{0, 1\}$ as its guess of the value of b. In particular, $\mathcal{A}$ utilizes the following simple decision rule:

$$b' = \begin{cases} \text{if } M1_i^{Tb} = M1_i^{T0} & b' = 0 \\ \text{otherwise} & b' = 1 \end{cases}$$

Hence we have:

Adv $_A^{\text{UPriv}}$ (k) =| pr (b' = b)–pr (random flip coin) |= | pr $(b' = b)$ - $\frac{1}{2}$ |=|1 - $\frac{1}{2}$| =$\frac{1}{2}$

Proof: According to the protocol, we have the following equations:

$$M1_i^{T0} = PRNG(EPC_{s,i}^{T0} \oplus N_{RI}) \oplus K_i^{T0} \tag{5}$$

$$M1_i^{Tb} = PRNG(EPC_{s,i}^{Tb} \oplus N_{RI}) \oplus K_i^{Tb} \tag{6}$$

Note that $\mathcal{T}_0$ does not update its secrets in the **Learning phase** and uses the same secret key K_i in both **Learning** and **Challenge phase**. Now we have the following result:

If $\mathcal{T}_b = \mathcal{T}_0 \Rightarrow M1_i^{Tb} = PRNG(EPC_{s,i}^{Tb} \oplus NR1) \oplus K_i^{Tb} = PRNG(EPC_{s,i}^{T0} \oplus NR1) \oplus K_i^{T0}$

$$= M1_i^{T0} \tag{7}$$

4   Revised Protocol

In order to eliminate the mentioned vulnerabilities in 3.1 and 3.2 subsections, we can modify the message $M1$ as: $M1 = PRNG(EPC_s \oplus N_R \oplus P_i) \oplus K_i$. Although the cited vulnerabilities are fixed by the above modification, the traceability problem still will be unsolved. Hence, we need to construct the message $M1$ as following: $M1 = PRNG(EPC_s \oplus N_R \oplus N_T) \oplus K_i$ to provide a secure protocol against all cited attacks.

4.1 Security Analysis

Now, we analyze the security of the revised protocol as following.

Untraceability: Due to the fact that N_T is a random and fresh value, the tag's responses are different whenever an adversary sends query and therefore, the adversary is unable to trace a tag.

Backward untraceability: If an adversary knows EPC_s and N_R in worth case, he cannot recognize any previous interactions by a tag inasmuch as he does not know N_T.

RevealEPC_s: Since EPC_s is constant and its length is short, the mentioned attacks in 3.1 subsection happened successfully. We have added the random and fresh value N_T in construction of $M1$ to remove these flaws. As a result, when an adversary wants to reveal EPC_s, he has to perform 2^{48} calculations rather than 2^{16}. It is a noticeable improvement in SRP security.

5 Conclusion

In this paper, the significant security flaws in the Yeh et al. mutual authentication protocol were showed. We presented a powerful and practical attack on SRP which reveals the permanent secret value of the target tag. This attack leads to tag and reader impersonation and desynchronization attack on the protocol. Moreover, we proved that this protocol did not provide *untraceability* and *backward untraceability*. Our privacy analysis has been presented in a formal privacy model. Finally, to eliminate all cited vulnerabilities, we revised the SRP protocol and constructed the message M1 in a new way.

Acknowledgment

This work was partially supported by Iran National Science Fund (INSF)-cryptography chair and research institute for ITC, Tehran, Iran.

References

[1]   Transport for London, Oyster card,
      http://www.oystercard.co.uk
[2]   Michelin Embeds RFID Tags in Tires. RFID Journal,
      http://www.rfidjournal.com/article/articleview/269/1/1/
      (accessed January 17, 2003)
[3]   Hoepman, J.-H., Hubbers, E., Jacobs, B., Oostdijk, M., Schreur, R.W.: Crossing Borders: Security and Privacy Issues of the European e-Passport. In: Yoshiura, H., Sakurai, K., Rannenberg, K., Murayama, Y., Kawamura, S.-i. (eds.) IWSEC 2006. LNCS, vol. 4266, pp. 152–167. Springer, Heidelberg (2006)
[4]   EPCglobal Inc., http://www.epcglobalinc.org/
[5]   EPCglobal Inc., EPCTM Radio-Frequency Identity Protocols Class-1 Generation-2 UHF RFID Protocols for Communications at 860 MHz – 960 MHz version 1.1.0, Available at [4]
[6]   Lim, C.H., Kwon, T.: Strong and robust RFID authentication enabling perfect ownership transfer. In: Ning, P., Qing, S., Li, N. (eds.) ICICS 2006. LNCS, vol. 4307, pp. 1–20. Springer, Heidelberg (2006)
[7]   Van Deursen, T., Radomirovic, S.: Attacks on RFID protocols. Cryptology ePrint Archive, Report 2008/310 (2008), http://eprint.iacr.org/
[8]   Ouafi, K., Phan, R.C.-W.: Traceable privacy of recent provably-secure RFID protocols. In: Bellovin, S.M., Gennaro, R., Keromytis, A.D., Yung, M. (eds.) ACNS 2008. LNCS, vol. 5037, pp. 479–489. Springer, Heidelberg (2008)
[9]   Peris-Lopez, P., Hernandez-Castro, J.C., Estevez-Tapiador, J.M., Ribagorda, A.: Vulnerability analysis of RFID protocols for tag ownership transfer. Computer Networks 54, 1502–1508 (2010)

[10] Chien, H., Chen, C.: Mutual Authentication Protocol for RFID Conforming to EPC Class 1 Generation 2 Standards. Computer Standards & Interfaces 29, 254–259 (2007)
[11] Konidala, D.M., Kim, Z., Kim, K.: A simple and cost-effective RFID tag-reader mutual authentication scheme. In: Proceedings of Int'l Conference on RFID Security, RFIDSec 2007, pp. 141–152 (2007)
[12] Kulseng, L., Yu, Z., Wei, Y., Guan, Y.: Lightweight mutual authentication and ownership transfer for RFID Systems. In: Proceedings of IEEE INFOCOM 2010, pp. 1–5 (2010)
[13] Chien, H.Y.: SASI: A new ultralightweight rfid authentication protocol providing strong authentication and strong integrity. IEEE Transactions on Dependable and Secure Computing 4(4), 337–340 (2007)
[14] Song, B., Mitchell, C.J.: RFID authentication protocol for low-cost tags. In: Proc. of Wisec 2008, pp. 140–147 (2008)
[15] Duc, D.N., Park, J., Lee, H., Kim, K.: Enhancing security of EPCglobal Gen-2 RFID tag against traceability and cloning. In: The Symposium on Cryptography and Information Security (2006)
[16] Han, D., Kwon, D.: Vulnerability of an RFID authentication protocol conforming to EPC Class-1Generation-2 Standards. Computer Standards & Interfaces 31, 648–652 (2009)
[17] Peris-Lopez, P., Hernandez-Castro, J.C., Estevez-Tapiador, J.M., Ribagorda, A.: Practical attacks on a mutual authentication scheme under the EPC Class-1 Generation-2 standard. Computer Communications 32, 1185–1193 (2009)
[18] Habibi, M.H., Gardeshi, M., Alagheband, M.R.: Attacks and improvements to a new RFID Authentication protocol. In: Proceedings of Third Workshop on RFID Security: RFIDsec Asia 2011, China (2011)
[19] Phan, R.C.-W.: Cryptanalysis of a New Ultra lightweight RFID Authentication Protocol – SASI. IEEE Transactions on Dependable and Secure Computing 6(4), 316–320 (2009)
[20] van Deursen, T., Mauw, S., Radomirović, S.: Untraceability of RFID protocols. In: Onieva, J.A., Sauveron, D., Chaumette, S., Gollmann, D., Markantonakis, K. (eds.) WISTP 2008. LNCS, vol. 5019, pp. 1–15. Springer, Heidelberg (2008)
[21] Habibi, M.H., Gardeshi, M., Alagheband, M.R.: Cryptanalysis of two mutual authentication protocols for low-cost RFID. International Journal of Distributed and Parallel Systems 2(1), 103–114
[22] Yeh, T.-C., Wang, Y.-J., Kuo, T.-C., Wang, S.-S.: Securing RFID systems conforming to EPC Class-1 Generation-2 standard. Expert Systems with Applications 37, 7678–7683 (2010)
[23] Avoine, G.: Adversarial model for radio frequency identification. Cryptology ePrint Archive, report 2005/049, http://eprint.iacr.org/2005/049
[24] Juels, A., Weis, S.A.: Defining strong privacy for RFID. In: Proceedings of PerCom 2007, pp. 342–347 (2007), http://eprint.iacr.org/2006/137
[25] Vaudenay, S.: On Privacy Models for RFID. In: Kurosawa, K. (ed.) ASIACRYPT 2007. LNCS, vol. 4833, pp. 68–87. Springer, Heidelberg (2007)
[26] Ouafi, K., Phan, R.C.-W.: Privacy of recent RFID authentication protocols. In: Chen, L., Mu, Y., Susilo, W. (eds.) ISPEC 2008. LNCS, vol. 4991, pp. 263–277. Springer, Heidelberg (2008)

A SMS-Based Mobile Botnet
Using Flooding Algorithm

Jingyu Hua⋆ and Kouichi Sakurai

Department of Informatics, Kyushu University
{huajingyu,sakurai}@itslab.csce.kyushu-u.ac.jp

Abstract. As a lot of sophisticated duties are being migrated to mobile
phones, they are gradually becoming hot targets of hackers. Actually,
during the past few years, It has appeared many malware targeting mobile phones and the situation is getting worse. Under this circumstance,
we may ask a serious question: whether can those infected phones be
organized to a botnet? In this paper, we present a design of such a botnet using Short Message Service (SMS) as its Command and Control
(C&C) medium. We cover all the aspects of the botnet design including
the stealthiness protection, the topology selecting and the botnet maintaining. Our simulations show that in our proposed SMS-based botnet
a newly issued C&C message can be covertly propagated to over 90%
of the total 20000 bots within 20 minutes based on a simple flooding
algorithm. Moreover, in this process each bot sends no more than four
SMS messages and the botnet is robust to both random and selective
node failures. Thereby, we demonstrate that the proposed mobile botnet
is indeed a serious threat on the security of the mobile computing environment. For this reason, we further explore several effective defense
strategies against such a botnet. In doing so, we hope to be one step
ahead of the hackers to discover and prevent this upcoming threat.

1 Introduction

1.1 Background and Motivation

During the past few years, a significant evolution has taken place in the field
of smart phones: firstly, their computing power is growing rapidly: some smart
phones like iPhone have already outperformed the early desktop. Secondly, as
the popularization of 3G and near future's 4G, they are also getting closer to
the desktop in the communication capability. For these reasons, more and more
sophisticated applications like financial markets, online banking, etc. are being
migrated to the smart phones from the traditional PCs. Then, smart phones are
inevitably becoming the next hot targets of the hackers with the constant rising
of their business values.

In fact, since 2004 many malware targeting mobile phones have already
emerged. These worms or viruses can propagate and infect vulnerable smart

---

⋆ Supported by the governmental scholarship from China Scholarship Council.

C.A. Ardagna and J. Zhou (Eds.): WISTP 2011, LNCS 6633, pp. 264–279, 2011.

phones through all kinds of mediums including Internet [1,2], Storage Cards [3], SMS [4], MMS [5], and even some local wireless protocols like Bluetooth [6,7]. Based on this, people may ask a serious question: can those infected mobile phones be carefully organized into a botnet by the hackers as they did in the PC world? For this question, although by now there's no major outbreak of mobile botnets, most researchers believe that the answer is positive: mobile botnets will appear sooner or later [8,9,10,11] and it's just a matter of time.

If the mobile botnet is unavoidable, it becomes quite meaningful for us to investigate the potential technologies that can be used to construct them from the perspective of the hackers. By doing so, we can get our defense strategies ready before the real outbreaks of mobile botnets and avoid being left behind again by the hackers as we really did in the desktop battlefield. In this paper, we follow this motivation to evaluate whether the Short Message Service (SMS) can be used to construct an effective mobile botnet. We choose to study SMS because of two reasons: firstly, as a mandatory function SMS is supported nearly by all the existing phones. It is text-based and system-independent. So the hackers can utilize this service to propagate commands among heterogeneous platforms. Secondly, SMS is quite simple and reliable: all you need is a phone number, and you can immediately send the corresponding phone a message with a very small error rate. Therefore, SMS may provide the hackers an ideal C&C medium.

1.2   Related Works

In 2009, Traynor et al.[11] propose using a mobile botnet to launch a DDoS attack against the core infrastructure of the cellular network. Their simulation and analysis demonstrate that their attack can cause nation-wide outages with even a single-digit infection rate, which teaches us a good lesson about the astonishing destructive power of mobile botnets. However, their work does not discuss how to construct a mobile botnet in details, especially how to construct an efficient C&C medium.

The first detailed work in the mobile botnet construction is done by Kapil et al [12]. They investigate the possibility to construct and maintain a mobile botnet via Bluetooth. In their design, botnet commands are propagated via Bluetooth when those infected mobile phones move into each other's radio range. Through several large-scale simulations based on some publicly available Bluetooth traces, they demonstrate this malicious infrastructure is possible. However, since this botnet is highly relied on the human mobility, its real performance is hard to guarantee especially when the density of hijacked phones is not high: according to their simulations, a command can only reach 2/3 of the bots even after 24 hour in a botnet with 100 bots.

Zeng et al. [13] later propose another mobile botnet using SMS to implement a Kademlia-like P2P network as its C&C channel. However, because Kademlia is quite complex, too many SMS messages are required to send for a bot to locate and get a command. According to their simulations, even in a small botnet with 200 nodes, on average 20 messages are needed to send for a single command lookup. In addition, since the nodes in this botnet don't know when a new command will be issued, they have to probe continually, which also wastes a lot of messages. As we known, all the SMS messages are under the monitoring of telecom operators and they may also cost money. Sending too many abnormal messages will make the botnet prone to being detected both on the service provider side and the user side.

Recently, Mulliner et al.[23] also investigate several methods to construct a mobile botnet. They first introduce a SMS-only C&C which uses the tree as the underlying topology. This topology suffers an obvious drawback that when one node fails, all its subnodes are isolated from the botnet and can no longer receive any commands. As a result, the botmaster has to continually broadcast ping messages to locate the failed nodes and then repair the tree, which brings great side effects to the stealth and the feasibility. They then introduce another improved SMS-HTTP hybrid C&C, which first hangs command SMS messages on some website and then informs several random selected bots to download and send them. The weak point is that although those SMS messages are encrypted, they may still disclose the destination bots because the decryption keys are embedded in the URLs. In addition, those random selected nodes are also prone to being captured because they may send unusual high number of SMS messages if the botnet is very large.

1.3   Challenging Issues

Generally, the hackers have to overcome the following challenges to design an effective SMS-based mobile botnet:

(1) The proposed botnet should have an efficient C&C architecture, in which a command issued by the botmaster can reach most of the bots in a short time. What's more, for security reason each bot should only send a small number of SMS messages in this process.

(2) Because all the SMS messages are under the monitoring of the telecom operators, we need special measures to disguise the botnet messages as the legal ones to evade being filtered out.

(3) Once a botnet is constructed, we need special mechanisms to maintain it. This mainly involves two issues: Firstly, the botmaster usually wants to master the runtime statuses of their controlled bots. Thereby, besides a command propagation channel, we need another reporting channel from the bots to the botmaster. Secondly, the botmaster has the requirement to update the malware distributed on the bots regularly. The sizes of these updates usually greatly exceed the maximum payload of a single SMS message, so we need an extra updating mechanism.

1.4   Our Works and Contributions

In this study, we mainly focus on investigating the above challenges to develop a proof-of-concept SMS-based mobile botnet in advance of the hackers. In particular, we make the following contributions:

(1) We propose a proof-of-concept SMS-based mobile botnet. It uses SMS to propagate C&C messages based on a simple flooding algorithm. We discuss how to guarantee the stealth of this botnet both on the user side and the service provider side by combining the data-encryption and the data-hiding.

(2) We do simulations to evaluate the performance of our proposed botnet with different topologies. We find that in the Erdos-Renyi random graphs the propagation of commands can be very fast and robust to both random and selective node failures. In particular, a message can reach over 90% of the total 20000 bots within 20 minutes from any node. And each node sends no more than 4 messages in this process.

(3) We then present a method to construct the desired random graph topology for our botnet under the help of an internet server. We also introduce a mechanism to maintain the constructed botnet by associating our mobile botnet with a traditional PC botnet.

(4) Based on the above, we demonstrate that it's entirely possible to utilize SMS for Mobile Botnet Command and Control. Therefore, in the end of this paper we explore several potential defense strategies against this mobile botnet.

2   The Overview of the Proposed SMS-Based Botnet

In this section, we present the overview of our proposed SMS-based mobile botnet with the sample in Fig. 1. For simplicity, we neglect technical details here and just show our basic idea.

In our proposed botnet, each compromised smart phone, namely bot is made to maintain a partial list of the other peers as its virtual neighbors. For instance, in the sample botnet in Fig.1, the bot $P1$ maintains a peer list ($A2, A6$), where $A2$ and $A6$ are the phone numbers of $P2$ and $P6$, respectively. By doing so, $P1$ gets to know that $P2$ and $P6$ also belong to the botnet and it is enabled to directly send them SMS messages. Then, the botnet commands are propagated in this special architecture based on a modified flooding algorithm: The botmaster can first send his command to any node via SMS. And then, for each node, whenever it receives the new command, it is made to continually select uncommunicated neighbors as the destinations to forward this command via SMS until the forwarding count reaches a pre-defined upper bound.

Here, two things we have to point out. Firstly, the bots do not use the group messaging to forward their received commands. Instead, we make them forward a command to their neighbors one by one with random time intervals. We make this decision because the use of group messaging will provide the service provider extra detection signatures. What's more, with this mechanism the number of forwardings may be also reduced: while a bot is waiting for the next forwarding window, it may receive the same command from a bot it is planning to forward the command to. As a result, these redundant forwardings can be avoided. Secondly, since sending SMS messages may cost money, we have to limit the number of forwardings made by each bot. Otherwise, if too many messages are required to send to propagate one command, a bot will face a high risk of being

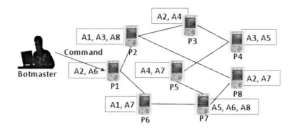

Fig. 1. An example of our proposed SMS-based mobile botnet

noticed while its user receives an unexpected high bill. That's why in the above we introduce a upper bound for the forwarding times of each bot.

If this simple botnet is made true, we will get a complete P2P botnet: each node is equivalent and there's no centralized infrastructure. In addition, because each bot only knows a limited number of others, the resistance of this botnet to the bot capture is high: de-infection of one bot only discloses its neighbors, which brings limited effects to the whole botnet. Now, let's discuss the details of this SMS-based mobile botnet in the following sections.

3   Stealthiness Study

As we known, the long live of a botnet is relied on its stealthiness, i.e., the ability to work without being noticed by the defenders. Therefore, at first we discuss the stealthiness of our proposed SMS-based botnet. This mainly involves two aspects: the stealth on the user side and the stealth on the service provider side.

On the user side, the most important thing is to enable the bot code to send and receive SMS messages carrying botnet commands without being noticed by the users. Besides, the bot code itself as well as the related processes and resources should be also hidden from the users. This requires us to implement a rootkit on the compromised mobile OSs. This is hard but not impossible. Recently, Papathanasiou and Percoco [14] introduced a method to implement a Linux KLM-based rootkit on Google's Android platform. Based on their work, we implement a prototype rootkit that can hijack the system call table to cover our malicious behaviors including secret message sending and receiving. The only problem is that we haven't thought of any elegant ways to persist this rootkit to make it survive from the reboots. This is quite important because mobile phones subject to frequent reboots. In addition, as we said before, because SMS message may cost money each bot should only send a limited number of messages in the process of command propagation. Otherwise, they face a high risk of being perceived when their users have to pay an abnormally high bill. We will show in the next section that by carefully selecting a topology for our botnet a command can quickly reach over 90% of the total 20000 bots in 20 minutes with each bot sending no more than four messages, which is quite stealthy.

On the service side, since all the SMS messages go through the gateways of telecom operators, the stealth is much more difficult to guarantee. In the traditional networks, since different subnets are administrated by different organizations, it's difficult to uniformly deploy a defense system against some security events even if the system is proven effective. However, in the cellular network, the situation is totally different. All the communications in this network are usually monitored by only one telecom operator. It's easy for them to quickly popularize a defense system within the whole network. For this reason, the C&C messages of our mobile botnets should never be broadcasted in their original forms. Otherwise, once one message forwarded by a bot is recognized as a botnet command, it will be easy for the telecom operators to compose a signature to filter out all these messages and further detect all the infected mobile phones. Hence, more complicate technologies are needed to guarantee the stealth of our bontet on the server side.

Our solution is to encrypt the C&C messages before they are transmited. We make each pair of neighbors share a unique secret key. And then commands sent from one node to another are encrypted and decrypted with their unique key. By doing so, the same command forwarded by different nodes to different destinations will appear in different forms. As a result, even if a command is captured by the service provider, it's still impossible for him to create a uniform signature to filter out all the command messages sent by different bots. Hence the stealth is greatly improved. However, this solution suffers a critical drawback: after the encryption, the obtained SMSs become random texts that are greatly different from those normal messages. So we further utilize some text steganography algorithms[15,16] to convert those ugly cipertexts to texts more closer to the natural language. Fig. 2 shows such an example. After being encrypted with the Rijndael cipher [17], the command "SYN F 233.123.23.45/23 10/8/20 12:30", which informs the bots to launch a SYN attack against 233.123.23.45/23 at 12:30 on August 20, 2010, will become unreadable random texts. However, if we further convert the ciphertext with the Stego! steganographic algorithm [16], we can obtain a stegotext that at first glance looks like a English text. Therefore, it will become more difficult for the service provider to determine the presence of a botnet command within a SMS message in a short time.

4   Topology Study Based on Simulation

As shown in Fig. 1 the proposed SMS-based botnet can be regarded as a graph $G = (V, E)$, where V is the set of nodes and each node is corresponding to a bot; E is the set of edges and for arbitrary two nodes $v_1, v_2 \in V$, they are linked ($\exists e_{ij} = (v_i, v_j) \wedge e_{ij} \in E$) if and only if their phone numbers are contained in each other's neighbor list. Obviously, the efficiency of the command propagation is closely related to the topology of the botnet graph. Therefore, in this section, we construct different topologies to study their different performances based on some simulations. By doing so, we hope to find an efficient topology for our SMS-based mobile botnet.

Fig. 2. Steganography Example

4.1   Simulation Setup

We mainly study three common topologies: Erdos-Renyi random graphs [18], Barabasi-Albert scale-free graphs [19] and Watts-Strogatz small world graphs [20]. We choose to study these three graphs because they are the most common complex networks in our world and also hot candidates in the design of traditional PC botnet [21].

All the topologies were implemented in the C programming language with the igraph C library [22]. We generated twenty graphs for each topology. And all their average node degrees are set to 6. We choose this value because it makes our simulated graphs become approximated connected graphs (The largest connected components covers more than 99% of the nodes). This is a necessary condition for a command to be eventually propagated to most of the nodes in the botnet. The simulations were driven by discrete events in seconds. When a node receives a command in an event, it will register new forwarding events in a central event queue one by one until the forwarding times reach a pre-set bound b. In each event, the node randomly selects an un-communicated neighbor as the target to forward this command. The time interval between two continuous forwarding events is a random value between $[60s, 120s]$. All the results for each topology presented in the following are the averages of the data obtained from the simulations on their own twenty graphs.

4.2   Simulation Results

We select three key measures to compare the effectiveness of the three topologies: Reachabilities from nodes, Influence of the forwarding Bound and Resistance to node failures. We present the details and the comparison results below:

Reachabilities from nodes: with our decentralized C&C infrastructure, the botmaster can issue his command to the botnet from any node within the botnet. Therefore, a key performance measure is the distribution of the reachabilities from different nodes in our botnet by an appointed time. Here, the reachability from a node at time t refers to the percentage of nodes that a command can

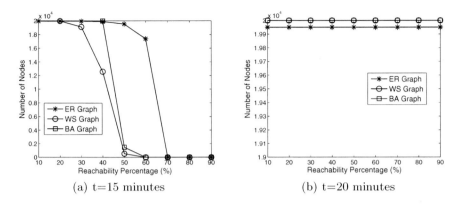

(a) t=15 minutes   (b) t=20 minutes

Fig. 3. Inverse cumulative distributions of the reachabilities after 15 and 20 minutes

reach by t from that node. In our study we use $I(r,t)$, the inverse cumulative distribution of the reachability to quantify this measure. It represents the number of nodes whose reachabilities at time t are larger than r.

Fig. 3 presents the simulation results of $I(r,t)$ in the three topologies when $t = 15$ and 20 minutes. These simulations assume no forwarding bound and no node failure. We can find that the efficiency of our botnet is very high in this case: no matter which of the three topologies is selected, a command can reach over 90% of the total nodes in 20 minutes from almost any node. In particular, the ER random model outperforms the other two: nearly 100% of the nodes in the ER model can make a 50% reachability within 15 minutes, while in the WS graphs and BA graphs no more than 2000 nodes can achieve this. In our opinion, this is quite reasonable: firstly, compared with the ER graph, the nodes in the WS graph show a property of high local clustering. As a result, the command forwardings made by local neighbors in this topology are more prone to conflict, which greatly reduces the propagation speed of commands. Secondly, the node degrees in the BA graph follow a power law distribution which means that some nodes in this topology having much higher degrees compared with others. As a result, these nodes attract many redundant forwardings because they are connected by more nodes. Thus, the command propagation in this topology is also slowed down.

Influence of the forwarding Bound: as we said before, to guarantee the stealth of the botnet, we introduce an upper bound for the forwarding times of one command on each node. Although this may greatly affect the command propagation in our botnet, it is necessary at some time. For instance, in our first simulation without forwarding bound, we found some nodes in the BA model sent more than 20 messages for one command, which have been enough to cause the attention of their users. Hence the success of our botnet is based on the premise that commands can be well disseminated even if the forwarding times are constrained to a small value on individual bots. So we did more simulations to study the impacts of the forwarding bound in the three topologies. Fig. 4

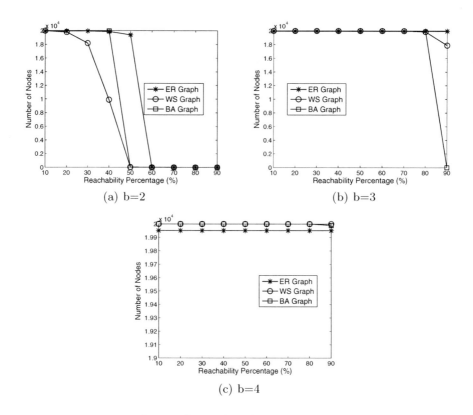

Fig. 4. Effects of the forwarding bound

presents the simulation results of $I(r,t)$ at the time of 20 minutes while the forwarding bound is set to 2, 3, 4, respectively. We can find that the ER random model is least affected by the forwarding bound: the reachabilities of most nodes in this topology can still exceed 90% after 20 minutes so long as the forwarding bound is no less than 3. For the other two topologies, although they are more affected, the effects of the forwarding bound can be also removed when $b \geqslant 4$. Since the cost of four SMS messages are too small to draw the attention of the users, we conclude that the stealth of our mobile botnet is high.

Resistance to Node Failures: by now, all our simulations make an assumption that all the nodes in the botnet are active and work correctly while the botmaster issues a command. However in reality, hijacked smart phones may be turned off by their users, be out of energy or even be disinfected and removed from the botnet forever. In all these cases, the bots will become inactive and lose the ability to receive and forward messages temporarily or perpetually. This is so called node failures. Obviously, the resistance to these node failures is critical to the success of a mobile botnet. Therefore, we do further simulations to test the performance of the three topologies when node failures happen. In the first test,

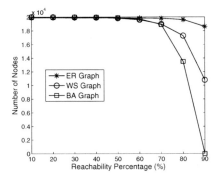

Fig. 5. Resistance to random node failures

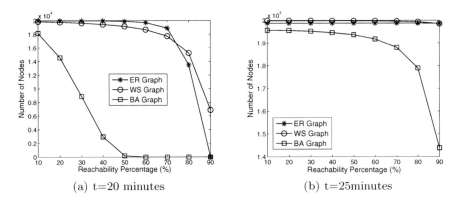

(a) t=20 minutes   (b) t=25minutes

Fig. 6. Resistance to selective node failures

we randomly removed 10% of the nodes from the botnet before each simulation. And then we observe the command propagation within the remained botnet. The simulation results are shown in Fig. 5. We can find that in the ER Graph the reachability can still exceed 90% from most of the nodes in 20 minutes; however, in the WS Graph only half of the nodes can make this and the situation in the BA Graph is even worse: the maximal reachability percentage can only exceed 80% if the start node is carefully selected. Therefore, we know that the ER random topology is more robust to the random node failures compared with the scale free and the small world topologies. Beside random node failures, we also test the resistance of the three topologies to the selective node failures. In this test, instead of random removing, we removed 10% of the nodes that are the most connected (i.e., nodes with the highest degrees). The simulation results for this case are shown in Fig. 6. Obviously, the influence is enlarged. In the ER Graph no node can reach 90% of the other nodes in the botnet within 20 minutes now and only about 70% of the nodes can achieve a reachability of 80%. The situation in the WS Graph is a little better: there are still around 7000 nodes that can make a reachability percentage over 90%. Compared with them, the situation in the BA Graph is much worse: less than 4000 nodes (20%) can achieve a reachability of 40%. We then extended the simulation time to 25 minutes. At this time, almost all the nodes in the ER Graph and the WS Graph can achieve a reachability larger than 90%. However, in the BA Graph the situation is still worse: only less than 4000 nodes can bypass a reachability of 80%. Thereby, the ER Graph and the WS Graph are less affected by the selective node failures.

Conclusion: based on the simulations and analysis above, we can conclude that in general the ER model is appropriate to build our SMS botnet. Under this topology with 20000 nodes, if each node knows 6 other peers on average, a command can be propagated to over 90% of the nodes in 20 minutes from any node. And in this process no more than 4 messages are required to send on each node. It's also robust to both random and selective node failures.

5   Botnet Construction

In the last section, we know that the ER random graph is a suitable topology for our SMS-based mobile botnet. So in this section we introduce a mechanism to construct this topology. We do not discuss the ways to infect mobile phones but simply assume that a number of mobile phones have already been compromised. What we concern is how these mobile phones get to know each other and finally form a botnet with the random graph topology.

Our proposal utilizes an internet server to help the construction. In this scheme, we first set up a helper server on the internet. And then when a mobile phone is infected by the malware of the botnet, it is made to actively connect to the helper server through internet to register itself and get a list of neighbors assigned by the server. Of course such kind of communication should be also hidden from the users under the help of our rootkits. The details of the above construction process are shown in Fig. 7, which can be divided in to four steps:

1. For a specific node (mobile phone) n_i, after being infected, it registers itself on the helper server by informing its phone number.

2. The helper server replied to n_i with a unique handshake sign s_i and a neighbor set L containing $\frac{dm}{N}$ nodes randomly selected from the infected phones that have already registered on the server. The handshake sign s_i will be used later by other bots to start a neighbor making process with this node. We denote by d, m, N the expected average degree of the botnet, the current count of registered phones and the expected population of the botnet, respectively. For each element $j \in L$, it consists of two parts: its phone number and its handshake sign s_j. The server will refuse further registration once the total number of the registered infected phones reaches N;

3. After receiving the reply, n_i begins to make neighbors with those nodes appeared in L one by one. This is done by sending them their specific handshake signs via SMS.

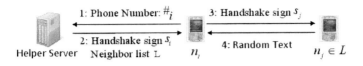

Fig. 7. Construction Protocol

4. When a node n_j receives its handshake message from n_i, it knows that it has been selected as a neighbor of n_i by the helper server. It then replies to n_i with a random selected normal message from its inbox or outbox. And several bytes at a fixed location in this message will be used as the secret key for the future communication between n_i and n_j. Based on this scheme, we can obtain a SMS botnet with the ER random graph topology, which is strongly desired. The proof for this assertion is given as follows:

Proof. Assume n_i is the i-th node that registers on the helper server. Then, for each earlier registered node n_j that $j < i$, it is selected as a neighbor of n_i with the probability $\frac{1}{i-1} \cdot \frac{d(i-1)}{N} = \frac{d}{N}$; i.e., in the generated topology graph the probability that n_i is connected with n_j ($j < i$) is $\frac{d}{N}$. On the other hand, for each latter registered nodes $n_k, k > i$, n_i will be selected as its neighbor with the probability $\frac{1}{k-1} \cdot \frac{d(k-1)}{N} = \frac{d}{N}$; i.e., in the generated topology graph the probability that n_i is connected with n_k ($k > i$) is also $\frac{d}{N}$. Thereby, we obtain the conclusion that the generated topology is our desired random graph. And the average degree is d.

For this construction mechanism, we have to notice that the introduced helper server may become the single failure point of the whole botnet especially when the infected mobile phones connect to it via the cellular network. Because once this server is disclosed, the telecom operators can easily create a signature based on the destination IP or URL to capture all the following infected phones trying to register themselves. To deal with this problem, the botmaster can take the following measures:

(1) Instead of using the cellular network like 3G, make the bots first search for available WiFi access points to communicate with the helper server. Compared with the cellular network, WiFi is much more stealthy because all the incoming and outgoing data are out of the monitoring of the telecom operators.

(2) Limit the time period for the construction stage. When the botnet size reaches an expected value or the time exceeds a predetermined threshold, directly refuse the later registration and even remove the server.

(3) Use a popular Internet service like HTTP to communicate between the server and the bots. In addition, all these communications should be encrypted.

(4) Use multiple helper servers instead of just one. This increases the hardness of the filtering.

6 Botnet Maintaining

Another major challenge in the design of a botnet is how to maintain a botnet after it is constructed. This involves two aspects: first, the botmaster may want to learn the runtime statuses of his controlled bots, such as how many bots are online, the results of an attack, etc. Therefore, in addition to an effective C&C channel, the botmaster also needs an effective report channel. Second, for 'security' reason, the botmaster has to update bot codes regularly. Therefore, we also have to design an effective updating mechanism.

It's difficult to fulfill these two tasks simply relied on SMS. For the botnet reporting, it's a process of information aggregation. If the botmaster collects bot reports via SMS messages, the used mobile phone will be quickly overwhelmed by a mass of messages and be noticed by the defenders. For the botnet updating, the data required to transfer usually greatly exceed the maximum payload of a single SMS message. So it's also unsuitable to deliver the updates via SMS.

As we known, after a long time developing, the traditional PC botnets usually have implemented some mature channels to collect and distribute data among their controlled bots. Therefore, if we can associate our mobile bots with some PC bots, the traditional PC botnet can help to maintain the mobile botnet. Our maintain mechanism showed in Fig. 8. is based on this idea. First of all, the botmaster has to collect a set of PC zombies that are visible on the internet, which means remote computers can actively connect to them if a malware installed on them listens on some ports. These zombies do exist because many network firewalls allow inbound connections to some special ports like 80. With this set, when the hijacked phones register themselves on the helper server, we assign each of them such a zombie. Then, after being equipped with a special malicious daemon these zombies can be used to collect reports and deliver updates for the botmaster: when the botmaster wants to learn the runtime information of the mobile botnet, he first issues a report command to the mobile botnet via the SMS

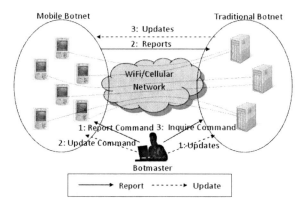

Fig. 8. Maintaining of the SMS-based mobile botnet

channel. After receiving the command, the smart phones are made to covertly connect to their assigned PC zombies to upload their information. Then, the botmaster can collect these information by commanding the PC botnets. Similarly, when the botmaster wants to update their malware, he first distributes the updates to the PC zombies through the C&C channel of the PC botnet. And then he issues an update command in the SMS botnet to ask the hijacked phones to download the updates from their associated zombies.

In the process of maintaining, we may take the following measures to increase the stealth of our mobile botnet:

(1) The same as in the construction process, bot phones should try to use WiFi instead of cellular network to communicate with their internet peers.

(2) The communication between the bot phones and the PC zombies should be encrypted with individualized keys, which means different pairs of phones and zombies use different encryptions.

(3) The mobile bots should change their associated PC zombies regularly.

7   Defense Strategies

The modeling and simulation in the previous sections have shown that it's entirely possible to construct an efficient and stealthy mobile botnet using SMS as its C&C channel. We are not smarter than the hackers. They may also have discovered this powerful tool. Therefore, in this section we consider several defense strategies against this threat.

According to our analysis, the most effective defense strategy against out SMS botnet is to disable the ability of malware to send or receive SMS message without the knowledge of the users. The best way to achieve this is to add some non-software-controlled signals (ringing, light flash, vibration, etc.) on the hardware level to inform the users that their mobile phones are sending or receiving SMS messages. Now, when an infected mobile phone attempts to send a botnet command covertly, the user can learn it immediately. This mechanism can be also extended to defend other mobile malware that utilize sensitive resources like WiFi by introducing hardware signals for the uses of these resources.

The second defense strategy has to first develop some special honeypots to capture the malware installed on the bots. This should take the propagation method of the malware into consideration. If they spread via local wireless protocol like Bluetooth or WiFi, the defenders can distribute vulnerable honey phones in crowded places with their Bluetooth or WiFi modular open to wait for being attacked and installed malicious codes. If they spread via social engineering by sending spam mails or hanging horses on the websites, the defenders can actively visit URLs contained in the spam mails or malicious sites to download and analyze the malicious codes. Then, once the malicious codes of our botnet are captured, defenders can take at least two further measures to detect or disable the botnet. Firstly, as we introduced earlier, our botnet is constructed via a helper server on the internet. Therefore, the defenders can perform reverse engineering of the obtained malicious codes to extract the embedded IP address or the URL of this server and then deploy a targeted filtering signature on the internet access points in their controlled cellular network to detect all the bots trying to connect with this server. Secondly, the defenders can also simply run the malicious codes to infiltrate the botnet. Then they can learn all the neighbor bots as well as the associated PC zombies used to upload runtime information and download updates. So the defenders can keep the latest version of the bot codes. In addition, after infiltrating the botnet, the defenders can receive the newest command issued by the botmaster as those ordinary bots. Then if this command is to attack a specific server, phone or send spam, the defenders can quickly deploy corresponding filtering signatures in the appropriate places in the cellular network to detect and block all the infected phones that are launching these attacks.

8   Conclusion

In this paper, we aim to investigate the possibility to utilize SMS as a medium for the mobile-botnet command and control. For this purpose we design a proof-of-concept SMS-based botnet based on a simple flooding algorithm. We mainly study the performance of this botnet under three different topologies including the random graph topology, small world topology and the power law topology. According to our simulations, the random graph topology outperforms the other two. Within this topology, a newly issued command can reach over 90% of the total 20000 bots in 20 minutes and no more than 4 messages are required to send for each bot in this process, which is quite efficient. This topology is also robust to both random and selective node failures. We then discuss how to construct and maintain this botnet. Based on these studies, we obtain the conclusion that the SMS-based botnet is indeed a serious threat on the security of the mobile computing environment. Therefore, we further explore several defense strategies against this botnet.

References

1. Virus News of Kasperksy Lab. Popular Porn Sites Distribute a New Trojan Targeting Android Smartphones (2010),
   http://www.kaspersky.com/news?id=207576175
2. Porras, P., Saidi, H., Yegneswaran, V.: An analysis of the Ikee.B (Duh) iPhone botnet (2009),
   http://mtc.sri.com/iPhone/
3. Lelli, A.: Security Response: A Smart Worm for a Smartphone-WinCE.PmCryptic.A (2008), http://www.symantec.com/connect/blogs/smart-worm-smartphone-wincepmcryptica
4. Apvrille, A.: Symbian worm Yxes: Towards mobile botnets? In: 19th Annual EICAR Conference, France (2010)
5. Mulliner, C., Vigna, G.: Vulnerability Analysis of MMS User Agents. In: ACSAC 2006, Miami Beach, USA (2006)

6. F-Secure Corporation. Worm:SymbOS/Mabir.A (2005),
   http://www.f-secure.com/v-descs/mabir.shtml
7. Ferrie, P., Szor, P., Stanev, R.: Security Response: SymbOS.Cabir. Symantec Corporation (2007)
8. Vanhorenbeeck, M.: Mobile botnets: an economic and technological assessment (2008),
   http://www.daemon.be/maarten/mobbot.html
9. Flo, A.R., Josang, A.: Consequences of Botnets Spreading to Mobile Devices. In: 14th Nordic Conference on Secure IT Systems, Oslo (2009)
10. Campbell, M.: Mobile botnets show their disruptive potential. The New Scientist 204(2734) (2009)
11. Traynor, P., Lin, M., Ongtang, M., et al.: On Cellular Botnets: Measuring the Impact of Malicious Devices on a Cellular Network Core. In: CCS 2009, Chicago, USA (2009)
12. Singh, K., Sangal, S., Jain, N., Traynor, P., Lee, W.: Evaluating Bluetooth as a Medium for Botnet Command and Control. In: Kreibich, C., Jahnke, M. (eds.) DIMVA 2010. LNCS, vol. 6201, pp. 61–80. Springer, Heidelberg (2010)
13. Zeng, Y., Hu, X., Shin, K.G.: Design of SMS Commanded-and-Controlled and P2P-Structured Mobile Botnets. University of Michigan Technical Report CSE-TR-562-10 (2010)
14. Papathanasiou, C., Percoco, N.J.: This is not the droid you are looking for. In: DEF CON, vol. 18 (2010)
15. Singh, K., Srivastava, A., Giffin, J., et al.: Evaluating Email's Feasibility for Botnet Command and Control. In: DSN 2008 (2008)
16. Walker, J.: Stego!Text Steganography (2005),
   http://www.fourmilab.ch/javascrypt/stego.html
17. Daemen, J., Rijmen, V.: The Design of Rijndael: AES - The Advanced Encryption Standard. Springer, Heidelberg (2002)
18. Erdos, P., Renyi, A.: On random graphs I. Publicationes Mathematicae.15 (1959)
19. Barabasi, A.L., Albert, R.: Emergence of scaling in random networks. Science 286 (1999)
20. Watts, D.J., Strogatz, S.H.: Collective dynamics of 'small-world' networks. Nature 393(6684) (1998)
21. Davis, C.R., Neville, S., Fernandez, J.M., Robert, J.-M., McHugh, J.: Structured Peer-to-Peer Overlay Networks: Ideal Botnets Command and Control Infrastructures? In: Jajodia, S., Lopez, J. (eds.) ESORICS 2008. LNCS, vol. 5283, pp. 461–480. Springer, Heidelberg (2008)
22. Csardi, G.: The igraph library (2005),
   http://igraph.sourceforge.net/index.html
23. Mulliner, C., SeifertRise, J.P.: Rise of the iBots: 0wning a telco network. In: MALWARE 2010, France (2010)

FIRE: Fault Injection for Reverse Engineering

Manuel San Pedro[1], Mate Soos[2], and Sylvain Guilley[1]

[1] Institut TELECOM
[2] INRIA, Security Research Labs

Abstract. In this paper, we propose a new technique that uses fault injection to reverse-engineer a private block cipher implemented with an unknown S-box. The private algorithm we wish to retrieve differs from a known algorithm in the choice of the S-Box, which we find using a novel, fault-injecting technique. The main idea is to consider the components of the S-Box as the solutions of a linear boolean system, whose equations stem from the faults injected, using existing fault models. We focus on two well-known block ciphers, DES and AES, and prove it to be feasible to retrieve the the S-Box for both cases. We present the fault models used, the equations extracted from the faults injected, and analyse the final results. Given the detailed analysis, the technique can be applied with ease to most ciphers employing an S-box.

1 Introduction

According to Kerckhoffs's principle, a cryptosystem should be secure even if everything about the system except the secret key is public knowledge [9]. Even though this became a fundamental principle of modern cryptology, it is moderately common for companies and sometimes even standards bodies to keep the inner workings of a system secret [1,6]. We then talk about *security through obscurity*, or *black-box cryptography*.

Under Kerckhoffs's principle, cryptanalysis consists in retrieving the cipher key. But when dealing with security through obscurity, the goal is now modified to also retrieve information on the private algorithm. This is called reverse-engineering. Nowadays, with the omnipresence of embedded cryptography, it has become crucial to be able to perform attacks on electronic devices embedding unknown cryptosystems.

Previous attempts at reverse-engineering unknown cryptosystems were either through (electro-)optical means, such as the discovery of the MIFARE algorithm [6], or through the use of side-channel analysis [11]. Side-channel analysis was originally devised to find the secret key through the measurement of physical characteristics of the chip such as power intake. Guilley et al. [7] employed this technique to retrieve the internals of black-box ciphers. This is called the side-channel analysis for reverse-engineering (SCARE) attack.

In this paper, we present a new type of attack employing the principle of fault injection [2] to retrieve the unknown S-box of a black-box cipher. Fault injection was originally devised to retrieve the secret key through injection of faults into

C.A. Ardagna and J. Zhou (Eds.): WISTP 2011, LNCS 6633, pp. 280–293, 2011.

the chip executing the algorithm and observing the modified output. Our attack injects faults into the chip, collects the output from the chip, performs analysis of this data and finally converts the data into a set of equations in binary variables, which are finally solved using Gaussian elimination to retrieve the S-box. This new type of attack we call fault injection for reverse engineering (FIRE).

The rest of the paper is organised as follows. In Sect. 2, we describe the state of the art, such as physical attacks of cryptosystems and linear systems solving. In Sect. 3, we present a DES-based cryptosystem, and a FIRE attack on it. Then, in Sect. 4, we describe an AES-based cryptosystem, and its corresponding FIRE attack. Finally, in Sect. 5 we conclude this paper.

2   State of the Art

2.1   Physical Attacks on Cryptographic Systems

Most of the cryptographic algorithms used in serious applications are supposed to be secure against algorithmic attacks. However, they are implemented on physical components, and hence become vulnerable against physicals attacks. Once such algorithms are implemented, either on dedicated hardware or as software on a micro-controller, the different physical properties of the algorithm can be observed. Over the years, sophisticated attacks have been developed to attack cryptographic devices through such observations.

Side-channel attack. The physical implementation of a cipher may reveal useful information about the secret key in an indirect way. Kocher in [10] and in [11] published two novel attack techniques exploiting side channel leakage of cryptographic devices. Computation requires time, consumes power and causes electromagnetic radiations: all these are possible sources of information related to the secret key. These techniques are powerful, as they allow to reduce the complexity of a brute-force attack by several orders of magnitude. However, they require physical access to the device to collect the necessary measurements.

Fault-injection attack. Fault attacks is the active way of attacking the physical implementation of an algorithm. During the proper functioning of the device, the attacker perturbs it by injecting hardware faults which produce an erroneous (or *faulted*) output. The attacker then exploits this to retrieve secret information. As explained in [8], the most common ways to carry out such an attack are manipulating the supply voltage or the the external clock, or applying laser or X-ray beams.

The SCARE attack. More recently it has been shown ([3,5,7]) that side-channel attacks could be used to retrieve secret parts of private algorithms. This is called side-channel attack for reverse-engineering, or simply SCARE. when a side-channel is used to retrieve an S-box on a private block cipher such as DES or AES, the attacker studies the transition $y = \mathcal{SB}(x \oplus k)$. In a classical side-channel attack, $\mathcal{SB}$ is known and we wish to retrieve k. In SCARE, we assume to know k and wish to retrieve $\mathcal{SB}$.

2.2   Solving Linear Boolean Systems

If we consider an S-box as a boolean function $f_{n \to m}$ (i.e. a boolean function from $\{0,1\}^n$ to $\{0,1\}^m$), we can split it into m and $f_{n \to 1}$, called the *components*. Each one of the components will be considered as a vector $s \in \{0,1\}^{2^n}$, being the solution of a linear system in 2^n variables. Each one of the faults injected brings a certain l number of equations (depending on the fault model), that the component s must satisfy. This means that each component s is one of the solutions of the system in $\{0,1\}$ of l equations:

$$A \cdot X = B. \tag{1}$$

where A is a $l \times 2^n$ boolean matrix, and both X and B are vectors of 2^n elements.

The equations are of the form $\bigoplus_{i=0}^{2^n-1} a_i \cdot x_i = b_i$. Let $\mathcal{L}$ be the set of solutions of the system $\mathcal{L} = \{s \in \{0,1\}^{2^n} : A \cdot s = B\}$. Let us note that

$$s \in \mathcal{L} \Leftrightarrow \bar{s} \in \mathcal{L} \tag{2}$$

It stems from the fact that if α and β are boolean variables, then $\alpha \oplus \beta = \bar{\alpha} \oplus \bar{\beta}$. This property will be important for the rest of the study, since the minimum of candidates returned will be 2. To solve this linear system of equations, we have used the Sage software [14] to perform the Gaussian elimination, but any mathematical software is adequate for the job, as the matrices are typically quite small.

3   The Case of DES

We first give a description of a FIRE attack on a DES-like cryptosystem. Even if the attack has already been shown by Biham & Shamir in [2], it gives us a good foundation to proceed during the more complex case of a SPN such as AES in Sect. 4.

The Data Encryption Standard (DES) was developed in the 1970s by the National Bureau of Standards with the help of the National Security Agency. Its purpose was to provide a standard method for protecting sensitive commercial and unclassified data. IBM created the first draft of the algorithm, calling it LUCIFER. DES officially became a federal standard in November of 1976 [12]. DES is a symmetric cryptosystem, specifically a 16-round Feistel cipher. It has a 64-bit block size and uses a 56-bit key. From this key, 16 sub-keys are created and are used at each round. The input is split in two halves. The progression of the cipher is described in Fig. 1.

The round function, applied to a 32 bits register R and a 48 bits round Key K, $F(R,K)$, consists in the succession of 4 sub-functions: first, E is an expansion function applied to R which returns a 48 bits output. The key K is then XOR-ed to $E(R)$. S is the substitution function. It consists in 8 S-Boxes $\mathcal{SB}_0, \ldots, \mathcal{SB}_7$ each of which map a 6-bit input to a 4-bit output. A 32-bit permutation P is finally applied to the output of S.

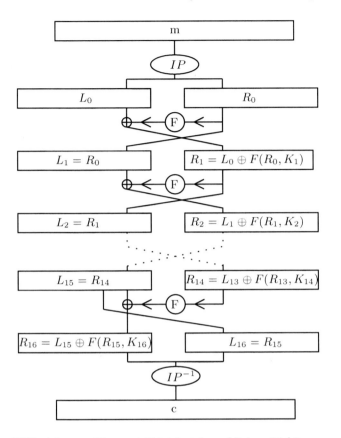

Fig. 1. The DES cipher, a 16-round Feistel cipher. IP is a 64 bit permutation. The round function applies F to the right half of the register, XORs the result to the left half, and exchanges the roles of the halves.

We consider the fault model introduced by Biham and Shamir in [2]: it assumes that the attacker is able to inject faults at the last round, round no. 15, on the right register R_{15}. We consider that the substitution function S has been modified and kept secret. We then wish to retrieve $\mathcal{SB}_0, \ldots, SB_7$, the 8 S-Boxes which compose it.

Let $c = (L_{16}, R_{16})$ be the correct and $c^\star = (L_{16}^\star, R_{16}^\star)$ be the faulty ciphertext, resulting from the same plaintext m and secret key K. If we consider that the secret key is not known but fixed to a certain value, we will not retrieve the exact S-boxes, instead we will retrieve the function $x \mapsto \mathcal{SB}_i(x \oplus k_i)$, where k_i is key input of the ith S-Box.

Without loss of generality, let us consider that the key is known for the attack, hence we can ignore it for our present discussion. We thus have:

$$R_{16} = L_{15} \oplus F(R_{15}) = L_{15} \oplus F(L_{16})$$
$$\text{and} \quad R_{16}^\star = L_{15} \oplus F(R_{15}^\star) = L_{15} \oplus F(L_{16}^\star).$$

hence we get:

$$R_{16} \oplus R_{16}^\star = F(L_{16}) \oplus F(L_{16}^\star)$$
$$R_{16} \oplus R_{16}^\star = P[S(E(L_{16}))] \oplus P[S(E(L_{16}^\star))]$$
$$P^{-1}[R_{16} \oplus R_{16}^\star] = S(E(L_{16})) \oplus S(E(L_{16}^\star)).$$

Since c and $c^\star$ are known, the only unknown register, L_{15}, disappears once R_{16} is XOR-ed with $R_{16}^\star$. The intrinsic design of Feistel block-ciphers allows us to have the knowledge of the fault injected, and its effect during the cipher, giving us the difference at the input and output of the S-Boxes. We note Δ_{in} and Δ_{out}, those differences:

$$\Delta_{in} = E(L_{16}) \oplus E(L_{16}^\star)$$
$$\Delta_{out} = P^{-1}[R_{16} \oplus R_{16}^\star].$$

where Δ_{in} and Δ_{out} are 48 and 32 bits long. However, if we focus on the ith S-box Sb_i for instance, we can consider Δ_{in}^i and Δ_{out}^i as 6 and 4 bits long. We know $x = E(L_{16})[6*i : 6*(i+1)]$, the 6 bits input of $\mathcal{SB}_i$ during the unaltered cipher, $x^\star = E(L_{16}^\star)[6*i : 6*(i+1)]$, the 6 bits input of $\mathcal{SB}_i$ during the faulty cipher. We have the relation:

$$Sb_i(x) \oplus Sb_i(x^\star) = \Delta_{out}^i.$$

Our goal is to retrieve Sb_i, which is a boolean function from $\{0,1\}^6$ to $\{0,1\}^4$. Let's consider it component-wise, i.e. as 4 functions from $\{0,1\}^6$ to

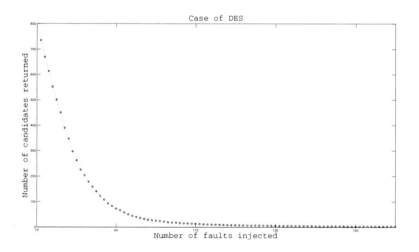

Fig. 2. Attacking component 0 of the first S-Box of DES: On the x axis, the number of faults injected, on the y-axis the mean of $\#\mathcal{L}_{1,0,x}$ after 1000 tries. In the end, we only have 2 candidates.

$\{0,1\}$: (s_0, s_1, s_2, s_3). From each injected fault, we must have:

$$\text{For } j = 0, \ldots, 3, \quad s_{j,x} \oplus s_{j,x^\star} = \Delta_{out}^i(j), \tag{3}$$

where $\Delta_{out}^i(j)$ is the jth bit of Δ_{out}^i. For each injected fault and for each component j, s_j must satisfy the previous equation. It is then added to the final system. We now have a distinguisher, we can define $\mathcal{L}_{i,j,N}$ as the set of candidates for the jth component of the ith S-box. Considering N fault injections, giving us $(x_k, x_k^\star, \Delta_{out,k})$ (k from 1 to N), we have:

$$\mathcal{L}_{i,j,N} = \{s \in \{0,1\}^{64} \text{ such that } \forall k, k \le N : s_{x_k} \oplus s_{x_k^\star} = \Delta_{out,k}^i(j)\}.$$

Simulating an error perturbing randomly one single input bit of an S-box of DES, we reach the final set of two candidates mentioned at eq. (4) after approximately 130 fault injections. Fig. 2 illustrates the mean progression of $\#\mathcal{L}_{1,0,N}$ with 1000 experiments. This attack converges to the expected solution, meaning that, since we have the property (2),

$$\exists n_0 \text{ such that } \forall n > n_0, \quad \mathcal{L}_{i,j,n} = \{s_j, \bar{s}_j\}. \tag{4}$$

Note that in order to fully retrieve the 8 S-boxes, one has to test both candidates for all the 32 components. This leads to an exhaustive search in 2^{32}, which is trivially feasible.

4   The Case of AES

AES is a widely used symmetric-key encryption by Daemen and Rijman [4], adopted as a standard by the National Institute of Standards and Technology of the US. It is based on a design principle known as a Substitution Permutation Network (SPN). AES has a fixed block size of 128 bits and a key size of 128, 192, or 256 bits. It operates on a 4×4 array of bytes, termed the state (where 1 byte = 8 bits). Most calculations carried out by the cipher are done in the finite field of $\mathcal{GF}(2^8)$.

The AES cipher is specified as a number of repetitions of transformation rounds, each round made up with 4 round transformations: SUBBYTES, MIX-COLUMNS, SHIFTROWS and ADDROUNDKEY. Note that the last round is exempt from MIXCOLUMNS.

Without loss of generality, since we consider that the cipher key is known, we set it to 0, and we also discard the final SHIFTROWS operation since it can trivially be inverted. Hence we only consider operations MIXCOLUMNS and SUBBYTES, as explained below in detail.

MIXCOLUMNS applies a linear transformation to a column of the state:

$$\text{MIXCOLUMNS} \left(\begin{bmatrix} x \\ y \\ z \\ t \end{bmatrix} \right) = \begin{bmatrix} 02 \ 03 \ 01 \ 01 \\ 01 \ 02 \ 03 \ 01 \\ 01 \ 01 \ 02 \ 03 \\ 03 \ 01 \ 01 \ 02 \end{bmatrix} \cdot \begin{bmatrix} x \\ y \\ z \\ t \end{bmatrix},$$

where the operations are performed in $\mathcal{GF}(2^8)$.

SubBytes is a non linear transformation which is applied to each byte of the state. It is traditionally implemented as a S-box, which can be seen as a boolean function $\mathcal{SB}$ from 8 bits to 8 bits. Note that SubBytes is a bijection.

$$
\text{SubBytes}\left(\begin{bmatrix} x \\ y \\ z \\ t \end{bmatrix}\right) = \begin{bmatrix} \mathcal{SB}(x) \\ \mathcal{SB}(y) \\ \mathcal{SB}(z) \\ \mathcal{SB}(t) \end{bmatrix}.
$$

In our attack, this function is unknown, and the goal is to retrieve it.

4.1   Fault Injection

Let us assume that we are able to inject a fault on one byte of the block, just before the last MixColumns, during the 9th round. The attack is column-wise, meaning that we only care about the column on which the fault is injected. For example, let us look at the first column of a regular cipher, from the last MixColumns until the end of the cipher. We have:

$$
\begin{bmatrix} \alpha \\ \beta \\ \gamma \\ \delta \end{bmatrix} \xrightarrow{\text{MC}} MC\left(\begin{bmatrix} \alpha \\ \beta \\ \gamma \\ \delta \end{bmatrix}\right) \xrightarrow{\text{SB}} \begin{bmatrix} x \\ y \\ z \\ t \end{bmatrix} = c. \tag{5}
$$

Now, the same data is processed, but with a fault ϵ injected before the last MixColumns. Fig. 3 illustrates the propagation of the error.

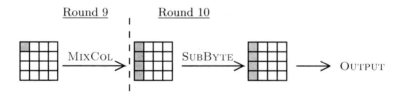

Fig. 3. Propagation of the fault on our simplified AES: we perturb a byte just before the last MixColumns. The error propagates to the whole column.

We thus have:

$$
\begin{bmatrix} \alpha \\ \beta \\ \gamma \\ \delta \end{bmatrix} \xrightarrow{\text{FI}} \begin{bmatrix} \alpha \oplus \epsilon \\ \beta \\ \gamma \\ \delta \end{bmatrix} \xrightarrow{\text{MC}} MC\left(\begin{bmatrix} \alpha \oplus \epsilon \\ \beta \\ \gamma \\ \delta \end{bmatrix}\right) \xrightarrow{\text{SB}} \begin{bmatrix} x^{\star} \\ y^{\star} \\ z^{\star} \\ t^{\star} \end{bmatrix} = c^{\star}. \tag{6}
$$

Now that we have a triplet $(c, c^{\star}, \epsilon)$. Let us examine how we could exploit Fault Injection to extract information on $\mathcal{SB}$. We start the attack from the ciphertexts, we retrieving $\mathcal{SB}^{-1}$, which is exactly the same since $\mathcal{SB}$ is bijective in SPNs.

We have, from eq. (5) and eq. (6):

$$
\mathcal{SB}^{-1}(c) \oplus \mathcal{SB}^{-1}(c^\star) = MC\left(\begin{bmatrix} \alpha \\ \beta \\ \gamma \\ \delta \end{bmatrix}\right) \oplus MC\left(\begin{bmatrix} \alpha \oplus \epsilon \\ \beta \\ \gamma \\ \delta \end{bmatrix}\right)
$$

$$
= MC\left(\begin{bmatrix} \epsilon \\ 0 \\ 0 \\ 0 \end{bmatrix}\right) = \begin{bmatrix} 02 \cdot \epsilon \\ \epsilon \\ \epsilon \\ 03 \cdot \epsilon \end{bmatrix},
$$

because MixColumns is linear. It translates into the system

$$
\begin{aligned}
\mathcal{SB}^{-1}(x) \oplus \mathcal{SB}^{-1}(x^\star) &= 02 \cdot \epsilon \\
\mathcal{SB}^{-1}(y) \oplus \mathcal{SB}^{-1}(y^\star) &= \epsilon \\
\mathcal{SB}^{-1}(z) \oplus \mathcal{SB}^{-1}(z^\star) &= \epsilon \\
\mathcal{SB}^{-1}(t) \oplus \mathcal{SB}^{-1}(t^\star) &= 03 \cdot \epsilon
\end{aligned}
\tag{7}
$$

4.2   Translation of the FI into Equations

Let us remind ourselves that $\mathcal{SB}^{-1}$ is a boolean function from $\{0,1\}^8$ to $\{0,1\}^8$. Considering it component-wise, i.e. as 8 independent functions from $\{0,1\}^8$ to $\{0,1\}$:

$$
\mathcal{SB}^{-1} = \{\mathcal{SB}_0^{-1}, \mathcal{SB}_1^{-1}, \ldots, \mathcal{SB}_7^{-1}\} \quad \text{with} \quad \mathcal{SB}_i^{-1} : \{0,1\}^8 \mapsto \{0,1\}\}.
$$

Now, $\mathcal{SB}_i^{-1}$ can be seen as a set of 256 boolean variables:

$$
\mathcal{SB}_i^{-1} = \{s_{i,0}, s_{i,1}, \ldots, s_{i,255}\}.
$$

If we consider bit-wise the equations given in (7) then for a fault injected, we know that, necessarily, for $i = 0 \ldots 7$, $\mathcal{SB}_i^{-1}$ has to satisfy

$$
\begin{aligned}
s_{i,x} \oplus s_{i,x^\star} &= (02 \cdot \epsilon)_i \\
s_{i,y} \oplus s_{i,y^\star} &= \epsilon_i \\
s_{i,z} \oplus s_{i,z^\star} &= \epsilon_i \\
s_{i,t} \oplus s_{i,t^\star} &= (03 \cdot \epsilon)_i
\end{aligned}
\tag{8}
$$

These four equations are to be manipulated according to the fault model, and used to build the final system that is solved with Gaussian elimination to finally give the solutions.

4.3   Random and unknown Faults

First, we discuss the fault model that is close to the one presented by Piret and Quisquater in [13]. The error is injected on the first byte of the state, just before the last MixColumns. It is random and unknown. By adding lines of the system (7), without any knowledge of the value of ϵ, we have:

$$SB^{-1}(x) \oplus SB^{-1}(x^\star) \oplus SB^{-1}(y) \oplus SB^{-1}(y^\star) \oplus SB^{-1}(t) \oplus SB^{-1}(t^\star) = 0$$
$$SB^{-1}(x) \oplus SB^{-1}(x^\star) \oplus SB^{-1}(z) \oplus SB^{-1}(z^\star) \oplus SB^{-1}(t) \oplus SB^{-1}(t^\star) = 0 \ ,$$

since $03 \cdot \epsilon \oplus 02 \cdot \epsilon \oplus \epsilon = 0$. The operations are made on $\mathcal{GF}(2^8)$.

Each one of the 8 components of SB^{-1} has to satisfy these equations. Now that we have removed ϵ, we can inject them into the system. Once solved, this system returns all the satisfying candidates, including the eight solutions. Considering N fault injections, giving us $(c_k, c_k^\star)$ (k from 1 to N), we can define the distinguisher $\mathcal{L}_N$ for the attack of SB^{-1}:

$$\mathcal{L}_N = \left\{ s \in \{0,1\}^{256} \text{ such that } \forall k < N, \ \begin{matrix} s_{x_k} \oplus s_{x_k^\star} \oplus s_{y_k} \oplus s_{y_k^\star} \oplus s_{t_k} \oplus s_{t_k^\star} = 0 \\ s_{x_k} \oplus s_{x_k^\star} \oplus s_{z_k} \oplus s_{z_k^\star} \oplus s_{t_k} \oplus s_{t_k^\star} = 0' \end{matrix} \right\}.$$

It so happens that after $n_0 \approx 400$ faults injected, we have a constant set of solutions $\mathcal{S}$:

$$\forall n > n_0, \quad \mathcal{L}_n = \mathcal{S}.$$

More precisely, the attack converges to a set $\mathcal{S}$ with 512 candidates. First we describe in detail this set $\mathcal{S}$, and then we discuss the possible conclusion of the attack through exhaustive search.

To account for the 512 solutions, we consider $\mathcal{S}$ as an *orbit* of the 8 components of SB^{-1}: we have always $SB_0^{-1}, SB_1^{-1}, \ldots, SB_7^{-1} \in \mathcal{S}$. But we also have $(0,0,\ldots,0)$ and $(1,1,\ldots,1)$ in $\mathcal{S}$ (they indeed satisfy all the equations brought by the distinguisher), we then state that:

Proposition 1. $u, v \in \mathcal{S} \Rightarrow u \oplus v \in \mathcal{S}$.

Proof. Without loss of generality, we shorten the definition of $\mathcal{S}$ to a single boolean equation, which does not change with the real context. For instance:

$$\mathcal{S} = \{s \in \{0,1\}^{256} \text{ such that } \quad s_y \oplus s_y^\star \oplus s_z \oplus s_z^\star = 0\}.$$

Now let $u, v \in \mathcal{S}$.

$$u_y \oplus u_{y^\star} \oplus u_z \oplus u_{z^\star} = 0 \text{ , and } v_y \oplus v_{y^\star} \oplus v_z \oplus v_{z^\star} = 0.$$
$$\text{Then } u_y \oplus u_{y^\star} \oplus u_z \oplus u_{z^\star} \oplus v_y \oplus v_{y^\star} \oplus v_z \oplus v_{z^\star} = 0.$$
$$\text{Then } (u \oplus v)_y \oplus (u \oplus v)_{y^\star} \oplus (u \oplus v)_z \oplus (u \oplus v)_{z^\star} = 0.$$
$$\text{Finally } u \oplus v \in \mathcal{S}.$$

We now can define $\mathcal{S}$ such that:

$$\mathcal{S} = \{a_0 \cdot SB_0^{-1} \oplus \ldots a_7 \cdot SB_7^{-1} \oplus a_8 \cdot (1, \ldots, 1), \quad a_i \in \{0,1\}\}.$$

We can remove from $\mathcal{S}$ the trivial solution $(1, \ldots, 1)$ and $(0, \ldots, 0)$: in fact, it is mandatory for a SPN S-box to be bijective, and it would not be the case if $(1, \ldots, 1)$ or $(0, \ldots, 0)$ was one of the components.

From this set, how can the full S-box be efficiently retrieved? We have 510 candidates that must be replaced into the correct position out of 8 possible choices. A naive exhaustive search would lead to $\mathcal{C}_8^{510} \times 8! \approx 2^{71}$ possibilities.

However, as we have already noticed, $\forall s \in \mathcal{S}, \bar{s} \in \mathcal{S}$. We can form 255 groups of elements of $\mathcal{S}$, each of them including a candidate and its complement. For an optimal exhaustive search, one has to select 8 of those groups, and then test the 256 possibilities. This would lead to $2^8 \times \mathcal{C}_8^{255} \approx 2^{57}$ possibilities to finish the attack. This computational complexity is moderately high, but can be achieved with a large set of modern GPUs and/or FPGAs, and is not out of reach of any major organisation such as multinational companies or governments. However, we also propose another solution by finishing the attack using the SCARE method.

4.4   SCARE Conclusion of a FIRE Attack

In this section, we propose a finishing of a FIRE attack when we are in the context described in Sect. 4.3. We have a set $\mathcal{S}$, of 510 candidates containing the 8 component of $\mathcal{SB}^{-1}$.

In order to use side-channel information to finish the attack, we use the curves of the DPA-Contest [15] to find $\mathcal{SB}^{-1}$. The context is the following. We have

- N power traces corresponding of the functioning of the components with known inputs/outputs/cipher keys.
- The set $\mathcal{S}$ of a reduced amount of candidates for the components of $\mathcal{SB}^{-1}$. Here, 510.

It is well-known that the power consumption of components strongly depend on the data processed, and more exactly the number of bit-flips completed. This number is given by the hamming distance between a register at a time t and $t+1$. We then talk about Hamming distance model. We study here the transition during the last SUBBYTES of the AES chiper.

For every candidates $s \in \mathcal{S}$, for every component j of $\mathcal{SB}^{-1}$, we compute what would be the hamming distance between c (which is known) and the state at the input of the last SUBBYTES, if we would have $s = \mathcal{SB}_j^{-1}$. We then use a distinguisher (Pearson's correlation) in order to measure the dependence between those hamming distances and the power traces.

On Fig. 4, the correlation traces resulting from the attack of the 7th component by using SCARE. This means that we are looking for $\mathcal{SB}_7^{-1}$ amongst the 510 members of $\mathcal{S}$. On the figure, by using 10000 traces, we clearly can identify $\mathcal{SB}_7^{-1}$ in red and bold, $\overline{\mathcal{SB}_7^{-1}}$, the symmetric below, and the 508 bad candidates, giving a correlation close to zero. An adversary able to perform fault injections on a component is very likely to be able to get a campaign of acquisition of power traces in order to conclude the attack this way. Hence it alleviates the burden on the attacker of making the exhaustive search in 2^{57} as munitioned at the end of Sec. 4.3.

Note that the SCARE attack is feasible here since we have a very restricted number of candidate for the solutions. When dealing with SCA, the number

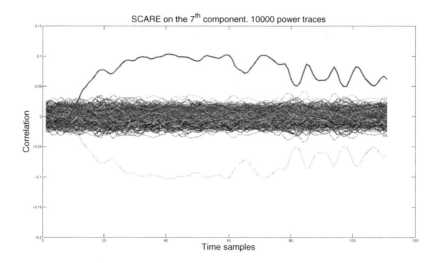

Fig. 4. SCARE on the 7th component of $\mathcal{SB}^{-1}$, with $N = 10000$ power traces. We have the 510 correlation traces: on the x-axis the time samples of the power traces, on the y-axis, the value of the correlation. We clearly identify here the solution (on the top) and its complementary (on the bottom)

of candidates to test is very important: 256 hypothesis to test when we want to retrieve a key byte, but 2^{2^8} hypothesis to test when we are looking for a single component of $\mathcal{SB}^{-1}$. Here the FIRE attack carried out most of the job by reducing the 2^{2^8} to 510.

On Fig. 4, we have the results with $N = 10000$ power curves. However, from $N = 5000$ curves (taken randomly from the ones available for the DPA Contest), the attack is feasible, meaning that we are able to extract the solutions.

4.5   Results with Various Fault Models and Contexts

In this section, we present several other realistic fault models, or context allowing us to perform a FIRE attacks.

Random and known faults. Let us consider the strongest fault model: we are able to inject a random and known fault during the cipher execution.

The advantage with this model, is that, since we know ϵ, we are able to target which one of the components of $\mathcal{SB}^{-1}$ we are attacking.

Considering N fault injections, giving us $(c_k, c_k^\star, \epsilon^k)$, $k = 1, \ldots N$, we can define the distinguisher $\mathcal{L}_{i,N}$ for the attack of the ith component of $\mathcal{SB}^{-1}$:

$$
\mathcal{L}_{i,N} = \left\{ s \in \{0,1\}^{256} \text{ such that } \forall k < N, \begin{array}{l} s_{x_k} \oplus s_{x_k^\star} = (02 \cdot \epsilon^k)_i \\ s_{y_k} \oplus s_{y_k^\star} = \epsilon_i^k \\ s_{z_k} \oplus s_{z_k^\star} = \epsilon_i^k \\ s_{t_k} \oplus s_{t_k^\star} = (03 \cdot \epsilon^k)_i \end{array} \right\}.
$$

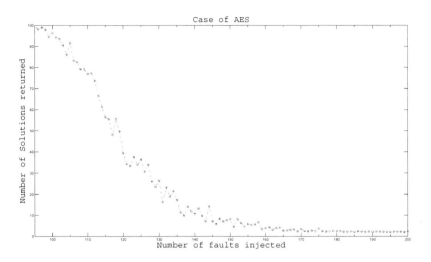

Fig. 5. Attacking component 0 of AES S-Box inverse. On the x-axis, the number of faults injected, on the y-axis the mean of $\#\mathcal{L}_{0,x}$ after 100 tries. In the end, we only have 2 candidates.

This model, combined with the technique described in Sect. 4.2, allows us to retrieve the full $\mathcal{SB}^{-1}$ in less than 180 faults injected. Fig. 5 illustrates the progression of $\mathcal{L}_{0,N}$, simulating an error occurring randomly on the first byte of the state just before the last MixColumns.

Stuck-at model. It has been shown that it is possible for an attacker to force a byte to a certain value, that it can choose. If we suppose that, just before the last SubBytes, one can force the first byte to a given value τ:

$$\begin{bmatrix} \alpha \\ \beta \\ \gamma \\ \delta \end{bmatrix} \xrightarrow{\text{FI}} \begin{bmatrix} \tau \\ \beta \\ \gamma \\ \delta \end{bmatrix} \xrightarrow{\text{SB}} \begin{bmatrix} x^\star \\ y^\star \\ z^\star \\ t^\star \end{bmatrix} = c^\star.$$

Hence he has access to $x^\star$ which is equal to $\mathcal{SB}(\tau)$. It leads to a trivial attack, since with 256 accurate *stuck-at* injections, one can retrieve the full S-Box.

Note that even one single *stuck-at* injection, we get a lot of information to bring into the system, if we decide do use different models during the attack.

In the case where it is not possible to inject a *stuck-at* fault at the input of the last SubBytes, but that it can be done just before the last MixColumns:

$$\begin{bmatrix} \alpha \\ \beta \\ \gamma \\ \delta \end{bmatrix} \xrightarrow{\text{FI}} \begin{bmatrix} \tau \\ \beta \\ \gamma \\ \delta \end{bmatrix} \xrightarrow{\text{MC}} MC\left(\begin{bmatrix} \tau \\ \beta \\ \gamma \\ \delta \end{bmatrix}\right) \xrightarrow{\text{SB}} \begin{bmatrix} x^\star \\ y^\star \\ z^\star \\ t^\star \end{bmatrix} = c^\star.$$

In that case, even if we know the value of τ, α is assumed to be random. But we have:

$$\exists \epsilon \in \mathcal{GF}(2^8) \text{ such that } \tau = \alpha \oplus \epsilon.$$

It hence leads to the fault model presented at Sec. 4.3, just as if we would have injected an unknown and random ϵ.

5 Conclusion

In this paper, we have introduced a new tool to reverse-engineer a private algorithm. This new FIRE attack allows us to retrieve the S-Box of private block-ciphers in a reasonable number of faults injected and under plausible and existing fault models. For the sake of practical demonstration, we have carried out the attack on two major ciphers, AES and DES, but the attack can be made to work on almost any cipher containing and unknown S-Box. In the case of the DES S-boxes, around 1000 Fault Injections are needed and a final exhaustive search in 2^{32} is necessary to fully retrieve all the 8 S-Boxes. For AES, under the most plausible model, around 400 fault injections suffice and lead to a finite set of 510 candidates. We can then either conclude the attack using exhaustive search in 2^{57}, or perform a data acquisition campaign and finish the attack using SCARE.

References

1. Anderson, R.: A5 (was: Hacking digital phones). Newsgroup Communication (1994)
2. Biham, E., Shamir, A.: Differential Fault Analysis of Secret Key Cryptosystems. In: Kaliski Jr., B.S. (ed.) CRYPTO 1997. LNCS, vol. 1294, pp. 513–525. Springer, Heidelberg (1997)
3. Clavier, C.: An improved SCARE cryptanalysis against a secret A3/A8 GSM algorithm. In: McDaniel, P., Gupta, S.K. (eds.) ICISS 2007. LNCS, vol. 4812, pp. 143–155. Springer, Heidelberg (2007)
4. Daemen, J., Rijmen, V.: The block cipher rijndael. In: Schneier, B., Quisquater, J.-J. (eds.) CARDIS 1998. LNCS, vol. 1820, pp. 277–284. Springer, Heidelberg (2000)
5. Daudigny, R., Ledig, H., Muller, F., Valette, F.: Scare of the des. In: ACNS, pp. 393–406 (2005)
6. Garcia, F.D., de Koning Gans, G., Muijrers, R., van Rossum, P., Verdult, R., Schreur, R.W., Jacobs, B.: Dismantling MIFARE classic. In: Jajodia, S., Lopez, J. (eds.) ESORICS 2008. LNCS, vol. 5283, pp. 97–114. Springer, Heidelberg (2008)
7. Guilley, S., Sauvage, L., Micolod, J., Réal, D., Valette, F.: Defeating Any Secret Cryptography with SCARE Attacks. In: Abdalla, M., Barreto, P.S.L.M. (eds.) LAT-INCRYPT 2010. LNCS, vol. 6212, pp. 273–293. Springer, Heidelberg (2010)
8. Hamid, H. B.-E., Choukri, H., Tunstall, D. N. M., and Whelan, C. The sorcerer's apprentice guide to fault attacks
9. Kerckhoffs, A.: La cryptographie militaire. Journal des Sciences Militaires IX, 5–83 (1883)
10. Kocher, P.C.: Timing attacks on implementations of diffie-hellman, rsa, dss, and other systems, pp. 104–113

11. Kocher, P.C., Jaffe, J., Jun, B.: Differential Power Analysis. In: Wiener, M. (ed.) CRYPTO 1999. LNCS, vol. 1666, pp. 388–397. Springer, Heidelberg (1999)
12. National Bureau of Standards. Data Encryption Standard (1977)
13. Piret, G., Quisquater, J.-J.: A Differential Fault Attack Technique against SPN Structures, with Application to the AES and KHAZAD. In: Walter, C.D., Koç, Ç.K., Paar, C. (eds.) CHES 2003. LNCS, vol. 2779, pp. 77–88. Springer, Heidelberg (2003)
14. Stein, W., et al.: Sage Mathematics Software, http://www.sagemath.org
15. VLSI Research Group TELECOM ParisTech. The DPA contest (2008/2009), http://www.dpacontest.org/

Hardware Trojan Side-Channels Based on Physical Unclonable Functions

Zheng Gong[1,*] and Marc X. Makkes[2]

[1] School of Computer Science, South China Normal University
Guangzhou, 510631, China
cis.gong@gmail.com
[2] Eindhoven University of Technology
P.O. Box 513, 5600 MB Eindhoven, The Netherlands
m.x.makkes@kr85.org

Abstract. The separation design and fabrication process in the semiconductor industry leads to potential threats such as trojan side-channels (TSCs). In this paper we design a new family of TSCs from physical unclonable functions (PUFs). In particular, a dedicated attack on the PRESENT block cipher is described by using our PUF-based TSCs. Finally we analyze the performance of our PUF-based TSCs and discuss other potential applications.

1 Introduction

With the rapid developments of semiconductor technology, integrated circuits (ICs) are fast becoming an overwhelming presence in our daily lives. Since information security attracts more and more concerns, security chips are widely used to provide hardware support of cryptographic algorithms and obtain trust computing bases. In most cases, it becomes theoretically infeasible to directly attack a well-analyzed cryptographic algorithm (e.g., AES) within a security chip by using traditional cryptanalysis. Although a security chip can resist the attacks at the algorithm level, the weaknesses in the implementation level might be analyzed for practical attacks. For instance, the side-channel information, such as differential time or power analysis, is widely investigated to break the security protection of embedded systems [11,13].

The original ideas of trojan side channel attacks and covert channels were first proposed by Simmons [15]. As an aggressive example of side-channel attacks, Lin *et al.* [7] introduced the concept of *trojan side channels* (TSCs). A TSC can be viewed as a malicious circuit that can compromise information from an embedded crypto core, afterwards it can send out the information via side-channel signals. Only the attacker who implements the TSC can decode the information. Although TSCs require extra hardware costs, it is hard to detect since

---

* This author's research was mainly performed while at DIES group, University of Twente, The Netherlands.

C.A. Ardagna and J. Zhou (Eds.): WISTP 2011, LNCS 6633, pp. 294–303, 2011.
© IFIP International Federation for Information Processing 2011

they usually occupy a negligible amount of area in the genuine IC. The current IC supply chain, such as outsourced manufacturing, also provides great opportunities to implant malicious circuits into the genuine IC to compromise their security. Nevertheless, many governments and agencies require that companies who use encrypted communications systems (e.g., mail services from Blackberry) to allow these institutions to recover encrypted information with a feasible effort. Normally this requirement leads to two options for vendors: either choose key escrow or weak design of cryptography. Implementing TSCs can match this requirement without relying on the above options.

On the other side, detecting flaws in the lithography process is usually done with extra hardware supports and it is often used to check if the functionality is correct. Verification of the functionality is often with some extra hardware attached to the IC. Recent developments showed that it is possible for an attacker to modify chip designs and add malicious circuits without changing the functionality. In the literature, many approaches have been proposed for trojan hardware detection, such as visual inspections, test patterns to find unexpected behavior, side-channel and path delay profiles [3]. Currently, it is still infeasible to detect a large amount of security chips whether they have been affected by a trojan hardware with very small gate counts. In order to keep the TSC undetectable, it is also crucial to blind the side-channel information for other parties except the original attacker. In [7], Lin *et al.* suggest to use a LFSR for encoding. This results a practical problem that every chip implemented with the same LFSR will output the same stream. Therefore, if anyone resolves the polynomial that constructs the LFSR, it will be straightforward to decode the information from every TSC based on this LFSR.

In 2001, Pappu *et al.* [12] introduced the concept of *physical unclonable functions* (PUFs, also known as physical random functions). Since it is practically impossible to model, copy, or control the IC manufacturing process variations, PUFs can make chips unique and effectively unclonable. In this paper we propose a new familty of TSCs based on PUFs. The advantages of using a PUF-based TSC are two-fold: 1) for every TSC, it is unnecessary to be implemented with different LFSRs (or keys) but a PUF with the same circuits to blind its side-channel information. The one-wayness of the PUF protects the side-channel information can only be decoded by the attacker who implemented the TSC. 2) An attacker can trace the side-channel information from a certain chip by using the physical unclonable property of PUFs. It also means mathematically modeling one chip for recovery will be useless to other chips. We propose a PUF-based TSC attack on the **PRESENT** block cipher to show the relatively negligible hardware implementation cost compared to genuine ICs.

The remainder of the paper is organized as follows: Section 2 reviews the preliminaries for TSCs and PUFs, Section 3 first describes a generalized model for PUF-based TSC attacks, after which propose a PUF-based TSC attack on the **PRESENT** block cipher, Section 4 discusses other applications of PUF-based TSCs, and Section 5 concludes the paper.

2   Preliminaries

2.1   The Trojan Side-Channel Model

It is widely accepted that a well-defined model must be formalized on the system that requires analysis. In [7], Lin *et al.* introduces the parties and activities that are involved with the Trojan Side-Channel (TSC) model. Here we will refine the TSC model from a more general perspective of the TSC scenario.

Entities & Activities. A TSC can be used either by a malicious attacker or by an anti-counterfeiting analyzer. Without loss of generality, we call the party who implants the Trojan hardware into the circuits *tracer* $\mathcal{T}$, and the party who attempts to detect those TSCs *evaluator* $\mathcal{E}$. For malicious applications, $\mathcal{T}$ will try to hide the usage of TSCs, while $\mathcal{E}$ will try to verify the correctness and integrity of circuits. For anti-counterfeiting usages, $\mathcal{T}$ will try to expose the side-channel information of TSCs, while $\mathcal{E}$ will try to discover and hinder the leakage by TSCs. Except for the implanted TSCs, we assume that the genuine ICs are tamper-resistant and no other side-channels can be found by $\mathcal{T}$. $\mathcal{E}$ can extensively test the functionality of the genuine ICs and capture the signals leaked out by TSCs.

Requirements. To evaluate its implementation quality, a TSC must obey the following conditions.

- *Circuit properties*:
  - Imperceptibility. Compared to the genuine IC, a TSC must only increase a negligible area of logic gates to reduce the possibility of detections by evaluators.
  - Conformity. A TSC must not affect the correctness and integrity of the genuine ICs. Moreover, the timing properties of the genuine ICs (e.g., cycles for an encryption/decryption) will not be affected overtly by an implanted TSC.
- *Signal properties*:
  - Blindness. Except for tracers who implanted the TSC, side-channel information leaked out by a TSC must be blind to other parties. That is to say, evaluators cannot distinguish the difference between information leaked out by TSCs and bits from a pseudorandom number generator.
  - Latency. To avoid the detection, a TSC will be latent unless it is triggered with a certain condition predefined by tracers. The trigger must be imperceptible from extensive functionality testing of the genuine ICs.

2.2   Physical Unclonable Functions

It is known that PUFs exploit the physical characteristics of the silicon and the IC manufacturing process variations to uniquely characterize each and every silicon chip. The unclonability property comes from the fact that a PUF consists of a finite number of random components, which is infeasible to exactly control over the manufacturing process. Each PUF uses these random components to map *challenges* to *responses* (CRPs). A challenge is a stimulus that is applied to the PUF and a response is the reaction of the PUF obtained through measurements. Due to the complex interaction of the stimulus with the physical microstructure of the device, each PUF will trigger a response that is highly unpredictable and unique. PUFs are often used to setup secure channels between devices. At the manufacturing process the manufacturer creates a set of CRPs with a PUF and hands them over to user. Therefore, a user can set a secure channel using the CRP by sending a challenge C to the PUF. Since the response R of the PUF is also known to the user, it can be used as a shared secret key for secure communication.

In the literature, many types of PUFs have been proposed based on different physical properties. By using the position of light as the challenge, Pappu *et al.* [12] proposed a PUF based on the scattering of light when shining a laser on a bubble-filled transparent epoxy wafer. In [6], Lim *et al.* introduced a new family of PUFs based on arbiters (APUF). An APUF consists of two identically configured delay paths that includes a number of switches. The switches are set by the stimulus and determine a unique path that signals have to travel. In order to generate response bits for an APUF, a signal is activated simultaneously on both delay paths. At the end of the delay paths there is an edge triggered flip-flop which determines the fastest signal by outputting a signal bit.

3   PUF-Based TSC Attacks

3.1   A Paradigm on PRESENT

The key objective of a TSC is to compromise key information from a crypto engine without altering or delaying the process of the genuine IC. Altering or delaying might reveal the existence of the TSC to evaluators. When a tracer $\mathcal{T}$ exploited the side-channel information, $\mathcal{T}$ will first decode the information to the original message. By retrieving the saved CRPs of the implanted PUFs, $\mathcal{T}$ can identify which IC leaked out the side-channel information, and then recover the compromised key information. In [7], Lin *et al.* adapted the concepts from spreads-spectrum communications (also known as code-division multiple access (CDMA)) to distribute the compromised bits as a covert channel to $\mathcal{T}$. For simplicity, we also choose it as the leakage circuit for PUF-based TSCs. Figure 1 depicts a generalized model for PUF-based TSC attacks.

Since TSCs also require signal blindness, traditional PUFs are not resource-efficient for ensuring the randomness of long length CRPs. Here we propose a new variant of PUF which is suitable for TSCs. Basically, our design (see Figure 2) is constructed from a combination of a *feedback shift register* (FSR) and a number of APUFs. The FSR can store a bit string with the length C and shift P bits in every cycle. Each APUF consists of C switch elements, and the number of APUFs is P. The FSR provides each APUF with an identical challenge, as the output of the APUFs is inserted back in the FSR and is sent out over the

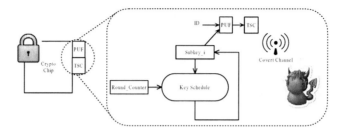

Fig. 1. PUF-based TSC attacks

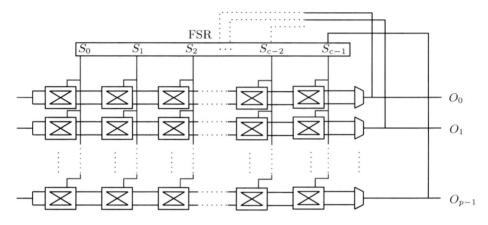

Fig. 2. A new variant of TSC based on PUFs. The top rectangle is a c-bit shift-register. The register is shifted by p-bits per cycle. Each bit is tapped and used to set the set the switch components of the PUFs. The output O_i produced by the PUFs are feedback to the shift-register and XORed with the keybits.

covert channel. We denote that a PUF-based TSC with only a single APUF to be a serial PUF-based TSC.

Initially, the FSR is loaded with a unique identifier (ID). To prevent the detection caused by the power usage, the PUF-based TSC processes and transmits key information (Key) at the same time as encryption occurs. In order to transmit the side-channel information, we suggest the following format for the covert channel.

$$\text{PUF(ID)}||\text{PUF(Key)}|| \cdots \text{PUF(ID)}||\text{PUF(Key)} \cdots$$

Using this format $\mathcal{T}$ can first decode the signal and retrieve the PUF(ID) which can be looked up in the list of devices. Afterwards, $\mathcal{T}$ can decode the PUF(Key) because the CRPs of each APUF are stored (to a database) beforehand. The length of an APUF (i.e., the number of switches) determines the storage requirement per device.

For a PUF-based TSC, the security and performance of a given structure determine its area costs. The first parameter is the length of the APUF which regulates the security of the structure. The second parameter is the number of APUFs which determine the performance of a PUF-based TSC by clock cycles. The gate equivalents (GE) of the PUF-based TSC also relies on the implementation of the cryptosystem. In [10], Ozturk *et al.* showed that a PUF with a 64-bit challenge and a single bit response using a tri-state APUF can be implemented in 351 gates. We will consider smaller challenges in our PUF-based TSCs for the imperceptibility.

PRESENT. At CHES 2007, Bogdanov *et al.* proposed an ultra-lightweight block cipher which is named PRESENT [2]. PRESENT is an example of an SP-network and consists of 31 rounds. The block length is 64 bits and two key lengths of 80 and 128 bits are supported. The hardware requirements for PRESENT are competitive. Using the *Virtual Silicon* (VST) standard cell library based on *UMC L180 0.18μm 1P6M Logic Process* (UMCL18G212T3), PRESENT-80 and PRESENT-128 are estimated to require 1570 and 1886 gate equivalents, respectively [2]. Since Bogdanov *et al.* do not expect the 128-bit key version to be used until a rigorous analysis is given, the term PRESENT means the 80-bit key version in hereafter. A high-level algorithm of the round function of PRESENT is depicted in Figure 3.

$$generateRoundKeys(k) \rightarrow \{k_1, k_2, \cdots, k_{32}\};$$
for $i = 1$ *to* 31do
  $addRoundKey(\text{STATE}, k_i);$
  $sBoxLayer(\text{STATE});$
  $pLayer(\text{STATE});$
end for
$addRoundKey(\text{STATE}, k_{32}).$

Fig. 3. The round function of PRESENT

The key schedule. PRESENT uses a hardware-efficient key schedule to avoid the scheduling weaknesses, which may be used for the related-key attack and the slide attack. The user-supplied key is stored in a key register K and represented as $k_{79}k_{78} \cdots k_0$. At the i-th round, the leftmost 64-bit of the current key register becomes the subkey $K_i = k_{79}k_{78} \cdots k_{16}$. Subsequently, the key register K is updated as follows.

- Cycling left shift 61 bits such that $[k_{79}k_{78} \cdots k_0] = [k_{18}k_{17} \cdots k_{20}k_{19}]$,
- The leftmost 4 bits are passed through the PRESENT S-box such that $[k_{79}k_{78}k_{77}k_{76}] = S[k_{79}k_{78}k_{77}k_{76}]$,
- The round counter value is XORed with bits $k_{19}k_{18}k_{17}k_{16}k_{15}$.

Based on the key schedule of PRESENT, we can design a lightweight TSC as follows. For each round, TSC will try to leak out the rightmost 4 bits of K. Since the key register is cycling left shift 61 bits, the rightmost 4 bits will not repeat themselves within 21 rounds (as illustrated in Figure 4). Thus we can obtain the whole key bits after 21 rounds of PRESENT. Since only the leftmost 64 bits in the key register will be used in the addRoundKey algorithm, compromising the rightmost 4 bits will not imply any unexpected behavior or path delay on PRESENT.

$$Round\ 1 : k_{79}k_{78}k_{77}k_{76} \cdots \underline{k_3k_2k_1k_0}$$
$$Round\ 2 : k_{18}k_{17}k_{16}k_{15} \cdots \underline{k_{22}k_{21}k_{20}k_{19}}$$
$$Round\ 3 : k_{37}k_{36}k_{35}k_{34} \cdots \underline{k_{41}k_{40}k_{39}k_{38}}$$
$$Round\ 4 : k_{56}k_{55}k_{54}k_{53} \cdots \underline{k_{60}k_{59}k_{58}k_{57}}$$
$$\cdots$$
$$Round\ 11 : k_{29}k_{28}k_{27}k_{26} \cdots \underline{k_{33}k_{32}k_{31}k_{30}}$$
$$\cdots$$
$$Round\ 21 : k_{59}k_{58}k_{57}k_{56} \cdots \underline{k_{63}k_{62}k_{61}k_{60}}$$

Fig. 4. Key Scheduling of PRESENT

Instead of recovering a full-length key, a parameterized approach can be used to lower the length of sending bits via side channels. Similar to the above attack on PRESENT, one can carefully choose a combination of key bits and rounds for a TSC. For instance, we can make a TSC that leaks 4 bits in each round and stops after 11 rounds. After 11 rounds of PRESENT, we can obtain 40 bits of the original key and execute an exhaustive search for the rest of 40 bits key. The exhaustive search only requires a time complexity of about $O(2^{40})$, which can be executed in minutes on current PCs. Consequently, a PUF-based TSC attack on PRESENT can be implemented as follows.

1. Send a pre-distributed identifier ID as the challenge to the PUF, obtain the response $r_1 = \text{PUF(ID)}$.
2. Eavesdrop each of the rightmost 4 bits of 11 rounds subkeys from the underlying PRESENT encryption/decryption. Input the compromised bits C to PUF, obtain the response $r_2 = \text{PUF}(C)$.
3. Encode the complete message $R = r_1 || r_2$, which will be sent by the covert channel.

Although the key scheduling algorithm of PRESENT has no security problems so far under cryptanalysis, our proposed attack endangers its security in practical implementations. We note that the above attack on PRESENT can also be extended to other ciphers designed with a "simple" key scheduling algorithm. If a key scheduling algorithm has a low non-linear complexity (i.e., mainly relies on linear operations such as bit shifts), a TSC attacker can easily recover the entire secret key by eavesdropping a few bits of the subkey in each round. If TSC attacks are considered in the adversary model, the non-linearity of the key schedule should be carefully strengthened by algorithm designers.

3.2   Performance Analysis

To estimate the lower-bound GE of our PUF-based TSC, we take the formula $P \cdot (5 \cdot C + 4) + 4 \cdot C$ where C is the length of the challenge and P is the number of the APUFs. Our lower-bound GE estimation is based on the implementation of PUF-based TSC in *Xilinx ISE Design Suite 12.2*. If we consider a 24-bit challenge for the PRESENT implementation where 4 key bits are snooped per cycle, the lower-bound of GE of the PUF-based TSC can be 592 gates. It is possible to lower the GE by lowering the number of APUFs. Table 1 gives an overview of the performance of implementations that are derived from different parameters of the PUF-based TSC. The results start with a low-area and low-performance implementation (serial PUF-based TSC), to a high-area and high performance implementation (TSC with 4 APUFs). It is obvious from the results that performance comes at a cost in area and storage while the length of APUF only significantly results in storage requirements.

Table 1. The performance our PUF-based TSCs

	TSC width (bit)	FSR length (bit)	CRPs storage	Performance in cycles	Area in GE
Serial PUF-based TSC	1	24	16MB	68	220
TSC with 2 APUFs	2	24	32MB	34	344
TSC with 4 APUFs	4	24	64MB	17	592
Serial PUF-based TSC	1	36	420MB	80	328
TSC with 2 APUFs	2	36	840MB	40	512
TSC with 4 APUFs	4	36	1.68GB	20	880

3.3   Evaluation

The Imperceptibility of a PUF-based TSC heavily depends on the size of the genuine chip. If a chip only contains gates nearly or below a thousand level, the TSC can be easily spotted. Our proposed TSC requires 592 gates, where as PRESENT requires 1570-1886 gates. This is almost 30-40% of the area of the attacked cipher. In [1], Agrawal *et al.* comments the that hardware trojans are detectable if the size of the trojan is more than 0.01% of the floorplan. But if a chip has thousands of gates, or a million chips need to be examined, spotting the TSC becomes increasingly difficult. Moreover, we recognize that it is a possible and clever way to hide this type of TSC in a protection mesh, such as in smartcards. In [14] Ruhrmair *et al.* presented a modeling attack on PUFs by using *linear regression* to a mapping a large amount of challenges to responses and deriving a model of the PUF. But in our PUF-based TSC attacks, the challenge for the PUF is derived form the round key. For an attacker to construct an key such that specific bits are set in the round key, it is infeasible to build a modeling attack on such CRPs of a PUF.

Besides that PUFs are well known and easily implementable in FPGAs [8,9], Devadas *et al.* showed in [5] how PUFs can be practically implemented in ASICs. Since our PUF-based TSC heavily relies on the implementation of PUFs, it can also be feasibly implemented even on a large scale. Although its feasibility and imperceptibility still require deeper investigation, our PUF-based TSC has many advantage over the TSC presented by Lin *et al.* [7]. Firstly, our PUF-based TSC can provide unpredictable outputs that are related to physical unclonability, which increases the blindness and the uniqueness of side-channel information. Secondly, PUF-based TSCs can be parameterized by the consideration of performance and resource limitations. This gives a high level of adaptability as shown with the attack on PRESENT. Note that our PUF-based TSC attack on PRESENT can be extended for other block ciphers with a similar bit-shifting key schedule.

Although Lin *et al.* [7] have not described how to activate the TSC in their proposal, here we provide a possible design for triggering the PUF-based TSC. Since PRESENT has a round counter for 31 rounds key schedule, while our proposed attack only requires the leakage bits of 11 rounds, a possible trigger can start the PUF-based TSC between $0 \leq i < 20$ where i is the round counter. The number i is variable and can be selected attacker at the manufacturing stage. This trigger requires some additional administration (i.e., 4 bits per PUF-based TSC) as the attacker needs to know which key bits of which round are sent.

4   Other Applications

Except direct attacks on key recovery, PUF-based TSCs can be used in many other applications. Two interesting examples are described as follows.

Personal communication eavesdropping. Nowadays, mobile devices are widely secured with cryptographic algorithms. If a PUF-based TSC is implanted to a certain user's device, a tracer can not only eavesdrop side-channel information, but can also identify such signals sent from a certain device that belongs to a certain user.

Parameterized backdoor. Some countries have restrictive regulations on the exporting of security chips, which impose that only chips lower than a certain security level can be shipped. Our parameterized TSC on PRESENT shows it can also be used as a factor to lower the security level of a tamper-resistant chip and therefore matches those exporting limitations.

5   Conclusion

In this paper we introduced a new type of flexible TSC based on PUFs. A dedicated PUF-based TSC has been proposed for attacking PRESENT. Compared to Lin et al.'s original proposal, our PUF-based TSCs cleverly uses the physical unclonability to obtain the blindness of side-channel information. The implementation results support that PUF-based TSCs can also be lightweight in logic gates, which is an important factor for the imperceptibility of TSC circuits. In future, we are interested in designing PUF-based TSCs on other cryptographic primitives that are practically used in security chips.

Acknowledgement. We would like to thank many anonymous reviewers for their valuable comments. The first author is supported by NSFC (No.6170217), National "863" Program of China (No. 2009AA01Z418) and National "973" Program of China (No.2007CB311201).

References

1. Agrawal, D., Baktir, S., Karakoyunlu, D., Rohatgi, P., Sunar, B.: Trojan detection using IC fingerprinting. In: IEEE Symposium on Security and Privacy, pp. 296–310. IEEE Computer Society, Los Alamitos (2007)
2. Bogdanov, A.A., Knudsen, L.R., Leander, G., Paar, C., Poschmann, A., Robshaw, M.J.B., Seurin, Y., Vikkelsoe, C.: PRESENT: An ultra-lightweight block cipher. In: Paillier, P., Verbauwhede, I. (eds.) CHES 2007. LNCS, vol. 4727, pp. 450–466. Springer, Heidelberg (2007)
3. Chakraborty, R.S., Wolff, F.G., Paul, S., Papachristou, C.A., Bhunia, S.: Mero: A statistical approach for hardware trojan detection. In: Clavier and Gaj [4], pp. 396–410
4. Clavier, C., Gaj, K. (eds.): CHES 2009. LNCS, vol. 5747. Springer, Heidelberg (2009)
5. Devadas, S., Suh, E., Paral, S., Sowell, R., Ziola, T., Khandelwal, V.: Design and implementation of PUF-based unclonableRFID ICs for anti-counterfeiting and security applications. In: IEEE International Conference on RFID, pp. 58–64 (2008)
6. Lim, D., Lee, J.W., Gassend, B., Edward Suh, G., van Dijk, M., Devadas, S.: Extracting secret keys from integrated circuits. IEEE Trans. VLSI Syst. 13(10), 1200–1205 (2005)
7. Lin, L., Kasper, M., Güneysu, T., Paar, C., Burleson, W.: Trojan side-channels: Lightweight hardware trojans through side-channel engineering. In: Clavier and Gaj [4], pp. 382–395
8. Merli, D., Stumpf, F., Eckert, C.: Improving the quality of ring oscillator pufs on fpgas. In: WESS, p. 9. ACM, New York (2010)
9. Morozov, S., Maiti, A., Schaumont, P.: An Analysis of Delay Based PUF Implementations on FPGA. In: Sirisuk, P., Morgan, F., El-Ghazawi, T., Amano, H. (eds.) ARC 2010. LNCS, vol. 5992, pp. 382–387. Springer, Heidelberg (2010)
10. Ozturk, E., Hammouri, G., Sunar, B.: Physical unclonable function with tristate buffers. In: IEEE International Symposium on Circuits and Systems, pp. 3194–3197. IEEE, Los Alamitos (2008)
11. Paar, C., Eisenbarth, T., Kasper, M., Kasper, T., Moradi, A.: Keeloq and side-channel analysis-evolution of an attack. In: Breveglieri, L., Gueron, S., Koren, I., Naccache, D., Seifert, J.-P. (eds.) Sixth International Workshop on Fault Diagnosis and Tolerance in Cryptography, FDTC 2009, Lausanne, Switzerland, September 6, pp. 65–69. IEEE Computer Society, Los Alamitos (2009)
12. Pappu, R., Recht, B., Taylor, J., Gershenfeld, N.: Physical One-Way Functions. Science 297(5589), 2026–2030 (2002)
13. Popp, T., Kirschbaum, M., Mangard, S.: Practical attacks on masked hardware. In: Fischlin, M. (ed.) CT-RSA 2009. LNCS, vol. 5473, pp. 211–225. Springer, Heidelberg (2009)
14. Rührmair, U., Sehnke, F., Sölter, J., Dror, G., Devadas, S., Schmidhuber, J.: Modeling attacks on physical unclonable functions. In: Al-Shaer, E., Keromytis, A.D., Shmatikov, V. (eds.) ACM Conference on Computer and Communications Security, pp. 237–249. ACM, New York (2010)
15. Simmons, G.J.: The prisoners' problem and the subliminal channel. In: CRYPTO, pp. 51–67 (1983)

Formal Analysis of Security Metrics and Risk*

Leanid Krautsevich[1], Fabio Martinelli[2], and Artsiom Yautsiukhin[2]

[1] Department of Computer Science, University of Pisa, Pisa, Italy
{krautsev}@di.unipi.it
[2] Istituto di Informatica e Telematica, Consiglio Nazionale delle Ricerche, Pisa, Italy
{fabio.martinelli,artsiom.yautsiukhin}@iit.cnr.it

Abstract. Security metrics are usually defined informally and, there-fore, the rigourous analysis of these metrics is a hard task. This analysis is required to identify the existing relations between the security metrics, which try to quantify the same quality: security.

Risk, computed as Annualised Loss Expectancy, is often used in order to give the overall assessment of security as a whole. Risk and security metrics are usually defined separately and the relation between these in-dicators have not been considered thoroughly. In this work we fill this gap by providing a formal definition of risk and formal analysis of relations between security metrics and risk.

1 Introduction

Quantification of security is a problem which has gained much attention recently [7,10,24,25]. The results of such quantification are needed for various purposes. First of all, the classical purpose is to understand how secure the system is and to determine if additional security controls are required [7,10]. The second purpose is to compare the level of security of a system with others [17,21]. Nowadays, Service Oriented Architecture becomes more and more popular. Therefore, quantification of security is required for advertisement of a good protection level of a service, for accurate stating the quality of protection level in service level agreements, and for selection of the most suitable and secure services [12,3,21].

There are a number of security metrics which are used in order to analyse the strength of security systems [7,10,20,17,21]. Although these metrics are widely used in security literature none of them (even a finite set of such metrics) can give a complete view of security strength. Moreover, the relations between the metrics, their contribution to the overall level of protection, and sensitivity are unclear. In other words, we do not know which metric is the best approximation of security level. Without this knowledge we appear in a situation when usage of different metrics leads to very different decisions.

Risk analysis is the most widely used method for analysing the complete picture of security state [23,2,5]. The main goal of this analysis is to compute the amount of possible losses which are caused by occurrences of various threats.

---

* This work is partially supported by FP7-ICT-2009-5 NESSOS and FP7-ICT-2009-5 ANIKETOS projects.

C.A. Ardagna and J. Zhou (Eds.): WISTP 2011, LNCS 6633, pp. 304–319, 2011.

Although this technique is not perfect [10,22], it has many advantages: the technique is general enough to be applied to any system, its results provide the complete vision of security, it helps to justify investments in security, and such justification is understandable for financial managers and general directors.

Currently, security metrics and risk exist apart from each other and the relation between these indicators, although assumed, is not specified. On the other hand, risk is supposed to be one of the most general security indicator. Thus, risk already must incorporate some security metrics, but it is unclear *how* different metrics contribute to the overall risk value. Moreover, risk analysis is blamed for providing results with low precision and consuming huge amount of time [10]. In some situations, usage only of security metrics contributing to the overall risk value may facilitate the analysis and make a preliminary assessment.

1.1 Contribution

In our previous work [13] we provided a formal description of various security metrics which relate only to a system (out of context) and investigated the relations between them. We have found that though some metrics are influenced by other metrics, in a wide sense, the existing metrics measure distinct aspects of security. On the other hand, the metrics must contribute to the overall security level. In contrast, in this work we have the main goal to establish the relation between security metrics and the most general and high-level way of security assessment – risk analysis. The formal model we propose explicitly connects various security metrics and indicates how they contribute to the overall assessment. Note, that we do not provide a new security assessment method, but analyse the existing ones.

The paper is organised as follows. In Section 2 we recall our definition of perfectly secure system, which we defined in [13], and describe our attack model. Section 3 is devoted to our formal definition of risk. Section 4 establishes the connection between the probability of successful exploitation of an attack and two types of cost. We analyse contributions of existing metrics to risk in Section 5. Related work (Section 6) and Conclusion (Section 7) conclude the paper.

2 Background

Definition 1. *Let $\mathcal{S}$ be a process modelling behaviour of a system and $\mathcal{X}$ a process modelling behaviour of an attacker. A system and an attacker perform some actions $a_l \in A$ and move from one state to another one. We denote a trace of actions accomplished by a system or an attacker as γ ($\gamma \in \Gamma$). $\gamma' \bullet \gamma'_{\mathcal{X}}$ denotes that one trace of actions is merged with another one in any way preserving the order of events. We say that the system is (perfectly) secure if and only if*

$$\forall \mathcal{X}, \ \forall \gamma, \ \mathcal{S} \xrightarrow{\gamma'} \mathcal{S}' \ \wedge \ \mathcal{X} \xrightarrow{\gamma'_{\mathcal{X}}} \mathcal{X}', \ \gamma = \gamma' \bullet \gamma'_{\mathcal{X}}$$
$$\mathcal{S}\|\mathcal{X} \xrightarrow{\gamma} \mathcal{S}'\|\mathcal{X}' \Rightarrow P_{sec}(\mathcal{S}'\|\mathcal{X}') = \emptyset \quad (1)$$

Function $P_{sec}(\mathcal{S}'\|\mathcal{X}')$ returns the set of possible threats (attacker's goals) which may occur in the reached state $\mathcal{S}'\|\mathcal{X}'$ when the system and the attacker work in parallel. In other words, the attacker has achieved a state where some malicious actions are possible and valuable assets can be compromised (e.g., the attacker has access to a database). A set of possible attackers is **X**. We define an attacker $\mathcal{X}$ simply as a set of possible traces the attacker can launch against the system. We write $\gamma \in \mathcal{X}$ to show that a specific attacker knows the trace (attack). We also use $a \in \gamma$ notation to denote that action a is contained in trace γ. A trace of events is denoted in the following way preserving the order of actions: $\gamma = a_1 \circ a_2 \circ \cdots \circ a_n$. To avoid ambiguity, we always use index l for actions, i for attacks, j for attackers.

In this work we extend our previous model and consider security of a system in a specific context. In our current model context includes protected assets and possible attackers. In particular, we need the amount of possible losses, caused by affecting valuable assets, and preferences of attackers.

For our new model we need a more detailed formal model of attacker.

Definition 2. *An attacker is a process which is characterised by the following tuple:* $\mathcal{X} = < \Gamma, goal, skill, res, money >$, *where Γ is a set of attacks the attacker can launch against the system; goal is the goal of the attacker[1]; skill - the level of skills the attacker possesses; res - the amount of resources the attacker is willing to spend to achieve its goal; money is the amount of money the attacker is ready to spend in order to make an attempt to compromise the system.*

Here we would like to consider money (*money*) and resources (*res*) required for an attack apart. In our model, money are needed for buying the tools without which the attack is impossible (e.g., in order to crack a safe a special drill is required). When the attacker starts its attack he spends some resources in order to achieve its goal. The more resources are spent the more chances for success the attacker has (e.g., the more time a bugler spends for studying and attempting to open a lock the more probably he will be able to open the safe). Sometimes money and resources can be considered as one parameter, but for understanding the different nature of these expenditures we consider them as two distinct sets. In the sequel, any attribute of a specific attacker is used with a corresponding index. For example, a set of possible attacks and amount of available resources for an attacker $\mathcal{X}_j$ are represented as Γ_j and res_j correspondingly.

Considering every attacker separately is an impractical approach. Usually similar attackers considered as one collective entity, or an attacker profile. We assume that all members of the same group of attackers have the same goal. For example, cyber terrorists are aimed at shutting down a system for a long time, cyber thieves (hackers) - at receiving economical benefits, insiders - at committing a fraud. Thus, we group the attackers according to their goals assuming that the attackers which have the same goal have also the same skills and resources (i.e., we assume small dispersion). Sometimes, there are attacker profiles which

---

[1] In our model every attacker has only one goal.

have the same goal but should be grouped differently (e.g., terrorists which usually have high skills and large amount of resources, and vandals, who simply behave as hooligans and have very limited amount of resources). Such groups can be separated, and this separation will not affect our further discussions.

3   Formal Definition of Risk

Let the total number of attackers be $|\mathbf{X}| = N^{\mathbf{X}}$ and number of attacks available for attackers $\mathcal{X}_j \in \mathbf{X}$ is $|\Gamma_j| = N_j^{\Gamma}$. Now, let a number of attacker profiles be $N^{\mathbf{X},pr}$ and each profile j has $|\mathcal{X}_j| = N_j^{\mathbf{X}}$ attackers ($N^{\mathbf{X}} = \sum_{j=1}^{N^{\mathbf{X},pr}} N_j^{\mathbf{X}}$).

Definition 3

$$\forall \mathcal{X}_j \in \mathbf{X}, \forall \gamma_i \in \Gamma_j, \ \exists \gamma' \ \mathcal{S} \xrightarrow{\gamma'} \mathcal{S}' \wedge \mathcal{X} \xrightarrow{\gamma_i} \mathcal{X}',$$

$$\mathcal{S}\|\mathcal{X} \xrightarrow{\gamma' \bullet \gamma_i} \mathcal{S}'\|\mathcal{X}' \Rightarrow P_{sec}(\mathcal{S}'\|\mathcal{X}') \ni goal_j$$

$$Risk(\mathcal{S}) = \sum_{j=1}^{N^{\mathbf{X},pr}} N_j^{\mathbf{X}} \times \sum_{i=1}^{N_j^{\Gamma}} p^v(\gamma_i, \mathcal{X}_j) \times p^t(\gamma_i, \mathcal{X}_j) \times d(\gamma_i, \mathcal{X}_j) \qquad (2)$$

where $p^v(\gamma_i, \mathcal{X}_j)$ is the probability of successful execution of attack γ_i by $\mathcal{X}_j$;

$p^t(\gamma_i, \mathcal{X}_j)$ is the probability of selection of attack γ_i by $\mathcal{X}_j$;

$d(\gamma_i, \mathcal{X}_j)$ is the damage which $\mathcal{X}_j$ causes by successfull execution of γ_i.

Note, that an attacker which is going to attack the system has to select one of the available attacks leading to achievement of its goal. Therefore, we have complete probability space here: $\forall \mathcal{X}_j, \ \sum_{i=1}^{N_j^{\Gamma}} p^t(\gamma_i, \mathcal{X}_j) = 1$. On the contrary, probability of successful execution of an attack does not depend on other attacks, but only on the attacker and the attack. Therefore, the complete probability space for the probability of successful execution of attack γ_i by $\mathcal{X}_j$ is $p^v(\gamma_i, \mathcal{X}_j)$ and $\neg p^v(\gamma_i, \mathcal{X}_j)$.

If we know that a randomly taken attacker belongs to group $\mathcal{X}_j$ with probability $p_j^{\mathbf{X}}$ we can find the number of attackers in this group if the overall amount of attackers is known.

$$N_j^{\mathbf{X}} = N^{\mathbf{X}} * p_j^{\mathbf{X}} \qquad (3)$$

Naturally, $\sum_{j=1}^{N^{\mathbf{X},pr}} p_j^{\mathbf{X}} = 1$

Proposition 1. *Definition 3 is a fine-grained form of the classical formula for computation of risk (annualised losses) [6,10]:*

$$Risk(\mathcal{S}) = \sum_{j=1}^{N^{\mathbf{X},pr}} ARO_j * SLE_j \qquad (4)$$

Where ARO_j is annual rate of occurrences of threat j ($goal_j$) and SLE_j is single loss expectancy of threat j.

Proof: First, we consider ARO_j. ARO_j gives us the average number of successful attacks which realise threat j. Let p_j^{real} be the probability that the next attack is successful in realisation of threat j. Then, the *number* of successful attacks can be found if a number of all attackers (attempts to compromise the system) and probability p_j^{real} are known $ARO_j = N^{\mathbf{X}} \times p_j^{real}$. To execute an attack an attacker has to *select* the threat and then *successfully realise* it. Therefore, expanding p_j^{real} ARO_j can be seen as $ARO_j = N^{\mathbf{X}} \times Vuln_j \times Threat_j$, where $Vuln_j$ is the average probability that threat j is *successfully realised*; $Threat_j$ is the probability that threat j is *selected*.

The selection of threat j is equivalent to the probability that the selected attacker is from profile j (recall that a "threat" and an "attacker goal" in our work are synonymous), therefore, $Threat_j = p_j^{\mathbf{X}}$. Using the probability theory we can compute the average probability that a concrete threat will be successful if we know all attacks which lead to realisation of this threat (goal). This set of attacks is the same set that a specific group of attackers knows.

$$Vuln_j = \sum_{i=1}^{N_j^\Gamma} p^v(\gamma_i, \mathcal{X}_j) \times p^t(\gamma_i, \mathcal{X}_j) \tag{5}$$

SLE_j is the expected damage in case threat j occurs. Note, that SLE_j is the average damage with *the condition that the attack is successful*. Indeed, in practice, the average damage is computed using the data collected from previous occurrences of threats. Therefore, we need to use *conditional* probabilities for computation of the average damage. Thus, the probability that attack γ_i has successfully occurred with the condition that at least one attack realising threat j has occurred is $p(\gamma_i/\Gamma_j) = \frac{p(\gamma_i)}{p(\Gamma_j)}$, where $p(\gamma_i)$ is the probability that attack γ_i is successfully executed, and $p(\Gamma_j)$ is the probability that one attack out of Γ_j has been successful. Thus, the formula for computation of SLE_j is the following:

$$SLE_j = \sum_{i=1}^{N_j^\Gamma} \frac{p(\gamma_i)}{p(\Gamma_j)} \times d(\gamma_i, \mathbf{X}_j) = \sum_{i=1}^{N_j^\Gamma} \frac{p^v(\gamma_i, \mathcal{X}_j) \times p^t(\gamma_i, \mathcal{X}_j) \times d(\gamma_i, \mathcal{X}_j)}{\sum_{i=1}^{N_j^\Gamma} p^v(\gamma_i, \mathcal{X}_j) \times p^t(\gamma_i, \mathcal{X}_j)} \tag{6}$$

Now, if we multiply and divide at once the part of formula 2 after the first sum by $\sum_{i=1}^{N_j^\Gamma} p^v(\gamma_i, \mathcal{X}_j) p^t(\gamma_i, \mathcal{X}_j)$ and substitute $N_j^{\mathbf{X}}$ as shown in Equation 3:

$$Risk(\mathcal{S}) = N^{\mathbf{X}} \times \sum_{j=1}^{N^{\mathbf{X},pr}} [p_j^{\mathbf{X}} \times$$

$$(\sum_{i=1}^{N_j^\Gamma} p^v(\gamma_i, \mathcal{X}_j) \times p^t(\gamma_i, \mathcal{X}_j)) \times \frac{\sum_{i=1}^{N_j^\Gamma} p^v(\gamma_i, \mathcal{X}_j) \times p^t(\gamma_i, \mathcal{X}_j) \times d(\gamma_i, \mathcal{X}_j)}{\sum_{i=1}^{N_j^\Gamma} p^v(\gamma_i, \mathcal{X}_j) \times p^t(\gamma_i, \mathcal{X}_j)}] \tag{7}$$

Finally, using Equations 5 and 6 and recalling that $Threat_j = p_j^\mathbf{X}$ we get:

$$Risk(\mathcal{S}) = N^\mathbf{X} \times \sum_{j=1}^{N^{\mathbf{X}.pr}} Threat_j \times Vuln_j \times SLE_j = \sum_{j=1}^{N^{\mathbf{X}.pr}} ARO_j \times SLE_j \quad (8)$$

$\square$

4   Probability vs. Cost

Cost of attack is a metric which is often used for analysis of security. Cost is considered as a one-time payment which an attacker has to make in order to exploit a vulnerability. An example could be the average amount of money required for bribing an employee in order to get access to the network or to buy information about an unknown vulnerability on a black market [21]. Such model is not entirely correct. First, one-time payment is usually an indispensable condition, but not a sufficient one. Possessing the information about an existing vulnerability and required tools do not always imply its successful exploitation. Second, in many cases different amount of investments may result in different probabilities of success. For example, the higher the bribe the higher the probability it is accepted. Third, in contrast to the real world criminals (e.g., buglers or thieves), hackers do not often need special equipment, but a computer, tools (likely, simply downloaded) and access to the Internet (or to the internal network). In other words, exploitation of most of vulnerabilities often does not require one-time investments.

Therefore, in this paper we propose to consider two types of cost: a fixed cost (C^f) and a changing cost (C^c). The first cost is the common one-time investment. Such investment is required to allow the attacker to make an attempt to exploit a vulnerability. The changing cost is the investment which influences the probability of successful exploitation of a vulnerability. Such investment is often only the time the attacker devotes to exploitation of a vulnerability. We can express this time in currency by simple multiplication of the time spent by the cost of an hour of the attacker (a way of transformation does not affect the further discussion). The idea behind this cost is the following one: anyone can exploit a vulnerability spending some time trying to do this (see, for example, the work of E. Jonsson and T. Olovsson [11] where even unskilled attackers were able to compromise the system after considerable time).

In order to model such dependency we can use either lognormal [18] or Weibull distributions. Both these distributions are used for modelling faults. In our case we can see the problem as how long the system withstands an attack. We also can apply multiplicative degradation argument here. In every small amount of time an attacker gets a tiny amount of knowledge about how to exploit a vulnerability. In this case system is "degrading" until it is broken. Such degradation is modelled by lognormal distribution [1].

We define the probability of successful execution of action a_l as a function of cost C_l^c and specific for the attacker profile (attacker skill level): $p^c(a_l, \mathcal{X}_j) = F_{j,l}(C_l^c)$, where $F_{j,l}$ is some distribution function (the exact formula, although desirable, is not important for the further discussion). We assume that this function depends on such attributes as, e.g., hardness of the exploitation of a_l and skill level of the attacker $(skill_j)$. The function returns the probability that the action will be successful when at most C^c amount of resources is spent.

Definition 4. *The probability of successful attack is the maximal probability to accomplish successfully all required actions, if the overall sum of resources spent for the overall attack is equal to the amount of resources the attacker has.*

$$p^v(\gamma_i, \mathcal{X}_j) = max\{ \prod_{\forall a_l \in \gamma_i} F_{j,l}(C_l^c)| \sum_{\forall a_l \in \gamma_i} C_l^c = res_j\} \qquad (9)$$

The fixed cost is used for defining the set of attacks available for the attacker:

$$\Gamma_j = \{\gamma_i \mid \exists \gamma', \mathcal{S} \xrightarrow{\gamma'} \mathcal{S}' \wedge \mathcal{X} \xrightarrow{\gamma_i} \mathcal{X}',$$

$$\mathcal{S}\|\mathcal{X} \xrightarrow{\gamma' \bullet \gamma_i} \mathcal{S}'\|\mathcal{X}' \Rightarrow P_{sec}(\mathcal{S}'\|\mathcal{X}') \ni goal_j \wedge \sum_{\forall a_l \in \gamma_i} C_l^f \leq money_j\} \qquad (10)$$

Minimal cost of attack (see Definition 11) has sense only for the fixed cost (C^f), but as we noted, possessing this amount of money does not always guarantee successful exploitation. The changing cost (C^c) simply cannot be minimal because even with a little effort an attacker has a chance (but a very small chance) to achieve its goal. Example could be the password cracker who finds a strong password after a couple of attempts by sheer luck.

5   Relation between Metrics and Risk

First, we define four levels of relations which can be established between two metrics. For brevity, lets call the metric which we observe and use for defining the dependency as a *dependee metric*, when the metric which behaviour we would like to determine as a *depender metric*.

Definition 5. *Let $\mathcal{S}$ and $\hat{\mathcal{S}}$ be the system before and after some changes. Correspondingly, $M(\mathcal{S})$ and $M(\hat{\mathcal{S}})$ are values of a dependee metric for the two versions. We can denote a depender metric as a function which depends on the dependee metric $f(M(\mathcal{S}))$ or $f(M(\mathcal{S}), M_1(\mathcal{S}), ..., M_n(\mathcal{S}))$ depending on how many dependee metrics are required for the computation. Let also $\triangle M(\mathcal{S})$ be the simplest change of the dependee metric $M(\mathcal{S})$ such that no other changes may occur at the same time.*

Level 1. *Weakest monotonicity. There is a weakest monotonicity relation between a depender and dependee metrics if the smallest increases of dependee metric cause the corresponding changes of the depender metric, while all other parameters required for computation of the depender metric are left the same. Formally,*

$$If\ M(\hat{\mathcal{S}}) = M(\mathcal{S}) + \triangle M(\mathcal{S})\ ,\ M(\hat{\mathcal{S}}) > M(\mathcal{S}) \Rightarrow$$

$$f(M(\hat{\mathcal{S}}), M_1(\hat{\mathcal{S}}), ..., M_n(\hat{\mathcal{S}})) > f(M(\mathcal{S}), M_1(\mathcal{S}), ..., M_n(\mathcal{S})) \qquad (11)$$

$$\forall k,\ M_k(\hat{\mathcal{S}}) = M_k(\mathcal{S})$$

Level 2. *Weak monotonicity. There is a weak monotonicity relation between two metrics if any resulting changes of dependee metric allows to judge about changes in the depender metric. All other parameters required for computation of the depender metric are left the same. Formally,*

$$M(\hat{S}) > M(S) \Rightarrow f(M(\hat{S}), M_1(\hat{S}), ..., M_n(\hat{S})) > f(M(S), M_1(S), ..., M_n(S)) \tag{12}$$

$$\forall k, \ M_k(\hat{S}) = M_k(S)$$

Level 3. *One-way monotonicity. Changes of dependee metric imply corresponding changes in the depender metric, even if we consider different systems (other parameters, if any, may change as well). Formally,*

$$M(\hat{S}) > M(S) \Rightarrow f(M(\hat{S})) > f(M(S)) \tag{13}$$

Level 4. *Equivalence. Changes of dependee metric imply corresponding changes in the depender metric, and visa versa:*

$$M(\hat{S}) > M(S) \Leftrightarrow f(M(\hat{S})) > f(M(S)) \tag{14}$$

The four levels are defined for monotonically increasing functions only for simplicity. Monotonically decreasing functions can be also used by the definitions (simply change $M(\hat{S}) > M(S)$ to $M(\hat{S}) < M(S)$).

Naturally, the first two levels are more relevant for considering the relations when a depender metric is a function of several dependee metrics, while the last two levels are applicable when only one dependee metric is required. Knowing what kind of relations exists between two metrics an analyst is able to predict changes of a more complex metric observing changes in another one (more easy to collect). Every monotonic relation can be either *sensitive* or *insensitive*.

Definition 6. *Sensitive relation notices every change in the dependee metric behaviour. A monotonic relation is insensitive otherwise.*

For example, weak monotonicity is *sensitive* if

$$M(\hat{S}) > M(S) \Rightarrow f(M(\hat{S}), M_1(\hat{S}), ...) > f(M(S), M_1(S), ...) \tag{15}$$

and insensitive if

$$M(\hat{S}) > M(S) \Rightarrow f(M(\hat{S}), M_1(\hat{S}), ...) \geq f(M(S), M_1(S), ...) \tag{16}$$

Now, our goal is to find how changes in security metrics affect risk level.

Number of attacks.

Definition 7. *We define* number of attacks *metric as the number of possible sequences of actions which contain the minimal number of actions required for satisfaction of attacker's goal.*

$$N_{att}(S) = |\{\gamma_i' \mid \exists \mathcal{X}_j \in \mathbf{X}, \ \gamma_i' \in \Gamma_j' \ \exists \gamma', \ S \xrightarrow{\gamma'} S' \land \ \mathcal{X}_j \xrightarrow{\gamma_i'} \mathcal{X}_j' \land$$

$$S \| \mathcal{X}_j \xrightarrow{\gamma' \bullet \gamma_i'} S' \| \mathcal{X}_j' \Rightarrow P_{sec}(S' \| \mathcal{X}_j') \ni goal_j \land \tag{17}$$

$$\nexists \hat{\gamma}_i', \hat{\gamma}, \ \gamma_i' = \hat{\gamma}_i' \bullet \hat{\gamma} \ \land \ S \| \mathcal{X}_j \xrightarrow{\gamma' \bullet \hat{\gamma}_i'} S' \| \mathcal{X}_j' \Rightarrow P_{sec}(S' \| \mathcal{X}_j') \ni goal_j \}|$$

Proposition 2. *There is only the insensitive weakest monotonicity between risk and number of attacks metric (Level 1).*

Proof: Consider two cases. The first case is when all Γ_j contain only the attacks the attackers can afford (see Equation 10). Thus, the attack can be executed (otherwise $\gamma_i \notin \Gamma_j$) and $p^v(\gamma_i, \mathcal{X}_j) \neq 0$; can be selected, even with very small probability, (otherwise $\gamma_i \notin \Gamma_j$) and $p^t(\gamma_i, \mathcal{X}_j) \neq 0$; and has some impact on the system (otherwise we do not consider it as an attack $\gamma_i \notin \Gamma_j$ and $d(\gamma_i, \mathcal{X}_j) \neq 0$. Thus, if the number increases ($\triangle N_{att}(\mathcal{S}) > 0$) more summands $(p^v(\gamma_i, \mathcal{X}_j) \times p^t(\gamma_i, \mathcal{X}_j) \times d(\gamma_i, \mathcal{X}_j))$ will contribute to the overall risk and the risk level increases. If the number decreases then less summands contribute to the risk and the risk level decreases. Note, the change of risk because of several changes in number of attacks is unpredictable (because the value of the summands is unknown).

In the second case we assume that some attacks are too expensive for attackers. Thus, there are attacks with 0 impact and the situation when $\triangle f(N_{att}(\mathcal{S})) = 0$ is possible and new summands are not added/deleted when number of attacks metric changes. Thus, in some situation the relation is insensitive. $\qquad\square$

Maximal probability of success. In this paper we provided a new definition for probability of successful exploitation shown in Equation 18 (using $p^v(\gamma_i', \mathcal{X}_j)$ from Equation 9).

Definition 8. *This metrics is simply the maximal probability of successful exploitation of one of possible attacks.*

$$P^{max}(\mathcal{S}) = max\{p^v(\gamma_i, \mathcal{X}_j) \mid \forall \mathcal{X}_j, \gamma_i \in \Gamma_j\} \qquad (18)$$

Proposition 3. *Risk is an insensitive weak monotonic function of maximal probability of success (Level 2).*

Proof: Maximal probability of success $P^{max}(\mathcal{S})$ is just one of the probabilities of execution used for computation of risk. Therefore, if $P^{max} = p^v(\gamma_q, \mathcal{X}_z)$ for an attack γ_q ($\gamma_q \in \Gamma_z$) conducted by attacker $\mathcal{X}_z$ we can see the Equation 2 as

$$Risk(\mathcal{S}) = \sum_{j=1}^{N^{\mathbf{X}, pr}} N_j^{\mathbf{X}} \times \sum_{\forall i \neq q} p^v(\gamma_i, \mathcal{X}_j) \times p^t(\gamma_i, \mathcal{X}_j) \times d(\gamma_i, \mathcal{X}_j) +$$
$$\sum_{\forall j \neq z \,.\, \gamma_q \in \Gamma_j} N_j^{\mathbf{X}} \times p^v(\gamma_q, \mathcal{X}_j) \times p^t(\gamma_q, \mathcal{X}_j) \times d(\gamma_q, \mathcal{X}_j) +$$
$$N_z^{\mathbf{X}} \times P^{max} \times p^t(\gamma_q, \mathcal{X}_z) \times d(\gamma_q, \mathcal{X}_z) \qquad (19)$$

Thus, clearly, if $P^{max}(\mathcal{S})$ increases/decreases the overall risk decreases/increases only if all other parameters are left the same (Level 2). Note, that if the attack with maximal cost is too costly for the corresponding attackers than no changes will be noticed. $\qquad\square$

Shortest attack.

Definition 9. *The shortest attack metrics indicates the length of an attack which contains less actions than others.*

$$L^{min}(\mathcal{S}) = min\{L(\gamma_i) \mid \forall \mathcal{X}_j, \gamma_i \in \Gamma_j\} \tag{20}$$
$$where \; L(\gamma) = n \; iff \; \gamma = a_1 \circ a_2 \circ \cdots \circ a_n$$

Proposition 4. *There is only the insensitive weakest monotonicity between risk and the shortest attack metric (Level 1).*

Proof: The shortest attack $L^{min}(\mathcal{S})$ affects only the probabilities which correspond to the same attack γ_q $\{p^v(\gamma_q, \mathcal{X}_j), \forall j\}$. If the shortest attack becomes longer/shorter the corresponding probabilities will decrease/increase according to Definition 8. We isolate all the affected summands in Equation 2.

$$Risk(\mathcal{S}) = \sum_{j=1}^{N^{\mathbf{X}.pr}} N_j^{\mathbf{X}} \times \sum_{\forall i \neq q} p^v(\gamma_i, \mathcal{X}_j) \times p^t(\gamma_i, \mathcal{X}_j) \times d(\gamma_i, \mathcal{X}_j)$$
$$\sum_{\forall j \, . \, \gamma_q \in \Gamma_j} N_j^{\mathbf{X}} \times p^v(\gamma_q, \mathcal{X}_j) \times p^t(\gamma_q, \mathcal{X}_j) \times d(\gamma_q, \mathcal{X}_j) \tag{21}$$

Thus, only the second sum descreases/increases when L^{min} increases/decreases. Note, that the shortest attack affects probabilities of success only if it has been either increased or decreased (not both at the same time) because of different magnitudes of changes in the probabilities. In other words, we have relation of Level 1. And, again, the change is noticeable only if the attack is not too expensive.   □

Percentage of compliance. Some authors propose to measure security according to its compliance with a standard (e.g., ISO 17799[2] [8]). Percentage of compliance is often used as an indicator [4].

Definition 10. *Check list is a set of actions recommended for a system $\Gamma^{cl} \subseteq \Gamma$. Let a set of satisfied items in the list be $\Gamma^S = \{\gamma | \gamma \in \mathcal{S} \; \wedge \; \gamma \in \Gamma^{cl}\}$. The check list metric is the following ratio*

$$CLM(\mathcal{S}) = |\Gamma^S|/|\Gamma^{cl}| \tag{22}$$

Proposition 5. *There is only the insensitive weakest monotonicity between risk and the percentage of compliance metric (Level 1).*

Proof: Since we consider a static system we will not take into account the requirements related to a process of security maintenance. Lets also assume that adding a new countermeasure does not have any negative effect on security of the system. We already have shown in [13] that this metric is not sensitive because some suggested countermeasures could be ineffective in a concrete system.

---

[2] Currently, the standard has been extended and is called ISO 27000 family.

Every security mechanism may work in three ways:

1. reduce the probability of successful exploitation of some vulnerabilities (e.g., password generation policies) – $p^v(\gamma_i, \mathcal{X}_j)$;
2. reduce the amount of attackers willing to perform a specific attack (e.g., monitoring mechanisms). Such security mechanisms have double effect:
   (a) reduce the probability of attack selection $p^t(\gamma_i, \mathcal{X}_j)$ and
   (b) reduce the total amount of attackers $N_j^{\mathbf{X}}$ which know the attack;
3. reduce the possible impact (e.g., back up mechanisms) $d(\gamma_i, \mathcal{X}_j)$.

Reduction of amount of attackers caused by installation of a new security mechanism causes redistribution of p^t-s, since $\sum_{\forall i} p^t(\gamma_i, \mathcal{X}_j) = 1$. In this article, we follow the strategy common for risk assessment methodologies: some attackers are no longer a threat for the system. We do not consider a more complex scenario when an attacker changes its mind and tries another attack [22]. Such analysis requires deeper understanding of how probabilities of selection are determined using behaviour of attacker. We are going to consider this issue in the future work.

Current redistribution of probabilities is connected only with reduction of one probability of selection caused by $\triangle CLM(S)$. In order to simplify mathematics and avoid re-computation of the probabilities, for our proof is enough just to imagine that we have a bogus attack with risk 0, but its probability of selection is a non-zero value $p_0^t > 0$. Thus if some $p^t(\gamma_i, \mathcal{X}_j)$ has been reduced by $\triangle p^t$ we simply add this value to the zero attack: $p_0^t + \triangle p^t$. In such a way we reduce only the summands which correspond to attack γ_i and, as a result, the risk reduces.

For reduction of other parameters (probability of successful exploitation and impact) similar to arguments for the shortest attack metric we can separate the summands which are affected by new countermeasures (or by deletion of countermeasures). The separated summands decrease if new countermeasures are installed and, thus, risk decreases.   □

Minimal cost of attacks. As we have shown in Section 4 minimal cost makes sense only for the fixed cost.

Definition 11. *Minimal fixed cost of attack can be see as:*

$$C^{f,min}(\mathcal{S}) = min\{ \sum_{\forall a_l \in \gamma_i} C_l^f \mid \forall \mathcal{X}_j, \gamma_i \in \Gamma_j \} \tag{23}$$

Proposition 6. *Risk is an insensitive weak monotonic function of minimal fixed cost metric (Level 2).*

Proof: This cost affects only the process of selection of available attack paths (see Equation 10). In other words, the attack which had a minimal cost value may become too expensive for an attacker if the minimal cost value increases. In this case, the formula for risk loses one non-negative summand and risk decreases. Note, that if the increase in the cost is small and the attacker still can use the attack risk level is left the same.   □

Average probability of penetration.

Definition 12. *In order to find the average probability of penetration for the whole systems we should first find the average probability for an attacker profile and then find the average probability of penetration among the attacker profiles.*

$$P^{avg}(\mathcal{S}) = \sum_{j=1}^{N^{\mathbf{X},pr}} p_j^{\mathbf{X}} \times \sum_{i=1}^{N_j^{\Gamma}} p^v(\gamma_i, \mathcal{X}_j) \times p^t(\gamma_i, \mathcal{X}_j) \qquad (24)$$

Proposition 7. *There is only the sensitive weakest monotonicity between risk and the average probability of penetration metric (Level 1).*

Proof: Although this metric uses the same components as risk does, there is no direct relation between risk and this metrics. Effects of changes of p^t and p^v have been discussed in the proof for percentage of compliance metric. Increase of number of attackers of one kind $(p_j^{\mathbf{X}})$ increases the average probability of penetration and risk (see Equations 2 and 3). In general, without knowledge of exact magnitudes of changes in several probabilities we cannot correctly predict behaviour of risk level, since risk is weighted with impact. Thus, we have a relation of Level 1. Since risk reacts on the change of every parameter required for P^{avg} the relation is sensitive. $\qquad \square$

Attack surface metric. Attack surface metric (ASM) [17] is defined as follows.

Definition 13. *Let us have 3 assets which can be affected by an attack:* method (m), data items (d), channel (c). *Let us know the damage-potential level of every asset* $dam^p(\gamma)$ *and the level of privileges required for execution of attack* γ_i $priv(\gamma_i)$ *(maximal difference in level of privileges among required actions of the same attack). Then, for every system we can assign the following tuple* $ASM(S) = \langle Risk^m, Risk^c, Risk^d \rangle$ *where*

$$Risk^m = \sum_{\forall \gamma_i \in \Gamma^m} \frac{dam^p(\gamma_i)}{priv(\gamma_i)}; \quad Risk^c = \sum_{\forall \gamma_i \in \Gamma^c} \frac{dam^p(\gamma_i)}{priv(\gamma_i)};$$

$$Risk^d = \sum_{\forall \gamma_i \in \Gamma^d} \frac{dam^p(\gamma_i)}{priv(\gamma_i)}). \qquad (25)$$

where $\Gamma^m, \Gamma^c, \Gamma^d$ *are the sets of attacks leading to compromise of the corresponding asset.*

Proposition 8. *Attack surface metric is equivalent to risk with a number of assumptions (Level 4).*

Proof: Since there are three values required for computation of ASM we also can compute risk for three possible damages separately. Assume that there are no attacks on the system others than the ones targeting the three assets $(N^{\mathbf{X},pr} = 3)$. The authors assume that the metric does not depend on the attacker. Thus, we do the same assumption for our risk formula. The authors also assume that the damage-potential value is proportional to the real value of loss, and the required level of privileges is reversely proportional to the probability to perform the attack: $dam^p(\gamma_i) = z1 * d(\gamma_i)$ and $priv(\gamma_i) = z2/p^v(\gamma_i)$. Here we have to make another assumption: all assets of the same class have the same cost and an attack required the same level of privileges have the same probability to be successful. Finally, we get almost the same formula we have for risk, but one compound: threat level. In other words, we also need an assumption that all attacks are equally frequent ($\forall \gamma_i\ p^t(\gamma_i) = p^t$). Now we can rewrite equation 2 using the assumptions we already made:

$$Risk(\mathcal{S}) = \sum_{j=1}^{N^{\mathbf{X},pr}} N_j^{\mathbf{X}} \times \sum_{i=1}^{N_j^{\Gamma}} p^v(\gamma_i) \times p^t(\gamma_i) \times d(\gamma_i) =$$

$$\sum_{j=1}^{N^{\mathbf{X},pr}} N_j^{\mathbf{X}} \times \sum_{i=1}^{N_j^{\Gamma}} p^t \times z2/priv(\gamma_i) \times dam^p(\gamma_i)/z1 = p^t \frac{z2}{z1} \times$$

$$(N_m^{\mathbf{X}} \sum_{\forall \gamma_i \in \Gamma^m} \frac{dam^p(\gamma_i)}{priv(\gamma_i)} + N_c^{\mathbf{X}} \sum_{\forall \gamma_i \in \Gamma^c} \frac{dam^p(\gamma_i)}{priv(\gamma_i)} + N_d^{\mathbf{X}} \sum_{\forall \gamma_i \in \Gamma^d} \frac{dam^p(\gamma_i)}{priv(\gamma_i)}) \quad (26)$$

Here we have the overall risk, while ASM does not combine the three values together. We can do the same considering the three summands separately. $\square$

Summary. In order to summarise the results we collect the findings in Table 1. We can see that most metrics have only the lowest level of relation with risk (weakest monotonicity). Thus, usage of only these metrics in order to predict the behaviour of risk level is impractical, although, changes of these metrics do contribute to changes of risk. Maximal probability and minimal fixed cost could be used for prediction of risk behaviour, but only if the corresponding attacks are considered. Such situation happens if attackers always select the most probable or less costly attack. Finally, we see that attack surface metric is equivalent to computation of risk, but relies on very strong assumptions. Moreover, most relations are insensitive and, thus, changes of the metrics do not always indicate change of risk.

Table 1. Relations between metrics and risk

Metric	Relation level	Sensitivity
Number of attacks N_{att}	Level 1	No
Maximal probability P^{max}	Level 2	No
Shortest attack L^{min}	Level 1	No
Minimal fixed cost $C^{f,min}$	Level 2	No
Avg. probability of penetration P^{avg}	Level 1	Yes
Attack surface ASM	Level 4	Yes
Percentage of compliance CLM	Level 1	No

6   Related Work

Most security metrics are defined informally. Such definition leads to many uncertainties in the actual meaning of the metrics. Informal definitions also do not allow to analyse metrics, find overlapping and relations between them. Unsurprisingly, NIST stated that one of the future directions in security metrics should be definition of formal models for security metrics [9].

An example of formally defined metric could be the attack surface metric [15,17]. The authors formally defined the notion of channels (attack path) introducing the notion of exit points and described how the metric is computed. In our work, we adapted the model of the authors to our model and formally proved that this metric is equivalent to risk, if the specified assumptions are taken into account. Nevertheless, the focus of our paper is formal analysis of large number of existing metrics, while the authors of attack surface metric focus on definition of this metric.

The authors of papers on attack graphs are also often use formal models. Moreover, a number of security metrics are defined for evaluation of a system based on attack graphs are: probability of successful attack [26], minimal cost of attack [20], minimal cost of reduction [27], shortest path [19]. The formal model is usually applied to the definition of the graph itself and only rarely used for the definition of metrics (e.g., [20]). In contrast, our work has the primary focus on formal definition and analysis of metrics.

Another example of formally defined metric is "mean time to failure" metric by Madan et al. [14]. This metric assumes that only one-step attacks are possible, when we consider multi-step attacks.

In our previous work [13] we formally modelled and defined several security metrics which measure security system out of the context. The metrics were analysed in order to check if some of them provide the same evaluation. We have found that in general metrics are mostly independent, but in specific cases some metrics can be used interchangeably. In this work, we formalised risk and have shown how these (and some other) metrics contribute to risk.

7   Conclusion

In this paper we formalised risk analysis. We have shown how existing security metrics relate to this the most general security evaluation. We can see that all metrics play only a small role when the overall risk is computed. Thus, we make a conclusion that none of single metrics is enough to predict behaviour of the risk value. The only metric which is as general as risk is the attack surface metric, but it relies on many strong assumptions. In this work we considered probability of successful execution of an attack as a function of cost. We have not identified which function must be used, but have shown that other approaches fail to model the relation between these two metrics correctly.

Currently, we consider a very generic attacker model. Our future work is to consider behaviour of attackers and determine models for computation of probabilities of attack selection. Introducing the behaviour of attackers (e.g., adapting

Dolev-Yao model for assessment of systems) will enhance our attacker model and will allow us to analyse different strategies of attackers. The probability of attack selection is often left out of the scopes of existing approaches and we are going to make some progress to fill this gap.

References

1. Bae, S.J., et al.: Degradation models and implied lifetime distributions. Reliability Engineering & System Safety 92(5), 601–608 (2007)
2. Butler, S.A.: Security attribute evaluation method: a cost-benefit approach. In: Proceedings of the 24th International Conference on Software Engineering (ICSE 2002), pp. 232–240. ACM Press, New York (2002)
3. Casola, V., et al.: A SLA evaluation methodology in Service Oriented Architectures. In: Proceedings of the 1st Workshop on Quality of Protection, Milan, Italy. Springer, Heidelberg (2005)
4. Eloff, M.M., von Solms, S.H.: Information security management: An approach to combine process certification and product evaluation. Computers & Security 19(8), 609–698 (2000)
5. Gordon, L., Loeb, M.: The economics of information security investment. ACM Transactions on Information and System Security 5(4), 438–457 (2003)
6. Gordon, L.A., Loeb, M.P.: Managing Cybersecurity Resources: a Cost-Benefit Analysis. McGraw-Hill, New York (2006)
7. Herrmann, D.S.: Complete Guide to Security and Privacy Metrics. Measuring Regulatory Compliance, Operational Resilience, and ROI. Auerbach Publications (2007)
8. ISO/IEC. ISO/IEC 27002:2005 Information technology – Security techniques – Code of Practice for Information Security Management (2005)
9. Jansen, W.: Directions in security metric research. Technical Report NISTIR 7564, National institute of Standards and Technology (2009)
10. Jaquith, A.: Security metrics: replacing fear, uncertainty, and doubt. Addison-Wesley, Reading (2007)
11. Jonsson, E., Olovsson, T.: A quantitative model of the security intrusion process based on attacker behavior. IEEE Transactions on Software Engineering 23(4), 235–245 (1997)
12. Karjoth, G., et al.: Service-oriented assurance comprehensive security by explicit assurances. In: Proceedings of the 1st Workshop on Quality of Protection, Milan, Italy. Springer, Heidelberg (2005)
13. Krautsevich, L., et al.: Formal approach to security metrics. what does "more secure" mean for you? In: Proceedings of the 1st International Workshop on Measurability of Security in Software Architectures. ACM Press, New York (2010)
14. Madan, B.B., Goseva-Popstojanova, K., Vaidyanathan, K., Trivedi, K.S.: A method for modeling and quantifying the security attributes of intrusion tolerant systems. Performance Evaluatin Journal 1-4(56), 167–186 (2004)
15. Manadhata, P., Wing, J.: Measuring a system's attack surface. Technical Report CMU-TR-04-102, Carnegie Mellon University (2004)
16. Manadhata, P., Wing, J.M.: An attack surface metric. Technical Report CMU-CS-05-155, School of Computer Science. Carnegie Mellon University (2005)
17. Manadhata, P.K., et al.: An approach to measuring a systems attack surface. Technical Report CMU-CS-07-146, School of Computer Science. Carnegie Mellon University (2007)

18. Mullen, R.: The lognormal distribution of software failure rates: application to software reliability growth modeling. In: The Ninth International Symposium on Software Reliability Engineering, pp. 134–142 (November 1998)
19. Ortalo, R., et al.: Experimenting with quantitative evaluation tools for monitoring operational security. IEEE Transactions on Software Engineering 25(5), 633–650 (1999)
20. Pamula, J., et al.: A weakest-adversary security metric for network configuration security analysis. In: QoP 2006: Proceedings of the 2nd ACM Workshop on Quality of Protection, pp. 31–38. ACM Press, New York (2006)
21. Schechter, S.E.: How to buy better testing. In: Davida, G.I., Frankel, Y., Rees, O. (eds.) InfraSec 2002. LNCS, vol. 2437, pp. 73–87. Springer, Heidelberg (2002)
22. Stewart, A.: On risk: perception and direction. Computers & Security 23(5), 362–370 (2004)
23. Stoneburner, G., et al.: Risk management guide for information technology systems. Technical Report 800-30, National Institute of Standards and Technology (2001)
24. Swanson, M., et al.: Security metrics guide for information technology systems. Technical Report 800-55, National Institute of Standards and Technology (2003)
25. Vaughn, R.B., et al.: Information assurance measures and metrics - state of practice and proposed taxonomy. In: Proceedings of the 36th Annual Hawaii International Conference on System Sciences (January 2003)
26. Wang, L., et al.: An attack graph-based probabilistic security metric. In: Proceeedings of the 22nd Annual IFIP WG 11.3 Working Conference on Data and Applications Security, pp. 283–296. Springer, Heidelberg (2008)
27. Wang, L., et al.: Minimum-cost network hardening using attack graphs. Computer Communications 29(18), 3812–3824 (2006)

STORM - Collaborative Security Management Environment

Theodoros Ntouskas, George Pentafronimos, and Spyros Papastergiou

Department of Informatics, University of Piraeus,
Karaoli & Dimitriou 80, 185 34 Piraeus, Greece
{tdouskas,gpentas,paps}@unipi.gr

Abstract. Security Management is a necessary process in order to obtain an accurate security policy for Information and Communication Systems (ICS). Organizations spend a lot of money and time to implement their security policy. Existing risk assessment, business continuity and security management tools are unable to meet the growing needs of the current, distributed, complex IS and their critical data and services. Identifying these weaknesses and exploiting advanced open-source technologies and interactive software tools, we propose a secure, collaborative environment (STORM) for the security management of ICS's.

Keywords: Security Management, Risk Management, Vulnerability Assessment tools, Security Tools, Collaboration.

1 Introduction

The most critical and sensitive data of the organizations is hosted in their Information and Communication Systems (ICS). Degradation, interruption or impairment of their ICS has serious consequences on safety, loss of sensitive data, loss of reputation or loss of service making security management one of the most important organizational concerns [2]. Current ICSs are distributed; complex and multidimensional resulting to the fact that security management is a cooperative obligation requiring the involvement and participation of all ICS participants.

Existing security management (e.g. ISO-15408 [31], ISO-17799 [32], ISO-27001 [33], ISO-27002 [34]) and risk assessment (e.g. Cobra [12], CRAMM [13], EBIOS [17]) tools do not enable collaboration and they do not consider all aspects (technological, business, legal, economical) that influence the evaluation of the ICS threats and vulnerabilities leading to incomplete and ineffective security management, with generic security policies and incomplete security procedures.

The risk management for current complex organizations (e.g. large-scale infrastructures, critical infrastructures, large enterprises) requires many interviews with all participants in order to identify the architecture of the ICS, the assets, and their interdependency, risks and criticality (from an organizational, technological, legal, business and economical perspective).

Furthermore, it does not exist an automated collaborative tool embedding security standards, methodologies, tools and guidelines that continuously guide and train the participants in the security management in order to:

C.A. Ardagna and J. Zhou (Eds.): WISTP 2011, LNCS 6633, pp. 320–335, 2011.
© IFIP International Federation for Information Processing 2011

– Perform risk assessment for risk identification
– Conduct vulnerability assessment
– Execute penetration tests/scenarios
– Implement appropriate countermeasures
– Design security policy and procedures
– Design security business continuity and disaster recovery plans

The aim of this paper is to contribute to the above challenge by providing a collaborative security management tool (STORM) which provides:

– **Innovative collection of security knowledge.** Using the STORM environment the necessary information will be collected from all participants, minimizing the gathering time, reducing costs for the organizations and most importantly taking into account the security knowledge of all participants of the ICS in order to obtain an accurate security policy.
– **Secure dependable and collaborative environment.** By the use of STORM modules, the governance of complex organizations will be able to establish and maintain a secure cooperate environment for their local and external users.

STORM is a prototype of a new generation, collaborative, innovative security management environment, which will be able to provide the necessary level of confidentiality, reliability, interactivity and interoperability of the organizations and their ICS's. The proposed STORM environment is an open and cost effective approach that is based on widely used collaborative web 2.0 technologies such as wikis, blogs, RSS and forums.

The rest of the paper is organized as follows: Section 2 describes existing standards and methodologies for Security Management and analyzes the ICS complexity. Section 3, describes the STORM architecture and its basic components. Finally, Section 4 draws conclusions.

2   State of The Art

Security Management is a continuous and systematic process of identifying, analyzing, handling, reporting and monitoring operational risks of an organization [6][18]. Security Management is an important governance and administration procedure aiming at the protection of an organization from internal and external risks that would negatively affect the achievement of its operational objectives.

Current ICS's are characterized by growing complexity, distribution of their Information System (IS) (network, hardware, software, human resources) in various locations (rooms/buildings/cities) and by the plethora of electronic services. In addition, these complex ICS's interact, interwork and their business become dependent on other organizations (e.g. providers, partners, banks, insurance companies, Tax authorities). They have a large number of users (internal, external administrators, users, providers), and they face a growing number of different types of spatial and temporal dispersion effects of attacks.

Despite the growing need for effective security management within the organizations, the existing security-related methodologies, standards and frameworks are inadequate to meet the above needs of current ICS in a holistic and integrated way. More specifically:

- Existing security management standards/frameworks/methodologies for the establishment of corporate security governance (e.g Cobit [11], ITIL [10], ValIT [56], ISO-17799 [32], ISO-27001 [33], ISO-27002 [34]), have not been implemented in a tool since they present specific limitations. They usually define principles and provide only guidelines mostly in the form of recommendations rather than strict rules that should be followed.
- Existing risk management methodologies (i.e. Cramm [13], Octave [43], ISO-15408 [31]) and their automated tools (e.g. Cramm [13], Cobra [12]) are costly, they require numerous and time consuming face-to-face interviews with all the administrators, not allowing collaboration, resulting to the insufficient collection of all available security knowledge of all participants.
- Most of available methodologies and frameworks for security testing [4], [52], [60], [50], [46], [25], [8] describe test cases and they indicate tools that can be used in each test providing merely a description of their capabilities. Nevertheless, the tracing and the correct configuration of the required vulnerability assessment tools is a time consuming process which requires specific expertise. Therefore, there is a need for consolidated vulnerability assessment information pertaining to the proper configuration and installation of the VA tools as well as the provision of an integrated VA environment that offers a comprehensive and large collection of security-related tools.
- Disaster Recovery and Business Continuity standards (i.e. BS 25999-1 [9], BCI GPG [7], ITIL V3 [10], HB 292 -2006 [24]) are unable to meet the needs of the current distributed IS's since they have not been implemented in an automated tool.
- The renewal, updating and awareness of these security documents (security policy, Disaster Recovery and Business Continuity plans) is done manually every time something changes in the ICS or in the security procedures which are costly and time consuming processes requiring a variety of organizational resources.

Therefore, there is an imperative need for continuous, collaborative, holistic and effective security management of the ICS. The proposed STORM environment, described in the following sections is an open, cost-effective, collaborative approach to security management.

3   STORM Collaborative Environment

Because of the changing conditions under which an organization operates today (distributed, complex and diverse technological environment, globalization, economic crisis), the implementation and maintenance of an accepted level of ICS security is requiring a planned and organized task. STORM contributes to the creation, enhancement, monitoring and assessment of the security of the information and communication systems providing an innovative, interactive collaborative environment that encompasses a bundle of primitive services which allow the organization to:

- identify and depict the ICS infrastructure;
- identify the applying security policies, procedures, standards and guidelines;
- specify, evaluate and classify daily risks and threats of the ICS continuously collecting the security knowledge of all operational ICS participants (administrators, users, providers);
- recognize the impacts (business, economical, technological, legal) of upcoming incidents on the operations of the ICS;
- execute technical vulnerability assessment with live scenarios (based on accepted vulnerability assessment methodologies and techniques) identifying at real time the security needs of the ICS;
- select reliable and appropriate countermeasures to achieve the confidentiality, availability and integrity of data;
- on-line generation/formulation/monitor/renew/update all the security documents (security policy, Business Continuity and Disaster Recovery Plans);
- continuously monitor new laws, standards and best practices.

In order to achieve these, the STORM collaborative environment is composed of four layers as depicted in the following Figure.

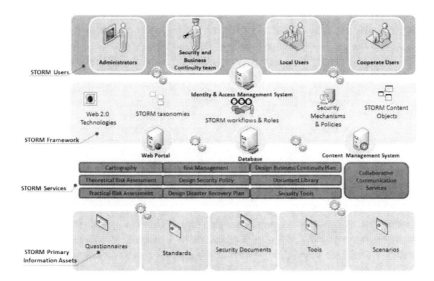

Fig. 1. STORM collaborative environment

STORM architecture, its basic components and their functionalities, are described in the following sections.

3.1   STORM Architecture and Services

STORM aims to become the harbinger of a new generation security management tool for ICS, stimulating the collaboration among all stakeholders. Figure 1 depicts the proposed architecture that encompasses the core participants and entities distributed in four distinct layers as follows:

Layer 1 - STORM Users: This first layer consists of the four groups of users namely, Security and Business Continuity Team, Administrators, local Users, external users. Considering the fact that local and cooperate users may not perceive critical security factors (e.g. threats, vulnerabilities, impacts) the same way as security experts, different access privileges to the STORM services have been applied to the aforementioned user groups. Remarkably, only the members of the Security and Business Continuity Team are responsible for properly and adequately providing initial content to the system and specifically all the primary information assets comprised at Layer 2 of its architecture, that are necessary for harmonizing security management procedures.

Layer 2 - The STORM Framework: The main components and the individual systems that comprise the core STORM environment.

Layer 3 - STORM Services: At this layer, an integrated bundle of security services is provided that aids the organization to apply an accurate, reliable and flawless corporate security management of ICS.

Layer 4 - STORM Primary Information Assets: All related standards, methodologies, best practices, related legislation are the assets of the STORM; typical examples are: Business Continuity and Disaster Recovery Standards, Security Management Standards methodologies, Risk Analysis questionnaires, Vulnerabilities scenarios, Security Policy, Disaster recovery/Business Continuity plans, Disaster Scenarios. These assets are structured documents in STORM Document Library.

3.2   Layer 1 - STORM Users

The STORM participants as described in Layer 1 are the following:

– The administrators of the IS who continuously inform the collaborative tool with all the necessary information (technical instructions, manuals, samples of business continuity and disaster recovery plans, international standards, best practices, open source security tools and scenarios etc.), create the questionnaires and the necessary recovery forms, define the responsibilities of users, control and renew the lists of the installed software and hardware of the information system.
– The members of the security and business continuity team, make an assessment of the criticality of services, analysis and evaluation of risks, risk management using appropriate countermeasures and implement all the procedures of the security policy. They are able to continuously be informed

with the new standards and best practices and apply them directly on the system.

- Local users of information systems (e.g. accounting user etc) will be able to actively participate in the collaborative security process, find information on technical and security procedures and as a result any difficulties may be treated effectively. Also they will be trained/informed about all the security procedures through the STORM communication module (with wiki/forum/polls).
- Cooperate users which cooperate with the organizations (e.g. custom offices, banks, agencies, suppliers, service providers, other organizations) can be informed about security rules and conditions for safe interconnection and access to the information systems of the organizations. In this way there will be safeguards put in place, minimization of threats, and trust in the quality of services.

3.3 Layer 2 - The STORM Framework

The STORM framework consists of two central entities. The fist is the Identity and Access Management (IAM) System which properly specifies and enforces security and privacy policies, used to control access to STORM services. IAM incorporates security mechanisms and policies that enhance the STORM platform with proper authentication and authorization properties and Single-Sign-On (SSO) procedures, enclosing end-user's preferences and requirements. Based on the above procedures, different user roles (administrators, local users etc.) have access to specific STORM services according to their business needs and requirements. This component is based on open source Open SSO [44].

The second major entity of the framework is STORM System that is comprised of the following components:

- **Web portal:** A Web Interactive System, which provides secure access to security related information and content, retrieved and processed from diverse sources, in a unified and user-friendly way. This system is based on collaborative Web 2.0 technologies and automated, open, interactive and reliable technological tools (such as collaborative forums, blogs, Wikis etc.). The STORM system will actually provide a consistent look and feel with secure access control and procedures for the integrated applications of the project. The STORM Web portal will serve as a unified secure access and presentation point to the full range of security services.
- **Enterprise Service Bus (ESB):** ESB is essentially a lightweight messaging framework integrating different technologies, devices and data transfer protocols, ensuring that different systems and applications communicate through a common channel to exchange information with other organizations.
- **Business Process Modelling (BPM):** It undertakes the responsibility to monitor, manage, analyze and implement the business logic of complex and distributed workflows of the services provided by the STORM system.

- **Decision Support System (DSS):** DSS facilitates the combination of a set of information in order to solve problems and reach tactical and strategic decisions in several security and privacy issues. These decisions can be considered more in the form of suggestions and recommendations rather than strict injunctions that should be followed. The users will be able to modify, complete, or refine these decision suggestions according to their needs. Representative example is the definition of a security and privacy risk mitigation strategy taking into consideration the enterprise financial status and the applied countermeasures.
- **Ontologies and Semantic Structures (Knowledge Base):** A collection of semantic structures (notably ontologies/taxonomies) modelling the STORM content as well as their semantic relationships will be designed, implemented and integrated within the STORM system. Thematic, security and privacy related ontologies/taxonomies will be defined to better organize the various quantities of the assets stored in the repository. These will bring context to words, topic areas and search results, providing a hierarchical structure of asset categories, from general to specific. We conveniently call the set of semantic structures of the STORM system, as the STORM Knowledge Base.
- **Content Management System (CMS)** responsible for creating, editing, management and publication of all the primary and processed content in a consistent and structured way. It consists of:
  - advanced content management tools (e.g. rich text editors, live page editing and scheduling, and advanced document managers) in order to provide the STORM friendly environment;
  - intuitive front end user interfaces that share a set of common characteristics to promote user friendliness and accessibility;
  - functionality for collecting, organizing and managing content from multiple sources (e.g., databases, repositories) and multiple formats;
  - STORM taxonomies for better access to the STORM primary assets and content.
- **STORM Repository:** All STORM primary assets (all related standards, methodologies, best practices, legislation, Risk Analysis questionnaires, Security Policy, Disaster recovery/Business Continuity plans) are stored in a repository.

All the aforementioned elements are the backbone infrastructure of the STORM framework. They will be combined in an effective way to establish a highly agile automation Services Oriented Architecture (SOA) environment that can boost both re-engineering and the integration of a set of security and privacy related services that will be described in the following section.

3.4   Layer 3 - STORM Services

The services offered by STORM (Layer3) are depicted at the figure 2 and described in detail as follows:

Cartography module: The main objective of this module is to describe critical information and communication systems in order to depict all their security-related aspects. These aspects are not confined only to technical issues, but they are also concerned with the business processes in which the systems are embedded. In order to describe the information and communication systems, STORM has adopted and integrated an object modeling approach based on the ISO Reference Model for Open Distributed Processing systems (RM-ODP) [57] standard in combination with the Unified Modeling Language (UML). The RM-ODP offers a general framework and a reference model based on five different viewpoints that identifies the crucial characteristics that qualify the systems while the UML provides the notation for representing the identified features.

The five viewpoints as described by RM-ODP and adopted by STORM are the following:

- *Enterprise viewpoint.* A viewpoint of the system and its environment that focuses on the technical guidelines and policies associated with the system as well as the system's purpose of operation, scope and business requirements. Also, it deals with aspects of the enterprise such as its organizational structure, which affect the system.
- *Information viewpoint.* A viewpoint which specifies and describes the information structure of the system. Specifically, it focuses on the information that is stored, processed and exchanged in the system.
- *Computational viewpoint.* A viewpoint which focuses on functional decomposition of the system into objects which interact at interfaces.
- *Engineering viewpoint.* A viewpoint which describes the way different objects of the system interact with each other as well as the resources required for this communication.
- *Technology viewpoint.* A viewpoint which focuses on the individual hardware and software components which compose the system.

The proper and accurate analysis and representation of the information and communication systems aid the early discovery of security vulnerabilities, inconsistencies and redundancies in these systems.

Theoretical Risk Assessment Module: providing the following functionality:

- *Online Forms* for user identification (responsibilities, roles etc.), asset identification (servers, routers, switches, applications, databases etc), reporting of their interdependencies with other systems, description of applications, detailed record of operational procedures.
- *Collaborative Questionnaires.* Embedded online questionnaires for the accomplishment of:
  - IT assets (software and hardware) identification
  - impacts determination (based on various security scenarios related to availability, integrity and confidentiality loss),
  - threats, vulnerabilities and risk identification.

The posted questionnaires are filled in by all participants and are collected and analyzed by the corresponding users through charts .The participants, answering

Fig. 2. STORM Security Management Services

the questionnaires, will be able to give their knowledge from their own perspective (e.g. deficiencies, security incidents, backup procedures, countermeasures of their department). This allows the accumulation of objective information that can be used as input for the execution of the risk analysis and risk management procedures in an effective and efficient manner.

Vulnerability (Practical Risk) Assessment module: This module consists of the following three subcomponents:

1. *Methodologies repository.* An inventory of the most wide-used and accepted vulnerability assessment (VA) methodologies and frameworks (i.e. OWASP [4], OWASP Code review [52], NIST SP800-42 [60], Special Publication 800-115 [50], Penetration Testing Framework (PTF) [46], OSSTMM [25], ISSAF [8])defined and released by the standardization bodies and the research communities. This acts as a reference point of existing methods for network and web application security testing and assessment as well as for forensics analysis.

2. *Tools Repository.* An inventory of open source and freeware tools that can be used in combination with the VA methodologies and frameworks for the deployment of specific security tests. A set of tools-related information concerning installation guides for various operating systems, links to sources codes and executable files as well as expert notifications about capabilities, problems and limitations is also provided.

   Within STORM, the VA tools are divided in the following categories taking into account the provided functionality:

   – Reconnaissance and Discovery: information gathering from publicly available sources and online databases such as IP registries, DNS information, public web sites and search engines (e.g. Dnsmap [15], DNSPredict [16], Fierce [22], Metagoofil [39], Gooscan [23]).
   – Network Mapping: acquisition of detailed information about the targets (e.g. Hping3 [27],Nmap [41], TCPtraceroute [54], P0f [47], Zenmap [62], Httprint [28]).

- Vulnerability Identification: discovery and enumeration of candidate vulnerabilities of the examined systems (e.g. OpenVas [45], W3AF [59], Nessus [40]).
- Penetration/Exploitation: exploitation of specific vulnerabilities aiming at gaining unauthorized access to the target systems (e.g. MEF [38], ExploitDB [21]).
- Privilege Escalation: gaining privileged access to the compromised systems (e.g. Hydra [29], [35], Medusa [37]).
- Further Enumeration: discovery of further information (e.g. passwords, network mapping) (e.g. EtterCap [20], Wireshark [61])
- Maintaining Access: establishment of covert channels, back door installation and deployment of rootkits (e.g 3proxy [1], ProxyTunnel [48], TinyProxy [55]).Digital Forensics Analysis: preservation and analysis of digital evidence (e.g. Autopsy [5], [14], Sleuth [51], Volatility [58]).

In addition, a VA environment (VA platform) has been configured and is available in STORM providing a user-friendly access to a comprehensive and large collection of security-related tools ranging from sniffers and traffic analyzer to web scanner and WEP/WPA cracking. The preconfigured environment is a Linux distribution based on Debian 5 that is available as a Live DVD. This allows the potential users either to boot the platform directly from any portable media or to install it to the hard disk or even to run it as a virtual machine. Configuration guidelines of the platform are also available strengthening the trust of the potential users. The main aim of this inventory is to assist individuals and organizations to establish a well-defined security "laboratory" environment enabling them to perform self-assessment in order to improve the security level of their infrastructure.

3. *Lesson Learned Repository.* This component acts as an inventory of common attacks. Its main objective is to bring into focus some of the theoretical and practical concerns of the most common threats. In this context, a comprehensive description of a set of attacks is provided covering all their aspects including exploitable security flaws, applied scenarios, tools which can be used, as well as mitigation recommendations and countermeasures that can be adopted. The attacks have been categorized as follows:

- Network Attacks: include any methods, processes or means used to maliciously attempt to compromise the security of a network. Representative examples of this type are Distributed Denial of Services attacks, Spoofing attacks, Eavesdropping etc.
- Application Attacks: include any methods, processes or means used to maliciously attempt to compromise the security of an application. Injection (e.g. sql, soap, ldap), Cross-Site Scripting (XSS), Buffer Overflow attacks are examples of this type.

In addition, a number of case studies that can be considered as lesson learned can be provided in STORM. These are more in the form of challenges rather than strict rules that must be followed. The challenges are discriminated in two types. The first concerns case studies of attacks' deployment (e.g. Distribution Denial of Service (DDoS), Denial of Service (DoS)) aiming at the evaluation and validation of the security controls and countermeasures that are integrated in an infrastructure. The impact of the attacks on the target is calculated and recorded in the system as it has to be the prime consideration for further investigation. The second type of case studies gives the opportunity to the potential users (individuals and organization) to analyze the attacks and post their findings in STORM CMS. The challenges concern a wide range of forensic issues such as the detection and analysis of suspicious software/malware, hash analysis, image analysis, partition recovery, signature analysis, file header reconstruction, password recovery, registry analysis, steganography and encryption. Furthermore, the results of case studies conducted within the activities of a set of national initiatives such as HONEYNET [26], CERT Exercises Handbook [19] can be also analyzed and presented in depth in the system. In this way, the users learn not only about the threats, but also how to deploy and analyze them.

Risk Management module: This module via online forms and library aid the organization for the selection of the appropriate taking into account the result of the risk assessment procedure. All participants will be able to give their opinion by using the communication module and agree or propose their new countermeasures.

Security Policy Module: This module provides the appropriate functionality for the design and creation of the security policy of the organization using the collaborative forms that are embedded in this STORM module. In addition, all the information related to security policies, procedures, guidelines, rules and responsibilities and credentials at the information and communication systems and services are also available and accessible by all the corporate users via this module.

   Administrators and security team will edit and update this module so all the other users of the organization will be able to find information about the security procedures, rules and their responsibilities and credentials at the applications and services.

Disaster Recovery (DR) / Business Continuity (BC) Module: The aim of this module is to provide the functionality required for the design and creation of BC and DR plans. It also contains all the disaster recovery procedures and relevant information such as responsibilities and contact information that are necessary in case of disaster or an emergency event. Further, the module provides forms for building of possible disaster scenarios and for real time responsibilities assignment. More detailed, there have been implemented forms for:

- user responsibilities,
- contact details,
- supplier contact details,
- incident report,
- incident handling,
- recovery procedures,
- backup infrastructure and procedures

Collaborative Communication Services: Provision of a group of communication services.

- Forum for exchanging ideas about security topics or reach consensus on evaluation of risks. This will help all participants to find quickly solutions about daily security or other problems so they will solve their difficulties quick. Also they will be able to discuss about security problems, accept or not the proposed countermeasures or recommend their security safeguards.
- Polls so users will be able to discuss critical security issues allowing them to reach solutions in a collaborative, cost and time effective manner.
- Wiki, based on which, all users will be able to find or propose their own solutions regarding security issues or find details about risk assessment, risk management and vulnerability and the security policy of their organization, so they will be able to solve any difficulty directly.
- Interactive user screens which are used for collaborative risk management and for reporting protection measures.

3.5 Layer 4 - STORM Primary Information Assets

STORM users will be able to perform various actions depending of their roles e.g. local and cooperate users will be able to access the STORM assets which support the STORM services as described in Section 3.4. In particular the following assets will be included: the cartography analysis report of the organization as produced in the Cartography module; the risk assessment questionnaires provided by the Theoretical risk assessment module; all the security related information pertaining to the technical vulnerability assessment (VA) i.e. methodologies, open source and freeware VA tools, installation guides, VA scenarios, case studies; the countermeasures proposed by the Risk management module; security corporate documentation i.e. security policies, Disaster recovery, Business continuity Plans as generated by the Security Policy and the DR/BC modules respectively.

4   Implementation

The development and integration of the main components of the STORM framework is based on the innovative integration of mature technological solutions and tools as follows:

- *Social Networking Tool:* A social networking open source solution that is based on Symfony Framework [53] has been adopted and integrated in the STORM system. This solution is an open source software platform available for social networking that provides a number of Web2.0 components such as, Document Library, Team Calendar, Wikis, Blogs, Forums (Message Boards), Private Site and separate secured areas, Instant Messaging, Announcements & Alerts and Email.

- *Content Management System:* The management of the content, documents, files, information and data related to the security services provided by the STORM system is performed by a CMS solution based on the Symfony Framework [53].
- *Business Process Management (BPM):* A holistic business process management tool, ADONIS [3], has been adopted for the composition of an integrated SOA environment. The tool utilizes notations like Business Process Execution Language (BPEL) standards in order to enable modelling, composition and deployment of service workflows. This tool is also be used in order to implement the Decision Support System that shall be integrated in the system.
- *SOA Environment:* An open SOA strategy has been adopted based on XML technologies and web services-based standards and will be followed for the design, development and implementation of the STORM system. For the integration of the middleware infrastructure [36] (i.e. application servers, enterprise service bus) an Open Source Enterprise Server, has been deployed that hosts the SOA environment.
- *Identity Management System (IMS):* The STORM framework has incorporated a solution, Open SSO platform [44], that provides core identity services such as strong authentication and authorization mechanisms as well as support and implement a transparent single sign-on (SSO) procedure.

As indicated in the brief analysis of STORM main technological components, the proposed integration framework is totally based on open-source technologies and software tools, rendering the final product (STORM Environment) a cost-effective and easily adopted innovative solution. This critical characteristic could be also considered as the fundamental benefit and added value of STORM, given that nowadays, key organisational decision makers and business managers (e.g. CIOs, CISOs, CFOs, etc.) are seeking urgently and massively, in a constantly evolving pace, for more efficient and cost-effective risk management solutions in order to reduce operational costs and resist the existing economic crisis. Especially in cases where security is falsely considered as a secondary need and disregarded due to the required additional costs (outsourcing to security consulting companies to perform risk assessment and management activities), an efficient solution that is able to provide reliable risk assessment and management services at extremely low cost is considered as an indispensable property.

Achieving this, STORM constitutes an innovative security management platform that is able to confront and effectively manage the trade-off between low cost and security management expertise by harnessing corporate knowledge, leveraging existing infrastructures and boosting work productivity.

5   Conclusions - Future Work

STORM is an open, innovative, collaborative security management environment, which can used in various organizations (from large organizations hosting critical infrastructures to SMEs and mEs) in order to effectively address their security and privacy needs.

The STORM environment has been proposed [42] as the preferred solution in order to provide security management services to the port Information systems. It will also be implemented in the S-PORT project [49] funded by the National research program "Cooperation" (NSRF 2007-2013) of the GSRT (General Secretariat for Research and Technology Development Department) in three Greek commercial Ports (Piraeus Port Authority S.A., Thessaloniki Port Authority S.A, Municipal Port Fund Mykonos).

STORM has also been selected as the appropriate architecture for policy making in collaborative environments and it will be implemented in the E.C. FP7 project ImmigrationPolicy2.0 [30].

Acknowledgements. The authors would like to thank the GSRT for funding the S-Port project, and the E.C. for funding the ImmigrationPolicy2.0 project. Finally we thank the S-Port and ImmigrationPolicy2.0 partners for their contributions.

References

1. 3proxy, http://tools.securitytube.net/index.php?title=3proxy
2. Abele Wigert, I., Dunn, M.: An inventory of 20 national and 6 international critical infrastructure protection policies. In: Wenger, A., Mauer, V. (eds.) International CIIP Handbook 2006, vol. 1. ETH, Zurich (2006)
3. ADONIS, http://www.adonis-community.com
4. Agarwwal, A., Bellucci, D., Coronel, A., DiPaola, S., Fedon, G., Goodman, A., Heinrich, C., Horvath, K., Ingrosso, G., Liverani, R.S., Kuza, A., Luptak, P., Mavituna, F., Mella, M., Meucci, M., Morana, M., Parata, A., Su, C., Sureddy, H.S., Roxberry, M., Stock, A.: Owasp testing guide v3.0 (2008),
   http://www.mare-system.de/whitepaper
5. Autopsy: Autopsy forensic browser,
   http://www.sleuthkit.org/autopsy/index.php
6. Basel Committee on Banking Supervision: Sound practices for the management and supervision of operational risk. BSI, Basel, Switzerland (2001)
7. BCIGPG: A management guide to implementing global good practice in business continuity management. In: Good Practice Guidelines 2007. (BCI GPG) Business Continuity Institute (2007)
8. Brunner, M., Dilaj, M., Herrera, O., Brunati, P., Subramaniam, R.K., Raman, S., Chavan, U., Rathore, B.: Information systems security assessment framework (issaf) draft 0.2.1 (April 2006), http://www.oissg.org/downloads/issaf-0.2/
   information-systems-security-assessment-framework-issaf-draft-0.2.1/
   view.html
9. BS25999-1: Business continuity management. British Standards Institute
10. Clinch, J.: Itil v3 and information security, ogc white paper (May 2009), http://
    www.best-managementpractice.com
11. COBIT4.1: It governance control framework. IT Governance Institute (2007),
    http://www.isaca.org
12. COBRA Methodology: Security risk analysis and assessment,
    http://www.riskworld.net/method.htm

13. CRAMM: Ccta risk analysis and management method, cramm version 5.2 information security toolkit (2003), http://www.cramm.com
14. ddrescue, http://freshmeat.net/projects/ddrescue/
15. Dnsmap, http://unknown.pentester.googlepages.com
16. DNSPredict, http://johnny.ihackstuff.com/downloads/task
17. Ebios: Expression des besoins et identification des objectifs de securite (2004), http://www.ssi.gouv.fr
18. ENISA: Risk Management: Implementation principles and Inventories for Risk Management/Risk Assessment methods and tools (2006)
19. ENISA: Cert exercises handbook. European Network and information Security Agency (2008), http://www.enisa.europa.eu/act/cert/support/exercise/files/handbook
20. EtterCap, http://ettercap.sourceforge.net/
21. ExploitDB, http://www.exploit-db.com
22. Fierce, http://ha.ckers.org/fierce/
23. Gooscan, http://johnny.ihackstuff.com/
24. HB292-2006: Handbook: A practitioners guide to business continuity management. Standards Australia, GPO Box 476, Sydney, NSW 2001, Australia (2006)
25. Herzog, P.: Osstmm:introduction and sample to the open source security testing methodology manual (osstmm 3 lite). Institute for Security and Open Methodologies (ISECOM) (August 2008), http://www.isecom.org/osstmm/
26. Honeynet: Honeynet project, http://www.honeynet.org/
27. Hping3, http://gd.tuwien.ac.at/www.hping.org/hping3.html
28. Httprint, http://net-square.com/httprint/
29. Hydra, http://www.thc.org
30. ImmigrationPolicy2.0, http://www.immigrationpolicy2.eu/
31. ISO/IEC:15408-1: Information technology - security techniques - evaluation criteria for it security – part 1: Introduction and general model (2005), http://www.iso.org
32. ISO/IEC:17799: Information technology - security techniques - code of practice for information security management (2005), http://www.iso.org
33. ISO/IEC:27001: Information technology - security techniques - information security management systems - requirements (2005), http://www.iso.org
34. ISO/IEC:27002: Information technology - security techniques - code of practice for information security management (2005), http://www.iso.org
35. John the Ripper, http://www.openwall.com/john/
36. Karantjias, A., Stamati, T., Martakos, D.: Advanced e-government enterprise strategies & solutions. International Journal of Electronic Governance (IJEG), Special Issue on Methodologies, Technologies and Tools Enabling e-Government 3, 170–188 (2010)
37. Medusa, http://www.darknet.org.uk/2006/05/
38. MEF: Metasploit exploitation framework, http://www.metasploit.com/
39. Metagoofil, http://www.edge-security.com/metagoofil.php
40. Nessus, http://www.nessus.org/nessus/
41. Nmap, http://www.insecure.org/nmap
42. Ntouskas, T., Polemi, N.: A secure, collaborative environment for the security management of port information systems. In: Proceedings of the Fifth International Conference on the Internet and Web Applications and Services, ICIW 2010, pp. 374–379. IEEE Computer Society Digital Library, Barcelona (2010)
43. OCTAVE: Octave method implementation guide version 2.0. Carnegie Mellon University (June 2001), http://www.cert.org/octave

44. OpenSSO8.0, `https://opensso.dev.java.net/public/use/index.html`
45. OpenVas: Open vulnerability assessment system, `http://www.openvas.org/`
46. Orrey, K., Lawson, L.J.: Penetration testing framework(ptf) v0.21, `http://www.vulnerabilityassessment.co.uk`
47. P0f, `http://lcamtuf.coredump.cx/p0f.shtml`
48. ProxyTunnel, `http://proxytunnel.sourceforge.net/`
49. S-PORT: S-port project, `http://s-port.unipi.gr/`
50. Scarfone, K., Souppaya, M., Cody, A., Orebaugh, A.: Technical guide to information security testing and assessment. Special Publication 800-115, `http://csrc.nist.gov/publications/nistpubs/800-115/SP800-115.pdf`
51. Sleuth Kit (TSK), `http://www.sleuthkit.org/sleuthkit/`
52. Stock, A.V.D., Lowery, D., Rook, D., Cruz, D., Keary, E., Williams, J., Chapman, J., Morana, M.M., Prego, P.: Owasp code review guide v1.1 (2008), `https://www.owasp.org`
53. Symfony: Symfony framework, `http://www.symfony-project.org/`
54. TCPtraceroute, `http://michael.toren.net/code/tcptraceroute/`
55. TinyProxy, `http://tinyproxy.sourceforge.net/`
56. ValIT: Enterprise value: Governance of it investments-the val it framework 2.0. IT Governance Institute (2008), `http://www.itgi.org`
57. Vallecillo, A.: Rm-odp: The iso reference model for open distributed processing, dintel edition on software engineering, pp. 69–99 (March 2001)
58. Volatility: Volatility framework, `https://www.volatilesystems.com/`
59. W3AF: Web application attack and audit framework, `http://w3af.sourceforge.net/`
60. Wack, J., Tracy, M., Souppaya, M.: NIST SP800-42:Guideline on Network Security Testing - Recommendations of the National Institute of Standards and Technology. NIST Special Publication 800-42, `http://www.iwar.org.uk/comsec/resources/netsec-testing/sp800-42.pdf`
61. Wireshark, `http://wireshark.org/`
62. Zenmap 4.60, `http://nmap.org/zenmap/`

Trust Agreement in Wireless Mesh Networks

Andreas Noack

Horst Görtz Institute for IT-Security
Ruhr University Bochum

Abstract. Establishing a trust relationship in decentralized wireless mesh networks (WMN) is an open question to date. In MANETs and cable bound meshed networks (like the Internet) there are a lot of proposals and solutions for trust establishment and for authentication.

In this paper we examine those existing solutions and analyze them for their applicability to wireless mesh networks.

We investigate the special demands of WMN, show the differences to existing network types and finally propose a trust agreement scheme that is particularly adapted to WMN.

Keywords: Wireless Mesh Networks, Trust Agreement, Reputation, Authentication, Authorization, Web of Trust.

1 Introduction

Imagine a group of wireless users in a city. These users are interconnected and some of them provide services like internet access or even an email service. Usually, the provider of a service does not want to offer his service to the whole world but only to a limited group of trusted users. On the other side there are users who only want to rely on trustful services, since no customer would like to use an email provider who eavesdrops on all his emails. The demand for a trust management system emerges.

Identification or at least the recognition of other users is an important issue for trust relations, because one can only have trust relations to users that you are able to authenticate. Authentication has been discussed widely for the classical internet and mobile ad-hoc networks (MANETs) [4][5]. But as far as we know, there is no feasible solution for authentication, recognition nor for trust establishment of nodes in Wireless Mesh Networks (WMN), which differ in several points from MANETs. WMN consist of static nodes, which have no computational nor battery power constraints and are able to do WiFi typical throughputs (11M, 54M, 300M) between neighboring nodes.

Wireless mesh networks are the "missing link" between the classical internet and mobile ad-hoc networks. Nodes in a MANET are mobile, whereas nodes on the internet are completely stationary. Wireless mesh networks are located in between, as the backbone of a WMN is mainly stationary. Nevertheless the availability and reachability of nodes is not nearly as good as on the internet due to wireless communication. Wireless interference has a big influence on the links and plays therefore a big role in wireless mesh networks, as it does in MANETs.

C.A. Ardagna and J. Zhou (Eds.): WISTP 2011, LNCS 6633, pp. 336–350, 2011.

In practice, wireless mesh networks can be found in community networks like SeattleWireless [2] or MIT Roofnet [1], industry projects (e.g. metalworking industry) and even military projects. Most of these networks grow irregularly while being bound to a specific environment, thus we cannot assume a clear network structure in most cases. We therefore assume that a WMN is a decentralized network without a central node that is reachable all the time (due to the limited reachability in WMN).

In this paper, we propose a protocol scheme for trust establishment that is optimized for wireless mesh networks. There are several solutions in the MANET and peer-to-peer world that support reaching the goal, e.g. offline CAs with hierarchical trust structure, virtual or distributed CAs (e.g. with threshold cryptography), ID-based key agreement, reputation management systems, the web of trust technique and many more [12][13][10][9].

We discuss the existing approaches regarding their feasibility for wireless mesh networks and conclude with a new trust agreement scheme for wireless mesh networks that combines and extends the most feasible ideas.

2   Differences to MANETs

Our contribution is particularly directed to wireless mesh networks. In order to delimitate our results from MANET solutions, we outline the essential differences between MA-NETs and WMN.

Mobile ad-hoc networks consist of a loose aggregation of mobile nodes. This means, the wireless link quality and also the link duration is fluctuating very randomly. When a node's link disconnects or a new link is established, the routing topology changes. Therefore it is not assured that each node can be reached at any time. Wireless mesh networks also rely on wireless links, but their nodes are more or less static in their position. Therefore the link duration is notably longer, although the link quality may fluctuate due to wireless interference. The frequency of topology changes in WMN is more similar to the internet than to MANETs and thus the proposed authentication mechanisms can be optimized for longer living connections.

Moreover most MANETs (e.g. sensor networks, VANETs and many more) are based on simple hardware components, so that there is usually limited computation power and sometimes even a limited energy supply, i.e. we have battery powered devices. These limitations are not present for WMN, leading to the capability of performing longer and more complex computations.

Due to the minor mobility of WMN nodes and no power limitations, WMN nodes can be equipped with more than one radio interface, using different wireless channels. This leads to far higher bandwidth as can be provided by MANETs, since half-duplex effects can be avoided and wireless interference is reduced.

2.1   Technical Design Goals

We design a trust establishment scheme that is particularly adapted to wireless mesh networks. For optimal compliance with this kind of network, the design has to be influenced by the advantages and restrictions that are provided by WMN.

The desired scheme should make use of local broadcasts, since they are cheap in wireless networks due to the wireless propagation of the signals.

In contrast to cable bound networks, we have higher packet loss rates in wireless networks because of wireless interference, range constraints and thereof resulting route changes. Usually, the occurence of packet loss in wireless networks is not uniformly distributed which results in phases with a good link and phases where nearly no packet passes through the network. It is sensible to minimize the number of messages to compensate the packet loss effect by having shorter sending periods. But if there is a connection, we are normally able to retrieve a high throughput in WMN (several radios, several channels, more transmit power than in MANETs). A good choice for the packet size is therefore near the maximum transfer unit (MTU), for the reason that the currently given throughput should not be limited by protocol overhead. To prevent packet fragmentation which would introduce a higher dropping probability (for the aggregated packet) and the need for a more complex retransmission mechanism, the packet size should obviously not exceed the MTU.

Furthermore the design has to consider a decentralized structure where no particular node can be a single point of failure, since wireless links (meshed wireless links are even worse) are not reliable in comparison to wired links.

As distinguished from MANETs, we have a much greater computation power and memory, while having no power constraints. This allows us to use complex mathematics like asymmetric cryptography, also elliptic curve based cryptography is imaginable. Trivial parts like an integrated clock or persistent memory, which can be absent in low cost devices, are furthermore assumed to be available in WMN devices.

Finally there is a further important point that will influence the design of the trust establishment scheme: The differentiation between important and and less important nodes. Important nodes are nodes that forward a lot of userdata, e.g. nodes that are located in the middle of the network or right before an internet uplink. These nodes obviously need a higher trust level than less important nodes that are e.g. located at the border of the network and do not forward any foreign data.

3   Related Work

On the way to our goal there are some issues to solve, e.g. there is the need for recognizing other users, since it is not possible to establish trust relations with a group of users that cannot be distinguished. This can on the one hand be handled by recognition techniques (e.g. a self signed public key pair) and on the other hand by common authentication schemes. In this section we give an overview about existing approaches for authentication from neighbouring research fields like the internet communication, MANETs and peer-to-peer networks.

- An *authentication server*, i.e. an AAA server or online certification authority (CA), authenticates clients to a wireless network. Cheikhrouhou et al. [3] and Lin et al. [8] proposed schemes that realize authentication between clients and authenticators (i.e. border gateways, access points). Both proposed schemes need an online Trusted Third Party (TTP) in the background for authenticating clients and authenticators. These schemes do not provide mutual authentication between the clients.

– An *offline certification authority* (CA) issues public key certificates for each user. Each user is then able to verify public key certificates from other users by verifying the certification chain up to the CA. This idea is widely spread on the internet and in the MANET world [12][13][7]. The CA can either be inactive or offline as long as no user joins or leaves the group. If a new user wants to join, a certificate must be issued. If a user leaves the group, a certificate revocation is required to preserve the consistency of the authentication process.

– A *distributed* or *virtual CA* issues public key certificates for each user, e.g. with the techniques from threshold cryptography [7]. A group of $k + 1$ randomly chosen CAs (or users) cooperates issuing or revoking a certificate for a certain user. Thus, revocation is possible without a particular TTP. Since for each new certificate or revocation a group of users (virtual/distributed CA) must cooperate, the solution is quite complex (in comparison with other solutions) and the deployed network protocol may need several rounds to complete. One proposal is given by Noack et al. [10].

– *Symmetric keys* for each pair of users. Each user shares a pairwise symmetric key with each other user of the network, leading to a large number of keys (exponential in the number of users). Certificate revocation lists or similar approaches are not needed, because single keys can be invalidated easily. Consider that when a new user joins or an active user leaves, all other users have to perform one key operation.

– *ID-based private keys* issued by an on demand CA. An on demand CA issues a private key (matching to the user's public key) for each new user. The special point is that everyone can compute the public keys of all users by using a common public value and the user's ID. Since everyone can compute the public keys and does not have to obtain them from a certain source, revocation is a challenging task. Zhang et al. proposed an ID-based authentication and billing scheme [14].

– *Self computed public key pairs* (e.g. self signed certificates) allow users to be cryptographically recognized. This idea can be extended with *trust agreement schemes*, like the web of trust technique, to add authentication due to transitive trust relations. However, for initial trust relationships there is the need for a trusted channel, i.e. a phone call to compare the public key fingerprints of each other. In completely autonomous networks without user interaction the trusted channel phase can be replaced by a multifactor authentication (i.e. public key certificate, MAC address, neighbourhood, behavior fingerprinting, cryptographic token, etc.).
The revocation of trust values can be handled by the trust agreement mechanism itself, similar to a certificate revocation.

– *Reputation management* schemes are used to classify the behavior or the grade of authentication of particular users. The global reputation of a particular user is calculated by the aggregation of votes by other users. Nithyanand et al. proposed a privacy preserving reputation management scheme for peer-to-peer networks [9]. Kamvar et al. introduce the EigenTrust reputation management algorithm to peer-to-peer networks, which helps to eliminate inauthentic files in file-sharing networks [6]. On the internet, reputation systems are also very common (i.e. ebay.com, amazon.com, etc.) [11], whereby the idea that is behind reputation management still remains untouched.

Wireless mesh networks have a decentralized structure that enables an autoconfiguration and self-healing ability. To preserve these abilities, a trust agreement or an authentication scheme (as a part of it) should not depend on a single party leading to a single point of failure.

Keeping this in mind, three techniques remain suitable for wireless mesh networks:

(1) a virtual or distributed CA that issues public key certificates,
(2) the use of self signed public key certificates with trust agreement mechanisms as trust anchor and
(3) a decentralized reputation management scheme.

However, virtual/distributed CAs need at least $k+1$ cooperating users to perform operations, whereas trust agreement and reputation management schemes do not have such restrictions. Therefore a mixture of trust agreement and reputation management turns out to be appropriate for a wireless network that does not provide full reachability of the nodes at any time.

4   Trust Agreement

Trust between users is an important point in wireless mesh networks. Only if a trust relationship is given, confidentiality and integrity make sense. Informally spoken, trust has a recognition (or authentication) part and a valuing part. Recognition is needed for being able to distinguish a user from other users which is obviously very important for trust relationships. The latter part of trust is a valuing part, used to express how trusted a user is.

Definition 1. *Trust Agreement means the establishment of trust relationships between all users of a group, whereby a trust relationship is the recognition of a particular user and a value that describes, how trusted this user is.*

In this section, we introduce a trust agreement technique to establish trust relations in WMN. To create a common trust base, we use direct as well as transitive trust relations between particular peers and combine them to a common view. The final goal is to create a trust network, in which each of the mesh networks' peers are included and each peer has a trust opinion of all other peers.

We proceed with a distinction of Trust Agreement and Web of Trust, which are important to not confuse with each other. Later on we present our idea of abstract trust requirements, define trust in WMN and propose a technical solution for creating trust in a network. All the steps are combined to a full trust agreement scheme in section 5.

4.1   Trust Agreement vs. Web of Trust

Trust agreement and web of trust are completely different concepts for dealing with trust in a network. The most important difference between trust agreement and web of trust is the trust view on the network. With trust agreement, one common trust view for all users is computed, whereas each user in a Web of Trust has its own trust view on the network.

Both solutions have advantages: Web of Trust is closer to reality, since it is natural that trust to a certain person is different for two independent persons. Usually your wife has a higher trust in you than a randomly chosen person from the street. Trust agreement, however, creates one global trust value for each user. Though this is not a realistic circumstance, trust agreement has some crucial advantages over web of trust. Firstly, if trust opinions on one user differ very much, the relevance of these opinions decreases for all other participants, since they probably do not have the ability to choose the right opinion. This is a general problem of trust, which is adapted by the web of trust technique and which can only be handled with a complete (transitive) trust view or a sensible average function. Secondly, most users do not know every other user of the network from the beginning. An initial trust value has to be assumed for unknown users. Trust agreement solves this by providing a sensible initial trust value for each user that was computed in a collective manner. After becoming an active participant of the network, you are able to influence the agreed trust value of a certain user with own trust impressions. Thirdly, if the system is operated autonomously, we require a simple system for authentication or recognition. Web of trust is problematic, since it does not provide a single trust view on the network that would be needed to create a robust network. Different trust opinions on one user can lead to divergency problems, e.g. a fully authenticated path for Alice may not be authenticated for Bob.

Therefore the best tradeoff is providing a trust agreement scheme that provides a globally agreed trust value for each user. This is what we are proposing in the following.

4.2   Abstract Trust Requirements

Wireless mesh nodes have different trust requirements concerning their position in the mesh network graph. We are beginning with the assignment of abstract trust requirement levels to different positions in the WMN. The idea of differentiating several positions in the network is similar to the different roles of autonomous systems in internet routing (stub, multi-homed and transit AS).

We assign numbers between "1" and "3", whereby a higher number means a higher trust requirement. Nodes with only one edge are mesh participants, who do not forward any data from other nodes. Since their responsibility and trustworthiness is quite low, they just need a low trust requirement (indicated by "1" in figure 1).

Nodes with at least two edges have a higher trust requirement, because they are forwarding data from other nodes. We distinguish between nodes, for which an alternative path exists and nodes, that cannot be avoided by at least one

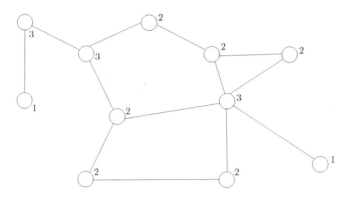

Fig. 1. Abstract trust requirement levels in a WMN

other node. So we introduce two trust requirements: "2" for routing nodes that can be circumvented and "3" for routing nodes without an alternative path.

Trust requirements are allocated on behalf of the amount of foreign data that passes a node. We think that it is very important to care for the honest handling of foreign data, which is transmitted in cleartext in the most practical wireless mesh networks to date. Thus we only refer to security and exclude availability and performance in this paper. Of course a reduced availability of a node will have impact on its trust value, but only because of a shorter availability time.

Additionally to the given trust requirements we provide an extended version in Appendix A.1, introducing a more practical and precise classification.

4.3   Definition of Trust in Wireless Mesh Networks

There are two different understandings of trust in wireless mesh networks: local and global. Local trust (later used as trust assignment) is the reputation meaning, one has towards a particular user. Global trust is the final trust level, a user gains after aggregating all local trust values.

In this section, we define the composition of trust in general. By our definition, trust in wireless mesh networks consists of two parts:

Definition 2. *Trust in wireless mesh networks is determined by a trust tuple* (α, θ). $\alpha \in \mathbf{N}^+$ *represents the authentication and* $\theta \in \mathbf{R}^+$ *the grade of authorization.*

The first part is the recognition or authentication part which is necessary to distinguish nodes from each other. Recognition means that every node has a distinct cryptographic attribute (e.g. a self signed certificate) that proves his binding to a self chosen identity. Authentication extends this by creating a cryptographic binding to an approved identity. Actually, authentication and recognition are binary decisions, because there are always only two possibilites: you have identified a user or you have not. After all, the authentication value α is determined by the addition of all binary authentication results. However, the value of α (if greater than one) is not the determining part of the trust level, it just represents the number of nodes who authenticated a certain node.

The second part of trust is a valuing component, namely how trusted a user is. We call this part authorization value, since it will be used to authorize users to become part of the network. Later on, the authorization value can also be used for choosing the best (most trustful) route for a packet through the network, if our scheme is combined with a source routing algorithm. Authorization is expressed by the real value θ.

4.4   Creating the Trust Network

Trust agreement bases on a simple reputation assignment and signing mechanism with the following basic idea:

If a particular user U_i trusts another user U_j with $i \neq j$ (local trust), U_i creates a trust assignment $T_{ij} = (\alpha_{ij}, \theta_{ij}, VD)$ and broadcasts this assignment together with a corresponding signature σ_i (signed with U_i's private key SK_i).

- $\alpha_{ij} \in \{0, 1\}$ represents the recognition/authentication from U_j towards U_i as a binary value ($1 \rightarrow$ trusted, $0 \rightarrow$ untrusted). However, an authentication is always a binary decision, since there are only two possibilities: U_i knows U_j or not. Revocation can also be handled with α_{ij}; its value has to be 0 in that case.
  In autonomous networks, recognition of other users is usually used instead of a full authentication. In this case, α_{ij} is 1 if the user U_i has made any experiences with user U_j, else α_{ij} is 0. If a full authentication scheme is used, U_i has to fetch an authentication evidence of U_j. This can be done by a personal meeting of both users, a comparison of the public key fingerprints by phone, a multifactor authentication or via many other ways.
- $\theta_{ij} \in \{0 \dots \theta_i\}$ is the grade of authorization given by the user U_i to the user U_j. The upper bound of the issued authorization value is fixed by the user U_i's own (global) authorization value.
- VD (Validity Date) represents the date, when the given trust assignment expires. Therefore, trust assignments have to be refreshed regularly. A trust assignment with a posterior Validity Date replaces previous ones.

Definition 3. *A valid trust assignment (local trust) for user U_j issued by U_i consists of a vector $T_{ij} = (\alpha_{ij}, \theta_{ij}, VD)$ and a signature σ_i over this vector T_{ij}. The signature σ_i is computed with the secret key SK_i of U_i. Furthermore the trust assignment must have the following properties:*

1. *The validity date VD must not be expired.*
2. *The authentication value α_{ij} must be 1 (if no revocation is intended).*
3. *If the issued authorization value θ_{ij} is intended to increase the authorization value of U_j: The issuer U_i's authorization value θ_i is bigger or equal than the receiver's θ_j plus the trust assignment's θ_{ij}. ($\theta_i \geq \theta_j + \theta_{ij}$)*
4. *If there is a trust assignment with $\alpha_{ij} = 0$, all trust assignments T_{kj} from U_k with $(\theta_k < \theta_i) \wedge (VD_{kj} < VD_{ij})$ are invalid.*

A trust assignment T_{ij} with an authentication value $\alpha_{ij} = 0$ is called revocation assignment. If a revocation assignment T_{ij} was issued to U_j, all trust assignments T_{kj} from U_k with lower authorization levels ($\theta_k < \theta_i$) *and* shorter validity dates ($\mathrm{VD}_k < \mathrm{VD}_i$) become invalid.

The global trust value of a particular user U_j is computed from all trust assignments (local trust) intended to him. A valid trust assignment contains a valid (not expired) VD and is signed from a user with a higher trust level, to prevent fraud. All valid trust assignment tuples are summed up component-wise, whereby each single authorization value θ_{ij} is multiplied with a coefficient ω before.

The coefficient ω is necessary in order to prevent a user U_i from transfering his complete trust to another user U_j, thus creating a more or equally trusted user than himself. ω is defined as $\frac{1}{s}$, whereby s equals the average number of ascertained trust assignments in the whole wireless mesh network.

Definition 4. *A user U_j's global trust value is computed as:*

$$(\alpha_j, \theta_j) := (\sum_{\forall i: U_i \in S} \alpha_{ij}, \quad \sum_{\forall i: U_i \in S} \omega \cdot \theta_{ij})$$

whereby S is the set of users U_i who issued valid trust assignments.

Each wireless mesh network has a founder $\mathcal{F}$, who plays a distinguished role in the trust agreement scheme. The founder $\mathcal{F}$ has the highest authorization level $\theta_{\mathcal{F}}$ of the network and due to the design of our scheme, no one is able to reach that level if $\mathcal{F}$ does not transfer his trust level directly. If the founder $\mathcal{F}$ leaves the network, the user with the highest trust level becomes the new founder. Trust assignments from $\mathcal{F}$ are summed up directly, without applying ω, to allow the network to grow faster.

Only summing up the particular trust assignments is the simplest and also the most obvious approach. Actually this might not be the best solution, so we give another (more complex) approach in Appendix A.2.

5   Trust Agreement Scheme

In this section, we define a full trust agreement scheme for wireless mesh networks in two steps: a startup phase to create a trust network from scratch and a subsequent phase for normal operation. We make use of the trust agreement technique introduced in the previous section and combine this with trust requirements for particular node positions in wireless mesh networks.

5.1   Startup

Each wireless mesh network is initiated by a founder node $\mathcal{F}$ resp. $U_{\mathcal{F}}$. All nodes U_i that are directly connected to $\mathcal{F}$ (not yet providing connectivity for other nodes) need a trust level of "1" according to the trust requirements from section 4.2.

Then, if an authentication scheme is used, $U_{\mathcal{F}}$ interacts with his neighbor nodes U_i, determining their identity e.g. with a multifactor authentication method. An example for a multifactor authentication may be the verification of: public key fingerprint + MAC/IP address + position in the network + hardware hash. If a recognition scheme is deployed, $U_{\mathcal{F}}$ only requests the identifying attributes (including a proof of possession) of his neighbor nodes U_i.

$U_{\mathcal{F}}$ issues trust assignments $T_{\mathcal{F}i} = (\alpha_{\mathcal{F}i}, \theta_{\mathcal{F}i}, \text{VD})$ and a signature $\sigma_{\mathcal{F}}$ for each, whereby $\alpha_{\mathcal{F}i}$ is 1, $\theta_{\mathcal{F}i}$ is at least 1.0 (depending on the designated trust requirement for the node) and VD a date in the future.

5.2 Normal Operation

From now on, our trust agreement scheme is able to work decentralized, that means an operation without the founder. The trust agreement scheme is operating according to the following conditions:

(1) **IF** Authorization value θ_i at date $D_{\text{near future}}$ < trust requirement
    THEN
    Request trust assignments T_{ji} from surrounding nodes U_j.
(2) **IF** Authorization value θ_j of neighbor U_j < trust requirement
    THEN
    Exclude U_j from routing.
    Do not join network, if U_j provides the only connectivity.
(3) **IF** U_j behaves dishonestly, i.e. dropping or manipulating packets
    THEN
    Reduce assigned trust to U_j by sending a new T_{ij} with lower θ_{ij}.
(4) **IF** U_j behaves trustworthy for a time period $P_{\text{threshold}}$
    THEN
    Raise assigned trust to U_j by sending a new T_{ij} with higher θ_{ij}.
(5) **IF** Revocation assignment T_{ij} was issued to U_j
    THEN
    Trust assignments T_{kj} from U_k with $(\theta_k < \theta_i) \wedge (VD_{kj} < VD_{ij})$ have to be renewed.

Trust assignments T_{ij} are broadcasted through the whole network, enabling all nodes to compute a complete trust view over the mesh network. To make the network more robust, each node broadcasts his own trust value at regular intervals: $H_i := (\alpha_i, \theta_i, \text{VD})$ and a corresponding signature σ_i.

If a trust assignment T_{ji} (intended for U_i) does not reach all hosts, the provided H_i value by U_i will differ from the computed trust value on these (non reached) hosts. In this case, all trust assignments intended for U_i can be requested directly from U_i, who saves them locally.

Both time values $D_{\text{near future}}$ and $P_{\text{threshold}}$ are to be chosen in respect to the practical scenario and the security requirements.

6 Security Considerations

We outline the security of the presented scheme with an informal security proof. At first we give an overview about possible attacks on our scheme, followed by how our scheme is able to resist those attacks. Consider an adversary $\mathcal{A}$ as a probabilistic Turing machine, who has control over all communication channels.

(1) **Trust incrementation.** An adversary gains a higher authorization level by spoofing trust assignments (adressed to him).
(2) **Mutual trust incrementation.** n adversaries increase their authorization levels in a mutual way to gain a higher impact on the mesh network.
(3) **Malicious behavior.** An inside adversary revocates randomly or distributes bad trust assignments to trustful nodes.
(4) **Revocation circumvention.** When an adversary is revocated, he blocks the revocation messages by trustful nodes to stay alive in the mesh network.
(5) **Adding virtual aversaries.** One or a group of adversaries add new virtual adversaries, simulating their whole communication, to infiltrate the network.
(6) **Denial of service.** An adversary exhausts the node's computation power by forcing them to do diffcult and/or multiple computations like signature creation or signature verification.

For resisting the above mentioned attacks, our scheme provides several security mechanisms. In the following, we describe these counter-measures.

(1) **Trust incrementation.** A trust assignment $T_{i\mathcal{A}}$ needs a valid signature σ_i to become valid. Since we can assume that an computational bounded adversary $\mathcal{A}$ is not able to forge a digital signature from an uncompromised user U_i, we conclude that this attack cannot be successful.
(2) **Mutual trust incrementation.** Due to definition 3 (property 3), the issuer's authorization level is always greater or equal than the reveiver's authorization level. We follow that the highest authorization level within a group of adversaries cannot be increased without interaction of external nodes (i.e. trustful users).
Consider k adversaries and $\theta_{\max}$, the authorization level of the most trusted adversary in the group. The maximum trust level, an adversary is able to gain, is: $(k-1) \cdot \frac{\theta_{\max}}{\omega}$.
(3) **Malicious behavior.** If an adversary revocates a trustful member U_i, all issuers of trust assignments to U_i with a lower authorization level than the adversary have to renew their trust assignments towards U_i. Random revocating can thus result in a denial of service attack, leading members with low authorization levels to trigger the authentication process (with U_i) over and over again. Therefore, if their authentication process returns a positive result, the revocation of the adversary will be valued as misbehavior and the adversary's authorization level will be reduced.
The same applies for exaggerated reduction of authorization levels.

(4) **Revocation circumvention.** Trust assignments have a validity date (VD). When this date expires, the authentication process must be renewed (and a new trust assignment must be issued). Thus blocking of revocation assignments does work as long as the other trust assignments towards the adversary are not expired. Remark that trust and revocation assignments are broadcasted through the whole network, so blocking particular messages is not a simple task.

(5) **Adding virtual aversaries.** If one or a group of adversaries create virtual members, the authorization levels of these virtual members are bound by the adversaries' authorization levels, since the adversaries are the only group members who assign trust assignments to the(ir) virtual members. The adversaries impact on the whole mesh network is not raised due to their virtual members, since their own authorization level cannot be increased by their virtual members.

Nevertheless, the problem of virtual members cannot be removed nor detected (despite from some timing or physical aspects), if a virtual member simulates the normal behavior of a trustful mesh network member.

(6) **Denial of service.** To reduce the effect of denial of service when verifying bogus data, we propose RSA with a small public exponent as signature algorithm, since verification is very efficient in this case. Then, signature creation by a trustful user should only be done, if the requestor is authenticated successfully.

Further, all users U_i can make a guess (based on the validity date of their last sent trust assigment T_{ij} to user U_j), when the next request by U_j should arrive. If the request is not received within this time range, U_i may deny to create a new trust assignment T_{ij}.

7   Evaluating the Behavior of other Nodes

In general, evaluating the behavior of other nodes and finding an appropriate trust estimation is not a trivial problem. Although we just have dealt with a general trust agreement solution in this paper, we want to outline shortly, how a behavior evaluation can look like.

There are two major cases to consider: A wireless mesh network with human interaction and an autonomously operated network.

With human interaction, trust assignments can be based on personal experiences with other network participants. This can be the case in community networks like SeattleWireless [2] or MIT Roofnet [1]. The trust opinion towards another user can be influenced by the confidentiality on the forwarded data, he provides. If your neighbor suddenly knows personal facts about you, that you have e.g. communicated via e-mail, you will probably lower his authorization level. Furthermore if you note that your data is not forwarded properly (maybe due to the ratio between forwarded and generated packets) or there is another misbehavior according to section 6, you will do the same. Increasing a trust level is done when noticing an ordinary behavior for a longer time period.

The case is much more complicated in an autonomously operated network, since there is no user interaction. Trust opinions can be based on non malicious behavior (see security considerations) and other actions that can be rated automatically. This is e.g. a reduced reliability when forwarding data, or the modification of data. In order to realize an automatic estimation of a neighbor's trust level, it is recommendable to deploy a local intrusion detection system (IDS).

8   Conclusion

We have presented the first trust agreement scheme that is especially designed for wireless mesh networks. The scheme can be operated in autonomous WMN to establish and maintain a trust relationship between the nodes of the network. Trust in wireless mesh networks consists of an authentication and an authorization part, whereby the first part is the number of nodes who authenticated a particular node and the latter part is used to value the behavior resp. misbehavior of a node.

An important part of our presented scheme is the introduction of abstract trust requirements for different positions of nodes in the network. Obviously, a node that forwards a lot of data from other nodes, needs more trust than a node that does not forward any data. Combining the new trust definition for WMN and the trust requirements, we propose a scheme that withstands a variety of attacks. An informal security proof concludes our contribution.

Future work is to analyze the behavior and misbehavior of mesh nodes in practice and to create rules for categorizing their behavior to be able to react with appropriate trust assignments. There is up to now no concrete proposal for an automated authentication process using a multifactor authentication (i.e. location based, fingerprint of public key, MAC address, hardware hash, etc.). Additionally it is open work to create more exact trust requirements for wireless mesh networks, as it is started in appendix A.1.

References

1. Mit roofnet (2010), http://pdos.csail.mit.edu/roofnet/doku.php
2. Seattlewireless (2010), http://www.seattlewireless.net
3. Cheikhrouhou, O., Laurent-Maknavicius, M., Chaouchi, H.: Security architecture in a multi-hop mesh network. In: 5th Conference on Safety and Architectures Networks, SAR 2006, Seignosse, Landes, France (2006)
4. Eschenauer, L.: On trust establishment in mobile ad-hoc networks. Masterthesis, The Center for Satellite and Hybrid Communication Networks (2002)
5. Eschenauer, L., Gligor, V.D., Baras, J.S.: On trust establishment in mobile *ad-hoc* networks. In: Christianson, B., Crispo, B., Malcolm, J.A., Roe, M. (eds.) Security Protocols 2002. LNCS, vol. 2845, pp. 47–66. Springer, Heidelberg (2004)
6. Kamvar, S.D., Schlosser, M.T., Garcia-Molina, H.: The eigentrust algorithm for reputation management in p2p networks. In: Proceedings of the 12th International Conference on World Wide Web, pp. 640–651. ACM, New York (2003)

7. Kim, Y., Mazzocchi, D., Tsudik, G.: Admission control in peer groups. In: NCA 2003: Proceedings of the Second IEEE International Symposium on Network Computing and Applications, p. 131. IEEE Computer Society, Washington, DC, USA (2003)
8. Lin, X., Ling, X., Zhu, H., Ho, P.-H., Shen, X.S.: A novel localised authentication scheme in ieee 802.11 based wireless mesh networks. Int J. Security and Networks 3(2), 122–132 (2008)
9. Nithyanand, R., Raman, K.: Fuzzy privacy preserving peer-to-peer reputation management. Cryptology ePrint Archive, Report 2009/442 (2009), http://eprint.iacr.org/
10. Noack, A., Spitz, S.: Dynamic threshold cryptosystem without group manager. International Journal of Network Protocols and Algorithms 1(1), 108–121 (2009) ISSN: 1943-3581
11. Resnick, P., Kuwabara, K., Zeckhauser, R., Friedman, E.: Reputation systems. ACM, New York (2000)
12. Stritter, B., Wahl, T.: Schlsselverwaltung und -verteilung. Seminarwork, TU-Darmstadt (2004)
13. Walter, F.: Authentifizierungsstrategien in mobilen adhoc-netzen. Seminarwork, Universität Tübingen (2004)
14. Zhang, Y., Fang, Y.: A secure authentication and billing architecture for wireless mesh networks. Wireless Networks 13(5), 663–678 (2006)

A   Extension for the Authentication Scheme

In this section, we give some proposals for the extension of the introduced trust agreement solution for mesh networks. We begin with an advanced abstract trust requirement scheme that allows a higher granularity.

A.1   Abstract Trust Requirements

It is obvious that nodes in the middle of the mesh network will forward more messages than nodes located at the margin. Given random pairs of nodes, the probability is above average (*Idea*: Pick a random node and partition the network into two halfs. The probability is $\frac{1}{2}$ that a second node is located in the other half. When picking n pairs of nodes, $\frac{n}{2}$ of them will communicate through the middle.) that they communicate through the middle.

Therefore it is smart to expect a higher trust from nodes in the middle of the mesh network than from nodes at the margin. For wireless mesh networks with internet gateways, this is even more complicated, since the communication will not be uniform as supposed in the former case. Nodes near the internet gateway and especially the internet gateway itself need a far higher trust requirement since they are forwarding the majority of the data. In addition to the introduced trust requirement values from section 4.2, we propose new values between "1" and "4": Nodes at the margin need less than "2", nodes in the middle need a trust level near to "3" and nodes in the near of an internet gateway need even more than "3". The internet gateway, however, should not have a trust level below "4".

A.2   Another Approach for Computing Global Trust

Definition 4 (section 4.4) shows how to compute a user's global trust value by summing up the particular local authorization levels and multiplying with the factor ω. This was the most obvious approach. However, there is a whole research field about optimizing trust aggregation e.g. in peer-to-peer, social networks and many more scenarios.

We head to the solution from Nithyanand et al. [9] who dealt with reputation management in peer-to-peer networks. They propose the ordered weighted average (OWA) function for the computation of the global reputation (global trust in our case). The advantage of this solution in comparison to our approach is that lower trust values become more weight, thus creating a more conservative scheme. We redefine Definition 4 as follows:

Definition 4*. *A user U_j's global trust value is computed as:*

$$(\alpha_j, \theta_j) := (\sum_{\forall i: U_i \in S} \alpha_{ij}, \ \frac{\sum_{k=0}^{|S|} sort_k(\{\theta_{ij}\}, \forall i: U_i \in S) \cdot W_k}{s \cdot \sum_{k=0}^{|S|} W_k})$$

whereby S is the set of users U_i who issued valid trust assignments. s is the average number of ascertained trust assignments to the mesh nodes. The function $sort_k$ arranges all input values from the lowest to the highest value and returns the k'th element of this array.

Last but not least there is the weight function W undefined. In [9], the weight function W_k realizes that lower values have a higher impact. We present two alternatives for the weight function W:

$$W_k = W(k) = \sqrt[d]{|S| - k + 1}$$

whereby $d \in \mathbf{Z}_{>0}$. d lowers the impact of the weight function by moving the results closer to 1 and must be chosen in respect to the practical scenario.

The previous solution just achieves that lower values have a higher impact. Another approach is to weight the particular trust assignments by the relation of the transmitted authorization value and the maximum that could have been transmitted.

$$W = \frac{\theta_{ij}}{\theta_i}$$

To prevent recursions, θ_i must be assumed as a fixed value and may not depend on the global trust level of U_j (which is currently computed). If there is no value for θ_i yet, the maximum authorization value used in the network is used for θ_i. The advantage of this solution is that for each trust assignment the intention of the issuing user, whether this is a very positive or quite negative assignment, is included.

Actually, to provide even better results, both proposals can be combined.

Secure E-Auction for Mobile Users with Low-Capability Devices in Wireless Network

Kun Peng

Institute for Infocomm Research

Abstract. The existing secure e-auction schemes are shown to be too costly for users using mobile devices in wireless network as they heavily depend on costly asymmetric cipher. A new secure e-auction efficient enough for devices with low computation capability and limited communication bandwidth is designed in this paper. Most of its operations are symmetric cipher computations and the only asymmetric cipher operations it needs for a bidder are several multiplications. With so high efficiency, its still achieves the normal security properties of secure e-auction.

1 Introduction

E-auction is a popular e-commerce application to distribute resources. In e-auction applications, the bids are often sealed for fairness and security. More precisely, the bidders seal their bids and submit them to one or more auctioneer, who then open the bids and determine the winner. In sealed-bid e-auction applications, the following security properties are usually desired.

- Correctness: the auction result is determined strictly according to the auction rule, while no bid is ignored or tampered with.
- Fairness: all the bidders make their unique choice at the bidding phase and cannot change their bids afterwards such that no bidder can take advantage over other bidders.
- Robustness: in abnormal situations (e.g. at presence of invalid bid), the auction can still run properly.
- Privacy: no secret information (e.g. the losing bid) except for the auction-result is revealed. More precisely, the auction transcript including all the published information in the auction can be simulated by a party without any secret knowledge but the auction result such that the simulating transcript is indistinguishable from the real auction transcript.
- Verifiability: operations of the bidders and the auctioneer(s) can be verified to detect invalid operations.

Usually, multiple auctioneers are employed to share the bid-opening capability such that if the number of malicious auctioneers is not over a threshold, the auction is guaranteed to be correct and private. An obvious solution to protect privacy in e-auction is secure multiparty computation (called secure evaluation

C.A. Ardagna and J. Zhou (Eds.): WISTP 2011, LNCS 6633, pp. 351–360, 2011.

in [11]) as e-auction can be regarded as computation (evaluation) of some secret inputs (the bids) to obtain an output (the auction result). Secure-multiparty-computation-based solution to e-auction includes a few schemes [9,5,4,3,2,8]. As analysed in [11][1], these schemes are not efficient as they employ general multi-party computation techniques designed to evaluate any function. In comparison, special techniques designed to handle e-auction only are usually more efficient. A very popular such method is homomorphic bid opening [6,7,1,10,14,12,11,15]. With this mechanism, each bidder employs a homomorphic encryption algo-rithm or a homomorphic secret sharing algorithm to seal their bids, while the auctioneers exploit homomorphism of the encryption algorithm or secret sharing algorithm to open the bids collectively instead of separately so that no losing bid is revealed. Homomorphic e-auction schemes usually employ binary search to determine the winning bid and are more efficient than the e-auction schemes employing the costly downward search [17,19,20,16,13].

To the best of our knowledge, the existing secure e-auction schemes heav-ily depend on asymmetric cipher in bid sealing, bid opening and verification of validity. So attempts to improve their efficiency are limited by an unchange-able fact: asymmetric cipher operations like bid encryption and decryption and zero knowledge proof usually cost some exponentiations whose bases, exponents and multiplicative moduli are hundreds of bits long. Such exponentiations and large integers involved in them lead to much higher cost than symmetric cipher operations in both computation and communication and they are inevitable in asymmetric-cipher-based e-auction. So, the existing secure e-auction schemes are not suitable for applications with critical requirements on efficiency.

With the development of wireless network and mobile computation-and-communication devices like mobile phone and smart cards, more and more users of e-auction hope to bid using wireless mobile devices in a wireless network. Such devices usually have much lower computation capability and communi-cation bandwidth than the normal computers in high-speed networks. So the existing secure e-auction schemes cannot meet this new trend in e-auction ap-plication. Therefore, if security cannot be compromised in e-auction of mobile users, a more efficient secure e-auction scheme needs to be designed.

The only solution to break the efficiency limit of the existing secure e-auction schemes and design efficient e-auction for mobile users using wireless mobile devices is replacing asymmetric cipher with symmetric cipher. A symmetric-cipher-based e-auction scheme is proposed in this paper. Most operations in it are based on symmetric cipher and the only asymmetric cipher operations for a bidder are several multiplications. No costly exponentiations in asymmetric cipher is needed. With such a strict requirement on efficiency, it still achieves the security properties desired in secure e-auction. Our new e-auction scheme is proposed in two steps. An unverifiable prototype is proposed in Section 2 and it is optimised to be verifiable in Section 4. The new e-auction scheme can

---

[1] It is shown in [11] that the most recent and efficient secure-multiparty-computation-based e-auction scheme [8] is less efficient than some homomorphic e-auction schemes.

be applied to auction applications with critical requirements on efficiency and mobile users can use it to bid in a wireless network.

2   An Unverifiable Prototype

The parameters and symbols used in our e-auctions schemes are as follows.

- There are m auctioneers $A_1, A_2, \ldots, A_m$ and n bidders $B_1, B_2, \ldots, B_n$.
- Integer t smaller than m is the trust threshold such that cooperation of at least t auctioneers is necessary to open any bid.
- The biddable prices are denoted as $P_1, P_2, \ldots, P_L$ in descending order.
- $E_k()$ and $D_k()$ denote the encryption algorithm and decryption algorithm using key k of a symmetric cipher like AES, where the key space, message space and cipher space of them is Z_δ.
- ρ is the largest prime no larger than δ.
- $H()$ is a one-way and collision-resistent hash function to map a long message to Z_ρ.
- $H'()$ is a one-way and collision-resistent hash function to map a long message to Z_δ.
- p_j and q_j are secret large primes chosen by A_j, who publishes $N_j = p_j q_j$. As a asymmetric cipher parameter, each N_j should be larger than any key of the symmetric cipher, which is s useful property.

The unverifiable e-auction protocol is as follows.

1. Initial Phase
   (a) Each B_i chooses $k_{i,j}$ for every A_j, the session key to communicate with A_j. He sends it to A_j in the form $(a_{i,j}, b_{i,j}) = (r_{i,j}^2 \bmod N_j, \ k_{i,j} \oplus H'(r_{i,j} \bmod N_j))$ where $r_{i,j}$ is randomly chosen from Z_{N_j}.
   (b) Each A_j calculates his session keys $k_{i,j} = b_{i,j} \oplus H'(a_{i,j}^{1/2}) \bmod N_j$ for $i = 1, 2, \ldots, n$ using his knowledge of p_j and q_j.
2. Bidding and bid opening
   The auctioneers cooperate to run a binary search for the winning price among the biddable prices. The binary search starts at $P_{L/2}$ and the auctioneers test whether there is any bidder willing to pay that price. If there is, the search goes on to the higher prices; otherwise it goes on to the lower prices. Next search step is just like the previous one, starting in the middle and going on to one side. As the binary search goes on, the searched range of prices becomes smaller and smaller and finally the search ends at the highest price any bidder is willing to pay. The search at a price P_l on the binary searching route is as follows.
   (a) Each B_i chooses his bid at that price: $b_{i,l}$. If he is willing to pay P_l, $b_{i,l}$ is random positive integer in Z_ρ; otherwise it is zero.
   (b) Each B_i builds a polynomial $f_{i,l}(x) = \sum_{j=0}^{t-1} \alpha_{i,l,j} x^j \bmod \rho$ where $\alpha_{i,l,0} = b_{i,l}$ and $\alpha_{i,l,j}$ for $j = 1, 2, \ldots, t-1$ are random integers chosen from Z_ρ.
   (c) Each B_i sends every A_j an encrypted bid share $c_{i,l,j} = E_{k_{i,j}}(f_{i,l}(j))$.

(d) Any t auctioneers can cooperate to calculate the sum of the all the bids at P_l as follows where the set of the indices of the participating auctioneers are denoted as S.

    i. Each A_j calculates $s_{j,l} = \sum_{i=1}^{n} D_{k_{i,j}}(c_{i,l,j}) \bmod \rho$.

    ii. The auctioneers cooperate to calculate $s_l = \sum_{j \in S} s_{j,l} u_j \bmod \rho$ where $u_j = \prod_{k \in S, k \neq j} k/(k - j) \bmod \rho$.

(e) If $s_l > 0$, the search goes to the higher prices; otherwise it goes to the lower prices. Finally, the binary search stops at a price P_L, which is the winning price.

3. Winner identification

The auctioneers opens all the bids at P_L

$$b_i = \sum_{j \in S} s_{i,L,j} u_j \bmod \rho \text{ for } i = 1, 2, \ldots, n.$$

A bidder B_i is a winner if $b_i > 0$. If there is only one winner, he wins the auction. If there are multiple winners, the final winner is determined according to a tie-breaking algorithm. Depending on the concrete auction application, the tie-breaking algorithm may differ. For example, it may employ the first-come-first-win strategy or ask the winners to bid again in a new round of auction.

This prototype is called Protocol 1. It actually employs Shamir's threshold secret sharing based on a polynomial [18] to share the bids among the auctioneers. When the auctioneers and the bidders are honest, Protocol 1 can work and the correct winning price and winner can be found as illustrated in Theorem 1, which is based on homomorphism of polynomial-based threshold secret sharing defined in Definition 1.

Definition 1. *In Shamir's threshold secret sharing, suppose $\beta_{1,1}, \beta_{1,2}, \ldots, \beta_{1,m}$ are shares of β_1 and $\beta_{2,1}, \beta_{2,2}, \ldots, \beta_{2,m}$ are shares of β_2. Then $\beta_{1,1} + \beta_{2,1}, \beta_{1,2} + \beta_{2,2}, \ldots, \beta_{1,m} + \beta_{2,m}$ are shares of $\beta_1 + \beta_2$. More generally, if $\beta_{i,1}, \beta_{i,2}, \ldots, \beta_{i,m}$ are shares of β_i for $i = 1, 2, \ldots, n$, then $\sum_{i=1}^{n} R_i \beta_{i,1}, \sum_{i=1}^{n} R_i \beta_{i,2}, \ldots, \sum_{i=1}^{n} R_i \beta_{i,m}$ are shares of $\sum_{i=1}^{n} R_i \beta_i$ where R_i is any integer.*

Theorem 1. *In Protocol 1, if the bidders and auctioneers are honest, with an overwhelmingly large probability s_l is non-zero if and only if there is at least one bidder willing to pay P_l.*

In Protocol 1, all the bids are shared among the auctioneers and every share is encrypted. So no losing bid is revealed if the employed encryption algorithm is secure and the number of malicious auctioneers is smaller than t. So correctness of auction is achieved in Protocol 1 when the auctioneers and bidders are honest and its privacy is achieved under a threshold thrust assumption. For each bidder, the only operations in asymmetric cipher are m instances of session key distribution, each costing a square. For each auctioneer, the only operations in asymmetric cipher are n instances of session key extraction, each calculating a square root. All the other operations are efficient symmetric cipher operations. Moreover, most of the integers transfered in the communication of Protocol 1 are ρ-bit integers used in symmetric cipher, which are much shorter and cost much less communication than the integers used in the asymmetric-cipher-based e-auction schemes. So high efficiency is achieved in Protocol 1 and it can be applied to mobile bidders with limited computation capability and communication bandwidth. However, when there are dishonest auctioneers and bidders, they can break robustness of Protocol 1 using the attacks described in Section 3.

3   Attacks by Dishonest Auctioneers and Bidders

As the operations of neither the auctioneers nor the bidders are verified in Protocol 1, they may deviate from Protocol 1 and launch some attacks. An obvious attack is for a malicious auctioneer to tamper with the bid shares to lead the auction to an incorrect result. For example, at a price P_l which no bidder is willing to pay, a malicious auctioneer A_j can publish a random $s_{j,l}$ in Z_ρ. As $s_{j,l}$ is randomly distributed in Z_ρ, the secret reconstructed from t shares including it, namely the opened sum of bids at P_l, is non-zero with a probability $1 - 1/\rho$, while the sum of the bids at P_l should be zero as every bidder submits zero at that price to indicate their unwillingness to pay. Under this attack, the auctioneer will declare a winning price higher than the highest bid and cannot find any winner at the that price, and so the auction fails. In this attack, the malicious auctioneer have some other options. For example, he can tamper with the bid share of a bidder at P_l as well to help the bidder to change his bid and win the auction. Moreover, the malicious auctioneer can use a changed bid share to make s_l discovered as zero in secret reconstruction while there is some positive bid at P_l.

One or more dishonest bidder can attack Protocol 1 as well. For example, a malicious bidder may submit a set of inconsistent shares to the auctioneers such that some subsets containing t of them hold shares of zero and some subsets containing t of them hold shares of an positive integer. Usually this attack happens at a high price and a malicious bidder can carry it out as follows to break fairness of the auction.

1. The malicious bidder expects that he can win an auction by bidding P_μ, while the highest price he is willing to pay is a higher price P_ν.
2. He submits his bids at all the prices normally except at P_ν. More precisely, he submits and shares a positive integer at the prices no higher than P_μ and zero at the prices higher than P_μ except for P_ν, while at P_ν, he shares zero among some auctioneers and positive integers among other auctioneers.
3. If the malicious bidder wins the auction at P_μ (e.g. P_ν is not on the binary search route or the auctioneers carrying out bid opening at P_ν get shares of zero from the malicious bidder), the malicious bidder does nothing. If P_μ is not high enough and another bidder submits a positive bid at a price higher than P_μ, the malicious bidder can dispute the auction result and claim his

winning at P_ν. More precisely, if P_ν is higher than the other bidders' positive bids, the malicious bidder claims winning at P_ν and ask the auctioneers sharing zero from him to carry out bid opening at P_ν to recover the malicious bidder's positive bid.

Even if this attack can be detected afterwards and the malicious bidder may be punished, this attack is still harmful as it makes the auction liable to two possible auction results depending on which t auctioneers participate bid opening. Actually, malicious bidders have more options in their attacks, some of which are even simpler and more effective. For example, two malicious bidders can even attack Protocol 1 without collusion of any auctioneer to break its fairness as follows.

1. Two colluding bidders B_μ and B_ν submit and share among the auctioneers d and $\rho - d$ respectively at the highest price they are willing two pay. At other biddable prices, they bid normally (e.g. only submitting non-zero bids at the prices no higher than their expectation of winning bid).
2. After bid opening, if either B_μ or B_ν wins, they accept the auction result and do nothing. If another bidder wins at a price lower than the highest price they are willing two pay, they claim winning and publish their bids at the highest price they are willing two pay to prove their claim.

The two attacks by malicious bidders allow them to win the auction at a price as low as possible while keeping their right to win at a higher price when being challenged by other bidders. This obviously violate fairness of sealed-bid auction, which does not allow any bidder change or choose his bid after bid submission. The attacks in this section shows that robustness of protocol is weak.

4   Verifiable E-Auction for Capability-Limited Mobile Bidders

If the operations of the auctioneers and bidders are verified, the attacks in Section 3 can be prevented. So Protocol 1 can be optimised into a verifiable e-auction protocol to achieve stronger robustness. Of course, high efficiency and suitability for mobile bidders with limited computation capability and communication bandwidth cannot be compromised. More precisely, costly asymmetric cipher operations like zero knowledge proof cannot be adopted in the optimisation. Our optimisation employs several efficient verification mechanisms to detect dishonest behaviours of the bidders or auctioneers. Firstly, the shares of the bids are verified by the auctioneers to guarantee their validity and consistency. More precisely, besides the bid another random integer is shared at every biddable price by each bidder among the auctioneers and the two sets of shares are randomly combined such that validity of the combined shares can guarantee validity of the bid shares with an overwhelmingly large probability. Secondly, the bids from all the bidders are randomized before they are summed up such that no matter how the bidders choose the integers in their bids, the sum of the randomized bids at any price is zero if and only if all the bids at that price are zeros with an overwhelmingly large probability. Thirdly, bid opening is verified against the public commitments of the bidders about their bids such that cheating auctioneers carrying out invalid bid opening can be detected with an overwhelmingly large probability except that all the auctioneers participating in bid opening are dishonest. The optimised e-auction protocol is described in details in the following.

1. Initial phase is not changed and the session keys $k_{i,j}$ for $i = 1, 2, \ldots, n$ and $j = 1, 2, \ldots, m$ are exchanged between the bidders and auctioneers.
2. Bidding and bid opening
   The auctioneers cooperate to run a binary search for the winning price among the biddable prices like in Protocol 1. The search at a price P_l on the binary searching route is as follows.
   (a) Each B_i chooses his bid at that price: $b_{i,l}$. If he is willing to pay P_l, $b_{i,l}$ is random positive integer in Z_ρ; otherwise it is zero.
   (b) Each B_i builds a polynomial $f_{i,l}(x) = \sum_{\kappa=0}^{t-1} \alpha_{i,l,\kappa} x^\kappa \bmod \rho$ where $\alpha_{i,l,0} = b_{i,l}$ and $\alpha_{i,l,\kappa}$ for $\kappa = 1, 2, \ldots, t - 1$ are random integers chosen from Z_ρ.
   (c) Each B_i builds a polynomial $g_{i,l}(x) = \sum_{\kappa=0}^{t-1} \gamma_{i,l,\kappa} x^\kappa \bmod \rho$ where $\gamma_{i,l,\kappa}$ for $\kappa = 0, 1, \ldots, t - 1$ are random integers chosen from Z_ρ.
   (d) Each B_i publishes encrypted bid shares $c_{i,l,j} = E_{k_{i,j}}(f_{i,l}(j))$ for $j = 1, 2, \ldots, m$.
   (e) Each B_i publishes another set of encrypted shares $c'_{i,l,j} = E_{k_{i,j}}(g_{i,l}(j))$ for $j = 1, 2, \ldots, m$.
   (f) $w_{i,l} = H(c_{i,l,1}, c_{i,l,2}, \ldots, c_{i,l,m}, c'_{i,l,1}, c'_{i,l,2}, \ldots, c'_{i,l,m})$ for $i = 1, 2, \ldots, n$ are challenges to validity of bidding and bid opening.
   (g) Each B_i publishes $\phi_{i,l,j} = w_{i,l}\alpha_{i,l,j} + \gamma_{i,l,j} \bmod \rho$ for $j = 0, 1, \ldots, t - 1$.
   (h) Each A_j verifies that his share from B_i is valid as follows.
       i. He calculates $s_{i,l,j} = D_{k_{i,j}}(c_{i,l,j})$.
       ii. He calculates $s'_{i,l,j} = D_{k_{i,j}}(c'_{i,l,j})$.
       iii. He verifies

$$w_{i,l}s_{j,l,j} + s'_{j,l,j} = \sum_{\kappa=0}^{t-1} \phi_{i,l,\kappa} j^\kappa \bmod \rho. \tag{1}$$

   If the verification fails, A_j claims that B_i has sent him an invalid bid share. He publishes $k_{i,j}$, $s_{i,l,j}$ and $s'_{i,l,j}$ such that any one can verify failure of (1) and that $s_{i,l,j}$ and $s'_{i,l,j}$ are shares sent to A_j by B_i. This public verification can detect dishonest bidders, who are kicked out and their bids are deleted.
   (i) After the shares are verified and only valid shares are kept, any t auctioneers can cooperate to calculate the sum of the all the bids at P_l as follows where the set of the indices of the participating auctioneers are denoted as S.
       i. Each auctioneer A_j in S calculates $s_{j,l} = \sum_{i=1}^{n} w_{i,l}s_{i,l,j} \bmod \rho$.
       ii. Each auctioneer A_j in S calculates $s'_{j,l} = \sum_{i=1}^{n} s'_{i,l,j} \bmod \rho$.

    iii. Each auctioneer A_j in S publishes $S_{j,l} = H(s_{j,l}, s'_{j,l})$.

    iv. After $S_{j,l}$ for $j = 1, 2, \ldots, m$ are published, each auctioneer A_j in S publishes $s_{j,l}$ and $s'_{j,l}$.

    v. It is publicly verified $S_{j,l} = H(s_{j,l}, s'_{j,l})$ for $j = 1, 2, \ldots, m$. Any auctioneer failing to pass the verification is required to publish $s_{j,l}$ and $s'_{j,l}$ again. Any auctioneer cannot provide correct $s_{j,l}$ and $s'_{j,l}$ is replaced by one of the $n - t$ stand-by auctioneers.

    vi. $s_l = \sum_{j \in S} s_{j,l} u_j \bmod \rho$ and $s'_l = \sum_{j \in S} s'_{j,l} u_j \bmod \rho$ are calculated where $u_j = \prod_{k \in S, k \neq j} k/(k - j) \bmod \rho$.

    vii. I can be publicly verified

$$s_l + s'_l = \sum_{\kappa=0}^{t-1} (\sum_{i=1}^{n} \phi_{i,l,\kappa}) j^\kappa \bmod \rho. \tag{2}$$

The auction continues only if the verification is passed. If the verification fails, another set of t auctioneers is selected to carry out bid opening. If at least t auctioneers are honest, correct bid opening is obtained.

  (j) If $s_l > 0$, the search goes to the higher prices; otherwise it goes to the lower prices. Finally, the binary search stops at a price P_L, which is the winning price.

3. Winner identification is not changed and all the bids at the winning price are opened to identify the winner(s).

This optimised e-auction protocol is called Protocol 2. It can detects dishonest behaviours of bidders and auctioneers and achieve robustness. Theorem 2, Theorem 3 and Theorem 4 illustrate that invalid operations in bidding and bid opening in Protocol 2 can be detected by the receiving auctioneer. More precisely, Theorem 2 shows that invalid bid sharing by any malicious bidder can be detected by the auctioneers with an overwhelmingly large probability; Theorem 3 shows that no matter how the bidders choose the integers in their bids the auction result is correct with an overwhelmingly large probability if the auctioneers carries out bid opening honestly; Theorem 4 shows that invalid bid opening operation can be detected with an overwhelmingly large probability.

Theorem 2. *If (1) is satisfied for a bidder B_i with a probability larger than $1/\rho$ at a price P_l, any share $s_{i,j,l}$ from that B_i at the price P_l is guaranteed to be the jth share generated by a unique polynomial.*

Theorem 3. *If the auctioneers follow Protocol 2 to recover s_l, $s_l = 0$ iff $b_{1,l}, b_{2,l}, \ldots, b_{n,l}$ are all zeros with an overwhelmingly large probability.*

Theorem 4. *Unless all the t auctioneers in S are dishonest, satisfaction of (2) with a non-negligible probability guarantees that the auctioneers strictly follow Protocol 2 to recover s_l.*

All the additional verification operations in Protocol 2 are symmetric cipher operations, which are efficient in both computation (using simple calculation) and communication (transferring short integers). So they do not increase cost of the e-auction scheme significantly. Therefore, like Protocol 1, Protocol 2 is an efficient e-auction protocol suitable for mobile users with limited computation capability and communication bandwidth.

5   Conclusion

The secure e-auction scheme proposed in this paper satisfies the desired security properties in e-auction and is very efficient. Most of its operations only involve symmetric cipher so are efficient in both computation and communication. The only asymmetric cipher operations needed in the new e-auction scheme are several squares for a bidder and some calculation of square root using knowledge of factorization of multiplicative modulus for an auctioneer. In comparison, the existing secure e-auction schemes [9,5,4,3,2,8,17,19,20,16,13,6,7,1,10,14,12,11,15] cost a lot of modulo exponentiations in asymmetric cipher operations for both the bidders and auctioneers and transfer large integers used in asymmetric cipher. So our e-auction scheme is especially suitable for e-auction schemes requiring both strong security and high efficiency like e-auction in wireless network with mobile users who use mobile wireless devices with limited computation capability and communication bandwidth.

References

1. Abe, M., Suzuki, K.: $M+1$-st price auction using homomorphic encryption. In: Naccache, D., Paillier, P. (eds.) PKC 2002. LNCS, vol. 2274, pp. 115–124. Springer, Heidelberg (2002)
2. Cachin, C.: Efficient private bidding and auctions with an oblivious third party. In: The 6th ACM Conference on Computer and Communications Security (1999), http://www.tml.hut.fi/~helger/crypto/link/protocols/auctions.html
3. Cramer, R., Damgård, I.B., Nielsen, J.B.: Multiparty computation from threshold homomorphic encryption. In: Pfitzmann, B. (ed.) EUROCRYPT 2001. LNCS, vol. 2045, pp. 280–299. Springer, Heidelberg (2001)
4. Jakobsson, M., Juels, A.: Mix and match: Secure function evaluation via ciphertexts. In: Okamoto, T. (ed.) ASIACRYPT 2000. LNCS, vol. 1976, pp. 143–161. Springer, Heidelberg (2000)
5. Juels, A., Szydlo, M.: A two-server, sealed-bid auction protocol. In: Blaze, M. (ed.) FC 2002. LNCS, vol. 2357, pp. 72–86. Springer, Heidelberg (2003)
6. Kikuchi, H., Harkavy, M., Tygar, J.D.: Multi-round anonymous auction. In: Proceedings of the First IEEE Workshop on Dependable and Real-Time E-Commerce Systems, pp. 62–69 (June 1998)
7. Kikuchi, H., Hotta, S., Abe, K., Nakanishi, S.: Distributed auction servers resolving winner and winning bid without revealing privacy of bids. In: Proc. of International Workshop on Next Generation Internet (NGITA 2000), pp. 307–312. IEEE, Los Alamitos (2000)
8. Kurosawa, K., Ogata, W.: Bit-slice auction circuit. In: Gollmann, D., Karjoth, G., Waidner, M. (eds.) ESORICS 2002. LNCS, vol. 2502, pp. 24–38. Springer, Heidelberg (2002)

9. Naor, M., Pinkas, B., Sumner, R.: Privacy perserving auctions and mechanism design. In: ACM Conference on Electronic Commerce 1999, pp. 129–139 (1999)

10. Omote, K., Miyaji, A.: A second-price sealed-bid auction with the discriminant of the p-th root. In: Blaze, M. (ed.) FC 2002. LNCS, vol. 2357, pp. 57–71. Springer, Heidelberg (2003)

11. Peng, K., Boyd, C., Dawson, E.: A multiplicative homomorphic sealed-bid auction based on goldwasser-micali encryption. In: Zhou, J., López, J., Deng, R.H., Bao, F. (eds.) ISC 2005. LNCS, vol. 3650, pp. 374–388. Springer, Heidelberg (2005)

12. Peng, K., Boyd, C., Dawson, E.: Optimization of electronic first-bid sealed-bid auction based on homomorphic secret sharing. In: Dawson, E., Vaudenay, S. (eds.) Mycrypt 2005. LNCS, vol. 3715, pp. 84–98. Springer, Heidelberg (2005)

13. Peng, K., Boyd, C., Dawson, E., Viswanathan, K.: Non-interactive auction scheme-with strong privacy. In: Lee, P.J., Lim, C.H. (eds.) ICISC 2002. LNCS, vol. 2587, pp. 407–420. Springer, Heidelberg (2003)

14. Peng, K., Boyd, C., Dawson, E., Viswanathan, K.: Robust, privacy protecting and publicly verifiable sealed-bid auction. In: Deng, R.H., Qing, S., Bao, F., Zhou, J. (eds.) ICICS 2002. LNCS, vol. 2513, pp. 147–159. Springer, Heidelberg (2002)

15. Peng, K., Bao, F.: Efficiency improvement of homomorphic E-auction. In: Katsikas, S., Lopez, J., Soriano, M. (eds.) TrustBus 2010. LNCS, vol. 6264, pp. 238–249. Springer, Heidelberg (2010)

16. Sako, K.: An auction protocol which hides bids of losers. In: Imai, H., Zheng, Y. (eds.) PKC 2000. LNCS, vol. 1751, pp. 422–432. Springer, Heidelberg (2000)

17. Sakurai, K., Miyazaki, S.: A bulletin-board based digital auction scheme with bidding down strategy -towards anonymous electronic bidding without anonymous channels nor trusted centers. In: Proc. International Workshop on Cryptographic Techniques and E-Commerce, pp. 180–187. City University of Hong Kong Press, Hong Kong (1999)

18. Shamir, A.: How to share a secret. Communication of the ACM 22(11), 612–613 (1979)

19. Suzuki, K., Kobayashi, K., Morita, H.: Efficient sealed-bid auction using hash chain. In: Won, D. (ed.) ICISC 2000. LNCS, vol. 2015, pp. 183–191. Springer, Heidelberg (2001)

20. Watanabe, Y., Imai, H.: Reducing the round complexity of a sealed-bid auction protocol with an off-line ttp. In: STOC 2000, pp. 80–86. ACM, New York (2000)

Privacy Respecting Targeted Advertising for Social Networks

Christian Kahl[1], Stephen Crane[2], Markus Tschersich[1], and Kai Rannenberg[1]

[1] Goethe University Frankfurt, Chair of Mobile Business & Multilateral Security,
Grüneburgplatz 1, 60629 Frankfurt am Main, Germany
[2] Hewlett-Packard Labs, Long Down Avenue, Stoke Gifford, BRISTOL BS34 8QZ UK
{Christian.Kahl,Markus.Tschersich,
Kai.Rannenberg,PICOS}@m-chair.net, Stephen.Crane@hp.com

Abstract. Online Social Networks form an increasingly important part of people's lives. As mobile technologies improve accessibility, concerns about privacy and trust are more apparent as advertising becomes a critical component of most social network's economic model. In this paper we describe the PICOS project's research into privacy preserving advertising options for social networks. We introduce an architecture that includes new concepts and technologies specifically designed to improve privacy and trust as well as advertising opportunities within social networks.

Keywords: Communities, Identity Management, Mobile Advertising, Mobile Marketing, Mobile Social Networks, Privacy, Trust.

1 Introduction

Online social networks[1] such as Facebook, MySpace, and LinkedIn, provide communication services that support the activities of virtual and real world communities (cf. [1], [2], [3]). Nowadays people spend increasing amounts of work and leisure time in using these services for professional and private collaboration and communication purposes. Mobile communication also allows the provision of services that make use of context information (e.g., location, time), thereby enabling a deeper integration of peoples' virtual (mobile) and real world communities (e.g., Loopt, Junaio, match2blue)[2]. Advertising, as a specific marketing activity, is an important way for social network providers to generate revenues, and is hence an integral part of many providers' business models. However, while classical online display advertising is focused on the more general target groups, with advertising activities in social networks often lacking success [2, 22, 23], advertisers are now looking for greater assurance that targeted audiences will be interested in their offerings. Social networks are especially attractive for targeted advertising and viral marketing campaigns [18].

---

[1] Also referred to as "social communities". If not stated otherwise, both terms are used synonymously in this paper.

[2] www.loopt.com, www.junaio.com, www.match2blue.com

C.A. Ardagna and J. Zhou (Eds.): WISTP 2011, LNCS 6633, pp. 361–370, 2011.
© IFIP International Federation for Information Processing 2011

However, the inclusion of personal information regarding users in these activities raises questions about user privacy and the use of their personal data. The desire by users for privacy within social networks on the one hand, and the need for advertising in these social networks on the other hand, creates a certain tension between the interests of the involved stakeholders. A balance needs to be achieved between these partially diverging interests of the involved parties, namely users, advertisers and the social network provider [3].

1.1 Research Question and Approach

Consequently, a new approach to identity management in social networking services is required in order to meet the stakeholders' different needs. Within the PICOS project[3], we had the goal to develop such a new approach to identity management that would enhance trust, privacy and identity management aspects of social networking services, while at the same time enabling 3rd party services including marketing and advertising.

PICOS started with a phase of preliminary activities, including the analysis of related contemporary research and an investigation of the context of communities (e.g., legal, technical and economic aspects) (c.f. [9], [10], [3]). Based on requirements of three exemplary mobile communities (anglers, online gamers, taxi drivers), we designed a community platform architecture including concepts to address the gathered requirements [5]. The developed concepts were implemented as prototype community platform and community applications, which we subsequently tested in user trials and evaluated with regard to trust, privacy, usability, ergonomics and legal issues (c.f. [17]).

This paper reports on the PICOS community platform architecture [5], focusing in particular on the targeted advertising component[4]. The following section provides a brief overview of the PICOS architecture and its concepts. Section 3 focuses on the advertising component, as a part of the architecture. Section 4 briefly provides details about the prototypical implementation of the architecture and the advertising component implementation in particular. Section 5 provides an overview of related work and section 6 concludes and indicates aspects for further research.

2   PICOS Architecture

The PICOS architecture has been designed to satisfy the needs of several stakeholders, and in so doing minimise the tensions around privacy and trust that would otherwise discourage contributions from any or all parties' involvement in the community. To address the users requirements, the architecture consists of components which provide different functionalities (concepts).

PICOS functionality is delivered as a service. Services could be hosted locally, but in the case of PICOS they are hosted centrally. In this client-server topology, clients (e.g. smart phones) process local services but rely on the social network for shared services and for services that are too demanding (in terms of computing and storage resources) for the client to host.

---

[3] The research leading to these results has received funding from the European Community's Seventh Framework Programme (FP7/2007-2011) under grant agreement n° 215056.
[4] For a more general overview of the PICOS architecture, see further [17].

2.1 Stakeholders

In situations where personal information is being shared, it is common for the various stakeholders to have different opinions about the use of the data. In social networks these stakeholders are:

- Members/users: The subject of the personal data.
- Community providers: Community service and/or communications provider.
- Community operators: The entity responsible for the operation of the community.
- 3rd parties: E.g. advertisers, regulators, external service providers.

2.2 Components and Concepts

The PICOS architecture comprises a number of new concepts designed to enhance user privacy. The overall intention is to provide users with tools that help them manage their visibility within and outside of the community. The three main categories of concepts are:

Enhanced Identity Management. Based on the concept of mobile identity management [11], the PICOS architecture supports users in managing the disclosure of their current position and mobile identity in communities. E.g. *Sub-communities* help users in selectively sharing personal information, as they represent a restricted area in which the sharing of content is limited to a sub-group of community members. *Partial Identities* [12] allow users to create different identities for use in different contexts and purposes. With the help of Partial Identities users are able to have a set of several identities in a single community, and decide for each identity what personal information they want to disclose.

User controlled Information Flows. A balance is needed between revealing (publishing) personal information in order to use functionalities provided by the community, and maintaining a degree of privacy [3]. *Location Blurring* gives users the enhanced ability to hide their exact position without being completely invisible to others. It foresees the obfuscation of a user's position on a map at various levels. The users can control, who is able to see their exact and their blurred position. *Privacy Policies* enable users to selectively define policies that control who is allowed to see which kind of personal information.

Privacy Awareness Support. Managing privacy by means of Partial Identities is a complex task. The *Privacy Advisor* component is designed to provide guidance on privacy related matters that may affect members as they interact with the community. Privacy (and trust) is subjective, and it is often difficult to find a single 'right answer' to questions and concerns about privacy. Hence, the Privacy Advisor is context sensitive and provides hints in specific situations that involve users' personal information (e.g. disclosure of location information, registration and profile management). It warns users when disclosure of information might place their privacy at risk.

3 The Advertising Component

The advertising component enables advertising activities to be carried out with due consideration of context and users' privacy preferences, managed by the aforementioned concepts. The foundation for this component was initially outlined in [24]. Within PICOS we targeted an exemplary application that was extended to include this advertising approach, resulting in a concrete social network service solution that gives users control over the use of their personal data. This unique approach is part of our community platform architecture and within one of our community application prototypes (gaming community prototype).

3.1 Approach

Communication can be regarded as one of the main activities conducted in social networks [32]. Hence, in order to include marketing (and in particular advertising) activities into social networks, these activities need to be integrated into the context of the communication processes, in order to be able to receive the attention of the participating users [24, 25]. Advertising can contribute to the communication in two ways: First, advertisers can provide targeted communication (targeted advertising) to social network users (Business-to-Consumer communication (B2C)). Second, advertisers can support the communication between users (viral marketing) (Consumer-to-Consumer communication (C2C)). While the targeting of advertising activities provides a benefit to the targeted users [2, 33], at the same time viral marketing is used in existing social networks[5] to benefit from the intensive social interactions between users. By supporting both in a novel way, communication between marketers and users is tailored more to an individual user's needs and is consequently more relevant. Further, users are encouraged to communicate with each other about such relevant advertisements [20, 21].

3.2 Component Elements

To support B2C and C2C communication processes, the social network provider acts as an intermediary between advertisers and users. This ensures that personal data of users is neither given to 3rd parties nor that 3rd parties have any direct access to it. Instead, the social network provider (e.g. a game developer in the case of the gaming community example) serves both the advertisers and the consumers, while respecting their specific interests (e.g. privacy of users).

Support of B2C communication. In order to support direct communication between advertiser and user, the social network provider needs to identify the users for which a particular advertisement might be relevant. He thereby conducts a matching operation between the users (consumers) and advertisers (represented by advertisements), based on profile, context and communication information. More targeted advertisements generally receive more attention by users, especially with regard to mobile usage scenarios [27, 36]. On the other hand, users can set their privacy preferences (e.g. using privacy policies and blurring settings) in response to the purpose of targeted

---

[5] See e.g. Facebook Advertising (www.facebook.com/advertising).

advertising. This enables social network provider to respect privacy preferences and satisfy users' needs for relevant advertisements, while at the same time enabling advertisers' to fulfil their interests and reach their target audience.

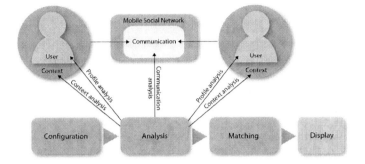

Fig. 1. The process to support targeted advertising (B2C) (Based on [24])

The whole process of supporting B2C communication can be divided into four steps, which are reflected in the design of the PICOS advertising component as follows (Figure 1).

Configuration. The advertising component provides a graphical interface, which allows configuring different advertising activities. As similarly described in e.g. [28, 29, 35] the advertiser can configure, which message he wants to deliver and whom he wants to target. Hence, the dimensions the advertiser needs to configure are the advertisement itself and the target profile. The form of an advertisement can be a selection of different types, e.g. banners, pop-up, etc. By defining the attributes of the target profile, the advertiser can describe his targeted users. Example: Target Profile: "male, 20-35 years, within 2 km around my shop, between 12 h and 18 h, key word in communication: 'lunch'"

The advertiser can configure how many attributes need to be equal in order to achieve a "matching" of target profile and user profile. For each attribute, the advertiser can also configure if this attribute needs to match in every case. In such a situation, no matching can be achieved if these "necessary" attributes are not fulfilled. E.g., if a user needs to be at least 18 years of age in order to receive an advertisement.

Analysis. In order to determine which advertisement might be relevant for which user, information about the user is needed, which is gathered from the user profile, the context and communications/interactions with other users [24]. The user profile contains attributes such as age, interests and favourite locations. The context is mainly described by the current location of the user (as geo-coordinates) in combination with the time and information which might be derived from the location (e.g. current weather conditions at this location). Communications could be all kinds of interactions in which a user communicates with other users, e.g. directly (mailing or chatting) as well as indirectly (e.g. via contributions in sub-communities). Such additional information, which has not been combined in previous approaches in a similar way, allows a more precise characterization of users and to draw conclusions about what users are doing, in addition to who they are. The gathered information leads to a dynamic user profile, which contains the profile, the context and communication information about the user.

Matching. The dynamic user profile characterises the user in his current context. In the "Matching" process the dynamic user profile and the target profiles are compared.

There are different ways to realise such matching in an actual implementation, and which of these ways is chosen might depend on various economic, organisational or technical reasons. In our case a comparison of attributes is conducted. If a pre-defined number of attributes are equal, a match is given. In the approach described by [24], the matching additionally contains a comparison between the communicating users. This is to identify similarities and common interests between them and present matching advertisements not only to one but to both of them.

Display. In the final step of the process, the actual advertisement needs to be shown to the identified matching users. In practice this also includes further considerations regarding the users' device. It might be necessary to adapt the advertisement due to technical specifications or limitations of particular devices and/or operating systems.

Support of C2C communication. The support of C2C communication is based on the principle of viral marketing, that is to initiate a marketing message and let it spread from one user to other users (who distribute it further) like a virus [cf. 18]. The goal here is to establish and support such a viral (marketing) process.

In literature and practice there is a varying understanding about how viral marketing works in detail [26]. In many social networks viral marketing is conducted by introducing a product or brand to the community (e.g. with a related profile or group on Facebook). The difference in our case is that viral marketing is designed to work in a targeted way, in order to address several opinion leaders who further spread the message [16]. This process comprises the following steps:

Configuration. As in B2C support the advertiser has various options to configure an advertisement and to describe the targeted users, including targeted characteristics (e.g. age, interests). The configuration also includes options regarding the form of the delivery (e.g. pop-up, text message, etc.).

The distinctiveness is that the advertiser defines the characteristics of the "key users", which should be addressed in order to further spread the advertisement. These users are regarded as opinion leaders, which have a stronger influence on their social surrounding [21, 26]. Depending on the actual advertisement which shall be delivered, there are different definitions of who the "key users" are, e.g. users who are very active with regard to communication, or users who have many relationships to other users (friends) or certain characteristics (e.g. a certain age). The definition of key users might also be a combination of such different characteristics.

Analysis & Matching. The analysis of user information (profile, context, communication) leads to a dynamic user profile, consisting of profile, context and communication information, as described previously. In the "matching" step, the characteristics of the key users (target profile) are compared to the dynamic profile of a user. The difference to the Matching process for targeted advertising is that only a limited number of matching users are addressed, namely the key users. These users are the users which match best with the target profile and fulfil the mentioned characteristics of key users.

Seeding. This phase includes the actual delivery of the advertising message to the identified key users, the so-called "seeding", in order to allow them to pass on the delivered message. Depending on how an advertisement is configured the form of delivery may vary. To support the action of forwarding (spreading) of the delivered message, advertisements need to contain a possibility to immediately and easily share them with other users (e.g. context Link on a specific site, Banner with possibility to forward, etc.).

Triggering. The whole viral marketing process is intended towards the viral distribution of the advertisement. Hence, an important part in this approach is not only to identify adequate users and provide them with the advertising message, as described before, but also to provide or support a motivation to these Users to forward advertisements they receive [30]. One step to support this is already the targeting itself, considering that we aim to provide only highly relevant advertisements to users. Further, an already existing intrinsic motivation of users to forward advertised messages, can be supported by the availability of technical possibilities, which allow and simplify a further recommendation to other users (e.g. "forward" button).

4 Prototypical Implementation

The PICOS architecture is a service oriented architecture consisting of 1) access and user management features, and 2) service delivery features. The current J2ME[6] based embodiment consists of a set of hosted web-based services, which implement the described concepts.

The advertising component is implemented based on the example of "commercial points of interest" (CPOI), e.g. cafés, shops, etc. For these CPOI's, a target user profile can be defined for some exemplary attributes (e.g. age). A matching is realised by comparing the attributes between this profile and profiles of users within a certain proximity of the CPOI. Under consideration of users' privacy preferences, advertisements are provided to matching users. The PICOS Privacy policies enable users to select the information which may be used for advertising. A recommendation mechanism further allows supporting user-to-user communication (C2C). Therefore a recommendation button is directly integrated in an advertisement.

5 Related Work

The aspect of privacy in online social networks is discussed intensively in the research area (cf. e.g. [13, 14, 15]), but there with focus on online social networks usually not considering the special aspects of mobile social networking services.

---

[6] Java 2 Platform, Micro Edition (http://www.oracle.com/technetwork/java/javame/overview).

Other projects, such as PRIME[7], PrimeLife[8], PEPERS[9] and DAIDALOS[10], have carried out work in this area. However, their work was focused on different aspects, e.g. on privacy and identity management in general (PRIME, PEPERS, DAIDALOS) or privacy in communities but not with regard to a specific application domain (PrimeLife). There are also some concepts in theory and practice which aim to help the user with regard to privacy. For instance, the "Privacy Bird" from AT&T[11] advises users on the privacy of website, using a P3P[12] policy matching algorithm. The Trustguide[13] research confirmed that openness backed up by education, which together provide enhanced understanding and awareness, engenders trust. This is particularly true when applied to situations involving privacy.

Regarding work in relation to the advertising approach, there are a few publications that focus on this aspect with regard to social networks. While some address general aspects, such as business models [4, 25], many focus on the application of viral marketing in the context of communities (e.g. [6, 7, 8, 31]). As mentioned, [24] is concerned with a deeper integration of marketing into the communication processes within social networks, and provides the basis for the advertising approach described in this paper.

6   Conclusion

The PICOS Architecture serves as a basis for integrating privacy enhancing concepts and advanced advertising into (mobile) community infrastructures. The architecture enables providers, users and involved 3rd party stakeholders to provide and use privacy enhancing social networking features. The advertising approach adopted by the architecture shows how a deeper integration of advertising is possible in (mobile) social networks and how the tension between diverging interests of the involved stakeholders can be addressed. The prototypical implementation of the PICOS architecture has further shown the feasibility of enclosed concepts such as those focused on in this paper. The currently ongoing analysis and evaluation of the PICOS user trial results will give additional insights on this.

Nevertheless, further research on the integration, usage and benefits of the concepts, and in particular advertising in social networks, remains a challenge for advertisers and social network providers. Much research in this area considers specific aspects of marketing or advertising. However, holistic approaches are needed in order to consider the different stakeholders in social networks and the factors which influence the success of marketing activities. In one of our next steps our research activities will focus on specific application scenarios, considering the diversity of social networks and as well the diversity of products and brands which are subject to marketing.

---

[7] www.prime-project.eu
[8] www.primelife.eu
[9] www.pepers.org
[10] www.ist-daidalos.org
[11] www.privacybird.org/e
[12] www.w3.org/P3P/
[13] http://trustguide.org.uk/

References

1. Nielsen: Critical Mass - Worldwide State of the Mobile Web. Nielsen Mobile (2008)
2. Nielsen: Global Faces and Networked Places - A Nielsen report on Social Networking's New Global Footprint. Nielsen (2009)
3. Liesebach, K., Scherner, T.: D2.4 Requirements. Public Deliverable of EU Project PICOS (2008),
   http://www.picos-project.eu/Public-Deliverables.29.0.html
4. Hoegg, R., et al.: Overview of business models for Web 2.0 communities. In: Proceedings of Workshop 'Gemeinschaften in Neuen Medien', pp. 33–49. TUD Press, Dresden (2006)
5. Crane, S.: D4.2 Architecture v2. Public Deliverable of EU Project PICOS (2010),
   http://www.picos-project.eu/Public-Deliverables.29.0.html
6. Leskovec, J., Adamic, L.A., Huberman, B.A.: The Dynamics of Viral Marketing. ACM Trans. Web 1, 1 (2007), Article 5
7. Kempe, D., Kleinberg, J., Tardos, É.: Maximizing the Spread of Influence through a Social Network. In: Proceedings of Ninth ACM SIGKDD International Conference on Knowledge Discovery and Data Mining (SIGKDD 2003), Washington, DC, USA (2003)
8. Hartline, J., Mirrokni, V.S., Sundararajan, M.: Optimal Marketing Strategies over Social Networks. In: Proceedings of the International World Wide Web Conference Committee 2008 (WWW 2008), Beijing, China, April 21-25 (2008)
9. Schrammel, J., Köffel, C., Weiss, S., Kahl, C.: D2.2 Categorisation of Communities. Public Deliverable of EU Project PICOS (2008),
   http://www.picos-project.eu/Public-Deliverables.29.0.html
10. Kosta, E., Dumortier, J.: D2.3 Contextual Framework. Public Deliverable of EU Project PICOS (2008),
    http://www.picos-project.eu/Public-Deliverables.29.0.html
11. Müller, G., Wohlgemuth, S.: Study on Mobile Identity Management, Public Deliverable of EU Project FIDIS (2005),
    http://www.fidis.net/fileadmin/fidis/deliverables/
    fidis-wp3-del3.3.study_on_mobile_identity_management.pdf
12. Hansen, M., Berlich, P., Camenisch, J., Clauß, S., Pfitzmann, A., Waidner, M.: Privacy-Enhancing Identity Management. Information Security Technical Report 9(1), 35–44 (2004)
13. Chew, M., Balfanz, D., Laurie, B.: Undermining Privacy in Social Networks. In: Web 2.0 Security and Privacy (in conj. with IEEE Symposium on Security and Privacy) (2008)
14. Adu-Oppong, F., Gardiner, C.K., Kapadia, A., Tsang, P.P.: Social Circles: Tackling Privacy in Social Networks. In: Proceedings of the 4th Symposium on Usable Privacy and Security (SOUPS 2008), Pittsburgh, Pennsylvania, July 23-25 (2008)
15. Hiltz, S.R., Passerini, K.: Trust and Privacy Concern Within Social Networking Sites: A Comparison of Facebook and MySpace. In: Proceedings of AMCIS 2007 (2007)
16. Dobele, A., Lindgreen, A., Beverland, M., Vanhamme, J., van Wijk, R.: Why pass on viral messages? Because they connect emotionally. Business Horizons 50(4), 291–304 (2007)
17. Kahl, C., Böttcher, K., Tschersich, M., Heim, S., Rannenberg, K.: How to Enhance Privacy and Identity Management for Mobile Communities: Approach and User Driven Concepts of the PICOS Project. In: Rannenberg, K., Varadharajan, V., Weber, C. (eds.) SEC 2010. IFIP Advances in Information and Communication Technology, vol. 330, pp. 277–288. Springer, Heidelberg (2010)
18. Kotler, P., Armstrong, G.: Principles of Marketing, 11th edn. Prentice-Hall, New Jersey (2006)

19. Kollmann, T.: E-Venture, 1st edn., Gabler, Germany (2006)
20. Schulz, S., Mau, G., Löffler, S.: Virales Marketing im Web 2.0. In: Kilian, T., Hass, B., Walsh, G. (Hg.) Web 2.0 – Neue Perspektiven im E-Business, pp. 249–268. Springer, Heidelberg (2007)
21. Dobele, A., Toleman, D., Beverland, M.: Controlled infection! Spreading the brand message through viral marketing. Business Horizons 48(2), 143–149 (2005)
22. Study on Social Network Adertisements. Linkshare (2009), http://www.netimperative.com/news/2009/august/social-network-ads-2018failing-to-engage-users2019 (retrieved on 2010-06-08)
23. IDC Report. U.S. Consumer Online Attitudes Survey Results, Part III: Social Networking. IDC (2008), http://www.idc.com/getdoc.jsp?containerId=214899 (retrieved on 2010-06-08)
24. Kahl, C., Albers, A.: Towards reasonable Revenue Streams through Marketing in Mobile Social Networks. In: Proceedings of the Multikonferenz Wirtschaftsinformatik (MKWI), Göttingen, Germany (2010)
25. Palmer, A., Koenig-Lewis, N.: An experiential, social network-based approach to direct marketing. Direct Marketing: An International Journal 3(3), 162–176 (2009)
26. Phelps, J.E., Lewis, R., Mobilio, L., Perry, D., Raman, N.: Viral Marketing or Electronic Word-of-Mouth Advertising: Examining Consumer Responses and Motivations to Pass Along Email. Journal of Advertising Research 44(4), 333–348 (2004)
27. Ho, S.Y.: Opportunities and challenges of mobile personalization: An exploratory study. In: Newell, S., Whitley, E.A., Pouloudi, N., Wareham, J., Mathiassen, L. (eds.) Proceedings of 17th European Conference on Information Systems (ECIS 2009), Verona, Italy, pp. 1211–1222 (2009)
28. Albers, A., Kahl, C.: Prototypical Implementation of an Intermediary Platform for Context-sensitive Mobile Marketing Applications. In: Proceedings of the 14th Americas Conference on Information Systems (AMCIS), Toronto, Canada (2008)
29. Commercialisation of Context-sensitive Mobile Attention in Mobile Media Markets - Design Recommendations for Mobile Marketing Providers, Schriften zum Mobile Commerce und zum Mobilfunk, Verlag Dr. Kovač, Hamburg, Germany
30. Pousttchi, K., Turowski, K., Wiedemann, D.G.: Mobile Viral Marketing - Ein State of the Art. In: Bauer, H.H., Dirks, T., Bryant, M.D. (Hrsg.) (eds.) Erfolgsfaktoren des Mobile Marketing. Strategien, Konzepte und Instrumente, pp. S.289–S.304. Springer, Berlin (2008)
31. Subramani, M., Rajagopalan, B.: Knowledge Sharing and Influence in Online Social Networks via Viral Marketing. Communications of the ACM 46(12), 300–307 (2003)
32. Carroll, E.: Success Factors of Online Social Networks. The University of North Carolina, Chapel Hill, USA (2007)
33. Ho, S.Y., Kwok, S.H.: The Attraction of Personalized Service for Users in Mobile Commerce: An Empirical Study. ACM SIGecom Exchanges 3(4), 10–18 (2002)
34. Schmidt, A., Beigl, M., Gellersen, H.-W.: There is more to Context than Location. Computers and Graphics 20, S.893–S.901 (1998)
35. Hristova, N., O'Hare, G.M.P.: Ad-me: Wireless Advertising Adapted to the User Location, Device and Emotions. In: Proceedings of 37th Hawaii International Conference on System Sciences, Hawaii, USA (2005)
36. Beales, H.: The Value of Behavioral Targeting (Study), Networked Advertising Initative (2010)

Privacy Protection for Smartphones: An Ontology-Based Firewall

Johann Vincent, Christine Porquet, Maroua Borsali,
and Harold Leboulanger

GREYC Laboratory, ENSICAEN - CNRS
University of Caen-Basse-Normandie,
14000 Caen, France
{johann.vincent,christine.porquet}@greyc.ensicaen.fr,
{maroua.borsali,harold.leboulanger}@ecole.ensicaen.fr

Abstract. With the outbreak of applications for smartphones, attempts
to collect personal data without their user's consent are multiplying and
the protection of users privacy has become a major issue. In this paper,
an approach based on semantic web languages (OWL and SWRL) and
tools (DL reasoners and ontology APIs) is described. The proposed semantic firewall takes its decisions (authorize or forbid some action) on
the basis of a set of privacy protection rules grounded on two ontologies respectively modeling identity of mobile phone's users and privacy
policies. To validate this ontology-based approach, a proof of concept
involving a real privacy threat scenario is implemented in Java and the
porting of the semantic firewall to the Android platform is outlined.

Keywords: Privacy protection, ontologies, smartphones, semantic
firewall.

1 Introduction

In the past few years, the mobile market has rapidly evolved from feature phones
to smartphones [1]. It is assumed that the smartphone market will continue to
grow in the upcoming years [2]. That evolution is impacting the mobile application market. In particular, the distribution model is progressively switching
from a market controlled by telecom operators to online markets such as the
App Store or the Android Market. The result of this opening is the recent boom
in the number of mobile applications. Since many of these applications are collecting personal data with or without the consent of the user [3], the issue of an
enhanced protection of the user's privacy must be addressed.

In this paper, we claim that an ontology-based firewall can effectively protect
the user's digital identity and personal data. Ontologies provide a shared vocabulary, which can be used to model a domain, that is, the type of objects and/or
concepts that exist, together with their properties and relations [4]. Thanks to
an explicit knowledge representation of the data requested by any mobile application, the firewall can determine whether the application requests are permitted
or forbidden, according to predefined customized security policies.

C.A. Ardagna and J. Zhou (Eds.): WISTP 2011, LNCS 6633, pp. 371–380, 2011.
© IFIP International Federation for Information Processing 2011

This paper is organized as follows. In section 2, several ontologies for digital identity and privacy protection mechanisms are reviewed and discussed. In section 3, our approach to achieve privacy protection for smartphones is detailed: the global architecture of the firewall is described, as well as the two distinct ontologies that have been specified and implemented in OWL language [5]: one dealing with digital identity and the other with privacy concerns. In order to explain how the proposed firewall responds to a common privacy threat, a basic scenario using policy rules expressed in SWRL [6] (Semantic Web Rule Language) language is explained step by step and the porting of the semantic firewall to the Android platform is oulined. Conclusions and future work are given in section 4.

2 Related Works

2.1 Protection on Smartphones

To protect their operating systems from malicious software, operating system developers have implemented various protection mechanisms. On iOS or Black-Berry OS for instance, applications are made available to customers after going through an agrement process that verifies that they do not contain unwanted code. Android also encourages developers to sign their applications with a trusted certificate but it is not mandatory.

In addition to this signature mechanism, Android and BlackBerry prompt the user with a manifest during the installation process. This manifest shows the permissions granted to the application and the user must accept them in order to install the application. The problem with that kind of protection is that users tend to accept the manifest without really assessing all its consequences. The BlackBerry OS tries to address this issue by allowing a modification of the permissions for each application outside the installation process.

However, to our knowledge, there is no real-time privacy protection mechanisms implemented on current platforms that can prevent an application to access specific data.

2.2 Identity Ontologies

Before building a semantic firewall that can efficiently protect users from privacy breaches, an exhaustive record of all the data that need to be protected must be done. Thanks to their declarative form, ontologies are the best way to explicitly represent the manifold digital identity of users that are juggling daily with several avatars, nicknames, passwords, telephone numbers, email accounts, homepages and so on.

On social networks, countless people are describing themselves and part of their private life on their home page. FOAF (Friend Of A Friend) uses W3C's RDF technology to represent such information as an ontology [7]. The core of FOAF describes characteristics of people and social groups, the networking being achieved thanks to the *foaf:knows* property. In addition to the FOAF core terms, one can also describe Internet accounts, mailboxes, homepages etc. This general-purpose ontology is well suited for social network identities but it lacks information regarding mobile phone identities.

Some of this missing information can be found in the vCard file standard format for electronic business cards. vCards contain the user's personal and professional affiliation, address and geolocalisation, email, URLs, photos, logos and even audio clips. They can be attached to email messages, directly embedded in web pages (hCard microformat for (X)HTML) or represented into XML/RDF. The corresponding ontology can be found in [8]. Thanks to that ontology, it is possible to specify fine grained information, for instance indicating that a phone number is also a fax number or telling which email address should be given preference to others.

2.3   Privacy Protection Ontology-Based Policies

A policy is an enforceable, well-specified constraint on the performance of a machine-executable action by a subject in a given situation. Web semantic languages are particularly suited for representing, reasoning and enforcing policies. Thanks to policies, it is possible to adapt the behaviour of a complex system without changing pieces of code. In [9], three approaches are compared and discussed: Ponder, Rei and KaoS. Only the last two are ontology-based and are both written in OWL language.

Rei [10] proposes an application-independent ontology to represent the concepts of rights, prohibitions, obligations and policy rules. It also includes a general class describing the action to be performed, together with preconditions, target objects and results. KaoS has been developed within the broad context of multiagent and distributed systems. It is a complete framework for domain and policy services. Among KaoS features, there is a GUI called KPAT (KAoS Policy Administration Tool) allowing people to manually specify, analyze, and modify authorization and obligation policies, thus hiding the complexities of OWL from end-users. Policy decisions are performed by so-called *Guards* that store precompiled policies and maintain a history of actions. KAoS framework is a very rich environment. However, a simplified framework without the multiagent paraphernalia would better suit our needs.

3   Our Approach

Our objective is to create a semantic firewall between the applications and the private data of the smartphone owner. We use ontologies to represent both the concepts of identity and personal data and also to model privacy policies. The proposed firewall relies on those ontologies to block or authorize a request. A request consists in some actions performed by an agent on another agent data. In our model, the applications are issued by a service provider and we consider that the data requests are made on its behalf.

3.1   Architecture

The global architecture (Figure 1) is grounded on a smartphone ontology written in OWL that includes two ontologies: the ontology designed to represent privacy policies and the ontology of the digital identity stored in the mobile. The firewall is in charge of populating the smartphone ontology with the individuals corresponding to the specific request. When a request is made, the firewall processes the request by calling the description logic reasoner (DL reasoner) in charge of inferences. These inferences are performed according to a set of policy rules written in SWRL. Our algorithm is inspired by the SOUPA algorithm [11]; three cases can occur after classification:

1. There is no policy to manage the request. The firewall then applies the default rule, which can be either liberal (all actions permitted) or conservative (all actions forbidden).
2. Two or more policies are in conflict. As in the first case, the default rule is applied.
3. An adapted policy exists. It is applied and the action is classified either as permitted of forbidden.

The interactions between the service provider and the firewall are described on the sequence diagram of figure 2. The firewall first identifies the service provider that makes the request. The firewall successively registers the service provider and the request by creating them as individuals in the ontology. Then, the DL reasoner is launched to classify the concepts of the ontology and decide the type of action (permitted/forbidden). Finally, if the action is permitted, the firewall provides the appropriate data and logs the request in the ontology for history purposes.

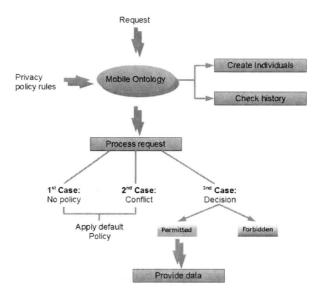

Fig. 1. Flowchart of the semantic firewall

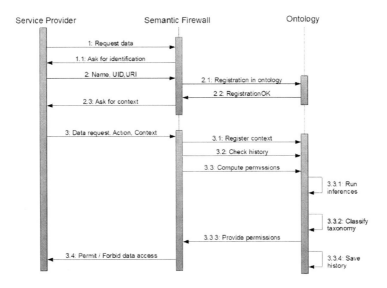

Fig. 2. Sequence diagram of the semantic firewall

3.2   Ontology of Identity on Smartphone

The ontology of identity on smartphone describes the concepts on which the privacy rules are applied. We have defined the following classes and properties:

- name, first name, date of birth and place of birth;
- contact information: postal address, phone number, email address;
- location data: GPS, IP address, Cell Id;
- IMSI: International Mobile Subscriber Identity;
- IMEI: International Mobile Equipment Identity;
- directory of contacts;
- certificates and cryptographic keys.

   These concepts are organized under three main classes: the *Agent* that can either be an individual or an organization, the agent's *IdentityInformation* and the agent's *Data*. The building of this ontology was done with the Protégé-OWL editor [12]. We also used Protégé to populate the ontology with individuals such as telecom operators and personal data.

3.3   Lightweight Ontology for Privacy Policy

To model privacy policies applied to smartphones, a lightweight ontology (figure 4) was built with Protégé. The two main classes of this ontology are *Policy* and *Action*. A policy controls an action, is created by an agent and has a date of creation. An action has the following attributes: date of the action, actor, context in which the action is performed and finally the data on which it is performed.

These information are used to manage the history of the request. As previously mentioned in the architecture description, that ontology is the key element for the classification of action in two categories: permitted or forbidden. We used the Pellet DL reasoner [13] plugin for Protégé to check that this classification is accurate. Due to the fact that the two classes *PermittedAction* and *ForbiddenAction* are not disjoint, in case of conflict, the action will be classified under both. That is how our firewall detects conflicts.

3.4   Rules for Privacy Protection

The firewall is based on the application of privacy rules defined in SWRL. This rule format was chosen because it is both supported by Protégé and the DL reasoner. The rule base is stored appart from the ontology. Rules are separated from the ontology in order to make the addition of new rules and maintenance easier. Listed below are some rules in the case of a liberal default policy which explains why they all are forbidding rules.

Rule 1: Forbid any action made by a service provider with an invalid certificate.

```
[policy1: (?s rdf:type id:ServiceProvider) , (?a rdf:type id:Action),
(?c rdf:type id:InvalidCertificate), (?s id:hasCertificate ?c)
-> (id:policy1 id:forbids ?a)]
```

Rule 2: Forbid access to location data if the service provider is SP1.

```
[policy2: (?a rdf:type id:Action), (?a id:hasActor id:SP1),
(?d rdfs:domain id:LocationData), (?a id:hasTarget ?d)
-> (id:policy2 id: forbids?a)]
```

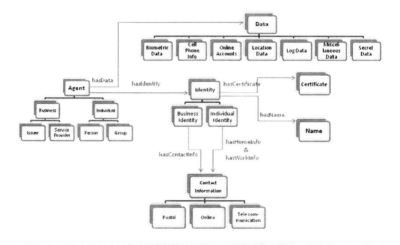

Fig. 3. Digital identity ontology for smartphones

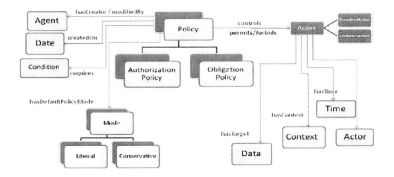

Fig. 4. Privacy ontology for smartphones

Rule 3: Prevent a service provider form obtaining postal address if it has already gathered the phone number.

```
[policy3: (?a rdf:type id:Action), (?c rdf:type id:ServiceProvider),
  (?a id:hasActor ?c), (?d rdfs:domain id:Postal), (?a id:hasTarget ?d),
  (?c id:hasHistoricTarget id:phoneNumber1) -> (id:policy3 id: forbids ?a)]
```

3.5 Validation

Privacy threat scenario

To demonstrate the interest of an ontology-based firewall, we devised a privacy threat scenario in which we want to prevent the collection of location data (GPS, IP address and wireless information) from a service provider (SP2). Our experimentation was conducted in three steps. First, the SWRL rules corresponding to our scenario were written. In our case, only one rule is required, since the IP address, wireless information or GPS are all subclasses of *LocationData*:

```
[policy5: (?a rdf:type id:Action) (?a id:hasActor id:SP2)
  (?d rdfs:domain id:LocationData) (?a id:hasTarget ?d)
  -> (id:policy5 id:forbids ?a)
```

Then, all the individuals needed by the scenario were created under the Protégé editor: SP2 as an instance of *ServiceProvider*, the user as an instance of *Person* with all his location data and SP2's request under the *Action* class. The rule base was launched within Protégé and policy rule number 5 was triggered. The DL reasoner was then executed to classify individuals. As explained before, the classification under the *ForbiddenAction* class confirmed that SP2 was not allowed to collect location data.

Proof of concept

A proof of concept of our firewall was implemented as a client/server application. We chose the client/server approach because we wanted to mimic a real

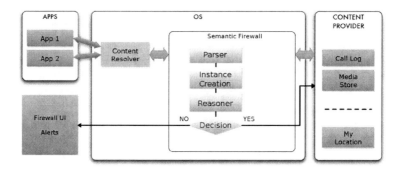

Fig. 5. Android porting of the semantic firewall

access scenario where the application (client) requests the data through a firewall (server). Both the client and the server are developed in Java since it is widespread for mobile phone programming. The Java language is also interesting because it supports specific API, such as JENA [14], for ontology interactions. The server was developed to be as generic as possible while the client was designed to match our test case. However, a graphical user interface was added on the client side to allow the tuning of the request parameters.

Our tests were done on a standard PC and they validate our approach by successfully preventing the access to any location data. The two ontologies (94ko) contain around fifty classes and a hundred object/data properties. In our tests, with five policy rules and around twenty individuals, the execution time is less than 100ms which is reasonable for a mobile usage.

Smartphone architecture

The next step of our work was to implement the semantic firewall on an actual smartphone based on the Android OS. Due to the specific nature of the Android smartphone platform, our client/server application had to be adapted. The major modifications to our firewall are described in the next paragraphs.

First of all, we chose the Android platform as it is free and allows modifications of the operating system. In fact, the operating system is the mandatory entry point of any data request made by any application. It thus appeared to us as the perfect place to implement our semantic firewall. Moreover, Android is also written in JAVA and a JENA API porting is available: AndroJENA [15]. Finally, the way to exchange data is centralized on Android as every request has to go through a single class: *ContentResolver*.

The major modification we had to make to our initial model was to review the way an application requests data. In our PC proof of concept, we made the simplistic assumption that the requests made on the client-side could be processed on-the-fly by the semantic firewall. It is unrealistic to hope that application developers will follow such an approach. To address this issue, a parser was added to the semantic firewall. It is charge of extracting from the request an <actor, action> pair and of providing a default context of execution. The actor, action and context of execution are then reified as instances of our ontology and fed to the DL reasoner. The new firewall complying with the Android specifications is described on Fig. 5.

4   Conclusions and Future Work

As semantic web techniques, languages and tools are coming of age, developing ontology-based applications is getting more straightforward. This paper demonstrates that it is possible to build a convincing prototype of semantic firewall for smartphones. The proposed firewall answers a growing concern: data collection without the user's explicit consent. It takes advantage of the expressiveness of OWL. Thanks to the Open Data Movement [16], more and more ontologies are available and can be reused and adapted to fit specific needs. Our application makes the most of the powerfulness of DL reasoners: all useful inferences are made by the classification mechanism. Policy rules are defined declaratively and separately from the ontologies. Thus the addition of new rules is made easier. The firewall is implemented in Java, using the Jena ontology API and response times to requests are less than what was expected, the call to the DL reasoner, being the most time-consuming operation.

Future works will mainly focus on extensive unit testing of our Android porting. Only once the functioning of the semantic firewall is satisfactory can we focus on the delicate issue of the storage of the ontology. Since smartphones are coupled with an embedded SIM card [17], one has to decide whether the whole ontology, or only part of it, can be stored directly on the SIM card. In particular, we think that the Smart Card Web Server technology [18] can be a promising solution for allowing some part of the handset operating system to be interfaced with the embedded SIM card ontology. The use of SWRL to write policy rules may also change, since RIF (Rule Interchange Format) has recently become a W3C Recommendation (june 2010) [19].

Acknowledgements

The authors gratefully acknowledge the sponsorship by SFR, the French second-largest wireless telecom operator. We especially want to thank Jean-Philippe Wary, initiator of the project at SFR.

References

1. Gartner. Gartner says worldwide mobile phone sales grew 17 per cent in first quarter 2010 (May 2010)
2. Gartner. Android to become no. 2 worldwide mobile operating system in 2010 and challenge symbian for no. 1 position by 2014 (September 2010)
3. Lookout. The app genome project (July 2010), http://blog.mylookout.com/2010/07/introducing-the-app-genome-project/

4. Allemang, D., Hendler, J.: Semantic web for the working ontologist. In: Effective Modeling in RDFS and OWL. Morgan Kaufmann, San Francisco (2008)
5. McGuinness, D.L., Van Harmelen, F., et al. Owl web ontology language overview. W3C recommendation, 10:2004–03 (2004)
6. Horrocks, I., Patel-Schneider, P.F., Boley, H., Tabet, S., Grosof, B., Dean, M.: Swrl: A semantic web rule language combining owl and ruleml. W3C Member submission, 21 (2004)
7. Brickley, D., Miller, L.: Foaf vocabulary specification 0.98. Namespace document, FOAF Project (August 2010), http://xmlns.com/foaf/spec/20100809.html
8. Iannella, R.: Representing vcard objects in rdf/xml, 12 (2001), http://www.w3.org/Submission/vcard-rdf/
9. Tonti, G., Bradshaw, J.M., Jeffers, R., Montanari, R., Suri, N., Uszok, A.: Semantic web languages for policy representation and reasoning: A comparison of kAoS, rei, and ponder. In: Fensel, D., Sycara, K., Mylopoulos, J. (eds.) ISWC 2003. LNCS, vol. 2870, pp. 419–437. Springer, Heidelberg (2003)
10. Kagal, L., Paolucci, M., Srinivasan, N., Denker, G., Finin, T., Sycara, K.: Authorization and privacy for semantic web services. IEEE Intelligent Systems, 50–56 (2004)
11. Chen, H., Finin, T., Joshi, A.: The soupa ontology for pervasive computing. In: Ontologies for agents: Theory and experiences, pp. 233–258 (2005)
12. What is protégé-owl? http://protege.stanford.edu/overview/protege-owl.html
13. Sirin, E., Parsia, B., Grau, B.C., Kalyanpur, A., Katz, Y.: Pellet: A practical owl-dl reasoner. Web Semantics: Science, Services and Agents on the World Wide Web 5(2), 51–53 (2007)
14. Carroll, J.J., Dickinson, I., Dollin, C., Reynolds, D., Seaborne, A., Wilkinson, K.: Jena: implementing the semantic web recommendations, pp. 74–83 (2004)
15. Androjena. Jena android porting (2010), http://code.google.com/p/androjena/
16. Bizer, C., Heath, T., Berners-Lee, T.: Linked data-the story so far. International Journal on Semantic Web and Information Systems 5(3), 1–22 (2009)
17. TS ETSI. 102 221:" uicc-terminal interface: Physical and logical characteristics". ETSI Standard (2010)
18. Urien, P.: Internet card, a smart card as a true internet node. Computer Communications 23(17), 1655–1666 (2000)
19. Kifer, M.: Rif overview. W3C Working Group Note (2010)

A Study on the Security, the Performance and the Penetration of Wi-Fi Networks in a Greek Urban Area

Savvas Mousionis, Alex Vakaloudis, and Constantinos Hilas

Department of Informatics and Communications,
Technological Educational Institute of Serres,
Terma Magnisias, 62124, Serres, Greece
{mousioniz,avakaloudis}@hotmail.com, chilas@teiser.gr

Abstract. This paper presents a study on the expansion of urban Wi-Fi networks and the degree of users' awareness about their characteristics. It involves an experiment contacted at the area of Serres, a Greek city of around 70,000 inhabitants. The findings revealed that although the number of Wi-Fi networks is quite high, their owners are unaware of their technical settings. As a result many networks remain either unlocked or with WEP encryption while many adjacent networks use the same channel thus reducing their performance.

Keywords: Wi-Fi networks usage, wireless security, war driving, urban networks.

1 Introduction

It has been around seven years since the introduction of Asymmetric Digital Subscriber Line (ADSL) as a high speed Internet access service in Greece. Despite the initial reluctance by home users to upgrade their previous dial-up connections to ADSL, currently a large number of Greek homes or enterprises connect to the internet through ADSL. It is a mainstream practice for providers to supply a wireless modem/router/access point for every new connection, mainly in the form of a subscription gift. This has gradually filled Greek cities with Wi-Fi networks. These devices typically use the 802.11b/g protocols with a 100mW antenna at 2.4 GHz. Transmission occurs in one of 13 overlapping channels [1].

The present paper explores the use of the resulted Wi-Fi networks which in turn provides clues for the degree of user awareness on wireless security. The main tool used in this research is the method of war driving [2]. War Driving is the act of searching for Wi-Fi wireless networks by a person in a moving vehicle using a Wi-Fi equipped computer, such as a laptop or a PDA. It is similar to using a radio scanner, or to the ham radio practice of DXing.

War driving is a play of words on the older term war dialing, which is automatically calling various telephone numbers to look for any that have a modem attached. War dialing, in turn, comes from the 1983 movie War Games now

C.A. Ardagna and J. Zhou (Eds.): WISTP 2011, LNCS 6633, pp. 381–389, 2011.
© IFIP International Federation for Information Processing 2011

written in the cult lore of computer geek circles. In the movie a young cracker (Matthew Broderick) is using war dialing to look for games and bulletin board systems. However, he inadvertently ends up with a direct connection to a high-level military computer that gives him control over the U.S. nuclear arsenal [3].

The paper proceeds as follows. The next section defines the hypotheses of the experiments, its subjects, methods and materials and the problems that occurred during its execution. Section 3 lists the results, while in the last section the outcomes of our work along with suggestions for improvements and future work are discussed.

2   Description of the Experiment

2.1   Motivation and Hypotheses

The survey discussed in this paper has two objectives. The first one is to investigate the penetration of Wi-Fi networks considering the provincial city of Serres as a case study. The outcome may not only be used to demonstrate their wide spread but also to confront the reluctance of home users to operate a wireless network due to health considerations. Measurements of the Signal-to-Noise Ratio (SNR) will confirm that the whole city is covered by a number of wireless networks. Therefore, if someone is surrounded by neighbors owning Wi-Fis, she is already exposed to some RF radiation anyway. Moreover, this RF exposure is normally thousands of times below international standards [4].

Our second objective is to examine the manner of usage of Wi-Fi networks and to demonstrate the ignorance of their owners when it comes to simple security of performance settings. The knowledge, for example, to choose the type of encryption or to adjust the Wi-Fi channel is important for the good operation of a network, yet the vast majority of wireless access point (WAP) users are either oblivious or inconsiderate when it comes to their network.

Although WiFi technology security vulnerabilities are well known, the extent of these vulnerabilities may be surprising. War driving may identify many potential points of entry [5].

2.2   Subjects

Serres is the capital of the Serres Prefecture located in the Central Macedonia Periphery of Greece. The city has a population of around 70,000 inhabitants (56,145 in the last official census of 2001) and is an important trade centre for tobacco, grain, and livestock. In our view, it represents a sound choice for an experimental subject since it reflects the average situation regarding wireless networks in Greece. It is situated in a location which is neither near the cutting-edge capital (Athens) nor one found in less developed places. For the better interpretation of results, we divided the city into the following areas:

- City centre: The area where mainly commercial shops or companies exist. Wireless networks in this area are expected to have been setup by professional technicians.

- Around the city centre: A residential area with few shops or companies.
- Suburban and densely populated: A residential area with block of flats of four to six floors.
- Suburban and sparsely populated: The outskirts of the city, a residential area with houses.
- Student area: The area around the technical university (T.E.I. of Serres) populated with students. Some of them study in the Informatics and Communications Department, hence a higher degree of technical expertise and involvement is expected from them.
- Difficult to approach: The area consisting of the hills around the old part of the city with old houses and narrow roads.

2.3 Methodology and Tools

The method used to carry out the experiment is war driving, in other words, driving around the city and stopping regularly to discover wireless networks. The density of these stops is specified by:

- The surrounding area: In densely populated areas stops are every 10–15m since networks of the top floors must be discovered and the number of expected networks is high. On the other hand, in sparsely populated areas the scheduled stops are around 20–30m.
- The surrounding environment: Parked coaches and large trees hinder the discovery of networks.

The tool used is Network Stumbler which is a widely used tool that provides all required information [6]. This is the WAPs MAC address and SSID which were used to identify unique networks, the communication channel, the encryption standard, the type of the device, e.g. WAP or station, and the SNR.

Regarding the first objective of our experiment we measure:

- The number of unique Wi-Fi networks at each stop. The uniqueness requires checking if a network has appeared in adjacent measurements.
- The SNR of each network and the maximum SNR for each point of measurement.

For the use of Wi-Fi networks we examine the following parameters:

- The encryption used, i.e. no encryption, WEP, WPA and WPA2. In the case of unencrypted networks we also try to login to the administration console to check if the user has changed the default username and password
- The SSID used, i.e. if it is the default one or it has been altered
- The Wi-Fi channel to which the network is adjusted.

From a legal perspective, there is no restriction of examining wireless networks broadcasting in a public place, especially for academic purposes. Moreover, we have just searched for the existence of wireless networks in a non-intrusive way, with no ulterior motive. Adding to this, no attempt was made to interfere or jam the wireless traffic nor did we try to correlate the networks or their traffic with specific persons. We, also, do not publicize the exact location and owner of the individual insecure APs. What is illegal is the unauthorized access to a wireless network in order to steal internet access, steal information, alter the network's configuration or commit other computer crimes. As a result, for networks that were found unlocked, our action stopped to the point of examining whether the user still uses the default security settings. We want to stress out that this may not always be legal in other countries.

2.4   Problems

Although war driving seems to be a time-consuming, yet straightforward process, a number of issues appeared during its execution. Stopping even for one minute in the city centre is not always permitted or it may cause the annoyance of other drivers. Consequently, it may take a few attempts to take a single measurement. Likewise, a stop on a street with parked cars on each side causes interruption of the traffic. Furthermore, some streets are one-way traffic which increases the time needed to reach a desired point. Finally in the difficult to approach section, driving must be very cautious to avoid damaging the car. There were cases where war driving turned out to be war walking.

Since the experiment took place during the summer, the leaves of the trees were a source of reduced SNR values. Hence, the measurement should not take place at points below or nearby large trees.

Finally, an updated map had to be used since the city is expanding and an outdated map was inconsistent with the real picture; for instance there were sections of roads that had been widened or even replaced by squares or round-abouts.

All the above, while solvable, increased the expected time planned for each session of war driving.

3   Results

The war driving part of the experiment took place over the three summer months of 2010. It took 14 sessions of 10 hours each to cover the whole city. The processing of the results included printing the screenshots of Network Stumbler, identifying unique networks along with their maximum SNR.

Overall, 1021 measurements were made and 5374 Wi-Fi networks were found (Table 1). From the 677 (12.6%) unlocked ones, 268 had retained the default access to the administration console. As regards the use of encryption 840 (15.6%) networks were using WEP, 3782 WPA and just 75 WPA2. 3728 were still using the default SSID and the rest 1646 had changed their SSID. The average SNR for each measurement point was 34.2 dB. Considering that WEP encryption is only little better than no encryption we see that almost one third of the networks are susceptible to eavesdropping.

The channels used for Wi-Fi are separated by 5 MHz in most cases but have a bandwidth of 22 MHz. As a result channels overlap and it is possible to find

Table 1. Number of Wi-Fi networks found at each of the areas described in subsection 2.3

Area	Unlocked	WEP	WPA	WPA2	Default SSID	Altered SSID	Total
City Centre	103	68	521	52	459	285	744
Around City Centre	181	276	1186	13	1199	457	1656
Densely populated	167	235	820	10	867	365	1232
Sparsely populated	64	63	217	0	258	86	344
Student Area	41	81	211	0	1199	457	1656
Difficult to approach	121	117	827	117	730	335	1065
Total	677	840	3782	75	3728	1646	5374

Table 2. Active networks per channel

1	2	3	4	5	6	7	8	9	10	11	12	13
1575	40	34	38	45	2296	50	45	57	42	1107	12	33

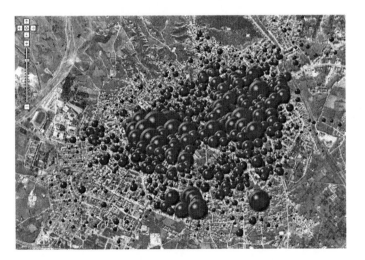

Fig. 1. Positioning and population of Wi-Fi networks. The size of the spheres correlates to the number of networks.

a maximum of three non-overlapping channels. Therefore, if there are adjacent pieces of WLAN equipment that need to work on non-interfering channels, there is only a possibility of three.

In Table 2 the channel usage of the surveyed networks is shown. Channels 1, 6 and 11 do not overlap with each other and are the preferred choices when setting up a WAP. Channel 6 is usually the default factory setting. The findings

Fig. 2. Wi-Fi coverage of the city. Measured SNR values are visualized by the size of the sphere.

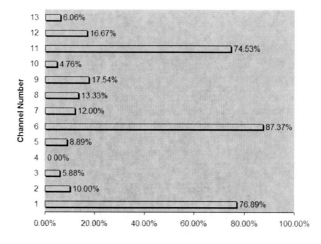

Fig. 3. Percentage (per channel) of neighboring networks that were found using the same channel

in Table 2 coincide with the common practice. Interestingly, there are WAPs set up to work on channels other than the three most common.

In Fig. 1 the position of the discovered networks in the city is depicted. The number of identified networks at each location is visualized by means of spheres of variable sizes. The size of each sphere correlates to the number of networks at the point. In Fig. 2 the SNR measurements at each position are visualized. One may observe that the city seems covered with Wi-Fi signals. In Fig. 3 the findings of Table 2 are further clarified. The bar chart displays the possibility two or more adjacent networks to use the same Wi-Fi channel.

4   Conclusions and Discussion

4.1   Interpretation of Results

This experiment demonstrated that a medium-sized city (for Greek standards of population) is almost fully covered by Wi-Fi networks. The only blank points where squares or the outer limits of the city. The number of unique networks discovered is translated to one network per around 11 inhabitants. This indicates a good penetration of the wireless technology plus that there is still room for more networks to be added. It also illustrates a wide-spread interest of people in Greece for wireless internet access.

As the number of base stations and local wireless networks increases, so does the RF exposure of the population. Recent surveys have shown that the RF exposures from base stations range from 0.002% to 2% of the levels of international exposure guidelines, depending on a variety of factors such as the proximity to the antenna and the surrounding environment. This is lower or comparable to RF exposures from radio or television broadcast transmitters [4].

Our measurements of the SNR also confront the fear of not installing a home wireless network because of health risk concerns [7]. If a specific apartment is surrounded by Wi-Fi networks, it is already susceptible to their electromagnetic radiation. However, considering the very low exposure levels and research results collected to date, there is no convincing scientific evidence that the weak RF signals from wireless networks cause adverse health effects [4].

An important question, left to be answered, is whether users actually access the Internet over a wireless and not over a wired medium. In other words, we can not be sure whether all the discovered networks serve their purpose or are idle.

On the issue of configuring a Wi-Fi network, our evaluation of the experiment's results is carried out under the perspective that the performance and security of wireless networks are topics of general interest, regularly brought up in ordinary discussions. Users are concerned with security and desire faster internet access.

At the same time, the basic configuration of a wireless access point is a procedure that does not require advanced technical expertise or understanding of the wireless technology. In addition, most devices are shipped, by the ISPs, with manuals detailing simple settings alterations e.g. how to change the channel or to apply encryption. And while encryption or Wi-Fi channel numbers are notions whose exact meanings are unknown to the common user, the provided web-based interfaces are simple enough to facilitate their management.

Nevertheless, our survey revealed that despite the importance of security and the easiness for its application, very few users are confident enough to change their WAP settings. As a result, only 1.4% encrypts their data with WPA2. The only exception to this rule is the city centre where 7% of the networks use WPA2. Even though this can be explained by the higher number of business related networks, these are usually setup by specialized technicians and hence this percentage should have been much higher. No WAP using WPA2 was found in the student populated area which took us by surprise as we expected to find more technically competent users there.

It was found that around 70% of Wi-Fi networks are encrypted with WPA. We assume that this is because WPA is the default encryption for the devices preset by Greek ISPs in the last couple of years. Older subscribers still use the unsecured WEP or no encryption at all.

Another evidence of security unaware users is the number of default SSIDs found. Keeping the default SSID can not be considered as a security risk on its own, but it prompts a potential hacker to try to penetrate to such a network. Default SSIDs provide clues about the apparatus model and imply that there is a good possibility that the default administration authentication has also been kept.

The ignorance of users is further exposed when it comes to channel collisions, i.e. the use of the same Wi-Fi channel by many neighboring networks. It is found that when interference exists, the throughput of the system is reduced. It therefore pays to reduce the levels of interference to improve the overall performance of the WLAN equipment. Although users crave for faster internet access they do not take the corresponding actions. Our survey shows that in 87% of the cases another nearby network was using the same channel. This causes interference among such networks and reduces their throughput.

4.2   Relation to other Works

To our knowledge no similar experiment has been contacted in Greece. A study on war driving in Dartmouth college campus is published in [8], while the Professional Information Security Association (PISA) of Hong Kong reports the findings of war driving in Hong Kong and Macau [9].

The first one is a survey that focus primarily on the accuracy of the WAP position estimation and the impact it has on pervasive-computing applications that depend on knowledge of user location. The article also comments on the effect of using estimated WAP locations in computing AP coverage range and estimating interference among WAPs.

The findings of the second survey are similar to ours, although it was made 3 years earlier (2007). An increasing adoption of encryption settings was identified although 72% of the encrypted sites used WEP. Also, more that 40% of the WAPs kept the default SSID settings while 20% of the rest used individual/family names or organization names as their SSID.

Also, RSA, the security division of EMC^2 Corporation, has commissioned annual research over the past seven years, as part of its campaign to promote and improve best practices in wireless security [10].

4.3   Impact for Practitioners

The fact that Wi-FI APs come with WPA encryption on their default settings has improved the overall security of home networks. We propose a similar approach to be adopted regarding the Wi-Fi channel setting. Randomizing the assigned channel per WAP will reduce the probability of interference and thus will improve performance.

It should be noticed that although all manufacturers provide advanced security measures in their appliances such as modifiable network identifier names and passwords, address filtering, firewalls and WPA to protect wireless networks, it is the consumer who must make the final steps in order to install, configure and adjust all features for maximum security. Thus, it would be very helpful to spare a few pages in user manuals with detailed step-by-step guides on security and performance.

The ignorance or fear to manipulate device settings seems to be apparent in the behavior of professional technicians as well and this is a situation that has to be addressed.

4.4   Research Agenda

The same experiment will be repeated next year to examine changes in the penetration of networks and the use of channels/encryption so as to find out any progress in these issues. We also plan to perform similar experiments in other cities in order to compare the relation of the public to wireless networks in different areas. The parameter of checking MAC filtering will also be added.

References

1. IEEE: IEEE 802.11: Wireless LAN Medium Access Control (MAC) and Physical Layer (PHY) Specifications (2007),
   http://standards.ieee.org/about/get/802/802.11.html
2. Wireless LAN Security, 802.11/Wi-Fi Wardriving and Warchalking,
   http://www.wardrive.net/
3. Brown, S.: WarGames: A Look Back at the Film That Turned Geeks and Phreaks Into Stars. Wired Magazine 16, 08 (2008)
4. World Health Organization: Electromagnetic fields and public health, Base stations and wireless technologies, Fact sheet N304 (2006)
5. Berghel, H.: Wireless infidelity I: war driving. Communications of the ACM 47(9) (2004)
6. Network Stumbler, web site http://www.netstumbler.com/
7. Bale, J.: Health fears lead schools to dismantle wireless networks. The Times, November 20 (2006)
8. Kim, M., Fielding, J.J., Kotz, D.: Risks of using AP locations discovered through war driving. In: Fishkin, K.P., Schiele, B., Nixon, P., Quigley, A. (eds.) PERVASIVE 2006. LNCS, vol. 3968, pp. 67–82. Springer, Heidelberg (2006)
9. Fong, K.K.K., Ho, A.: PISA & WTIA's Hong Kong & Macau War-Driving Report 2007, Professional Information Security Association Seminar: Live! Wi-Fi Attack and Defense (2008)
10. RSA wireless security surveys, http://www.rsa.com/node.aspx?id=3268

Author Index